PEREGRINE BOOKS

THE LIFE OF HENRY JAMES
VOL. I: 1843–89

'The greatest literary biography of our time' – A. L. Rowse

Since 1953, when the first part was published, Leon Edel's life of Henry James has been the subject of increasing critical acclaim. It now appears in Penguins in a 'definitive edition' of two volumes.

The first volume takes in James's boyhood and youth in New England, the 'passionate pilgrimage' to Europe and his life in America and then Europe until 1889. It was at this time that much of his best work was done, including *The Portrait of a Lady*, *The Bostonians* and *The Princess Casamassima*. Like Orwell and T. S. Eliot, Henry James was reluctant to open his life to biographers, but Professor Edel, in what amounts to an object-lesson in the art of biography, has masterfully uncovered the life of a man whose contribution, by precept and practice, to English literature was enormous.

*

Leon Edel is a fellow of the Royal Society of Literature, a member of the American Academy of Arts and Letters, a past president of P.E.N. (U.S.) and, after occupying the Henry James Chair of English and American Letters at New York University, he was named to the Citizens Chair of English at the University of Hawaii, which he now holds.

LEON EDEL

·

THE LIFE OF
HENRY JAMES

·

Volume I: 1843–89

PENGUIN BOOKS

Penguin Books Ltd, Harmondsworth, Middlesex, England
Penguin Books, 625 Madison Avenue, New York, New York 10022, U.S.A.
Penguin Books Australia Ltd, Ringwood, Victoria, Australia
Penguin Books Canada Ltd, 41 Steelcase Road West, Markham, Ontario, Canada
Penguin Books (N.Z.) Ltd, 182-190 Wairau Road, Auckland 10, New Zealand

—

First published in Great Britain by Rupert Hart-Davis in 3 volumes
(*Henry James: The Untried Years, 1843–70*; *Henry James: The Conquest of London, 1870–82*;
Henry James: The Middle Years, 1882–95), 1953, 1962, 1963
First published in this edition in Peregrine Books 1977

—

—

Made and printed in Great Britain by
Hazell Watson & Viney Ltd,
Aylesbury, Bucks
Set in Linotype Pilgrim

Contents

CONTENTS

CONTENTS

Preface to the Definitive Edition

Mr Lawrence Durrell called his four-part novel of Alexandria a quartet: emulating him, I have fallen into the habit of speaking of my five-part life of James as a quintet. And while my work came out *seriatim* over a period of twenty years, it is here presented as if played at a single concert, each movement following the other in the prescribed way. A biographer – especially a modern biographer – is primarily a storyteller; in this he differs from his illustrious predecessor, James Boswell, who liked to pretend he wasn't telling a story at all, but only letting Dr Johnson speak for himself. Artless Boswell! I often wonder what he would do if he were placed in the modern library of quite another Johnson – Lyndon B. – in Texas and how he would rummage among the millions of pages, the videotapes and photographs, the endless memorabilia, the clutter of a President's days? The modern biographer, as I often say, must melt down his materials or he will smother the reader if he is not smothered himself.

Henry James lived for seventy-three years and had a large career. He wrote for fifty years. He had known all literary Europe. I had to deal with a celebrated cast, Flaubert, Zola, Turgenev, George Eliot, Trollope, Meredith, a procession of prime ministers, and even Queen Victoria, perched maternally over the nineteenth century; and after her, 'fat Edward' – as James called him – and the era of Bennett and Moore and Wells and the nascent Bloomsbury. Henry James left New York, his birthplace, when it was a provincial city, and lived a full life in London, Paris, Rome. He looms large in American literature which is but 200 years old; but no less large in the 300-year history of the modern novel in which he pre-empted such a distinguished and law-giving place. I said as much when I wrote the first movement of my quintet. He was massive and I needed a large stage.

People used to ask, during the years of my writing of this work, 'When will we have your next volume?' The conversation always came, at such a moment, to a stop. 'How near are you to the ending?' One friendly critic in *The Times Literary Supplement* exclaimed 'How long, Leon, how long!' I could only shake my head. I never knew. Some thought I was being evasive or secretive. I really never knew. The quintet had its own schedule. It had long periods of gestation. I often did other things – wrote other books, – edited, gave lectures, travelled. The quintet never revealed its plans to me in advance. What I learned was that one's art or craft (whatever biography may be) can't afford to be impatient. If I forced the matter and tried to write a page, it was usually a hodge-podge. The quintet had a mysterious organic growth.

When I say this, I suppose I make some people think I was living inside Henry James's skin all these years. This was never true, save when I was at my writing desk; and even then I was what psychologists call a 'participant-observer'. I had to *feel* what I was writing; I had to identify with my people, in one way or another, but I had also to take my perspective, be analytical, distant, see my subject not as one to whom I was rendering homage, but as a living person whose sense of humour was as boundless as his egotism, whose mannerisms could irritate as well as amuse. The solemn, unsmiling countenance; the Johnsonian bulk and authority; but earlier the eager young American distinctly, but discreetly, 'on the make' in London society, and still earlier, the passionate, troubled youth, walking the sands of Newport dreaming of fame, fortune and glory.

It is the perspective that is the true measure of a biographer. Many of my critics have overlooked this important element in my work. They think I 'invested' my being in Henry James because my work was of long duration; as one critic, trying to be generous, worded it, I had performed 'a rare act of total imaginative bestowal'.

There was a practical 'investment' in my subject, of course; but my imaginative 'bestowal' was not in Henry James: it was in my beloved art of biography. This critic had no sense of the enormous appeal to me of the biographical process, the real 'fun' of the doing, the messing about in archives, as it seemed, the journeys into attics, palazzos, far-away *maisons de campagne* for bundles of letters and diaries and the interviews with James's contemporaries. I have a memory, as I write, of Bernard Shaw at 70, white-bearded, red-cheeked in a corduroy jacket, pacing his study in Whitehall Court, forgetting the young man seated in a large chair who has been asking questions about the theatre of the '90s, launching into a discourse, a splendid private lecture, on 'the dreary nineteenth-century fatalism and pessimism' of Henry James and George Eliot. They should have been socialists. They should have tried to create brave new worlds instead of bringing up old family ghosts. And I remember Edith Wharton, at her Pavillon Colombe near Paris, looking at me amusedly out of her hazel eyes, playing with her Pekinese while she talked of Henry James : 'The man was greater than his works, much greater – and that is saying a good deal.'

My work on James has had four phases. I originally wrote of him in a piece of academic juvenilia; this became, years later, my little book *The Psychological Novel*. Then there was a second phase, when I tried to run down James's unhappy years in the theatre. This led me to Shaw, Granville Barker, Elizabeth Robins, some elderly drama critics and surviving actresses; and the result was a Paris dissertation, written in French, *Henry James: Les Années Dramatiques* of 1932 (when I was 25). It is now a rare book, because very few copies were printed, just enough for the libraries as required of a degree candidate in France. Henry James's executor read this book and liked it; he gave me permission to edit James's bad plays as a 'study in failure' and priorities in the James family papers. But the depression and the war intervened; and almost twenty years after my Paris book – during which I bestowed my imagination on journalism, broadcasting, and (as much of it as is allowed) on soldiering – I brought out my edition of James's complete plays. After this long hiatus in my life of letters, which had started in the 1920s, I found that publishers were asking for a biography of James. I set to work, having had, in spite of the long interval, a head start. Thinking back on the sprawl of my work, I have totalled up my actual writing time. It comes surprisingly to little more than six years. My first volume *The Untried Years* was written between 1950–52 and published in 1953; the next two volumes *The Conquest of London* and *The Middle Years* were written during 1960 and 1961; *The Treacherous Years* 1967–8 and *The Master* 1969–71.

If this was my writing time, what did I do between my forties and my sixties when the quintet was coming into being? I have already suggested that I did many things. A biographer has his own life to lead as well as the lives of his subjects. There had been my researches, of course. There were trips abroad, some for work, some for holiday; there were non-Jamesian enterprises. There were longish periods when I was forced to reap the practical benefits of my reputation, such as it was – teaching, barnstorming, visiting colleges, making public appearances. Journalists have created a charming and fanciful legend of Leon Edel breathing, sleeping and eating Henry

James for forty years. To be sure my name has become associated with his, and we figure together on many title pages, for I edited his complete tales as well as his plays, and I wrote many prefaces for his novels and collections of his prose.

I have said that this life of James had an organic growth. I originally estimated it would take four years to write. But when I completed the first 'movement', my publisher was all for printing it at once. It was a viable book – why not? This made me very nervous. What if I should find a new batch of letters? What if I hadn't clearly understood my man's character? What if I wanted to rewrite a chapter? I told myself however that if I really believed in what I had written, that is in my estimate of James's character and personality, and if I really had captured his childhood and youth and first maturity, my problem was simply to show in the sequel his continued growth and development. New material might make for a richer or more detailed picture; yet the 'dynamic' of his character remained and evolved with his art. *The Untried Years* was enthusiastically received in America and England and my serialization was launched. It created many unforeseen problems.

I had not anticipated the deluge of James letters which followed. At one moment I had 2,000 holographs on my desk, mailed in from many parts of the world by generous readers. I won't speak of the tension induced by thought of fire hazards, or the friendly way in which my favourite cat managed always to lie right on top of great batches of them, as if to keep them warm for me. When I had finished, I had read not only the family archive at Harvard, where there are at least 7,000 letters, but as many again scattered in many places. The new material had to be assimilated; my solution was to use a 'retrospective' method – in a word, a form of 'flashback'. I saw no reason why this could not legitimately serve the ends of biography as it does the writer of fiction. I taught myself how to recapitulate, to summarize, to plan transitions from volume to volume, to watch my pacing, and I decided that my ideal form would be the scenic, the episodic. Instead of freezing myself into chronology, I sought a kind of Proustian flexibility, moving backward and forward in time, as Mr Durrell was doing during the same period in his fictional quartet. The 'serialization' caused me to test all sorts of technical devices; I built thematically and used symbolic and archetypal analogies. The effect of this was to avoid that piling up of the documentary which is the bane of many first-rate biographies. I showed, without breaking my story-line, the evolutionary process of James's art as well as the process of his aging. The reader could feel he was growing up with James, conquering the literary world, growing old and achieving mastery. James was one of the few American artists to have an old age: so many burned themselves out by 30 or 40.

The art of biography, as I have practised it, is the art of 'leaving out' and this has helped get rid of a great deal of clutter. It hasn't prevented critics (who should know better) from saying I have put every last detail in. If I had, I would have a full-fledged Wagnerian *Ring* instead of a quintet. The biography's organic wholeness has made the task of preparing it for its Penguin form difficult – yet not as difficult as one might imagine. There could be no question of abridgment. The themes are too closely interwoven: and it is dangerous to cut such threads. But what was possible was to remove the redundancies, the 'overlap', the machinery of multi-volume structure, and the verbal fat – my recapitulations which reminded readers of what had gone before.

This edition has given me what James called 'the better chance' – the opportunity to remove or alter passages that time had rendered obsolete. I could also get rid of early prolixities. I nowhere scrupled to rewrite a sentence or a chapter if I felt my text susceptible of improvement. At the same time I incorporated such new material as was relevant – and revelatory. For this reason I call this harmonized quintet my 'definitive' edition – it is as definitive as any biography can be. I have re-divided my five parts into twelve sections. Indeed, I treated the whole text as if it were a newly-written manuscript, requiring the normal revisions an author makes to achieve 'wholeness', economy and lucidity.

*

If I were asked what it has meant to write the James quintet, I would say that it has meant the excitement of finding the material, and then the far greater excitement of discovering an ideal form for it. There was the constant shaping of a 'work in progress'. I tried to make the reader see my subject, *feel* the stages of his life. I sought to write a narrative that gives an illusion of a living person and not a *papier-mâché* figure built of documents. My personal reward lay in the imagination of form and structure – the only imagination a biographer can be allowed.

Those who want to know my sources and read my acknowledgements will find them in the five-volume form. The present version is intended for readers who want a continuous and uninterrupted story. I have however supplied an index without which no biography can be said to be complete.

LEON EDEL

Honolulu, 1975

BOOK ONE:
THE UNTRIED YEARS
1843–69

Part One:
Interrogation of the Past

I

The Spectral Eye

THE James family was founded in America by an Irish immigrant who arrived in the United States immediately after the Revolution. He was a Protestant from County Cavan, William James. His father had been a William, and among the thirteen children the immigrant fathered in the New World there was still another William and also a Henry, who in turn became the father of still another William and of a Henry, a philosopher and a novelist. The names had become dynastic symbols, as if the family were a royal line and there were a throne to be filled.

Henry James, the novelist and grandson of the enterprising William who had fared across the seas, was to plead often against the confusing proliferation of Williams and Henrys; and doubtless his passion for finding the right names for his fictional characters stemmed from a sense that wrong names had been bestowed within his family experience. It was difficult to have an identity if one's Christian name as well as one's surname was a family tag pinned to the cradle of a helpless babe.

Family legend has it that the founder of the line, who was eighteen when he set foot in the New World in 1789, brought with him a 'very small sum of money', a Latin grammar and a desire to visit the fresh battlefields of the Revolutionary war – a desire he appears to have promptly gratified. He found employment as a clerk in a New York store, and two years later was able to open his own establishment. In 1793 he settled in Albany, then a thriving town of 5,000 inhabitants set in frontier country. In the three decades that followed he lived – in fact helped to create – the traditional American success story. He purchased land in upper New York State and in Manhattan; he ventured into activities as diverse as banking and the manufacture of salt in Syracuse. He became an influential power on the upper Hudson (his novelist grandson bestowed the name of Hudson on his first important hero); and in due course the name of James was given to a street in Albany, another in Syracuse and to Jamesville, New York. He was one of the staunchest pillars of the Presbyterian Church and prominent in civic affairs; he was chosen to deliver the official oration at the completion of the Erie Canal and he was a trustee of Union College, Schenectady. He died rich and honoured on 19 September 1832, and the Albany *Argus* said, 'Turn where we may, and there are the results of his informing mind – his energy – and his vast wealth.'

His wealth was vast even in terms of the later period of 'tycoons' and multi-millionaires. William of Albany left an estate valued at $3,000,000 to be divided among his eleven surviving children and his widow, Catharine Barber, who outlived him by twenty-seven years. And he left them a legacy of rigid Presbyterianism against which the elder Henry James rebelled all his life. This son was punished in the will with an annuity of $1,250 a year. The will also invested the trustees with wide powers to supervise the lives of the heirs 'with a view to discourage prodigality and vice and furnish an incentive to economy and usefulness'.

The children of William of Albany rose against this attempt of their father to police their lives from beyond the grave. They went to court, Henry among them, and the will was broken. In the division, the elder Henry James received property that yielded him about $10,000 a year. He found himself, as he remarked, 'leisured for life'.

I

The elder Henry James was the fourth son of William of Albany's third marriage, the first wife having died in childbirth and the second two years after her marriage. He was a sensitive boy, strong of limb and keen of mind, with an abundance of healthy animal spirits. The father, preoccupied with his ever-growing business empire, found little time for his numerous progeny, save to exercise (and catechize) them in the rugged Presbyterian manner. The elder Henry, in later years, recorded his memories of Sundays in the Albany household in which the children were taught

not to play, not to dance nor to sing, not to read storybooks, nor to con over our school lessons for Monday even; not to whistle, not to ride the pony, nor to take a walk in the country, nor a swim in the river; nor, in short, to do anything which nature specially craved.

'Nothing is so hard,' the old man added, ruefully looking back at his childish self of those long Albany Sundays – 'nothing is so hard for a child as *not-to-do*.'

Yet the child is ever resourceful, and the observant, out-going little boy in that large family found compensations and solutions. One was to arrive at church early on Sundays in order to occupy the corner of the large family pew next to the window. He combined entertainment with a brave appearance of piety. The window-blind had a reachable cord and tassels to be set a-swinging; in the street (barred to traffic after the manner of the time for the duration of the Holy Service) he could watch the picturesque parade of irreligious strollers in their Sunday finery enjoying a Sabbath idleness. And always, just about the time the sermon began, there was an added touch of colour. Opposite the church stood the dwelling of a Justice of the Peace, and every Sunday the housemaid would appear and shake out the crumb-cloth over the side of the steps. She did this unhurriedly and nonchalantly, studying the passers-by – and studied in turn by the small boy at the church window. 'I was unfeignedly obliged to the shapely maid for giving my senses so much innocent occupation when their need was sorest,' the elder Henry wrote decates later. 'Her pleasant image has always remained a figure of my memory ... the fresh, breezy, natural life she used to impart to those otherwise lifeless, stagnant, most unnatural Sunday mornings.'

The Devil could stalk the streets of Albany, and sow temptations even more serious than a glimpse of a shapely maid through a church window. When the senior Henry was ten – he later confessed this to one of his sons – he used to stop every morning on his way to school at a shoemaker's shop near his father's house for a nip of raw gin or brandy. The ritual was renewed in the afternoon. This was not, he said, an occasional thing but habitual. If, on the one hand, it was a way of being a manly little fellow among drinking and card-playing schoolmates, it was also a way of defying God the Father who had created dull Sundays and the other father who, in that important Albany household, was virtually a god.

The son pictured William of Albany as a stern and uncompromising parent. What is more, Henry felt himself a helpless victim of parental disregard. 'I cannot recollect that he ever questioned me about my out-of-door occupations, or about my companions, or showed any extreme solicitude about my standing in school.' Nor does his mother seem to have filled the gap. She was 'a law only to our affections', 'a good wife and mother, nothing else – save, to be sure, a kindly friend and neighbour'.

These were the senior Henry's feelings about his father and

mother recalled in old age. The available evidence tends to show that within the stern Calvinistic frame of their house at State and Green Streets, and later North Pearl Street, the parents distributed much love, devotion, parental solicitude and parental anger, accompanied by the usual moments of gaiety and joy as well as the storms, rivalries and tempests of passion that are to be found in a numerous family in which big and little egos clash. Henry Senior, sensitive and reflective, clearly felt himself pushed aside; and we can judge how unhappy the boy must have been by the words his older self set down : 'I was never so happy at home as away from it.'

If happiness lay away from home it was because home early became for the young boy a place where competition with his brothers and sisters was intense and where the two fathers – the prosperous and busy corporeal William of Albany and the invisible Almighty – kept him under their gaze and *not-to-do* echoed through its rooms. Years later, in speaking of some of his contemporaries, the elder Henry James invoked spy and detective images to characterize them. Emerson had 'no sympathy with nature' but was 'a sort of police-spy upon it ... He is an uncommonly sharp detective, but a detective he is and nothing more'. Similarly, Hawthorne 'had the look all the time, to one who didn't know him, of a rogue who suddenly finds himself in a company of detectives'. There spoke a man who all his life felt himself spied upon. The dark, silent night, for the small Albany boy, 'usually led in the spectral eye of God, and set me to wondering and pondering evermore how I should effectively baffle its gaze'.

To baffle the detective gaze of a suspicious Calvinistic Deity, to find a benign and friendly God, this was to be the troubled quest of Henry James Senior. And it was to leave its mark upon his gifted sons.

2

Away from home lay wood and field. Venturing into the world of Nature he could at least provisionally shake off the vocal prohibitions of the house in North Pearl Street. 'The dawn always found me on my feet,' he wrote when he was old, 'and I can still vividly recall the divine rapture which filled my blood as I pursued under the magical light of morning the sports of the river, the wood or the field.' For the son of William of Albany the days 'bowled themselves out one after another, like waves upon the shore, and as a general thing deafened me by their clamour ... the common ore of existence perpetually converted itself into the gold of life in the glowing fire of my animal spirits ... I lived in every fibre of my body'.

There came a day when the dawn did not find him on his feet and when it seemed indeed that Divine punishment had finally been visited upon him for all his sins.

He was 13 and attending Albany Academy. On summer afternoons the boys would meet one of their teachers in the park in front of the Academy to combine learning with sport. One of their favourite pastimes was balloon-flying. The power was supplied by air heated by a flaming ball of tow saturated with spirits of turpentine. When one of the balloons ignited, the ball would drop and the mass of fire would be rapidly kicked about until extinguished.

On one such afternoon some of the turpentine splashed over Henry's pantaloons. The balloon rose, caught fire; the ball dropped, the boys swooped down upon it. A sharp kick sent the flaming mass through the window of a nearby stable. Quick to realize the danger, Henry rushed into the barn and climbed to the hayloft. In stamping out the ball of fire his turpentine-soaked trousers were ignited.

The burns he suffered were severe. In one leg 'a morbid process in the bone' set in which 'ever and anon called for some sharp surgery'. It was sharp indeed in the era before anaesthesia, when liberal doses of whisky may have dulled but did not eliminate the terror of the knife. The robust boy survived the primitive surgery of the 1820s; but when he left his bed long months after the accident he had lost his leg. It had been amputated above the knee. For two years on his back he had been face to face with the spectral eye. He would no longer be able to pursue the sports of the river, the wood or the field. He was wedded, henceforth, to the pavement or wherever an artificial limb, first of wood and later of cork, could take him; largely, he had to rely on the easy conveyance of horse and carriage. For him, forever, the smoother walks of the cities rather than the free latitudes of the country.

A curious and important thing happened, however, during this time. He discovered that both his father and mother were not as unmindful of his existence as he had believed. He remembered his mother, candle in hand, sleep-walking at night, coming to his bedside during his illness, covering his shoulders, adjusting his pillow, 'just as carefully as if she were awake'. He recalled his father's agony, standing by his son while the surgeons did their work; his sympathies were 'so excessive that my mother had the greatest possible difficulty in imposing due prudence upon his expression of it'. He could say thus that 'my father was weakly, nay painfully, sensitive to his children's claims upon his sympathy; and I myself, when I became a father in my turn, felt that I could freely sacrifice property and life to save my children from unhappiness'. In recording this he reveals to us that, where sensibility was concerned, his mother possessed greater self-control than his father.

He would have remembered William of Albany as an 'indifferent parent' if the accident had not revealed 'his tenderness to me ... so assiduous and indeed extreme as to give me an exalted sense of his affection'. However, the original struggle with his father was never resolved. The years of his illness offered compensations – at best poor ones – for a more serious handicap. But *not-to-do* was now a law because he simply couldn't do. To the frustrations imposed in childhood by Father was added the frustration imposed by an arbitrary act of God. It had deprived him of freedom to roam with his fellowmen. If he felt himself belatedly appreciated, surrounded by doctors and attending anxious parents (and later tutors), he also felt increasingly that there existed between man and the God of his father 'a profound natural enmity'. The thoughtful boy had time, during those long months, to daydream and to read, and to develop a feverish mental life which had to be a substitute for physical activity. With this he mastered a rhetorical, vigorous, aggressive eloquence, that was to be transmitted to his four sons and to his daughter – picturesque phrases, conceits, elaborate flights of the imagination, a mordant wit, as if some fragment of the knife that had pierced his bone had remained in his mind: all this became part of the dismembered young man who one day found himself, at the end of his adolescence, erect again, facing the world on a solitary foot.

3

The elder Henry James entered Union College, Schenectady, in 1828, in conformity with William of Albany's wishes, and asserted his recovered manhood by becoming a spirited young blade, if one can use such a term for a young man-about-town of Schenectady of that era. Liberated from his bed of sickness – and from home – he in-

dulged himself freely in un-Presbyterian luxuries: cigars, smart
clothes, books of an undevout character, oysters. William of Albany
had always kept the loose change for the household expenses in a
drawer of his dressing-table, and when Henry, at 7 or 8, had incurred
expenses by constant frequentation of a confectioner's shop down
the street (and later the informal 'bar') he relieved himself of his debt
by two or three times borrowing freely 'without any thought of
making restitution'. This surrender to Satan remained with him as a
disturbing memory. When he ran up debts, however, at Schenectady,
there was no convenient drawer into which he could plunge his hand
for some silver. Instead, he quite simply gave his creditors drafts on
his opulent parent.

A letter from William of Albany to a friend has survived, in which
the explosive paternal anger emerges in short, breathless sentences.
Henry had

so debased himself as to leave his parents' house in the character of a
swindler etc. etc. – details presented today – are the order which I enclose as a specimen of his progress in arts of low vileness – and unblush-
ing falsehood ... a fellow from Schenactady was after him today for 50
to 60 dollars – (in a note I understand) for segars and oysters.

All this, William of Albany concluded, would certainly 'lodge him
in a prison'. The elder Henry's novelist son, alluding to this episode
as a 'misunderstanding, if not ... a sharp rupture', recalled that there
had been a tradition that his father 'had been for a period quite
definitely "wild"'. The father didn't, however, end up in prison. He
ran away to Boston instead.

It was not an easy pilgrimage for a one-legged man in the days
when there was no railroad from Albany to the city of his flight.
But he made his way to New England, and it is interesting to note, in
the light of the later legend that the Jameses were New Englanders,
that this was the father's only departure from the Hudson Valley in
his youth. He was not to return to Boston, save for brief trips, until
much later, when his children, also natives of the Hudson Valley,
were advancing towards manhood.

In Boston he found a position as a proof-reader, lodged himself
comfortably, and enjoyed the society of the city's first families,
where he was cordially received. The Boston excursion is important
only as it underlines the break between father and son; and although
he later established a truce with Albany and went back to Union

College (he graduated from it in 1830), Henry neither completely placated his parent nor made peace with his own troubled spirit. He attempted the study of law, in accord with his father's wishes; he participated for a spell in the editing of an Albany publication; but he was eternally restless and volatile.

The death of his father only exacerbated the emotional problems fixed in the sturdy young man who now had a comfortably filled purse, yet did not know where to turn. Seeking to understand his misgivings over religion and to comprehend his relationship with God, the elder Henry gravitated to the Princeton Theological Seminary – almost as if to do penance to the ghost of his father. This was in 1835, three years after William of Albany's death. The gesture of submission to the Deity of William did not last long. How could so intense a rebel accept religion, conformity, blind belief? And yet the conviction of God's supernatural being 'was burnt into me as with a red-hot iron'. He has left a vivid picture of his disturbed state of mind :

I doubt whether any lad had ever just so thorough and pervading a belief in God's existence as an outside and contrarious force to humanity ... I am sure no childish sinews were ever more strained than mine were in wrestling with the subtle terror of his name. This insane terror pervaded my consciousness more or less ... made me loath at night to lose myself in sleep, lest his dread hand should clip my thread of life without time for a parting sob of penitence, and grovel at morning dawn with an abject slavish gratitude that the sweet sights and sounds of Nature and of man were still around me.

He had escaped being 'thoughtful, anxious' and the weary slave of terror during his juvenile years. Now he carried his anxieties with him and a perpetual feeling of guilt. He abandoned his theological studies, he settled in New York, he married and became a father; but he remained troubled, as one who had never found quite what he was looking for – nor known quite what he sought. He derived some solace from the friendship of Ralph Waldo Emerson, whom he met shortly after his marriage, and in the marks of respect men began to pay him for his fervour of speech, his intensity, his incisive wit, his devotion to the Scriptures.

In 1843, when his second son – the subject of this biography – was only six months old, he took his family abroad to England. There, in one horrible hour, came the crisis foreshadowed in all the years of his conflict. After that came revelation.

Vastation

IT came (in the image used by his son years later in another but related context) like some beast in the jungle that had long crouched within him for the spring. He had spent the winter in and out of London, meeting Carlyle and the writers and free-thinkers who frequented the sharp-tongued Scotsman's home in Chelsea. He had worked for long hours and days at his desk, seeking an answer in the pages of Genesis to the struggle between physical well-being and Calvinistic spiritual well-being. He had settled his family in Frogmore Cottage, next to the residence of the Duchess of Kent, in Windsor Great Park. His health was good, he was in cheerful spirits, he was interested in his work. It seemed to him that at last he could make some contribution to an understanding of the word of God.

I

One day, towards the end of May 1844, the elder Henry James ate a good meal and remained at the table after his wife and boys had left it. The afternoon was chilly and there was a fire in the grate. He gazed contentedly into the embers, 'feeling only the exhilaration incident to a good digestion'. Relaxed, his mind skirting a variety of thoughts, he suddenly experienced a day-nightmare. It seemed to him that there was an invisible shape squatting in the room, 'raying out from his fetid personality influences fatal to life'. A deathly presence thus unseen had stalked from his mind into the house. Or was this again the sense of being spied upon, this time the spectral eye of the Devil?

He recognized that 'to all appearance it was a perfect insane and abject terror, without ostensible cause' – but it was terror nevertheless and not to be reasoned or talked away. 'The thing had not lasted ten seconds before I felt myself a wreck; that is, reduced from a state of firm, vigorous, joyful manhood to one of almost helpless infancy.' He kept his seat in that room – haunted with the terror of his mind – wanting to run like a child to the foot of the stairs and shout as if calling for his mother, or to the roadside to 'appeal to the public to protect me'. He did neither. He remained motionless, 'beat upon by an ever-growing tempest of doubt, anxiety and despair', until he was able to struggle to his feet and confide the 'sudden burden of inmost, implacable unrest' to his wife.

He consulted eminent physicians. They told him he had overworked his brain and urged upon him open air, cheerful company, a water-cure. The elder Henry obeyed; however, his curious and active mind brooded on his illness. He went to an English watering-place, where the waters did not help but where he was struck by the pastoral beauty of the countryside; and we find him wishing himself a sheep, grazing on a 'placid hillside' and 'drinking in eternal dew and freshness from Nature's lavish bosom'. Later he muses also on the 'heavenly sweetness in the soul of a patient over-driven cab horse, or misused cadger's donkey'. Thus this intellectual now sought identity with the animals, the lowly creatures, subdued and passive – and beaten – servants of man. He discovered that he no longer wanted to study the Scriptures. He became convinced that he had never really wanted to discover Scriptural truth, 'but only to ventilate my own ability in discovering it'. He experienced a sense of 'my downright intellectual poverty and dishonesty'. – He wondered that he could have even pretended to an ability to ferret out the word of God. 'Truth must *reveal itself* if it would be known.' He mentions also that his depression and despair were such that to go for a walk or to sleep in strange surroundings called forth an effort such as might be required to plan a military campaign or write an epic.

The amputation had been a physical ordeal when the boyish frame could triumph over the shock. The second experience, twenty years after the first, was a collapse of mental well-being. Evil, to put it in theological terms, in that shape that squatted invisible, had come to reveal to the elder Henry James that he must not question the word of God but await the Truth of Divine Revelation. On psychological ground, we might say that he was suffering from nervous exhaustion after years of inner doubt. The terror of defying Fathers and escaping spectral eyes was finally too much for him. He chose the one escape possible : return to the innocence of childhood.

I had nevertheless on the whole been in the habit of ascribing to the Creator . . . an outside discernment of the most jealous scrutiny, and had accordingly put the greatest possible alertness into his service and worship, until my will, as you have seen – thoroughly fagged out as it were with the formal, heartless, endless task of conciliating a stony-hearted Deity – actually collapsed.

The time had come in the life of the elder Henry James to make his peace with the gods, household and universal, so that he should have to conciliate neither; for if the task were endless, life would lose its meaning; he would live forever on the edge of the abyss. That way lay madness. Within him the will to live, the will to manhood, eventually triumphed over the distintegrating forces of a divided self. The revelation came in unexpected form through the medium of a mother-like figure whose name has been preserved for us only as that of Mrs Chichester.

2

She lived in the vicinity of the watering-place and was considered by the elder Henry to be 'a lady of rare qualities of heart and mind, and of personal loveliness as well'. One day she asked him what had brought him to seek a water-cure. Her sympathetic inquiry provoked a ready response; he poured out the story of his visitation in all its horror. She listened attentively and then she spoke to this effect:

It is, then, very much as I had ventured to suspect from two or three previous things you have said: you are undergoing what Swedenborg calls a *vastation*; and though, naturally, you yourself are despondent or even despairing about the issue, I cannot help taking an altogether hopeful view of your prospects.

The words were balm for Henry James. He inquired about Swedenborg – he had never read him. Mrs Chichester explained that the *vastation* was, in Swedenborgian thought, one stage in the regenerative process of man – awakening, purgation, illumination – and that a new birth for man was the secret of Divine Creation and Providence. She admitted she was but an amateur in these matters, but the elder James had heard enough. He journeyed post-haste to London and purchased two of Emanuel Swedenborg's works – *Divine Love and Wisdom* and *Divine Providence*. The doctors had warned him not to exercise his brain; he began therefore by merely nibbling at the books. This he found a torture; his interest grew 'frantic'; finally he threw caution to the winds and plunged in. He said later that his heart divined even before his intelligence seized the truth he found in Swedenborg. His strict Swedenborgian readers agreed; they said that Henry James projected into Swedenborgian thought many of his own beliefs and ideas. The Swedish seer provided the ailing man with a kind of mental healing that strengthened and saved and altered the course of his life. For what, in effect, had the motherly Mrs Chichester told Henry but that what had happened to him had happened to other men, that he could undergo rejuvenation, that he must not be afraid of confronting God, his father, for God intended him to be reborn. Henry formulated it himself: 'I had no doubt that this being or self of mine ... came originally as a gift from the hand of God; but I had just as little doubt that the moment the gift had left God's hand ... it became as essentially independent of him in all spiritual or subjective regards as the soul of a child is of its earthly father.' And independence of his earthly father was what he needed to effect his cure, even though his father had been dead for more than a decade. His novelist son was to recall later that his father never travelled without the red-bound Swedenborgian volumes in his luggage; he remembered them as a 'majestic array' forming 'the purplest rim of his library's horizon'. With the discovery of Swedenborg the senior Henry 'passed rapidly into that grateful infinitude of recognition and application which he was to inhabit for the rest of his days'.

He discovered finally that there was for him a God residing in infinite wisdom and love. Since Man was made in God's image, Man too could dispense love and wisdom. Henry James began to lecture and give of himself in brilliant talk, in friendship and at times in an almost ecstatic devotion to his family. He no longer struggled with the Deity of Discipline and Absolute Obedience. He could now remake the God of his father – and by the same token his father, too – in his own image. He could *be* his father. In this manner he found a God that corresponded with his own expansive spirit. Emanuel Swedenborg contributed to his spiritual liberation, teaching him that

God's great work was wrought not in the minds of individuals here and there, as my theology taught me, but in the very stuff of human nature itself, in the very commonest affections and appetites and passions of universal man, a transforming, redeeming, regenerating work, which shall lift all mankind into endless union with God.

3

Henry James had found the New Heaven. Now in Charles Fourier he found the 'scientific insight' for the new life on earth. Fourier furnished 'disclosures of the harmonies which are possible to humanity, in every sphere whether of its passions or active administration, as stamped with God's own truth'. Fourier's 'practical' social science could in a sense be read as complementing the doctrine of Swedenborg. Man made in the image of God had God-given instincts. To inhibit them, as civilization did, was to violate the will and the intention of God. 'Every appetite and passion of man's nature is good and beautiful, and destined to be fully enjoyed,' James wrote in consonance with Fourier, whom he began to read and study while he was still recovering from the *vastation*.

Fourier's ideas had taken firm hold of America in those early decades of the nineteenth century. 'We are all a little wild here with numberless projects of social reform,' Emerson wrote to Carlyle in the autumn of 1840. 'Not a reading man but has a draft of a new Community in his waistcoat pocket.' In 1846, two years after Henry James's discovery of Swedenborg, the French social thinker had an estimated 200,000 followers in the United States. His proposals to establish communal societies, social units (*phalanxes*), from which competition might be banished and an harmonious social order achieved, constituted an enlargement of the very ideas which the Transcendentalists at Concord were preaching – the fuller realization of Man. We know that some twenty years after the elder Henry's first reading of Fourier his name was still respectfully invoked in the James family. Henry Junior's boyhood friend, Thomas Sergeant Perry, recalled that 'it was near Lily Pond [in Newport] that we long discussed Fourier's plan for regenerating the world. Harry had heard his father describe the great reformer's proposal to establish universal happiness and like a good son he tried to carry the good news further.'

The future novelist was a very small boy when his father, turning from the self-centred analysis of his relations with God, began to contemplate society around him. As with Swedenborg, he adapted Fourier (and we might add Rousseau) to his needs. These doctrines sufficed for a lifetime. The elder Henry's last book, published three years before his death, reflected this marriage of Society and God;

it bore the title *Society the Redeemed Form of Man and the Earnest of God's Omnipotence in Human Nature*. His son William later said that he had devoted his life to the elaboration of 'one single bundle of truths', a fresh conception of God and of our connection with Him. Evil for the father were the constraints which civilization put upon the individual; they prevented him from fulfilling his God-given destiny, since the individual owes all he has to his inheritance and to the society in which he is born. 'Make society do its duty to the individual, and the individual will be sure to do his duties to society.' With this the elder James had supreme confidence that God would not fail man in his hour of need. He looked to the day when 'the sexual relations will be regulated in every case by the private will of the parties; when the reciprocal affection of a man and a woman will furnish the sole and sufficient sanction of their material converse'. To a correspondent he wrote : 'Let us permit divorce whenever the parties desire it, in order that the name of marriage may be utterly dissociated with the idea of bondage.'

4

His life after his return to America was no longer an exhausting battle with himself, although his mercurial temperament remained unchanged. A growing family of four boys and a girl testified to his fertility, and now his writings began to multiply. He published them at his own expense. They never reached a wide public. They contain evidence of a continual self-questioning and an unfinished search for inner harmony; they reflect the welling up of emotion that sometimes clouded logic and reason, yet they constitute a body of religio-social thought essentially 'Jamesian' with the stamp of the father's individual rhetoric. He could throw off quaint conceits : 'If the Deity were an immense Duck capable only of emitting an eternal quack we of course should all have been born web-footed, each as infallible in his way as the Pope, nor ever have been at the expense and bother of swimming schools.' His style at its best is pithy, enthusiastic, good-humoured; yet it is recondite. William Dean Howells observed that his interpretations of Swedenborg, 'which sentence by sentence were so brilliantly suggestive, had sometimes a collective opacity which the most resolute vision could not penetrate'. Howells observed that Mr James in writing *The Secret of Swedenborg* had kept the secret very well.

He lectured, he indulged in polemic, he even had a few disciples.

He was universally respected and became a local celebrity among the élite of New York and New England. He was a friend of Greeley, Ripley and Dana. Through Emerson he came to know the Transcendentalists – Margaret Fuller, William Ellery Channing, Bronson Alcott. Thoreau called on him when Henry Junior was in his cradle; Thackeray came to see him during an American tour. He had a host of transatlantic Swedenborgian friends, most notable of these being J. J. Garth Wilkinson, a London doctor and writer. James was considered a genial and eminently likeable man. Emerson said he had 'heroic manners', found in him a 'serenity like the sun', and considered his lectures 'brilliant'. Thoreau, after first calling on him, said he had never been 'more kindly and faithfully catechized'. He found him 'patient and determined to have the good of you'. Carlyle discovered 'something sly and skittish in the man, but a brave heart intrinsically, with sound, earnest sense, with plenty of insight and even humour'. And again Howells :

His written style had traits of bold adventurousness, but it was his speech which was most captivating. As I write of him I see him before me : his white bearded face, with a kindly intensity which at first glance seemed fierce, the mouth humorously shaping the moustache, the eyes vague behind the glasses; his sensitive hand gripping the stick on which he rested his weight to ease it from the artificial limb he wore.

The elder Henry James, on his side, was an unusually affectionate man. He began always by liking; but often the great of his time, from their position of authority, seemed to him like gods, fathers, dictators, and hidden hostilities in Henry Senior's nature would escape from the tip of his tongue or his pen. Even the benign Emerson was not spared. Henry James could see him as 'a soul full of doors and windows' and find that an 'unmistakable breath of the morning encircles him, and the odour of primeval woods'; he could call him, also, a 'man without a handle'. Bronson Alcott, with whom he had sharp verbal tilts, was once informed that he was 'an egg, half-hatched'. He had seen Carlyle as 'an artist, a wilful artist', yet finally he wrote in disillusion that he was the child of Mother Eve's 'most melancholy old age', who 'used to bury his worn, dejected face in her penurious lap, in a way so determined as forever to shut out all sight of God's new and better creation'. On renewed acquaintance the Scotsman was 'the same old sausage, fizzing and sputtering in his own grease'.

A man who could caricature with so free a hand had a compelling need to trim his fellow mortals to the measure of himself. 'My intelligence is the necessary digestive apparatus for my life,' he once said, and indeed the regenerated Henry James fed hungrily upon all that came within his purview. His contemporaries felt that he lived too much by his intelligence; and there remained something rather ineffectual about him – he seemed so much an addict of talk without thought for action; a dream of a utopia seemed to suffice. He appeared to conceive of society as a kind of happy anarchy. The personality moulded in the Albany household, with the strong effervescent spirit of Ireland in his mind and speech, conditioned by the accident, 'leisured' by the enterprise of the immigrant father, was a passive intellectual. He could lecture on art, on property, on democracy, on theology, but he remained fundamentally aloof from the core of action. Thus he never interested himself in the details of Fourier's planning, embracing only his ideas on the brotherhood of man and exalting his general principles. His opponents might indeed have applied to him the strictures he applied to Carlyle. One of them, having something of Henry's verbal gifts, did attack him as belonging to the

class of purely ideal reformers. men who will lounge at their ease upon damask sofas and dream of a harmonic and beautiful world to be created hereafter, a mere *jet d'eau* of aspiration, reaching a higher elevation at some point than any other man, but breaking into spray and impalpable mist, glittering in the sun, and descending to earth with no weight or mechanical force to effect any great end.

The elder Henry continued to lead an inner life, sallying forth among men, but returning quickly to his hearth to be at his greatest ease next to his wife who mothered him as she mothered her offspring.

5

Henry James was married, four years before his *vastation*, to Mary Robertson Walsh, sister of a fellow-student at Princeton Seminary. The Walshes were a prosperous family, as stoutly Presbyterian as the Albany Jameses. They were descended from Hugh Walsh, an Irishman of English extraction who came from Killyleagh, County Down, in 1764 and settled at Newburg, New York, and from a Scotsman, Alexander Robertson, who arrived in the United States on the

eve of the Revolution and attained civic prominence in Manhattan.
The future mother of a cosmopolitan novelist and a great American
philosopher was a woman of sterling domestic virtues, strongly
Calvinist and of a down-to-earth literalness of mind. She and her
younger sister Catherine Walsh would sit in the family parlour at No.
19 Washington Square and listen to the strange and vivid eloquence
of the young Albany scion, as he expounded his unorthodox religious views; and the flame of his words warmed the inscrutable
Mary Walsh as they did her handsome sister. Both were charmed
and spellbound. In due course he proposed to the elder sister and was
accepted. The drama in this wooing is lost to us; but it is reflected in
the novelist's works. Catherine Walsh became a member of the
James household, lived and travelled with her sister's family and
was in every way a second mother to the James children if not a
second wife to the elder Henry. Lively, spirited, with much wit, she
was more outgoing than her elder sister. She married, late in life,
but perhaps she had waited too long, for shortly afterwards she and
her husband parted and she resumed her perpetual role of the family
aunt among her kinsfolk.

In later years, in talk with Emerson, the elder James told him that
on seeing Mary Walsh 'the flesh said It is fc me, and the spirit said
It is for me'. So successful was he in weaning Mary Walsh from
orthodoxy that she consented to a purely civil marriage. 'To mark
the rueful rupture,' her son wrote, 'it had invoked one evening, with
the aid of India muslin and a wondrous gold head-band, in the
maternal . . . "parlours" [of No. 19 Washington Square] . . . the secular nuptial consecration of the then Mayor of New York – I think Mr
Varick.' The evening was 28 July 1840. The mayor was not Mr
Varick but Isaac Leggett Varian. The bride was 30, her husband 29.

They did not set up house immediately. There were spacious
family houses in Albany and New York to accommodate the newly-
married. They spent some time near Catharine Barber James. Then
they moved briefly into No. 5 Washington Square, and thereafter
lived at the Astor House, the great new hotel of Manhattan of that
day. Here the first son was born in January of 1842, and it was probably this which prompted the elder Henry to seek a more permanent
home. He purchased No. 21 Washington Place for $18,000 from his
younger brother, John James – a brick house a block off the Square,
near Green Street. By March the family was installed. This was the
month the elder Henry met Ralph Waldo Emerson for the first time

and, it is said, brought him home to see the new-born babe, named William after the grandfather.

A year later, directing Thoreau how to find him in Washington Place, Henry James described the street as running from the Square to Broadway, 'flanked on one corner by the university and on the opposite by a church'. In this home, within a stone's throw of these symbols of organized religion and systematized scholarship – from which he was always to remain aloof – was born on 15 April 1843, 'another fine little boy', as the father proudly announced to Emerson. 'Tell Mrs James,' Emerson replied, 'that I heartily greet her on the new friend, though little now, that has come to her hearth.'

3

Keystone of the Arch

MARY JAMES, the wife and mother, moves with so quiet a step for so brief a space through the pages of her son's copious memoirs that we glimpse only a phantasmal form and catch only a distant echo of her voice – as if it were drowned in the clamour of her children and the undisciplined eloquence of her husband. The senior Henry spoke of her 'sleepless' sense of justice, and Henry Junior described as 'soundless' her 'all-saving service and trust'. Her daughter Alice spoke of her 'selfless devotion'. *Soundless, selfless, sleepless*, linked with such words as justice, service, trust and devotion, convey an image of an august and omniscient personage walking with unheard step through a household where justice and mercy had to be dispensed even-handed and with generosity among contending factions. Implied also was a figure devoted and loyal, vigilant and unrelaxed. It was as if she simply 'embodied the unconscious essence of wife-and-motherhood', her daughter said. 'She was our life, she was the house,' Henry Junior wrote in his notebook just after her death. He added, 'she was the keystone of the arch'.

I

The picture that has come down to us describing Mary James as 'self-effacing' suggests a weakness or at least an impassivity that clearly did not exist. To have been the 'keystone' of the James family arch required strength and firmness and an ability to control and weather high emotional tempests. This Mary James appears to have been able to do all her life. Holding 'a firm rein', she wrote once in a letter to her son Wilkinson, 'is especially my forte'. It was. She was a strong woman, strengthened by the worship of her husband and the love of her four sons and daughter, who accepted her not only as their devoted mother but also as the exalted figure of their father's veneration. It was the age of Victoria in England, and the image projected from over the seas of a Supreme Queen reigning with a Consort was thoroughly familiar to the little Jameses.

Mary James seems to have governed with a certain grace and a quiet unperturbed dignity. Her domain itself was, however, far from quiet. Two accounts of meal-times in the James household, when the boys were in their teens, give us a picture not only of a commingling of food and disputation, but also of the happy turbulence that could prevail : Garth Wilkinson makes a remark and is challenged by his younger brother Robertson. Henry Junior emerges from his silence to defend Wilky. William joins in. Finally the father seeks to act as moderator. Ralph Waldo Emerson's son Edward, who described this scene went on to say that the voice of the moderator

presently would be drowned by the combatants and he soon came down vigorously into the arena, and when in the excited argument the dinner knives might not be absent from eagerly gesticulating hands, dear Mrs James, more conventional, but bright as well as motherly, would look at me, laughingly reassuring, saying 'Don't be disturbed, Edward; they won't stab each other. This is usual when the boys come home.'

'I remember,' writes another witness, E. L. Godkin, the founder and editor of the *Nation*, 'it was not unusual for the sons to invoke humorous curses on their parent, one of which was that "his mashed potatoes might always have lumps in them !"'

Mary James was quite equal to this family rivalry which emerged in the presence of eye-witnesses, and even to the stormier tussles and bursts of open warfare at other times. The mother has left us a vivid piece of testimony of the infantile struggle for power which takes us back into the James family nursery in Albany. In 1846 she wrote to Mrs J. J. Garth Wilkinson, her third son's English godmother :

Your little Wilkie has come out for himself since the birth of little Rob. He seemed thereupon to take the hint, and seeing that he was about to be shoved off, concluded to let us see how well he could take care of himself. He began to walk when the baby was two weeks old, took at once into his own hand the redress of his grievances which he seems to think are manifold, and has become emphatically the *ruling* spirit in the nursery. Poor little soul! my pity I believe would be more strongly excited for him were he less able or ready to take his own part, but as his strength of arm or of will seldom fails him, he is too often left to fight his own battles.

Allowing for possible maternal embellishment, we are given the impression that Mary James followed a not always happy policy of *laissez-faire* in the nursery. Indeed the battles continued far beyond infancy.

For relaxation I go to the Jameses, the parents are away, and those unhappy children fight like cats and dogs [wrote T. S. Perry when he was a student at Harvard and the James boys in their late teens]. The other evening I went there, and stayed for about an hour and a half, during 3/3 of which time Willie [Harry?] was trying to obtain solitude in the library, with the rest of the family pounding at the door, and rushing in all the time. He so far forgot himself at one time as to try to put and lock me out of the house. It was a terrible sight, and I can assure you I pitied poor Harry, and asked him to come and stay with me.

The James residence was rarely tranquil while the boys were growing up.

2

A photograph of Mary James, taken two years before her death when she was 70, shows a woman in the characteristic pose of resigned elderly maternity: the black taffeta trimmed with lace and the greying hair parted in the middle upon which has been mounted the carefully-composed lace cap; the hands are folded, the lips pursed to a single, hard line. The nose is prominent, the eyes are keen, the forehead is high. If we make allowance for the fact that sitting for one's photograph then was a somewhat more intense matter than it is today, her countenance suggests a purposeful, strong-willed and determined woman. Her daughter Alice remembered her as the central source of comfort and security in the family:

Father's sudden return at the end of thirty-six hours – having left to be gone for a fortnight – with Mother beside him holding his hand, and we five children pressing close round him 'as if he had just been saved from drowning' and he pouring out as he alone could the agonies of desolation through which he had come.

And we glimpse her in middle life in a few casual words set down by William James in a letter: 'Mother is recovering from one of her indispositions, which she bears like an angel, doing any amount of work at the same time, putting up cornices and raking out the garret-room like a little buffalo.'

Mary James herself left this brief self-sketch in a letter to William: 'The poor old Mater wears well I am happy to say; strong in the back, strong in the nerves, and strong in the legs so far, and equal to her day.' She was indeed equal; and the emphasis must be placed, perhaps, on the phrase 'strong in the nerves'.

During the early years of the marriage the family tore up its roots continually. Henry Junior later spoke of himself and his brothers and sister as having been 'hotel children'. In addition to moves between New York and Albany there were two trips to Europe, major undertakings at that time, with sojourns in England, France and Switzerland. The young children had to be cared for under conditions of travel far-removed from the modern transatlantic liner; the stage-coach and carriage were still important adjuncts to the primitive railroads. Mary James always had domestic help, and took an American nursemaid with her to Europe when the children were small. She also engaged French maids, governesses, tutors. In addition, she was aided by her only sister, as we have seen, the 'Aunt Kate' of Henry James's letters and memoirs. Her lot as mother was eased considerably by her husband's comfortable means; but there were always responsibilities and worries, illnesses and accidents.

Despite these cares there were the compensations of a busy maternal life: she took justifiable pride in her growing children; she was surrounded by affection; she was devoted to her husband and wrote of him with deep feeling: 'All that he has to say seems so good and glorious and easily understood to him, but it falls so dead upon the dull or sceptical ears who come to hear him.' She participated in his dream of a Heaven on Earth. Her novelist son described her as always sitting on the steps of her husband's 'temple' of Swedenborg, which stood in 'the centre of our family life', catching the 'reverberations of the inward mystic choir'. Apparently the reverberations sufficed. The father once said that his wife had not been 'intellectually speaking' a 'liberal education' to him – but, he added, 'she really did arouse my heart'.

3

In her later years Mary James wrote every Sunday morning to her
scattered sons, dispensing brief, factual reports of the local happenings in Cambridge, interlarding counsel with concern about health
and with affectionate platitudes, and in general revealing those attributes we would associate with a 'typical' American mother who has
a firm hold on her family. She speaks in one of these of 'my pen
which runs so fluently and lovingly every *Sunday* ... over a full
sheet, sometimes more'. The letters are indeed fluent, but literal, the
spelling not always certain, the formulations homely, prosaic, the
handwriting precise, sharp, thin. 'God bless you my darling boy and
help you to be manly and generous in your intercourse with one
another and with all about you.' 'All are well – Father has gotten
over his sleeplessness and Aunt Kate is flourishing.' 'Deal honestly
with yourself and with us, and try and observe closely what effect
perfect rest has upon you, and act accordingly.' 'Harry went to Newport for a few days, Mrs Frank Shaw is there. Your Boston friends
keep you *au courant* of what is going on there. There is no news
here. Love from all.'

Not all her letters had such a homely air. She could smother Henry
with maternal solicitude and denounce William, during his prolonged period of ill-health, as a too-articulate hypochondriac. 'The
trouble with him is that he *must express* every fluctuation of feeling
and especially every unfavourable symptom,' she wrote to Henry.
'He keeps his good looks, but whenever he speaks of himself, says
he is no better. This I cannot believe to be the true state of the case,
but his temperament is a morbidly hopeless one, and with this he has
to contend all the time, as well as with his physical disability.' In a
later letter she says: 'If, dear Harry, you could only have imparted
to him a few grains of your own blessed hopefulness, he would have
been well long ago.' Her characterization of her eldest son at a difficult point in his life has a quality that we cannot associate with a
'self-effacing' mother, any more than we can the possessiveness she
showed towards her second son. She tells him shortly after he has
settled in London that what is lacking in his life is the affection she
could give him were he at home, 'your life must need this succulent,
fattening element more than you know yourself'. Since she cannot
be with him in England, she offers him the familiar motherly counsel

that he take a wife: 'You know Father used to say to you, that if you would only fall in love it would be the making of you.' There was, however, a great measure of truth in the father's insight: it would take his son a lifetime to learn to love.

When William was 26 and travelling in Germany, the admonition came from Quincy Street: 'Beware dear Willy of the fascinations of Fräulein Clara Schmidt, or any other such artful charmers. You know your extreme susceptibility, or rather I know it, so I say *beware.*' And when Henry at 30 was travelling in Italy and Switzerland, he still received counsel: 'You will without doubt fall some day soon into the arms of Mrs Lombard and Fanny, who I am told are to spend the summer in Montreux. They are both I imagine great invalids, so avoid committing yourself further than you can help with them.' Or she might simply complain, 'Another mail dear Harry, and no letter. I am trying not to be anxious.'

There was something strong-yet-yielding, firm-yet-soft about Mary James. Behind the façade of 'selflessness' was a quiet method of holding the 'firm rein' of which she boasted. She was, in Henry's words, 'our protecting spirit, our household genius', and yet there was an ambiguous quality about her protection. She could voice opposition to her children's ideas or plans, yet if in turn she was firmly resisted, she could yield with confusing promptness. She was inconsistent in her firmness; and this firmness itself was in contradiction to her husband's theory that children should be 'free and uncommitted'. A parental tug-and-pull upon the emotions of their offspring that was alike irrational and anxiety-provoking gives a deep significance to Henry James's remark in later years that in childhood 'we wholesomely breathed inconsistency and ate and drank contradictions'. When he was younger he did not find this 'wholesome'. On the contrary, it showed a too generous contempt for facts. His life would be a long search to understand the ambiguous world of his childhood.

4

In retrospect Henry James was conscious of 'our sense of her gathered life in us and of her having no other'. He also describes his mother as the 'so widely open yet so softly-enclosing lap' of his father's 'liberties and all our securities'. Thus in the junior Henry's picture the mother envelops the family, the father disappears in her 'enclosing lap', the children are taken up in her softness and she becomes all-encompassing. 'She *was* he, *was* each of us,' he wrote after she had been dead thirty years. 'She was patience, she was wisdom, she was exquisite maternity,' he had written at the time of her death. This is an exaltation of the mother to a supremacy not uncommon in American households. Nevertheless, it is striking that both Henry and William James, who talked often of their father in later years, had little to say of their mother. And when Henry came to write of his parents in *Notes of a Son and Brother* he gave her only a few ambiguous paragraphs. His nephew, William's eldest son, inquired into the reason for this; the answer was: 'Oh! my dear boy – that memory is too sacred.'

The memory undoubtedly was 'sacred'. Yet the remark could also have been an evasion, for the brief passages concerning the mother in the autobiographies reveal to some extent Henry James's difficulty in seeing her as she really was. He asks questions, he wonders, he justifies, but mainly he idealizes. We may speculate that he experienced difficulty simply because he was emotionally confused by his memories, and rather than record the confusion, he took refuge in the 'sacredness' of the tomb. The confusion, however, emerges in spite of himself, and nowhere more sharply than when he begins to muse about her identity. 'The only thing I might well have questioned ... was the possibility on the part of a selflessness so consistently and unabatedly active, of its having anything ever left *acutely* to offer.' He refers to this also as her 'inaptness for the personal claim' and leaves us wondering how much Mary James did 'offer'. He tries to explain: 'She lived in ourselves so exclusively with such a want of use for anything in her consciousness that was not about us and for us, that I think we almost contested her being separate enough to be proud of us – it was too like our being proud of ourselves.' It is almost as if he were saying that without her family Mary James ceased to have an identity.

She makes her sole appearance in *Notes of a Son and Brother* as a 'pipeline' or conveyor of 'Father's ideas' to her son – ideas he held himself 'little framed to share'. It was the way in which she listened to her husband that gave them some meaning for Henry Junior. He pictures Mary James as a support 'on which my father rested with the absolute whole of his weight'. She listened with the 'whole of her usefulness' and also 'the whole of her tenderness' and 'with a smoothness of surrender that was like an array of all the perceptions'. She had a 'complete availability'.

Henry Junior saw his father as living only by his mother, and what he observed as a small boy was borne out for him when fully grown. After his mother's death, the father was incapable of going on without her: 'he passed away or went out, with entire simplicity, promptness and ease, for the definite reason that his support had failed'. It showed the son 'more intimately still what in this world of cleft components one human being can yet be for another, and how a form of vital aid may have operated for years with such perfection'. However much Henry Senior was an individual in his own right, robust and essentially active, what struck the small boy was his dependency on Mary James. He gives us a vivid glimpse of a little parental drama. The children were allowed to go to ballets and plays but not to the elder Henry's lectures. He remembered his mother putting him to bed and then leaving with the father. Henry Junior climbs down to the parlour in the 14th Street house and from the window watches the departure. There is a little act of pantomime at the carriage door. By the light of the street lamp the father produces from a coat-tail pocket his lecture notes and shakes them in the face of his companion. The mother is the central figure in the pantomime. It is she, earnest and confident, who makes sure that the father has forgotten nothing.

It was the father who, at Christmas, weakened and gave his children a snatched view of the packaged gifts making them promise not to tell their mother. It was to the father that little Alice wrote: 'We have had two dear letters from you and find you are the same dear old good-for-nothing homesick papa as ever.' His homesickness was but one of the established family jokes. Henry Junior remembered that 'we all used brutally to jeer at him; and I doubtless as hard as the rest'. The son records a crucial instance.

The happiest household pleasantry invested our legend of our mother's fond habit of address, 'Your father's *ideas*, you know—!' which was always the signal for our embracing her with the last responsive finality (and, for the full pleasure of it, in his presence). Nothing indeed so much as his presence encouraged the licence.

This was more than 'oedipal' – it was alliance with strength against what seemed to him weakness.

'We were delightedly derisive with her,' Henry adds, 'even about pride in our father.' William James participated in such occasions as well. Once when the father was at work on one of his abstruse volumes, he sketched the frontispiece for it: a picture of a man flogging a dead horse! The household pleasantries, however bright and funny, had a brutal directness.

Before the little boy's observant eyes there was this ever-present picture of ambiguity and reversal of relation: a father strong, robust, manly, yet weak and feminine, soft and yielding, indulging his children at every turn; and a mother, strong, firm, but irrational and contradictory. Ralph Touchett, musing about his parents in *The Portrait of a Lady*, thinks 'His father as he had often said to himself, was the more motherly; his mother, on the other hand, was paternal, and even, according to the slang of the day, gubernatorial.' In the guise of fiction it was much easier for James to be candid: and behind the elaborate formulations of *Notes of a Son and Brother*, this is, in effect, what he is trying to say to us in his old age.

5

The future novelist accepted the queenship of his mother and her authority; it was less easy to understand the strange light in which a reversal of parental roles placed the father. The portrait Henry James drew of his father in *Notes of a Son and Brother* sixty years later reflects the ambiguity a child would experience in discovering the male parent in such a situation. Behind a warm show of affection, reflecting his conscious feelings towards the senior Henry, we catch his uncertainties. Every now and again the father peeps from behind his son's flowing sentences as an ineffectual old man; and Henry occasionally slips in an undesigned word of contempt. 'Our dear parent', we find him saying at one point, 'could have told us very little, in all probability, under whatever pressure what had become of anything.' He 'could answer with the radiant when one challenged him with the obscure', he also responded 'with the general when one pulled at the particular'. It was a matter of concern to the little Henry that he could not give his father a paternal identity that conformed with the identity of other fathers. The senior Henry seemed unlike them in more respects than that of his missing limb. Henry Junior pressed him to say how he could describe him to his schoolfellows. 'Say I'm a philosopher, say I'm a seeker for truth, say I'm a lover of my kind, say I'm an author of books if you like; or best of all, just say I'm a student.' This was hardly helpful; other boys could describe their fathers as merchants, doctors or lawyers.

The father listed no occupation for himself in the New York directory until 1854–5 when he finally inserted 'author' after his name.

We have no evidence of Henry's feelings concerning his father's
amputated state.* He makes no allusion to it save as 'a grave accident in early life' in A Small Boy. In Notes of a Son and Brother,
however, he does specify that the accident 'lamed him for life'. In
this volume he equates the lameness with his father's inability to be
a large literary success. In fact he begins the portrait of the elder
Henry with the observation that his writings brought him 'no ghost
of a reward'. He then goes on to describe the good qualities in his
prose but criticizes him for not having a characteristic 'style'. 'I so
suffered ... under the impression of his style, which affected me as
somehow too philosophic for life, and at the same time too living ...
for thought.' It is 'monotonous' and 'verbally repetitive', and he
records a 'shade of irritation' at finding it 'narrow', devoid of
imagery and above all lacking in variety. And he wonders whether
there is any relationship between his father's crippled state and his
apparent vagueness.

Henry decides that there is. 'The two acceptances melt together
for me – that of the limits of his material action, his doing and
enjoying, set so narrowly, and that of his scant allowance of "public
recognition" or of the support and encouragement that spring, and
spring so naturally and rightly,' from a message 'richly and sincerely
urged'. The novelist knew he had far out-distanced his father. What
he overlooked was how successful, within its limits, his father's
life had been, despite his accident, what resources of fortitude and
optimism he had, even if his books were obscure.

6

From the daydreams recorded in his notebooks, from his tales, from
his observations in the memoirs, we can fathom the effect on the
young Henry of this view of the parental relationship which remained with him throughout his life. At some stage the thought
came to him that men derive strength from the women they marry,
and that conversely women can deprive men both of strength and
life. Mothers – women – apparently were expected to give them-

* William James's interest in amputated persons is attested by a paper
entitled 'The Consciousness of Lost Limbs' (Proceedings of the American
Society for Psychical Research, Vol 1, No. 3).

selves wholly, submerge themselves (he uses the word *availability* twice in describing Mary James) in their family. Men used women, were propped up by them and sometimes could not go on living after they were dead. Women could control the lives of men, and this he believed had happened to his father. A father demanded the mother's complete attention ('the whole of her usefulness ... the whole of her tenderness'). Similarly, women could command the abject worship of men.

This led to further considerations. What happens to anyone who gives himself to another? To love – was not that to renounce? Did not the mother give all of herself? What did she have left *acutely* to offer? Selfless, sleepless, soundless ... ('there are few things more soundless,' Henry wrote in one of his novels 'than a deep devotion'). Is the man therefore a threat to the woman in a love relationship? (It was clear enough to him that the woman could be a threat to the man.) Would the man collapse and become weak (like the senior Henry) if he ever allowed himself to love a woman? To be a man and to take a woman for wife – was that not something to be feared? In the James family annals there seemed to be answers: women were strong and survived their men, or if they did not, then somehow the men could not continue to live. The man seemed doomed. Grandmother James had lived on in triumphant old age reading the lady novelists with a tall candle set straight between her eyes and the page. Mary James was strong – the father revealed this by all his words and deeds – and when she died the sacred fount from which the father had derived life and strength was dried up. There was his mother's Cousin Helen, whose husband was a 'spectral spouse', a 'dim little gentleman'. Once a seafaring man, he walked the length of his two parlours as if they were the deck of a ship; and Cousin Helen ruled her wards, Albert and Henry, with an iron hand. On all sides strong-minded women swallowed up their men.

Henry James did not reason in this fashion : but these equations emerge as fictional themes : and in particular what we might call the 'vampire theme', elaborated in three of his works, early, middle and late, recording the observed reality of his father's subservience to his mother and the perhaps less consciously observed fashion in which she in turn took strength from him. In *De Grey: A Romance*, written when he was 26, an old family curse destines brides of the De Greys to early death. When the curse is resisted it is reversed : De Grey himself must die. The prospect of marriage proves fatal in this case for the man. In *Longstaff's Marriage*, written at 35, Longstaff is dying of his love for Diana but recovers miraculously when she rejects him; then it is she who fades and dies. The prospect of marriage can prove fatal to a man unless the woman is removed. Then it is fatal to the woman. And finally in the short novel of Henry James's fifty-seventh year, *The Sacred Fount*, the theme attains its full morbidity: an acute and hyper-sensitive observer spends a week-end in a country house studying what he believes to be the way in which couples deplete one another. From *Roderick Hudson* to *The Ambassadors* and in the tales the permutations and combinations of this situation are played out: the observer is obsessed by the relationships between people, as if the little Henry, looking at his father and mother, and the ever-present Aunt Kate, never quite grasped what occurred between them. Mothers in James's novels are sometimes the negative and long-suffering Mrs Hudsons or the permissive Mrs Millers, or sometimes terrifying creatures who dominate the lives of their progeny. Both types mirror the two aspects of Mary James. Fear of women and worship of women: the love-theme plays itself out in striking fashion throughout Henry James's work. And usually love, in these fictions, as one critic has put it, is 'a deterrent to the full life'. It is more: it is a threat to life itself.

In a list of names he set down in his notebooks when he was 50, Henry James included that of 'Ledward', and then, as was often his custom, he improvised several variants, Ledward-Bedward-Dedward-Deadward. This appeared to be a casual rhyming of led-bed-dead. It was, in effect, a highly condensed statement springing from Henry's mind of the themes of *De Grey*, *Longstaff*, *The Sacred Fount* or that story of Mérimée's he liked so much in his youth, *La Vénus d'Ille*. To be led to the marriage bed was to be dead.

Henry James accordingly chose the path of safety. He remained celibate.

Mere Junior

THE male child born in 1843 in Washington Place was named Henry after the father, even as his elder brother had been named William after the grandfather. For the next forty years he was destined to be known as Henry James Junior. All his works, up to and including *The Portrait of a Lady*, carried the junior label on their title-pages. Throughout his life Henry volubly protested against the parental failure to let him have a distinctive name and (by the same token) an identity of his own. He pleaded with vehemence against the conferring of juniorhood upon a 'helpless babe'. When William James's second son was about to be named William (the first having been promptly named Henry), the novelist sent a fervent plea from London to Cambridge adjuring his brother to cut short the dynastic confusion. William, however, paid no heed. The new William James grew to manhood, married, had a son. And the novelist, by now an Olympian of three score and ten, promptly renewed his plea, this time in 2,000 vigorous words, against a practice to which he could never be reconciled. He had argued that the name given to a child can affect his whole life. Now he couldn't 'but feel sorry that you are embarking upon that unfortunate *mere* junior. I have a right to speak of that appendage – I carried it about for forty years ... disliking it all the while, and with my dislike never in the least understood or my state pitied.' The 'interminable career of the tiresome and graceless "Juniors" ' clearly could not be arrested in the James family.

As late as 1882, the year of the elder Henry's death, the father and son were being taken for one another, since they both wrote and published and on occasions appeared in the same table of contents of the *Atlantic Monthly*. This resulted on one occasion in a critic incongruously congratulating Mr Henry James on his travel essay *Roman Rides* written in his 'usually charming graceful style' and on 'another article in quite a different vein entitled "Modern Diabolism", which he found very original'. Mary James quite justifiably commented to her son, 'You will each soon be groaning under this double weight of honour.' It was not, however, the confusion of names that really agitated the novelist. Some sons are proud to bear their father's given name. Deeply emotional reasons as well as practical ones are reflected in his acute feelings. Foremost among these was his struggle in that family of competing egos to find his own identity. William's name recalled the long-dead Albany grandfather. Garth Wilkinson James, born after Henry in 1845, honoured an English Swedenborgian. Robertson, the youngest boy, born in Albany in 1846, was named after the maternal grandfather. Henry alone had a shared name. The word 'junior' had a diminishing sound. His dislike of the 'appendage' is evident in the signature he evolved up to the time of his father's death. Use of the 'Jr' often caused him to curtail the first name to an initial. At first the 'Jr' was quite legible. As the years passed it was finally reduced to a mere curved stroke over which floated a seemingly inexplicable dot.

I

Readers of Henry James's novels and tales can discover at every turn the writer's predilection for second sons. Sometimes he kills off elder brothers or turns them into villains; sometimes his hero is an only son, usually with a widowed mother. He confers on them an ideal fatherless and brotherless state. In his memoirs he has told us how 'parentally bereft cousins were somehow more thrilling than parentally provided ones'. They constituted his first childish conception of the possibilities residing in their 'enviable lot to be so little fathered and mothered'.

Henry James's first hero, in *Roderick Hudson*, is the second son of a Virginia slaveholder. His 'ugly-faced' elder brother has been killed in the Civil War. (In later editions of the novel, Henry indulgently altered the description to 'plain-faced'.) 'I have to fill a double place,' Roderick explains. 'I have to be my brother as well as myself ... I was the curled darling ... I stayed indoors to be kissed by the ladies while he made mudpies in the garden ... he was worth fifty of me.' Significantly Roderick, on arriving in Rome, executes first a statue of Adam and then one of Eve. Having created the father and mother of the race, he identifies himself promptly with their eldest son. Abel doesn't interest him. 'I have been thinking lately of making a Cain, but I should never dream of making him ugly. He should be a very handsome fellow, and he should lift up the murderous club with the beautiful movement of the fighters in the Greek friezes who are chopping at their enemies.' Valentin de Bellegarde, in *The American*, embodies grace and romantic charm; he is a second son; his elder brother, the Marquis, is a monument of fatuity and corruption. Owen Wingrave, in the ghostly tale, has an elder brother who has been committed to an asylum; his father was killed by a sabre-thrust in India. Morgan Moreen of *The Pupil* is the sensitive and perceptive member of a mendacious family whose firstborn, Ulick Moreen, is anaemic and ineffectual, with a 'buttonhole but feebly floral and a moustache with no pretensions to type'. Nick Dormer in *The Tragic Muse* is a second son, whose brother, a peer, devotes himself to the hunt. It is Nick who must stand for parliament, where his father ruled for many years. And in his late novel, *The Wings of the Dove*, James gives us a concrete reflection of the feeling of fraternal inferiority which he harboured. Kate Croy lives in 'a state of abasement as the second born, her life reduced to mere inexhaustible sisterhood'.

For Henry, life in the James family was a state of inexhaustible brotherhood, as if William 'had gained such an advantage of me in his sixteen months' experience of the world before mine began that I never for all the time of childhood and youth in the least caught up with him or overtook him'. William was

always round the corner and out of sight, coming back into view but at his hours of extremest ease. We were never in the same schoolroom, in the same game, scarce even in step together or in the same phase at the same time; when our phases overlapped, that is, it was only for a moment – he was clean out before I had got well in.

The image of an absent, elusive, distant William persisted to the end. The novelist 'seems often to think that my father is here, *tho' not in the same room*', William's eldest son wrote during Henry James's last illness. The novelist's memoirs promptly establish the difference between himself and his elder brother: it is the refrain of the autobiographies – sometimes good-humoured, sometimes a trifle mocking, but filled often with self-pity and 'abasement'. The titles of the memoirs, *A Small Boy and Others* and *Notes of a Son and Brother*, reflect Henry's need to put himself into the forefront. What he described as 'an attempt to place together some particulars of the early life of William James' emerged as autobiography. Henry responded to an overwhelming need to make himself the subject of the book. It is Henry who is the Small Boy; and it is Henry, not William, who looks at us from the Matthew Brady daguerreotype which serves as frontispiece – looks at us with a gentle, quiet stare from bright boyish eyes, his hand resting on his father's shoulder. By the end of the volume the Small Boy has reached his teens, and the account of William remains to be written; the broad background of their common childhood has been brilliantly established but this, however, on Henry's, not William's terms.*

A second volume thus became necessary. Once again Henry takes the foreground. *Notes of a Son and Brother* are, of course, Henry's notes. He argued that the only honest picture he could give of William and his father was in the light of his own observation and relationship to them, and he freely altered the texts of their letters, from which he quoted. He was yielding, however, to dictates deeper than those of the craft of authorship. The dictates were of a psychological order and they are revealed in the contents of the two volumes: Henry's buried sense of his subordinate position alike to father and brother. The terms in which he talks of his father, a mixture of admiration, mild indulgence and depreciation, and of his brother, a mixture of affection and praise always coupled with humility, tell a story the author never intended us to know, nor was fully aware of himself.

2

We are confronted with brotherly rivalry at the start of *A Small Boy* when Henry is brought crying and kicking to the primary school in the Dutch House in Albany – that house which James affectionately describes in the opening of *The Portrait of a Lady*. Isabel Archer's revolt against attending school is not explained by her creator; but in *A Small Boy* he is quite clear why little Henry James, aged 5 or 6, kicks and screams in front of the yellow-painted colonial structure. His rage is provoked by the discovery that William is there ahead of him, seated at his desk, serene and 'in possession'. Henry's vocal retreat left William 'once for all already there, an embodied demonstration' that Henry was foredoomed to arrive always 'belatedly and ruefully'.

The infantile Henry rebelled; the adolescent sought equality when he and William were in Geneva. He attained it when he was able to attend the Academy where William had been enrolled ahead of

* Usually accurate in dating events, the novelist errs in giving the date of William's birth in this book – 9 January instead of 11 January 1842.

him; then, during their young manhood, at Newport, he picked up pencil and paint-brush, seeking to emulate his senior who was studying art in William Morris Hunt's studio (William drew 'because he could, while I did so in the main only because he did'). Later still, when William went to Harvard, Henry follows him. His brother's pasture always seemed greenest until he actually reached it and then, feeling himself 'outclassed', he turned away in search of his own.

The terms in which he describes his descent upon Harvard at 20, written half a century later, show that the old rivalry persisted. William was studying medicine, and Henry, briefly at the Law School, could have created an independent career. He describes William's easy faculty for taking hold of an environment; he demonstrates his alert qualities of mind and his sociability. He conveys, however, under guise of a generous inferiority, his own anxieties.

'At Cambridge, of course' – and the 'of course' denotes inevitability – 'I was further to find my brother on the scene and already at a stage of possession of its contents that I was resigned in advance never to reach; so thoroughly I seemed to feel a sort of quickening savoury meal in any cold scrap of his own experience that he might pass on to my palate.' He fed himself on 'the crumbs' of William's feast and on 'the echoes of his life'. The tribute to William is generous, the self-portrait curious. It lends emphasis on the one hand to the respect inspired in him by his brother's *savoir-faire*; it suggests also a distinct humility. There were many ways in which the 70-year-old Henry James could have sketched his relationship to William; and yet the picture evoked, even if we accept it as whimsicality or irony or euphemism, is that of a grovelling beggar picking up cold scraps and crumbs from a brother's table and finding life in 'echoes' of his senior's occupations. This indeed is the complete abasement of younger brotherhood. Henry does not stop there. He remembers that he wished to live, if only 'by the imagination, in William's adaptive skin'. He thus characterizes himself as unadaptive, aloof, lacking in William's social qualities, and expresses clearly what he has always wanted to be – his elder brother.

3

William had been taken first to the theatre while little Henry was left at home by the lamplight in a 'vivid vigil' to imagine the stage and the actors and to nurse 'my view of paternal discrimination'. William presided authoritatively over boyish games. William put Henry in his place with '*I* play with boys who curse and swear!' when Henry proposed to accompany him. Henry didn't curse and swear. And the old man, remembering his elder brother's broad insult, looked sadly at his younger self and added: 'All boys I rather found were difficult to play with.'

This was not the only remembered instance in which William aggressively put his younger brother in his place. The philosopher recalled later in life how Henry, combining authorship with attempts at drawing, sketched a mother and child clinging to a rock in the midst of a stormy ocean. Beneath the drawing he wrote: 'The thunder roared and the lightning followed.' We might pause here over Henry's choice of subject: the image of a child clinging to a mother in the fearsome surroundings of a tempest. But it was not the fear and dependency which arrested the scientifically-minded William. That Henry should put thunder before lightning was a meteorological blunder inviting high derision. With all the weight of his seniority, William pounced upon the brother's work and tormented him to such an extent that Henry promptly enacted a portion of his story. He ran for maternal protection. William was punished for a too enthusiastic display of exact knowledge at Henry's expense. The incident ended in triumph for the younger brother and emphasized the elder's overlordship. It may well explain in part, the reticence and secrecy with which Henry surrounded his literary efforts early and late. There had been too many prying brothers, too much merciless criticism and childish lampooning. Garth Wilkinson, who was in turn Henry's junior (and described by him as my 'extremely easy yokefellow and playfellow') reported to T. S. Perry in 1860 from Geneva, 'Harry has become an author I believe for he keeps his door locked all day long.' Apparently at 16 and 17 the feud continued, for Wilky also reported that 'Willy and Harry had been getting along very well indeed this last winter', which suggested other winters when the getting along went less well. William would continue to the end of his life to be a sharp and not always friendly critic of Henry's work.

4

We are indebted to T. S. Perry for a significant glimpse of James at Newport, 'when we got to the house and the rest of us were chattering, Henry James sat on the window-seat reading Leslie's *Life of Constable* with a certain air of remoteness'. There lay escape from the frustrations of his juniorhood: in books, in the imagination, in writing. He couldn't draw like William, but he could read books about art and artists. He couldn't act, or felt that he couldn't, but he could invent stories about himself doing some of the things his brother did. William could be impulsive, filling each moment with imagination translated into action. Henry, possessing an equal capacity for action, translated it into imagination. There was a virtue in immobility: he could observe, and his memory clung tenaciously to all that he saw. They might urge upon him greater activity; he sat back and looked, looked at everything with the calm yet seeing eyes of childhood and the aid of his fostered and stimulated imagination. It is no surprise that he attached so much importance to his eyes – that the heroes with whom he most identified were those endowed with the finest perception. He gave first place always to the 'observer' in his fiction and to his 'point of view'.

The evidence of Henry James's life points to a curiously paradoxical element in his personality: he was an active and masculine individual who, finding direct action impossible in his brother's presence – and with this, direct expression of his individuality – achieved this activity and individuality through a prodigiously creative and highly productive art only when he could put an ocean between himself and William. The small boy cultivated a quiet aloofness; nothing would happen to him if he withdrew and used his eyes and his mind in that turbulent family. Inside the little mind great worlds were created, great achievements, great aggressions planned. He confessed late in life that his favourite fairy-tale in childhood was *Hop o' my Thumb*. Is he not the merest of mere juniors and yet the greatest of little adventurers? Youngest of seven boys, and yet a monument of resourcefulness, deserted with his brothers by his parents, he takes charge – becoming thus Senior instead of Junior – outwits the ogre, obtains possession of the Seven League Boots and ends up as the benefactor of his entire family, including his unhappy parents. 'It is the vague memory of this sense of him,' James wrote, as some small precious object, like a lost gem or a rare and beautiful insect on which one might inadvertently tread, or might find under the sofa or behind the window-curtain, that leads me to think of Hop o' my Thumb as my earliest and sweetest and most repeated cupful at the fount of fiction.

But it was not Hop o's *smallness* alone that counted; it was that, being tiny, he conquered worlds. And Henry James, inexhaustible younger brother, making himself small and quiet among the other Jameses, turned into the depths of himself to fashion a fictional world based on the realities around him in which elder brothers were vanquished, fathers made to disappear, mothers put into their place. But it was not as easy as all that. Such daydream accomplishments – and aggressions – had their concomitant fears and anxieties and guilts within the outwardly serene little boy. Yet in this fashion, by seeking to control his environment, suppressing his hostilities, electing the observer's role rather than the actor's, he was able to act in his own highly personal way and conquer. He came to be his mother's favourite son. He was called 'angel'. At the time of his parents' death he had achieved international celebrity; he had surpassed his elder brother who was to win renown some fifteen years after Henry's first novel was published. The elder Henry, shortly before his death, wrote to the son who bore his name: 'I can't help feeling that you are the one that has cost us the least trouble, and given us always the most delight.'

The victory within the family was complete. But beyond the family lay the great outer world, hard and competitive, and it would have to be faced in a new struggle – a renewal of the old. One could cease writing Junior after one's name and still have to go on contending with the problems of being second son. And he was to discover that the mask of immobility, the manoeuvre to control the environment, did not always succeed. Sometimes people and surroundings defied control. Nevertheless, a large personality had been moulded in this difficult familial process – and an artist as well.

5

Notes on a Nightmare

No chapter has greater fascination in the records of Henry James's childhood than the one in *A Small Boy and Others*, in which the novelist describes his rambles in Paris with his brother and his first visits to the Luxembourg and the Louvre. In the middle of this chapter James sets a nightmare, dreamed many years later, which he relates to these rambles and to this early time of life. He begins by describing his long walks with his brother from the Champs-Élysées, along the quays, past the bookstalls and print-shops to the Rue de Seine; their progress up that familiar street into the old Rue de Tournon, the relatively short street leading to the Luxembourg, not only the seat of the Senate but also the museum of modern works of art. He remembers the cobbles of the Rue de Tournon, then a little grass-grown and the Café Foyot at the top; and he looks at 'the high grey-headed, clear-faced, straight-standing old houses'. As was his custom in his later years he gives these houses a voice. They seem to say, 'Yes, small staring *jeune homme*, we are dignity and memory and measure, we are conscience and proportion and taste, not to mention strong sense too.' He puts us back into the 1850s, pictures himself and William in tall hats and black gloves, wandering in the thick air of Imperial Paris, which still retained some of its pre-revolutionary streets. The houses represented 'Style'; they looked down upon himself and William 'with conscious encouragement'. He was then 12; William 14.

He remembers William always carrying a sketch-book and drawing people and objects which caught his eye. They pause in the Luxembourg before Couture's large canvas of the 'decadent Romans', the picture of the hour, and James muses on this painter, touched lightly and only once by fame. Couture is recalled perhaps because James later met him and visited his studio, and because he taught William Hunt, the Boston painter, who for a while taught William at Newport. Henry remembers also seeing landscapes, and repeats the names of Troyon, Rousseau, Daubigny and Lambinet, the latter recalled vividly in *The Ambassadors*, where James would endow his hero with walks in Paris not unlike those of his own childhood.

He especially recalls William's deep admiration for Delacroix at a time when that artist was not yet widely known. Henry said he felt his importance – 'was sure of it, I must properly add, but as an effect of my brother's sureness'. And then he speaks of another painting involving two brothers, Delaroche's *Les Enfants d'Édouard*, the princelings in the Tower and describes 'the long-drawn odd face of the elder prince, sad and sore and sick, with his wide crimped side-locks of fair hair and his violet legs marked by the Garter and dangling from the bed'. He remembers other paintings by this artist, always historical : 'the headsman, the bandaged eyes and groping hands, of Lady Jane Grey' and the 'noble indifference of Charles the First' while being insulted by the Puritan soldiers. These are pictorial memories of dishonoured and beheaded royalty : and Henry wondered why his brother did not attempt to sketch these but stayed always with what he could learn from Delacroix. He writes these memories to show how he and William were undergoing an education in 'style', but at the same time reveals his own interest in pictures with a 'story' in them; indeed, pictures of high drama. Power is mingled with the thought of style, and power seems to have supreme and tragic issue – the murdered Princes, and the beheaded Lady Jane Grey and Charles I.

From this, his transition in his memoirs is directly to the Louvre where the pictures, the palace itself, the sense of power and glory and style 'overwhelmed and bewildered me'. It was as if they had gathered there into a vast and deafening chorus;

I shall never forget how – speaking, that is, for my own sense – they filled those vast halls with the influence rather of some complicated sound, diffused and reverberant, than of such visibilities as one could directly deal with. To distinguish among these, in the charged and coloured and confounding air, was difficult – it discouraged and defied; which was doubtless why my impression originally best entertained was that of those magnificent parts of the great gallery simply not inviting us to distinguish. They only arched over us in the wonder of their endless golden riot and relief, figured and flourished in perpetual revolution, breaking into great high-hung circles and symmetries of squandered picture, opening into deep outward embrasures that threw off the rest of monumental Paris somehow as a told story, a sort of wrought effect or bold ambiguity for a vista, and yet held it there, at every point, as a vast bright gage, even at moments a felt adventure, of experience.

At this moment he continues 'I felt myself most happily cross that bridge over to Style constituted by the wondrous Galerie d'Apollon'. Here he 'inhaled little by little ... a general sense of *glory*. The glory meant ever so many things at once, not only beauty and art and supreme design but history and fame and power, the world in fine raised to the richest and noblest expression.' In his own mind he extends the idea of the glories seen in the Louvre to his vision of 'the local present fact, to my small imagination, of the Second Empire'. If it was a diminished echo of Napoleon, it still was 'amply radiant and elegant'. James then asks himself how childhood imbibes the sense of such matters, or as he puts it 'who shall count the sources at which an intense young fancy (when a young fancy *is* intense) capriciously, absurdly drinks?' Keeping up the image he speaks of the effect 'of a love-philtre or fear-philtre which fixes for the senses their supreme symbols of the fair and strange'. At this point in the narrative Henry James, with his recall of his first vision of the Galerie d'Apollon, remembers 'what a precious part it played for me' when he awakened years later, in a summer dawn, 'to the fortunate, the instantaneous recovery and capture of the most appalling yet most admirable nightmare of my life'.

Love and Fear. Fair and strange. Admirable and appalling. We weigh these balanced opposites and note that to Apollon and Napoleon we must now add another word – *appalling*. Here is a consonance of syllable and association which emerges in this closely-woven chapter of reminiscence : Apollon-Napoleon-Appalling, the last word many times reiterated; and these words can be read as art, grandeur, love, power glory, conquest, terror – fright perhaps at the vaulting ambition of his own imagination.

The small boy was in the Paris of the Second Empire; the name of Napoleon was still heard everywhere even if the tradition had shrunk to the nature of Charles-Louis Napoleon. Henry saw the pageantry of this era – with its suggestion of 'the generations and dynasties and armies, the revolutions and restorations they had seen come and go' – as represented in the paintings at the Luxembourg. The small boy watched the infant Prince Imperial taking his airing in the Champs-Élysées and in the Tuileries, and his progress through Paris to Saint-Cloud 'in the splendid coach that gave a glimpse of appointed and costumed nursing breasts and laps, and beside which the *cent-gardes*, all light blue and silver and intensely erect quick jolt, rattled with pistols raised and cocked'. He remembered the public holiday of the Prince's baptism at Notre-Dame, the fête of

Saint-Napoléon, which he was later to rediscover in the pages of Zola's *Eugène Rougon*, wondering whether the French novelist had been in the same crowds, a future creator of fiction like himself.

The sense of that interminable hot day, a day of hanging about and waiting and shuffling in dust, in crowds, in fatigue, amid booths and ped-lars and performers and false alarms and expectations and renewed re-actions and rushes, all transfigured at the last, withal, by the biggest and brightest illumination up to that time offered even the Parisians, the blinding glare of the new Empire.

Napoleon represented, in a Europe in which he was but thirty-five years dead, the glory of a recent and heroic past. If in the Louvre – the Louvre of Napoleon, the Gallery of Apollo – Henry James found his initiation to Style, then Style remained associated for him thereafter with power. Were not many of the works of art in the great Palace the fruit of Imperial conquest? When James years later recalled the apartment in Paris where he wrote the first portion of *The American*, he remembered 'the light of high, narrowish French windows in old rooms, the light somehow, as one always feels, of "style" itself'. The rooms, we know, were in an old house close by the Place Vendôme with its Napoleonic column recording the great victories of the post-revolutionary era. Style itself, intensity of tone, the 'high homely style' of an older day, is evoked in *The Ambas sadors*, where Strether's first call on Madame de Vionnet in the Rue de Bellechasse 'reveals as a background of the occupant, some glory, some prosperity of the first Empire, some Napoleonic glamour, some dim lustre of the great legend.'

2

He is defending himself, in terror, against the attempt of someone to break into his room. He is pressing his shoulder against a door and someone is bearing down on the lock and bolt on the other side. Suddenly the tables are turned. Terror is defied. Nightmare is routed. It is Henry who forces the door open in a burst of aggression – and of triumph. Now he is no longer afraid. Now he is triumphant. He experiences an extraordinary sense of elation. The figure had tried to appal him. But now it is appalled. The pursuer, the attacker, be-comes the pursued.

Routed, dismayed, the tables turned upon him by my so surpassing

him for straight aggression and dire intention, my visitant was already
but a diminished spot in the long perspective, the tremendous, glorious
hall, as I say, over the far-gleaming floor of which, cleared for the occasion of its great line of priceless *vitrines* down the middle, he sped for
his life, while a great storm of thunder and lightning played through the
deep embrasures of high windows at the right. The lightning that revealed the retreat revealed also the wondrous place and, by the same
amazing play, my young imaginative life in it of long before, the sense of
which, deep within me, had kept it whole, preserved it to this thrilling
use; for what in the world were the deep embrasures and the so polished
floor but those of the Galerie d'Apollon of my childhood? The 'scene of
something' I had vaguely then felt it? Well I might, since it was to be the
scene of that immense hallucination.

For Henry the

lucidity, not to say the sublimity, of the crisis had consisted of the great
thought that I, in my appalled state, was probably still more appalling
than the awful agent, creature or presence, whatever he was, whom I
had guessed, in the suddenest wild start from sleep, the sleep within my
sleep, to be making for my place of rest.

Sublimity was indeed the word for this 'immense hallucination'.
And with Henry James's fidelity to inner memory he proceeded to
recall the component which perhaps caused him to speak of a 'fear-
philtre' as well as a 'love-philtre'. He recognizes the effect upon his
perceptions of the great rooms of the Louvre; he sees them as 'educative, formative, fertilizing' and 'in a degree which no other "intellectual experience" our youth was to know'. The strange nightmare,
'the quite heart-shaking little prevision' of it he recognized – beginning to associate to the dream in a very modern way, as if in anticipation of Freud – went back to his first visit in 1855 to the Galerie
d'Apollon with his brother. The two boys had been entrusted to the
family courier, Jean Nadali, as their guide and he remembers that,
'appalled but uplifted', he clung to Nadali's arm. He had already told
how the scene had become a deafening chorus; but in his further
memories he begins to name pictures, and the first picture he names,
with its components of nightmare terror, heroism, and brilliance is
Géricault's *Radeau de la Méduse*, the great symbolic picture, in its
concreteness, of the raft of life. He names other works, but singles
out Géricault and the works of David (the latter depicting the glories
of Napoleon) as the pictorial landmarks of 'Style'. He then asks himself without pursuing it too far, why there had been 'under our

courier's protection and in my brother's company' a sense of 'alarm' as well as one of 'bliss'.

The bliss in fact I think scarce disengaged itself at all, but only the sense of a freedom of contact and appreciation really too big for one, and leaving such a mark on the very place, the pictures, the frames themselves, the figures within them, the particular parts and features of each, the look of the rich light, the smell of the massively enclosed air, that I have never since renewed the old exposure without renewing again the old emotion and taking up the small scared consciousness.

The 'alarm' he decides was that of a boy receiving more impressions than he could absorb; and this brilliant chapter of memory and recreation ends with his feeling that 'the great premises' of the Louvre had served as the starting point for his lifetime adventure. The pictures and painters that were representative of art – Veronese, Murillo's 'moon-borne Madonna', Leonardo's 'almost unholy dame with the folded hands', and others, spoke for France and Europe and spoke to America, 'history as a still-felt past'. He pictured his young sensibility rubbing against the great palace of the Louvre as a cat invokes 'the friction of a protective piece of furniture'.

These were the 'vague processes' of picking up an education. His brother had not agreed with him – his brother being scientific concluded this was no kind of education at all 'I was so far dissentient, I say, that I think I quite came to glorify such passages and see them as part of an order really fortunate.' And he likened the experiences to silver and gold threads perhaps 'casually interwoven' but into a very fine tissue. It sufficed that he had learned and lived and created, and he recognized the difficulty of unravelling the tissue.

3

The threads cannot be unravelled: old dreams become mere fables when divorced from the dreamers. Yet the suggestive, interpretive mind of Henry James has given us ground for some speculation about a dream that by its very allusions and depths springs from the central myths of Henry James. Clear at least, in its first part, is the picture of himself as threatened – who can tell by whom? – the 'mere junior' surrounded by admonishing governesses, a permissive father, an often stern ambiguous mother, above all a hyper-active elder brother. William seems to be with him, for the scene is set in the Louvre; and William has been sketching and studying and appreciating. The 'sublime' synthesis links the Gallery of Apollo and the Paris of the new Napoleon. *Apollon* and *Napoléon* – pronounced in French, the names sound almost alike – Apollo representing the glory of art and Napoleon the symbol for 'history, fame, power'. But with this, as we have seen, James recurrently uses the word 'appalling' which strikes the note of fear and alarm. The three words encapsulate the emotions James conveys to us in his dream-narrative – the nightmare of aggression implicit in the drive to power of a Napoleon, the glory of the arts personified in Apollo and also an Emperor, as patron, instigator and collector of art. And with this the sense of being appalled – for these words also evoke the grandeur and nightmare of history, the ferocities and primitive agonies (depicted by Géricault), the mixture of heroism and terror, the love-philtre which can be death (when did love-philtres lead anywhere but to tragedy?) and the fear-philtre which is the fear of the over-whelmed small boy, clutching the arm of his guide, and amid histori-cal glories keeping pace with his older brother.

The remarkable element in the nightmare resides in Henry's con-quest of fear and the guilt of his aggression. And, as we read his description of the great chase along the gallery in the Louvre, amid thunder and lightning, as of Zeus, we can remember Henry's saying of William, 'We were never in the same schoolroom, in the same game, scarce even in step together or in the same phase at the same time.' We remember also his earlier account of William 'when our phases overlapped ... it was only for a moment – he was clean out before I had got well in'. And the language of pursuit had been used earlier. 'I never for all the time of childhood and youth in the least caught up with him or overtook him. He was always round the corner and out of sight.' Then, at the end of his dream, there is the mention of the older brother waving aside the art-viewing and street-wandering in Paris as non-educative, while the younger brother incorporates these memories into the immediate 'fact' of the Second Empire, where the banners still waved and the eagles still flew. The artist sees the panorama of his childhood as an exposure to history and to Style, which is synonymous with glory; to beauty and art and fame and 'supreme design', which become power and grandeur.

There is evidence that Henry James may have had this 'dream-adventure', as he called it, in 1910 when he was himself old and ill and William was dying. It was a kind of gathering in of the essence of his life, the story of his art and his rivalry with his brother and the way in which he had conquered fear and family pressures. There was one difference between the dream and the facts of his life. In the wishful dream his conquest was achieved by direct counter-attack, by pursuit. In his life it was he who fled; his conquests were by persistence, indirection, secrecy. Napoleon had used the sword. Henry James used the subtle pen. James left his homeland; his real home was the Galerie d'Apollon. By the power of created art, James achieved a victory over the 'appalling' of life. We can see this in his tale of *The Jolly Corner* where (as in the dream) the elderly American goes in pursuit of the ghost (of himself 'as he might have been'). But when he encounters the apparition, he falls in a faint. Curiously enough James, in recalling this story in his notebook, did not tell it in this way. He told his dream instead.

my hero's adventure there takes the form so to speak of his turning the tables, as I think I called it, on a 'ghost' or whatever, a visiting or haunting apparition otherwise qualified to appal *him*; and thereby winning a sort of victory by the appearance, and the evidence, that this personage or presence was more overwhelmingly affected by him than he by *it*.

4

When he was 17, and the hours of his last youthful stay in the Old World had shrunk to but a handful, Henry James slipped from his bed on the fifth floor of his hotel (it bore appropriately the name of Hôtel des Trois Empereurs) in the Rue de Rivoli. It was a September morning and he looked out upon Paris from the balcony. There was the wide open Place du Palais Royal with a ceaseless swarming movement in it. On one side was a cab station with the drivers asleep on the top of their box-like fiacres, while their horses stamped and whisked their tails. He had seen soldiers parade there, with a mixture of waddle and swagger. Across the way loomed the new wing of the Louvre. Set into the great palace wall were the statutes of Napoleon's young generals – Hoche, Marceau, Desaix. At that moment

what it somehow came to was that here massed itself the shining second Empire, over which they stood straight aloft and on guard, like arch-angels of the sword, and that the whole thing was a high-pitched wonder and splendour, which we had already. in our small gaping way, got into a sort of relation with ... we were present at something it would be always after accounted a privilege to have been concerned with, and that we were perversely and inconsiderately dropping out of it.

The moment of French history now mingled with personal history.

It meant, immensely, the glittering régime, and *that* meant in turn, prodigiously, something that would probably never be meant quite to any such tune again : so much one positively and however absurdly said to one's self as one stood up on the high balcony to the great insolence of the Louvre and to all the history, all the glory again and all the imposed applause, not to say worship, and not to speak of the implied inferiority, on the part of everything else, that it represented.

The Louvre again is Napoleon and his generals, and *gloire* and style – the supreme palace of the Western World, 'the most peopled of all scenes not less than the most hushed of all temples'. It was the Temple of Apollo and the Palace of Napoleon and the Palace of Art which in the end 'became mixed and interchangeable with the House of Life'.

Part Two:

Scenes from a Boyhood

6

The Two Squares

I

HENRY JAMES always said that his earliest memory was of the Place Vendôme in Paris, with its column celebrating the victories of Napoleon. He had been taken to England when he was six months old. France was visited during the following year. The James family returned to America in 1845 and ten years elapsed before they went abroad again. This means that Henry's remarkable 'recollection' of the Place Vendôme dated from his second year.

As he set it down, he remembered he was still 'in long clothes' seated on his Aunt Kate's lap in a carriage opposite his father and mother; he was 'impressed with the view, framed by the clear window of the vehicle as we passed, of a great stately square surrounded with high-roofed houses and having in its centre a tall and glorious column'. When he spoke of this later in childhood, his parents compared notes in surprise. Neither Albany nor New York had such a square, nor was there anything like it in London, where he had been taken at an even earlier age. 'Conveyed along the Rue St Honoré while I waggled my small feet, as I definitely remember doing, under my flowing robe, I had crossed the Rue de Castiglione and taken in, for all my time, the admirable aspect of the Place and the Colonne Vendôme.'

Was this the loom of memory at work, weaving backward and forward among things seen early and late? Whether the brilliant infant had really absorbed and remembered so concretely we cannot know. What we do know is that his awakening consciousness was first exposed to Europe. It was there that he emerged from the cradle and began to assimilate the world around him. We know also that he had a precocious memory and a tenacious one.

Henry James reached the age of recognitions and perceptions during the period of his father's *vastation*, in a small cottage between the Great and Little Parks at Windsor, fronting the entrance to the Little Park, within the range of vision of Queen Victoria herself from her great castle windows. 'Willy and Harry,' the senior Henry wrote to his mother in Albany, 'from the nursery windows may hold delightful converse with the sheep and cattle browsing beneath.' They also had the view of the long broad meadows of the Park, 'dotted with the noblest oaks of England'. It is not surprising that when Henry returned to England at 26 he had a deep sense of rediscovering the familiar; or that beneath noble trees on wide lawns the opening pages of Isabel Archer's story invite us to join in the English ceremony of afternoon tea. The infant had been taken from the edge of cart-crowded Broadway in New York across an ocean and had opened his eyes before the august beauty of the English countryside at the very spot where it was designed to regale the eyes of a queen. Memories of the English, the European, ambience – the colour and tone of the buildings, the grandeur of squares and boulevards – inevitably remained.

2

If the novelist's first glimpses of the world were European, his emerging consciousness caught hold, on native grounds, of another square in the city of his birth which was to give its name to one of his best-known works. In the early pages of *Washington Square* he allows himself a striking autobiographical digression or what he calls a 'topographical parenthesis', almost as if he wanted to make certain that his own identity with that Square would be permanently enshrined in a work of art.

I know not whether it is owing to the tenderness of early associations, but this portion of New York appears to many persons the most delectable. It has a kind of established repose which is not of frequent occurrence in other quarters of the long, shrill city; it has a riper, richer, more honourable look than any of the upper ramifications of the great longitudinal thoroughfare – the look of having had something of a social history. It was here, as you might have been informed on good authority, that you had come into a world which appeared to offer a variety of sources of interest; it was here that your grandmother lived in venerable solitude, and dispensed a hospitality which commended itself alike to the infant imagination and the infant palate; it was here that you took your first walks abroad, following the nursery-maid with unequal step, and sniffing up the strange odour of the ailanthus-trees which at that time formed the principal umbrage of the Square, and diffused an aroma that you were not yet critical enough to dislike as it deserved; it was here, finally, that your first school, kept by a broad-bosomed, broad-based old lady with a ferule, who was always having tea in a blue cup, with a saucer that didn't match, enlarged the circle both of your observations and your sensations.

He telescopes events. If he had not been writing this reminiscence within a fictional frame he might have specified that his 'first walks abroad' were indeed 'abroad'. He is alluding here of course to his first walks in Manhattan from his maternal grandmother's home, to which the James family briefly went on their return to America when little Henry was 2½. We note also in these few lines the role the novelist quite properly gives to the small nose and palate, infantile avenues to discovery. Concerning the school he has left us other recollections. It was not his first: the Dutch House in Albany had provided the official beginning of his education after his original rebellion. His teacher was a Miss Bayon, or Bayhoo; he remembered only the sound of her name. The school in the Square was a later and better-remembered affair, presided over by a Mrs Daly in one of the small red houses on the south side of Waverly Place. Stout, red-faced, apparently Irish, Mrs Daly viewed her little pupils as 'so many small slices cut from the loaf of life and on which she was to dab the butter of arithmetic and spelling, accompanied by way of jam with a light application of the practice of prize-giving'. The ferule alluded to in the Jamesian parenthesis was bestowed by him on a different teacher in *A Small Boy*, a tall spare lady named Miss Rogers, whose face was framed in ringlets and who wore a light blue dress. She 'beat time with a long black ferule to some species of droning chant or chorus in which we spent most of our hours'.

These were but three of a series of ladies who administered 'small vague spasms of school' to the future novelist. But before his schooling began there were further displacements. The elder Henry had brought his wife and two boys back from Europe after the residence at Windsor. Mary James was then carrying her third child, born in New York on 21 July 1845, and named Garth Wilkinson. A few months later the father gravitated anew with his family towards his mother in Albany. He resided at No. 50 North Pearl Street, a few doors away from Catharine Barber James, who lived at No. 43, and from his brother Augustus and his family, who lived at No. 47. Here the James family remained until 1847 and here Mrs James gave birth to still another son, Robertson, on 29 August 1846.

7

A Flavour of Peaches

WHEN Henry Junior in later years spoke of 'infantile Albany' he meant his third and fourth years spent near his grandmother in a veritable settlement of Jameses. Catharine Barber James ('the most democratic person by temperament I ever knew', the senior Henry said of her) lived in the large old-fashioned house which her grandson later described in the opening pages of *The Portrait of a Lady*. She exercised

within the limits of the family a high hospitality ... There was a constant coming and going ... grandmother's sons and daughters and their children appeared to be in the enjoyment of standing invitations to arrive and to remain, so that the house offered to a certain extent the appearance of a bustling provincial inn kept by a gentle lady who sighed a great deal and never presented a bill.

Catharine James's grandfather had been a judge of the Court of Common Pleas and her father and two uncles had served in the Revolutionary Army. One uncle was detailed by George Washington to be an aide to Steuben. John Barber, Catharine's father, returned from the battlefields to his native Montgomery, Orange County, New York, to become an associate judge of the County Court, a member of the State Legislature and a church elder, a post he held for fifty years. Late in life Henry James sought, after his long residence in England, to discover some shred of English ancestry in his family among his Scottish–Irish antecedents. He represented Catharine Barber James as providing 'for us in our generation the only English blood – that of both her own parents – flowing in our veins'. The novelist was seeking to mould fiction into fact. Catharine Barber's grandfather came from Ireland and he married a Jeannet Rhea or Rea of Montgomery who is nowhere listed as English in the James family annals.

2

All Henry James's memories of Albany had a flavour of peaches. There were certain 'capital peach trees' in the great expanse of garden behind the grandmother's house and the small boy required no urging to do justice to them. For Isabel Archer in the early pages of *The Portrait of a Lady* peaches and Albany are synonymous, and in Henry James's third story, published when he was 23, the heroine makes an entrance bearing 'a plate of early peaches'. In *A Small Boy* he remembers mounds of Isabella grapes and sticky Seckel pears. But ah the 'peaches *d'antan*' !

bushels of peaches in particular, peaches big and peaches small, peaches white and peaches yellow, played a part in life from which they have somehow been deposed; every garden, almost every bush and the very boys' pockets grew them; they were 'cut up' and eaten with cream at every meal; domestically 'brandied' they figured, the rest of the year, scarce less freely – if they were rather a 'party dish' it was because they made the party whenever they appeared, and when ice-cream was added, or they were added *to* it, they formed the highest revel we knew. Above all the public heaps of them, the high-piled receptacles at every turn, touched the street as with a sort of southern plenty ... We ate everything in those days by the bushel and the barrel, as from stores that were infinite.

In matters of food the small boy was inevitably less discriminating than his later fictional characters. The small boy would not have been satisfied with the *omelette aux tomates* and bottle of straw-coloured Chablis consumed by Lambert Strether and Madame de Vionnet on the Paris quayside. He ate large quantities of ice-cream at every turn; he swallowed hot cakes and sausages and molasses on the hospitable porch of a neighbour, when the family was back in New York; doughnuts were consumed on Broadway when young Henry wasn't using his pennies for the more tempting fare offered at Barnum's Museum, and waffles 'by the hundreds' were eaten after school ('the oblong farinacious compound, faintly yet richly brown, stamped and smoking, not crisp nor brittle, but softly absorbent of the syrup dabbed upon it'). There were 'small amber-coloured mounds of chopped cocoanut or whatever other substance, if a finer there be'. Later, on the Continent, there were to be the melting *babas* and criss-cross apple tartlets with other delights of the French pastry-shops. At 70 Henry seemed to be smacking his lips over his hearty boyish appetite.

He remembered more than the peach-trees in Albany, although these always came first to mind: the swing on the covered piazza to the rear of his grandmother's house, the long garden sloping down to the stable, the library of William of Albany, full of books 'with frontispieces' which the child climbed on a chair to take down, guided in his selection chiefly by the pictures; the 'office' beyond the library with its musty smell and ancient pieces of furniture, and the school-house across the street from which came the 'hum of childish voices repeating the multiplication table'. Albany constituted the first stage in the novelist's experience of his native land; and the scene was crowded with the faces of the James clan at its most numerous before separations and deaths – already begun – cut its ranks and dimmed the fading splendour of the merchant-founder's domain.

8

58 West 14th Street

IN 1847 the James family moved back to New York, and here Mrs James gave birth on 7 August 1848 to her fifth and last child, a daughter, named Alice. After a brief residence at 11 Fifth Avenue in a house later razed to make way for the Brevoort Hotel, the elder Henry settled his brood in the then fashionable 'uptown' residential neighbourhood near Union Square – first in a rented house and then at No. 58 West 14th Street near Sixth Avenue, in a building which he purchased. It was not a new mansion; the plasterer and the paperhanger were summoned and little Henry watched the yellow-grained paper with a pattern of dragons and sphinxes being applied to the walls. The New York of *A Small Boy and Others*, in which the future novelist roamed between his fifth and twelfth years, was largely constituted for him by the area between Sixth and Fifth Avenues down to Washington Square and up eastward to Union Square which, in that era, was enclosed by a high railing, had a fountain and was presided over by a solitary amateur-looking policeman, 'a strange superannuated, dilapidated functionary, carrying a little cane and wearing, with a very copious and very dirty shirt front, the costume of a man of the world'. This was the 'old liquor-scented, heated-looking city, the city of no pavements', with the 'blistering summers' recorded on its face. On the corner of Eighth Street the boyish nostrils eagerly sniffed the warm smell of the bakery with its cookies, cream cakes and pies; on the corner of 15th Street and Fifth Avenue he remembered a great mansion which seemed to him the finest in New York. As the boys grew older New York widened for them. There were excursions downtown to the theatres of Chambers Street or Park Place and walks up and down Broadway and the farther reach of 42nd Street beyond which everything was clearly suburban. New York was a city of mixed buildings, vacant lots filled with weeds, theatrical billboards and wooden fences. The squares were fenced, there were poplars in the important thoroughfares, and stray pigs and poultry wandered in the side-streets. The grass plots in front of City Hall were known as 'the park', Hoboken was a 'genteel resort' and the rotunda of Castle Garden echoed with the warble of precocious Adelina Patti, while earlier all New York had talked of Jenny Lind.

He was in the 'small warm dusky homogeneous New York world of the mid-century'. The house on 14th Street was large and well-furnished. In the winter evenings the fires burned brightly in the hearth and little Henry spent intervals before bedtime looking at pictures and reading books. In the front parlour there was a large painting of a Florentine view by Thomas Cole; the rear parlour boasted still another Italian scene, a Tuscany landscape by Lefèvre, over the sofa; between the two rear windows stood the bust of a Bacchante with vine leaves in her hair and her breasts imperfectly covered. Certain visitors pronounced the marble lady rather 'cold' for a Bacchante.

Henry remembered Mr Emerson seated on the sofa in the rear parlour between his parents, in the dusk before the lamps were lit, 'elegantly slim, benevolently aquiline'. The great man showed an interest in the small boy, inviting him to draw nearer off the hearth-rug, and the 'sweetness of the voice and the finish of the speech' established for the future novelist the fact that the human tone could evoke personality and arouse feeling. In the library one day he saw Mr Thackeray who had come to America to lecture on the English Humourists of the Eighteenth Century. Henry was dressed after the fashion of the time in a tight jacket adorned in front with a row of brass buttons; hovering near the door of the sun-filled

library, he heard himself summoned by the enormous English gentleman: 'Come here, little boy, and show me your extraordinary
jacket.' Thackeray peered through and over his spectacles alike at
garment and boy. He then carefully explained to Henry that if he
were to go to England he would be addressed as 'Buttons'.

It is possible from these fragmentary reminiscences to put together the house at 58 West 14th Street – parlours front and back,
a sunny library, a guest room (known to the little Jameses as Mr
Emerson's room), bedrooms for the four boys and for Alice, the
maternal and paternal quarters, the attic in which theatricals were
staged by the enterprising William, and servants' quarters as well
as a large old-fashioned kitchen below stairs. The childhood of Henry
James was spacious in home and in city, a world rich and various,
wrapped in outward security and 'floating in such a clean light social
order'. Henry could 'dawdle and gape' at his ease and observe to his
heart's content. Old New York was to remain with him all his life
and he was to situate it in his work long after it had changed its face
and wedged itself up the island into the era of the automobile and
the skyscraper.

9

Picture and Scene

I

BETWEEN the front parlour windows in the 14th Street home stood
a piece of furniture which housed volumes of Gavarni's caricatures,
a set of Béranger enriched by steel engravings, and the four tall folios
of Joseph Nash's *Mansions of England in the Olden Time*. Here on
winter afternoons, in the fading light and the glow of a red fire, the
small boy lay on his stomach on the drawing-room hearth-rug studying the Nash pictures, all unaware that some day he would be an
honoured guest in England's mansions; in Gavarni he delighted in the
pictures of the sturdy Frenchwomen who came to life on the page
and resembled the short-skirted Mlle Delavigne, one of his teachers.
(He was later to characterize Gavarni as 'the wittiest, the most
literary and most acutely profane of all mockers with the pencil'.)
And here he read *Punch*. Between his seventh and twelfth years the

front parlour was associated with Henry's discovery of wider horizons than those embraced by Broadway and Union Square, Chambers Street and the big brown house at 18th Street where he sometimes admired the two or three little elegant cows, the nibbling fawns and other 'browsing and pecking and parading creatures'.

Every year Henry's parents talked of going again to Europe; every year they just as surely changed their minds. Meanwhile, all England seemed to unfold from the pages of *Punch* but mainly London – the names of London streets and theatres, Kensington Gardens and Drury Lane, the sound of Piccadilly seemed to be there, people riding in the Row, cabmen and costermongers, little pages in buttons, bathing-machines at the seaside, small boys in tall hats and Eton jackets, elaborately dressed gentlemen hunting foxes, pretty girls in striped petticoats with their hair dressed in the shape of mushrooms. Long before he had seen it, he was acquainted through Leech's drawings with the aspect of Baker Street in December. He was to discover in due course that if *Punch* had represented London to him, London in turn was *Punch*. Everything looked familiar once he was able to pace the great city, everything seemed to have been drawn by Leech.

The transition from pictures in books to pictures in galleries was made early. New York at the mid-century favoured large canvases and bright colours – as large 'as the side of a house and of a bravery of colour and lustre of surface that I was never afterwards to see surpassed'. The Düsseldorf School, as exemplified in the work of Leutze's celebrated painting of Washington crossing the Delaware, commanded the market, and its paintings were almost constantly on exhibition on Broadway, in a 'disaffected church where gothic excrescences and an ecclesiastical roof of a mild order helped the importance'. The first exhibition of the Leutze painting was an occasion never forgotten; the James family attended in force, taking the crosstown omnibus on 14th Street at an hour of the evening when Henry was usually in bed. There it was, the painting, in a 'wondrous flare of projected gaslight', with little Henry taking in 'the sharpness of the ice blocks ... the sickness of the sick soldier .,. the protrusion of minor objects ... the strands of the rope and the nails of the boots ... above all ... the profiled national hero's purpose', which seemed to be that of 'standing *up*, as much as possible, even indeed of doing it almost on one leg'. The Father of the Country was thus promptly identified with Henry's own father.

Less thrilling was another evening spent at Bryan's Gallery of

Christian art, viewing a collection of 'worm-eaten diptychs and triptychs, of angular saints and seraphs, of black Madonnas and obscure Bambinos', all certified 'primitives'. He heard later that this collection fell under suspicion and he believed it consisted largely of frauds and fakes. 'I have never since stood before a real Primitive,' he wrote, 'a primitive of the primitives, without having first to shake off the grey mantle of that night.'

What is clear from these early memories is the extent to which 'picture' entered into the experience of the young Henry; he was to link it to 'scene' that he learned also as a boy to watch on the stage; and he was to seek a wedding of picture and scene in his novels. In fact, at the end, he tended to see his own life as a series of images and scenes, 'the only terms in which life has treated me to experience ... I cherish the moment and evoke the image and repaint the scene'.

2

His father had taken him to visit an uncle on his estate at Rhinebeck, on the Hudson, Linwood – one of the most beautiful sites on the river. He remembered peaches, roses, grapes, the hum of insects, a wide view, 'great bright harmonies of air and space', taken in from an eminence overlooking the Hudson. One evening little Henry had the company of his cousin, Marie, who was a year older than he was. Small, brown, with shining black eyes, she was an object of special interest because Henry had heard she was 'spoiled'. The James boys had never been spoiled. It gave her a romantic status; he only half understood the meaning of the term. His uncle, Augustus James, at a given moment, remarked with some emphasis that it was Marie's bedtime. The words must have fallen with some weight; by implication it was probably Henry's bedtime, too. Marie objected. There was an emphatic rejoinder from Uncle Augustus. Marie appealed to her mother, and Henry, then 11, heard these sharp words which were emphatically registered: 'Come now, my dear; don't make a scene – I *insist* on your not making a scene!'

That was all the witchcraft the occasion used, but the note was none the less epoch-making. The expression, so vivid, so portentous, was one I had never heard of – it had never been addressed to us at home; and who should say now what a world one mightn't at once read into it? It seemed freighted to sail so far; it told me so much about life. Life at these intensities clearly became 'scenes'; but the great thing, the immense illumination, was that we could make them or not as we chose.

'Picture' and 'scene' would become a part of Henry James's essential terminology of fiction.

3

After pictures came books. Visits to the bookstore, 'fondest of my father's resorts', were frequent. Even before he could read young Henry sniffed the fresh paper and the printer's ink – he called it the 'English smell' because so many of the books were imported from England. The small boy learned to read early. He remembered that he accompanied his father one summer's day on a visit to the New York *Tribune* in Nassau Street, where the elder Henry usually called on his friend Horace Greeley. Here Henry Junior was impressed by a conversation about the French theatre and of tales of a new great town springing up in the west, a conglomeration of shanties and wooden plank sidewalks called Chicago. Someone handed his father a volume by Solon Robinson, a staff member of the paper. It was called *Hot Corn*. Little Henry promptly wanted to get his sensitive nose into the book but one of the men suggested that the volume wasn't for little boys. A glance at the book, with its lurid pictures of New York slum life (*The Story of Little Katy* who sold hot corn on Manhattan's sidewalks, *The Rag Picker's Daughter* and *Wild Maggie*), explains why. Henry Junior at 70 remembered the 'soreness of the thought that it was I rather who was wrong for the book'. This, to say the least, was 'somewhat somehow humiliating'. He never read *Hot Corn*, although the title remained with him long after the book was forgotten.

As a consolation he was given Maria S. Cummins's *The Lamp-lighter*, then enjoying great vogue on both sides of the Atlantic, and it was suggested to him that this was a 'grown-up' book. In his memoirs Henry James suggests that the small boy wasn't fooled. He had his reserves as to whether such a book could be 'really and truly grown-up', although he confessed that the tale of the little orphan adopted by the lamplighter with its pathos and moralizing received an 'absorbed perusal'. Something else happened, however, to give young Henry his real taste of what a novel could be.

10

An Initiation

I

ONE day when the family had fled the New York heat and was
staying at New Brighton, on Staten Island, the elder Henry accompanied by Henry Junior took the boat to New York to do a number
of chores. These included the usual visit to the bookstore where the
father purchased a number of volumes, including a novel for the
mother's reading. This book was handed to young Henry to carry.
They made their way back to the boat and the small boy clambered
into the little cabin or sitting-room for the brief journey. Here he
turned the book's pages. It was called *The Initials* and was by a
woman with the picturesque name of the Baroness Tautphoeus. 'It
came over me with the very first page,' he later wrote, 'assimilated
in the fluttered little cabin ...' that '*The Initials was* grown-up.'

It is easy to see, even today, what appeal the first page of this
novel by Jemima Montgomery, Baroness Tautphoeus, had for the
young Henry. It has an atmosphere not unlike the first page of *Daisy
Miller*: a young Englishman named Hamilton has alighted at a
Munich inn and is taking a sophisticated view of his continental
surroundings. In a few minutes an 'international' situation develops,
a mysterious note, merely initialled, is delivered, and in due course
Mr Hamilton has met the proud German beauty Hildegarde and her
sister Crescenz and the book, with a freshness and lightness that
have not faded from its pages after a century, carries us into mas-
querades and suppers, visits to little towns (even to Berchtesgaden
long before its garish moment in history), inspection of cloisters and
monasteries, hare hunts, the Hôtel d'Angleterre in Frankfort (how
many Hôtels d'Angleterre Henry was to stay at in later years!). The
Baroness was an Irishwoman who had married a Chamberlain to the
King of Bavaria and was one of a group of English writers of her
time who skilfully illuminated foreign manners for Anglo-Saxon
readers. She is entirely at home abroad, and little Henry, aged 11,
seems to have felt himself at home also in her pages. What was a
sentimental story of an orphan and a lamplighter compared to a tale,
romantic and witty, set in the Bavarian Alps, containing a lurid

suicide, a struggle of lovers against cruel fate, even a quasi-elope-
ment in which, however, the hero observes all the niceties after
registering the heroine at a Mainz hotel and being taken for her
husband. 'I will go at once across, and if there be any rooms to be
had, not quite on the other end of town, I shall not return until
morning.' The precision of the 'not quite at the other end of the
town' could only be an anticipation of the early writings of Henry
James Junior.

2

Henry James discovered that day on the New Brighton boat what
real fiction could be, fiction sophisticated and written with a bright,
facile charm,

the history of the long-legged Mr Hamilton and his two Bavarian beauties,
the elder of whom, Hildegarde, was to figure for our small generation as
the very type of the haughty as distinguished from the forward heroine
(since I think our categories really came to no more than those). I
couldn't have got very far with Hildegarde in moments so scant, but I
memorably felt that romance was thick round me – everything, at such
a crisis, seeming to make for it at once.

The 'romance' that took the small boy from fiction to a 'scene'
from life was his discovery that 'lurking' in the same public cabin
sitting-room were two little girls whom he recognized as the 'Boon
Children' of the New York stage, scheduled to perform that evening
at the New Brighton Pavilion. Thus Henry, not quite the long-legged
Mr Hamilton, could fancy himself as being 'in relation' with two
beauties, not quite Bavarian. They had come down to the cabin
supervised by a female in whom 'the strain of the resolute triumphed
over the note of the battered'. They lurked 'out of more public view
as to hint that they weren't to be seen for nothing'.

The Boon Children were weary and sleepy, and young Henry
'found the histrionic character and the dramatic profession for the
first time revealed' to him. He was fascinated yet somehow afraid.
The girls were frightening in their assurance, their lack of interest
in anything and anybody; they expressed 'melancholy grace and a
sort of peevish refinement, yet seemed awfully detached and indifferent, indifferent perhaps even to being pinched and slapped, for
art's sake, at home'. Even after, Henry James was to have a certain
contempt for actors and actresses – exception made for such per-

sonages as Fanny Kemble or Elizabeth Robins in whose lives the stage had only a partial role. He considered actors 'self-exhibitionistic' creatures. This, however, did not lull his admiration for their art or his love of the theatre.

The Boon Children seemed unaware of young Henry's presence. He thought of himself quite as one of the 'little louts' peeping through a hole in the canvas of a tent at two circus performers. Looking at the Boon Children constituted adventure enough on that historic day – historic in the sense of providing a capital initiation. Henry discovered that experience existed alike in the pages of a book and in the life around him: that fiction at such moments became life and life could be fiction.

II

The Dickens Imprint

His mother had told him it was bedtime. But the small boy was as reluctant as all small boys are to obey when there is a visitor in the house. An Albany cousin had arrived and the elders were gathered in the library; the cousin was to read aloud the first instalment of Mr Dickens's new novel, David Copperfield.

Henry feigned a withdrawal upstairs but retreated instead to cover in the library, 'the friendly shade of some screen or drooping table-cloth'. Behind this protection, doubled up and hugging the carpet, he listened. He listened holding his breath as the story unfolded. Finally the tense cord 'snapped under the strain of the Murdstones' and the elders assembled in the room became aware of a loud sobbing.

This time he was effectively banished to bed. But the 'ply then taken was ineffaceable'. Dickens was woven into the fabric of the young Henry's life. The familiar characters were emerging freshly then in magazine and volume and were also being thrown hastily upon the stage by play-tinkers seeking to give bodily form to the Micawbers and Scrooges, Pickwicks and Copperfields, Oliver Twists and Paul Dombeys whose very names assured a full house. In his later writings Henry alluded to Dickens always in charmed retrospect, yet he never devoted a critical article to him. He wrote of George Eliot and Anthony Trollope, he devoted articles to Robert

Louis Stevenson and even a late essay to Thackeray, but Dickens figured in reminiscence rather than criticism, and only once did he review one of his novels. When James was invited to contribute the Dickens volume to the English Men of Letters series for which he wrote the Hawthorne, he hesitated for a long time and finally declined. Dickens 'laid his hand on us in a way to undermine as in no other case the power of detached appraisement ... he entered so early into the blood and bone of our intelligence that it always remained the better than the taste of overhauling him'. So Dickens remained 'hoarded in the dusty chamber of youth'. Henry preferred it that way. To deal with Dickens as a novelist and craftsman would have been quite another matter; about Dickens's art and sense of life Henry James was to have distinct reservations and they are incorporated in the remarkable review he wrote, as a young man, of *Our Mutual Friend.*

In that same chamber of youth and sentiment were hoarded the memories of the dramatized Dickens, the actor Burton as 'a monstrous Micawber, the coarse parody of a charming creation, with the entire baldness of a huge easter egg and collar-points like the sails of Mediterranean feluccas'. This memory and that of Lizzie Weston as Smike in *Nicholas Nickleby* 'all tearful melodrama' was retained through the years as a striking portrait of 'Nicholas's starved and tattered and fawning and whining protégé'. Decidely, the 'force of the Dickens imprint, however applied, in the soft clay of our generation' resisted 'serenely the wash of the waves of time'.

12

At the Theatre

WHEN he saw the Dickens plays he was already an inveterate theatre-goer of 9 or 10. Henry James's theatrical memories are a striking part of *A Small Boy and Others* whose 400 pages cover only the first fourteen years of his life. Yet one-eighth of these is devoted to a detailed recounting of nights at the play – pantomimes viewed in early childhood, old theatrical billboards with their lurid synopses of the plays and the picturesque names of the stage folk, excursions to the theatres of New York and later of London and Paris. William was taken to the theatre first. Henry tells that story twice, in separate books: and since he names the play to which he was not taken (Charlotte Cushman in *Henry VIII*), we can estimate, from the date of her performance, that at 7 little Henry was not considered quite ready for the theatre. But at 8 the curtain rose on what was to be a lifetime of theatre-going.

James believed that his first play was *A Comedy of Errors*. The work was read to him during the day and he recalled the 'sacred thrill' once inside the theatre before a green curtain that refused to go up. 'One's eyes bored into it in vain, and yet one knew that it *would* rise at the named hour, the only question being if one could exist till then.'

Young Henry was taken to all the leading theatres of the time – Burton's, the Broadway, the National, Wallack's Lyceum, Niblo's Gardens and Barnum's, attached to the 'Great American Museum'. It was the era when many theatres, in the lingering Puritanism, still masqueraded as gardens, lecture rooms, lyceums, baptized with innocent titles while openly plying their lively and profane trade.

At Burton's, in Chambers Street, he saw such familiar farces as *The Toodles* and *The Serious Family*; at the Broadway the super-spectacle of *The Cataract of the Ganges* or *The Rajah's Daughter* (with a cataract of 'real water') and the popular *Green Bushes*; at Wallack's the clever comedies of Dion Boucicault (then written Bourcicault), *London Assurance* and *Love in a Maze*. Always there is the vivid recollection of the actors: William Burton, as Aminadab Sleek, Mr Toodles or Paul Pry, 'his huge person, his huge fat face and his vast slightly pendulous cheek, surmounted by a sort of elephantine wink, to which I impute a remarkable baseness'; Madame Ponisi, the Oberon of *A Midsummer Night's Dream*, 'representing all characters alike with a broad brown face framed in bands or crowns or other heavy headgear out of which cropped a row of very small tight black curls'; Madame Céline Celeste 'straight out of London' in *Green Bushes* 'whose admired walk up the stage as Miami the huntress, a wonderful majestic and yet voluptuous stride enhanced by a short kilt, black velvet leggings and a gun haughtily borne on the shoulder, is vividly before me'; Miss Julia Bennett 'fresh from triumphs at the Haymarket ... in a very becoming white bonnet, either as a brilliant adventuress or as the innocent victim of licentious design, I forget which, though with a sense somehow that the white bonnet, when of true elegance, was the note at that period of the adventuress'. We can multiply examples of these crowded recollections, sometimes accurate in all details, sometimes mistaken, as when he assures us he saw Fanny Wallack in *London Assurance* 'as Lady Gay Spanker, flushed and vociferous, first in a riding-habit with a tail yards long and afterwards in yellow satin with scarce a tail at all'. Fanny Wallack's last appearance in America was in June 1852 and *London Assurance* was not produced at Wallack's until 1854 with Rosa Bennett as Lady Gay.

Henry went to one important drama that was to remain a landmark in the American theatre for successive generations. In November 1853 Barnum mounted his production of *Uncle Tom's Cabin* at his Broadway Museum and here the boy saw the play for the first time with Emily Mestayer, red-faced, 'her swelling bust encased in a neat cotton gown', giving an intrepid and graceful performance of Eliza's flight across the ice. This was an abridged version with a happy ending. Later, Henry saw the full version in six long acts at the National – eight tableaux and thirty scenes – an evening particularly remembered because it happened to be the occasion of his first theatre party. He was able to play the role of critic: he could compare the two versions. He was certain the second Eliza was less dramatic than Miss Mestayer: but the ice-floes at the National seemed more genuine than Barnum's obvious carpentry. And Henry James, writing of this evening late in life, felt that the occasion was all the richer for him in that its humour and melodrama and pathos were collectively shared. He was absorbed as much by the junior audience as by the play. The little sophisticates had gone to *Uncle Tom's Cabin* with some detachment but found themselves swept along by the play's strong currents. It was initiation into social as well as aesthetic adventure.

13

... And Others

I

THE United States at that time consisted for Henry James of 'the busy, the tipsy and Daniel Webster'. The 'busy' were all around him – and there was no shortage of the 'tipsy'. He knew that people went to offices and stores (though his father never did) and that they made money – yet the process of making it was forever a mystery to him, money-conscious though he was from his earliest days. He later came to give New York's uptown and downtown special meanings related to money. Downtown was the world of the money-makers that he didn't know and couldn't write about. Uptown represented leisure, largely feminine (since the males were downtown making the money), and this world was usable in his books.

Early in life there came to him faint echoes of the Mexican War; he caught a glimpse of an uncle in uniform and later was introduced to Winfield Scott on Fifth Avenue. Then he remembered two uncles arriving at their Fifth Avenue apartment, just before the family moved into 14th Street, to announce excitedly to his father the triumph of the revolution of 1848 in France and the flight of Louis-Philippe. Henry was 6 when the country reverberated to the discovery of gold in California, but the Jameses had their eyes turned towards Europe as the covered wagons moved westward. These major events had reality for the boy only as stories told by persons around him, as news broadcast by word of mouth on the Avenue. Beyond the perpetual circle of relatives he began to pay attention to an ever-widening group of callers at his father's house. There were artists, Thomas Hicks, A. J. H. Duganne, C. P. Cranch, Felix O. C. Darley and they talked of others, names that had common currency then, Cropsey, Cole, Kensett, Ives, Powers, Mozier. There were writers, George Curtis, Parke Godwin, George Ripley, Charles Dana, Rufus Griswold and N. P. Willis, with talk of Bryant, Washington Irving, Poe and the familiar Mr Emerson. He remembered meeting Washington Irving on the steamboat to Fort Hamilton. Irving told his father that Margaret Fuller had been drowned with her husband and child off Fire Island in the foundering of a ship during the storm of two days before.

Thus gradually was constituted an atmosphere around the small boy and his brothers and sister, in which figured people doing things, men with reputations, a world of books, talk of art. Closest to Henry Junior were the maternal and paternal relatives; he dubs them 'a company of characters' and proceeds to sketch them in his memoirs in a brilliant series of profiles. They are the *Others* outside his immediate family in the title of his autobiographical volume. Mainly there are cousins on all sides, even as we find them later in his novels in groups and clusters, people one could or could not be 'in relation with' and who are also 'other'. 'Everyone was a little someone else,' he wrote in a late story. In *A Small Boy* he tells us that he was 'constantly eager to exchange my lot for that of somebody else, on the assured certainty of gaining by the bargain'. He is careful at the same time to explain that this was not 'jealousy'. In contemplating the qualities of his orphaned cousins in particular he reveals how low a value the small boy placed on himself; and, when this is the case, it does not permit any such acute passion as jealousy. His desire to be 'somebody else' was the equivalent of a small boy's view, he explained, of sweets through a plate glass window. The glass will never melt. To be 'other, almost anyhow, seemed as good as the possible taste of the bright compound wistfully watched in the confectioner's window; unattainable, impossible, of course'. Therefore, jealousy wasn't involved. Accepting the idea of the unattainable meant also removing himself from competition. 'I never dreamed of competing – a business having in it at the best for my temper if not for my total failure of temper, a displeasing ferocity. If competing was bad, snatching was therefore still worse, and jealousy was a sort of spiritual snatching.'

Little Henry thus reduced himself to his favourite pastime of watching. He observed his relatives closely. William of Albany's family had been large; and there were maternal relatives as well. The human material close to the future novelist was abundant.

2

They pass before us in a series of sketches and portraits; they constitute a 'chronicle of early deaths, arrested careers, broken promises, orphaned children'. The father's relatives to whom he alludes in this fashion receive less notice than the mother's; and the mother's are all 'strong' females, holding their men under their thumbs, from Great-Aunt Wyckoff, 'an image of living antiquity ... that I was never to see surpassed', to Cousin Helen, his mother's cousin, with her 'fine old New York ignorance and rigour'. The Great-Aunt sat for Juliana Bordereau in *The Aspern Papers*, 'throned, hooded, and draped' wearing a green eye-shade. Cousin Helen with her suppressed husband could have been the inspiration for *Georgina's Reasons*. Cousin Helen's husband was described as a 'dim little gentleman' and a 'spectral spouse'. He is also a 'shade of nullity', 'a blank', 'a zero' and a 'natural platitude'. But Henry makes it clear that it is Helen who has utterly reduced him to this status. He was

'Mr' to his own wife. This seemed to Henry to sum up the situation.

Henry frequently went to the Fourteenth Street 'other house' (where he remembered reading *Oliver Twist*) and saw Helen's husband in his shipboard pace, from the street-end to the piazza at the back; he wore neckclothes that seemed to elongate his neck and was partially bald, with his hair standing up on both sides. Here the small boy also used to see Albert Wyckoff, Cousin Helen's nephew, who seemed an independent spirit since he was among those neither fathered nor mothered; yet in the end Cousin Helen sufficed for both. The husband talked often of the grand tour he would some day make. Finally, after half a century, he sailed for England. The shock was too much for him. There was a 'snap of the tense cord ... he just landed and died'. Helen also had charge of Henry Wyckoff, her brother, and of his ample fortune. She gave him a dime a day on the theory that he was 'not to be trusted' with money. When finally his guardian died after almost half a century of this discipline, he naturally failed to rise to his estate. 'He did feel rich, just as he felt generous; the misfortune was only in his weak sense for meanings.' Henry James decided that not his pocket but his imagination had been starved. Years later Henry Wyckoff became the subject of the novelist's stage comedy, *The Reprobate*.

The small boy saw only the beginning of these stories of his relatives, but he lived to be present also at their endings. There were other cousins and uncles who died almost before their lives began : Minny Temple, the second daughter of the senior Henry's second sister, Catherine James, a bright Albany cousin known briefly to the small boy, but later destined, on re-acquaintance at Newport, to play a large role in his life; Gus Barker, the second son of Jeannette or Janet James, Catherine James's oldest sister, whose mother died giving birth to him. A guerrilla's bullet cut him down at 21 during the Civil War and we capture him, during his brief bright life, through Henry Junior's eyes, clad in the uniform of the military school he was attending and much admired by his cousin, 'the most beautifully-made athletic little person, and in the highest degree appealing and engaging'; and again without uniform, in fact without clothes, 'perched on a pedestal and divested of every garment', being drawn by William James in Hunt's studio at Newport. Henry kept William's sketch; presently, it was all that remained of the genial Gus.

There was Gus's brother, Bob Barker, with his promise as a sculptor; Johnny James, with a talent for music cut short by death; the four uncles, Augustus, John, Edward and Howard, the first presiding in grandeur over Linwood, the last three figuring as customers of Mrs Cannon who sold ties, collars and the essence known in old New York as 'Cullone', somewhere near Fourth Street; little girl cousins encountered in Paris; Vernon King with his European background and his sad end – a tale told twice in *A Small Boy* : the conflict between Vernon, the blond-bearded short-of-breath dandy of Paris and Newport and his mother Charlotte who had Southern sympathies; Vernon's promise not to return to battle after he was wounded in the Civil War, his violation of the promise; his untimely end at Richmond or Petersburg and his burial at Newport under a stone that makes no allusion to his soldier's death.

The dimmest ghost of all perhaps was the memory of Aunt Ellen King James, 'softly spectral' with ringlets, who died at 26 – when Henry was 6. This was in Albany and he remembered a call at her house in Elk Street, the memory being fixed mainly by the fact that she had married Smith Thompson Van Buren, the son of a President of the United States. The visitable past of the James family could lead Henry even to the White House.

Part Three:

The Nostalgic Cup

14

Theory of Education

IN the history of literature and in the lives of a majority of the nineteenth-century novelists, Church and School figure as twin institutions colouring their childhood and casting shadows, for good or bad, across the adult years. The discipline of the spirit and of the mind was imposed by precept and sermon in those rigorous decades or firmly injected by the broad and generous application of strap and ferule. In how many novels do we sit with the struggling hero or heroine through interminable Sunday mornings – such as those commemorated by Henry James Senior – and long classroom hours over Latin and sums? The era of *The Way of All Flesh* and Wackford Squeers left Henry Junior relatively untouched. Although he was born, as we have seen, in a house hard by a church and a university he grew up unencumbered by religion or formal education. The elder Henry, remembering his joyless childhood, shrank from anything that would be 'narrowing' for his children. A cheerful anarchy characterized the schooling of the little Jameses. As for the Church, Henry himself described his relations with it as 'pewless'.

I

'What church do you go to?' his schoolmates challenged. Little Henry was as bereft of an answer as he was when asked to name his father's profession.

It was colder than any criticism, I recall, to hear our father reply that we could plead nothing less than the whole privilege of Christendom, and that there was no communion, even that of the Catholics, even that of the Jews, even that of the Swedenborgians, from which we need find ourselves excluded. With the freedom we enjoyed, our dilemma clearly amused him: it would have been impossible, he affirmed, to be theologically more *en règle*.

To have all the churches and all the religions was really to have none. And this may explain why Henry James, during early adult life, indulged in periods of intense church-going, as if to compensate for past omissions. At 20 he wrote from New York to T. S. Perry that he had filled two Sundays with the sermon of a Presbyterian preacher and visits to a revival meeting and to 'a congregation of the new dispensation'. The Presbyterian preacher aroused particular curiosity because he had officiated in a church attended years before by Henry's mother. 'Darkly must her prospect of Heaven have been obscured!' mused her son. 'The old man is now 80, but he still finds strength, with great reinforcements of tobacco-juice, to fulminate against back-sliders and evil-doers. I may emphatically say he gave us hell.'

From this divine Henry went on to hear Mrs Cora V. Hatch in an Astor Place basement. A committee, selected on the spot, decided upon her subject: 'The Evidence of the Continued Existence of the Spirit after Death'. Cora, after invoking Divine aid, began to speak in 'a string of ... arrant platitudes', and we promptly recognize the type of female oratory we shall encounter thirty years later in *The Bostonians*. At the 'congregation of the new dispensation' he listened to 'a grand oration (tremendous) from the female on the right and singing from her on the left'. Henry was taking his father's account of their universal church membership literally. His taste in church services was to remain ecumenical.

Church-going for Henry, whether in London or while paying country visits in later life, was essentially a social phenomenon rather than a religious experience. 'James's churches of any denomination,' one critic has remarked, 'are a humane crystallization of the scene – moments, aspects, tones, with little sectarian dispute to disturb the atmosphere.' On Sundays, in his stories, we walk across the English countryside, past the old tombstones into the old small church whose bell long before has musically been chiming through the hollow. Here dramatic incidents sometimes occur: the ghost of Sir Edmund Orme suddenly stands in the pew, or little Miles demands that he be sent back to school. If Henry James can be said to have had a personal religion, it was a mysticism compounded of meditation and communion with spirits and forces vaguely discerned yet acutely felt, in a dim intuitional 'beyond'. On the one hand he accepted the supremacy of reason and on the other he inclined towards Pascalian intuition. He worshipped in solitary visits to churches and cathedrals much after the manner of his strange protagonist in *The Altar of the Dead*. By middle life he had a series of shrines – the shrine of art, tradition, morality, his own religion of beauty and the 'religion of consciousness' – a worship almost pagan, were it not so highly sophisticated; he invoked the 'powers and forces and divinities to whom I've ever been loyal', including the guiding spirit of his writing-table, whom he familiarly addressed as *mon bon* – the unseen but felt power within him that was his creative god. This, combined with the curious private prayers he wrote out in his notebooks – more invocation to the special Jamesian Muse than prayer – constituted the 'religion' of the novelist. He never seems to have prayed to a specific Deity in his writings, and his admiration for Catholicism was exclusively for that portion of it which provided for 'retreat', meditation, communion with a Deity – a Deity of his own choosing (much like his father's), together with a delight for the colour of Catholic ritual. *The Great Good Place* was a monastery of the mind.

For Catholicism as a functioning religion, and for some of its manifestations, as he saw them at Rome, he occasionally had the word of a Protestant born if not bred. The absence of formal religion in his upbringing did stimulate a curiosity about religious experience; he wondered, for instance, at the absence of clergymen in the James household, although he found them present in most English novels read as a boy; but he did have the case of his father and the revolt against Calvinism. During his boyhood he was exposed at the most to his father's talk of Swedenborg, his diatribes against organized religion and an occasional Sunday reading of the Scriptures. He was exposed much more to religious *feeling* than to religion itself. This resulted in his reviewing in later years such works as Père Chocarne's *Inner Life of Father Lacordaire* or Count de Falloux's *Life and Letters of Madame Swetchine* – works in which the religious sentiment is paramount. Henry James complained that Daudet in *L'Évangéliste* not only did not understand Protestantism, but lacked any 'natural understanding of the religious passion'. That 'province of the human mind', James added, 'cannot be *fait de chic* – experience, there, is the only explorer'. Through his father he had had this experience. Nevertheless, the 'religious passion' is generally absent from his novels. It was not absent from his life, where it was constantly being translated, in full measure, into his art.

2

'School' was present in Henry's life with much greater regularity than Church. First there were the 'educative ladies' – the long line that began with Miss Bayou or Bayhoo. They included a Miss Sedgwick, a Mrs Wright (Lavinia D.), a Russian lady with an accent whose name was forgotten, a Mlle Delavigne, who taught French, and a Mrs Vredenburg, who maintained a summer school at New Brighton on Staten Island. Then, when he was 10, he was sent to the Institution Vergnès in lower Broadway, 'a sordidly *black* interior'. It occupied the first and second floors of a building past which stage-coaches and horse-cars rattled and heavy carts were painfully dragged and where he could hear the 'promiscuous human shuffle of New York'. M. Maurice Vergnès was an old and rather irritable individual, or seemed to be to the young Henry, and the school swarmed with small homesick Cubans and Mexicans. The entire staff of this institution was 'constantly in a rage'.

I remember infuriated ushers, of foreign speech and flushed complexion – the tearing across of hapless 'exercises' and *dictées* and the hurtle through the air of dodged volumes; only never, despite this, the extremity of smiting. There can have been at the Institution no blows instructionally dealt – nor even from our hours of ease do any such echoes come back to me. Little Cubans and Mexicans, I make out, were not to be vulgarly whacked – in deference, presumably, to some latent relic or imputed survival of Castilian pride ... In Vergnès air at any rate I seem myself to have sat unscathed and unterrified – not alarmed even by so much as a call to the blackboard; only protected by my insignificance.

In due course the elder James, always experimenting, removed William and Henry to the greater establishment of Mr Richard Puling Jenks at 689 Broadway, where they were pupils during 1853–4 – that is, during Henry's eleventh year. Mr Jenks was a rotund, bald man with a *barbiche*, who nursed his ferule and whacked occasionally, although Henry had no recollection of ever being the recipient of so much attention. Mr Coe was the drawing-master, tall, white-haired and affecting a great cloak. What impressed little Henry was that so tall an individual produced such miniature drawings, 'as if some mighty bird had laid diminutive eggs'. Mr Coe, he added, laid his 'all over the place', and Henry in his old age could remember the very smell of the tiny panels he painted. He taught the boys to draw crooked cottages, feathery trees, browsing beasts.

The third member of the Jenks faculty was the writing-master, Mr Dolmidge, 'a pure pen-holder of a man' who taught the boys how to make complicated flourishes. The school itself was recalled by Henry as a couple of

middling rooms, front and back, our close packing, our large unaccommodating stove, our grey and gritty oilcloth, and again our importunate Broadway ... Up out of Broadway we still scrambled – I can smell the steep and cold and dusty wooden staircase; straight into Broadway we dropped – I feel again the generalised glare of liberation ... we must have knocked about in Broadway, and in Broadway alone, like perfect little men of the world; we must have been let loose there to stretch our legs and fill our lungs, without prejudice either to our earlier and later freedoms of going and coming.

The stove scorched without warming and Henry wondered how he could have been put into a school with such a 'deficiency of landscape'. For Henry there had been nothing comparable to the playing-fields of Eton, only the dusty, noisy streets of old New York.

In the following year they changed schools yet again. This time, Henry recalled, they were moved to the establishment of 'Forest and Quackenboss' at Fourteenth Street and Sixth Avenue. However, no such school is given in the New York directory of that year although two teachers list their names as Quackenbos. George P. Quackenbos lived at 292 Henry Street and George C. at 124 Leroy; a William Forrest is listed as a teacher in the 1854–5 directory at 71 West 14th Street, which would be near Sixth Avenue at that time. At any rate, Henry studied with a Mr Forest or Forrest, a massive individual in a black dress-coat and white neckcloth, and found him 'the driest of all our founts of knowledge'. William had Mr Quackenbos – the two teachers may have occupied the same premises – and was lost on upper floors, in higher classes, in real pursuits'. We gather that in this class Henry day-dreamed much over the prospect of Europe.

3

Henry James Senior's theory of education was comparatively simple. He feared pedantry and rigidity; he had a horror of dogma and of moral judgements. He wanted to spare his children the sufferings of his own boyhood. His solution was to throw them into many schools and to let them find their own feet. He reasoned that there was Divine Truth in the world and this the children were bound to discover under Divine Guidance. 'The literal,' Henry Junior said, 'played in our education as small a part as it perhaps ever played in any ... Method certainly never quite raged among us.'

The father's desire to surround his boys with 'an atmosphere of freedom' was itself surrounded by contradictions. When William at one point expressed a desire to go to Union College, his father burst out that colleges were hotbeds of corruption where it was impossible to learn anything. Later, he agreed to William's attending Harvard. When Henry first expressed a desire to follow William, the father said it was 'wholly unpracticable'. Some months later, in a different mood, he informed Henry there was no obstacle to his going. 'To have deprecated the "college course" with such emphasis,' his son reflected, 'only so soon afterwards to forswear all emphasis and practically smile, in mild oblivion, on *any* Harvard connection I might find it in me to take up, was to bring it home, I well recall, that the case might originally have been much better managed.' This was still another instance of having to breathe inconsistency and drink contradiction.

The 'theory' – if the elder James's ideas on education can be called anything so formal – produced in young Henry the feeling that he had been given no standard by which to judge the facts of the life he saw around him. He felt himself forced, he reasoned much later, to pay attention to everything, and by this process could seek to bring order, reason and common sense into the world's chaos. The senior Henry gave him, he felt, no sense of values save to realize the value of *all* life and *all* experience. At one point the novelist likens his brother and himself to Romulus and Remus, disowned by the parent, thrown into the Tiber of life, left to flounder as best they could, and called upon to build Rome – that is, to have the right answers to the Divine Truth which the father affirmed was all around them. The novelist reasoned that this free-and-easy mode of education – or absence thereof – was the best thing that could have happened to him: it made him 'convert' – everything had to be translated into his own terms and rendered in the light of his own inner resources. He had a need for order, for design, for apprehending – and later communicating – the world around him. In a sense the circle came full round: William of Albany sought to impose discipline and order on the senior Henry; the elder Henry carefully refused to impose such order upon his novelist son, who in the end imposed it, as a consequence of inner needs, upon himself – with the aid always, however, of his mother's greater rigidity and firmness.

Reflecting in his old age on the years spent in the New York classrooms, Henry was struck by his isolation, in the midst of 'elbowing and kicking' classmates. The little boy was as shy in class as at home. He neither attracted attention nor was molested by his thoroughly down-to-earth schoolfellows. He gives the impression that he was perturbed by this, yet at the same time aware of the ground upon which he stood as a little observer of the human scene. 'I lived and wriggled, floundered and failed, lost the clue of everything but a general lucid consciousness (lucid, that is, for my tender years) which I clutched with a sense of its values.' This lucid consciousness enabled him to remember the appearance and the dress of his teachers, the smell of the classrooms, the aspect of bustling Manhattan in which he moved. He had an eye for detail, for picture, for scene – and sensual awareness from the first. There was 'self-abandonment ... to visions' in the obscure classrooms, and in doing this he carried on 'in the midst of the actual – an existence that somehow floated and saved me even while cutting me off from any degree of direct performance, in fact from any degree of direct participation, at all'.

He 'converted'. The small boy's imagination could make

all pastors and masters, and especially all fellow-occupants of benches and desks, all elbowing and kicking presences within touch or view, so many monsters and horrors, so many wonders and splendours and mysteries, but never, so far as I can recollect, realities of relation, dispensers either of knowledge or of fate, playmates, intimates, mere coevals and coequals.

What the small boy could do was to endow them with the wonder of his imagination; far from indulging in a flight from reality, he achieved something that did not exist at all for his fellow-pupils.

They were something better – better above all than the coequal and coeval; they were so thoroughly figures and characters, divinities or demons, and endowed in this light with a vividness that the mere reality of relation, a commoner directness of contact, would have made, I surmise, comparatively poor.

Henry's conclusion was that 'no education avails for the intelligence that doesn't stir in it some subjective passion and that on the other hand almost anything that does so act is largely educative'. There remains indeed the significant fact that not all little boys possess a subjective passion.

15

The Thames and the Seine

HENRY JAMES the elder had been settled only a few months in the house on 14th Street when he began to speak of taking his family abroad. This time, however, he did not move precipitately. The project was discussed for six years. Meanwhile the small boy and his brothers were able to push down roots in Manhattan. As early as August 1849, when Henry was 6 the father wrote to Emerson a since much-quoted letter about his boys and their education. The family had grown, the 14th Street house required enlargement, a country place was needed for the hot summers. 'These things look expensive and temporary to us, besides being an additional care,' the father wrote,

and so, looking upon our four stout boys, who have no play-room within doors, and import shocking bad manners from the street, with much pity, we gravely ponder whether it would not be better to go abroad for a few years with them, allowing them to absorb French and German and get a better sensuous education than they are likely to get here. To be sure, this is but a glimpse of our ground of proceeding – but perhaps you know some decisive word which shall dispense us from further consideration of the subject.

This was indeed a large request, and Emerson's reply was a model of tact. 'I hear with some terror that you are going to Europe, I who never see you ... New York looked available and intelligent whilst I knew you were in it.' Years later, Henry Junior, quoting from the letter to Emerson in his memoirs, amended the words 'get a better sensuous education than they are likely to get here' to read 'get such a sensuous education as they can't get here'. In this way he proclaimed the absence of proper facilities in America for 'sensuous' schooling and at the same time sought to create the impression that his father's decision to go abroad was not an arbitrary act but one of necessity.

In 1851, the debate was still going on in the elder Henry's mind. 'We are still talking of Europe for the boys,' he wrote to Dr Wilkinson. To Edmund and Mary Tweedy, he wrote, 'We may go to foreign parts ... and educate the babies in strange lingoes.' But they remained in New York, from year to year, with Europe always on the horizon. Finally, however, the decision was taken and the preparations made. On the evening of 26 June 1855 the elder Henry wrote to S. G. Ward, 'We are having a golden sunset to pace our last evening at home.' The next day he marched aboard the S.S. *Atlantic* of the Collins Line with his wife and five offspring and a French maid, Annette Godefroi, who came from Metz. The great adventure, the 're-exposure' to Europe, 'to air already breathed and to a harmony already disclosed', was begun. Henry Junior was then twelve.

The 'nostalgic cup', he wrote years later, 'had been applied to my lips even before I was conscious of it'. He had been 'hurried off to London and to Paris immediately after my birth and then and there, I was ever afterwards strangely to feel, that poison had entered my veins'. The nostalgic cup was about to be offered to him again or, in another image which he also used, the golden nail was to be driven in once more, this time not into an infant kicking his feet in his flowing child's robe on someone's knee in the Place Vendôme, but to a keen-eyed little product of Manhattan, alert to the wonders of the world.

I

They disembarked at Liverpool on 8 July 1855 and forty-eight hours later Henry was sitting beside a coachman on a vehicle piled high with luggage and packed with his brothers and sister, gaping at the spectacle of London. The remainder of the stay in the capital of mid-Victorian England was a memory only of a curtained four-poster bed in the Euston Hotel. Henry suddenly developed chills and fever, an after-effect of the sojourn on Staten Island the previous summer. He remained in bed 'with the thick and heavy suggestions of the London room about me ... and the window open to the English [July] ... and the far-off hum of a thousand possibilities'.

A few days later the James boys were on a balcony of the Hôtel Westminster in the Rue de la Paix, looking at the Paris of the Second Empire. It was at this moment that Jean Nadali took Henry and William to the Louvre for their memorable first visit. The curious small boy remembered also that across the street from the hotel he could see one of the capital's famous dressmaking establishments, busy young women sewing far into the night. The James family did not linger long in Paris. They pushed ahead whenever Henry's fever and chills subsided. They took the railway to Lyon and, at the Hôtel de l'Univers, Henry spent more time in bed. The hours in this hostelry prepared him, he felt, for the French *vie de province* in the pages of Balzac. There was no railway between Lyon and Geneva, and the father engaged two travelling-carriages to complete the journey. They set forth with young Henry stretched out on an improvised couch, formed by a plank across two seats and a small mattress fortified by cushions, and with an elaborate retinue – a costumed postillion, the black-moustached Nadali and the fresh-coloured, broad-faced Mlle Godefroi. For Henry this was 'the romance of travel'. He was to yield to it, in one form or another, all his life.

And so while in the United States new generations of Americans were striking westward, the James family, products of the eastern seaboard, pushed still farther east, across an ocean, to travel in this elaborate fashion over the Franco-Swiss highways into the Alps. Henry James would not write about prairie schooners but he would write about Americans spending the fruits of their native wealth in Europe and riding in travelling-carriages through Switzerland. The capital event of this journey, during which the young Henry sat propped among his pillows like some young princeling, was 'an hour that has never ceased to recur to me all my life as crucial, as supremely determinant'. The carriages mounted and mounted, and at one point there was a halt at the doorway of an inn in the cool sunshine. Henry munched cold chicken and surveyed the scene. The village street was unlike any that he had ever observed: it was hilly and opened on a fresh, a significant, in fact an epochal, revelation: a castle and a ruin.

The only 'castle' Henry knew was an elaborate villa with towers at the New Brighton summer resort; and he had never before encountered a ruin. Below the slope he spied a woman at work, attired in a black bodice, a white shirt, a red petticoat, a pair of sabots, the first peasant he had ever seen. Here was a 'sublime synthesis' of Europe for the future novelist, and it was as such that he remembered it: a castle (with a tower), a ruin, a peasant woman in sabots engaged in field labour. Memories came to little Henry of books, of lonely readings in 14th Street; now imagined scenes focused into reality.

'Europe mightn't have been flattered, it was true, at my finding her thus most signified and summarized in a sordid old woman scraping a mean living and an uninhabitable tower abandoned to the owls ... It made a bridge over to more things than I then knew.' The young Henry James – or the old Henry James recalling the past – had fixed on the symbols of 'Europe' selected by Goethe in his *Poems of Wisdom* dedicated to America :

> America, you fare much better
> Than this old continent of ours.
> No basalt rocks your land enfetter,
> No ruined towers.

The memory of that day was embodied by Henry James some years later in one of his early stories, written when he was 26 and on the verge of his first adult journey to Europe. In *Gabrielle de Bergerac* there is the castle of Fossy, lifting its 'dark and crumbling towers with a decided air of feudal arrogance from the summit of a gentle eminence in the recess of a shallow gorge ... offering the hospitality of its empty skull to a colony of swallows'. The hero talks as if he had been reading Goethe : 'It's haunted with the ghost of the past. It smells of tragedies, sorrows, cruelties.' The heroine speaks of knights and ladies, a lover on bended knee, a moat sheeted with lilies, all the trappings of feudal romance. The young man isn't interested. Could he have counted on being a Knight in that old order? The reality is that he would have been a 'brutal, senseless peasant, yoked down like an ox, with my forehead in the soil'.

'I should have liked to live in those old days,' sighs the heroine. And her young lover answers : 'Life is hard enough now.'

High on the road into Switzerland that day Henry James glimpsed the romance and the ruin of Europe, the contradictions of past and present, the symbols human and material of the old feudal order. This was more education than he had ever received in Broadway or Washington Square.

2

In Geneva the James family established itself during August of 1855 in an old house, the Villa Campagne-Gerebsow, sublet by an invalid Russian lady who assigned five or six rooms to her guests and kept a wing for herself. The grounds led to the junction of the Arve and the Rhône. The garden was whitened with orange-blossoms. There was a view of Mont Blanc. All this for ten dollars a week, the elder James triumphantly announced in a wordy letter to the New York *Tribune*. The Russian lady could be seen regularly in her *chaise-longue* under a mushroom hat and green veil in a corner of the garden. Henry watched her from afar. Wilky, more gregarious, made her acquaintance and reported to Henry on her identity and history. In most of his tales of Switzerland later, shadowy Russian ladies figure in the background, sometimes alluded to as 'tartaresses'.

He was still spending feverish days in bed. William, Wilky and Bob were placed at a Swiss boarding-school, the Pensionnat Roediger at Châtelaine, where Henry was scheduled to join them upon his recovery. The elder Henry extolled the school in a second letter to the *Tribune* for having a playground as big as Washington Square and providing the young with gymnastic facilities; he also praised the participation of the teachers in the boyish games, was deeply impressed by the absence of rowdyism, the cultivation of the arts, the staging of concerts; in subsequent letters he stressed the fact that the students were given a large measure of freedom on Sundays. The James parents attended one of the Sundays at the school. There was a grand dinner at five in the afternoon, followed by singing and dancing; the senior Henry was pleasantly struck by a Sabbath converted into a day of 'pure festivity'.

Henry Junior recalled the spaciousness of the Geneva villas, the cool houses, the green shutters, the placid pastoral scenes, the great trees, the afternoon shadows and the polyglot character of the school, where a babble of English, French, German and Russian was constant. The boys were to be sent at first to the Institution Haccius, a celebrated establishment dedicated to teaching languages to young Americans – but the father changed his mind when he discovered that the American language 'reigned there almost unchallenged'. The stay in Switzerland, begun with such parental enthusiasm, was soon curtailed. In fact, by the time the father's enthusiastic letters were appearing in the *Tribune* he was writing his mother that Swiss schools were 'over-rated'. He and his wife had decided 'home tuition' would be best for the children. This was in late September, two months after they had arrived in Geneva.

Early in October the elder Henry decided to spend the winter in London. 'We had fared across the sea,' Henry Junior wrote, 'under the glamour of the Swiss school in the abstract, but the Swiss school in the concrete soon turned stale on our hands.' This time without a courier, but with a new Swiss governess, they clambered aboard the big postal coach between Geneva and Lyon, 'vast, yellow and rumbling.' It was wholly filled by the Jameses. To the last there was a note of romance: an expatriate cousin, Charlotte King, emerged from a rural retreat and ran alongside the carriage pleading with the conductor to slow up, *rien que pour saluer ces dames*. The coach didn't slow down much, but the enterprising Charlotte achieved her brief, breathless visit with her ambulatory relatives and 'dropped as elegantly out as she had gymnastically floated in'.

Two days later they were in Paris. Then, late one evening, tired and hungry, they were in London, at the Gloucester Hotel close to Berkeley Square, where they ate cold roast beef, bread and cheese and washed it down with ale, while an exuberant father extolled the English scene: 'There's nothing like it after all.' From here they moved into a small house at No. 3 Berkeley Square and then, after a month and before their first English Christmas, into a furnished house in St John's Wood above Regent's Park, No. 10 Marlborough Place, where they had Dr J. J. Garth Wilkinson and his family as neighbours. 'You have a home-feeling in London,' the elder Henry wrote to his mother.

3

On 14 November 1855, an advertisement appeared in *The Times* of London. 'To teachers. – The advertiser wishes to engage a tutor, by the month, for three or four hours a day, who is competent to give his boys instruction in Latin, and the ordinary branches of an English education. None but well qualified persons need apply. Address H.J., 3, Berkeley-square, between 5 and 7 in the evening.' The father selected from an overflow of candidates, a fresh-complexioned, long legged, cleared-eyed, Scot with a tendency to trip over his legs, Robert Thomson (James spelled it Thompson in his memoirs). Thomson engaged rooms in Titchfield Terrace along Regent's Park, over a baker's shop to be near his charges, and from morning until noon he taught them – exactly what, Henry could not remember. He recalled only that Thomson gave him as a reward a copy of Lamb's *Tales from Shakespeare*; that he pitched ball with the boys in the large garden of their house; and on days when they did their work in his rooms, at recess time, a little girl, looking like a Dickens orphan, would come up from the shop with a big stale cake which the young Jameses speedily consumed.

Thomson did not confine education to books or ball-playing. He took the boys on long rambles – the length of Baker Street, the landmarks of the English novelists, the Tower, St Paul's, the Abbey, not to speak of Madame Tussaud's. Years later, Henry discovered that the warmly-remembered Scottish tutor, after leaving his American pupils, taught still another future novelist, and a later friend, Robert Louis Stevenson.

Their French was not neglected. Mlle Amélie Cusin, who had come from Geneva to London, carefully officiated over the family's use of the Gallic tongue. She was but one of 'a longish procession of more or less similar domesticated presences' whose ghostly names Henry retained: Mlle Cusin, Augustine Danse, Amélie Fortin, Marie Guyard, Marie and Félicie Bonningue, Clarisse Bader. Mlle Danse, 'her of the so flexible *taille* and the so salient smiling eyes' was 'the most brilliant and most genial of irregular characters'. She was abruptly dismissed, however; someone hinted she had been an 'adventuress'. That made adventuresses interesting for Henry. He had admired Mlle Danse's 'sophisticated views' and she had shown the James children much 'solicitude'. He likened her to a distinguished governess of fiction, Becky Sharp.

They haunted the Pantheon in Oxford Street studying the vast canvases of Haydon; they visited Marlborough House and looked at the works of Maclise, Mulready, Landseer, David Wilkie and Charles Leslie. Maclise's *Play-Scene in Hamlet*, with Ophelia looking as if she were cut in silhouette out of white paper, pasted on the canvas, attracted Henry; he 'gazed and gazed again' at Leslie's *Sancho Panza and the Duchess*. They went also to the Royal Academy and saw the fresh flowering of the Pre-Raphaelites – exemplified in Millais's *Vale of Rest*, his *Autumn Leaves* and his *Blind Girl*.

Playgoing in London was an elaborate ceremony, a ride through foggy tracts of the town from St John's Wood to the West End. The British capital offered the excitement of the Christmas pantomime

and Charles Mathews, Frederick Robson, Alfred Wigan and Charles
Kean. The 'momentous' event of the London stay was Kean's production of *Henry VIII*. For weeks afterwards the James children
sought to reproduce in water-colours Queen Katharine's dream-
vision of beckoning and consoling angels. 'The spectacle had seemed
to us prodigious – as it was doubtless at its time the last word of
costly scenic science.' The stunted Robson, his hoarse voice, his
grotesque delivery, fascinated the children; he leered and snarled; he
would grind his teeth and roll his eyes; he created comedy and painful intensity for the young Americans. At the Olympic, Henry saw
Tom Taylor's *Still Waters Run Deep* with Wigan; Mathews he saw
in *The Critic*. He remembered the nights at the Olympic in Wych
Street, approached through squalid slums, an 'incredibly brutal and
barbarous' avenue to the make-believe of the theatre.

For Henry the London people themselves offered a wide field of
observation. They had an 'exuberance of type' and a wealth of costume – postmen in their red frock-coats and black beaver hats,
milk-women in shawls and enormous boots, footmen hooked behind
coaches, grooms with riders in the Park. He remembered in particular one evening, a return from the Continent to London with his
father, a long ride in a Victorian four-wheeler westward from the
station at London Bridge. It was June : the evening light lingered
softly; there were swarming crowds. The gas-lit patches of street
seemed like the London of Cruikshank (and, as he later recognized,
of Hogarth). The Artful Dodger and Bill Sikes and Nancy were in
the streets that night; Henry caught a glimpse from the cab window, as a framed picture, of a woman reeling backward from a blow
to the face given her by a man. Violence – that side of life excluded
from his novels – was not unfamiliar to him. There were 'embodied
and exemplified "horrors" ' in the streets – and 'horrors' was added
to Henry James's special lexicon of words surrounded by quotation
marks, that is, words having special meanings and associations for
him. To narrow the meaning was to be specific. To use the word
'horrors' and leave it at that, was to suggest *all* the horrors a reader
wanted to imagine.

4

From the London of the 1850s to the Second Empire was a small jump – yet it was a progress to another world. St John's Wood was abandoned in the early summer of 1856 in favour of the French capital. The James boys said good-bye to Robert Thomson and in due course were entrusted to Monsieur Lerambert, who was apparently as good a teacher although more aloof. They lived first in a house rented from an American who divided his time between Louisiana and France. Henry remembered glassy floors, a perilous staircase, redundant mirrors, clocks, ormolu vases, white-and-gold panels, brocaded walls, sofas and chairs in red damask. Lerambert was spare and pale; he wore a tight black coat and spectacles and came from the Rue Jacob on the Left Bank, where he lived with his mother and sister. He had written a volume of meditative verse which the great Sainte-Beuve had sympathetically noticed. They spent long sleepy mornings in a pavilion on the Champs-Élysées between the Rond Point and the Rue du Colisée. The windows opened on a clattery, plashy court. They rendered La Fontaine into an English that was admired and commended by his parents. In the afternoons there was the wonderful Mlle Danse with her smiling eyes to take the boys for walks along the Champs-Élysées. She devoted herself mainly to Henry and the younger brothers. She wasn't interested in William, whom she considered rather an *ours* – a bear – because he insisted on precise and scientific answers. She was fondest of the youngest, *l'ingénieux petit Robertson*. Henry was beyond the age when children delight in mere puppets; nevertheless he relished Guignol and Gringalet on the Champs-Élysées; more than this he relished Mlle Danse's Paris; she 'vouchsafed us all information for the free enjoyment – on the terms proper to our tender years – of her beautiful city'. It was not then as beautiful as it is today. Baron Haussmann had not yet cut his boulevards through the slums. It was the old Paris, the Paris of the Revolutions, with its little streets and small squares and its lively citizens. In the Paris of the Second Empire the eye could take in the Tuileries and the grandeur of the Arch while cafés and houses with gardens and terraces were to be discovered along the Seine in a kind of 'dusty ruralism' that merged with the Bois. The Jardin d'Hiver 'looped itself at night with little coloured oil-lamps, a mere twinkling grin upon the face of pleasure'. Beyond the Arch was the beginning of suburb, and the two lodges of the *octroi* stood guard on either side, suggestive of revolutions and re-storations. The young Empress, 'more than young, attestedly and agreeably *new* and fair and shining', was constantly to be seen riding in state. The father's contemporary report of their view of royalty was:

We saw the Empress yesterday promenading *en voiture*, and shortly after the Emperor [with] his American swagger. Certainly it is a high compliment to our country that he should thus adopt one of its most distinctive institutions. We see the infant hope of the Empire every bright day, of which we have had a great many lately.

He added: 'On the whole then we are too well off here, to think of returning just yet.' Paris of that era had a 'homely grace', and the Jameses set up their fireside for another winter abroad. By September 1856 they had left the plush house for an apartment at No. 19 Rue d'Angoulême-St Honoré (now Rue de la Boëtie), with many windows from which Henry could survey the full flow of life of his *quartier*: the inevitable *boulangerie*, the *crémerie*, the *épicerie*, the *écaillère* or oyster-lady, the blue-frocked workers and stout or spare cabmen, all thoroughly *bavard* and critical, as their descendants are to this day; the *marchand de bois* with his neat faggots and logs stacked around him, and so on, the whole series of local shops, sociable and domestic, that made up the individual streets of the French capital.

From this Paris Henry still maintained his links with New York. His earliest boyhood letter extant is a missive still in its narrow envelope addressed in a bold hand to Master E. Van Winkle, 14 st, N. York. The recipient, Edgar Van Winkle, son of a lawyer, lived two doors from the Jameses and 'walked in a maze of culture' – at least so Henry remembered him. 'Dear Eddy,' it runs, with a brevity the novelist was seldom to achieve in his later correspondence, 'As I heard you were going to try to turn the club into a Theatre. And as I was asked w'ether I wanted to belong here is my answer. I would like very much to belong. Yours Truly H James.'

In Paris the staunch little playgoers were reduced to the level of circuses – the perpetual *Cirques d'Été* and *d'Hiver* and the Théâtre du Cirque. The plays in the French capital were, as Henry put it, 'out of relation to our time of life ... our cultivated innocence'. The plays of Manhattan, and even of London, had been directly addressed to such innocence. Out of this Paris he remembered only a couple of plays with Rose Chéri and Anaïs Fargueil; and of hearing the name of Rachel invoked with awe. There remained with him, however, the memory of a walk with some girl cousins who had more ready access to the French theatre than he had and who related how many times they had seen Madame Doche in *La Dame aux Camélias* and what floods of tears she made them weep. For Henry James the name of Dumas *fils* forever evoked the distant memory of little girls in the Palais-Royal giving a curious aesthetic role to the handkerchief in the theatre, and the memory, too, of the strange beauty of the title, and the complete unawareness, shared by himself and his cousins, of the social position of the lady of the expensive flowers.

During the autumn of 1856 Henry and William began their long walks through Paris that led them to the Luxembourg and the Louvre. In due course Monsieur Lerambert was dropped by the father in favour of a Fourierist school discovered in the Rue Balzac, the Institution Fézandie. M. Fézandie was bald, with a melancholy eye and a delicate beard. The school was frankly experimental; it was part *pension*, part class-room. Elders of both sexes and of many nations were taught French side by side with the children. Henry saw 'ancient American virgins', 'long-haired and chinless compatriots', a host of young Englishmen finding the food at the *pension* 'rotten' and speaking of everyone within view as 'beggars and beasts' – expressions 'absent from our domestic, our American air'. Here Henry became familiar with the *pension* as institution, such as he was later to study in the pages of *Le Père Goriot*. In particular, he met those Americans abroad he himself was to portray and satirize in his early works.

Dictation was read to the mixed class by M. Bonnefans, who seemed to Henry to go all the way back to the Revolution. He was contemptuous of Americans and ridiculed their pronunciation of the all-important word *liberté*. They pronounced it *libbeté*, and M. Bonnefans would, with a show of r's like a drum-roll, demonstrate how it should sound. Bonnefans was a candid, if whispering, 'subversive', opposed to the monarchy and as full of dark hints about police spies as some of James's characters in *The Princess Casamassima*. Bonnefans would recite with bravado from *Le Cid*

Nous nous levons alors!

and in the process would move from a crouch to a leap. It was from instructors such as these, as well as from the constant reading of French novels, that Henry gained his extraordinary fluency in the French language.

4

The family moved into still another apartment in the spring of 1857, this time at No. 26 Rue Montaigne – a large and costly establishment which required many servants. Mary James estimated her annual household expenses here at $2,200. That summer they went to Boulogne-sur-mer, where they set up house at No. 20 Rue Neuve Chaussée. Boulogne had a large English colony: blue-jacketed British schoolboys, little English ladies with mushroom hats, English water-colourists. Henry assiduously explored the town of Colonel Newcome and its waterfront, with its fishermen and boatmen, and acquired impressions that were to find their way into his first anonymously published story a few years later. He studied the fishing-boats, tramped over the cobbles, visited the Napoleonic monument. He seems to have been a regular customer at the English lending library, kept by a Mr Merridew, who supplied him with Victorian three-deckers. 'Henry is not so fond of study, properly so-called, as of reading,' his father wrote that autumn. 'He is a devourer of libraries, and an immense writer of novels and dramas. He has considerable talent as a writer, but I am at a loss to know whether he will ever accomplish much.' The elder Henry's attitude both towards William's early ambition to be a painter and Henry's youthful literary strivings tended to be depreciatory. Art was frivolous, vain, 'narrowing', in a world possessing the fundamental truths of science and religion. But he was of fixed mind also that 'whatever befalls my dear boys in this world, they and you and I are all alike, and after all, absolute creatures of God, vivified every moment by Him, cared for every moment by Him, guided every moment by an infallible wisdom and an irreproachable tenderness'.

Since Henry was 'an absolute creature of God', he was allowed to continue his reading even as William was allowed to study art. At the same time both were made aware of parental disapproval of their choice of pursuit. This was not, psychologically speaking, a happy situation. We have no record of Henry's readings, but his constant allusions to novels and novelists, letter-writers and biographers, in his early criticism, could be made only by one saturated with literature, and especially fiction, both in French and English.

There came a day in Boulogne – it was in September of 1857 – when Henry developed symptoms of illness and remained in his bed through the afternoon with the sounds of the port floating in through half-open windows. As daylight waned he was conscious of mounting uneasiness, a sense of being increasingly unwell. He tumbled out of bed to summon help and then knew only the 'strong sick whirl of everything'. It is with this dramatic moment, 'the gravest illness of my life', that the novelist concludes his account of the *Small Boy and Others*. 'My Harry has been very ill with typhus fever,' the elder James wrote to a friend, 'but he is now better, and we hope the best results. He was for several days delirious, and he is now extremely weak and low.' To Albany he wrote that 'we trembled more than once for the issue'. He called in an Irish homeopathic physician named Macoubrey, who carefully ministered to Henry. The rest of the stay in Boulogne was a dreary blur. He was in bed the better part of two months.

By the end of October when Henry was convalescent, the Jameses moved back to Paris. Now, for the first time, the children heard whispers of financial difficulties. The elder James had taken his family abroad during a period of booming American prosperity. The era of railroad expansion had begun; during their first year abroad 3,400 new miles of rail were laid. Land speculation was at its height; business inflated itself in anticipation of new markets and much of the inflation rested on credits dispensed by unstable banks. In the summer of 1857 loans began to contract under the effects of an unfavourable trade balance, rail stocks began to fall, a great insurance and trust company went bankrupt and a characteristic American 'crash' was under way.

Its effect on the senior Henry was marked. To a brother he wrote:

It is something new for us to feel anxious for the future ... I wrote to Ma to ask you and Augustus and Howard to aid her to contribute as large a sum as you can, to be put to my credit at Samuel G. Ward's in Boston. We shall get home as soon as we can command the means ... Was ever anything clearer than that these commercial disasters inflict the widest *social* disease in the community? The lack of the sentiment of brotherhood – the prevalence of self-seeking – this is the disease of the common mind.

This was on 28 October, and within the week Mary and Henry James, Sr., had made their plans. In Paris they were paying 800 francs a month for their elaborate apartment in the Rue Montaigne; they would retrace their steps to Boulogne, where they could find adequate quarters for as low as 200 francs a month. Instead of a retinue of servants and tutors they would do with one or two, and the children could attend the local schools. For forty dollars a month the education of all the children would be assured, including music and dancing. The father wrote to a friend on 2 November 1857,

We have been very nearly sent home by these dreadful commercial disasters on the other side. As it is I think we shall consult duty by retracing our steps to Boulogne, and passing the winter there ... it is a most agreeable place, with good schools and a capital market, and a population much more manly, or rather more womanly (for it is of those remarkable fisherwomen that I speak particularly) than that of Paris.

Later that winter, when they were installed again in Boulogne, at No. 29 Grande-Rue, in smaller and less elegant quarters than those of the preceding summer, the elder Henry wrote to the same correspondent, 'The children wish you a merry Christmas. They have no idea as yet, poor souls, that Christmas can ever be otherwise than merry to every one. – We *have* lost some of our income by the crash at home ..., I don't know where another year may find us.' It is doubtful whether teenage children, as observant and sensitive as the young Jameses, would have been as innocent and as unworldly as their father painted them. The changed circumstances were not concealed; the sudden frugality of their parents was obvious and they were aware of transatlantic happenings. The anxieties of this time were remembered by Henry – remembered over the decades – and they emerged in the poignant tale of *The Pupil*, describing an itinerant American family in Europe, under perpetual financial embarrassment. In the tale it is a second son who suffers from the spectacle of the mendacity of his parents and their happy-go-lucky habits. While these parents bear no resemblance to the novelist's, the plight of young Morgan recaptures the anguish of an adolescent for whom the world has no anchors, and who thus remains afloat among uneasy values and unrelieved anxieties.

For a while, still convalescent from his typhus, Henry was assigned a tutor at home, a Monsieur Ansiot, whom he described later as 'a form of bland porpoise, violently blowing in an age not his own'. For all his dreariness, his greasy texts (extracts of classical writers), his 'drowsy lapses and honest aridities', M. Ansiot left something with his young pupil, a 'working' sense of *le vieux temps*, a glimpse of a past world.

At the Collège Impérial Henry found himself no longer a young aristocrat, privately tutored, but a member of a class made up of the sons of local shopkeepers, mechanics, artisans and fishermen. He remembered in particular the son of the local pastry-cook, a youth with a pug-nose named Coquelin, whom he would later admire on the stage of the Théâtre Français and entertain in London – the inimitable creator of Cyrano de Bergerac.

A winter at Boulogne sufficed for the parents. If the children now had a schoolful of playmates, the adults tended to find restricted opportunities for social life. And the elder Henry was again fretting about his children's education, his chronic excuse for displacement. 'I have no doubt from all I can gather,' he wrote to his mother, 'that our own schools are ... much superior to the European schools.' After that it was inevitable that the Jameses would turn westward again. They remained at Boulogne until the end of the school year. Robertson James recalled the Commencement. His memory was characteristic of his sense of isolation and self-pity in that family :

Boulogne-sur-mer and the Collège Municipale and its stone vaulted ceiling where Wilky and I went and failed to take prizes. But the day when the Mayor of the City distributed these I do remember, and somehow I think that tho' it was not a prize we both had souvenirs or a reward of some kind – for I recall a beautiful book with gold figures. But around the mayor who stood on a platform with great civic splendour and officials in uniform, I see yet the fortunate scholars ascend the steps of his throne, kneel at his feet, and receive crowns or rosettes, or some symbol of merit which we did not get. The luck had begun to break early!

They had been abroad three years. The young Henry was now a sturdy youth of 15. Early in the summer of 1858 – the depression in America was running its short-lived course – the family set sail, their destination, for the first time, New England.

16

Newport Idyll

THEY went to live in Newport, Rhode Island, then a quiet seaside perch to which the elder Henry James was drawn by the presence of his old friends Edmund and Mary Tweedy, foster-parents of his nieces, the four orphaned Temple girls. 'We are settled very comfortably at Newport for the present,' the father wrote that summer.

Mary is very well, though still concerned about many things, such as inkspots in children's shirts and rents in their trousers, which deflect her from the strait path of conjugal rectitude and devotion. The boys however are as good as good can be, inside of their shirts and trousers, and utterly abandoned to the enjoyment of their recovered liberty, boating and fishing and riding to their hearts' content. They have not fairly recommenced their studies.

Little more than a year later, he was writing:

I have grown so discouraged about the education of my children here, and dread so those inevitable habits of extravagance and insubordination which appear to be characteristic of American youth, that I have come to the conclusion to retrace my steps to Europe, and keep them there a few years longer. My wife is completely of the same mind, and though we feel on many accounts that we are making personal sacrifices in this step, the advantages to the children are so clear that we cannot conscientiously hesitate. I am a good patriot but my patriotism is even livelier on the other side of the water.

Abroad the children went again with their indefatigable parents to Switzerland and later to Germany, and then they once more returned to Newport. The novelist, in his old age, reviewing these itinerant chapters of his life, found them disturbing. The restless crossings of the Atlantic seemed to testify too eloquently to a lack of purpose in his father — and they made for confusion in the narrative. It was artistically more satisfying, in writing his reminiscences, to keep the family in Europe for a full five years and then return them, once and for all, to America. He explained his reasoning to his nephew, the oldest son of William James, one day (23 August 1913) at Lamb House. The nephew made a record of the conversation:

H.J. at lunch said 'There is one thing about your father's early life in respect to which you mustn't give my *Small Boy* away. I've covered over the fact – so overcome am I by the sense of our poor father's impulsive journeyings to and fro and of the impression of aimless vacillation which the record might make upon the reader – that we didn't go to Europe twice, but once. I've described our going abroad the first time, and am saying that the year '60 found us back at Newport.

The nephew noted that this struck him as 'a ridiculous subjectivity on the part of a biographer' (Henry in reality was writing not biography but autobiography). He told his uncle

I was surprised by his feeling so and that it seemed to me that it made a real difference to a boy in the fifties (or now) whether he was brought up solidly for five or six years in Europe after the age of thirteen, or whether he was dipped for fifteen months in the middle of the period into his native American bath. Uncle H. rather pooh-poohed this, saying 'Yes, if you want to be very *analytical*; but nothing happened in that fifteen months. The family went abroad in '55, came to Newport for the summer of '58, took a house for the summer and another for the winter, went to Europe again in late summer or autumn '59 and returned to America in '60.'

The nephew noted:

Uncle H. evidently has a very lively consciousness of his father's vacillations and impulses – as if the possibility of going home or going to Europe, going from one place to another, were always in the air and often realized to the disturbance of his, Uncle H.'s, equanimity. He is also evidently self-conscious about the fanciful and inconsequent explanations and reasons which his father used to give to people, who expressed surprise or made inquiries.

There is no doubt that the 'equanimity' of the young boy was disturbed, and this malaise was still present in the old man. In a letter written to T. S. Perry at the time of the publication of *Notes of a Son and Brother*, the novelist confessed that he suppressed the 1859 journey to Europe to avoid giving the impression that his father was 'too irresponsible and too *saccadé* in his generous absence of plan and continuity'. He added that he found himself, in his memoirs, enumerating 'so many choppings and changes and interruptions and volatilities (as on our parents' part, dear people) in our young education that the aspect of it grew in a manner foolish on my hands'. Consequently he simply 'dropped, for worry-saving, certain stitches'. But first, their stay in Newport.

I

After their sojourn by the Thames and the Seine, after the galleries, palaces, schools, *pensions* and theatres of the Old World, the James boys finally set foot in New England. A reasonably brief ocean voyage had brought these sons of the Hudson Valley from the Second Empire of Louis Napoleon to the America of President Buchanan. They arrived at a time when the slavery issue was entering an acute phase. Lincoln was about to begin his debates with Douglas. The stage was being set, the historic forces were at play, for a great and bloody civil war. These things were of the future. For the moment their return to America – or to the rim of America – was a return to happy native conditions, the re-discovery of certain cousins now grown up like themselves, and the making of new and important friendships. Henry felt in later years that Newport was 'the one right residence in all our great country'. The old town seemed indeed, with its crooked streets and small buildings, its old wharves, its historic cemeteries, its associations with Bishop Berkeley, to be a bit of Europe or an European outpost on the soil of America.

Newport was more: it was a corner of the eighteenth century that had lingered into the nineteenth. It possessed in the 1850s a 'quaint shabbiness'. Thames Street recalled the lately deserted London, the great houses faced the sea and behind them lay the Avenue along which Henry James often strolled and where stood in their grey nudity, in contrast to the elaborate modern dwellings, the shingled boxes that had been the dwellings of another day. Newport had a landscape and a seascape; it had, indeed, some of the characteristics of the European watering-places, and for the little James pilgrims, freshly returned from far-away lands, it served as an ideal stepping-stone to reconciliation with their homeland. The James boys had been 'disconnected' from America; Newport seemed the 'one marked point of reattachment'. It had an active social life; there was a colony of artists; old American families lived in the town; there were cultivated elderly gentlemen and ladies, and a vast summer population of elegant wives with their children sent away from overheated New York or Boston to enjoy sea breezes while husbands wilted bravely in their offices. Old-fashioned streets echoed to the footfalls of attractively dressed young women. There was, above all, a constant vision of land and sea, more sea than land. There were walks to be taken along moss-clad rocks and over sand-choked grass with the ocean a constant companion. There were a 'thousand delicate secret places dear to the disinterested rambler'. In his late book *The American Scene* there is almost a rhapsodic note – certainly a lyrical one – as James comes upon Newport after a fifty-year interval and remembers 'far-away little lonely, sandy coves, rock-set, lily-sheeted ponds, almost hidden, and shallow Arcadian summer-haunted valleys with the sea just over some stony shoulder: a whole world that called out to the long afternoons of youth'. The afternoons were long indeed.

2

Henry James revisited Newport in 1870, a decade after his first re-sidence there, when he was already launched on his career, to write a travel paper for the *Nation*. He wrote, 'I suffer from knowing the natural elements of Newport too well to attempt to describe them. I have known them so long that I hardly know what I think of them.' Thirty-five years later, again revisiting the spot, he wrote *The Sense of Newport* and observed that he had known the place 'too well and loved it too much for description or definition'. It wasn't, however, until three years before his death, when Newport was half a century distant, that he explored the role of the town in his young creative consciousness that began to find itself there in 1858 and 1860.

For Henry James the place was to have always a 'shy sweetness', and one suspects that the words betrayed his own state of feeling. 'Shy' probably refers to his first encounters with young women; the female population of Newport was large. But it also expresses the sense Henry James had being an 'outsider' in America and different from Americans. He could not be a part of an American society 'where the great black ebony God of business was the only one re-cognized'. He had known only the other gods: the gods of art, of culture, of educated talk, the life of the spirit. He understood New-port was devoted to people like his father 'leisured for life'. He is concerned over his idleness in a national community energetically attending to material things in the months before the Civil War. He recalls that as a boy he 'felt it tasteless and humiliating that the head of our little family was *not* in business'. Everyone else in America seemed to be. For him Newport represented 'disconnection' not only from Europe but from America itself.

This was his feeling late in life as he surveyed his early years. At the time, disconnected though Henry James undoubtedly was by temperament and upbringing, and by his long deep draught from the nostalgic cup, he felt for Newport itself a deep attachment. His roots, pulled up when they were tender, from the banks of the Hudson, here found new and fresh American earth. Taken abroad once more by his ever-restless father, they accepted the fertilization of Europe but resisted, for the time, the transplanting. His letters reflect a nostalgia for Newport and the Newporters, 'surrounded with a halo, in my mind which grows brighter and brighter', and again, 'Geneva has endless lovely walks, but I think Lily Pond, Cherry Grove, Purgatory, Paradise and Sprouting Rock (how I delight to write the names) ... how I wish I was going to migrate there.' In Europe, during these years of his emergence into young manhood, he had been able to make only casual friends; how could he do more in the capricious moves from place to place and school to school? The James boys were thrown a great deal upon each other's company. The elder Henry was aware of this; the boys had been 'all along perfectly starved on their social side'. Newport filled a serious gap in Henry's life; for museums and galleries, books and theatres and lonely European promenades he could substitute at last important human ties. Henry Junior was young enough and sufficiently adaptable, to live himself into Newport's life and to attach himself to new-found friends. When the time came to go abroad once more it was difficult to leave.

3

Two friendships formed by Henry James at Newport embraced letters and art and exerted a deep and enduring influence. Thomas Sergeant Perry was perhaps the first and closest friend; two years younger than Henry, and also a second son, he lived even more than the future novelist in a world of books. John La Farge, the painter, was seven years older. He proved to be an extraordinary mentor, sensitive and devoted, especially during the later phase of Henry's Newport residence. Both Perry and La Farge nourished Henry's mind and spirit at a crucial time. La Farge could guide Henry into the world of the painter; Perry was a companion with whom there could be a constant exchange of ideas and books. He had a formidable ancestry: his mother was a direct descendant of Benjamin Franklin;

his father was a son of Commodore Oliver Hazard Perry, who won the victory on Lake Erie in 1813, and a nephew of Commodore Matthew Calbraith Perry, who opened Japan to the west. Young Perry was precocious and passive, with a tendency to substitute books for action; and he was a faithful companion. Henry James's tribute to him, in *Notes of a Son and Brother*, describes him as a great lumberjack of the library, felling volumes and sets of volumes as if they were trees in a forest, absorbing whole literatures at a time. The Redwood Library loomed large, and its name may have suggested the lumber-image. It was the pride of Newport, with its fifty-foot-long reading-room, windows at each end, a dome, and more than 100 paintings on its walls. This was not the Galerie d'Apollon, but it was a haven for the literary Henry.

T. S. Perry met the James boys in June or July of 1858, shortly after they had settled in Newport. He used to box with William, he was a friend of the genial Wilky, who was his own age, but he was for the most part with Henry. His diary, carefully kept over years, discloses how often they were together, in and out of school. The latest educational institution to which Henry was committed was the Berkeley Institute, headed by the Rev. William C. Leverett, curate of Newport's Trinity Church, who was addicted as much to delivering orations on things 'as such' – his favourite expression – as to coming to grips with the concrete. Perry remembered that Henry James was an 'uninterested scholar'. The school was located in the Masonic Building and contained a large study room and 'recitation rooms'. One day a week they declaimed pieces from Sargent's *Standard Speaker*. 'H.J. in his books speaks without enthusiasm of his school studies,' Perry recalled, 'but he and I read together at Mr Leverett's school a fair amount of Latin literature. Like Shakespeare he had less Greek.'

John La Farge carried about him the aura of 'Europe'. He was of French descent, a Catholic of ample means and wide horizons. His father, like Henry's grandfather, had amassed a Hudson Valley fortune, in real estate, and he had been brought up in the same compact old New York as the future novelist. Like Henry he had lived in Paris but with the difference that in the capital he had glimpsed the literary élite, encountered through a relative of his mother's, the critic Paul de Saint-Victor. He could speak of Sainte-Beuve, Baudelaire, Flaubert and the Goncourts with a certain impassive familiarity.

La Farge shared with Henry the latest copies of the *Revue des Deux Mondes* as they arrived in their salmon-coloured wrappers. The artist had sketches of European scenes, water-colours of Breton peasants, costumes, interiors, bits of villages and landscapes. He took Henry on long rambles across the rocks. And he filled the afternoons with a full measure of talk, and more than this, ideas. He acquired with young Henry 'an authority ... that it verily took the length of years to undermine'.

Perry too remembered their walks. 'A thousand scrappy recollections of the strolls still remain,' Perry wrote at 80 after Henry James was dead, 'fragments of talk, visions of the place.' Near Lily Pond they talked one day of Fourier. Another time they were full of their reading of Ruskin; Henry devoted himself to the 'conscientious copying of a leaf and very faithfully drew a little rock that jutted above the surface of Lily Pond ... We read the English magazines and reviews and the *Revue des Deux Mondes* with rapture'.

The first part of the Newport idyll lasted from early 1858 until the autumn of 1859. Presently the Jameses were in New York again and (it was 8 October 1859) Henry was writing to his Newport friend Sargy, 'You see by the date that this is our hour for sailing ... I can scarcely sit still to write this and feel myself thinking much more of what I leave behind than what I expect to find ... Goodbye to you and every body and every thing! Yours very truly H. James Jr.'

17

The Rhône and the Rhine

ONCE again the Jameses turned their faces eastward. The steamship *Vanderbilt* made the crossing in eleven days of unrelieved bad weather. They landed at Le Havre and spent a day, 'plenty of time to find out what a nice little place it is' (remaining just about as long as Caroline Spencer in James's *Four Meetings*). They spent two days in Paris revisiting familiar places. Five days after landing they were in Geneva.

The James family had gone abroad in 1855 'with an eye to the then supposedly supreme benefits of Swiss schooling', and had ended up by the Thames and the Seine. Now, four years later, they had retraced their steps to the city of Calvin and of Rousseau, and, we might add, of Gibbon and Madame de Staël and Voltaire. Henry and Mary James took rooms in the Hôtel de l'Écu at the edge of the rushing Rhône. The two younger sons were placed in the Pensionnat Maquelin just outside Geneva; Alice remained with the parents. William enrolled at the Academy which later became the University of Geneva, and Henry was dispatched to the Institution Rochette – a preparatory school for engineers and architects!

I

This was perhaps the most curious of all of Henry James's miscellaneous schools. As he put it many years later, he had been 'disposed of under a flattering misconception of my aptitudes'. He found himself among students whose goals were far removed from literature; he was called upon to study mathematics, and his brave attempt to make some sort of showing was 'mere darkness, waste and anguish ... it was hard and bitter fruit all and turned to ashes in my mouth'. What astounded him in later years was his failure to protest 'with a frankness proportioned to my horror'. And again, as before, he explains his ordeal as an under-estimation of self; he considered himself inferior to others in not being able to attack geometry and algebra. He was determined to overcome the inferiority. It was a hopeless battle. Henry withdrew or was withdrawn 'not even as a conspicuous' but 'only as an obscure, a deeply-hushed failure'.

The Institution Rochette was selected, and apparently with Henry's concurrence, because it was the best school in Geneva other than the Academy and the *Gymnasium*, neither of which he was qualified to enter. There is no evidence that the parents intended to make either an architect or an engineer of their second son. Henry might have been tutored at home, as in the past; this, however, would have provided no companionship and little opportunity for talking French. At the Rochette school he was cloistered with some twenty fellow-students for the greater part of the day, five and a half days a week. It was understood from the outset that he was not to receive the full pre-science training; as he put it to Perry, 'I am the only one who is not destined for either of the useful arts or sciences, although I am, I hope, for the art of being useful in some way.' In his letters to Perry, Henry kept up a bold front, assuring him repeatedly he was getting on 'very well'. By Easter it was clear that he wasn't; mathematics was clearly a waste of time, and without giving details Henry told Perry 'the yoke, if the expression is not too tragic, has been considerably lightened'. He had dropped all subjects at the Institution Rochette except German, French and Latin and he had arranged to sit in at a number of courses at the Academy instead. His bitter-sweet year in Geneva ended with his achieving a certain level of equality with his elder brother.

His letters to young Perry during these months give no suggestion of gloom; they are filled with the healthy observations of an unusually wide-awake young man of 17. Nowhere do they suggest that 'eternity of woe' James described in the opening pages of Notes of a Son and Brother. However, the contemporaneous account does not appear to be in contradiction with that written fifty years later. On the contrary, James's memory is accurate in the details. It was not to be expected that young Henry would pour out his woe to Perry; for him he recorded the more joyful aspects of his European stay with a zealous adherence to fact rather than to feeling. The year was certainly not one of unmitigated gloom, even if it was one of hard – and unsuccessful – study. As Henry puzzled it out towards the end of his life, his parents had 'simply said to themselves that I read too many novels, or at least read them too attentively – that was the vice'. Moreover, they had 'got me in a manner to agree with them'.

2

Geneva itself, as he described it later, was 'a strongly-featured little city, which, if you do not enjoy, you may at least grudgingly respect'. It had no galleries, museums or interesting churches, but it did possess a natural beauty; there were 'liquid sapphire and emerald' in the surface of Lake Leman, and the 'divinely cool-hued gush of the Rhône beneath the two elder bridges'. It must have seemed to Calvin, James mused, 'as one of the streams of the paradise he was making it so hard to enter'. The town itself presented a sordid aspect that nevertheless fascinated Henry when he first explored and described it to Perry with uncommon skill and concreteness that revealed a writer formed, a younger master of the resources and rhythms of English. 'Such dingy old streets and courts and alleys, black with age some of them are, steep and dirty, such quaint old houses, high and sombre are very picturesque.' The sentence may be lacking in completeness, but it has conjured up a picture. We can look with young Henry out of the window of the Institution Rochette, down into the street.

Perhaps you would like to know about my school. The building is wholly unlike that of the Berkeley Institute. It is a dilapidated old stone house in the most triste quarter of the town. Scarcely a soul passes by it all day, and I do not remember to have seen a wheeled vehicle of any kind near it since I've been there. Beside it is the prison and opposite the Cathedral of St Peter, in which Calvin used to preach. It seems to me that none but the most harmless and meekest men are incarcerated in the former building. While at my lesson in a classroom which looks out on the door, I have once in a while seen an offender brought up to his doom. He marches along with handcuffs on his wrists, followed by a gendarme in 'spick and span' uniform. The gendarme knocks on the door, which is opened by some internal spring, shoves in his charge, the door closes, the gendarme retraces his steps. What happens after the prisoner is inside I don't know, but as the only officer I have ever seen about the prison is a diminutive little porter with a most benign countenance, I am inclined to think that the most inoffensive subjects are sent to him to deal with.

We wonder how Henry knew the door opened by some internal spring; we may smile at the 'diminutive little'; but there is no denying the care and system of the narrative.

Henry rose at 6.30 in the winter dark; he breakfasted alone in the Hôtel de l'Écu. By eight, in the dawning light, he has reached the school. Four hours later he walks back for lunch. He is at his school bench again an hour later. At five he returns to the hotel. He dines; he studies till bedtime. And so it goes, from Monday to Saturday, with a half-day off on Thursday. During the Thursday afternoon he reads, he idles, he looks out of the hotel window, he explores the shops, he walks around the edge of the lake. He is very much alone. His brothers are scattered. He doesn't make friends with his schoolmates; he, an English youth and a young Russian, are the sole foreigners. He talks to his fellow-foreigners. The English youth 'is the only one with whom I have been able to become the least bit friendly. When I first went there no one spoke to me. I had to commence every conversation myself. I think that if a Frenchman had come to Mr Leverett's he would have been more hospitably received.'

On Sunday the family gathers at the Hôtel de l'Écu: Wilky and Bob come in for the day from the Pensionnat Maquelin; Alice is there; William on occasions mingles with them unless he can find 'livelier recreation'. Towards the end of the winter there seems to be a little more social life. Henry is going to parties. 'I go twice a week to a dancing school,' he tells Perry,

and seldom have I seen a more hideous collection of females than I do on these occasions. They all sit on benches ranged along one side of the room and the cavaliers stand up against the wall on the opposite side – for a fellow to sit down on one of their benches would be a most heinous crime. In the intervals of the dancing therefore we have occasion to contemplate them as they sit with their eyes modestly cast down upon the floor. I learned to dance because at the parties here that is the sole amusement,

and the young American with the ever-hearty appetite adds characteristically and patriotically, 'they do not even have supper but hand round little glasses of syrop and "helpings" of ice-cream about twice as large as a peach pit! Be thankful that you are born in our free and enlightened country.'

He is now liberated from his rigorous educational schedule; he has time for newspapers and magazines. The new *Cornhill Magazine*, edited by Thackeray, has arrived and he reads it avidly. ('Strokes of the great Victorian clock,' the old Henry James wrote, remembering the first issue which particularly brought him Trollope 'charged with something of the big Balzac authority.') He is now studying French literature and Natural Philosophy at the Academy (the selfsame Academy which Winterbourne, in the revised versions of *Daisy Miller*, attends: 'Winterbourne had an old attachment for the little capital of Calvinism; he had even gone, on trial – trial of the grey old "Academy" on the steep and stony hillside – to college there.') Henry was there 'on trial'. He listens to H.-F. Amiel, vaguely aware of him as a 'mild grave oracle'. With a bow to science he studies anatomy. 'I went the other day in company with half a dozen other students to see a dissection at the Hospital,' he tells Perry. 'It was a most unlovely sight. The subject was a strapping big gendarme who had died of inflammation of the lungs. The smell was pretty bad, but I am glad to say that I was not in any way affected by the thing.' William is invited to join the Société de Zoffingue, the Swiss student organization for 'brotherhood and beer'. He takes his younger brother with him to the village of Moudon near Lausanne, where they drink, smoke German pipes and sing. The local clergy participate. 'They drank as hard, sung as loud and gave as many toasts and jolly speeches as the most uproarious student.' The students swear allegiance with a great 'swilling down of beer, of grasping of hands, of clashing of rapiers, and of glorious deep-mouthed German singing'.

Despite the ups and downs of this winter, Henry has been quietly scribbling. Wilky, writing to Perry, reports seeing 'some poetical looking manuscripts lying on the table, and himself looking in a most authorlike way'. William had been reading aloud satiric odes to his sister Alice and other members of the family, and Wilky observes, 'The only difference there is between Willy and Harry's labours is that the former always shows his productions while the modest little Henry wouldn't let a soul or even a spirit see his.' Commenting on this, Perry wrote that Henry seldom entrusted his early efforts 'to the criticism of his family – they did not see all he wrote. They were too keen critics, too sharp-witted, to be allowed to handle every essay of this budding talent', and we might add there was too strong a fund of rivalry; if the senior Henry lampooned his contemporaries, his offspring lampooned one another. Perry adds that their comments on Henry's work

would have been too merciless; and hence, for sheer self-preservation, he hid a good part of his work from them. Not that they were cruel, far from it. Their frequent solitude in foreign parts, where they had no familiar companions, had welded them together in a way that would have been impossible in America, where each would have had separate distractions on his own. Their loneliness forced them to grow together most harmoniously, but their long exercise in literary criticism would have made them possibly merciless judges of Henry's crude beginnings.

Perry perhaps minimizes the fund of plain boyish high-spirits that prevailed, the usual competition among growing youngsters. He questioned Henry about Wilky's disclosure of his literary efforts and was told in reply: 'A fearful vengeance awaits Wilky's foolhardy imprudence in disclosing, as he did, my secret employment.' But he does not deny it. Perry having asked him what 'style of work' he is cultivating, he volunteers readily, 'I may reply that to no style am I a stranger, there is none which has not been adorned by the magic of my touch.' And as if to demonstrate to Perry his facility, he begins his next letter with an extravagant imitation of the eastern romances he has been reading as well as Thackeray, 'The morning broke! High into the vast unclouded vault of Heving rode the Awb of Day, chasing before it the fleeting clouds that enshroud the slumbers of men.'

And so on, describing the awakening of ''Enry James de Jeames' on his couch 'covered with the skin of a leopard, which he had killed with his own hands in the burning wastes of Arabia'. He stretches forth his arm, on which the 'cerulean veins swelled like ivy creepers round a giant oak and grasping a timepiece more glittering with brilliants than an eastern monarch's diadem he ... Nay – but a truce to this idiotic strain. This meaneth in plain English that your good friend Henry James Jr Esquire was awakened by the sun.' And so on. Perhaps Henry had not been boasting; he was not a stranger to many styles, and no stranger to good humour and geniality either. Of his studies that spring he told Perry not a word. But in *Notes of a Son and Brother* he remembered that he read Livy and Virgil with a Monsieur Verchère, Schiller and Lessing with a ruddy, noisy little German professor, and that he was 'almost happy' with M. Toeppfer, with whom he read Racine and who described for him Rachel's playing of *Phèdre*, her entrance 'borne down in her languorous passion by the weight of her royal robes – *Que ces vains ornements, que ces voiles me pèsent*!'

The Swiss spring was at hand and Henry practised swimming in the deep blue lake-water and enjoyed the Alpine views; he wandered along the verdant hedges, stopped to peer at the iron gateways up long avenues of trees leading to châteaux: he has trans-Atlantic thoughts. 'I suppose you will soon see the commencement of the annual migration to Newport,' he writes to Perry. 'How I wish I was going to migrate there.' Family plans, however, called for a summer at Bonn and a stay at Frankfort. Before going to Bonn, William and Henry went on a week's walking-tour through the mountains. They crossed the Mer de Glâce, went to the Canton du Valais by way of the Tête-Noir, and from Martigny, with the aid of a guide and a mule, they climbed the St Bernard. The scene as they neared the celebrated Hospice called forth this passage from the future novelist to Perry; at 17 he was distinctly beginning to master that 'spirit of the place' which he was to invoke in his later travel writings.

At about three hours distance from the hospice the scenery becomes most wild dreary and barren. Everything indicates a great elevation. The growth of everything but the enormous rocks is stunted – not a blade of grass or straggling mountain pine. The tinkling of the last cattle bell dies away, you see the last hardy Alpine sheep climbing over desolate heights which would seem to afford no nourishment and then you enter upon the snow which lies all the year round.

At the Hospice they are received by one of the Fathers, given warm slippers, hot broth and mutton, and sleep on the hard mattresses, 'apparently stuffed with damp sand'. In the morning they see the 'noble, majestic tawny' dogs which Henry observed had the same 'stately courtesy' as the Fathers themselves. Henry visits the morgue where the bodies of those found in the mountains are placed. 'As they cannot be buried they are stood around the walls in their shrouds and a grim and ghastly sight it is. They fall into all sorts of hideous positions, with such fiendish grins on their faces! faugh!' The region was mournful indeed, and Henry, with his sense of tone and colour writes: 'The sky is of a liquid twinkling sort of blue, and the gigantic grey and white rocks rise up against it so sharply-cut and so barren, and the stillness that reigns around and the apparent nearness of every object from the greater tenuity of the atmosphere!'

On the following day they go to Loèche-les-Bains and walk over naked and rugged terrain down narrow steep zigzags, ending their trip at Interlaken, where they meet, as scheduled, their father, mother, Alice and Wilky. Robertson had gone off with his teacher and classmates towards the Italian Alps, with Venice as his ultimate destination, after which he rejoined the family at Bonn. The Jameses travelled from Interlaken to Frankfort, sampling the hot springs and witnessing the gambling at Wiesbaden. Then they went by the Rhine to Bonn. The journey seemed pretty tame to Henry after Switzerland.

3

They arrived at Bonn in July of 1860. Henry and Wilky were installed in the *pension* of a Dr Humpert, Latin and Greek professor, situated at No. 190 Bonngasse, near the birthplace of Beethoven. William was housed with a Herr Stromberg, whose wife made fine pancakes and wrote tragedies. It was the elder James's wish that his sons should acquire a working knowledge of German during the coming weeks. He and his wife took rooms for themselves and Alice in a large mansion built like a feudal castle, looking across the broad expanse of river at the Seven Mountains – in reality a series of green hills. Henry found himself in characteristic Germanic surroundings. The Herr Doktor's family was composed of his wife, her sister, and his son Theodore. There were also five young German pensioners aged six to fourteen. The sister, Fräulein Stamm, reminded Henry of Hepzibah Pyncheon in *The House of the Seven Gables*, always wiping hock-glasses and holding them up to the light and bearing long-necked bottles and platters of food through the 'greasy rooms' of the house. 'This is an opportunity for me to see something of German life, in what would be called, I suppose, the middle classes,' Henry wrote to Perry. 'I naturally compare it with the corresponding life at home, and think it truly inferior. The women stop at home all day, doing the house-work, drudging, and leading the most homely and I should say joyless lives. I fancy they never look at a book, and all their conversation is about their pots and pans.' Fräulein Stamm wanted to know whether there was a king in America; her knowledge of his homeland was based, Henry discovered, on a reading of expurgated adaptations of Fenimore Cooper. Life, he found, was a round of German 'conversation' centring on the stereotyped amenities *Haben Sie gut geschlafen?* and *Wie geht's?* Henry made excursions, to nearby Godesberg, and to the Drachenfels across the Rhine, which they climbed in a party with Mary James riding a donkey for conveyance. There were picnics and walks on the Venusberg, in the early morning, and the pursuit in German orchards of pears, cherries and plums. He walked in old Germanic woods and enjoyed the long vistas of the river. He didn't learn much German, devoting most of the summer to a laborious translation of *Maria Stuart*, after being taken by his father one night in Bonn to see Adelaide Ristori in the play ('the vulture counterfeiting Jenny Wren' was the elder's verdict).

Although Henry enjoyed his Bonn experience, he was never to feel, as did William, a kinship with the German people and the German mind. When he revisited Germany in 1872 he satisfied himself once and for all that 'I can never hope to become an unworthiest adoptive grandchild of the fatherland. It is well to listen to the voice of the spirit, to cease hair-splitting and treat oneself to a good square antipathy.' He satirizes the Germans in a number of his tales. In only one tale did he create a sympathetic German – who collaborates, on artistic ground, with a Frenchman.

4

They had been at Bonn only a few days when the elder Henry James took an important decision, which his second son promptly and exuberantly communicated to Perry. 'I think I must fire off my biggest gun first. One-two-three! Bung-gerdee bang bang ...!!!

What a noise! Our passages are taken in the Adriatic, for the 11th of September!!!!!!! We are going immediately to Newport, which is the place in America we all most care to live in.' William James, after many misgivings and much inner debate, had confided to his father that he didn't want to be a scientist, as his parent had hoped. He felt his vocation to be that of a painter and he wanted to study with William Morris Hunt, the American artist, whom he had met earlier and who had a studio in Newport. The elder Henry re-expressed his misgivings about artists and writers. William argued with him: 'I am sure that far from feeling myself degraded by my intercourse with art, I continually receive from it spiritual impressions the intensest and purest I know. So it seems to me is my mind formed, and *I can see* no reason for avoiding the giving myself up to art *on this score*.' That summer at Bonn William was striking a blow not only for himself; he was, in effect, leading a family revolt against further wanderings and an education that reflected too much parental vacillations. Henry expressed this to Perry: 'I think that if we are to live in America it is about time we boys should take up our abode there; the more I see of this estrangement of American youngsters from the land of their birth, the less I believe in it. It should also be the land of their breeding.' He was to hold this view all his life. His own later expatriation, he felt, was the direct and logical outcome of his early 'estrangement'.

The father, writing to a friend on 18 July 1860, on the same day that Henry wrote to Perry, throws still further light on his decision.

The welfare of the other youngsters will, however, be as much consulted by this manœuvre, I am persuaded, as Willy's. They are none of them cut out for intellectual labours, and they are getting to an age, Harry and Wilky especially, when the heart craves a little wider expansion than is furnished it by the domestic affections. They want friends among their own sex, and sweethearts in the other; and my hope for their own salvation, temporal and spiritual, is that they may 'go it strong' in both lines when they get home. Early marriages are thought very bad as a prudential step here in Europe, but an immense deal of imprudence may yet be transacted in America with the happiest social and individual consequences.

We smile as we read that 'none' of the boys was cut out for intellectual labours; but the elder Henry was right in perceiving – at long last – that his children were starved for the companionship of their American peers.

The decision taken, the father promptly left Bonn ('where he can neither understand nor make himself understood', William wrote to Perry), and was joined in Paris by his wife and Alice, Robertson and Aunt Kate. They installed themselves in the Hôtel des Trois Empereurs to await the September sailing, while the other three sons completed their period of study at Bonn. If the senior Henry deplored Henry's addiction to novels, he nevertheless sent him copies of *Once a Week*, which had begun to appear a few months earlier, and in the pages of which his son first discovered Meredith and Charles Reade. William, reporting on life in Bonn, described Henry as working 'pretty stoutly' and resisting all week the temptation to read the periodical. 'Harry says he "wakes up every day from his lethargy to wish he was in Paris" instead of availing himself of the little time he has here ... [he] has not touched the *Once a Week* until today.' In another letter the eldest son announces, 'We are going to put Harry through a slashing big walk daily,' and reports that he indulges in wrestling matches with Wilky 'when study has made them dull and sleepy'. Henry himself was quite articulate about his German impressions. In August he wrote to his mother – it is the earliest extant letter to her – in a vein of filial amiability, describing excursions, conversations in the *pension*, the epistolary activities of his brothers, who 'are so free in their communications that I begin to suspect they simply despatch you blank sheets of paper, for what they can find to say about Bonn to fill so many pages is to me inconceivable'. His hostess and Fräulein Stamm

seem to think it is the exception in going to America not to be drowned and assurances to the contrary are received with uplifted eyes and hands and raised eyes and incredulous 'Ohs!' and 'Achs', and pious ejaculations. I wish we could take Madame Humbart [Humpert] to America with us as cook. She is by far the best one I ever saw. I wish you could come on and take a few lessons from her; I shall bring you a lot of receipts by which I shall expect you to profit next winter. I shall look for a *marked improvement* in the cookery department.

The graceful letterwriter was already formed; and, as for the German cooking, the time was to come when a more fastidious Henry would have the opposite of praise for Germanic cuisine.

Punctually on 1 September the three boys made the twelve-hour train journey from Cologne to Paris in a first-class carriage. They shared it with a French lady's-maid, valet and coachman, 'who chattered by the hour for our wonderstruck ears'. They gave Henry a glimpse in their talk on the one hand of 'servile impudence' and on the other of the life of the French upper classes. There were long stops at stations with trains going in the opposite direction carrying the French society of the time in its annual descent upon Homburg and Baden-Baden. He was to discover this society of the dying days of the Second Empire in the works of About and Daudet. During the day Madame la Marquise came to inspect her servants:

It was true that Madame la Marquise, who was young and good-natured and pretty without beauty, and unmistakeably 'great', exhaling from afar, as I encouraged myself to imagine, the scented air of the Tuileries, came on occasion and looked in on us and smiled, and even pouted, through her elegant patience; so that she at least, I recollect, caused to swim before me somehow such a view of happy privilege at the highest pitch as made me sigh the more sharply, even if the less professedly, for our turning our backs on the complex order, the European, fresh to me still, in which contrasts flared and flourished and through which discrimination could unexhaustedly riot.

'Europe' had begun for Henry James with the spectacle of a peasant, a castle, a ruin; it ended with this glimpse of 'happy privilege at the highest pitch' and his final view of the Louvre. They sailed on the Adriatic on the 11th, were in New York on the 23rd and a few days later Henry was pacing the sands of Newport with Sargy Perry. The 'nostalgic cup' had been filled to to the brim. His European adventure of childhood and young adulthood was at an end. Henry did not know it then, but this adventure had been but the prelude to what he would ultimately call his personal 'Americano-European legend'.

18

Palette and Pen

FOR their second and longest phase in Newport, the elder Henry James settled his family in a rented house at No. 13 Kay Street, near the Edmund Tweedys, and the son resumed the idyllic life from which they had been torn fifteen months before. They lived here for the next two years, until the spring of 1862, and then in a large stone house at the corner of Spring Street and Lee Avenue. Brief allusions in the youthful diary of Thomas Sergeant Perry give us

glimpses of their activities. 2 January 1861 : 'Went with Harry James
to the 40 Steps ... Went after dinner with Jno [La Farge] and Willie
J. to the Point.' 3 January : 'Down town then with Harry J. Met
Willie and with him to Belmont's.' 4 January : 'In the morning down
street with W.J. ... dined at the Jameses.' Saturday 5 January :
'Down street again with H.J.' And so the life went, a constant series
of excursions 'down street' and to the scenic points in Newport,
with abundant sociabilities. Perry later wrote that 'all the land and
shore beyond the Avenue was a wild pasture where the Jameses and
I were the sole inhabitants'. On Sunday 6 January : 'H.J. came to
church with me in the morning,' and then Perry boxes with Willie
till 1 p.m. On Monday he and Henry go to the Redwood Library. The
next day 'walked after school to the Big Pond nearly with H.J.' On
13 January a significant entry : 'To the Jameses. Introduced to and
to walk with their cousins, the Miss Temples.' Mary and Edmund
Tweedy, having lost their three children, had taken into their home
the four orphaned Temple girls, children of Catherine Margaret
James, the elder Henry's favourite sister and of Colonel Robert
Emmet Temple, a West Point graduate and a lawyer. Mrs Tweedy
was a daughter of Colonel Temple by a first marriage, and thus not
directly related to the Jameses. She was, however, always referred
to by Henry as 'Aunt Mary'.

William lost no time in starting to paint. Henry 'under the irresistible contagion' followed him to the studio of William Morris Hunt.
Apparently for the moment there was no thought of further schooling. Henry found the world of art, even though he participated in it
largely as a dabbler and observer, to be a 'rounded satisfying world'.
The experience gained here, together with his renewed friendship
with John La Farge, was to be carried over into his fiction. He was
on the easiest of terms with the men of the palette and the brush.

I

The studio on Church Street in Newport was filled with plaster casts
and canvases and the presence of the gaunt Quixote-like figure of
the American master. William Morris Hunt had been a pupil of
Couture, he had studied later with Millet in Barbizon. In Newport
he was the the artist to his finger-tips, the flowing beard, the velvet
jacket, the scarlet sash. There were two spacious rooms on the
ground floor where Henry was allowed to wander as he pleased, and

the large studio proper upstairs where William, not yet 20, worked with 25-year-old La Farge and Theodora Sedgwick, youngest sister of Mrs Charles Eliot Norton. Henry remembered sitting alone in one of the grey cold lower rooms, trying to draw by himself, and day-dreaming that his copy of a plaster cast of the uplifted face of Michelangelo's *Captive*, seen in the Louvre, might attract the attention of the Master. He remembered with gratitude an occasional friendly word, a gesture of kindness from Hunt. He felt that he was entering the temple of art 'by the back door' but remained on the threshold.

One day he crossed the threshold. Wandering upstairs, he discovered his handsome young cousin, Gus Barker, standing on a pedestal, a gay, neat model 'divested of every garment'. It was Henry James's first 'glimpse of ' "life" on a pedestal and in a pose'. The spectacle settled matters for him then and there. 'I well recall the crash, at the sight, of all my inward emulation – so forced was I to recognize on the spot that I might niggle for months over plaster casts and not come within miles of any such point of attack.' The students were working in pencil and charcoal. Henry watched closely. His brother's ease in reproducing the figure astonished him. There was no point, he decided, in seeking to emulate such skill.

Henry James pocketed his drawing-pencil and picked up his pen.

2

He had never really wanted to be an artist, and he now recognized his pursuit of art was in reality his pursuit of William. It is difficult to say whether his decision to return to his own pasture was as deliberate and as vivid as he makes it out to be in his memoirs. What we know is that he found someone who took him seriously as a writer. The family had made light of his addiction to novels; he had been teased and baited; his parents had tried to turn him from his world of dreams and books. He had, on his side, always imitated William. Now, in the friendly surroundings of Newport, he found in John La Farge a much-needed ally, friend, guide. La Farge was not only willing to talk to him about books and about writing; he listened; he bestowed, in effect, paternal sympathy, for he was older and knew the world. Henry remembered that at Newport in 1860 the future painter 'opened up to us, though perhaps to me in particular, who could absorb all that was given me'.

The painter was an attractive figure, riding on a chestnut mare across shining Newport sands, against a background of far sunsets, or emerging in cool white from top to toe, or wearing his artist's velvet jacket. Henry posed for him willingly. La Farge talked as he painted. There survives a portrait in oils which Henry James considered the best perhaps of La Farge's early exhibition of 'a rare colour sense'. The portrait sets the young Henry in sharp profile against an opaline background, in dark attire, austere, almost priestly, as if he were a young seminarist. The head is bent and pensive, the lips firm, the forehead straight and high; the painting suggests a sensuous youth set in colours that recall a stained-glass window. La Farge was indeed to become a master of this medium. He was to invent opaline glass; he developed a deep interest in architecture and in æsthetics; he lectured and wrote on art and left behind him vivid accounts of travel in the Far East and the South Seas. His interest in stained glass and cathedrals was to set his friend Henry Adams upon the exploration of Mont St Michel and Chartres. Thus John La Farge, who lived so large a creative life himself, fed the lives of two other creative personalities – the young Henry James and, in later life, Henry Adams. Adams considered La Farge 'among the best talkers of his time'.

For Henry James he opened 'more windows than he closed'. The windows he closed were those of the practice of painting. He let Henry daub, but encouraged him and even pushed him to write. He taught him that the 'arts were after all essentially one'. He gave Henry the sense of a young man who feels secure, 'a settled sovereign self'. And as Henry talked with him, he felt surer of himself. The painter introduced Henry to the world of Honoré de Balzac. Balzac was then but ten years dead, and Henry read him with such attention that years later, on reopening *Eugénie Grandet*, 'breathlessly seized and earnestly absorbed' under La Farge's instruction, he was 'to see my initiator's youthful face, so irregular but so refined, look out at me between the lines as through blurred prison bars'. The influence seems, in fact, to have been immediate, for T. S. Perry testifies to his writing at this time stories 'mainly of the romantic kind' in which the heroines were sophisticated and seemed 'to have read all Balzac in the cradle and to be positively dripping with lurid crimes'. Perry added that Henry began these extravagant pictures 'in adoration of the great master whom he always so warmly admired'.

La Farge also introduced Henry to the short stories of Prosper Mérimée; the future novelist found himself 'fluttering deliciously – quite as if with a sacred terror – at the touch of "La Vénus d'Ille"'. It 'struck my immaturity as a masterpiece of art and offered to the young curiosity concerned that sharpest of all challenges for youth, the challenge as to the special source of the effect'. James's later critical writings disclose how closely he studied his early models. In *Notes of a Son and Brother* he remembered that La Farge prodded him into translating Mérimée's tale of the ghostly Venus. He sent it to a New York periodical, 'which was to do me the honour neither of acknowledging nor printing'. In a reminiscence recorded in 1898 he spoke of having translated Mérimée's *Tamango* and *Matteo Falcone* and offering them to an illustrated weekly. He could recall 'the rejected manuscript cast at his feet again by the post, unroll, ironically, its anxious neatness'. Henry was to consider Mérimée's stories 'perfect models of the narrative'; they possessed a firmness of contour suggestive of hammered metal.

John La Farge was the first to prod Henry to a constructive writing effort and to insist that once his manuscript was completed, he do something with it. Perry testified that Henry went on to translate Alfred de Musset's *Lorenzaccio* and introduced into it scenes of his own. It was obvious that the youth needed no urging; what he did need was appreciation. He gives us an instance which reveals the extent to which La Farge filled a great want in his life. Browning's works had lain among his parents' books, but Henry had never ventured to read the poet. La Farge had only to invoke Browning and Henry fell upon the volumes immediately. Gathering these old memories, late in life, James throws in curious praise of La Farge at the expense of his parents. '*They*,' he noted, and he italicized the word, 'had not divined in us as yet an aptitude for that author.' This reproach does not appear to have been entirely justified. In the Lamb House library there was a copy of *Dramatis Personae* inscribed 'H. James Jr from his aff. Father. Aug. 20. 1864.' Earlier that year Henry also was given a copy of *Sordello* by his friend Perry. The copy is inscribed 'Henry James from T. S. P., Newport Mar. 2. '64.'

3

Henry James was in America in 1910 when John La Farge died at 75; and he was in Boston when a large commemorative exhibition of La Farge's work was held. The novelist, then 67, looked upon landscapes that suddenly 'laid bare the very footsteps of time'. As he stood there his mind wandered back to one incident which he recounted in his *Notes* with such evident pleasure that it reveals, more than anything else, the depth of the Newport – and the La Farge – attachment. 'There recurs to me,' Henry wrote,

... one of the smallest of adventures, as tiny a thing as could incur the name and which was of the early stage of our acquaintance, when he [La Farge] proposed to me that we should drive out to the Glen, some six miles off, to breakfast, and should afterwards paint – *we* paint! – in the bosky open air. It looks at this distance a mythic time, that of felt inducements to travel so far at such an hour and in a backless buggy on the supposition of rustic fare. But different ages have different measures, and I quite remember how ours, that morning, at the neat hostel in the umbrageous valley, overflowed with coffee and griddle-cakes that were not as other earthly refreshment, and how a spell of romance rested for several hours on our invocation of the genius of the scene : of such material, with the help of the attuned spirit, may great events consent to be composed.

La Farge arranged his easel and canvas, palette and stool, while Henry 'at a respectful distance' arranged his. He wondered, in recalling the incident, why it had been remembered and why it had 'really mattered'. It did indeed matter, he told himself, because there was 'in the vagueness of rustling murmuring green and plashing water and woodland voices and images' the hovering possibility that 'one's small daub might incur appreciation by the eye of friendship'.

This indeed was the true source of the spell, that it was in the eye of friendship, friendship full of character and colour, and full of amusement of its own, that I lived on any such occasion, and that I had come forth in the morning cool and had found our breakfast at the inn a thing of ineffable savour, and that I now sat and flurriedly and fearfully aspired.

To the old man, standing amid the works of his friend, the post-humous exhibition was filled with more scenes than were depicted on the walls. His debt to La Farge must not be measured in terms of 'influence'. He lived in the 'eye of friendship' – and it was a painter's eye. La Farge had appeared in Henry's life at a significant moment. The 'sovereign' self, the breakfasts near the Glen, the walks with La Farge and Perry, and other memories were to remain and merge with Balzac and Mérimée and Musset – and Browning. One has but to read the pages of *The American Scene* consecrated to Newport to understand what Henry James meant when he spoke of the 'time of settled possession' and the 'pure Newport time'. These were the richest hours of his young manhood, on the eve of national disaster.

Part Four:
The Vast Visitation

19

An Obscure Hurt

THE Southern guns opened up on Fort Sumter on 12 April 1861, and on 15 April – Henry James's 18th birthday – Lincoln issued his first call for volunteers. Presently T. S. Perry was noting in his Newport diary: 'April 27: We made bandages all evening.' 'April 28: After breakfast we all rolled bullets.'

Bandages and bullets! Abruptly the evidence of struggle confronted the young Henry James and his generation as the four epic years of passion, of 'blood and tears' (the words were written in juxtaposition by the novelist long before their modern use) began. There were 'hurrying troops' and a 'transfigured scene' and 'the interest of life and of death' that involved the whole question of national as of personal existence.

From the perspective of the twentieth century and two world wars the American Civil War seems in the long retrospect a local, if bloody, conflict in which battlefields bore familiar names and relatives could bring home the wounded and the dead after the carnage. In the spring of 1861 the moment, filled with excitement and terror, was unbelievable, and for young sensitive men such as Henry and William James it was unbearable. The paradise of paternal optimism and cheerfulness in which the Jameses had been reared, the free-ranging through countries, schools, books, galleries, was now at an end. On the brink of manhood they found themselves on the edge of the abyss, almost within earshot of the guns and in conflict whether they should go out and face them. Yet with the abrupt dawn of insecurity and grief, there was also the drama of war, the waving of banners, the bugle's blare, the marching of men. The James boys run to the Armoury to see the militia off. They are at the wharf to see the troops go by. And they see the ships returning, filled with the wounded.

Stirring deeds, patriotism, exaltation and also fear – and bafflement: a merging of the personal predicament and the national crisis; there were all these elements in the complex of emotion that young Henry felt in the dawn of the struggle for the Union. As war broke out in 1914, when he was an old man, he suddenly recalled the older time, 'the sudden new tang in the atmosphere, flagrant difference, as one noted, in the look of everything, especially in that of people's faces, the expressions, the hushes, the clustered groups, the detached wanderers and slow-paced public meditators'. The stretch of more than half a century had still left a sharpness : for Henry 'war' was to mean all his life the Civil War.

After Fort Sumter came the moment when North and South took a deep breath; then followed the Northern march on Richmond and in July the first battle of Bull Run. By then the North knew that the struggle would be difficult and perhaps long. The youths in Newport took their usual walks that summer; they watched the soldiers; they read the newspapers. On 4 July the elder Henry delivered the Independence Day oration at the invitation of his fellow-citizens. He entitled it *The Social Significance of Our Institutions* and displayed his rhetoric and eloquence; it was a vivid statement, surcharged with the emotions of the moment. From his criticism of the arrogance and the ignorance of the American wealthy and the British class-structure it was but a step to the denunciation of slavery.

Our very Constitution binds us, that is to say the very breath of our political nostrils binds us, to disown all distinctions among men, to disregard persons, to disallow privilege the most established and sacred, to legislate only for the common good, no longer for those accidents of birth or wealth or culture which spiritually individualize man from his kind, but only for those great common features of social want and dependence which naturally unite him with his kind, and inexorably demand the organization of such unity. It is this immense constitutional life and inspiration we are under which not only separate us from Europe, but also perfectly explain by antagonism that rabid hostility which the South has always shown towards the admission of the North to a fair share of government patronage, and which now provokes her to the dirty and diabolic struggle she is making to give human slavery the sanction of God's appointment.

In mid-July Henry and Sargy Perry went on a walking-tour in New Hampshire, climbing Mount Lafayette and Mount Washington and returning a week later to Newport, tired, cheerful, penniless. Perry noted : 'At and with Harry James to the Lily Pond. Lay on the grass and talked.' The idyllic life could, for the moment, still go on. It was during this month (and not a year later as he suggests in *Notes of a Son and Brother*) that Henry, again with Perry, went one afternoon 'to a vast gathering of invalid and convalescent troops, under canvas and in roughly improvised shanties' on the Rhode Island shore, at Portsmouth Grove. This was his 'first and all but sole vision of the American soldier in his multitude, and above all – for that was markedly the colour of the whole thing – in his depression, his wasted melancholy almost'. He talked with the men as he would later at Readville, when he visited his encamped younger brother Wilky; he strolled with them, sat by the improvised couches 'of their languid rest'. He drew from 'each his troubled tale, listened to his plaint on his special hard case' and emptied his pockets for them of whatever cash he had. In his memories he identified the image of himself on this occasion with Walt Whitman, 'even if I hadn't come armed like him with oranges and peppermints'. He felt himself under the spell of the same forces that later moved 'the good Walt' to his 'commemorative accents'. He sailed back to Newport that evening with Perry 'through the summer twilight ... the hour seemed by some wondrous secret, to know itself marked and charged and unforgettable'.

In September William entered the Lawrence Scientific School at Harvard, abandoning his study of art almost as abruptly as he had begun it a year earlier. It is impossible to judge what role the Civil War played in this decision; certainly it was difficult for William to remain painting in the studio under the pressures of the time. Wilky and Robertson had been put to school at Concord the previous autumn, at Frank B. Sanborn's pioneering co-educational Academy. Here the younger Jameses, then 16 and 15, found themselves class-mates of Emerson's son, Edward, and Hawthorne's son, Julian. Henry was left alone at Newport with his parents, his sister and Aunt Kate. He proposed to his father at this time that he also should go to Har-vard. The senior James brushed the suggestion aside and Henry stayed on, marking time while around him young men were spring-ing to the colours. In due course the two younger brothers enlisted, and before the war had run half its course two of Henry's cousins, young Gus Barker and William Temple, had died in battle.

Henry James has left us no concrete record of his thoughts and feelings in those early weeks of the war. We know only from later evidence that for him, as for many others, the call to arms provoked an acute depression. Temperamentally unsuited for soldiering, unable to endure violence, he had long ago substituted close obser-vation of life for active participation. He had from the first culti-vated passive resistance to competition with his brothers, and now he ran the risk of being called upon to take the field in direct assault upon brother Americans. In Henry James the universal conflict – the reluctance of the citizen-soldier in a democracy to shoulder arms against his fellow-men – merged with the conflict that arose within his constituted personality. If peacetime competition had for him a 'displeasing ferocity', what could he say of war?

The young man of letters experienced a certain amount of social pressure to which many of the youths of the time were subjected. This was reflected in verses such as Dr Holmes indited to 'The Sweet Little Man, dedicated to the Stay-at-Home Rangers', or his hortatory

> Listen young heroes! your country is calling!
> Time strikes the hour for the brave and the true!
> Now, while the foremost are fighting and falling,
> Fill up the ranks that have opened for you.

Nor was the senior Henry particularly helpful. While public sentiment pulled in one direction he pulled in the other. 'Affectionate old papas like me are scudding all over the country to apprehend their patriotic offspring and restore them to the harmless embraces of their mamas,' he wrote very early in the struggle. 'I have had a firm grasp upon the coat tails of my Willy and Harry, who both vituperate me beyond measure because I won't let them go. The coats are a very staunch material, or the tails must have been off two days ago, the scamps pull so hard.' It is difficult to tell from this letter whether the elder Henry is dramatizing the family problem for the benefit of his correspondent, or merely reflecting the indecision of himself and his sons. He goes on to write:

The way I excuse my paternal interference to them is, to tell them, first, that no existing government, nor indeed any now possible government, is worth an honest human life and a clean one like theirs; especially if that government is likewise in danger of bringing back slavery again under our banner: than which consummation I would rather see chaos itself come again. Secondly, I tell them that no young American should put himself in the way of death, until he has realized something of the good of life: until he has found some charming conjugal Elizabeth or other to whisper his devotion to, and assume the task, if need be, of keeping his memory green.

(This last sentence could almost be a note for a portion of Henry's Civil War tale *The Story of a Year*, which began with the engagement of the young hero, on the eve of his departure for the war, to a girl named Elizabeth.)

Almost two years after the war began there seems to have still been indecision among the elder sons. 'I may say,' the father wrote to his English friend Dr Wilkinson, 'that my two elder boys Willy and Harry, who have just come home from college, are thinking of going down to labour among the contrabands or now, thank God, the *freed* blacks. They have applied for places, but have as yet not heard of the success of their application.'

Nothing came of this project. The elder Henry's two letters suggest a parent understandably concerned; but it is difficult to say whether he reflects his own state of mind of that of his older sons. The letters do suggest that both Henry and William, at various times, entertained plans to participate in the nation's struggle. Their indecision was in part a reflection of the indecision of the entire North. Compulsory service was not instituted by the Lincoln administration until more than a year after the first appeal for volunteers. The reluctance of the citizenry to respond, after the first rush to the colours, was exemplified in the bitter opposition to the draft which was finally instituted in March 1863; and even then Henry James had the option of finding a substitute or simply paying $300, which would exempt him from service. The cry arose of 'a rich man's war and a poor man's fight', and the draft riots of July 1863 in New York counted a thousand killed or injured and bore testimony to the inequalities of sacrifice and the confusion of the time. Long before this, however, an incident had occurred in Henry James's life that was to colour the war years and the decades beyond.

I

Henry James tells us in *Notes of a Son and Brother* that at the 'same dark hour' as the Civil War he suffered a 'horrid even if an obscure hurt'. 'Scarce at all to be stated,' he says, 'the queer fusion or confusion established in my consciousness during the soft spring of '61 by the firing on Fort Sumter, Mr Lincoln's first call for volunteers and a physical mishap, the effects of which were to draw themselves out incalculably and intolerably.'

He called it a 'passage of personal history, the most entirely personal', which he nevertheless associated with the 'great public convulsion'. The mishap occurred during 'twenty odious minutes' and kept company 'with the question of what might still happen to everyone about me, to the country at large: it so made of these disparities a single vast visitation. One had the sense,' he adds,

of a huge comprehensive ache, and there were hours at which one could scarce have told whether it came most from one's own poor organism, still so young and so meant for better things, but which had suffered particular wrong, or from the enclosing social body, a body rent with a thousand wounds and that thus treated me to the honour of a sort of tragic fellowship.

The twenty minutes sufficed, James said, to establish a relationship with the world that was 'at once extraordinarily intimate and quite awkwardly irrelevant'. And he goes on :

I must have felt in some befooled way in presence of a crisis – the smoke of Charleston Bay still so acrid in the air – at which the likely young should be up and doing or, as familiarly put, lend a hand much wanted; the willing youths, all round, were mostly starting to their feet, and to have trumped up a lameness at such a juncture could be made to pass in no light for graceful.

(The use of the word 'lameness' reminds us of the father's missing limb.)

With this prelude he tells how during a Newport fire, 'jammed into the acute angle between two high fences', in an awkward position, he and others managed to make 'a rusty, a quasi-extemporized old engine' work sufficiently well to help put out what James characterized as a 'shabby conflagration'. What was interesting to him was that 'from the first' he did not doubt in the least the duration of the injury. He does not describe it, nor give any further details. In the ensuing passage he says that he tried to 'strike a bargain' with his ailing condition, and spent much time in bed or on a couch on the theory that rest would help. Also he did not mention it to his family. Since, however, it did not mend, he finally confided his trouble to his father and received prompt and sympathetic attention, although he felt that publicizing his hurt diminished the value of the comfort he was receiving. Early 'that summer', he goes on to say (apparently in the weeks immediately following Sumter), he accompanied his father to Boston 'for consultation of a great surgeon, the head of his profession there', who was also a friend of the elder Henry James.

This interview, Henry continues, 'settled my sad business', so that he was never afterward to pass the doctor's house without feeling the 'ironic smug symbolism of its action on my fate'. What happened was that the eminent surgeon made 'quite unassistingly light of the bewilderment exposed to him'. He gave no warnings; he treated Henry to a 'comparative pooh-pooh'. And Henry felt, ruefully, that he had to reckon on the one hand with his pain and on the other 'with the strange fact of there being nothing to speak of the matter with me'. He accordingly decided to act as if there wasn't – but he continued to suffer for many months. Speaking of the choice of a course of action, he says: 'I think of the second half of that summer of '62 as my attempt at selection of the best [alternative].' He decided once again that he would propose to go to Harvard. This time his father agreed.

2

This is all Henry tells us of the 'obscure hurt'. It is a queer tale – queer since he has mingled so many elements in it and at the same time thoroughly confused us about the time sequence. If the accident occurred at the 'same dark hour' as the outbreak of the Civil War – that is, in the 'soft spring of '61' – then the visit to the doctor 'that summer' must have taken place during the summer of 1861. But 'that summer' becomes, at the end of the account, the summer of 1862. The details as given by Henry are meagre; and they bristle with strange ambiguities: in his characteristically euphemistic manner he makes it sound at every turn as a matter grave and ominous while at the same time he minimizes its gravity.

The hurt is 'horrid' but it is also 'obscure'. It is a 'catastrophe' but it is in the very same phrase only a 'difficulty'. It is a passage of history 'most entirely personal', yet apparently not too personal to be broadcast to the world in his memoirs, even though when it happened he kept it a secret and regretted the necessity of making it known. It is also 'extraordinarily intimate' and at the same time 'awkwardly irrelevant'. This is perplexing enough. James compounds the mystery by giving no hint of the kind of hurt he suffered, although at various times during his life he complained of an early back injury, which he usually dated as of 1862. That he should have chosen to omit all specific reference to his back in his memoirs is significant; in some way he seems to have felt that by vagueness and circumlocution he might becloud the whole question of his non-participation in the Civil War. To the error of omission – 'error' because of the consequences of his reticence – must be added the effect of his elaborate euphemisms: the use of the words *intimate*, *odious*, *horrid*, *catastrophe*, *obscure* and the phrase *most entirely personal*. These had an effect not unlike that of the unspecified 'horrors' of *The Turn of the Screw*. His readers were ready to imagine the worst. James would, several years later, use language quite as portentous, to describe his then chronic constipation.

What, after all, is the most *odious*, *horrid*, *intimate* thing that can happen to a man? In the case of Henry James critics tended to see a relationship between the accident and his celibacy, his apparent avoidance of involvements with women and the absence of overt sexuality in his work. Moreover, his early tales deal with sexually ineffectual young men. As a consequence there emerged a 'theory' that the novelist suffered a hurt during those 'twenty odious' minutes which amounted to castration. In the April–June 1934 *Hound and Horn* issue, devoted entirely to Henry James, Glenway Wescott reports it almost as fact: 'Henry James, expatriation and castration ... Henry James, it is rumoured, could not have had a child. But if he was as badly hurt in the pre-Civil War accident as that – since he triumphed powerfully over other authors of his epoch – perhaps the injury was a help to him.' Stephen Spender quotes this passage in *The Destructive Element* and suggests that 'Castration, or the fear of castration, is supposed to preoccupy the mind with ideas of suicide and death.' He goes on to show how this is true of many of James's characters. Professor Spender, however, does have a second thought, and adds in a footnote: 'The rumour of castration seems exaggerated and improbable, but it seems likely that James sustained a serious injury.' F. O. Matthiessen in *The James Family* speculates that 'since Henry James never married, he may have been sexually impotent'. R. P. Blackmur equates James with the emasculated Abelard 'who, after his injury, raised the first chapel to the Holy Ghost'; so James, he adds, 'made a sacred rage of his art as the only spirit he could fully serve'. And Lionel Trilling, overlooking motivation, suggests that 'only a man as devoted to the truth of the emotions as Henry James was, would have informed the world, despite his characteristic reticence, of an accident so intimate as his'.

3

The most logical explanation of Henry James's blurring of the date of the hurt (the 'same dark hour' as the outbreak of the Civil War) is that it served to minimize his failure during the first six months to enlist with the other young men. To take his timing literally would fix the hurt as occurring in April or perhaps May of 1861. Had it occurred that spring, however, it is doubtful whether he would have climbed mountains in New Hampshire with T. S. Perry during July. Fortunately it is no longer necessary to speculate, since Perry comes to our assistance with specific dates. In a letter to James's nephew and executor, written shortly after the publication of *Notes of a Son and Brother* and alluding directly to the 'obscure hurt' passage, Perry wrote that 'the fire at West Stables was in the night of Oct. 28, '61'. Hence the particular incident occurred a full six months after Fort Sumter and three months after the first battle of Bull Run. The contemporary records of the fire are detailed. They include the newspaper accounts and the official report written by one of the firemen, now in the archives of the Newport Historical Society.

A high wind blew through the town on the night of 28 October, and some time between 10.30 and 11 a blaze was discovered in the large stable of Charles B. Tennant at the corner of Beach and State Streets. In a few minutes the entire stable was in flames amid the screaming of horses and the scramble of an alerted town that rushed to give aid and to see the spectacle. The wind carried the fire to an adjoining stable, and the flames threatened a newly-built residence. By the time the fire-fighters had brought Engine No. 5 down to the Tennant stable there was little hope of saving it. Four horses perished and a number of vehicles were destroyed, as well as substantial quantities of hay and grain.

The No. 5 engine had stopped en route at the Redwood Reservoir only to discover that the hose was not long enough to reach the scene of the fire. The engine accordingly was brought farther down and the requisitioning of wells in the neighbourhood began. Two wells were pumped dry in rapid succession. In the meantime the fire had begun to spread in the second stable; a dozen horses and an equal number of carriages were removed to safety, while a stream from other cisterns was directed on the house, which also caught fire. A small carpenter's shop was gutted and the fire-fighters tore down another dwelling, directly in the path of the flames. This helped to arrest the fire and to confine it, so that about 1 a.m., 'there being no sign of any fire by this time, we were ordered by the chief to return home which order was most willingly obeyed'. At the height of the fire, reported the Newport *Mercury*, 'clouds of sparks and smoke curled high up in the heavens and we have no doubt it was a great sight to the hundreds who congregated in the vicinity as idle spectators'. The Newport *Daily News* said that 'engine companies were on the ground and rendered all assistance in their power'. The loss was estimated by the press at $7,000. In terms of the time, the fire was much more than the 'shabby conflagration' pictured by Henry James.

The high wind and the shortage of water would explain Henry's role among the volunteers that night. Apparently all available pumping-engines were pressed into service, and the novelist spoke of having helped induce 'a saving stream to flow', probably that which kept the flames from the new residence. The accounts understand-ably make no mention of volunteers, since volunteer firemen were taken for granted in those days. There were no reports of any persons suffering injuries. Whatever hurt Henry received was suffered in silence as he testified; perhaps it went unnoticed and did not manifest itself until later.

Three days after the fire, on 31 October 1861, Perry's diary testifies to the fact that Henry James was well enough to travel. 'Thursday, Oct. 31 [1861] At recitation in morning. Harry has gone to Boston.' Perry by this entry identified (for James's nephew) the visit to Wil-liam that Henry mentions in *Notes of a Son and Brother*. A letter from William to the family after Henry returned to Newport speaks of the 'radiance of H's visit'. Had Henry suffered anything approach-ing serious injury he would have been in condition neither for journeying nor visiting; nor does it seem likely that William would have found the visit 'radiant'. Henry remained for a long week-end. On 5 November Perry's diary says: 'At school. Harry's before 12,' and on the next day Henry walked with his friend to Easton's Point.

The next few months are those to which Henry alluded when he spoke of his seeking 'to strike some sort of bargain' with his injury, and his date of the summer of 1862 – apparently early summer – for the visit to the eminent surgeon seems accurate. However limited medical knowledge may have been in that era, it is quite clear that there would have been no 'pooh-pooh' had the surgeon discovered a groin injury or a hernia. Hernia operations had been performed earlier in the century and any acute hurt would have been easily apparent to an experienced medical man. The 'obscure hurt' was obscure indeed.

4

Some years after the Newport fire Henry published a short story about a Civil War veteran who survives the conflict without physical injury but is stricken by illness at the end. The nature of the disorder is not disclosed; it is, however, 'deeply-seated and virulent'. The attending physician tells the hero, whose name is Colonel Mason, 'You have opposed no resistance; you haven't cared to get well.' Mason tries and is aided by an affectionate aunt who takes him to her home and gives him the care and attention of a mother. Staying with her is a beautiful niece, Caroline Hoffman, with whom Mason falls in love; he worships her, however, from afar; he gives her no intimation of his feelings. When he discovers that Miss Hoffmann has been wooed successfully by his own doctor he has a relapse. 'It's the most extraordinary case I ever heard of,' says the doctor as his patient dies. 'The man was steadily getting well.' And again : 'I shall never be satisfied that he mightn't have recovered. It was a most extraordinary case.' The story, entitled A Most Extraordinary Case, appeared in the Atlantic Monthly of April 1868, when Henry was 25.

The extraordinary case was as mystifying to the doctor as the obscure hurt was to Henry James. The doctor was, however, unaware of the subjective elements which caused Mason to give up the fight; and Henry James was unaware of the subjective elements which conditioned and at the same time obscured his hurt. He gives us a very positive clue in his final account when he asserts that 'what was interesting from the first was my not doubting in the least its [the obscure hurt's] duration'. This is a curious and significant admission. James claims foreknowledge or a feeling that his injury would have lasting effects. We can, of course, attempt to explain this in part by saying that James was an extraordinarily intuitive person. Still, to know in advance that the hurt would have a 'duration' is not intuition; it suggests a wish that the hurt might endure, or at least betrays an extraordinarily pessimistic frame of mind about it. It was a pre-judgement which the doctor in Boston did not in any way endorse. To understand the real ground for James's certainty of his hurt prolonging itself, we must reach back into the events of his father's life before he was born.

Fire had a particular meaning in the life of the James family. A fire in a stable had an even more special meaning. The senior Henry's cork leg had been the symbol through all Henry Junior's life of what could happen to someone who becomes involved in putting out a stable fire. It was an enduring injury. We can therefore speculate (and the evidence warrants it), that from the moment Henry hurt himself in circumstances analogous to those of his father, he felt his hurt too would have a long duration. And this is what happened. Henry was still experiencing his back-ache in middle life.

The theory that there was an unconscious identification with the father at the moment of the accident is reinforced by a similar identification which occurs in the account set down in old age. Describing his hurt as keeping 'unnatural' company with 'the question of what might still happen to everyone about me, to the country at large', Henry James said, as we have noted, that these 'marked disparities' became 'a single vast visitation'. His use of these words evokes for us that other word which seems almost a portmanteau version of *vast* and *visitation* – Henry James at the last could claim that, like his father, he also had had his *vastation*.

5

Two letters of William James's supply independent evidence. In 1867 William speaks of having 'that delightful disease in my back, which has so long made Harry so interesting. It is evidently a family peculiarity'. In the same vein, when Robertson James complained of a back-ache in 1869, William, by then a medical student, wrote 'even if we suppose that this recent matter of your back is a false alarm, yet in virtue of the sole fact of your fraternity with Harry and me, you must have a latent tendency to it in you'.

Edmund Gosse remembered that early in the 1880s he called on James in London and found him stretched on his sofa. James apologized for not rising to greet him. 'His appearance gave me a little shock,' Gosse testified, 'for I had not thought of him as an invalid.' James 'hurriedly and rather evasively declared that he was not that, but that a muscular weakness of his spine obliged him, as he said, "to assume the horizontal posture" during some hours of every day,

in order to bear the almost unbroken routine of evening engagements. I think,' Gosse added, 'this weakness gradually passed away,
but certainly for many years it handicapped his activity.' Seeing
James in 1886 Gosse noted : 'He had not wholly recovered from that
weakness of the muscles of his back which had so long troubled him,
and I suppose this was the cause of a curious stiffness in his progress,
which proceeded rather slowly.'

In 1899, when Henry was 56, he wrote to console his friend
Howard Sturgis, then ailing,

if you have a Back, for heaven's sake take care of it. When I was about
your age – in 1862! – I did bad damage (by a strain subsequently –
through crazy juvenility – neglected) to mine; the consequence of which
is that, in spite of retarded attention, and years, really of recumbency,
later, I've been saddled with it for life, and that even now, my dear
Howard, I verily write *with* it. I even wrote *The Awkward Age* with it;
therefore look sharp!

Three years later in a letter to Mrs Frank Mathews, a daughter of Dr
Wilkinson, he mentions a photograph of himself taken at Newport :
'I remember (it now all comes back to me) when (and where) I was
so taken : at the age of 20, though I look younger, and at a time
when I had had an accident (an injury to my back,) and was rather
sick and sorry, I look rather as if I wanted propping up.'

In the privacy of his notebooks, James wrote a passage of reminiscence on the occasion of his return to America in 1905, in
which he recalled a stay at Swampscott in 1866, where 'I was miserably stricken by my poor broken, all but unbearable, and unsurvivable *back* of those (and still under fatigue, even of these) years'. And
again in another notebook entry he recalled his

suffering tortures from my damnable state of health. It was a time of
suffering so keen that that fact might [claim?] to give its dark colour to
the whole period ... Ill-health, physical suffering, in one's younger years,
is a grievous trial; but I am not sure that we do not bear it most easily
then ... Some of my doses of pain were very heavy; very weary were
some of my months and years.

He alluded to his back-ache in an article published just seven
months before his death. Recalling how J. T. Fields, the Boston editor
and publisher, allowed him in the 1860s to read certain celebrated
works in page-proof, he remembered turning the ink-besmirched
pages of *Essays in Criticism*. 'I can still recover the rapture with

which, then suffering under the effects of a bad accident, I lay all day on a sofa in Ashburton Place and was somehow transported, as in a shining silvery dream, to London, to Oxford, to the French Academy, to Languedoc, to Brittany, to ancient Greece.'

6

In sum, the evidence points unquestionably to a back injury – a slipped disc, a sacroiliac or muscular strain – obscure but clearly painful as such injuries can be. Perhaps the letter to Sturgis best describes it, 'a strain subsequently neglected'. That the hurt was exacerbated by the tensions of the Civil War seems quite clear. Mentally prepared for some state of injury by his father's permanent hurt, and for a sense therefore of continuing physical inadequacy, Henry James found himself a prey to anxieties over the fact that he might be called a malingerer ('to have trumped up a lameness at such a juncture could be made to pass in no light for graceful'), and had a feeling that he was deficient in the masculinity being displayed by others of his generation on the battlefield. This is reflected in all his early stories and contributed to the quite extraordinarily literal assumption by some critics that Henry James 'castrated' himself. Yet even if we did not have the evidence of Henry James's activities immediately after the fire, or his repeated assertions, his physically active later life and his monumental production would in themselves undermine the legend. An invalid could not have accomplished what Henry James did between the ages of 21 and 73. He rode horseback, fenced, lifted weights (to fight off corpulence), took long daily walks and was an inveterate traveller, indulging in a prodigious expenditure of physical energy over and above his fecundity in creation, which in itself is deservedly legendary; he spent hours daily at his desk; he combined literary labour with a crowded and intricate social life. There was nothing of the eunuch about him either in appearance or action. Henry James himself, we suspect, would not have used the word *eunuch* so freely, as he did on occasions, to describe bad and unproductive writers, had he been physically one himself.

20

The Younger Brothers

IN Concord, where the major accents of Abolition had sounded, Garth Wilkinson and Robertson James now heard the more violent accents of the war. In 1862 Wilky, then 17, turned his back on the Sanborn school and sought a place in the Northern Army. A few months later Bob followed him.

The war emphasized a widening gulf between the four brothers that had been simply the result of their difference in age. Wilky and Bob were still busy with their schooling when William and Henry gained comparative liberty in Geneva. There the younger boys had been set apart in the Pensionnat Maquelin, returning to the family at the Hôtel de l'Écu usually on Sundays. A similar isolation from family occurred upon their return to America, in their prompt installation in Concord. Bob, in particular, had for some time 'strained much at every tether', Henry observed. He considered himself a foundling in the family; he talked of running off to sea. The war offered him a ready alternative. Their enlistment was a reflection of a youthful desire for action, freedom, adventure, and a response to strong anti-slavery sentiment to which they had been exposed both at home and at Concord; it was also a leap to manhood and the sudden achievement of a superior position in the family hierarchy. By one swift bound they surpassed their elder brothers; the focus of family interest turned upon them where it had previously treated them as juveniles and attached all importance to William's artistic and scientific career and Henry's bookishness. The younger brothers stepped into the bright and lurid light of war for their brief hour – and it turned out to be their only hour. Life after the Civil War was for them a long and painful anticlimax, while for William and Henry it marked a progression to careers and fame. The splitting apart within the family was permanent. The younger boys went their separate ways, first of heroism and then of frustration and suffering. Their story is a separate chapter in the annals of the James family, rich in idealism and courage, but also beclouded by pathos and decline.

The younger brothers sent vivid and excited letters from the field and gave Henry a continuing picture of the life of the soldier and the life of action. Here were Jamesian voices reporting the national catastrophe; Henry listened with deep emotion. He remembered visiting Wilky when he was in the 44th Massachusetts at Readville and marvelled that 'this soft companion of my childhood should have such romantic chances and should have mastered, by the mere aid of his native gaiety and sociability, such mysteries, such engines, such arts. To become first a happy soldier and then an easy officer was in particular for G.W.J. an exercise in sociability.' He remembered Readville as 'an interplay of bright breezy air and high shanty-covered levels with blue horizons, and laughing, welcoming, sunburnt young men'. Presently Wilky joined the dramatically-constituted 54th Massachusetts, the first regiment of coloured troops, headed by Colonel Robert Gould Shaw. Henry was ill the day they marched out of Boston – 28 May 1863 – 'to great reverberations of music, of fluttering banners, launched benedictions and every public sound'. That the moment seemed to him deeply important is shown by the fact that he twice describes it in his memoirs, even though he was not present.

I

On 1 July 1863, as the battle of Gettysburg was being fought, Henry paced restlessly in a Newport garden, with some New York cousins, 'neither daring quite to move nor quite to rest, quite to go in nor quite to stay out ... This *was*, as it were, the War – the War palpably in Pennsylvania'. Before the month was out the war was experienced in the James household in Newport. There had been a courageous assault by the Negro regiment on Fort Wagner in Charleston Bay with the guns of Sumter playing on them. The 54th withdrew after two-thirds of its officers and nearly half its men had been shot down or bayoneted within the fortress or before its walls. Shaw had died, leading his men, a bullet in his heart; and Wilky James, his adjutant, had received a wound in his side and a canister ball in his ankle.

It fell to William James many years later (in 1897) to pronounce a eulogy of Colonel Shaw and his men at the unveiling of the Shaw monument by Saint-Gaudens in Boston. William, drawing on Wilky's memories, described the forced marches in the rain, the hunger of the men as they lay

in the evening twilight against the cold sands of Morris Island with sea-fog drifting over them, their eyes fixed on the huge hulk of the fortress looming darkly three-quarters of a mile ahead against the sky, and their hearts beating in expectation of the word that was to bring them to their feet and launch them on their desperate charge.

He told of the fierce attack and finally described how the next day the rebels, having repulsed the assault, dug a ditch and threw into it the bodies of Shaw and his coloured soldiers. 'In death, as in life, then, the 54th bore witness,' said William James, 'to the brotherhood of man.'

Wilky James probably would have been among the dead had not a rescuing hand intervened. Reported missing in the struggle at Charleston was Wilky's closest friend in the Army, Cabot Russell, whose father promptly went in search of his son. He did not find him, but he discovered Wilky among the wounded and brought him north by boat to New York and thence to Newport, where, one August day in 1863, he appeared at the James residence with the wounded youth on a stretcher. They carried Wilky in, placing the stretcher just inside the door of the house. There he lay for days. The doctor ordered that he should not be moved. Henry in his old age remembered the moment of arrival as clearly as 'some object presented in high relief against the evening sky of the west' – with himself sitting beside the stretcher and Cabot Russell's father 'erect and dry-eyed at the guarded feast of *our* relief'. In Henry James's first signed story the bringing home of the young hero from battle is described, much as it occurred at Newport, and the heroine wonders, as Henry might have, whether the young soldier were not dead, 'Death is not thinner, paler, stiller.' A sketch of Wilky made by William at this moment shows him almost as one dead – open-mouthed, leaden-eyed, his cheeks sunken and his face covered with the stubble of his beard. 'Poor Wilky cries aloud for his friends gone and missing, and I could hardly have supposed he might be educated so suddenly up to serious manhood altogether as he appears to have been,' the senior Henry wrote to a friend at the same moment.

Wilky's recovery was slow, but he pulled through and with a fine show of strength returned to the field in 1864, rejoining his own regiment. In spite of his freshly-healed wounds he was able to ride and march and he participated in the entry into Charleston. He was present when the American flag was hoisted over Sumter.

In the meantime Robertson had been made a lieutenant in the 55th Massachusetts. While Wilky was recovering, he was at Morris Island building earthworks and mounting guns in the southern heat with rebel shells playing on the troops, so that they made for their breastworks 'like so many land-crabs in distress'. He suffered so serious a sunstroke during Seymour's raid on Florida that he was recommended for discharge. Instead, as soon as he had recovered, he took a staff post in the cavalry, and later returned to his regiment before Charleston. He participated in a heavy fight, made an heroic charge ('I rammed my spurs into my own beast, who, maddened with pain, caried me on through the line, throwing men down, and over the rebel works some distance ahead of our troops'). This earned him a captaincy. The 55th later was the first body of Northern troops to enter Charleston.

2

Re-reading the war letters when he was writing *Notes of a Son and Brother*, Henry re-experienced 'the places, the hours, the stilled or stirred conditions' in which he had originally absorbed them fresh from the front. These conditions, he said, 'settled for me into the single sense of what I missed, compared to what the authors of our bulletins gained, in wondrous opportunity of vision, that is *appreciation of the thing seen*'. Henry longed to live by his eyes 'in the midst of such far-spreading chances, in greater measure than I then had help to', and his role was reduced to 'seeing, sharing, envying, applauding, pitying, all from too far-off'.

The Civil War letters of his brothers form a logical bridge to Henry's later reading of war memoirs and Napoleonic lore. James would have given much to have been able to pass to vivid conquering action in his waking hours as he had done in his nightmare of the Louvre. He admired the active soldier: he shrank from the killing.

3

When the war was over, Wilky and Bob, imbued with the cause for which they had fought, embarked on a courageous if misguided venture: they set out to be plantation owners in Florida with paid Negro labour, as if the South no longer considered them 'enemy' once the last shot was fired. They struggled valiantly, risked their lives, lost large sums of money advanced them by their father, and finally gave up. The rest of Wilky's brief life was a series of efforts to find a place for himself in a disjointed America; sociable, as always, improvident, he drifted finally westward, worked as a railway clerk and died at 40 after a period of prolonged ill-health. Robertson lived into our century, a brilliant, erratic individual, gifted, witty, deeply unhappy. Henry called him 'our one gentleman of leisure'. He worked for a railroad for a while; he tried to paint, he wrote verse, he travelled; he experienced a series of religious conflicts much like his father – for a while he found solace in Catholicism, then he rebelled against the Church's authority and turned to the family religion, Swedenborgianism. The senior Henry's letters to him during these years are filled with brilliant exposition of his beliefs and with paternal counsel and solace. There were periods of heavy drinking and guilt, which Robertson expressed once in a pathetic poem that reveals his strength of feeling and insight into his own sense of desolation. He wrote in the cadences of Omar:

> With Wine I slept, and sleeping did not hear ...

> The night we live in, is the all of Fate,
> Oblivion's sleep will come, or soon or late;
> Drink deep! nor for some distant Heaven wait;
> And these, my friends, stayed on, until the Wine
> Was out – and then, they left me desolate.

> Nor did I wake for many an empty year
> Nor did I wish to wake, for very fear.

The poem is an amalgam of the self-pity and sorrow that recalled his boyhood. He died in the same year as William, in 1910, and Henry, mourning him, spoke of the 'vivacity of his intelligence, the variety of his gifts' and the 'easiest aptitude for admirable talk, charged with natural life, perception, humour and colour, that I have perhaps ever known'.

21

A Particular Divergence

THE doctor's pooh-pooh had offered Henry James neither cure nor the awkward solace of invalidism. To remain at home at such a moment, with nothing more to show than a back-ache, however painful, while the great hurricane of the fratricidal war swept the nation, could indeed 'pass in no light for graceful'. James felt acutely that he had to 'make some show of life ... when everyone was on the move'. He was, he told himself, 'no less exalted than wistfully engaged in the common fact of endurance', like the soldiers themselves. Moreover, he found himself, at this moment, isolated in his own family. The younger brothers were gone; William was in Cambridge. And now his boon companion Sargy Perry was about to enter Harvard. This was clearly no time to stay at home. In September 1862 Henry James accordingly journeyed from Newport to Cambridge and registered at the Harvard Law School. Looking back at his young collegiate self, he felt that his act was similar to that of a young man joining a mustered army.

The Cambridge campus was tented field enough for a conscript starting so compromised; and I can scarce say moreover how easily it let me down that when it came to the point one had still fine fierce young men, in great numbers, for company, there being at the worst so many such who hadn't flown to arms.

Thus at 19 the young cosmopolite, who had lived in New York, in London, in Paris, found himself at last on the Boston scene. Newport, 'with its opera-glass turned for ever across the sea', was at best a stepping-stone to America. Now he was in the Back Bay itself and its academic suburb of Cambridge, in that city which the consummate Brahmin, Dr Oliver Wendell Holmes, with a Bostonian complacency and civic pride that Henry was later to satirize, had characterized as 'the thinking centre of the continent'. New England had been only a domestic geographical designation to Henry James, something discovered as a boy in 14th Street through his reading of the Rollo books, or in the benign aspect of Mr Emerson. It had, however, acquired a certain reality in the persons of three playmates who lived down the street during those Manhattan years, Johnny,

Charley and Freddy Ward. They exhaled, for the young Manhattan-ite, an atmosphere of apples and cheese, nuts, pies, jack-knives, 'domestic Bible-reading and attendance at "evening-lecture" ', as well as fear of parental discipline 'and the cultivated art of defying it'. The Wards were tough little New Englanders who talked of 'squrruls', had warts on their hands, wore homespun and revealed 'a brave rusticity'. The words *rustic, rural, provincial* figure always in Henry James's picture of New England. He found Boston a 'rural centre even to a point at which I had never known anything as rural', and this was strange because the city was at the same time 'stoutly and vividly urban ... a town of history'.

One felt there the 'breath of the fields and woods and waters ... at their domesticated and familiarized stage' which Emerson had brought into the 14th Street parlour. New York might be described as 'vulgar' and 'homely', but the Puritan capital, with its plodding horse-cars and the afterglow of the great snowfalls, reflected 'the higher complacency' and at the same time was New England 'un-absorbed and unreconciled' – and also 'the most educated of our societies without ceasing to be that of a village'. In his later sketch of Emerson and in his book on Hawthorne, as well as in his tribute to those Brahmins who became his mentors and friends, Henry James never forgot that Nature, in New England, could inspire notes both lyrical and rhapsodic; its life constituted an 'achromatic pic-ture' of 'a plain, God-fearing society ... not fertile in variations'. Between the rectitude and morality of meeting-house and pulpit and the open fields and spreading elms there was that same disparity which the elder Henry had discovered between his Calvinistic home and the out-of-doors of his boyhood. The father, in fact, had once described John Calvin as 'a sort of model Bostonian'.

This was, however, Henry James's view of New England during his maturity and long after his saturation with Back Bay life and Cambridge. The process began with Harvard and was to continue for the next six years. It flowed ultimately into *The Bostonians* and *The Europeans* and largely as satire and irony penned by the grand-son of an Albany merchant, an immigrant, who could never recon-cile himself to the gentility of the Brahmins and the frugality of Concord; or the manner in which New England considered culture to be an arduous duty rather than a joy of life and of civilization. Yet within this environment he considered hostile to major creative art, lay the associations of his 'untried years', so that Cambridge and

Boston were regarded by him as repositories of old personal memories that had marked the launching of a career, *his* career. In the end his pictures of the old scenes are suffused with a kind of redeeming affection and tenderness. New England became a part of Henry James even though he resisted it.

I

Henry James had actually entertained the idea of a university education in Bonn, two years earlier, when he excitedly awaited his return to America. 'I wish,' he had written to Perry, 'although I've no doubt it is a very silly wish, that I were going to college.' He now had his wish. In his old age, however, it seemed 'odd' to him that he should have wanted to go, and odder still that he should have elected the study of law. Law, nevertheless, appears to have been for him the only acceptable alternative in 1862. Harvard was then a college of 1,000 students and thirty teachers. Nothing approaching 'liberal arts' existed, except the rhetoric and oratory taught by Francis J. Child or the French and Spanish taught by James Russell Lowell. Henry was neither rhetorical nor oratorical; he had no need to study French and no desire to study Spanish. The Divinity School, the core of the institution, could offer little to a young man neither philosophical nor religious. He certainly had no desire to join William at the Lawrence Scientific School. Once he had excluded the clergyman, the scientist, the doctor, what remained but the lawyer? The law was the one field which seemed eminently 'practical'. It represented 'life' and the 'world'. In reality it was the avenue of least resistance for a shy, observant young man who asked only to be just 'literary'. Harvard appeared to him 'detached from any such interest', but that mattered little. For literature he could go to the library at Gore Hall, or when at home he had only to open the door of the big square closet in the Newport house where the pink copies of the *Revue des Deux Mondes* were piled, 'with the air, row upon row, of a choir of breathing angels'. This had been his best school. He wanted no other.

Henry James lodged with William for a few days after his arrival in Cambridge until he found himself in Winthrop Square, in an old house with 'everything in it slanting and gaping and creaking'. His sitting-room commanded a view of distant hills, and in an alcove there was a large desk where 'even so shy a dreamer as I ... might perhaps hope to woo the muse'. In his short story *The Ghostly Rental*, written some years later, the young Harvard graduate lives 'in a great square low-browed room with deep window-benches', hangs prints on the walls and arranges his books 'with great refinement of classification' in alcoves beside a high chimney-shelf. We can imagine the young Henry doing this and taking 'long and sustaining sniffs' at the 'scented flower of independence'. William was close at hand, to be sought at will; T. S. Perry was as always a familiar companion. But now Henry had Boston and Cambridge to explore, and the privacy of his room to which he could return to watch the flushed sunsets and the cloud scenery. He had to 'rinse my mouth of the European after-taste *in order* to do justice to whatever of the native bitter-sweet might offer itself'.

Harvard's setting at this time was entirely rural. In a matter of minutes the student could find himself walking past little meadows and scrubby little orchards, encountering crooked little crossroads and studying solitary dwellings on long grassy slopes under tall New England elms 'with their shingled hoods well pulled down on their ears'. Divinity Hall, where William had rooms in 1863, was remembered through a haze of Indian summers, with the vista of the nearby Norton woods massed in autumnal scarlet and orange,

when to penetrate and mount a stair and knock at a door and, enjoying response, then sink into a window-bench and inhale at once the vague golden November and the thick suggestion of the room ... was to taste as I had never done before the poetry of the prime initiation and of associated growth.

'Europe' had faded and was supplanted by a rustic and homespun scene studied by the earnest young man with penetrating eyes, high forehead and carefully-parted and already-receding hair, who had become a cosmopolite without ever having been a provincial.

2

Henry joined William at meals three times a day at Miss Upham's board in her house at the corner of Kirkland and Oxford Streets. The young law student lost no time in translating the establishment into Balzac's Maison Vauquer, but agreed promptly that the Maison Upham, under the elms, had nothing of the sordid or sinister of its French counterpart and that 'in the matter of talk as talk we shone

incomparably brighter'. In fact it was 'a veritable haunt of conversation'. There was, of course, a major subject, the continuing war.
The 'torch flared sufficiently about Miss Upham's board', Henry remembered, but the spinster shoved it quickly away from her end of
the table with heavy sighs, as if hoping to extinguish the flame.
Henry sat beside William, who was brightly communicative, full of
life and always ready to help 'the lame dog of converse over stile
after stile'. There was little need to do this, for opposite sat Harvard's
Chaucerian and collector of ballads, Francis J. Child, round-faced,
cherubic, fair-haired, wearing gold-rimmed spectacles and filled with
discourse about the conduct of the war, his talk a 'darting flame'
when it came to the North's transatlantic enemies, and gravely
elegiac in keeping the memory of the young men who had gone
from his classes to war and death. Also at the table was John Ban-
croft, son of the historian, whom Henry had met at Newport; a
young fellow student of Henry's, Beach Vanderpool Jr and two
friends of William's, Joe May, son of a New York abolitionist, and
a young theological student named Salter, with dark moustache and
pointed beard, who looked like an old Spanish portrait and who was
New England at its 'sparest and dryest', and at the same time at its
wittiest.

If Henry went conscientiously to the lectures in Dane Hall in the
mornings – and he marvelled at the extent to which he faithfully
attended – it was because, he later felt, he could exercise his observer's role to his heart's content. The question of how people
looked and 'of how their look counted for a thousand relations' had
existed for him from early days. Here he had a classroom filled with
Americans to study at first hand. For the first time he found himself
among his peers in his native land; he sat in the rear of the audi-
torium, in the dusky half-smothered light coming from low windows, as if his classmates were actors on the other side of the
footlights. He felt that 'when one should cease to live in large
measure by one's eyes ... one would have taken the longest step
towards not living at all'. He sought to fix 'the weight, the interest,
the function' of his fellow-Americans. He wanted to get to know the
'types'. The law students at Harvard came from a prosperous section
of American society; this was apparent. They appeared to be stan-
dardized and homogenized New Englanders from Springfield or
Worcester, Providence or Portland. Yet now and again they flowered
into the 'special type'. Their very names, as we read them today, are

redolent of New England – Wentworth, Lathrop, Pickering, Young, Kirkland, Sargent – and readers will find them used in the American novels and tales of Henry James. Curiously enough, however, with the exception of Salter, who was William's friend, and not a law student, Henry does not single out any New England classmates for the vivid sketches of his young contemporaries which are woven into his memoirs. The three fellow-students whom he recalls and describes are, like himself, 'outsiders' – Beach Vanderpool Jr, 'incorruptibly and exquisitely dumb ... admirable, ineffaceable, because so essentially all *decipherable*' who came from New Jersey; an unnamed New Yorker, a 'finished fop' (identified by T. S. Perry as Sam D. Craig), a comedy figure, a caricature with a tight umbrella under his arm, a toy-terrier at his heels, and a monocle in his eye when it was not being used in his hand as 'a defensive crystal wall'. James admired his way of standing up to his classmates as an individual, never intimidated by their mockery and always consistent in maintaining the personality he had created. More important than either of these was a classmate designated as G. A. J., who reached 'westward, westward even of New York and southward at least as far as Virginia', whom we identify as George Abbot James (not however a descendant of William of Albany), marked by Henry from the first 'for a friend and taken for a kinsman' – sole member of the Harvard law class whose friendship the novelist retained in later life. G. A. J. could kindle 'bonfires of thought', and through him Henry could reach out, later to create a Westerner such as Christopher Newman or a Southerner such as Basil Ransom.

The novelist hangs before us also three vignettes of his law professors : Dr Theophilus Parsons, who sat beneath a 'huge hot portrait of Daniel Webster' discoursing in 'rich quavering accents', a provincial with accretions of unction, serenity, quality and homage to old superstitions; 'Governor' Emory Washburn, from the depths of whose rusticity there emerged candour 'as to his own pleasant fallibility', and Judge Joel Parker, with a tight mouth above an absent chin, representing 'dryness and hardness, prose unrelieved', perhaps, observed Henry, because he was most master of his subject.

Only once during the year does Henry James seem to have stepped out of his observer's role in the Law School, and this became 'a black little memory'. The Marshall Club staged a moot court and Henry agreed, or was assigned, to represent the 'defendant' in an arbitration suit. He found himself in 'a perfect glare of publicity' which frightened him into virtual silence. The opposing counsel won the case with ease. Henry retired in deep discomfiture over his failure to think quickly on his feet. James's nephew many years later, seeking to discover more about this incident, learned that a classmate, George Gray, was the 'judge' who found against the defendant, and that the case apparently was such that a real lawyer in a real court could have stood no chance of winning. We suspect, however, that Henry could not have won even the easiest case. He had not studied his law books with any assiduity and, aside from this brave display of himself before his class, his connection with Dane Hall – a building long since gone – remained 'as consistently superficial as could be possible' to one who was so 'restlessly perceptive'. Perceiving, James noted, had a distinct value; it 'kicked up no glare'. He invariably preferred to see rather than to be seen.

3

He went on long lonely rambles in Cambridge and Boston; he sat in Gore Hall reading Sainte-Beuve,* whom he discovered during that year, counting this as a 'sacred date' – sacred, he felt, in the development of any historic or aesthetic consciousness; he wandered occasionally into other classrooms, and on certain dark winter afternoons listened to James Russell Lowell discoursing by lamplight on English literature and Old French. The lectures were an 'unforgettable initiation', and the lamplight illuminated the bearded face and expressive hands of the stocky Yankee.

Henry was in Boston at the height of the Abolition fever. The question of slavery had touched him from his earliest days. He remembered how in 14th Street the Norcom family arrived from Kentucky with three sons, Eugene, Reginald and Albert, and set up a sausage-making contraption on their porch – pronounced by them 'poo'ch' – proceeding to dispense southern hospitality to the little Northern Jameses – hot cakes, sausages and molasses in prodigious quantities. They had brought with them precious pieces of property – two slaves, Davy and his mother, Aunt Sylvia (pronounced

---

*The Harvard College Library records show that James at various times borrowed Michelet, Carlyle, Voltaire, certain American writers including Charles Brockden Brown, Browning, Wordsworth, Schiller, Goldoni. Allowance must be made for the possibility that James drew some of these works for other members of the James family.

An'silvy). Davy became one of Henry's playmates, mingling in James family sports and talk until the day when both he and An'silvy quite suddenly disappeared. The slaves woke up to the fact that in the North they need not remain in bondage and one night made off 'beyond recall or recovery'. Little Henry, fresh then from his reading of *Uncle Tom's Cabin*, noted how the Norcoms were 'shocked at such ingratitude'. Henry had experienced at first hand a little of the crucial history of his time.

A milestone in this same history was his trip on New Year's day 1863 into Boston, through milling crowds, to the Music Hall, where an excited multitude celebrated Lincoln's Emancipation Proclamation with an uncommon Bostonian show of emotion. On the crowded platform was the old family friend, Mr Emerson, tall and spare, reading his *Boston Hymn* in ringing tones, the long-familiar voice. 'He who does his own work frees a slave,' Emerson had once written and now he rendered the thought into verse:

> Pay ransom to the owner
> And fill the bag to the brim.
> Who is the owner? The slave is owner
> And ever was. *Pay him!*

Other moments during his year at Harvard were bound to be less historic. However, in the private history of Henry James there was an evening when he travelled into Boston to the Howard Athenæum to see Maggie Mitchell in *Fanchon the Cricket*, translated from a German play which in turn was derived from a novel by George Sand. He had found that in the Boston audience there lingered the 'half-buried Puritan curse ... that intimation more than anything else perhaps of the underhand snicker', the 'implication of the provincial in the theatric air and of the rustic in the provincial'. Miss Mitchell had played the part up and down the United States – she 'twanged that one string and none other, every night of her theatric life' – and yet there was nothing stale about the charm she exercised upon the young law student. He returned entranced to his room in Winthrop Square and wrote Miss Mitchell a letter from which she should 'gather the full force of my impression'. Maggie reciprocated. She sent him an autographed 'acting edition' of the play, and Henry fancied himself quite the young Pendennis smitten by Miss Fotheringay.

The impression stimulated him to much more than a 'fan' letter.

He sat down at his desk in the alcove with his view of the distant hills 'to enroll myself in the bright band of the fondly hoping and fearfully doubting who count the days after the despatch of manuscripts'. His first piece of independent writing deemed fit for publication dealt with a play and an actress. He adds coyly that 'nothing would induce me now to name the periodical on whose protracted silence I had thus begun to hang'. We do not know whether this spontaneous piece of drama criticism was ever published. Le Roy Phillips's bibliography of Henry James's writings lists nothing earlier than 1864 and in that year only criticism. But in December 1864 Wilky was writing from the front, 'Tell Harry that I am waiting anxiously for his "next". I can find a large sale for any blood and thunder tale among the darks.' Some time between his departure from Harvard in 1863 and the appearance of his first unsigned criticism in the *North American Review* in the autumn of 1864 the young writer found his literary feet and took the path from which he would never stray.

Was this the turning-point in Henry James's life? An editor, many years later, asked him to tell of that crucial moment. James turned the matter over in his mind, as a few unpublished pages among his papers testify. He had brought away from the Law School 'certain rolls of manuscript that were quite shamelessly not so many bundles of notes on the perusal of so many calfskin volumes'. These were notes of another sort. He told himself, 'I must then, in the cold shade of queer little old Dane Hall, have stood at the parting of my ways, recognized the false steps, even though few enough, already taken, and consciously committed myself to my particular divergence.'

Henry James goes on in the fragment to say that he wondered whether 'my youth *had* in fact enjoyed that amount of drama'. He couldn't be sure. The fragment breaks off at this point, leaving us without a final answer. However, James's recollections of his Harvard year contain no mention of a conscious choice between law and letters. He drifted into the law school and he nowhere mentions how or when he drifted away from it. He was as ill-fitted for the law as he had been for his 'scientific' studies at the Institution Rochette. Dane Hall may not have marked a 'turning-point' so much as the turning of a corner. There were to be no more 'false steps'.

22

Ashburton Place

THE Civil War, as with all wars, was a time of terminations – and beginnings. The Emancipation Proclamation marked the triumph – and the end – of the Abolitionist cause. Boston had never lacked causes or their advocates, but this cause had been at once the noblest and the most deeply felt. It had engaged common sympathies. Men had laid down their lives to defend it; with it nineteenth-century New England touched its highest note of compassion and humanity. In intellectual Boston the war marked the end of an era of 'radicalism' and a return to old conservative virtues. Not that New England 'radicalism' had ever been very radical; it reflected, however, in the mid-century, a certain enlightenment, a kind of Athenian glory – the dazzle of marble in the sun at high noon – and now the long afternoon had begun. The elder Henry James, arriving on this scene from Newport, was impressed, as an outsider might be, by the geniality, intelligence and high-mindedness of the Bostonian élite; he did not, however, allow their virtues to blind him to their complacency and self-assurance. The Brahmins struck him, at moments, as 'simmering in their own fat and putting a nice brown on one another'.

His son was to say many brilliant if unkind things about the Bostonians and to enshrine them and their city in a long and distinctly unpopular novel; but at 21 he found life in the Back Bay full of interest. For him, too, the period was one of terminations and beginnings. Despair engendered by war and ill-health now gave way to a feeling of hope and elation. The senior Henry and his wife moved to No. 13 Ashburton Place in Boston from a Newport that had become too lonely for them, and William and Henry were returned to the family hearth. The house, of red brick, set on a granite basement, was as substantial as Boston itself. Henry had a large green-shuttered room on the third floor overlooking the Place, and here he was able to establish his working relationship with 'the small inkpot in which I seemed at last definitely destined to dip'. The very words Ashburton Place in later years were tinted with memories of coming-of-age, 'the days, the hours, the seasons, the winter skies and darkened rooms of summer ... the old walks, the old efforts, the old exaltations and depressions'. 'Ah the things and the people, the hours and scenes and circumstances, the *inénarrables* occasions,' 'the sense ... of particular little thrills and throbs and day-dreams ... of un-forgettable gropings and findings and sufferings and strivings and play of sensibility and of inward passion'. In Ashburton Place Henry James heard the news of Grant's victories and the surrender at Appo-mattox. Here – on his 22nd birthday – the shrill cry reached him of an outraged and grieving America standing at the bier of the assas-sinated President. Here, too, one morning, word came that Haw-thorne had died. Half-dressed, on the edge of his bed, in the dim light that filtered through the green shutters, he found himself yield-ing 'to the pang that made me positively and loyally cry'. And here, in these same surroundings, he one day counted the first earnings of his pen, a dozen greasy dollar bills.

It was the springtime of his life, and his memories were of Boston springs, a dropping down from Beacon Hill for 'those premonitary gusts of April that one felt most perhaps where Park Street Church stood dominant, where the mouth of the Common itself uttered promises, more signs and portents than one could count'. The two years at Ashburton Place were festive, a kind of prolonged cele-bration, as if he were moving 'through an apartment hung with garlands and lights'. He came of age here in more ways than one: he became a writer.

I

When the young literary aspirant arrived on the Boston scene in 1864 – as distinct from the collegiate scene in Cambridge of the pre-vious year – the *Atlantic Monthly* was seventeen years old and the *North American Review* almost fifty. The *Atlantic* was under the editorship of James T. Fields, a friendly, hospitable and benevolent individual, deeply attached to his mission of publisher. He and his wife were 'addicted to the cultivation of talk and wit and to the in-genious multiplication of such ties as could link the upper half of the title-page with the lower'. Fields was a collector of literary relics, autographs, rare editions, and his house by the Charles was a verit-able 'waterside museum'. The Fieldses maintained a salon ('so far as salons were in the old Puritan city dreamed of') in which were received the élite of the literary and artistic world from both sides of the water. They were host to Dickens and to Thackeray, to every distinguished visitor who came to Boston and to all the Brahmins; and it was not long before the young Henry found himself welcomed as a writer of promise, having Sunday supper opposite the celebrated Mrs Stowe, who had a 'nonchalance of real renown' to the eyes of a youth seeking renown. It was Fields who, in due course, published Henry James's first fiction in the *Atlantic*, while complaining of his 'strain of pessimism'. 'What we want,' said Mr Fields, with perfect truth, 'is short, *cheerful* stories.' Henry was ready to admit years later that he had been 'precociously dismal' and that he was striking a note alien to a society that was fundamentally optimistic and which had its eyes upon transcendent things. The future novelist took the writing of fiction more seriously than any writer in that society – a society which tended to give first place to poetry, the sermon and the essay, rather than the novel. James Russell Lowell characterized the limits of the writer in New England when he asserted, 'Let no man write a line that he would not have his daughter read,' and Henry James was to complain bitterly that American magazines sought to reduce him to the intellectual level of 'adolescent maidens'.

Henry James in his modest way began to introduce into the bookish air of the Puritan city a sense of reality distinct from the romances of the time. The young outsider could only, at this stage, stand in the shadow of the celebrities of Boston and Cambridge – none save Mrs Stowe were novelists – who by the end of the Civil War were reaching comfortable middle-age and had become New England oracles as well as men of letters. Oliver Wendell Holmes, the 'autocrat' and wit, was 55 when the Jameses appeared in Boston. Longfellow was 57, and Lowell 44. Fields, their publisher, was 47. Longfellow and Lowell were buried too far between book-covers to want to look at any life beyond the pleasing perspective they had from their study windows in their ancestral homes, where at night the sound of the cricket and grasshopper from lawn and garden was the sole voice of the outer world to reach them. Lowell, it is true, stirred uneasily later, on becoming a diplomat, and acknowledged that books were 'good dry forage' and that after all 'men are the only fresh pasture'. The New England élite fell roughly into two classes : the men who, like Emerson and Thoreau, had built a philosophy in communion with the out-of-doors, and the urban Brahmins, sons and grandsons of clergymen, whose creativity was fed by the creativity of the past. They were, most of them, but one generation removed from the pulpit. They still tended to preach. Hawthorne alone among the writers had expressed, for Henry James, the passive, haunted, imaginative side of the transplanted Puritan. Lowell was the antithesis of this: he represented New England prosperity and good health linked to a facile and erratic literary talent. A haze of cigar-smoke surrounded him, and he was always digging into books for recondite information.

Longfellow, who in Henry James's eyes had found 'the large, quiet, pleasant, easy solution' in life and literature, had absorbed heavy doses of German culture and derived inspiration from a variety of European models. He looked to the past, an unreconstructed romantic, whose work James found 'remarkably even, neither rising above nor falling below a level ruled as straight as a line from a copy-book'. The youngest of the Brahmins in 1864 – he was 37 – was Charles Eliot Norton, son of a celebrated Biblical scholar, a friend of Ruskin, an art scholar, a lover of Italy. In his home, Shady Hill, which like Lowell's Elmwood was a Cambridge landmark, Norton had collected his trophies and spoils of Europe, and in his long library he worked on his translation of Dante and carried out his 'civilizing' mission, an apostle of Old World culture in the New World. The word 'civilization' was often on his lips, and Henry James remarked, in a late tribute, that the 'representative of culture' had in those days 'a great and arduous mission requiring plentiful courage as well as plentiful knowledge, endless good humour as well as assured taste'.

In 1864 Norton and Lowell undertook to rescue the middle-aged *North American Review* from the staleness into which long-established periodicals often decline. And on 30 July of that year Henry James addressed to the editors from Ashburton Place a two-sentence letter, one of the least distinguished but most significant of his early epistolary efforts. 'Gentlemen,' he wrote, 'I take the liberty of enclosing a brief review of [Nassau W.] Senior's *Essays on Fiction* published in London a few months ago. Hoping that you may deem it worthy of a place among your Literary Notices, I remain yours respectfully Henry James Jr.' This done, he left to spend the summer at Northampton, Massachusetts.

2

The choice of Northampton seems to have been dictated in part by its being in that era a comfortable health resort. Henry spoke of the town as 'my small square patch of the American scene' when he put it into the opening pages of *Roderick Hudson*. It was, he wrote, the 'only small American *ville de province* of which one had happened to lay up, long before, a pleased vision', and he thought of the way in which Balzac, in his *scènes de la vie de province*, had 'done' Saumur, Limoges and Guérande. He didn't pretend to 'do' it – there wasn't much to do with it and he felt, indeed, that he had failed in his emulation of the French master. The town has since grown, but when Henry James visited it in 1864 – he prolonged his stay there from early August to December – it was a small New England settlement, with broad country streets and old white houses framed by box hedges and set off by high elms. Situated near an elbow of the Connecticut River and not far from Mount Holyoke, it provided Henry with a place of relaxation and rest, a spot where he could take a 'water-cure' and be near woods and rocks, red cedars, pines, 'beauty sufficient for an artist not to starve upon it', as he said in his preface to *Roderick*. In that novel he introduces briefly those classical Balzacian figures, the town lawyer and the local clergyman; there is a picnic near the river such as James might have taken part in with his summer acquaintances, and a sense of calm and dreamy peace which Rowland Mallet, the reflective observer, relishes – and from which Roderick, the artist, wants to escape. The choice of Northampton in James's first important novel was deliberate and autobiographical, as nearly all his choices of scene were. In this town Henry James, the American artist, was driving his pen in more professional fashion than ever before; it was therefore a fitting town in which to launch his fictional artist, and to impart to him those thoughts about the role of the creator in American society which Henry pondered as he walked through the American night and looked at the moon through the lofty elms.

Nine days after dispatching his manuscript to the *North American Review* he had his answer. The article was accepted – accepted with a show of enthusiasm that was flattering and with a prompt demand for more. He replied that he would enjoy writing other literary notices if the books came 'within my narrow compass', and he added, 'I am frequently in the way of reading French works.' Among the reviews he wrote at Northampton was one of Harriet Elizabeth Prescott's *Azarian* and Mrs A. M. C. Seemuller's *Emily Chester*. Before he returned to Boston his notice of Senior's essays was published in the October issue of the *Review*. He arrived at Ashburton Place to find a request from Norton for a review of T. Adolphus Trollope's *Lindisfarne Chase* and did this for the January issue which contained three of Henry's reviews, all of them unsigned. 'I do *not* desire to notice novels exclusively,' Henry wrote to Norton,

although I confess that that kind of criticism *comes most natural*. Other books which are not books of erudition, I shall always be glad to do my best for. Nothing would please me better, however, than to notice the novels of the next quarter in a lump, as you propose; so you may send me whatever appears in that line.

It was during December 1864 that Henry James went out to snow-bound Cambridge in response to an invitation from Norton and spent a memorable half-hour with him in his library at Shady Hill. He always considered this moment as 'a positive consecration to letters'. The winter sunshine touched the bookshelves and pictures of the Dante scholar 'with I know not what golden light of promise, what assurance of things to come : there was to be nothing exactly like it later on – the conditions of perfect rightness for a certain fresh felicity, certain decisive pressures of the spring, *can* occur, it would seem, but once'.

The friendship formed that day was to endure for decades and to embrace Norton's immediate family and his sisters as well. It is doubtful whether it ever became intimate. Charles Eliot Norton did not inspire in Henry great warmth of feeling; he was a dry, self-contained demanding individual; but a deep respect was there and the common ground of their love for the cultural riches of the Old World. Henry's letters to him are among his best : they contain a large body of extra-literary comment on political events abroad, as well as discussion of art, morality, Christianity and criticism in apparent response to questions raised by Norton. Always, the American art scholar remained for Henry the man who had opened to him one of the first doors to the world of letters. The *North American Review* paid Henry James $2.50 a page; his first review netted twelve dollars. He had a sense of being launched, the first member of the family of the elder Henry James to have gone out into the world and taken a step towards earning his way.

3

Henry James's book review, which had received such prompt acceptance, dealt with the art of fiction. It marked in every way an extraordinary début as a critic for one destined to become a master of the
art – almost as if, on the threshold of his career, he must consciously
commit to print a theory of the novel he was to elaborate and prac-
tise during the next half-century. What Henry's readers did not
know was that the anonymous writer was not talking of fiction in a
vacuum; that he had published at least one tale and was writing
others soon to see print.

The essay is distinctly young and yet singularly mature. Its youth
is proclaimed by its dogmatism, its attempt to demolish in cutting
phrases, its forced mannerisms and above all by the desire of the
writer to conceal his years. 'Certain young persons,' he says at one
point and 'youthful critics will be much more impartial at middle
age' – as if he knew all about middle age. It is doubtful, however,
whether the casual reader of 1864 would have noticed this; he would
have been impressed rather by the remarkable range of the writer's
reading and his original ideas on the art of the novel, whose form,
then, was rarely discussed. He speaks as one who has been dissecting
novels to determine how they were written, who feels that the time
has come to set down if not an 'Anatomy of Fiction', at least some
suggestive thoughts on the subject. His first paragraph strikes the
note for his entire career :

We opened this work with the hope of finding a general survey of the
nature and principles of the subject of which it professes to treat. Its title
had led us to anticipate some attempt to codify the vague and desultory
canons, which cannot, indeed, be said to govern, but which in some
measure define, this department of literature. We had long regretted the
absence of any critical treatise upon fiction. But our regret was destined
to be embittered by disappointment.

Here spoke the man of the future who was to write an historic
paper on *The Art of Fiction* and who was to codify, in his late prefaces, those 'laws' of the novel which had at least governed his own
work. In this first essay he confined himself to making a few simple
points which today may seem banal but which in their time were
striking affirmations of the power and resources of the fictional
form : fiction is a reflection of life; 'even the most photographically

disposed novels address pre-eminently the imagination'; the public must be approached from its own level and not be preached at; fiction must become 'self-forgetful', not seek to instruct or to edify. It must, like *Waverley*, 'prove nothing but facts'. Men and women must be represented as they are, as motivated living creatures, not puppets .'Fiction?' queries the young man in discussing Sir Walter Scott's novels,

These are triumphs of fact. In the richness of his invention and memory, in the infinitude of his knowledge, in his improvidence for the future, in the skill with which he answers, or rather parries, sudden questions, in his low-voiced pathos and his resounding merriment, he is identical with the ideal fireside chronicler. And thoroughly to enjoy him, we must again become as credulous as children at twilight.

In demanding this evocation of reality even in such flights of the historic imagination as Scott's, Henry James ticks off the founders of the novel and rejects them: Richardson, Fielding, Smollett are 'emphatically preachers and moralists'; *Tom Jones* 'is like a vast episode in a sermon preached by a grandly humorous divine; and however we may be entertained by the way, we must not forget that our ultimate duty is to be instructed'; Richardson is 'neither a romancer nor a story-teller; he is simply Richardson'. Most important of all, for the light they throw on the young aspirant, are his asides, which show him at grips with the form:

For our own part, we should like nothing better than to write stories for weary lawyers and schoolmasters. Idle people are satisfied with the great romance of doing nothing. But busy people come fresh to their idleness. The imaginative faculty, which has been gasping for breath all day under the great pressure of reason, bursts forth when its possessor is once ensconced under the evening lamp, and draws a long breath in the fields of fiction.

And so he defines the function of the novelist as an artist who must meet distinct needs of certain readers and at the same time know his job.

From the first Henry shows sensitivity over the selection of names. 'It is often enough to damn a well-intentioned story, that the heroine should be called Kate rather than Katherine; the hero Anthony rather than Ernest.' Doesn't a novelist grow weary grinding out 'false persons and events'? He puts the question on behalf of the craftsman and answers it as if he has been grinding them out for years, the best novelist is the busiest man. It is, as you say, because I 'grind out' my men and women that I endure them. It is because I create them by the sweat of my brow that I venture to look them in the face. My *work* is my salvation. If this great army of puppets came forth at my simple bidding, then indeed I should die of their senseless clamour. But as the matter stands, they are my very good friends. The pains of labour regulate and consecrate my progeny. If it were as easy to write novels as to read them, then, too, my stomach might rebel against the phantom peopled atmosphere which I have given myself to breathe.

In Boston, at 21, Henry James was approaching fiction more consciously and with greater deliberation than any American novelist before him; the need to put the house of fiction in order and the need for precept, canon, codification, is clearly in evidence. Later it was to be expressed in a series of tales about misunderstood writers, groping for an ideal world.

Nearly all the early unsigned notices written between 1864 and 1866 in the *Review* and the *Nation* show the young reviewer devoting himself almost exclusively to the novel. He lectures such writers as Miss Prescott and Miss Alcott on the need to create living characters, give them 'a body, a local habitation, a name', but more than this reminds them : 'The reader who is set face to face with a gorgeous doll will assuredly fail to inspire it with sympathetic life. To do so, he must have become excited and interested. What is there in a doll to excite and interest?' He advises the novelists to read Mérimée, to learn from the pages of Balzac how to set a scene and launch a drama, and to study the realism of George Eliot. His concern is always with the reader who must be introduced to an atmosphere 'in which it was credible that human beings might exist, and to human beings with whom he might feel tempted to claim kinship'. The novelist must not describe, he must *convey*; characters once launched must *act* in certain ways consistent with their personality; the artist must not finger his puppets as a child besmudges a doll, he must endow them with their individuality and with life. Balzac is held up as an example of the 'scientific' novelist concerned with 'the facts of things'. James also lectures the novelists on their use of words. He chides Miss Prescott for such phrases as 'vermeil ardency' or such alliteration as 'studded with starry sprinkle and sputter of splendour'. The novelist must use prose concretely : 'You construct your description from a chosen object; can you, conversely, from your description, construct that object?'

Whatever doubts and hesitancies Henry James had about his personal abilities he had none whatever about how fiction should be created. In a society addicted to happy-endings, he was a confirmed realist; in an age when the novel was generally regarded as an inferior form of art he had a profound faith in it as 'history' and as 'fact'. We glimpse the certitudes of his craft in a journal entry, made by Louisa May Alcott who in 1865 published her first novel *Moods*, which Henry in due course tartly reviewed. Miss Alcott came to Boston and dined in Ashburton Place. She found Henry Jr all very friendly. 'Being a literary youth he gave me advice, as if he had been 80, and I a girl.' She adds, as if in extenuation, 'My curly crop made me look young, though 31.' The truth was that Henry, just turning 22, offered her important counsel, if we are to judge by his review of *Moods*. He observes there is no reason 'why Miss Alcott should not write a very good novel, provided she will be satisfied to describe only that which she has seen'. Elsewhere he remarks that the writing of a novel requires neither travel nor adventure nor sightseeing, 'it is simply necessary to be an artist'.

At every turn he discloses the extent of his reading. Reviewing Miss Braddon's *Lady Audley's Secret*, he invokes the names of Wilkie Collins, Mrs Radcliffe, Horace Walpole, George Eliot, George Sand, Hawthorne, Jane Austen, mentions the *Oresteia*, *Macbeth*, *Blackwood's Magazine* (of which he was an inveterate reader) and *Denis Duval*. He reviews *Felix Holt* and forgives George Eliot her 'clumsily artificial' plots because she delineates character, possesses human sympathy, poetic quality, microscopic observation, morality, discreet humour and exquisite rhetoric. As he nears his 23rd birthday he reviews Dickens's *Our Mutual Friend* with a sense that the master has written himself out; the young Henry had seldom read 'a book so intensely *written*, so little seen, known, or felt', and concludes that Dickens knows men rather than *man* and that 'it is one of the chief conditions of his genius not to see below the surface of things'. As such he is the 'greatest of superficial novelists'. Dickens, the young critic finds, reconciles readers to the commonplace and to the odd, but he lacks an overall philosophy, a capacity for generalizing the given case and so raising it to the level of the greatest art. The Dickens review is perhaps the most meditated of all Henry's early writings. He is freeing himself of an early idol. He is not intimidated by greatness. What is important for him is his search for a viable theory of fiction.

This theory was derived not only from his close reading of novels. It bespoke a long saturation with French literature, largely through the medium of the *Revue des Deux Mondes*. A young man who had been carefully reading Sainte-Beuve and Taine, Schérer and Montégut, was equipped with serious critical tools; and a young man who had read – and studied – the major French novelists as well as the minor, from Balzac to George Sand and Flaubert, as well as Edmond About, Octave Feuillet, Victor Cherbuliez, inevitably had standards of form, of style, of grace, of subtlety, that did not exist in the as yet brief history of American criticism. The imprint of France was strong upon Henry James's early writings, both in his critical pieces and his fiction. The young Henry James had more theory in his head and a wider embrace of European models than any novelist then writing in the United States – and he had not yet written a novel himself.

4

He had not written a novel but he was assiduously writing fiction. It has always been assumed that Henry James made his début as a critic and then as a writer of short stories. The reverse occurred and the tale always regarded as his first – *The Story of a Year* – was in reality the first to which he signed his name. It had a significant anonymous predecessor. A full year before the publication of *The Story of a Year* Henry wrote to Perry (in March 1864) that the printer's devil had been knocking at his door. 'You know,' he wrote, 'a literary man can't call his time his own.' This suggests the publication of something more than a book review, and a few sentences later he proposes that he use Perry's mail address for correspondence with the *Atlantic* editors about a story. 'I cannot again stand the pressure of avowed authorship (for the present) and their answer could not come here unobserved. Do not speak to Willie of this.' The old victim of fraternal criticism still felt himself vulnerable. But his letter reveals something more: that there had been 'avowed authorship'.

A chance remark in a letter, written by a Newport friend of the Jameses, enables us to identify what was doubtless Henry James's first published but unsigned tale, and thus advance by a year the formal beginning of his literary career. Mrs George De Kay, mother of the future poet and critic Charles De Kay, wrote to her son, then at school, on 29 February 1864:

Miss Elly Temple has just come in looking very fresh and pretty – Henry James has published a story in the February Continental called a Tragedy of Errors. Read it. Smith Van Buren forbade Elly to read it! which brought a smile of quiet contempt to Harry's lips but anger and indignation to those of Miss Minnie Temple.

Smith Van Buren was exercising an uncle's prerogative over one of his orphaned nieces. And Henry James's look of 'quiet contempt' marked perhaps the first – and certainly not the last – time in his long literary career during which he stood accused of writing stories unfit for young girls to read. The February 1864 issue of the *Continental Monthly*, a journal devoted to literature and national policy, contains a twelve-page tale, unsigned, entitled *A Tragedy of Error*. It is clearly from the early pen of Henry James Junior: French phrases flower on every page (and those to which Henry was particularly addicted); and the tale fits, more accurately than any of the other early tales, the account of his friend Perry, that at Newport Henry wrote stories in which the heroes were villains and the heroines seemed to have 'read all Balzac in the cradle and to be positively dripping with lurid crimes'.

The tale begins in the best manner of a French romance: 'A low English phaeton was drawn up before the door of the post office of a French seaport town. In it was seated a lady, with her veil down and her parasol held closely over her face. My story begins with a gentleman coming out of the office and handing her a letter.' Thus the drama – apparently at Le Havre – is launched. The lady gives the gentleman her parasol to hold, lifts her veil to show 'a very pretty face' and 'such persons as were looking on at the moment saw the lady turn very pale'. We note the 'such persons as were looking'. Enter the first Jamesian observer! He is seeking to cut the umbilical cord binding him to his story.

Hortense Bernier's paleness was caused by the contents of the letter. Her husband is returning. She must act, for she has taken a lover in his absence. She has 'half a mind to drown myself', she tells Louis de Meyrau, but ends by making a pact with a brutal boatman to drown her husband instead. The details are arranged with care. The boatman will meet the arriving vessel beyond the breakwater the next morning and offer to row her husband ashore. It will be simple to do away with him en route.

'You want me to finish him in the boat?'
No answer.

'Is he an old man?'
Hortense shook her head faintly.
'My age?'
She nodded.
'*Sapristi!* it isn't so easy.'
'He can't swim,' said Hortense, without looking up; 'he – he is lame.'
'*Nom de dieu!*' The boatman dropped his hands.

The dénouement is swift. Hortense has not counted on her lover deciding on his own course of action. He goes aboard the ship in the early dawn to greet the husband, only to discover that Bernier has already had himself rowed ashore. He finds a waiting boat, however, and seats himself in it. He asks the boatman to take him to the Bernier house. 'You're just the gentleman I want,' says the boatman.

Meanwhile Hortense Bernier is pacing nervously in her garden. The last paragraph administers the shock. She utters a cry. 'For she saw a figure emerge from below the terrace and come limping toward her with outstretched arms.'

5

Thus in the earliest of Henry James's stories a limping husband is married to a woman capable of strong and determined action – even to the point of seeking to destroy him. The tale's plot embodies the lameness of Henry's father and we are asked to assume that the lover, who is not lame, also cannot swim. But the narrative is lively, the talk vivid, and little touches at every turn show how precociously the young writer had studied his craft. There are calculated scenes, each with its own dramatic content : the Bernier maid, looking at Hortense through a keyhole, observes her swallowing brandy by the glassful and scanning the harbour with her opera-glass; the distracted woman's walk along the wharves; the boatman seizing a jug of milk from a boy and drinking it, thereby revealing himself to Hortense as a predatory person; the cautious conversation in which she becomes aware that he can be bought to commit a crime. The characterization of boatman, lover and of the heroine herself, is skilful for so young a writer. Louis de Meyrau's hard-headed egotism is revealed in his first remarks; we know he will be of no help to Hortense. As for the distracted wife, she is the first of a long line of 'bad heroines', capable of murder, yet exciting our sympathy. Kate Croy and Rose Armiger are dimly on the horizon.

A close analysis of the novelist's early tales has shown how they contain ideas and techniques basic to later Jamesian work. There is such a foreshadowing in this first tale. It is to be found in the series of interpolations, one of which has already been noted: 'such persons as were looking'. Again and again it is not Henry James who sees what goes on but always someone else: 'although to a third person it would have appeared', 'a wayfarer might have taken him for a ravisher escaping with a victim'. On the way to the boat Hortense walked 'as if desirous to attract as little observation as possible ... yet if for any reason a passer-by had happened to notice her ...' The third person, the observer, the wayfarer, the onlooker, the passer-by – and their testimony is presented objectively to the reader. The tradition James invokes is closer to Defoe than to his nineteenth-century contemporaries. At one point Henry James makes it clear that he wants us to consider that he is writing not fiction but the truth: 'Though I have judged best, hitherto, often from an exaggerated fear of trenching on the ground of fiction, to tell you what this poor lady did and said, rather than what she thought, I may disclose what passed in her mind now.' As if to add to the authenticity of his account the 20-year-old author inserts a gloss to 'It was perhaps fortunate for Hortense's purpose ... that she was a pretty woman.' A footnote elaborates: 'I am told that there was no resisting her smile; and that she had at her command, in moments of grief, a certain look of despair which filled even the roughest hearts with sympathy and won over the kindest to the cruel cause.'

There was conscious method in the narrative. The young man who talked of the art of fiction had the glimmerings of a design and a ruling theory. But many years were to elapse before he would begin to explain it to his readers.

6

Henry James had sailed confidently into Charles Eliot Norton's study as a critic. The publication of *The Story of a Year* seems to have been attended by greater difficulties. In a letter from Newport to T. S. Perry of 25 March 1864, Henry said he had been rewriting 'that modern novel I spoke of to you ... it is almost finished and will go in a day or two'. He added

On the whole, it is a failure, I think, tho' nobody will know this, perhaps, but myself ... it is a simple story, simply told. As yet it hath no name:

and I am hopeless of one. Why use that vile word novelette. It reminds me of chemisette. Why not say *historiette* outright? Or why not call it a bob-tale?

He tells Perry that he is sending the tale to the *Atlantic* and is asking the journal 'to send their letter of reject, or accept, to you'. In October, while staying at Northampton he received word from Perry that an answer had come, for he replied to him, 'The news ... was very welcome altho' as you say "not unmingled with misfortune". But I suppose I ought to be thankful for so much and not grumble that it is so little. One of these days we shall have certain persons *on their knees* imploring for contributions.' In the letter there is a sketch of a man representing the *Atlantic Monthly* kneeling before a haughty bearded individual. The letter suggests that there has been a qualified acceptance ('I ought to be thankful for so much'), either a request for a certain amount of rewriting or an encouraging rejection. The drawing illuminates the authorial situation; but it does suggest one other bit of biographical information – it would appear that by his 21st year Henry James had begun to grow the beard which he was to wear, after the fashion of the time, for the next thirty-five years, a thick, neatly-trimmed growth. The acquisition of the beard coincided with the decision of Henry's hero in *The Story of a Year* to 'crop my head and cultivate my chin'.

While no title is given in the letter, the words 'novelette', 'historiette', 'modern novel', could all be applied to the first acknowledged tale, which today we would call a long short story. It is, if we make allowance for its awkward moments and quaint formal expression, a story of considerable originality. The attention to detail revealed in the later notebooks of Henry James exists in this story; character is suggested by action and speech. Relationships are dramatically established; the goal is narrative precision. Henry doesn't tell us what year this is the story of, but General McClellan's picture figures on the heroine's table beside that of the hero; the hero is wounded on the Rappahannock River in Virginia, where young Gus Barker was shot down by a guerrilla in 1863, and this, it would seem, was the year James was writing about. The heroine reads Jane Porter's *Scottish Chiefs*, a story of strife between Scotland and England – an older North and South, albeit a struggle between sovereign powers, across the sea. The principal characters bear Scottish names: Elizabeth Crowe meets a Robert Bruce (and his sister Jane) and refers to him as her 'Scottish chief'. There is the maternal name of Robertson in the tale and also the Scottish name of Mackenzie. When we recall that Henry's mother provided the sole Scottish strain in the otherwise Irish family we are tempted to remark that Henry has linked his tale to his mother.

The three figures in the foreground were to reappear in many forms in James's later fiction – the determined mother, her ward or protégée or relative, and the young son in love, unsure of himself, fearing to assert himself, and if he does, paying for assertion by personal disintegration. Mrs Ford is a somewhat fiercer Mrs Garland, John Ford an ineffectual and inartistic Roderick, and Elizabeth a shallow Mary Garland. The situation recurs with quite other types in *The Portrait of a Lady* – Mrs Touchett, Isabel and Ralph. In this first tale the hero's mother, seated sewing, bites the end of her thread as if 'executing a human vengeance' when her son discloses to her his engagement to Elizabeth. The hero gives up the fight even before he goes off to war; he is certain he will die. 'My memory be hanged ... what rights has a dead man?' and he is as secretive as Henry himself. He wants his engagement to be a secret ('My dread of the horrible publicity which clings to all this business'), but he doesn't keep it from his mother. She has an advantage over the heroine, who believes her betrothal to be unknown. John Ford is brought back to his mother's door, like Wilky James, wounded in battle. He has no desire to live. And so he gives up the fight, and Lizzie, sitting at his bedside, is unaware that he sees her not as flesh but as stone. 'He lay perfectly motionless, but for his eyes. They wandered over her with a kind of peaceful glee, like sunbeams playing on a statue. Poor Ford lay, indeed, not unlike an old wounded Greek, who at dusk has crawled into a temple to die, steeping the last dull interval in idle admiration of sculptured Artemis.'

In this fashion Lizzie is converted into Artemis or Diana, goddess of the chase, the masculine-active yet all-mothering woman. In most of Henry James's early stories loved women are compared to statues. Only later does he become aware, if not of their flesh, at least of their heart and mind.

7

The Story of a Year appeared in the March 1865 issue of the *Atlantic Monthly*. The senior Henry wrote to Wilky that it was 'considered good' and that he was sending him a copy, 'so you can see his name in print'. Henry was launched, and just how successfully he could measure when there appeared at Ashburton Place a handsome, vigorous man, an Irishman, named Edwin Lawrence Godkin. He had arrived in New York in 1856 after serving in the Crimean War, and by 1865, at 34, had thoroughly identified himself with America and its future. A liberal in the school of Bentham and Mills, he was convinced that the time was ripe for the launching of a weekly publication which would reflect the changing times and particularly the pressing problem of the freed slaves. He enlisted the sympathies of Norton and other Bostonians and raised enough capital for immediate needs. In July 1865 the *Nation* began its long and illustrious career. Godkin was to make the journal a guiding force in a confused country; he called for integrity in high office, he sustained the principles of nineteenth-century liberalism and democracy and gave direction in the field of the arts to a level of criticism America badly needed. William James many years later described Godkin as 'the towering influence in all thought concerning public affairs', and said that 'indirectly his influence has certainly been more pervasive than that of any other writer'.

The purpose of Godkin's call at Ashburton Place was to enlist the services of the two Henry Jameses on behalf of the new publication. Vol. 1, No. 1 contains unsigned reviews by both father and son – Henry Junior reviews a novel by Henry Kingsley and Henry Senior Carlyle's *Frederick the Great*. From then on the junior Henry was a consistent writer for the *Nation*, first of reviews, later of travel sketches. For a brief period he was all but a staff member in New York; still later he was the *Nation*'s informal correspondent-at-large in England. In later years his contributions to the journal tapered off, especially after Godkin relinquished the editorship, yet his connection with it can be said to cover almost half a century. He remembered 'that winter at Ashburton Place, the winter following the early summer-birth of the confident sheet, fairly reeks for me, as I carry myself back to it, with the romantic bustle of getting my reviews of books off'. He got them off always too late to be able to read proofs, and his constant complaint was that there were typographical errors – these, it might be added, resulting almost exclusively from misreading of his handwriting.

'I was never "cut" that I can remember,' James wrote, 'never corrected nor disapproved, postponed, nor omitted, but just sweetly and profusely and plausibly misprinted.' A majority of the writings for this periodical were unsigned and it was only through the resource-fulness of James's first bibliographer, Le Roy Phillips, that they were identified and listed. This he was able to do in part by an examination of the *Nation*'s account-books, in which the payments made to James were faithfully recorded. The *Nation* was never an important source of income to the writer : nevertheless it paid him, in an era when the dollar could purchase a great deal, especially in Europe, enough to provide marginal funds. In having access to the *Nation*, James became, in effect, a significant commentator for his country-men on the latest books and pictures, occasional theatrical develop-ments and trends in literature abroad, as well as a purveyor of tid-bits of political intelligence.

In those early months Henry James reviewed two novels by Trollope and Dickens's *Our Mutual Friend*, discussed Miss Braddon, the mystery novel and the ghostly tale, and wrote a review of Walt Whitman's *Drum Taps*. The young critic was merciless. 'It has been a melancholy task to read this book, and it is a still more melancholy one to write about it.' He then proceeds to write about it without a touch of melancholy. His objections to Whitman were largely to the absence of ideas in his poetry : he found only 'flashy imitations of ideas'. James decidedly had been reading Matthew Arnold. Art, he informs Walt, 'requires, above all things, a suppression of oneself, a subordination of oneself to an idea. This will never do for you, whose plan is to adapt the scheme of the universe to your own limitations.' The time would come, years later, when James would recant this review and read Walt Whitman with profound emotion.

Henry James reflected in his remarks not only his youthful literary decorum but his sense of his personal inadequacies. Behind his ela-tion of 1865, the launching of his literary self in three important journals and his liberation from a troubled self-esteem, and a tend-ency to 'suppress' himself, lay old childhood anxieties. His early acceptance as a writer was a distinct piece of good fortune in giving him assurance and recognition. Had he found himself in a society less receptive, or in a time when old periodicals were not being over-hauled and new ones created, he might have had to face a much greater measure of discouragement than was his lot; and while this would not have submerged his creativity or affected his sense of his destiny, it would have delayed, we suspect, the launching of his career. He was ill-equipped to stand rebuff as his later experiences in the theatre would show; he was temperamentally unsuited for the more strenuous competition of the literary market-place. As it was, he made his literary début in a fashion devoid of frustration and distinguished in every way. He was to gain assurance as he continued to be published. Below the surface there remained fear of failure, and of being considered a failure.

23

Heroine of the Scene

IN 1884, while writing a letter to the editor of the *Atlantic Monthly*, Henry James made a series of slips of the pen. He was promising to write a serial for the following year and instead of 1885 he wrote 1865 at three different points in his letter. To have jumped backward in time by two decades – and not once but thrice – signifies the extent to which in his inner mind 1865 had an emotional importance for him. And this is corroborated by the exclamation recorded in his notebook late in life, 'Ah, the "epoch-making" weeks of the spring of 1865!' The spring was indeed epoch-making: in the national life the end of the Civil War and the discharge upon the face of the North of the great veteran army; in Henry James's private life, the year of his official début as a writer of fiction. It was also the year in which William James departed with a scientific expedition to the Amazon. Henry himself added William's sailing to the significant events of this significant year. William's departure left him, 'the more exposed, and thereby the more responsive, to contact with impressions that had to learn to suffice for me in their uncorrected state'.

To be 'uncorrected' yet able to respond the more fully and freely to impressions: this sense of suddenly-discovered emotional freedom made 1865 seem to Henry ever after an *annus mirabilis* and probably accounted for the thrice-repeated slip of the pen. At one stroke he was freed of the deep and frustrating anxieties engendered by the war; and at the same time he found himself elevated, at least temporarily, into the position of the elder brother, clear of the lingering sense of being subordinate and supervised. The new-found freedom bursts through the lines of memory: 'I literally came and went, I had never practised such coming and going.' To be at large suddenly in the New England world, a young man of talent who attracted attention, to have asserted himself as a creative writer and found favour, to have shed the shackles of the war, all this represented a kind of personal triumph, or series of triumphs.

'I had never practised such coming and going.' He paid repeated visits to Newport, spending happy days with John La Farge, who had married the sister of his friend Perry. He spent enthralling hours in Lawton's Valley, a short ride from Newport, with the 'Boston Muse' – Julia Ward Howe – who had written the *Battle Hymn of the Republic*; he visited, also at Newport, the Edmund Tweedys, '*their* house almost a second summer home to us'. At the Tweedys' lived the four cousins, the Temple sisters, and in particular Mary (Minny) Temple the younger, who for some time past had begun to assume an important place in Henry's life. He also went 'in particular, during summer weeks to the White Mountains of New Hampshire, with some repetition'. He does not tell us whom he visited in the White Mountains in *Notes of a Son and Brother*, but many pages later we discover that North Conway has almost, when recalled, 'the force for me of a wizard's wand ... the sense in particular of the August of '65 shuts me in to its blest unawareness not less than to all that was then exquisite in its current certainties and felicities'. The White Mountains were visited 'in particular with some repetition' during that summer for the same reason that Henry gravitated to the Tweedy house in Newport. Minny Temple spent the summer of 1865 in the White Mountains.

I

In 1865 Minny Temple was 20, the most radiant of his rediscovered Albany and New York cousins, 'a young and shining apparition', slim, graceful, with a 'wonderful ethereal brightness of presence'. She was lithe and active, possessed of restlessness of body and mind and a 'splendid shifting sensibility'. She was always interested in those around her; she liked to draw people out in talk; she always had questions and looked for answers; she had a fund of wit and a striking face – large eyes, an upturned nose, full lips, large but not unattractive teeth. She talked with a charming toss of the head and walked with the 'long, light and yet almost sliding steps' which Henry James imparted to several of his heroines. For him Newport was 'vocal with her accents, alive with her movements'. She remained for him always a dancing figure, possessing more humanity 'than any charming girl who ever circled round a ballroom'. In the end she became for him 'a disengaged and dancing flame of thought'.

She might have her flirtatious moments, but for a girl addicted to the ballroom she had a serious mind. In one letter to a friend she observed, 'Let us never give up one element of the problem for the sake of coming to a comfortable solution.' The observation is characteristic of the quality of her mind. She attracted to her young men who could not be satisfied by a pretty face alone. With Minny they could have the pretty face and wit and intelligence as well. She was courted, or at least admired, at this period, by a future philosopher, a future novelist, a future Supreme Court Justice and a future professor of law. In those Civil War years they were simply 'promising' youths drawn to Minny Temple's presence, making her, as Henry put it, 'the heroine of our common scene'. She was a heroine, he explained, not in the romantic sense of the word nor in the sense of seeking to dominate the scene.

She had beyond any equally young creature I have known a sense for verity of character and play of life in others, for their acting out of their force or their weakness, whatever either might be, at no matter what cost to herself; and it was this instinct that made her care so for life in general, just as it was her being thereby so engaged in that tangle that made her, as I have expressed it, ever the heroine of the scene. Life claimed her and used her and beset her – made her range in her groping, her naturally immature and unlighted way from end to end of the scale. She was absolutely afraid of nothing she might come to by living with enough sincerity and enough wonder.

He is here describing not only Minny but also the heroines in his fiction : Isabel Archer, Milly Theale and the central figure of a group of his tales, as well as the woman to whom he consecrated the most moving of his chapters of memory in *Notes of a Son and Brother*. 'Most of those who knew and loved, I was going to say adored, her,' Henry wrote in his memoirs. Henry *adored* Minny, and between adoration and love there can be a wide difference. The word explains why in the retrospect of half a century he spoke of her alternately as angel and human. He remembered her on the one hand as graceful and quick, 'all straightness and charming tossed head', and on the other as having 'noble flights and such discouraged drops'. To have flights one must have wings. It is not strange that in these circumstances he embodied his ultimate memory of Minny in *The Wings of the Dove*.

2

Among the young men back from the wars was the junior Oliver Wendell Holmes, a young law student William had met at Harvard, who became an intimate of Henry as well. The friendship with Henry was between a sharp-witted young man, all action and passion, touched with the fire of the conflict and thrice wounded by it, and a sedentary literary youth, psychically wounded by the same conflict, all hidden passion without physical action. Holmes was now sitting in Dane Hall under Henry's old professors. The future Supreme Court Justice was two years Henry's senior and a good deal more at ease socially, in particular with young women. 'Harry never lets up on his high aims,' Wendell later wrote to William James, admitting that *he* often did. He added, 'There are not infrequent times when a bottle of wine, a good dinner, a girl of some trivial sort can fill the hour for me.' Wendell was singularly pleasing to young ladies. His father pictured him reciting his war exploits as 'my white Othello with a semi-circle of young Desdemonas about him listening to the oft-told tale'.

Henry James had arranged his visit to the White Mountains for the end of July 1865 and he invited Wendell to join him. He set Minny Temple room-hunting for them but with the summer influx she could find only a single room, 'the only one in the place, high or low – far or near. This,' Henry exuberantly informed Wendell, 'the wretch who owned it refused to furnish with two beds; but she took it and when we get up there we can pull his own out from under him. At any rate we are sure of a shelter, and I will tell Minny T. to keep her "eye-peeled" for another room or another bed.' The room was $2.50 a week and meals were to be obtained nearby for $5 or $6 a week.

Holmes meanwhile had been busy with his social life and with the Harvard Commemoration at which James Russell Lowell read his deeply felt Ode to the Harvard dead, *Was dying all they had the skill to do?*

> In these brave ranks I can only see the gaps,
> Thinking of dear ones whom the dumb turf wraps,
> Dark to the triumph which they died to gain.

Henry James was to read the Ode many times in subsequent years and to find its lines charged with the overtones of 1865; each time it seemed to him 'more full and strong ... more august and pathetic'. That summer, however, only the echoes of the occasion reached him at Newport, and he wrote to Wendell, 'What adventures you must be having. What with the Commem., Gen. Meade and all the rest of it!' And he adds with a friendly jibe at Wendell's cheerful loquacity 'Pray don't tell the story to death before I see you.' On 1 August 1865, Henry travelled with Holmes up the coach road into the White Mountains, to North Conway. Holmes brought with him another young man fresh from the wars, a bearded fellow-student, already a friend of Minny's, John Chipman Gray, destined to become one of Harvard's most distinguished jurists, for many years a member of its Law Faculty.

The scene Henry paints in *Notes of a Son and Brother*, without divulging the identity of Holmes or Gray, is touched with the warm brush of memory, 'the fraternizing, endlessly conversing group of us under the rustling pines'. They talked of 'a hundred human and personal things'. It was 'high talk' in the 'splendid American summer drawn out to its last generosity', and he felt the talkers constituted 'a little world of easy and happy interchange, of unrestricted and yet all so instructively sane and secure association and conversation, with all its liberties and delicacies, all its mirth and earnestness'. They read the then fresh pages of Matthew Arnold, they talked of Browning and of George Eliot. In 1905, when Henry returned to this scene after an absence of forty years – returned by motor-car over the old coach road – he surveyed the valley of the Saco and painted it as 'the near ... the far, country of youth', physically there, yet recoverable only in memory. Much was changed in the man-made scene, but

the high rock-walls of the ledges, the striking sign of the spot, were there; grey and perpendicular, with their lodged patches of shrub-like forest growth, and the immense floor, below them, where the Saco spreads and turns and the elms of the great general meadow stand about like candelabra (with their arms reversed) interspaced on a green table.

The woods were a 'sacred grove', a place 'prepared for high uses, even if for none rarer than high talk'. The old Henry, on this revisited scene, found 'latent poetry – old echoes, ever so faint'. Forty years before, in similar woods and on similar meadows, he had walked with his Temple cousins and here, not far from Mount Washington's paternal face, had taken place a little drama, divided neither into scenes nor acts, and wholly without climax, that nevertheless touched off in Henry's mind stories to be relived early and late at his writing-desk.

3

The drama resided largely in Henry's mind. For what happened at North Conway during that August of '65 was simply that two young Civil War veterans, perhaps still in uniform, and Henry, gallantly attended the Temple girls, devoting themselves particularly to Minny. Henry, however, felt himself in a very special relationship to the veterans. The end of the Civil War, he noted in his memoirs, had transported from the battlefields 'a quantity of military life' and 'images of military experience' into the very drawing-rooms of New England. The bronzed, muscular young men had come back full of stories and were 'swamping much of the scene as with the flow of a monster tide'. Henry would not have used such words had he not felt himself swamped; and while he presented himself as 'the dreaming painter of things' seeking to absorb some portion of this common fund of history, he felt himself once more on a footing of inequality among his fellows. The 'very smell' of having served in the war, he wrote, seemed to his 'supersensitive nostril an emanation the most masculine'. The bronzed young men, fresh from the struggle, constituted a challenge to one, who had not been a soldier; he seems to have felt *his* masculinity diminished by their presence. Every uniform, every swordbelt and buckle, suggested a life of action that could never be a part of his life. He had put this very clearly in *The Story of a Year*: 'I have no intention of following Lieutenant Ford to the seat of war. The exploits of his campaign are recorded in the public journals of the day, where the curious may still peruse them. My own taste has always been for unwritten history, and my present business is with the reverse of the picture.' He was borrowing phrases from Balzac; he also set himself down as one whose action was imagining and observing.

The reverse of the picture was, for instance, Minny in earnest or witty talk with Lieutenant-Colonel Oliver Wendell Holmes Jr, and Judge Advocate John Chipman Gray Jr, while Henry, the 'mere junior', the civilian stay-at-home, looked on from the outer rim of talk. He could claim the prerogative of a kinsman, which he felt was a handicap; he was almost, in that group, a host; he felt he had a claim to special privilege because he had helped bring such a fine company together;

if we were just the most delightful loose band conceivable, and immersed in a regular revel of all the harmonies, it was largely by grace of the three quite exceptional young men who, thanks in part to the final sublime coach-drive of other days, had travelled up from Boston with their preparations to admire inevitably quickened.

He added:

I was quite willing to offer myself as exceptional through being able to promote such exceptions and see them justified to waiting apprehension. There was a dangling fringe, there were graceful accessories and hovering shades, but, essentially, we of the true connection made up the drama ... if drama we could indeed feel this as being, I hasten to add, we owed it most of all to our just having such a heroine that everything else inevitably came. Mary Temple was beautifully and indescribably *that*.

The heroine was there but the would-be hero was eclipsed; 'the interesting pair', Wendell and John, had a 'quantity of common fine experience that glittered as so much acquired and enjoyed luxury – all of the sort that I had no acquisition whatever to match'. He could only rejoice that his friends had so much to show to Minny, such 'brilliant advantage', even if he had 'none of my own' to offer. His was the consolation of the observer; with it, however, was the awareness – and it appears to have been acute – that his relationship to Minny in the circumstances was somewhat less than masculine. The 'emanation the most masculine' came from the veterans of the Civil War; and Henry testified later in a letter to William that with his bad back and tendency to invalidism, he had lived in the hope of regaining 'my natural lead', so that the friendship with Minny might have become 'more active and masculine'.

This was a recognition, an insight into the shortcoming of the relationship. It is doubtful, however, whether Henry would have acted otherwise, even if there had been no young men present to admire, to love, to adore Minny. A young man naturally shy and tending to hover in the background of any social situation, Henry in reality wanted only to worship Minny from a quiet and discreet – and we might add, safe – distance. Henry was as uncompetitive in affairs of the heart as in matters of literary import; he left it to others to seek the attention of Minny by direct approach, relying upon his radiated emotion to assert his own claim to attention. To sit back and observe his cousin, to worship her from afar, to give her signs of devotion at the right moment, this seems to have been the love stratagem of Henry – as it was of a number of his early young fictional heroes – those who do not go to the opposite extreme of tearing their passion frantically to tatters. He was too reticent and emotionally withdrawn to be an ardent wooer – to woo at all – too intellectual to accept romance on its own sentient terms; and he lived in an era when, particularly in his world, there was much greater reticence between the sexes. Henry James was in love, but it was love of an inner sort, the tormenting heart's rue, or that love which Voltaire framed in a conventional conceit when he sought to write a poem in English: *True love is best by silence known.* We might say that Henry loved Minny as much as he was capable of loving any woman, as much as Winterbourne, uncertain and doubting in his bewilderment, loved Daisy, or the invalid Ralph loved Isabel: a questioning love, unvoiced, unavowed.

True love is best by silence known. And such silence can have in it a component of fear. Love unfraid is not usually inarticulate; love afraid finds subterfuge in worship, adoration, a kind of desperate passive hope of acceptance that can reflect at the same time fear of rebuff. Henry James feared women and worshipped them. He hesitated to express his feelings lest he be turned away. For him women could be as chaste and beautiful – and unattainable – as Diana; or else they were another kind of huntress, harsh and predatory, literally dedicated to the chase – the chase of a husband – and thus to be fled.

Minny was not only a bright-burning flame, or Diana, chaste and beautiful. If the first object of a young man's affection usually has in her some of the attributes of the most familar female figure in his life, namely his mother, this was certainly true of Minny. Her very name, Mary, was his mother's; she was a kinswoman and she had a capacity, similar to Mary James's, for being all charm and simplicity while holding back certain feelings; she could 'relate' winningly to those around her with the familiar toss of the head and at the same time draw down a curtain of inscrutability. 'Heroine of the scene' she was for him, and the very word 'heroine' suggests the extent to which he exalted her. It is true that other young men were also under her spell. Gray later said Holmes loved her; Holmes said it was William James; and others said it was Gray, for whom she does seem to have shown considerable feeling. Some time later Henry wrote to

William : 'Every one was supposed, I believe, to be more or less in love with her,' and, while in this letter he denied that he was, he added 'I enjoyed *pleasing* her almost as much as if I had been. I cared more to please her perhaps than she ever cared to be pleased.' This is at once denial and avowal : for to want to please there must indeed be a fund of affection, and the abundant evidence of the memoirs, and of the place Henry James assigned to Minny alike in his life and in his work, testifies to her role as an object of his affection. The evidence is transparently written into a short story penned shortly after the episode in the White Mountains. It is so transparent, in fact, that he clearly was thinking of it when, in an eloquent passage devoted to his early short stories ('these secrets of the imaginative life'), he alludes to sending 'the most presuming of my fictional bids' to William Dean Howells. The first story he sent to Howells was a tale of two Civil War officers and a civilian. In the same passage he admits that his tales of that time

referred to actual concretions of existence as well as to the supposititious; the joy of life, indeed, drawbacks and all, was just in the constant quick flit of association, to and fro, and through a hundred open doors, between the two great chambers (if it be not absurd, or even base, to separate them) of direct and indirect experience.

The tale of *Poor Richard* sprang from direct experience.

4

This story, which Henry James wrote during the next year, was his fifth acknowledged tale. It appeared in the *Atlantic Monthly* in three instalments, June to August 1867 – one of the three tales he wrote about the Civil War. Its biographical interest resides in the central situation – that of a wealthy young heroine loved by three men, a Captain, a Major and a civilian, Richard Clare (his name was changed to Richard Maule in a later revision), a stay-at-home. While neither of the military men appears to resemble Holmes or Gray, the hero is endowed with the feelings of Henry James. He suffers from a deep sense of inadequacy, and though he pleads his love to Gertrude Whittaker in defensive and rough accents, he is conscious of his 'insignificance' in the presence of the military suitors.

The two officers were already slightly known to each other, and Richard was accordingly presented to each of them ... His companions displayed toward their hostess that half-avowed effort to shine and to outshine natural to clever men who find themselves concurring to the entertainment of a young and agreeable woman. Richard sat by, wondering, in splenetic amazement, whether he was an ignorant boor, or whether they were only a brace of inflated snobs ... He writhed and chafed under the polish of tone and the variety of allusion by which the two officers consigned him to insignificance; but he was soon lost in wonder at the mettlesome grace and vivacity with which Gertrude sustained her share of the conversation ... As he gulped down the sickening fact of his comparative, nay, his absolute ignorance of the great world represented by his rivals, he felt like anticipating its consequences by a desperate sally into the very field of their conversation. To some such movement Gertrude was continually inviting him by her glances, her smiles, her questions, and her appealing silence. But poor Richard knew that, if he should attempt to talk, he would choke; and this assurance he imparted to his friend in a look piteously eloquent. He was conscious of a sensation of rage under which his heart was fast turning into a fiery furnace, destined to consume all his good resolutions.

We cannot say now whether Henry, in the White Mountains, had similarly raged; however, helplessness and frustration seem to have been his lot, and the eloquence as well as minuteness with which he describes poor Richard's feelings have the vividness of personal experience. The little episode had become a dramatic situation which was to be carried over in due course to a major work as well. In *The Portrait of a Lady*, the heroine, Isabel Archer, modelled on Minny, also has three lovers – the invalid Ralph Touchett, Lord Warburton and Caspar Goodwood – and like her predecessor she marries none of them. Touchett, the invalid, has much in common with the ineffectual Civil War heroes; he assumes from the outset that he can never marry; he is the helpless and foredoomed lover of romance. Richard belongs to a somewhat different category. He expresses his love, but later loses interest in the heroine because she shows an interest in another man. She has stepped down from her exalted pedestal. In some respects Richard is a predecessor of Roderick Hudson and of Eugene Pickering. Gertrude, in *Poor Richard*, has little in common either with Minny or Isabel. She is that impossible type of woman James often created – neither interesting nor even good-looking, difficult to see as anything but wealthy and motherly. However, she is a moral force, and she loses this strength in the eyes of Richard when she accepts the mendacious Major.

Midway through the story Richard comes down with typhoid, an

illness Henry James was well qualified to describe. The Captain, who
has loved Gertrude in silence – in Henry's fashion – has gone off to
the wars and been killed; and when Richard recovers his health he
discovers that Gertrude, who has really loved the Captain, is now ill.
'I've got my strength again,' Richard exclaims, 'and meanwhile
you've been failing.' The Jamesian 'Vampire Theme' is here enunci-
ated for the first time. It was to form the subject of a full-length
story a year later, and would recur in stories early and late. Henry
had linked himself to Minny as he had seen his father linked to Mary
James. If she was the 'heroine of the scene', then he could not be the
hero. One or the other had to give way in Henry James's equation.
The time was to come when he would equate his improving health
with Minny's fading radiance. For the bright and shining flame of the
heroine of his scene was flickering.

Part Five:
The Complex Fate

24

Jacob and Esau

IN the Old Testament, Jacob and Esau are twins, born but a few minutes apart. Jacob emerges from the womb clutching the heel of his brother, as if determined to be as little behind him as possible. The elder of the two became the active one, a cunning hunter, favourite provider of venison for his father. The younger, a dweller in tents, a stay-at-home son, was beloved of the mother. Then one day Esau, driven by hunger, sold his birthright for a mess of Jacob's pottage. Later their father, Isaac, old and tired and near-blind, called upon his eldest son to bring him venison and to receive the paternal blessing. But while Esau hunted for the game with which to serve his father, Jacob, at the urging of his mother, supplanted him, donned his clothes, placed the skin of kids on his arms to give an effect of Esau's hairiness, and brought his father meat carefully prepared by the mother. When Esau returned and discovered that Jacob had usurped his place and received the blessing, he raised his voice and wept: 'He hath supplanted me these two times. He took away my birthright and behold, now he hath taken away my blessing.'

There was neither birthright nor need for blessing in the James family, but between the ancient archetypal drama of rivalry in the tents of Israel and the brothers' drama in Quincy Street there are parallels — although Quincy Street saw neither deliberate acts of usurpation nor overt fraternal struggles. The parallels are there because the ancient story touched eternal truths.

I

William James came back from Brazil in March 1866 and resumed his medical studies. Henry's back-ache revived with his brother's return. He spent an uncomfortable summer at Swampscott, on Massachusetts Bay, twenty miles north of Boston. He read a great deal and wrote very little. A fugitive memory of this time, recorded in his notebook, is that of

lying on my bed at Swampscott ... towards the summer's end, and reading in ever so thrilled a state, George Eliot's *Felix Holt* just out, and of which I was to write, and *did* write, a review in the *Nation* ... I was miserably stricken by my poor broken, all but unbearable, and unsurvivable *back* ... To read over the opening pages of *Felix Holt* makes even now the whole time softly and shyly live again.

William spent this summer as an intern in the Massachusetts General Hospital, and in the autumn the brothers were reunited under the family roof, which was moved from Ashburton Place to 20 Quincy Street, a large comfortable house, facing the Harvard Yard. This was to be the last home of the James Family. 'Home' for them had been houses, hotels, *pensions* in a chain of cities – Albany, New York, Geneva, Paris, London, Newport, Boston. Their longest residence in one house had been in 14th Street in New York. Now, in late middle age, the parents brought their wanderings to an end. Their sons were grown; the younger boys were conducting their experiment on their southern plantation. William, Henry and Alice were at home, but the older sons were restless. Alice, now a girl of 19, was highstrung and was soon to develop attacks of nervous prostration from which she suffered during the remainder of her life.

Now it was William James, the vigorous and active elder brother, who fell into a series of illnesses – back-aches, like Henry's, insomnia, eye-trouble, digestive disorders – a general state of exhaustion, nervousness and depression. The symptoms were to continue for several years and disappeared gradually as William found his way into a career, married and established his own home. In the spring of 1867 he interrupted his medical studies and left for Germany in search of health and to profit by research in German laboratories and study of the language.

Henry, on his side, showed prompt signs of improvement after William's departure. 'I have felt quite strong since you sailed,' he wrote his brother in May 1867; and eleven days later, 'I have been feeling essentially better since you left.' That same week their mother wrote to William that 'Harry does you the compliment of choosing the same cloth for a summer suit as you had last year'. It was almost as if, in the absence of the elder brother, Henry could step into his clothes – don, like Jacob, the raiment of Esau – and be, in role and in dress, the first born.

With Henry's improving health came resumed literary activity. He was so productive during the months of William's absence that he earned $800 by his pen. This was a comfortable sum in an era when a room cost a few dollars a month and a steak a few cents.

William on his side, who inquired into Henry's earnings, seems to have been troubled over his own inability to contribute, rather than use, the family's resources. In September of 1867, in Berlin, he tried his hand at a book review, sending it to Henry for revision and possible publication. 'I feel that a living is not worth being gained at this price,' he wrote and then, apparently sensing that this remark was inappropriate to one who *was* earning his living by his pen, he crossed out the 'not' in the sentence and substituted 'is hardly worth being gained'. He added: 'Style is not my forte and to strike the mean between pomposity and vulgar familiarity is indeed difficult.' (Henry could hardly have relished this view of the horizons of literary art – a middle course between vulgarity and pomposity.) 'Still,' William James went on, 'an' the rich guerdon accrue, an' but ten beauteous dollars lie down on their green and glossy backs within the family treasury, in consequence of my exertions, I shall feel glad that I have made them.' William wrote a few book reviews and articles under his brother's aegis and editing, and was paid for them on publication. He did not pursue this type of writing for long and was to emerge as a different sort of writer – of vivid and lucid scientific papers, works in psychology and philosophy; he achieved a vigorous, muscular style that abounded in image and example and created an effect of spontaneous talk. It was essentially his father's style but clearer, more direct, and disciplined.

In the autumn of 1868, after eighteen months abroad, William James returned from Europe. Henry promptly ceased to publish. His back-ache revived; he could bring himself neither to read nor write. Apparently the observation Henry had made about his new-found freedom and his 'uncorrected self', on William's departure for the Amazon, had become a pattern. When his elder brother was away, Henry could expand and flourish. The moment William returned, the inhibiting forces in their relationship, reduced Henry to inaction and even illness. Quincy Street did not seem capable of housing comfortably two geniuses at the same time.

Mary James, faced with two ailing sons, tended to exacerbate rather than ease the hidden psychological tensions. She had for a long time openly shown her preference for Henry, the quiet one, and not a little hostility towards William, the active and effervescent. She might fuss over Henry's aches and pains, to which the household was quite accustomed, but William's sudden acquisition of analogous symptoms she considered with a singular lack of sympathy. Her letters make quite free with his condition; he complains too much; he has a 'morbid sympathy' with every form of physical trouble; he worries excessively; 'he must express every fluctuation of feeling,' exclaims Mary James. Henry had taken illness with a kind of fatalistic resignation that made him easy to live with; the pronouncedly active William could be neither fatalistic nor resigned. Illness represented a sudden curbing of his energetic personality. He experienced his fluctuations of mood with a lack of reticence that was at the same time a voluble protest.

2

There was not much open rivalry between the two brothers. Had there been a healthy expression of their submerged feelings, had William, like Esau, raised his voice and wept that Henry was for the moment surpassing him in material achievement, or had Henry on his side not harboured a sense of guilt, there might have been flare-ups and scenes, but fewer symptoms. On the surface there was love and affection and mutual respect as well as close intellectual sympathy between the brothers. The affection, indeed, was far beyond that which usually exists between brothers as different temperamentally as were Henry and William. What happened was that the old brotherly equations of childhood, below the surface of the conscious and adult relationship, underwent a significant change. In 1866 a very important, and to William disturbing, reversal of role had occurred within the James family. Henry, the mocked and derided junior of old, who had secretly dispatched his manuscripts and used Sargy Perry's address to avoid family teasing, suddenly emerged as the only one of the four brothers who had his goal clearly in view and was proceeding towards it in a straight line. William, on the other hand, always sure of himself in the past, now appeared to be without fixed purpose. 'Much would I give,' he exclaimed to Wendell Holmes at this time, 'for a constructive passion of some kind.' Henry had long ago discovered such a passion. William, returning from South America, where he had believed himself to be the focus of family interest, discovered that Henry was in the centre of the scene, exciting admiration and approval as a promising young man of letters. Jacob had supplanted Esau. William's behaviour provides a striking series of clues to this disturbed fraternal state. Even before his Brazilian journey, and immediately after the

appearance of Henry's first writings in the *North American Review*,
he had dispatched to Norton a curious little note, that, for all its air
of innocent humour, illuminates his desire to emulate his younger
brother. 'My dear Mr Norton,' he began, 'As my friends and relations
seem to be successful in their attempts to draw a revenue from the
North American Review I am emboldened to try what I can do myself.' He proposes that he review Huxley's lectures on comparative
anatomy. It is significant that here, as in the later letter from Berlin,
William is concerned not so much about literary achievement as by
the fact that Henry could 'draw a revenue' from his writings.

William from the first constituted himself critic and judge of his
brother's writings, and delivered his verdicts and opinions, *ex
cathedra*. His criticisms at times took the form of a display of his
own literary virtuosity while demolishing his brother; on still other
occasions he praised unstintingly and eloquently. There was critical
discernment in what he said, but the form was often painful. He
criticizes Henry's 'want of heartiness'; he tells him his stories are
'thin'. They 'give a certain impression of the author clinging to his
gentlemanliness though all else be lost'; also there is 'want of blood
in your stories ... I think the same thing would strike you if you
read them as the work of another'. There was indeed something stiff
and precious in the style of the early tales; nevertheless, William was
throwing ice-water at Henry. During the weeks that followed, he
sensed that this was what he had done. 'I have the impression,' he
writes, 'I assumed a rather law-giving tone.' He reassures Henry. 'I
feel as if you were one of the two or three sole intellectual and moral
companions I have.' When he read *A Most Extraordinary Case* in the
April 1868 *Atlantic* he found better things in it, 'your style grows
easier, firmer, and more concise as you go on writing ... the face of
the whole story is bright and sparkling'.

3

In 1867 Henry, in a letter to William, mentioned he had received
'overtures' from the *Nation*. Since he was a regular contributor to
the journal this suggests that he had been offered a closer connection,
perhaps an editorial post. All we know is that the 'overtures' were
turned down. A year later Charles Eliot Norton asked him to become
an editor of the *North American Review*. Flattering this was, to a
writer in his middle twenties; the post held promise of regular earn-

ings. Yet he unhesitatingly declined. There seems to have been no self-questioning, no doubt. He had made up his mind what his career would be, and was not allowing himself to be deflected. Under no circumstances was he prepared to become a mere functionary, concerned with the writings of others. Just how confident a measure he had taken of himself we may judge from the manner in which he told Perry, 'I write little, and only tales, which I think it likely I shall continue to manufacture in a hackish manner, for that which is bread. They *cannot* of necessity be good; but they *shall not* be very bad.' To have doubted himself would have been to doubt his art. His training, self-organized, had been directed to making his pen proficient, his eye observant, his mind alert. When moments of decision came he made the right choice, perhaps because he consulted only his inner self. He never yielded to the false whispers of the immediate and the external. And because he had such deep underground sources of observation, training, knowledge and imagination and such faith in them, he moved implacably forward in spite of delays occasioned by his mode of life and uncertain health.

He showed indeed a strange inertia by remaining in the family home. If, in retrospect, he characterized these as his 'untried years', he seems at this time to have made singularly little effort to 'try' them. He was securely anchored in Quincy Street, looking enviously on while William and Wendell Holmes and Sargy Perry successively went abroad. 'Can Cambridge answer Seville?' queries Henry when Perry writes him from Spain. 'Can Massachusetts respond unto Granada?' Apparently it could at least voice envy. 'Bed-bugs? Methinks that I would endure even them for a glimpse of those galleries and cathedrals of which you write.'

Why did Henry James linger in Quincy Street long beyond the time when most young men leave home to make their own way in the world? His health had improved; he was self-supporting; the leading periodicals welcomed his work; his parents did not oppose his decisions. Nevertheless it is significant that he was 26 before he ventured abroad, and 32 before he finally cut the ties binding him to the family scene.

In a sedentary young man it was perhaps understandable that he should hesitate to alter the established course of his life. It required no effort to allow the days to glide by and to accept all the home-comforts provided by his doting mother. Yet it is clear that for Henry this existence was boring. The young man who looked eagerly across the sea to the literary world of London and Paris spoke of life in Quincy Street as being 'about as lively as the inner sepulchre'. To his brother abroad he complained: 'I haven't a creature to talk to ... How in Boston, when the evening arrives and I am tired of reading, and know it would be better to do something else, can I go to the theatre? I have tried it, *ad nauseam*. Likewise *calling*. Upon whom?' These then were the horizons of Henry James from 1866 until 1869 – his 23rd to his 26th years: the writing-desk, the book, the occasional play, the rare and usually disappointing social call, the journey by horse-car from Cambridge to Boston, a full and chilly evening's adventure among the city's deep snows or irksome and exhausting in the summer's heat.

Nor was this tone of complaint destined for his brother exclusively. 'I have a pleasant room, with a big soft bed and good chairs,' he wrote to Perry at the end of the summer of 1867, during which he boasted he had remained in Quincy Street without leaving it for a single night. But he added, invoking Tennyson, it was 'stiller than chiselled marble'. He was sure that before the end of another year 'I shall have had enough' of Cambridge. He found no friends among the new generation of students at Harvard; as for the amiable Brahmins – Lowell, Norton, Longfellow – they were 'not at all to my taste, for the bulk of my society'.

Was he really a fledgling who took longer than most to try his wings? Or was he a Jacob quite satisfied to dwell in tents and brew his literary pottage rather than roam afield? There is no doubt that one reason was that he was waiting his turn to go to Europe; his ample earnings were not yet sufficient to provide funds for travel, and his father, with the younger brothers on his hands, and with William to support abroad, does not seem to have been prepared at this time to keep two sons in Europe simultaneously. The question indeed would not present itself were it not for the tales Henry was writing during this time, and these, as before, offer us some insight into inner problems seeking a solution. Three tales were set down during William James's absence in Europe and each resolves itself into a similar situation. The first deals with the rivalry of two sisters for the hand of an Englishman who has come out to make his fortune in the colonies. The younger sister wins him, but her triumph is short lived; she dies in childbirth and, knowing how envious her elder sister is, obtains a promise from her husband that her trousseau, carefully locked away, will be kept for her daughter. The elder sister is now able to supplant the younger. She marries the widower and becomes the stepmother of the child. One bitter pill remains: she cannot put her hands on her sister's fine clothes. Finally she obtains the key to the trunk and like Bluebeard's wife opens the forbidden lock. Her husband finds her, at sunset, dead, with ten ghostly finger-marks on her throat, lying beside the satins, silks, muslins and velvet she will never wear. The tale is called *The Romance of Certain Old Clothes*. It was written, singularly enough, not long after Henry ordered from his tailor the suit of clothes made from the same cloth as William's suit of the previous summer.

A second tale was also ghostly and melodramatic. It was about young De Grey whose bride refused to accept the old family curse which doomed her, and in the process reversed it, so that instead of dying she found herself bringing about the death of her husband-to-be; 'she blindly, senselessly, remorselessly drained the life from his being. As she bloomed and prospered, he drooped and languished. While she was living for him, he was dying of her.'

But it was the third tale which crystallized this recurring theme of reversal of role and usurpation. *A Light Man* was one of the few early stories he esteemed sufficiently to revise and republish. It represented the first instance in which he used a technical device later to be developed to perfection: the device of self-revelation by the principal character, with the author never intervening to describe or elucidate; the reader must figure out all the implications of the narrative himself. Maximus Austin is a cheerful scoundrel, but we discover this only because James lets us read a few entries in his journal, where he candidly displays his improvidence, his opportunism, his dishonesty. He relates how he returns to America from Europe penniless; how Theodore Lisle, a friend of schooldays who treats him as if he were a brother, invites him to stay at the home of Lisle's employer, a wealthy eccentric. This man, brilliantly sketched, is weak, idiosyncratic, effeminate; combining in his personality both masculine and feminine traits, he acts as a kind of father-mother to both young men; indeed, he has known in the past the father of one and the mother of the other, and in this way another chain of invisible brotherhood is established between the two. The employer has drawn his will in favour of Theodore; but Maximus plays on the old man's erratic affections and receives from him the promise that he will make him the heir instead of his friend. The old will is destroyed; however, the would-be benefactor dies before he can write a new one. Not only has Max deprived Theodore of what might be considered his birthright – he has failed to obtain it for himself.

All three of these tales involve a reversal of role between two persons closely linked, and the supplanting of one by another : the elder sister becomes the wife of her dead sister's husband and dies herself when she would wear her sister's clothes. De Grey's bride becomes a vampire-like destroyer of the man destined to be her husband in order to save herself; Maximus seeks to usurp the place held by Theodore in the household of a wealthy man and to obtain the birthright destined for his friend. Usurpation is central to the three tales.

Had Henry usurped William's place? Their roles were certainly reversed. In a sense he was wearing William's clothes and he had stepped into William's shoes; in the family, in which he had for so long felt himself in a subordinate role, he had now achieved supremacy. While William was away he could be the first-born, with his brother's prerogatives of seniority. It was the same situation as the triumphal dream of the Louvre; there, too, roles are reversed, the pursued becomes the pursuer. We may speculate, therefore, that Henry clung to Quincy Street because there he could enjoy, over and above the general amenities of home, a sense of power unchallenged; all unaware he achieved a feeling of well-being during the long absences of his brother because he was alone and triumphant, even if at moments, as the stories showed, feelings of guilt caused him to dream that punishment is meted out to usurpers. Significantly, in these stories he seems to identify himself not with the younger or weaker individual, as in some of his tales, but with the elder and stronger, the *usurping* individual. And in each case the usurper pays with his life or with defeat,

William James, on his side, enjoying Europe, was experiencing feelings of guilt as well. 'It seems a sin to be doing such things while Harry is moping at home,' he wrote in his diary. And in a letter to his sister he uses the language of the Bible : 'I somehow feel as if I were cheating Harry of his birthright.' Thus the two brothers played out the drama of Jacob and Esau. The curious thing was that both cast themselves in the role of Jacob.

25

A Military Eye

CHARLES DICKENS came to Boston in November 1867 to begin those readings of his works which were to be acclaimed throughout America. On 18 November, when the tickets were put on sale, Henry turned up at the box office at 9 a.m. to find nearly 1,000 persons waiting. 'I don't expect to hear him,' he wrote to William. He expected even less to meet him.

A few evenings later Charles Eliot Norton was host at Shady Hill to the visiting celebrity. It was a brilliant dinner-party and the elder Henry James was among the guests. His son was invited to drop in later in the evening. The small boy who had hugged the carpet in 14th Street while he listened to *David Copperfield* was now 24.

Dickens stood there, a striking figure in conservative dinner attire, the sculptured beard, the handsome face, a 'face of symmetry yet of formidable character', a chiselled mask. The great novelist looked at young Henry 'with a straight inscrutability, a mercilessly *military* eye ... an automatic hardness ... a kind of economy of apprehension'. It all took place in a moment in that famous house thronged with the élite of Cambridge and Boston. Henry was stopped in a doorway and quickly introduced; Dickens gave Henry a solitary stare; he said nothing; they didn't shake hands.

Many years later Henry mused that had they spoken to one another there would have been but an exchange of platitudes, a perfunctory handshake. Dickens was being lionized; he was tired; Henry's face was but one of many in Shady Hill. What had taken place instead was this fixed look, acute and penetrating, of this 'mercilessly military eye', and the return of his look by the nervous young writer.

'I saw the master – nothing could be more evident – in the light of an intense emotion, and I trembled, I remember in every limb.' Feeling, however, did not blur Henry's recording eye. The 'exquisitely complicated image' remained, all the more vivid for not having spoken. 'How tremendously it had been laid upon young persons of our generation to feel Dickens, down to the soles of our shoes ... no other debt in our time had been piled so high.' And it was as 'a slim and shaken vessel of feeling' that Henry stood before the Master, then near the end of his life. Henry's father remembered the novelist as 'saintly'. His son found in him an 'essential radiance'.

These were the impressions Henry James read into that fixed moment and brief encounter. For one 'single pulse of time' they met – a novelist of the past, a novelist of the future.

26

Venus and Diana

I

THE young man in Quincy Street held back from the world, and this meant that he held back from women as well. He seems to have seen little of Minny Temple during the Cambridge years; there was only one more summer in the White Mountains, that of 1868, and he spent it at Jefferson, New Hampshire, in a 'great rattling tavern'. The Temples were not at Conway. He wrote to Minny's elder sister, Katherine, to congratulate her on her engagement, and discreetly inquired how Minny 'in that deep inscrutable soul of hers contemplates your promotion. It is a rare chance for Minny's cogitations – heaven bless her! If she could drop me a line I should be very glad to have her views.'

Minny was off at Newport, or New York, or suburban Pelham, where she now lived, in a gay whirl of parties, dances and concerts but wracked by cough and suffering occasional lung haemorrhages that subdued her dancing body and committed her to silence and rest. There is no evidence that Henry was aware of her condition; the immediate members of her family, in those medically primitive days, seemed to be without serious concern for her. She was away in the distance, removed from Henry, a remote Diana, chaste and active. Any closer view, any bubbling up of feeling between them, might have created problems for Henry. No feeling could bubble, however: Henry continued to hold himself aloof.

In Cambridge itself he saw a goodly number of women, saw them as creatures to be observed and chatted with at tea; and he formed a series of friendships with various spinsters, notably of the Norton entourage, that endured for many years: the elderly Miss Ashburners, Theodora Sedgwick, Grace and Jane Norton, Frances Morse, Elizabeth Boott. Of these, the friendship with Grace Norton appears to have been the most enduring; something in her personality, and in her troubled spirit, evoked a response in Henry James and inspired him to write to her certain of the most felicitous letters of his middle years: they are long, detailed, spontaneous, filled with a running account of his literary life, his readings, his evaluation of persons encountered in the social world. The 160 letters which Grace Norton preserved (he kept none of hers) are intimate, yet without a suggestion of any depth of intimacy. She, on her side, seems to have poured out her troubles to Henry and received advice, comfort, solace from him. It was largely a pen friendship, for they were, for years, separated by the Atlantic. As she grew old in Cambridge and Henry grew famous, his letters became one of the great facts of her life, and she used to read them to her friends 'with omissions' (William James once informed his brother) that suggested there were more deeply personal portions than was really the case. William once described her to Henry: she was growing stoutish, was plainly dressed, 'but her voice is still in the major key and her intelligence, sociability and goodwill as great as ever ... She still seems to retain her aversion and contempt for female society.' She was one of Henry's cherished links with his homeland all his life.

A younger friend, intermittently at Cambridge and Newport, was Elizabeth Boott, who was also a friend of Minny Temple. She was the daughter of a widower, Francis Boott, of the elder Henry James's generation, who had lived long in Italy. 'The easy-fitting Bootts,' Henry James once described them in a letter home. Lizzie had grown up a graceful, well-tended American-European girl, shy, reserved, proficient in languages and dabbling in art and music. Henry thought of her later as 'the admirable, the infinitely civilized and sympathetic, the markedly *produced* Lizzie', and she was to sit for the portrait of Pansy in *The Portrait of a Lady*, even as Frank Boott, an amateur composer, whose songs had a certain vogue, gave the novelist the figure, if not the cruel character, of Gilbert Osmond, Pansy's father. Henry saw the Bootts as 'inverted romantics'. They had had their Europe when they appeared on the Newport horizon, had it to the full, and could now taste of their homeland. Henry was to see much of Lizzie at home and abroad and to enjoy her modest company. This was one of the few friendships of his life with a woman of his own age. There is not a word in Henry's letters – which Lizzie carefully preserved – that suggests a closer intimacy.

In general Henry felt at Cambridge that the women he saw were 'provincial, common, inelegant'. They did not appeal to his fancy, he wrote Perry, but he did admit that 'perhaps I am grossly insensible'. Henry James could take the measure of his countrymen with a clear sense of their attributes and shortcomings. He could describe them; he could reproduce faithfully their conversation and their manners; he might even try to give a picture of their minds; his intelligence could grasp them – but what were they? Fine pieces of statuary, yes, he could say that and did, likening them in his early tales to Venuses and Dianas and Junos, frozen in stone. They were, when they aroused feeling, or were encountered in the flesh, creatures of mystery and consequently of danger. Unfathomable. Sometimes when they seemed to be Jezebels they turned out to be purer than the Boston snows; and sometimes a mask of purity covered women who, like Browning's *Last Duchess* is described as liking

> whate'er
> She looked on, and her looks went everywhere.

The description has its bias but the poem fascinated Henry. Later, when he had observed English girls, he might write that they were 'wholly in the realm of the cut and dried', and that they could not match the 'intellectual grace' or the 'moral spontaneity' of American girls.

Intellectual grace ... moral spontaneity. He might find a formula for them, without the certainty of emotional apprehension. What was his most celebrated story of some years later but that of a young man who tries unsuccessfully to fathom the innocent surface and unconventional behaviour of a young girl named Daisy?

2

When Henry James wasn't writing stories of usurpation, he wrote of the mystery of womankind, of young men trapped by wily females, of sad heroes betrayed, of curious men circling at a distance from the irrepressible *ewig Weibliche* of literary allusion. In his first acknowledged story the despairing hero goes off to the Civil War, in his dying moments he sees his fiancée as a goddess in a Greek temple. In his next story, *A Landscape Painter*, the heroine is the 'very portrait of a lady' – and her name is Esther Blunt! Her behaviour bears out her name. She marries the hero for his $100,000 a year. He had thought he had successfully concealed this important fact from her and was being loved for himself. 'It was the act of a false woman,' the landscape painter blurts out when he discovers the truth. 'A false woman?' Esther queries and then smiles: 'Come, *you* be a man!' This Henry must have felt was a little too blunt an ending; the heroine's name was changed on revision to Miriam Quarterman and her final speech to 'it was the act of any woman – placed as I was placed'. If this tale reflects considerable insecurity about personal worth it reflects also uncertainty about the trust-worthiness of women. Just how dangerous woman in flesh (or even in stone) could be to man we have seen from the vampire tale of *De Grey* or James's fascination for the French story *La Vénus d'Ille*, in which the statue of Venus, upon whose outstretched finger the hero has carelessly placed his engagement ring during a heated game of tennis, comes crashing into the bridal chamber to claim her 'fiancé' and crushes him to death. Lovers preyed upon one another, women preyed upon men; the supreme love of Venus could be all-destroying.

The sad hero of *The Story of a Masterpiece* discovers in the por-trait of his fiancée, which he commissions, disturbing qualities he had not discerned in her living self. Did she possess a 'certain vague moral dinginess'? Lennox is troubled until the night before his marriage; and then he finds a solution.

'Come,' he tells himself as he looks at the portrait, 'Marian may be what God has made her; but *this* detestable creature I can neither love nor respect.' Seizing a poiniard he thrust it 'with barbarous glee, straight into the lovely face of the image. He dragged it downward, and made a long fissure in the living canvas. Then, with half a dozen strokes, he wantonly hacked it across. The act afforded him an immense relief.' Here, at least, the symbolic murder removes the painting, not the woman.

In another tale, *Osborne's Revenge*, the lawyer hero determines to avenge his dead friend Robert Graham, who committed suicide because of a broken heart. He seeks the acquaintance of the young woman, Henrietta Congreve, assured by a mutual friend that she is a destructive siren. He feels a 'savage need to hate her'. To his surprise, he discovers she is a gentlewoman, of fine intelligence and feeling. He sees no sign of remorse in her, nor any awareness that she had contributed to his friend's death. She refuses to discuss Graham with him. 'I shall begin to think she's a demon,' he says. He also speaks of her as if she were a vampire, 'she drained honest men's hearts to the last drop and bloomed white upon the monstrous diet'. Yet if she did, it was behind a mask of goodness. 'Ideally she had been repulsive; actually she was a person whom, if he had not been committed to detest her, he would find it very pleasant to like.' He is puzzled that 'a woman could unite so much loveliness with so much treachery, so much light with so much darkness'.

Then he learns that the image he has compounded of Henrietta Congreve is false; in reality, she never jilted Graham and it was Graham who was over-attentive and volatile. She did not even know of his suicide and believed his death due to natural causes. Thus a woman who seemed a flirt and a vampire turns out to be noble and virtuous and innocent of all the designs attributed to her by the vengeful hero. The tale is that of a man seeking to understand a woman and discovering that he has been in error from start to finish. It speaks of a serious doubt : what if Henry's reading of women were wrong? He was aware, as this tale reveals, of the disparity between appearance and reality; and in its primitive fashion it is, therefore, a forerunner of future tales of bewilderment. It is also a story of a man's chronic difficulty with the opposite sex.

3

William James, in a letter from Dresden of 24 July 1867, urged Harry to 'read (if he wants to) an essay by Grimm on the Venus de Milo ... and compare it with the St Victor one. Both are imaginative rhapsodies, but how much solider the German! (if I remember right). It is worth reading, Harry.' We do not know whether Henry read the Grimm essay or how he would have described that of Saint-Victor. We do know that the latter was published in a volume entitled *Hommes et Dieux* in 1867, and that the book remained from then until the end of Henry James's life in his library. In the year before his death he scrawled his name on the flyleaf and below it affixed the dates '1867–1915', thereby commemorating the volume's long life on his shelves. Paul de Saint-Victor endows the Venus de Milo with many qualities that must have evoked a warm response in Henry James :

The ambiguous visage of the Sphinx is less mysterious than this young head so naive in appearance ... This is the Celestial Venus, the Venus Victorious, always sought, never possessed, as absolute as the life whose central fire resides in her breast ... She is the flame which creates and

which preserves, the instigator of great things and heroic projects ...
There is not an atom of flesh in her august marble ... she sprang from a
virile mind nourished by the Idea and not by the presence of the woman.
She belongs to the time when statues expressed the superhuman character and the eternal thought ... From what avenue of the centuries dost
come to us, O young Sovereign ... Who has not experienced on entering
the Louvre and the hall where the Goddess reigns, that sacred terror –
deisadaimonia – of which the Greeks spoke? Her attitude is proud, almost
threatening ... There are no bones in this superb body, nor tears in its
blind eyes, nor entrails in this torso ... Allow the charm to have its effect
... rest at the foot of the august marble, as if under the shadow of an
ancient oak. Soon a profound peace will course through your soul. The
statue will envelop you in its solemn lineaments and you will feel as if
you have been enlaced in its absent arms. It will elevate you quietly to
the contemplation of pure beauty.

William was right in speaking of Paul de Saint-Victor's subjective
reverie as rhapsodic; yet its substance corresponds to Henry James's
dream of fair women as beings beyond flesh – immortal Venuses,
chaste Dianas – translated into imperishable stone where they may
be contemplated by the eye and the mind as goddesses. A woman of
flesh and blood could be a source of grave anxiety and bewilderment.
In stone – or in death – she could be felt as beauty pure. One could
even allow oneself to be enlaced by her absent arms.

Venus, Diana – and Jezebel! There were many kinds of women in
this world, and a man had to be on guard lest his inner feelings make
him attribute things to them that in reality were not there; for
women added to their worldly appearance embellishments, trickeries
– and treacheries – that were at the same time elegance and luxury
and civilizing attributes. When Henry James in October 1868 reviewed a trifling book entitled Modern Women in the Nation, he
disliked the aggressive tone of the writer and came to the conclusion
that it was impossible to discuss and condemn modern women apart
from modern men. Their follies were all 'part and parcel of the
follies of modern civilization'. They also reflected 'with great clearness the state of the heart and the imagination of men. When they
present an ugly picture, therefore, we think it the part of wisdom for
men to cast a glance at their own internal economy.' This was of
course what had happened to Osborne. It suggested also that women
existed as images in men's minds and as 'patient, sympathetic, submissive' creatures willing to model themselves upon those very

images. Henry James would learn to portray women not as men had fashioned them but as persons. Greater ease with them, and closer study, never banished however his primitive fear of womankind. The debate would be carried into a long novel of his middle years.

27

The Two Georges

TWO women who had both chosen to call themselves George came to occupy a large place in Henry's life and not entirely because of their assumption of the masculine identification. George Eliot and George Sand figured prominently in Henry's little library in Quincy Street, beside Browning, Balzac, Sainte-Beuve, Gautier, Taine and Goethe. Both represented for him the art of fiction practised at a fine pitch, even if at opposite poles. He had met the name of George Sand as a boy in Thackeray's *Paris Sketch Book* and had later felt that this male novelist failed to appreciate his continental confrère. He remembered also that one of Margaret Fuller's first acts on arriving in Paris had been to bring her New England presence into the drawing-room of the Lady of Nohant; the encounter apparently made a deeper impression on Margaret than on George. Henry spoke of Madame Sand as having an overwhelming glibness and as being a 'great improvisatrice'. She contributed to literature the 'ardent forces of the heart'. It was true that she often, in Henry's view, cheapened passion ('she handles it too much; she lets it too little alone'). She took too technical a view of it at times. As he outgrew her, he continued to admire her flowing style and increasingly complained of her lack of form. In his late essays he was fascinated by the revelations of her private life, while finding it difficult to justify the way in which she paraded her private affairs in print. He devoted to George Sand during all his writing years seven essays and reviews.

George Eliot became a prime influence during his young manhood; the appearance of her works coincided with the years in which Henry was launching his own works. In the autumn of 1866, after reading 'in ever so thrilled a state' the newly-published *Felix Holt*, he contributed his first signed critical article, *The Novels of George Eliot* to the *Atlantic*. 'It was by George Eliot's name,' he wrote in his memoirs, 'that I was to go on knowing, was never to cease to know, a great treasure of beauty and humanity, of applied and achieved art, a testimony, historic as well as aesthetic, to the deeper interest of the intricate English aspects.' The emphasis undoubtedly belongs on the words 'applied and achieved art'. Her plots were forced and unsatisfactory; her endings clumsy and contrived; yet in *Felix Holt* he had found 'so much power, so much brilliancy and so much discretion' that she could be forgiven the tedium of her endless expositions. He was to admire *Daniel Deronda* and *Middlemarch* even more enthusiastically. George Eliot offered much to a young man seriously concerned with the novel-form, 'a style, the secret of whose force is in the union of the tenderest and most abundant sympathies with a body of knowledge so ample and so active as to be absolutely free from pedantry'.

In this essay, in its opening words, as with his first book review, Henry James shows us how he approached fiction when he was 23. 'The critic's first duty,' he began, 'in the presence of an author's collective works is to seek out some key to his method, some utterance of his literary convictions, some indication of his ruling theory. The amount of labour involved in an inquiry of this kind will depend very much upon the author.' The writer of these words would some day write a story called *The Figure in the Carpet* and would collect his own works in conformity with a 'ruling theory'. George Eliot was an author who invited critical search for her method; unlike Dickens and Thackeray she was 'also a good deal of a philosopher; and it is to this union of the keenest observation with the ripest reflection, that her style owes its essential force'. To George Eliot he devoted five essays or reviews between 1866 and 1878, the years of her greatest influence. But he did not return to her in his old age. His *Notes on Novelists* of 1914 has two papers on Balzac, one on Flaubert and one on Zola, three on George Sand, none on the English George.

In George Eliot mind prevailed over passion; in George Sand passion prevailed over mind. Both were voluble; both tended to moralize and philosophize to an inartistic degree, but George Eliot was 'solid' and George Sand was 'liquid' – and in his early writings it was the liquid Sand that proved inspiring; as he shed his early traces of romanticism, the last strong example of which was *The American*, George Eliot became an increasingly significant source of inspiration. By the time of *The Portrait of a Lady* she had quite surpassed her French colleague. Both writers represented for Henry also aspects of femininity – the Gallic George, virtually a man, yet possessed of those qualities of soft self-assertiveness that Henry cautiously admired; the English George possessing the feminine strength he had known from childhood in his mother, his grandmother, his aunt. He was to meet George Eliot, to meet and admire her; he was never to know George Sand save in the anecdotes of his friends in Paris – Turgenev, Flaubert, Goncourt, Pauline Viardot. *They* – the two Georges – never became for him Venuses or Dianas. If George Eliot, in spite of her assumed masculine name, had the true attributes of femininity, George Sand had the 'true male inwardness' and for Henry much more masculinity than her many lovers. She was virtually a man, yet she was not – Henry observed – a gentleman!

28

The Terrible Burden

ONE day in September of 1867 in Cambridge, when Henry James was 24, he wrote a long letter to his friend Perry, who was in Paris. It began in the characteristic vein of their correspondence. Since Perry was in France, Henry must write to him in French. The opening sentences contain a brave show of subjunctives, '*J'aurais bien mieux aimé que tu m'eusses parlé de toi, que tu m'eusses donné de tes nouvelles intimes.*' Then he lapses into English. He lists his readings; he affirms that English literature is in reality a vast unexplored field, 'especially when we compare it to what the French is to the French'. In a confiding mood he writes that 'Deep in the timorous recesses of my being is a vague desire to do for our dear old English letters and writers *something* of what Sainte-Beuve and the best French critics have done for theirs.' He dismisses this promptly as an 'arrogant hope'. Yet 'at the thought of a study of this kind, on a serious scale, and of possibly having the health and time to pursue it, my eyes fill with heavenly tears and my heart throbs with divine courage'. He looks forward to Perry's return, so that they may resume their old exchange of 'feelings and ideas'. And now the young man in Quincy Street suddenly drops the banter of their friendship. The serious writer who was being published and noticed in New York and Boston begins to speak, and what he says is sufficiently remarkable. It is 'by this constant exchange and comparison, by the wear and tear of living and talking and observing that works of art shape themselves into completeness'. And then :

When I say that I should like to do as Saint-Beuve has done, I don't mean that I should like to imitate him, or reproduce him in English : but only that I should like to acquire something of his intelligence and his patience and vigour. One feels – I feel at least – that he is a man of the past, of a dead generation; and that we young Americans are (without cant) men of the future. I feel that my only chance for success as a critic is to let all the breezes of the west blow through me at their will. We are Americans born – *il faut en prendre son parti*. I look upon it as a great blessing; and I think that to be an American is an excellent preparation for culture. We have exquisite qualities as a race, and it seems to me that we are ahead of the European races in the fact that more than either of them we can deal freely with forms of civilization not our own, can pick and choose and assimilate and in short (aesthetically &c) claim our pro-perty wherever we find it. To have no national stamp has hitherto been a regret and a drawback, but I think it not unlikely that American writers may yet indicate that a vast intellectual fusion and synthesis of the various National tendencies of the world is the condition of more import-ant achievements than any we have seen. We must of course have some-thing of our own – something distinctive and homogeneous – and I take it that we shall find it in our moral consciousness, our unprecedented spiritual lightness and vigour. In this sense at least we shall have a national *cachet*. I expect nothing great during your lifetime or mine perhaps; but my instincts quite agree with yours in looking to see some-thing original and beautiful disengage itself from our ceaseless fermenta-tion and turmoil. You see I am willing to leave it a matter of instinct. God speed the day.

He had had a vision during these solitary months in Cambridge, at the end of the long summer during which he had not budged from the paternal home : with remarkable prescience he had studied his native land and looked into himself and seen the future; for it was he who would deal 'freely with forms of civilization not our own'. He was to move out into that world between worlds in which he had spent the happy years of youth, turned in two directions, prepared to let 'all the breezes of the west blow through me at their will'. The letter to Perry was the view of a cultivated American, translated into cosmopolitan terms. James was determined from the first to be an American artist, determined to discover what his native land could offer his art. At the same time his ideal was that 'vast intellectual fusion and synthesis' which was to become the melting-pot dream of later decades. What he could not foresee in the Cambridge quiet of the 1860s was the great abyss that would open up between the tight little eastern society, which was the America of Henry James, and the floodtide of immigration and the growth of the industrial mammoth that followed the Civil War.

To Charles Eliot Norton he wrote, some time later, 'Looking about for myself I conclude that the face of nature and civilization in this our country is to a certain point a very sufficient literary field. But', he added, 'it will yield its secrets only to a really *grasping* imagination. This I think Howells lacks. (Of course *I* don't!) To write well and worthily of American things one needs even more than elsewhere to be a *master*. But unfortunately one is less!' And again to the same correspondent, 'It's a complex fate, being an American, and one of the responsibilities it entails is fighting against a superstitious valuation of Europe.'

The opening pages of *Roderick Hudson* echo this. On the eve of his departure for Europe, Rowland exclaims,

It's a wretched business, this virtual quarrel of ours with our country, this everlasting impatience to get out of it. Is one's only safety in flight? This is an American day, an American landscape, an American atmosphere. It certainly has its merits, and some day when I am shivering with ague in classic Italy I shall accuse myself of having slighted them.

James was not to slight the America of his young manhood. His Cambridge years were filled with close and studious observation of the life around him. Van Wyck Brooks told us that James admitted to being 'at sea' about his native land. But Brooks was arguing that Henry James had no native land. What the novelist really said was that 'it was a joke, polished with much use, that I was dreadfully at sea about my native land'. The joke arose among those who could not understand that the novelist chose a cosmopolitan path; it lay closest to his experience and furnished him with the richest material for his fiction. Henry was at sea, however, when it came to the country of Bret Harte or Mark Twain. In New York or Boston or rural New England, where all his early stories are set, he was in safe anchorage. He did not attempt to write of Europe until he could see it with adult eyes. His first thirteen tales – those to which he signed his name – deal exclusively with his homeland. He confined himself to the people of his particular world in America, those who lived the leisured cultivated life of Newport and Boston. His characters were either rich young men, dilettantes, artists, doctors, lawyers, unhappy Civil War veterans from the middle class, young heiresses, and in one instance a young gentleman farmer. He believed then, as he did all his life, that the writer must create out of 'lived' experience. He was to be accused in a later era of journalism of 'turning his back' upon whole areas of American life. Henry James was as incapable of writing of Howells's world, or Melville's, as Howells and Melville were of his. Distinctly an urban dweller, a product of the streets and squares of many cities, he could speak for the cities of the east. His first novel, *Watch and Ward*, was set in Boston; later in the Balzac–Zola manner he 'did' the city in a full-length work. The America and Americans he observed during the ten years between his adolescent return from Europe and his later journeys abroad remained with him all his life. Joined to his New York boyhood, his New England years had given him well-defined roots in his native land. He was alive to the virtues and shortcomings of his countrymen; he considered himself an American artist-in-the-making – with one important difference. Unlike some of his fellow-artists, he brought to his observation the cultivated cosmopolitanism of his early years. He could not accept his Americanism lightly; he had seen the world sufficiently to take nothing in it for granted. He had spoken of his 'complex fate'; he was later to speak of it as a 'terrible burden' which no European writer had to assume.

This was a further elaboration of the ideas he had expressed in his letter to Perry as well as a defining of his own special problem. When he began his travels at 26 he went to a Europe already familiar to him. He travelled also as a young man who had spent twenty-one years – including the formative years of his childhood – in the United States.

29

A Suburban Friendship

I

HE talked of these questions, of America and Europe and of his writing, with a new-found friend during these Cambridge years – a man seven years older than himself who admired his work and encouraged it and was himself a writer freshly returned from a stay in

Italy. This was William Dean Howells, who had just moved to Cambridge to become the assistant editor of the *Atlantic Monthly*.

In later years the legend grew that it was Howells who gave Henry his start in the world of letters. It was, as with all legends, partly true. Henry himself contributed to it by writing an open letter on the occasion of Howells's 75th birthday, saying,

You held out your open editorial hand to me at the time I began to write – and I allude especially to the summer of 1866 – with a frankness and sweetness of hospitality that was really the making of me, the making of confidence that required help and sympathy and that I should otherwise, I think, have strayed and stumbled about a long time without acquiring. You showed me the way and opened me the door; you wrote to me, and confessed yourself struck with me – I have never forgotten the beautiful thrill of *that*. You published me at once – and paid me, above all, with a dazzling promptitude; magnificently, I felt, and so that nothing since has ever quite come up to it ... you talked to me and listened to me – ever so patiently and genially and suggestively conversed and consorted with me.

Howells did not give Henry his start, and in that very summer of 1866 Henry had found in the *Galaxy* a fourth journal ready to print him; but what he was saying in his generous tribute was that Howells was the first editor to take him seriously as a writer of fiction and to see that he had a future. When Howells assumed his post at the *Atlantic* two of Henry's stories had appeared in it and a third had been accepted. Howells remembered that the first Jamesian tale to reach his desk was *Poor Richard* late in 1866. 'He was then writing also for other magazines; after that I did my best to keep him for the *Atlantic*,' Howells recalled. J. T. Fields had asked Howells whether the story should be accepted, and the new editor replied, 'Yes, and all the stories you can get from the writer.' When Howells was dying in 1920 he began to set down his early recollections of Henry, and the fragment he left starts with the words,

It is not strange that I cannot recall my first meeting with Henry James, or for that matter the second or third or specifically any after meeting ... All I can say is that we seemed presently to be always meeting, at his father's house and at mine, but in the kind Cambridge streets rather than those kind Cambridge houses which it seems to me I frequented more than he. We seem to have been presently always together, and always talking of methods of fiction, whether we walked the streets by day or night, or we sat together reading our stuff to each other.

Norton and Lowell at the *North American Review* were older men; they published Henry, but could hardly become his intimates. Godkin and his staff were in New York, and Henry's relationship to the *Nation*, while close, was essentially that of a reviewer who supplies his copy and is paid for it; his relationship with the *Galaxy*, just begun, was formal. At the *Atlantic* J. T. Fields had accepted Henry James as a promising young man to be encouraged among imposing Brahmins. Now, however, William Dean Howells, himself a would-be novelist, full of the memories of his Venetian years (where he had been American Consul during the Civil War, the reward for a campaign biography of Lincoln), proved to be an editor who could also be a friend; he was young enough and close enough to Henry's generation to understand him and have deep faith in his art and his future. 'Talking of talks,' Howells wrote in December 1866 to Edmund Clarence Stedman, the New York banker-poet,

young Henry James and I had a famous one last evening, two or three hours long, in which we settled the true principles of literary art. He is a very earnest fellow, and I think him extremely gifted – gifted enough to do better than anyone has yet done towards making us a real American novel. We have in reserve from him a story for the *Atlantic* which I'm sure you'll like.

Happy time, when in three hours they could settle the true principles of literary art! The story was *Poor Richard*. After it appeared Howells wrote to Norton that an adverse notice of the tale in the *Nation* made him feel unsure of Henry's public. The *Nation* critic wondered whether a character as loutish and belligerent as Richard would have 'entertained a doubt as to his inferiority' in the presence of the two Civil War officers and the heroine. He also noted that sex in James's stories 'is not only refined but subtle – an aroma, as it were'. He recognized Henry's fondness 'for handling delicate shreds of feeling and motives in the intricate web of character'. This prompted Howells to observe that 'James has every element of success in fiction. But I suspect that he must in a great degree create his audience' – a balanced and prophetic judgement. During this period Henry was noticed briefly – but decidedly noticed – on the strength of his few magazine appearances. If *Poor Richard* was criticized by the *Nation*, the same journal welcomed Henry James's next tale, *The Story of a Masterpiece*, asserting with an enthusiasm akin to Howells's, that 'within the somewhat narrow limits to which he confines himself Mr James is ... the best writer of short stories in

America'. This for a young man with only six signed tales to his credit. 'He is never commonplace,' said the *Nation*, 'never writes without knowing what he wants to do, and never has an incident or a character that is not in some way necessary to the production of such effects as he aims at.' Howells, in an appreciation written in 1882, recognized that Henry's work 'was at once successful with all the magazines'.

2

The friendship between Howells and James, the one destined to become a distinguished editor and writer of fiction, and ultimately 'dean' of American letters, the other America's cosmopolitan novelist and an innovator in fiction, lasted all their lives. The friendship was both professional and intimate. Their correspondence of almost half a century testifies to Howells's esteem from the first for his younger contemporary and an unswerving belief in his literary powers; there is, in some of his later letters, pride in Henry James's achievement and a genuine humility and awareness of his own narrower limits. They sent each other their novels. Henry always took pains to read and discuss Howells's work – and even on occasions to borrow suggestions from it. There was an interplay of influence between the two that in neither case was very significant, since their personalities markedly differed. Henry's strictures, expressed always in the kindest terms his feeling of Howells's artistic limitations; he was candid, but in a gentle and generous way. In letters to others, of the Cambridge circle, he allowed himself freer criticism.

'I sometimes wish ... for something a little larger, – for a little more *ventilation*,' he wrote to Howells in one instance while proclaiming that 'the merit and the charm quite run away with the defect, and I have no desire but to praise, compliment and congratulate you!' When he read *A Hazard of New Fortunes* he wrote to his brother :

I have just been reading, with wonder and admiration, Howells's last big novel, which I think so prodigiously good and able and so beyond what he at one time seemed in danger of reducing himself to, that I mean to write him a gushing letter about it not a day later than tomorrow ... His abundance and facility are my constant wonder and envy – or rather not perhaps, envy, inasmuch as he has purchased them by throwing the whole question of form, style and composition overboard into the deep sea – from which, on my side, I am perpetually trying to fish them up.

On the following day he wrote his letter to Howells 'You are less *big* than Zola, but you are ever so much less clumsy and more really various, and moreover you and he don't see the same things – you have a wholly different consciousness – *you* see a totally different side of a different race.' He then launched into this passage, anticipating a much later and finer imagining of the 'house of fiction' :

The novelist is a particular *window*, absolutely – and of worth in so far as he is one; and it's because you open so well and are hung so close over the street that *I* could hang out of it all day long. Your very value is that you choose your own street – heaven forbid I should have to choose it for you. If I should say I mortally dislike the people who pass in it, I should seem to be taking on myself that intolerable responsibility of selection which it is exactly such a luxury to be relieved of. Indeed I'm convinced that no reader above the rank of an idiot – this number is moderate I admit – can really fail to take any view that's really *shown* them – any gift (of subject) that's really given. The usual imbecility of the novel is that the showing and giving simply don't come off – the reader never touches the subject and the subject never touches the reader : the window is no window at all – but only childishly *finta*, like the ornaments of our beloved Italy – this is why as a triumph of *communication*, I hold the *Hazard* so rare and strong.

The praise is subtle and confined to that which Henry could honestly praise. He is saying, ever so gently, that the novel is limited, and implying that if it is a triumph of communication it is not necessarily a triumph of art. He had, much earlier (in 1870), expressed the same feeling, and in strong terms, to Grace Norton, writing after the appearance of Howells's *Their Wedding Journey* :

Poor Howells is certainly difficult to defend, if one takes a standpoint the least bit exalted; make any serious demands and it's all up with him. He presents, I confess, to my mind, a somewhat melancholy spectacle – in that his charming style and refined intentions are so poorly and meagerly served by our American atmosphere. There is no more inspiration in an American journey than *that*! Thro' thick and thin I continue however to enjoy him – or rather thro' thin and thinner. There is a little divine spark of fancy which never quite gives out. He has passed into the stage which I suppose is the eventual fate of all secondary and tertiary talents – worked off his slender primitive capital, found a place and a routine and an income, and now is destined to fade slowly and softly away in self-repetition and reconcilement to the commonplace. But he will always be a *writer* – small but genuine. There are not so many after all now going in English – to say nothing of American.

The letters Henry James wrote to Howells are large, full, literary, expressive of the busy and lively life he led abroad. They are filled with gossip, and in later years make of Howells a counsel in publishing matters and a sympathetic adviser on questions of his literary reputation. Some of the letters are slyly humorous and filled with gentle teasing – the friend who was to sit ultimately for the portrait of Lewis Lambert Strether. It is difficult otherwise to explain the extent to which Henry James went out of his way to raise the very subjects which the *Atlantic* editor sought carefully to keep out of his magazine – and indeed his life. James is describing an afternoon at Gustave Flaubert's: 'The other day Edmond de Goncourt (the best of them) said he had been lately working very well on his novel – he had got upon an episode that greatly interested him, and into which he was going very far.' Flaubert inquired: 'What is it?' Goncourt answered: 'A whore-house *de province*.' To which Howells rejoined in his next letter he thanked God he wasn't a Frenchman.

In the following letter Henry returned to the charge. He had been visiting in Paris the supposedly illegitimate daughter of an English peer, a certain Baroness:

She lives in a queer old mouldy, musty rez-de-chaussée in the depths of the Faubourg St Germain, is the greasiest and most audacious lion-huntress in all creation, and has two most extraordinary little French emancipated daughters. One of these, wearing a Spanish mantilla and got up apparently to dance the *cachacha*, presently asked me what I thought of *incest* as a subject for a novel – adding that it had against it that it was getting, in families, so terribly common.

In still another letter, and with unconcealed delight, James reported how a mother, after reading a novel by Howells, took elaborate precautions that it should not be read by her daughter. It seemed to James a pleasant irony that a novel by a writer seeking to keep his work 'wholesome', who pleaded for happy endings and simple romantic tales, should be forbidden a *jeune fille*.

3

The friendship between James and Howells was never more intimate than during its early years, when the two young men took suburban walks on Sundays to Fresh Pond, talking of their art and their ambitions, or when they sat, as they did one November day, in the thin pale sunlight, on the edge of a hotbed of violets at the Botanical Gardens, with Howells cheerfully punching his cane into a sandy path while the talk followed a spontaneous and meandering course. Howells could talk about Italian writers and about Italy, and then refer back to his native Ohio; he had had a childhood in a log cabin and had gone to work in his father's print-shop. Henry, the young patrician, could evoke old New York, and describe his innumerable relatives and his European boyhood. Howells remembered 'a walk late in the night up and down North Avenue, and of his devoting to our joint scrutiny the character of remote branches of his family and the interest in art. They were uncles and cousins of New York origin and of that derivation which gave us their whole most interesting Celtic race.' If Howells talked of Hawthorne, whom he had met, Henry talked of Balzac and of Sainte-Beuve, whom he hadn't, but whom he had closely read. And if Henry submitted to the *Atlantic* two rather Hawthorne-like tales, we are led to suspect it was to meet Howell's preferences at this time for the romance, and not necessarily because he had himself fallen under the American novelist's influence.

George Moore once remarked that Henry James went abroad and read Turgenev while William Dean Howells stayed at home and read Henry James. The remark was unkind but in a sense true. Henry was cosmopolitan; Howells was provincial. Howells wanted above all, during his early years, to become a Boston Brahmin. On his first visit to the American Athens he had been treated with marked respect by Lowell, Fields and Holmes; the memory of that time, and of his talk with other Bostonians and the great Concordians, was kept green all his life. He was later to reach toward realism and to flirt earnestly with socialism; yet his reach had sharp limits and his flirtation was on the sentimental side. Henry had more rigorous, if more conservative standards and more dazzling aims. The Brahmins revered by Howells were fallible humans – and sometimes rather boring – to Henry, who had known some of them from his early years. If Howells reached from Ohio to Boston, Henry was reaching from Boston towards Europe. To one of the Brahmins, Henry once tersely summed up his feelings about Howells's career. Five years after meeting him, the young novelist could write – still from Quincy Street – to Charles Eliot Norton :

Howells is now monarch absolute of the *Atlantic* to the increase of his profit and comfort. His talent grows constantly in fineness but hardly, I think, in range of application. I remember your saying some time ago that in a couple of years when he had read Sainte-Beuve &c. he would come to his best. But the trouble is he never will read Sainte-Beuve, nor care to. He has little intellectual curiosity, so here he stands with his admirable organ of style, like a poor man holding a diamond and wondering how he can wear it. It's rather sad, I think, to see Americans of the younger sort so unconscious and unambitious of the commission to do the *best*. For myself the love of art and letters grows steadily with my growth.

This was not only a candid evaluation of a literary friend : it was the expression also of Henry's own ambition and passion – to do the *best*, to surpass himself, to grow, to escape from the present into the future, to take as his models in his art those who had in his time come as near attaining what he deemed to be perfection. Henry was supremely confident that, when *he* found himself holding the diamond of his style and art he would know what to do with it.

BOOK TWO:

THE PASSIONATE PILGRIMAGE

1869–70

30

Departure

IN later years Henry James remembered how quiet the house had been when he called to say good-bye to Minny Temple. She entered the old spacious parlour in the day-time stillness with her swift sliding step and her old free laugh. He was aware that she had been ill; he did not know how seriously. She was slight, erect, thin, almost transparent. He remembered ruefully that he thought her delicate appearance 'becoming'.

The Henry James who, en route to Europe, journeyed in mid-February of 1869 to Pelham near New Rochelle to bid farewell to his cousin, was a quiet, grave young man, nearing 26, of medium height, with a brownish beard, receding hair, piercing eye and shy manner. He spoke in a well-modulated voice, without hesitancy (and without a stammer apocryphally attributed to him). He was witty and warm; his laughter was the laughter of a serious young man. He told Minny his plans. He would go to England, then to the Continent, perhaps to winter in Paris or to push southward to Italy, where he had never been. They agreed it was 'wholly detestable' that he should be voyaging off while she was staying behind. The doctors had talked to her about another climate. Rome had been mentioned. Perhaps the cousins would meet next winter in Rome. The idea charmed them.

There had always been a deep fondness between them. Minny's affection is expressed in old letters to friends and relatives, as when from Newport she writes, at 18 'I found dear old Henry here; he had come from Cambridge for a day or two *expressly* to see *me*, which renders me quite happy.' And again, 'Harry is as lovely as ever, verily the goodness of that boy passeth human understanding.'

They talked. She did not speak of her illness. Henry asked her whether she was getting enough sleep. 'Sleep,' she cried, 'oh, I don't sleep. *I've given it up.*' He remembered how she laughed at her little joke. They talked of writers. Minny had come to have 'an overpowering admiration and affection' – so she said – for George Eliot. Did Harry intend to meet her? Would he give her Minny's love? She would like very much to see that woman. Henry remembered

the toss of Minny's head, the 'bright extravagance of her envy', and
the amount of laughter that contributed to 'as free a disclosure of
the handsome largish teeth that made her mouth almost the main
fact of her face'. They parted gaily. Perhaps they *would* see each
other soon abroad. He would write.

'Harry came to see me before he sailed for Europe,' Minny wrote
to John Gray.

I am very glad that he has gone, although I don't expect to see him
again in a good many years. I do not think he will come back for a long
time. I hope it will do him good, and that he will enjoy himself, which
he hasn't done for several years, I think.

31

The Banquet of Initiation

CAMBRIDGE – and America – were finally behind him. He was to
have a new vision of Europe: the old, the boyhood memories had
turned grey, like faded ink. He was now making a fresh beginning.
As he looked over the wintry sea from the deck of the S.S. *China* –
it had put out from New York some ten days before, on 17 February
1869 – he could see the 'strange, dark lonely freshness' of the coast
of Ireland, homeland of his Albany grandfather. Then the black
steamers were knocking about in the yellow Mersey under a low sky
that almost touched their funnels. There was the promise of spring in
the air and 'the solemnity of an opening era'. He was, in a sense,
retracing ancestral footsteps – those of his grandfather and of his
father; even more he was about to retrace the footsteps of a small
boy who had seen and remembered so much and had dreamed he
would one day return.

I

He stepped ashore at Liverpool on a windy, cloudy, smoky day,
Saturday, 27 February. By the time he had brought his luggage to the
Adelphi Hotel in a hansom, it was two o'clock. In the deserted
coffee-room he drank his tea and ate his boiled egg and toasted
muffin, folding and re-folding the crisp copy of *The Times*, much
too excited to notice its contents. The damp dark light floated in

from the steep street; a coal fire glowed in the room's obscurity. The waiter who hovered attentively about him in full dress was a familiar figure. He had met him in Dickens, in Thackeray, in Smollett. There was a singular permanence to the memories of his childhood. 'The impressions of my boyhood return from my own past and swarm about my soul,' he wrote home a few hours after his arrival. 'I enjoy these first hours of landing most deeply.' The sense of change 'lies with a most comfortable weight on my soul'. Ten years had elapsed since the autumn morning when he had looked out of the window of the Hôtel des Trois Empereurs by the Louvre and bade farewell from its balcony to the Second Empire and to Europe.

He slept deeply that night, exhausted by his voyage, the excitement of arrival and the afternoon in Liverpool. He had planned to go to Chester on Sunday, but he overslept. When he arose he found he had missed the only train. The rain was coming down monotonously upon the gloomy shut-up city; the prospect of spending the day in Liverpool was unattractive. Henry snatched a hurried breakfast and caught the London train. It was a slow Sunday train. As it proceeded southward the weather lifted and Henry studied the land from his window as best he could while a solicitous Englishman in the same compartment, discovering that he was an American, volunteered information and counsel from which the bored young traveller finally escaped by feigning sleep. This, however, deprived him of the scenery. The train pulled into Euston station at dusk and Henry engaged a four-wheeler into which his luggage was piled. As he rode through the town to Morley's Hotel in Trafalgar Square, a hostelry recommended by his loquacious fellow-traveller, he was struck by the 'low black houses like so many rows of coal scuttles and as inanimate' and the occasional flare of light from the pubs. He found Morley's dingy enough, although his later description tended to coat the dinginess with glamour. 'What terrible places are these English hotels!' he exclaimed in a letter to his mother that evoked nostalgically the comforts of Boston's Parker House. There was, however, a warm fire in the coffee-room of Morley's Hotel and the heavy mahogany furniture gleamed in its light. In his room the large four-poster bed was lit up luridly by the bedroom candle, stuck in its deep basin. The shadows and silence made him think of *The Ingoldsby Legends*. To his mother he complained about the musty bedroom, the twopenny candle, the absence of gaslight. For the moment he felt homesick, as no doubt he was, although he may have been exaggerating for the benefit of Quincy Street. For the mood passed quickly enough. He sallied forth early next morning, purchased a pair of gloves, went down to the City, probably to take care of his letter of credit, and 'all history appeared to live again'. As he passed under Temple Bar and looked at the statue of Queen Anne on Ludgate Hill, lines from *Esmond* came into his mind. He took a memorable walk along the Strand – it lived for him forever after, like the famous boyhood walk from the Louvre to the Luxembourg – and old pages out of *Punch*, old drawings out of the *Illustrated London News*, came alive on all sides. He stopped at Mr Rimmel's establishment, and never quite forgot the scent of the particular hair-wash he bought that day from a slim, smiling young lady. He paused before the granite portico of Exeter Hall; he dallied before the shop-windows, resisting the temptation to buy everything. London, old and new, the city of boyhood memory, and of history, and of mid-Victorian reality, assumed an air of magnificence, a grand tone it was ever to have for him in spite of its slums and squalor, its dirt and darkness. 'The place sits on you, broods on you, stamps on you with the feet of its myriad bipeds and quadrupeds,' he wrote to his sister. He imagined it as a great Goliath, and this suggests that he must have thoughts of himself as a young David. He was to conceive of cities, and London in particular, as places to be besieged, conquered, possessed. He was to speak also of London as a great grey Babylon, and at the end of his life, he planned to write a brooding book about it; it fascinated him as did no other city in Europe. It was to become his home for twenty crowded years and a place of return for two decades after that. He was crushed at first under a sense of 'its inconceivable immensity'. He was to see it as 'a dreadful, delightful city', more delightful, however, than dreadful.

Charles Eliot Norton was in London with his wife and his sisters Grace and Jane. Norton introduced Henry to a young Englishman named Albert Rutson, who worked in the Home Office. Rutson told him there were furnished rooms available below those he occupied himself, and introduced him to his landlord, Lazarus Fox, a pensioned retainer of the Rutson family. Within three or four days of his arrival in London, Henry had transported his luggage from Morley's to No. 7 Half Moon Street, just off Piccadilly. He had dark rooms on the ground floor decorated with lithographs and wax flowers. He could hear the din at the end of the street, and as he stared into the fire 'a sudden horror of the whole place came over me, like a tiger-pounce of homesickness'. His rooms seemed 'an impersonal black hole in the huge general blackness'. London appeared 'hideous, vicious, cruel and above all overwhelming'. For a moment a grim fantasy of decay and death came to him, 'I would rather remain dinnerless, would rather even starve than sally forth into the infernal town, where the natural fate of an obscure stranger would be to be trampled to death in Piccadilly and his carcass thrown into the Thames.' He discharged this sense of powerlessness in the face of London into a letter to his mother, his feelings oscillating between lugubrious homesickness and the relish of his picturesque surroundings. He wished he were in Quincy Street 'with my head on mother's lap and my feet in Alice's!' However, he is soon lost in a description of his journey, the search for rooms, his encounters with landladies, 'hard-faced, garrulous ravening creatures encrusted with a totally indescribable greasy dingy dowdiness!' and finally his discovery of Mr Lazarus Fox.

My landlord is a very finished specimen and I wish you could see him. He is an old servant of some genteel family, who lets out his three floors to gentlemen and waits upon them with the most obsequious punctuality. He does everything for me – won't let me raise a finger for myself – is butler, landlord, valet, guide, philosopher and friend all at once. I am completely comfortable, save that his tremendous respectability and officiousness are somewhat oppressive. Nevertheless, in this matter of lodgings, esteem me most happy and fortunate.

Mr Fox was to be immortalized in the opening pages of the unfinished memoir *The Middle Years*.

Henry may have feared at first to venture out for dinner into the dark and forbidding streets of Victorian London, but presently, at the recommendation of Mr Fox, he found himself resorting with some regularity to the Albany – the name could not have been a happier one for the grandson of the first William James – a small eating-house in Piccadilly. It is incorporated into the opening pages of *A Passionate Pilgrim*, where it figures as *The Red Lion*. It had small compartments as narrow as horse-stalls, and the feeders sat against the high straight backs of the wooden benches so close to one another that they seemed to be waving their knives and forks under their respective noses as they ate their mutton chops. It was a primitive place, full of life and aspects that reminded him of the London of Boswell or Smollett and, we might add, Hogarth. Every face in the establishment was a documentary scrap, every sound was strong to the ear, and the scene that greeted him there was as definite as some of the Dutch paintings of low life.

Henry explored London strenuously from the first. A shipmate on the *China* had warmly urged him to go to Craven Street for lodgings. He was curious enough to inspect the quarter 'for atmosphere', and obtained an abundance of it. The effect of Craven Street 'was that it absolutely reeked, to my fond fancy, with associations born of the particular ancient piety embodied in one's private altar to Dickens ... the whole Dickens procession marched up and down, the whole Dickens world looked out of its queer, quite sinister windows'. It was the 'socially sinister' Dickens and the 'socially encouraging or confoundingly comic' which had significance for Henry here. Craven Street, with its dead end on the Thames, was packed 'to blackness with accumulations of suffered experience'. The future author of *The Princess Casamassima*, relishing the picturesque and the sense of the past, could open his eyes wide to the sinister aspects of the great Babylon as well.

2

The first phase of Henry's pilgrimage was in the fullest degree, as he put it, 'a banquet of initiation'. If his senses fed on London, he also discovered how sociable England could be when it is host to a cultivated young American provided with unusual credentials. With Norton's aid great personalities proved readily accessible. 'For one's self,' he noted forty years later, 'there all-conveniently had been doors that opened – opened into light and warmth and cheer, into good and charming relations.' The note of hospitality was struck with great promptness in his own lodging when young Rutson invited Henry to breakfast with him upstairs. There the American discovered a fellow-guest, the Hon. George Brodrick, son of Lord Midleton, like Rutson bewhiskered in the Victorian fashion; both were well-turned out by their tailors; they were charming, interested, curious. They ate fried sole and marmalade and seemed to know more about American politics than Henry. They questioned him closely about Grant's new Cabinet – the President having taken office at the beginning of that year – and Henry was at a loss to identify its members and to offer any tidbits of American political intelligence. He was distinctly more in his element when, two or three days after settling in his lodgings, Leslie Stephen, then 37, called to invite him to lunch on the following day, a Sunday. They had met originally in the home of Mr and Mrs Fields, in Boston. Stephen was a fellow contributor to the *Nation*; he wrote a fortnightly London letter. Jane Norton also was a guest. In the afternoon Stephen took his American visitors by the London underground to the Zoo in Regent's Park. In the evening Henry dined with the Nortons, and although tired out by the day's sociabilities, went with them, again by underground, to University College, to hear John Ruskin lecture on Greek myths. Three days later he dines once more with the Nortons, and meets Miss Dickens, the novelist's only unmarried daughter. The next day is memorable. He breakfasts – still with the Nortons – and meets Aubrey de Vere, the Catholic poet, who tells good stories 'in a light natural way'. He rests at home for a few hours, then joins Norton in Bloomsbury, and they go to call on William Morris. He is filled with curiosity : he has reviewed Morris's *The Life and Death of Jason* and *The Earthly Paradise* within the last year and a half, and feels him to be 'a supremely healthy writer' and 'a noble and delightful poet'. In the house in Queen Square he finds Morris, short, burly, corpulent, carelessly dressed, loud-voiced, with a nervous, restless manner and a business-like way of speaking. He says no one thing that Henry can remember, yet all he utters shows good judgement. Henry examines his handiwork – tiles, medieval tapestry, altar cloths – 'quaint, archaic, pre-Raphaelite' and exquisite. Above all he is enchanted by Morris's wife. 'Oh ma chère,' he writes to Alice, 'such a wife ! *Je n'en reviens pas* – she haunts me still.' She is a figure 'cut out of a missal – or out of one of Rossetti's or Hunt's pictures'. And when such a figure puts on flesh and blood she becomes 'an apparition of fearful and wonderful intensity'. 'Imagine,' Henry tells Alice,

a tall lean woman in a long dress of some dead purple stuff, guiltless of hoops (or of anything else, I should say) with a mass of crisp black hair heaped into great wavy projections on each of her temples, a thin pale face, a pair of strange sad, deep dark Swinburnian eyes, with great thick black oblique brows, joined in the middle and tucking themselves away under her hair, a mouth like the 'Oriana' in our illustrated Tennyson, a long neck without any collar, and in lieu thereof some dozen strings of outlandish beads – in fine complete.

They stay to dinner. Then Mrs Morris, suffering from a toothache, stretches out on the sofa with a handkerchief over her face while Morris reads an unpublished poem about Bellerophon from the second series of *The Earthly Paradise*. 'Morris reading in his flowing antique numbers a legend of prodigies and terrors ... around is all the picturesque bric-à-brac of the apartment ... and in the corner this dark silent medieval woman with her medieval toothache.' Thus was fixed in Henry's memory a corner of the pre-Raphaelite world; later he glimpsed another corner, Rossetti's studio, in 'the most delicious melancholy old house at Chelsea'. Henry regarded him as more poet than painter. He told La Farge he found the painter personally unattractive – 'I suppose he was horribly bored!' His pictures were 'all large, fanciful portraits of women ... narrow, special, monotonous, but with lots of beauty and power'. His chief model, Henry noted, was Mrs Morris. Henry also met during this time Edward Burne-Jones, destined later to become a warm friend.

A few days after meeting Morris, he dined at Denmark Hill with the great defender of the pre-Raphaelites, John Ruskin. To his mother he described him as 'scared back by the grim face of reality into the world of unreason and illusion', adding, 'he wanders there without a compass and a guide – or any light save the fitful flashes of his beautiful genius'. The young Henry was not overawed by the famous; the note-taker and the evaluator, the critical faculty, functioned as he made his way from dinner-table to dinner-table. Again at Ruskin's, it was the women-folk who interested him, Ruskin's two nieces, one a young Irish girl with 'a rich virginal brogue' and the other a Scotch lass. Even more than the nieces, 'I confess, cold-blooded villain that I am, that what I most enjoyed was a portrait by Titian – an old Doge, a work of transcendent beauty and elegance such as to give one a new sense of the meaning of art.' He was also shown his Turners and 'a beautiful Tintoret'.

He dines once more with the Nortons, and meets Frederic Harrison of the *Fortnightly Review*. He is always dining at the Nortons, not so much because of Norton himself, who tends to be over-protective and quasi-paternal, but because the Norton women are friendly and congenial. During his first days in London, he calls on his father's friend Dr Wilkinson, in the old remembered St John's Wood surroundings, and finds him a remarkable talker. For old times' sake he journeys to Brighton to see Wilkinson's daughter, Mary, named after his mother, now Mrs Florence Mathews. She had been one of his playmates during his boyhood days in St John's Wood. He visits the British Museum to see the Elgin Marbles 'the only thing to look at' for 'they vulgarize everything else'. Keats is in his mind. 'Had I the pen of an immortal bard I would comment with a Sonnet.' He visits the Kensington Museum and on a grey raw day he takes the penny steamer and rides on the Thames. He goes to Hampton Court and Windsor, Richmond and Dulwich; he walks on Hampstead Heath and Putney Common; he inspects towers and temples and cathedrals; he strolls endlessly through the National Gallery. 'I admire Raphael; I enjoy Rubens; but I passionately love Titian,' he reports to William. His *Bacchus and Ariadne* is 'one of the great facts' of the universe. One afternoon, as he studies the painting, he becomes aware that a little gentleman is talking vivaciously with another gentleman beside him – the little man with astonishing auburn hair 'perched on a scarce perceptible body' whom Henry promptly recognizes (having had a picture of him in Quincy Street) is the author of *Atalanta in Calydon*. 'I thrilled ... with the prodigy of this circumstance that I should be admiring Titian in the same breath with Mr Swinburne – that is in the same breath in which *he* admired Titian and in which I also admired *him*.'

3

He was in the 'best of health and spirits', he wrote to his mother after a month of this busy London life. He was exaggerating somewhat to assuage maternal concern; in reality, he had begun to suffer from a recurrent and debilitating costiveness which troubled him throughout his stay in Europe. He had suffered from it in America, but he now attributed it to over-indulgence at London eating-houses. In deference to his sluggish condition he went, in early April, to Malvern and took up residence in the therapeutic establishment of Dr Raynor, a medical man who affected a black velvet coat and an oily beard, but who inspired confidence. Dr Raynor's regimen consisted of a cold bath on rising, a walk to 'get up a reaction', breakfast at 8.30, another bath at noon, followed by another reactionary walk. Dinner was at two, and at five Henry took a running sitz-bath. Tea was at seven; and early bedtime was prescribed.

In the establishment Henry found himself in the company of a group of plain, civil, amiable if rather inarticulate Britons who read the *Telegraph* and the *Standard* by day and played cards by night; among them were several Indian Army officers with yellow faces and declining livers, a fox-hunting clergyman and a gentlemanly and indifferent squire. The baths do not seem to have been particularly helpful, and Henry enjoyed most of all the walks over the sloping pastures of the Malvern hills, 'a compendium of the general physiognomy of England'. It was April and the whole land had burst into spring.

The young man put into his pocket, as he walked to get his 'reactions', a rectangular sketch-book; for the first time since his Newport days with La Farge, he sketched hills and trees and spreading willows. He continued to sketch after leaving Malvern: there is a pleasant scene, drawn with hasty semi-professional strokes, of English field and stream and a distant Norman tower in which the austere chill of early spring is suggested. It is dated 'Near Tewkesbury, Gloucestershire, April 8 p.m. '69'. Another, drawn with some attention to architectural detail, is marked 'Old houses at Tewkesbury opposite Swan Inn where I supped'. A letter to William completes the picture: 'I took tea in a dark little parlour in the old Inn ... as I consumed my bread and butter and Ale, tried to sketch in the twilight one of the romantic, strangely tempered dwellings opposite.'

Henry spent three comparatively sedentary weeks at Malvern and then decided that what he really needed was 'plain physical movement'. He wrote to his father that he believed 'a certain amount of regular lively travel would do me more good than any further treatment or further repose'. He accordingly embarked on a tour of the England of valiant deeds in arms, the England of the old religion and the England of literature and scholarship. He visited Raglan Castle, Monmouth, Tintern Abbey and Chepstow; he went to Worcester by coach, to Gloucester and to Newport; he spent a day at Tewkesbury. He visited Salisbury and Ely, Blenheim and Winchester. At Oxford, bearing letters from Leslie Stephen and the Nortons, he dined in Hall at Christ Church, and at Lincoln was the guest of the rector, Mark Pattison, whom he described as a desiccated old scholar 'torpid even to incivility with too much learning', and his young wife, who was in riding-habit and, Henry believed, 'highly emancipated' and inclined to use slang of which Henry disapproved. The well-known Pattison, who would figure in later novels (not least as the possible 'original' of Casaubon in *Middlemarch*) and his young wife, offered James a distinct spectacle 'the dark rich scholastic old dining room in the college court, the languid old rector and his pretty little wife'. But he wondered whether an English woman could be emancipated 'except coldly and wantonly'. He found the evening 'slow'. A. Vernon Harcourt, tutor in chemistry, was his main Oxford guide. James dined in hall at Christ Church, quaffing strong ale from a silver tankard. Deeply stirred alike by their architecture, their quiet and their summer-term beauty, he wandered through the Oxford colleges, experiencing emotions that were to spill over into the vehement outbursts of Clement Searle in *A Passionate Pilgrim*. 'The whole place,' he wrote to William, 'gives me a deeper sense of English life than anything yet.' He lingered by New College's ancient wall; he spent a dreaming hour or two in St John's spacious garden; he walked in Christ Church meadow; Magdalen's eight-spired tower was 'the perfect prose of the Gothic'; the doorways of the colleges were monkish, the green quadrangles noble and hospitable. Oxford was 'a kind of dim and sacred ideal of the Western intellect -- a scholastic city, an appointed home of contemplation'. Yet he found strange imagery for it – touched by a mildly erotic note; the plain walls of the street-fronts suggested that the colleges were 'seraglios of culture and leisure' – they 'irritated' the fancy like the blank harem-walls of Eastern towns. In the college gardens, Henry wrote, he wanted to lie on the grass 'in the happy belief the world is all an English garden and time a fine old English afternoon'.

4

The little English tour lasted three weeks, after which Henry returned to London. Writing to Quincy Street, he reported his improved health and mentioned, among other things, that the trip had cost him £60 – a largish sum for a somewhat limited journey. Quincy Street was startled and disturbed. William promptly wrote on behalf of the elder Henry to say that 'it seems a pity to let such a sum go in a single escapade'. Drawing upon his own comparatively frugal experiences in Germany, he urged Henry to proceed to that country, where there was a 'really classical and cosmopolitan literature, compared to which French and English both seem in very important respects provincial'. The proposal was hardly to his brother's taste. Henry James had not gone abroad without a plan : he wanted to travel, he wanted to learn more about art, and he was determined to visit Italy. He hoped that in the process his health would continue to mend. He answered William that doubtless Germany would be beneficial to him but he had no desire to settle down and be a student : a life of movement in Europe seemed the best prescription for health and education. Still, he was worried lest his parents should

...nink him improvident. He accordingly wrote a long and troubled letter to his father.

To have you think that I am extravagant with these truly sacred funds sickens me to the heart and I hasten insofar as I may reassure you ... I have now an impression amounting almost to a conviction that if I were to travel steadily for a year I would be a good part of a well man ... As to the expenses of my journey, in telling that tale about the £60 I acted on gross misinformation. I was circulated for nearly three weeks and spent less than £25, seeing a very great deal on it. I am obliged, of course, on account of the seats, to travel first class. My constant aim is to economize and make my funds minister, not to my enjoyment – which may take care of itself – it wasn't assuredly for that I came hither – but to my plain physical improvement, for which alone I live and move ... I can't bear to have you fancy I may make light of your generosity.

He had spent during his eleven weeks in England £120, distributed among five weeks in London, three at an expensive water-cure and three in travelling. It covered the purchase of considerable clothing and articles of permanent use, but 'very little trivial, careless or random expenditure' except perhaps a large amount of cab-hire. 'I have treated you to this financial budget,' he added, 'as a satisfaction to myself rather than because I suppose you expect it.' He reminded his parents he was inclined to take his responsibilities 'too hard rather than too easy', and that he did not want his enjoyment of travel to be diminished by 'constant self-torturing as to expense'. In a word, he wanted a little more family faith in his ability to act responsibly.

This letter does not seem wholly to have satisfied Henry's mother. 'I was slightly disappointed,' he wrote to William,

at mother's reply in her last to my remarks about going to Scotland and at her apparent failure to suspect that it was not as a spree but as part of an *absolute remedy* that I thought of the journey ... That she should have thought it necessary to place a veto on my proposition, nevertheless proves the necessity of my thus defining my situation.

He defined his situation as a need to lay the foundations for an education in the great works of painting and sculpture 'which may be of future use to me'. He also had to make the most of the opportunity to visit the great cities and historic places on the Continent. This was no time for him to settle down to reading and study. He was now 26, and there would be time enough for that later. 'I shall hang on to a place till it has yielded me its drop of life-blood,' he said, explaining his artist's quest for the spirit of place. 'I promise you there shall be a method in my madness. In this way I hope to get a good deal for my money and to make it last a long time. How long I know not. When it is gone I shall come home,' and he added, 'a new man.'

Henry asked William not to read this letter to the family, but to use it as guide to his philosophy of travel. 'I feel,' he reiterated, 'that it is in my power to "do" any place quietly, as thoroughly as it can be done ... I have established it as an Absolute Certainty that I can't sit and read and between sitting and standing I know of no middle state.' He still had £867 in his letter of credit.

I want father and mother to write and say that they understand and approve my representations. They cannot overestimate my perfect determination to spend my money only as wisely as it was generously given and any future use I make of it will give me tenfold greater satisfaction for receiving beforehand some slight propulsion from them.

He added: 'I have no right to concern myself with what lies *au delà* this season of idleness: my present business – strange destiny! – is simply to be idle. I shall have no plans but from month to month.' Having called for a blessing on his plans, Henry lost no time in carrying them out.

5

He kept his promise to Minny Temple. 'I was much interested in your account of George Eliot,' she wrote to him during the summer of 1869. This particular account has not survived. There is another, however, written for Henry's father, of 10 May 1869, which records the impression the novelist made on him.

She is magnificently ugly – deliciously hideous. She has a low forehead, a dull grey eye, a vast pendulous nose, a huge mouth full of uneven teeth and a chin and jawbone *qui n'en finissent pas* ... Now in this vast ugliness resides a most powerful beauty which, in a very few minutes, steals forth and charms the mind, so that you end as I ended, in falling in love with her. Yes behold me literally in love with this great horse-faced bluestocking. I don't know in what the charm lies, but it is a thoroughly potent, an admirable physiognomy – a delightful expression, a voice soft and rich as that of a counselling angel – a mingled sagacity and sweetness – a broad hint of a great underlying world of reserve, knowledge, pride and power – a great feminine dignity and character in these massively plain features – a hundred conflicting shades of consciousness and simpleness – shyness and frankness – graciousness and remote indifference – these are some of the more definite elements of her personality. Her manner is extremely good tho' rather too intense and her speech, in the way of accent and syntax peculiarly agreeable. Altogether, she has a larger circumference than any woman I have ever seen.

On this first occasion, although agitated over the illness of one of G. H. Lewes's sons, she was still cordial and communicative. She talked of a recent trip to the south of France, the mistral, Avignon, the frequency in those foreign parts of 'evil faces; oh the evil faces'. George Eliot, in her black silk dress and lace mantilla attached to her head with the low-falling thickness of her dark hair, was 'illustratively' great – there was grace in her anxiety that day and 'a frank immediate appreciation of our presence'. He counted it the 'one marvel' of his stay in London – that he should have been admitted to her distinguished presence.

32

The Dishevelled Nymph

ENGLAND, he wrote to his family, had been 'a good married matron'. Switzerland, where he spent the summer, was a 'magnificent man'. Italy, which he reached late in the autumn of 1869, he found to be a 'beautiful dishevelled nymph'. He would take up his residence with the matron; but at regular intervals all his life he would pursue the dishevelled nymph.

I

In mid-May Henry crossed the Channel to re-discover the Continent. Boulogne looked as if he had left it yesterday, only it seemed much smaller. The Grand Hotel in Paris, where he stayed for a day while waiting for the train to Switzerland, was 'a complication of terrors'. He enjoyed the magnificence of the boulevards; they were too monumental and certainly, for Henry's Cambridge taste, over-lit at night. Too much 'flare and glare'. *Napoléon a tué la nuit*, he complained, adapting Hugo. Between noon and night Henry visited the Salon and strolled through the eternal Louvre. 'Oh the tumult and the splendour,' he exclaimed to his mother, 'the headlong race for pleasure – and the stagnant gulf of misery to be seen in two great capitals like London and Paris. Mankind seems like the bedevilled herd of swine in the Bible, rushing headlong into the sea.' Here spoke the voice of New England, through Henry, perhaps with a distant echo of grandfatherly Calvinism.

After this, Switzerland was calm, cool, quiet. Geneva was still the city of his youth. Henry took long walks over familiar boyhood paths, visiting Coppet, with its memories of Madame de Staël and the Ferney of Voltaire. He walked to Vevey to call on the ubiquitous Nortons, who were staying there, and he renewed acquaintance with the Castle of Chillon, to which Daisy Miller was to make her lively excursion a decade later. For a time he settled at Glion in a hotel-*pension* on the mountainside, above the castle. Finding him-self fit and strong, he began to tramp through Switzerland, as he had done in his youth. 'I feel,' he wrote to William, who was still ailing at home, 'as if every walk I take is a burning and shining light for your encouragement.' This was on 12 July 1869, when he was at Scheidegg. A month later at Lucerne he was glowing with a sense of well-being. 'The only thing worth now putting into words is just what I can't – the deep satisfaction in being able to do all this healthy trudging and climbing. It *is* – it *is* a pledge, a token of some future potency – Amen!'

His mother continued to caution him against extravagance, preaching economy alike in money and expenditure of physical resources. She now suggested that perhaps a winter in Paris, or even Germany, as William urged, might be more frugal (and sensible) than a winter of 'recreation' in Italy. Mary James had a way of putting forward such suggestions to her sons, tentatively yet firmly, and arousing in them a conflict of obedience; having decided on one course Henry was put in the position of having to rebuff his mother.

I duly noted your injunction to spend the summer quietly and econom-ically. I hope to do both – or that is to circulate in so far as I do, by the inexpensive vehicle of my own legs ... When you speak of your own increased expenses etc., I feel very guilty and selfish in entertaining any projects which look in the least like extravagance. My beloved mother, if you but knew the purity of my motives ... the only economy for me is to get thoroughly well and into such a state as that I can work ... A winter in Italy ... will help me on further than anything else I know of.

And he went on to say that in thinking of the proposed Italian sojourn as an occasion not only of physical regeneration but of serious culture too (culture of the kind which alone I have now at 26 any time left for) I find the courage to maintain my proposition even in the face of your allusions to the need of economy at home. It takes a very honest conviction thus to plead the cause of apparently gross idleness against such grave and touching facts. I have trifled so long with my trouble that I feel as if I could afford now to be a little brutal. My lovely mother, if ever I am restored to you sound and serviceable, you will find that you have not cast the pearls of your charity before a senseless beast, but before a creature with a soul to be grateful and a will to act.

Mary James, following her characteristic pattern, went to an opposite extreme. 'Take the fullest liberty and enjoyment your tastes and inclinations crave, and we will promise heartily to foot the bill. Italy will be just the place for you; and do not, I pray you, cramp yourself in any way to hinder your fullest enjoyment of it.'

2

By mid-August, at Lucerne, he had had his fill of Switzerland. 'What was Switzerland after all? Little else but brute nature, of which at home we have enough and to spare. What we seek in Europe is Nature refined and transmuted to art. In Switzerland what a pale historic setting; what a penury of relics and monuments! I pined for a cathedral or a gallery.' Thus muses his narrator in a story written shortly afterwards which catalogues his life at Lucerne.

One morning, at the beginning of September, he marked his luggage Milan and took the steamboat at Lucerne. He approached Italy across the Alps partly by coach and partly on foot. It was three years before the St Gothard tunnel was carved through the mountain and almost forty before the Simplon. Henry crossed the granite bridge over the Reuss and the Devil's Bridge high on the long monotonous St Gothard road. He tramped from Brieg over the Simplon up the Swiss side and down over the winding highway thirty-three miles to the frontier town of Isella and into Italy, 'warm and living and palpable', the Italy of the Romantics. 'If I could only write as I might talk I should have no end of things to tell you about my last days in Switzerland and especially my descent of the Alps,' he wrote to William a few days later, 'that mighty summer's day upon the Simplon when I communed with immensity and sniffed Italy from afar. This Italian tone of things which I then detected lies richly on my soul and gathers increasing weight.'

From home there came another missive. 'Since your last let. darling Harry,' wrote his mother,

I have had a new anxiety awakened in my too susceptible mind by thinking of you traversing alone those mountain solitudes. Of course I know you would not attempt any dizzy heights or any but well beaten tracks without a guide. But you might easily overestimate your strength and sink down with sudden exhaustion.

By the time Henry received this he was deep in Italy.

He felt he could never absorb and appropriate Italy as he had appropriated London and Oxford, and indeed all England, where he had felt himself breathing the air of home. His impressions were new and he had a sense of strangeness in that land where the late summer lingered in the north and the soft landscape wrapped him in quiet enchantment. He could not surrender completely to the 'Spirit of the South', but 'I nevertheless *feel* it in all my pulses'. And again, 'How beautiful a thing this month in Italy has been, and how my brain swarms with pictures and my bosom with memories.' He came to Maggiore and Como, and paused at the Hôtel Belle-Ville at Cadenabbia on Como's shore, 'the pink villas gleaming through their shrubberies of orange and oleander, the mountains shimmering in the hazy light like so many breasts of doves, the constant presence of the melodious Italian voice'.

From Cadenabbia Henry wrote a long letter to Alice, describing his walk into Italy. Imbedded in its pages there is a brief remark about his art, provoked by his sister's praise of the three-part tale of *Gabrielle de Bergerac*, which appeared that summer in the *Atlantic*. The story is laid in France before the French Revolution; it anticipated his re-discovery of Europe and now it struck him as 'amusingly thin and watery – I mean as regards its treatment of the Past'.

Since coming abroad and seeing relics, monuments, &c.. I've got a strong sense of what a grim old deathly reality it was, and how little worth one's while it is to approach it with a pen unless your mind is *bourré* with facts on the subject – how little indeed it is worth while at all to treat it imaginatively ... The present and the immediate future seem to me the best province of fiction – the latter especially – the future to which all our actual modern tendencies and leanings seem to build a sort of material pathway.

He was never again to write directly of the past. What he did try to describe was the *sense* of the past in men and women of the present.

3

He is in Milan, in the brooding heat, before Leonardo's *Last Supper*. 'I have looked at no other picture with an emotion equal to that which rose within me as this great creation of Leonardo slowly began to dawn upon my intelligence from the tragical twilight of its ruin.' The soul of the *Cenacolo* nevertheless survived ruin. He is moved almost as much by Raphael's *Marriage of the Virgin* in the Brera. He goes to the Certosa of Pavia, the Carthusian monastery south of Milan; he will visit many monasteries, wherever he finds them, to capture the spirit of quiet and retreat within them, to sit in their cloister out of the sun and meditate. And then, unhurried, he turns the pages of Italy's early history ... Brescia, Verona, Mantua, Padua, Vicenza, a chain of towns constituting his avenue to Venice, shabby, deserted, dreary, unclean, into which the sun pours fiercely, dead little towns yet how full of the past! how sentiment and passion had blossomed there! Henry James sat in the cafés and walked about with his Murray and his Baedeker – and in his pocket *La Chartreuse de Parme*. He is reading Stendhal for the first time, 'a capital observer and a good deal of a thinker'. In his later notes on Italian scenes he sprinkles such phrases as 'a feast of facts à la Stendhal' and 'innumerable anecdotes à la Stendhal'. At Verona he sits in the Caffè Dante in the Piazza dei Signori eating ices and chatting with his neighbours: three nights running he comes here to linger until midnight, experiencing the scene: the slender brick campanile, the white statue of Dante, the ancient palace – wherever he turns in Italy he finds 'a vital principle of grace', whether it is in the smile of a chambermaid or the curve of an arch. The palaces are old and faded, 'but the ghost of a graceful aristocracy treads at your side and does the melancholy honours of the abode with a dignity that brooks no sarcasm'. Art and piety here have been 'blind, generous instincts'. And at every step he feels 'the aesthetic presence of the past' and he gathers 'some lingering testimony to the exquisite vanity of ambition'.

Romance – the romance of antiquity on which had been superimposed the successive centuries – and Passion – such as he had found in George Sand and now in the Italy of Stendhal: this was what the special banquet of initiation in Italy meant for Henry James. It was as if this hot Italian sun and these dark shadows created by the venerable stones of old buildings alternately warmed and cooled his American blood, so that feeling could first melt and then be poured into the crucible of the intellect. The young intellectual from Quincy Street had become quite suddenly a sentimental and impassioned traveller. The *Italienische Reise* of Henry James imbued him with what he could only call at the moment '*the Italian feeling*'. It was he who italicized the words, and he was to devote many pages later to explaining and interpreting the Italy of those early years. In the writings about it the word 'passion' crops up at every turn, in letter, in sketch, in story.

4

He came into Venice toward the end of a mid-September day when the shadows began to lengthen and the light to glow. He caught the distant sea-smell, glimpsed the water, the domes, the spires, and then the brown-skinned white-shirted gondolier swept him through the water amid slimy brick, battered marble, rags, dirt, decay. It was not, however, Venice in its details, but Venice in its totality that fired his imagination. With Ruskin in his pocket he walked or floated through the city. From this first moment it became a golden link in the chain of cities that comprised Henry James's life, and one has only to read the pages devoted to Venice in *The Wings of the Dove* to discover how enduringly the spirit of the place had entered his being.

Some of his finest pages were written here in old palaces, in rooms fronting on the Grand Canal during long visits early and late. On this visit of discovery, he explored church and palace; he discovered Veronese, Bellini, Tintoretto. He devoted many hours contemplating the latter's two crucifixions and writing William long letters about him. The painter *felt* pictorially 'the great, beautiful, terrible spectacle of human life very much as Shakespeare felt it poetically'. He conceived his subjects scenically. He had boundless invention, passionate energy. 'I'd give a great deal,' Henry burst out, 'to be able to fling down a dozen of his pictures into prose of corresponding force and colour.' He admired Bellini and goes to out-of-the-way churches to look at his work. He is the first painter to make Henry feel there is such a thing as 'pure religious art'. He had always fancied it to be 'more or less an illusion of the critics'. Each of his pictures seemed to Henry James 'a genuine act of worship'.

He was to note later that 'it takes a great deal to make a successful

...erican, but to make a happy Venetian takes only a handful of quick sensibility'. He readily appreciated the plight of the Venetians.

In the narrow streets, the people are far too squalid and offensive to the nostrils, but with a good breadth of canals to set them off and a heavy stream of sunshine to light them up as they go pushing and paddling and screaming – bare-chested, bare-legged, magnificently-tanned and muscular – the men at least are an effective lot.

They were on better terms with life than many people who had better advantages. 'Not their misery, but the way they elude their misery, is what pleases the sentimental tourist.' For the tourist, the pleasures of the place were simple enough: fine Titians or Tintorettos, the ever-waiting windowless gloom of St Mark's, 'a great hoary shadowy tabernacle of mosaic and marble, an immense piece of Romanticism', the gondolas, and the relaxed café life in the Piazza. 'Everyone knows that the Grand Canal is a wonder: but really to feel in your heart the ancient wealth of Venice, you must have frequented these canalettos and campos, and seen the number and splendour of the palaces that stand rotting and crumbling and abandoned to paupery.' The mere use of one's eyes in Venice was happiness enough. Even the children, clamouring for coppers from the tourists, added to the tone, 'the handsomest little brats in the world', furnished with eyes that could signify 'the protest of nature against the meanness of fortune'. A little American, straight-haired, pale-eyed, freckled, duly 'darned and catechized', marching into a New England schoolroom, was often seen and soon forgotten. These children, playing 'on the lonely margin of a decaying world, in prelude to how bleak or to how dark a destiny', were remembered. It was a melancholy city – in a sense the most beautiful of tombs. However, gondolas spoilt one (he wrote William) for a return to common life. James's first stay in Venice lasted a fortnight. He frequented the cafés and studied the people; he went to the Lido – then a very natural place, with only a rough lane across the little island from the landing-place to the beach – and dined on the wooden terrace, looking at the sea and thinking how much this resembled Easton's beach at Newport. At the Academy he glimpsed the Bronsons, of Newport, not yet residents of Venice; she was destined to become his closest American-Venetian friend.

Early in October he turned his footsteps to Florence. From Lombardy and Venetia to Tuscany – to that Tuscany whose landscape had figured in the parlour in 14th Street – he travelled by e. stages, Padua to Ferrara, Bologna, the Parma of Stendhal, and finall, Firenze, in that time of the year when the sun is still hot, the evenings cool and the city's aspect softly jewelled in riverine and mountain setting.

Florence caught his fancy as no other city in Italy. The Tuscan palaces with their pure symmetry had for him the nobility of Greek architecture; there was less romantic shabbiness here than in the Lombardian and Venetian towns, and when it did occur, as in the group of old houses on the north side of the Arno, between the Ponte Vecchio and the Ponte Santa Trinità, it was, in the yellow light with mellow mouldering surfaces, 'the perfect felicity of picturesqueness'. Tuscany had nine years before been united to the new kingdom of Italy, and Florence had become its capital. Rome was still integrally Papal and the French troops of the Second Empire were its guards. Henry was in Italy during the last months of the great drama of the *Risorgimento*. The older, divided Italy, however, has a way of transcending the immediate political ferment and upheaval and facing the centuries unperturbed. In Florence, Henry spent his mornings at the Uffizi or the Pitti; he went on his regular walks; he explored the suburbs, the churches, the squares, the cafés, as in the other towns and cities. He accompanied Charles Eliot Norton on a villa-hunt: and confessing that Florence had its gloomy aspects, he nevertheless found in its architecture 'a charm inexpressible, indefinable'. It helped fasten his mind to Italian soil. He had casual encounters with Americans, known and unknown, chance meetings such as were to furnish the point of departure for future stories:

Yesterday I met at the Uffizi Miss Anna Vernon of Newport and her friend Mrs Carter, with whom I had some discourse; and on the same morning I fell in with a somewhat seedy and sickly American, who seemed to be doing the gallery with an awful minuteness, and who after some conversation proposed to come and see me. He called this morning and has just left; but he seems a vague and feeble brother and I anticipate no wondrous joy from his acquaintance.

It was from Florence, after a number of such encounters, that Henry delivered himself, in the year of Mark Twain's *Innocents Abroad*, of his view of the same innocents. William had asked Henry how the English compared with the Americans, and Henry replied,

the Englishmen I have met not only kill, but bury in unfathomable depths, the Americans I have met. A set of people less framed to provoke ɔnal self-complacency than the latter it would be hard to imagine. ᴛere is but one word to use in regard to them – vulgar, vulgar, vulgar. ᴛheir ignorance – their stingy, defiant grudging attitude towards everything European – their perpetual reference of all things to some American standard or precedent which exists only in their own unscrupulous windbags – and then our unhappy poverty of voice, of speech, and of physiognomy – these things glare at you hideously.

This passage has often been quoted as evidence of Henry James's intolerant and snobbish attitude towards his fellow-countrymen in Europe. Yet, placed beside the sentence which follows, the cry *vulgar, vulgar, vulgar*, can be seen only as the strong reaction of a cultivated young American, to whom Europe was a deep and life-enhancing experience, against frontier illiteracy and parochial horizons. Henry went on to say,

On the other hand, we seem a people of *character*, we seem to have energy, capacity and intellectual stuff in ample measure. What I have pointed at as our vices are the elements of the modern man with *culture* quite left out. It's the absolute and incredible lack of *culture* that strikes you in common travelling Americans.

James was to take up the story of the American abroad and play it out in all its variants. It was to remain his greatest subject. He was to feel, in the end, that there was no 'possibilty of contrast in the human lot so great as that encountered as we turn back and forth between the distinctively American and the distinctively European outlook'. As an artist and social satirist, James drew his Americans as he found them in Europe – and often the satire hurt. Mr Evans, the absinthe-drinking father of the heroine of *Travelling Companions*,

in many ways an excellent representative American. Without taste, without culture or polish, he nevertheless produced an impression of substance in character, keenness in perception, and intensity in will, which effectually redeemed him from vulgarity. It often seemed to me in fact, that his good-humoured tolerance and easy morality, his rank self-confidence, his nervous decision and vivacity, his fearlessness of either goods or men, combined in proportions of which the union might have been very fairly termed aristocratic.

Here is a foreshadowing of Christopher Newman and of Adam Verver. In those galleries and streets, cathedrals and cafés, along the well-beaten nineteenth-century paths in Europe, he met face to face the host of Americans, rich and poor, the struggling artists, the

wandering expatriates, the innocent young girls, who were henc
forward to walk across the pages of his fiction. Henry James had
found his great theme. But three years were to elapse before he
would recognize it.

5

Early in October, in Florence, James's health, which had shown constant improvement, took a turn for the worse. It was again not the
back-ache, but the condition which had led him earlier to Malvern.
On 7 October 1869, he wrote to William, then the newest of new
M.D.s, a long detailed letter which in the history of literature may
well be the most elaborate account of constipation extant. A week
later he began to ponder curtailing his trip and returning to Malvern
to take the waters. In due course William's reply arrived, filled with
medical generalizations and counsel. 'It makes me sick,' he wrote,
'to think of your life being blighted by this hideous affliction.' Writing to the younger brother, Robertson, William quite rightly
assumed that Henry would improve. 'I enclose you Harry's last
letter, which please return. This devilish constipation of his seems
the only trouble with him now, but I think it can be cured. He was
entirely free from it at Malvern and afterwards in England and is
only living from day to day in Italy, before going back there.'

For the time being, however, Henry had been reduced to a pathetic
state. He dragged himself about Florence uncomfortable in body,
unhappy in mind and deeply disturbed at the prospect of having to
leave Italy in a renewed search for health. On 26 October he wrote
William that his condition was 'unbearable'. He posted the letter
and began an easy stroll; he walked through the Roman Gate, passed
two rows of tenements and proceeded into the country. Three miles
beyond the gate he came to a hillside; on its summit he perceived a
Carthusian Monastery resembling a medieval fortress and 'lifting
against the sky, around the bell-tower of its gorgeous chapel, a kind
of coronet of clustered cells'. It was but five minutes of uphill climb
to gain its lower gate, past a clamouring group of deformed beggars
thrusting their stumps of limbs at him. He gained admission and
inspected the great proportions of the church, designed by the primitive painter, Andrea Orcagna. On a later visit, as perhaps on this
one, he was struck by the contrast between the opulence of the
church as a place of worship and the bareness of the monks' cells.

...e meaner the convent cell the richer the convent chapel. Out of poverty and solitude, inanition and cold, your honest friar may rise at his will into a supreme perception of luxury.' He visited the subterranean oratories and the funeral vaults, he looked at the dwellings of the monks in the great pillared quadrangles, lying half in the sun and half in the shade, with a tangled garden at the centre. The little chambers were cold and musty; the view, beyond the Arno and the clustered towers of Florence, magnificent. A second letter of the day to William shows a great calm, the descent of an inner peace. In *Roderick Hudson*, Rowland has such an experience after a visit to a Franciscan monastery situated not far from this one. 'On coming out,' Henry wrote to his brother, 'I swore to myself that while I had life in my body I wouldn't leave a country where adventures of that complexion are the common incidents of your daily constitutional : but that I would hurl myself upon Rome and fight it out on this line at the peril of my existence.' But just before he left for the papal city he paid a long meditative visit to the Medici tombs – Michelangelo's – 'the last word of Romantic art'. The 'warrior with the cavernous visage is absolutely terrible'. He shed sufficient sorrow 'to infest the universe'.

The weather had turned cold and there was much rain. He took reluctant leave and in the bleak dawn of 30 October 1869 he reached the Eternal City.

6

The letter Henry James wrote to William that evening after his first solitary day in Papal Rome was an ecstatic outburst, a page of exuberant rhetoric, as if he had to inscribe the emotion of the moment for posterity – which indeed he did. If he was overdramatizing himself and striking an attitude (as in so many of his letters home), this was understandable : the romantic spirit was strong in him, and to be in Rome was to visit History itself, to feel not only his own passion at the moment but the passions of the centuries. The letters home were written by a young man fully conscious of his literary powers. He could not resist 'writing' a subject to the hilt the moment he put pen to paper. The letters were destined, moreover, for an invisible recipient who would read them later in the American setting – himself. 'You mustn't let my letters bore you,' he wrote home. 'Don't read them if you don't feel like it – but keep them neverthe-

less. They will serve me in the future as a series of notes or ob-
vations – the only ones I shall have written.' The letters, therefore
are to be read not only for their epistolary qualities: they constitute
a working notebook, a repository of emotion and experience, stored
up for the future. Written with intensity and under the immediate
impress of the scene, they are long, vivid, reflective, a kind of continuing self-communion punctuated by bursts of appreciation and
exclamations of enthusiasm. It was not surprising that the elder
Henry sent them to Emerson, who read them with praise, and that
Norton read them to an approving Ruskin. On this evening in Rome
Henry wrote :

At last – for the time – I live! It beats everything : it leaves the Rome
of your fancy – your education – nowhere. It makes Venice – Florence –
Oxford – London – seem like little cities of pasteboard. I went reeling and
moaning thro' the streets, in a fever of enjoyment. In the course of four
or five hours I traversed almost the whole of Rome and got a glimpse of
everything – the Forum, the Coliseum (stupendissimo!), the Pantheon,
the Capitol, St Peter's, the Column of Trajan, the Castle of St Angelo –
all the Piazzas and ruins and monuments. The effect is something indescribable. For the first time I know what the picturesque is. In St
Peter's I stayed some time. It's even beyond its reputation. It was filled
with foreign ecclesiastics – great armies encamped in prayer on the
marble plains of its pavement – an inexhaustible physiognomical study.
To crown my day, on my way home, I met his Holiness in person –
driving in prodigious purple state – sitting dim within the shadows of his
coach with two uplifted benedictory fingers – like some dusky Hindoo
idol in the depths of its shrine. Even if I should leave Rome tonight I
should feel that I have caught the keynote of its operation on the senses.
I have looked along the grassy vista of the Appian Way and seen the topmost stone-work of the Coliseum sitting shrouded in the light of heaven,
like the edge of an Alpine chain. I've trod the Forum and I have scaled
the Capitol. I've seen the Tiber hurrying along, as swift and dirty as
history! From the high tribune of a great chapel of St Peter's I have heard
in the papal choir a strange old man sing in a shrill unpleasant soprano.
I've seen troops of little tonsured neophytes clad in scarlet, marching and
counter-marching and ducking and flopping, like poor little raw recruits
for the heavenly host. In fine I've seen Rome, and I shall go to bed a wiser
man than I last rose – yesterday morning.

James would temper these first enthusiasms. He would come to
see Rome less ecstatically as a muddy provincial city in which papal
power was shrinking even while he was visiting it. But he caught it
at the last moment of its old splendour – the romance of antiquity

ᴛe. 'A leaf out of the Middle Ages,' he wrote as he saw the Pope ᴀrive at a Church opposite his hotel, surrounded by cardinals and ambassadors. He remembered the Vatican draped in scarlet, the scarlet coaches of the cardinals, the monsignori in their purple stockings followed by solemn servants, the sobriety of the Papal newspapers, the traces that Lords Spiritual still presided by divine emanation over the rites of mere humans. The great meeting of the Ecumenical Council was taking place at this very moment; it would proclaim the dogma of Papal Infallibility in its final attempt to solidify the papacy, even as the Pope was moving into symbolic terrain. Instead of the City of Rome he would have only the City of the Vatican. But the first glimpse of Pius IX in his gilded coach remained; we can read it in *Roderick Hudson*.

Secular Rome, and above all antique Rome, touched Henry more profoundly. The Pantheon loomed out of its centuries with a 'delicacy' of grandeur; it seemed to him more worshipful than the most mysterious and aspiring Gothic. St Peter's was a 'first-class sensation'; he could feel 'the heart-beats of the Church'; but the Protestant side of Henry James turned away to admire the statue of Marcus Aurelius at the Capitol and he found in it – in consonance with Hawthorne – 'an audible personal voice'. As between 'that poor sexless old Pope' and the imperial Aurelian legs astride the splendid horse 'swinging in their immortal bronze' Henry James cried out to Quincy Street 'Here at last was a *man*!'

His health improved during his first weeks in Rome, almost as if the stimulus to his mind and senses ministered to physical wellbeing. He systematically visited all sections of the Holy City, churches, sculptures, ragged columns, ancient stones, shabby princely old palaces – Farnese, Colonna, Corsini, Doria – and then 'the great violet Campagna'. He was regularly at the Vatican museum; he spent hours in the Colosseum, then still filled with earth and flowers – a whole province of the picturesque. He watched the parade of priests, and the French troops supporting the Pope against the *Risorgimento* during these crucial months – troops soon to be diverted, at the first cannon-burst of the Franco-Prussian war. His rambles were solitary, filled with meditations. He was following the footsteps of Goethe and Stendhal and the English romantics – and Hawthorne. He visited the graves of Keats and Shelley in the Protestant Cemetery – with its grey pyramid inserted into the sky on one side and the dark cold cypresses on the other and the light

bursting out between them – the spot where he would bury Da̶
Miller, his little American girl among more famous pilgrims of th̶
non-Catholic world.

'I see no people, to speak of, or for that matter to speak to,' he
wrote home. Towards the end of his Roman stay, however, he met
some members of the American colony including the American
sculptor, William Wetmore Story, 'very civil and his statues very
clever'. In December he went to Naples and wandered sadly among
the excavations of Pompeii. He found Naples a 'barbarous' city but
enjoyed its museum. For Christmas he returned to Rome, having
made up his mind by this time that he would curtail his Italian
journey. He was still unwell. On 27 December, the day before he left
Rome, he went to San Pietro to bid farewell to Michelangelo's statue
of Moses, and decided that of all the artists who had wrought in
Italy he was the greatest. His energy, positiveness, courage, marked
him as a 'real man of action in art'. The *vigour* of the Moses, and
Michelangelo's willingness to 'let it stand, in the interest of life and
health and movement, as his *best* and his only possible' had a powerful appeal for Henry at this moment. For one whose ambition was to
be a man of action in art, the figure of Moses, leader of men, carved
in stone, could speak eloquently. In describing him to William,
however, and stressing his 'health and movement', he was to a
degree accentuating his own wish for similar health and strength –
and power – while meeting William on his critical ground. Indeed
the ensuing passage sounds much more like his brother than himself.

I'm sick unto death of priests and churches. Their 'picturesqueness'
ends by making me want to go strongly into political economy or the
New England school system. I conceived at Naples a ten-fold deeper
loathing than ever of the hideous heritage of the past, and felt for a
moment as if I should like to devote my life to laying railroads and
erecting blocks of stores on the most classic and romantic sites. The age
has a long row to hoe.

Next day he took the train for Assisi, and had there 'a deep delicious bath of medievalism'. He went on to Perugia and Siena and
thence to Florence, to which he bade a farewell of much greater
intensity than he had thought possible. He experienced at this
moment so much emotional pain that it remained with him for
years. In *A Little Tour of France* of fourteen years later Henry incorporated a direct passage of personal reminiscence which began
with his saying, as he came to write to Avignon, that he had been
there before.

¬all not soon forget the first [visit], on which a particular emotion set indelible stamp. I was creeping northward in 1870, after four months spent, for the first time, in Italy. It was the middle of January, and I had found myself unexpectedly forced to return to England for the rest of the winter. It was an insufferable disappointment; I was wretched and broken-hearted. Italy appeared to me at that time so much better than anything else in the world, that to rise from table in the middle of the feast was a prospect of being hungry for the rest of my days ... In this state of mind I arrived at Avignon, which under a bright, hard winter sun was tingling – fairly spinning – with the *mistral*.

A contemporary record of his feelings is preserved in a letter to his father written when he reached Genoa. 'The whole affair,' he said, speaking of his decision to leave Italy,

was brutally and doggedly carried through by a certain base creature called Prudence, acting in the interest of a certain base organ which shall be nameless. The angel within me sate by with trembling fluttering wings watching these two brutes at their work. And oh! how that angel longs to spread these wings into the celestial blue of freedom and waft himself back to the city of his heart ... Last night I spent – so to speak – in tears.

The city of his heart was Florence.

Only a few weeks before he had been daydreaming of staying in Italy until March and then going for the summer to Paris, Normandy, Brittany and perhaps thereafter on a little tour of the Low Countries and the Rhine. He had even contemplated spending the following winter in Dresden, where William had been two years before. Now he turned his face toward the winter sleet and drizzle of England. He was deeply depressed. He called this journey a 'tragical pilgrimage'. He regarded his decision as an act of courage, 'the deliberate, cold-blooded, conscious, turning of my back on Italy'. It required a great will to turn one's back upon a dishevelled nymph!

33

Minny Temple

THE dream that they – Henry and Minny – might meet in Rome had been only a dream. The months during which Henry had been discovering Europe and writing letters home that reflected new experiences and the growth of his imagination were months of serious illness for Minny. Of this Henry appears to have been unaware. He continued to have hopes of meeting her. Twice in September 1869 he asked his mother: 'What of Minny Temple's coming to Italy?' 'Is Minny coming abroad?' The record of his cousin's courage is preserved in the letters which she wrote to John Chipman Gray and which, late in life, he turned over to the novelist. They were incorporated by him into the final chapter of *Notes of a Son and Brother*, without, however, mention of Gray's name. Henry, with his compulsion during those final years to revise not only his own works but the writings of his father and of William, 'doctored' Minny's letters as well. But the story they tell remains unchanged. He kept four of Minny's letters to himself written during these months. *His* own to Minny do not appear to have survived.

I

In the weeks that elapsed after Henry's departure for Europe, Minny had frequent lung haemorrhages. She had lived her life with a restless intensity that did not abate even in her lowest moments; the doctors in those days knew little that could help. They prescribed quiet to that dancing spirit and she went to bed, at Pelham, at Newport or in Philadelphia, wherever she might be among her numerous relatives. Then, when she felt better, she would start a new cycle of visits, sleigh-rides, concerts, dances – followed by an inevitable relapse. Her letters to Gray speak of 'my old enemy hæmorrhage', and she tallies them for him : she had had 'seven big ones' on one occasion and several smaller. 'I can't stop them.' The voice is unresigned, helpless, yet full of courage. 'I mean to beat them yet.' She speaks freely of death, laughs at it with the free laughter of her 23 years. The haemorrhages stop. She makes plans to see *Faust*. The doctor orders her back to bed. Music excites her too much. She is in New ĸ. The doctor packs her back to Pelham. He listens to her lungs. e tells her they are sound. 'Either sound lungs are a very dangerous thing to have, or there is a foul conspiracy on foot to oppress me,' writes Minny from her bed. She rebelliously accepts the regimen of 'gruel and silence'. There has come a moment when she has no choice.

2

Her letters to Henry James are written with the same candour as those to Gray, although they are briefer and contain a considerable amount of family gossip absent from the others. 'I have had no more interesting news so far to give you but of my repeated illness, so I thought I would spare you,' she writes from Newport in June of 1869. 'My darling Harry,' she writes, and parenthesizes, 'You don't mind if I am a little affectionate now that you are so far away, do you?' She tells him that his last letter 'reached me while I was in the very act of having the third hæmorrhage of that day, and it quite consoles me, for them'. She adds, 'I still continue in my evil courses which, however, don't seem to have killed me, yet.' She had journeyed from Pelham to Newport to visit her aunt and to see Frank and Lizzie Boott. She plans to visit the Jameses in Quincy Street:

I shall miss you, my dear, but I am most happy to know that you are well and enjoying yourself. If you were not my cousin I would write and ask you to marry me and take me with you, but as it is, it wouldn't do. I will console myself, however, with the thought, that in that case you might not accept my offer, which would be much worse than it is now.

Had he seen George Eliot? 'Kiss her for me. But from all accounts, I don't believe that is exactly what one wishes to do to her. If I were, by hook or by crook, to spend next winter, with friends, in Rome, should I see you, at all?' And so she continues, in a half-flirtatious tone, with a slightly forced euphoria and an abundance of misplaced commas. At moments it is the prattling of a little girl counselling Henry not to be homesick, inquiring about his health, giving him gossip of her sisters. She signs herself 'always your loving cousin Mary Temple'.

Two months later, at Pelham, she writes of her younger sister's engagement, the birth of a baby to Kitty, her elder sister, and her continuing dream of going to Rome. 'Think, my dear, of the pleasure we would have together in Rome. I am crazy at the mere thought.

It would be a strange step and a sudden for me to take. ... I wo
give anything to have a winter in Italy. We must trust in Heave
and wait patiently.' She doesn't post this letter until a week later
when she adds,

The evening I wrote you I was enchanted with the project, but the next
morning I was disenchanted. I am really not strong enough to go abroad
with even the kindest friends. I have been ill nearly all week with a kind
of pleurisy, which makes me clearly perceive that it would never do for
me to be ill away from home, on the bounty of strangers for my nursing, See'st thou?

And she continues affectionately, 'My dearest Harry what a charming tale is *Gabrielle de Bergerac*, just as pretty as ever it can be. I am
proud of you, my dear, as well as fond – have you any special objections?'

During the summer of 1869, Henry's mother, writing to him from
Pomfret, contrasted Lizzie Boott with Minny, showing a marked
preference for the European-bred Miss Boott:

What a striking instance she is of what a careful and thorough education
can accomplish, perhaps I should add under the most favourable circumstances. Of course she never could have been formed as she is in America
... Look at Minny Temple in contrast with her. Minny has all the tastes
and capabilities naturally in a high degree, and look at the difference.
Minny writes that she gets up at 6 o'clock every morning and takes a
lesson in drawing. Perhaps she is beginning to work out her own salvation.

Mary James was chatting off the top of her head. The 'admirably
produced' Lizzie was precisely the kind of American-European girl
that Henry could convert into the delicate Pansy Osmond – and the
name he gave her completely describes her; but Minny's heroic
qualities and intensities seem to have escaped his mother. Minny
wasn't working out her salvation at this particular moment: she
was trying quite simply to *live*, even if the process meant early rising
for the sake of art – although we suspect that it was not exclusively
for art's sake that Minny was up at six. She was spending sleepless
nights. In those weeks Minny was living at a feverish pitch that
seemed to be a final endeavour to defy her fate. 'I have a cough
nearly all the time,' she writes Gray. Yet she continues her rounds
of visits. Her last letter to Henry is dated from Pelham, 7 November
1869. She had spent some days in Quincy Street and read some of
Henry's letters to William and to his father.

think that you should be ill and depressed so far away, just when
was congratulating myself that you, at all events, were well and happy,
nobody else was. Well, my dearest Harry, we all have our troubles in
this world – I only hope that yours are counterbalanced by some true
happiness, which Heaven sends most of us, thro' some means or other.
I think the best comes thro' a blind hanging on to some conviction, never
mind what, that God has put deepest into our souls, and the comforting
love of a few chosen friends.

She goes on to describe her Cambridge visit and talks much of
John Gray, who had come to see her at Pelham during a period of
pouring rain and shown much awkwardness in kissing her sister's
baby. 'He is a most noble gentleman in spite of his not knowing how
to kiss!' Upon reflection she adds, 'The foregoing has a depraved
sound. But I do indeed like him much – better as I know him better.'

In Cambridge, she had lunched twice with Lizzie Boott and talked
with John Gray, T. S. Perry, Wendell Holmes and Fanny Dixwell,
whom Holmes was to marry; and she had much light banter with
William James, of whom she was deeply fond. On 5 December
William wrote to Henry, 'M. Temple was here for a week, a fortnight since. She was delightful in all respects, and although very
thin, very cheerful.' He went on to describe her as 'a most honest
little phenomenon' and to say that she was 'more devoid of "meanness", of anything petty in her character, than anyone I know, perhaps, either male or female'.

Henry had written to Minny that gondolas reminded him of her
(the 'sliding step'?), and she wrote,

My dear, I hope you may henceforth *live* in gondolas, since gondolas
sometimes make you think of me – so 'keep a doin' of it' if it comes
'natural' ... I feel much better now-a-days. Good-bye, dear Henry –
'words is wanting' to tell you all the affection and sympathy I feel for
you. Take care of yourself, write soon. God bless you. Your loving
cousin, Mary Temple.

3

Affectionate these letters are, a mixture of tenderness and inconse-
quential chatter, the letters of a cousin who had known Henry from
her earliest years. They are not love-letters. The letters to Gray are,
in a reticent way, longer and more detailed and filled with much
discussion of the why of life; they are the communications of a

serious young lady to a serious young man. 'If morality and \
were the test of a Christian, certainly Christ would never h.
likened the kingdom of heaven to a little child, in whose heart is n
struggle, no conscious battle between right and wrong, but only un-
thinking love and trust.' She wonders whether she is 'hopelessly frivolous and trifling', or does this mean that she really doesn't *believe*,

that I have still a doubt in my mind whether religion *is* the one exclusive
thing to live for, as Christ taught us, or whether it will prove to be only
one of the influences, though a great one, which educate the human race
and help it along in that culture which Matthew Arnold thinks the most
desirable thing in the world? In fine is it the meaning and end of our
lives, or only a moral principle bearing a certain part in our development?

She goes to hear Phillips Brooks preach and doesn't find an answer.
He didn't say anything new or startling, 'though I believe I did have
a secret hope that he was going to expound to me the old beliefs
with a clearness that would convince me and for ever banish doubt'.
He didn't touch the real difficulties. 'I wonder what he really does
think about it all,' Minny writes, 'and whether he ever feels the reaction I feel about Thursday, which is sure to follow the enthusiasm
and confidence made by his eloquence and earnestness on Sunday.
Tomorrow will be Saturday, and I shall be glad when Sunday comes
to wind me up again.'

The time was coming when no amount of winding would help.
The 'old consolatory remark "Patience, neighbour, and shuffle the
cards" ought to impart a little hope to me, I suppose; but it's a long
time since I've had any trumps in my hands, and you know, that
with the best luck, the game always tired me'. It was now near the
end of January 1870, and Minny was indeed exhausted. The plan to
go to California had fallen through and she was depressed. And she
couldn't sleep. 'Oh yes,' she said to herself, and wrote it to John
Gray, 'here it is again; another day of doubting and worrying, hoping
and fearing has begun.' She describes this as the 'Demon of the Why,
Whence, Whither?' The doctors are giving her morphine in the hope
that it will help her sleep. It only makes her ill. 'I am sometimes
tempted to take a drop of "pison" to put me to sleep in earnest,' she
confesses.

'I had a long letter yesterday from Harry James from Florence —
enjoying Italy but homesick,' she writes to Gray. The letter was
apparently written during Henry's brief pause there as he was Eng-

ɔound. In the middle of February, Minny left Pelham for Man-
ɹtan in a state of great fatigue and weakness to consult Dr
ᴧletcalfe, an important specialist. She stayed with a cousin, who
urged her to allow her physician, a Dr Taylor, to examine her. Dr
Taylor had a brutal bedside manner. He sounded Minny's lungs and
said to her solemnly : 'My dear young lady, your right lung is di-
seased; all your hæmorrhages have come from there. It must have
been bad for at least a year before they began. You must go to
Europe as soon as possible.'

Minny then asked the doctor 'for the very worst view he had
conscientiously to take', but didn't mean definitely to inquire 'how
long I should live'. The doctor, however, understood her question,
and she was unprepared for his 'two or three years'. 'Well, doctor,'
Minny replied, 'even if my right lung were all gone I should make a
stand for my left,' and promptly fainted away. Dr Taylor revived
her and assured her that perhaps her case was not as bad as all that
and left. 'His grammar was bad,' Minny reported to Gray, 'and he
made himself generally objectionable.'

Dr Metcalfe brought reassurance the next day. He told Minny her
right lung was weaker than her left, which was quite sound, and that
the haemorrhages had kept it from actual disease. He said that if she
kept up her general health she might fully recover. He had known
a case ten times worse get entirely well. He recommended a trip to
Europe, 'so this last is what I am to do with my cousin, Mrs Post, if
I am not dead before June'.

She sat on the piazza at Pelham bundled up on this February day
scribbling her long letter to John Gray in pencil.

If I begin to be indifferent to the result I shall go down the hill quickly.
I have enough Irish blood in me rather to enjoy a good fight.

I feel the greatest longing for summer, or spring; I think I would like it
to be always spring for the rest of my life.

4

After Henry James had his last look at Florence, he travelled with an
aching heart to Genoa, where, on 14 January 1870, he wrote a long,
affectionate and philosophical letter to his father, telling him he
wasn't sure whether he was in a position to assess his parent's
notions 'with regard to the amelioration of society'. His year abroad
had convinced him, however, of the 'transitory organization of the

actual social body. The only respectable state of mind is to ⎯
stantly express one's perfect dissatisfaction with it'. His father ha⎯
apologized for sermonizing his son. Henry rejoined, 'Don't be afraid
of treating me to a little philosophy. I treat myself to lots.' And he
went on to tell him of his regret at leaving Italy. Three days later he
was at the Hôtel de Grande Bretagne in Mentone. From there he
went the following day by carriage to Nice. He visited Monte Carlo
and watched the play at the gaming tables; for a while he toyed
with the idea of staking a napoleon 'for that first time which is
always so highly profitable'.

Discretion triumphed; he turned instead to study the 'nobler face
of the blue ocean'. He enjoyed the French cooking and the play of
light and colour along the Riviera. Aboard the train from Nice to
Marseilles he fell in with an English consumptive and earned his
gratitude by showing him attention. When he reached Arles there
was a howling *mistral*; Avignon caught his fancy, but seemed tame
after Italy. On 27 January he was in Paris. He went to see *Frou-Frou*
with Desclée at the Gymnase, and for the first time he visited the
Théâtre Français where he saw a play by Molière. One couldn't
know Molière, he told his mother, until one had seen him done by
Regnier, Got and Coquelin; nor Augier without Mlle Favart. He spent
hours at the Louvre, he dined modestly, he returned in the evenings
to the Théâtre Français and read late into the night by the fire in his
hotel. He would have liked to linger in Paris – 'I should have learned
bien des choses at the Théâtre Français.' He recrossed the Channel
via Boulogne and went to the Charing Cross Hotel, where he
promptly re-acclimated himself by dining in the coffee-room off
roast beef, brussels sprouts and a pint of beer.

On 5 February, in a letter from London, he gave his mother an
accounting of his year's expenditures. He had been in Europe almost
eleven months and had drawn £379 of the £1,000 his father had
put at his disposal. He had not been extravagant, he said; perhaps
too many hansoms, but he had pampered himself in this respect
because of poor health. Apparently, only poor health could serve as
a sufficient justification in Mary James's eyes for such travels as
Henry had undertaken. He told his mother he wasn't a good econo-
mist and that he had purchased only a few clothes and half a dozen
books.*

* At least two of these were still in his library at the time of his death : Jules
Zeller's *Entretiens sur l'Histoire* (Paris, 1869) in which he inscribed his name

.y being unwell,' he explained, 'has kept me constantly from
.empting in any degree to rough it. I have lived at the best hotels
and done trips in the most comfortable way.' Nevertheless, he had
run through almost £400, and this seemed to him a large sum.
Everything would depend now on how things went at Malvern. If he
didn't feel better he would return home. Even if he improved, he was
inclined to return in the autumn. He would not be disappointed at
the curtailment of his grand tour; he had on the whole had a 'magnificent holiday'.

Eight days later he was at Malvern, living in a dingy bedroom and
summing up for William his Italian journey. He was convinced that
Florence 'has really entered into my life and is destined to operate
there as a motive, a prompter, an inspirer of some sort'. (This it did;
for here he began, three years later, his first important novel.) He still
liked England – the fields were vivid in their rain-dampened green
and 'ah! that watery sky, greatest of England's glories! so high and
vast and various, so many-lighted and many-shadowed, so full of
poetry and motion'.

Three more weeks passed and he was again writing to William
from Malvern. He was obtaining plenty of 'gentle emotions from
the scenery'. He had found no intellectual companionship, however,
among his fellow-patients at the thermal establishment. The women,
particularly, struck him as plain, stiff, tasteless in 'their dowdy beads
and their lindsey woolsey trains'.

'Nay, this is peevish and brutal,' he wrote. 'Personally (with all
their faults) they are well enough. I revolt from their dreary deathly
want of – what shall I call it? – Clover Hooper has it – intellectual
grace – Minny Temple has it – moral spontaneity.'

The name of Minny, and the present tense, slipped easily from his
pen as he wrote his letter in his rapid hand. The date of the letter
was 8 March 1870. On this very day Minny's tired, sick lungs had
drawn their last breath in the quiet house in Pelham, where little
more than a year before Henry had said the good-bye to her that was
destined to be their last.

---

and the date Florence, October 1869, and Charles de Brosses's *Lettres Familières*
(2 vols., Paris, 1869) in which he also signed his name, adding 'Rome, Nov.
1869'.

34

The Wings of the Dove

From Henry James's notebook, 3 November 1894 – twenty-four years after the death of Minny Temple:

Isn't perhaps something to be made of the idea that came to me some time ago and that I have not hitherto made any note of – the little idea of the situation of some young creature (it seems to me preferably a woman, but of this I'm not sure), who, at 20, on the threshold of a life that has seemed boundless, is suddenly condemned to death (by consumption, heart-disease, or whatever) by the voice of the physician? She learns that she has but a short time to live, and she rebels, she is terrified, she cries out in her anguish, her tragic young despair. She is in love with life, her dreams of it have been immense, and she clings to it with passion, with supplication. 'I don't want to die – I won't, I won't, oh, let me live; oh, save me!' ... If she only could live just a little; just a little more – just a little longer.

I

The heroine – the 'very heroine of our common scene' – was dead at 24, and Henry, contemplating the cold green landscape of Malvern through his tears, found himself trying to face the irreversible truth. Minny was '*dead* – silent – absent forever ... While I sit spinning my sentences she is dead.' He received the news on 26 March from his mother and replied to her on the same day. At moments his letter reads like a soliloquy, interrupted by a sharp cry of grief, and then the grief is submerged in a flow of memories and of self-solace – relief that Minny had not lived to suffer; in that light her death was 'the happiest fact of her career'.

'I have been spending the morning letting the awakened swarm of old recollections and associations flow into my mind – almost *enjoying* the exquisite pain they provoke,' he wrote. He experienced a feeling of 'absolute balm in the thought of poor Minny and *rest* – rest and immortal absence'. Life on a footing of illness and invalidism would have been impossible for that disengaged dancing flame.

It had come as a violent shock. 'Your last mention of her condition had been very far from preparing me for this. Minny seemed such a breathing immortal reality that the mere statement of her

..h conveys little meaning.' He scribbled the thoughts as they
..me to him. 'Oh dearest Mother! oh poor struggling suffering *dying*
creature!' He wanted all the details of her death, the last hours, the
funeral, 'any gossip that comes to your head … I have been raking
up all my recent memories of her and her rare personality seems to
shine out with absolute defiant reality. Immortal peace to her
memory!'

When he had written himself out, he took a long walk, and gradually the thought of her disappearance became familiar. He wished
they could have met in Europe; he would have liked to tell her many
things, to take up the talk where they had left off at Pelham. 'Poor
Minny! how much she was not to see!' He strolled across the fields;
the landscape assented stolidly enough to death, 'this vast indifferent
England which she fancied she would have liked. Perhaps!' Minny
was 'a plant of pure American growth', however; there was no telling what Europe would have meant for her.

He returned to his room and picked up his pen again. The writer
in him soliloquized best pen in hand. He had written in the first part
of his letter, 'It comes home to me with irresistible power, the sense
of how much I knew her and how much I loved her.' He now added:
'It is no surprise to me to find that I felt for her an affection as deep
as the foundations of my being, for I always knew it.' *Dear bright
little Minny*, his mother had written. He answered: 'God bless you
dear Mother, for the words … I am melted down to such an ocean
of love that you may be sure you all come in for your share.'

2

The letter to Mary James, written in the first moments of grief, reflects his immediate shock. The eloquent letter he wrote three days
later to William is long, self-conscious, rambling and repetitive, the
fruit of meditation and inner contradictions. Over and over, its refrain is that Minny can now be translated from reality into an image
of the mind. He had written to his mother, 'Twenty years hence –
what a pure eloquent vision she will be,' and now he reiterated, as
if talking to Minny, 'Twenty years hence we shall be living with
your love and longing with your eagerness and suffering with your
patience.' Minny now was 'a steady unfaltering luminary in the
mind rather than as a flickering wasting earth-stifled lamp'. And
again, 'Her image will preside in my intellect,' and still again, 'The

more I think of her the more perfectly satisfied I am to have her translated from this changing realm of fact to the steady realm of thought. There she may bloom into a beauty more radiant than our dull eyes will avail to contemplate,' and yet again, 'I could shed tears of joy far more copious than any tears of sorrow when I think of her feverish earthly lot exchanged for this serene promotion into pure fellowship with our memories, thoughts and fancies.'

From this his mood swings to a 'little decent passionless grief – a little rummage in our little store of wisdom – a sigh of relief – and we begin to live for ourselves again'. Minny alive was a creature of flesh and blood to be loved; and also, for Henry, a threat, as women were; Minny dead was an idea, a thought, a bright flame of memory, a statue – Diana! – to be loved and to be worshipped in complete safety, 'embalmed forever in all our hearts and lives'. She had been 'a sort of experiment of nature ... a mere subject without an object ... the helpless victim and toy of her own intelligence'.

The letter to William culminates in a passage describing what Minny had meant to Henry James – 'she *represented*, in a manner, in my life several of the elements or phases of life at large – her own sex, to begin with, but even more *Youth*, with which, owing to my invalidism, I always felt in rather indirect relation'. Every one, he said, was supposed to have been more or less in love with Minny. 'Others may answer for themselves : I never was.' It may be that Henry was making a fine distinction here; he had written to his mother that he loved Minny; this was different from being in *love* with her. One might love a cousin without being in love with her. He tells William :

Among the sad reflections that her death provokes for me, there is none sadder than this view of the gradual change and reversal of our relations : I slowly crawling from weakness and inaction and suffering into strength and health and hope : she sinking out of brightness and youth into decline and death. It's almost as if she had passed away – as far as I am concerned – from having served her purpose, that of standing well within the world, inviting and inviting me onward by all the bright intensity of her example. She never knew how sick and disordered a creature I was and I always felt that she knew me at my worst. I always looked forward with a certain eagerness to the day when I should have regained my natural lead, and our friendship on my part, at least, might become more active and masculine. This I have especially felt during the powerful experience of the past year.

At the end of his letter he repeats: 'I can't put away the thought that just as I am beginning life, she has ended it.'

3

This thought is the key to Henry's feelings at the moment of Minny's death. What he had observed from his earliest years and later recorded in his fiction had now become in his mind (for so he articulated it) a part of his own life – 'the gradual change and reversal of our relations'. But what *had* been his relation to Minny? He had not been engaged to her, as De Grey was to Margaret in the tale he had written two years earlier; nor had he been her avowed lover, like poor Richard, who had shouted his passion to Gertrude on the banks of the river. What mystic strength was he endowing himself with, that fed on Minny's weakness and grew ever greater? What transparent mental link had he forged with the image of his cousin to arrive at the equation that her loss was his gain? It was almost as if, in his mind, he had already imagined himself betrothed to her or even married. He was drawing up the eternal balance-sheet of the love and death as he had observed it, in which either the man or the woman, or both, were victims of a love relationship. While Richard had recovered from his typhoid fever, Gertrude had begun to waste away; in the story of De Grey the equation was reversible – one or the other had to die.

He said that twenty years hence Minny would be 'a pure eloquent vision'. She began to figure in Henry's short stories and novels long before the day when, a quarter of a century later, he made his first notebook entry of the theme for *The Wings of the Dove*. Seven years after Minny's death Henry wrote a curious tale that reads as if it stemmed directly from the letter to William on the death of his cousin. The story bears the title of *Longstaff's Marriage*. The heroine is named Diana – Diana Belfield – and she is as beautiful as the chaste huntress, with a 'tall, light figure ... a nobly poised head ... frank quick glance ... and rapid gliding step'. She has had many suitors; like the wakeful huntress she is 'passionately single, fiercely virginal'. Travelling abroad with her faithful companion, Agatha Gosling, she winters at Nice, and there daily on the promenade she finds herself being observed by a handsome young Englishman whose strongly masculine name she discovers to be Reginald Longstaff. He sits for a long time in the sun, a book in his pocket, staring at the sea – when he is not staring at Diana. Agatha believes that one of Longstaff's lungs is 'affected' and he is in Nice for his health. He is clearly a worshipper of Diana – but from a safe distance. He makes no effort to speak to her or to be introduced to her. The ladies fall into the habit of speaking of him as 'poor Mr Longstaff'. 'No one, indeed, knew, with certainty, that he was consumptive ... but unless he were ill, why should he make such a mystery of it?' Agatha wonders why he doesn't ask to be introduced. One day, however, he does summon the courage to speak to her. He tells her he is a dying man, and in the ensuing conversation Agatha becomes conscious that 'what he meant was simply that he admired her companion so much that he was afraid of her'. He explains that, because of his invalidism, 'to speak to her of what I felt seemed only to open the lid of a grave in her face'. He adds that he knows he will not recover, and asks Agatha to tell Diana after he is gone how much he loved her.

Shortly after this interview Longstaff's serving-man comes to announce that his master is dying, not of consumption but of love. Agatha urges Diana to go to see him, out of pity. 'What is Mr Longstaff to me?' replies the chaste Diana. When a second urgent request is received, however, she yields. She finds Longstaff in bed, as white as the sheets, and gravely ill. He makes an extraordinary proposal: nothing less than a deathbed marriage so that Diana may inherit his possessions, 'lands, houses, a great many beautiful things'. In exchange he would have 'a few hours in which to lie and think of my happiness'.

Diana is not unmoved by his sad mien, his deathly pallor, his plea. However, she has a down-to-earth reflection: 'Suppose, after all, he should get well.' Longstaff, overhearing this, moans softly and turns his face to the wall. Diana leaves. 'If he could die with it,' she observes coldly, 'he could die without it.' From that moment, however, she is uneasy and restless. She returns to America.

Two years pass and she summons Agatha to her. 'Will you come abroad with me again? I am very ill.' Later she tells her, 'I believe I am dying.' They wander across Europe, and Agatha Gosling observes the changes in her companion. 'The beautiful statue had grown human and taken on some of the imperfections of humanity.' One day in Rome, in St Peter's, Diana glimpses a healthy and completely recovered Longstaff. 'So you were right,' Agatha tells Diana. 'He would, after all, have got well.' Diana replies: 'I am right now, but I was wrong then. He got well because I refused him. I gave him a hurt that cured him.' Later Agatha meets Longstaff and discovers that he too attributes his cure to the 'miracle of wounded pride'. He is clearly no longer interested in Diana. She, however, is now in love with him and dying. She sends for him, He agrees to marry her on her deathbed. Unlike Longstaff, she does not recover. Love – and marriage – have been fatal to her. 'She loved you,' says Agatha, 'more than she believed you could now love her; and it seemed to her that, when she had had her moment of happiness, to leave you at liberty was the tenderest way she could show it.' The words *to leave you at liberty* come very close to Henry's words to William that Minny had passed away almost as if she had fulfilled her purpose – that of inviting him onward into the world.

The story was published in *Scribner's Monthly* in August 1878, a month after *Daisy Miller* appeared in the *Cornhill Magazine*. It is decidedly not in the happy manner of *Daisy*, although it is told with all the narrative charm Henry had mastered by this time. Weak in substance and art, it is strong in biographical content, since in it James worked into story-form the ideas expressed or implicit in the letters written after Minny's death. He had felt that there had been a reversal of his and Minny's relationship; he recovered and Minny died, and this is the story of Longstaff and Diana. What is striking in the tale is that Longstaff is afraid to express his love in the first instance, and that fear is a component of his illness. His later rationalization is that hurt pride contributed to his recovery: actually what did was the removal of the source of his great, brooding, disastrous anxiety. From the moment that Diana rejected him – from the moment that she had made it clear the relationship must remain that of a man to a statue – Longstaff no longer felt himself threatened. He was suffering, indeed, from the Jamesian malady to which we have already alluded, summed up in the names of his notebook, *Ledward, Bedward, Dedward*. So Henry's reiterated expression in his letter to William, stated in four different ways – that Minny had become a memory, a thought instead of a fact, an image, 'a steady unfaltering luminary in the mind' – was in reality an expression of relief that Minny had permanently been converted into an invisible statue, an object to be serenely contemplated, appreciated and even loved – through the opaque glass of memory; and this without the uncomfortable feeling that he ought, in the process of becoming 'more active and masculine', to do something about his feelings. Henry and Longstaff were one. And Minny's death, much as it brought deep personal grief and a sense of irreparable loss, brought also, in this curious buried fashion, a concealed emotional relief. Years later Henry was to re-embody the same situation in an even more morbid tale than *Longstaff's Marriage* – *Maud-Evelyn*, in which a 'hero' named Marmaduke renounces marriage in order to accept an imaginary marriage to a girl who has died; the dead girl's parents think of him as the man she would have married had she lived. He humours them and he more than humours himself; he substitutes a ghost for a flesh-and-blood wife. The dead Dedrick girl shapes and controls his life. Fear-ridden, shut in, he achieves the status of a widower with even less difficulty than Longstaff. The two tales, separated by a quarter of a century, tell the same story.

4

The ending of Henry James's long letter to William about Minny Temple is a summing up of all his feelings, expressed and re-expressed in a kind of Shakespearian tribute over the tomb of an unattainable Juliet or Ophelia:

Farewell to all that she was! How much this was and how sweet it was! How it comes back to one, the charm and essential grace of her early years. We shall all have known something! How it teaches, absolutely, tenderness and wonder to the mind. But it's all locked away, incorruptibly, within the crystal walls of the past. And there is my youth – and anything of yours you please and welcome! turning to gold in her bright keeping. In exchange, for you dearest Minny, we'll all keep your future.

The crystal walls of the past. Minny alive had been a constant reminder to Henry of his inarticulateness and his fear of asserting himself. Minny gradually sinking into decline could renew his strength. Dead, Minny was Henry's, within the walls of his mind. He could write – and it is almost in a tone of triumph – 'She has gone where there is neither marrying nor giving in marriage! no illusion and no disillusion – no sleepless nights and no ebbing strength.' In these balanced parallels – marrying and giving in marriage, illusion and disillusion, sleepless nights and ebbing strength – marriage and decline are again wrapped together, 'ledward-bedward-dedward'. He did not have to marry Minny and no one else could, neither John Gray, nor William, nor Wendell, none of the clever young men who surrounded her at Conway or in the ballrooms of New York. Minny was now permanently his, the creature of his imagination.

She became, nine years after her death, the heroine of *The Portrait of a Lady*. The hero of that scene, Ralph Touchett, dies of consumption (again a reversal of roles), but not before he has watched Isabel – whose last name is Archer and so suggests a kinship with the Archeress Diana – play out the drama of her life and make a mess of it. 'Poor Minny! how much she was not to see!' Henry had written to his mother. And to Grace Norton, 'She was a divinely restless spirit – essentially one of the "irreconcilables"; and if she had lived to great age, I think it would have been as the victim and plaything of her constant and generous dreams and dissatisfactions.'

In the novel Henry gave his heroine a chance to see the world and live out her dreams and disillusion. Isabel goes from Albany to England, to Italy, and sees all that Minny might have seen; she has much of the happiness Minny might have had, is surrounded by a group of lovers strangely parallel to the lovers in *Poor Richard*, becomes the step-mother of Pansy Osmond (sketched from Minny's friend Lizzie Boott), and is the victim of her own bright intensities. Courted by the three lovers, one disqualified by invalidism, she chooses a fourth and ruins her life.

In the years between *The Portrait* and *The Wings of the Dove* there was a curious story, a pot-boiler, written for a newspaper syndicate, and therefore intentionally sensationalized by James. In *Georgina's Reasons* there figures a girl named Mildred or Milly Theory, who dies of consumption and her older sister Kate. Milly Theory is a pale shadow of the future Milly Theale; and Kate in no way resembles Kate Croy of *The Wings*. (That a Kate should be placed beside the two Millys is not surprising, for Minny's elder sister was Katherine, commonly known as Kitty.) Again Minny's ghostly figure had passed across Henry's desk, and she returned finally at the turn of the century, to be converted into the ultimate flame-like creature of his fiction. The theme of *The Wings* was the reverse of that of *The Portrait*. The earlier novel had grown from the speculation 'What sort of life would Minny have had?' The later novel was the fictional rendering of her actual ordeal.

'Death, at the last, was dreadful to her; she would have given anything to live.' And when Milly Theale, the 'dove', has folded her wings, Kate Croy and Merton Densher confront one another. Milly's money makes possible at last their long-deferred marriage. Kate, however, is no longer sure of Densher.

'Your word of honour that you're not in love with her memory.'

'Oh – her memory!' Densher exclaims.

Kate makes a high gesture. 'Ah don't speak of it as if you couldn't be ... *Her memory's your love. You want no other.*'

So it was with Minny Temple and Henry James.

35

Return

HENRY JAMES recrossed the Atlantic in the spring of 1870, eager to be home. Fifteen months had elapsed since his visit to Pelham, the most crowded and dramatic of his life. Minny had been laid to rest next to her father and mother in Albany Rural Cemetery, and Henry seems to have observed the prescription of his letters : a little decent grief, 'a sigh of relief – and we begin to live for ourselves again'. The hallowed memories had no relation to the continuing reality; and reality for him was the determination to recover his health and become a great American novelist.

In the first days at Malvern after receiving the news of Minny's death he had had a bad relapse. His back-ache returned, and he rushed to London to consult a specialist. He was told that he had indulged excessively in hip-baths and given himself 'a sort of inflammation' in the kidney region. Dressing the balance between remaining abroad and returning home he decided that the most economical road to recovery lay through Quincy Street. In London a meeting with his Aunt Kate, who had been travelling abroad, provoked an acute fit of homesickness. They sailed on 30 April, on the *Scotia*.

By the time he reached Cambridge – on 10 May – he was so much improved that the comparatively new Dr William James, who examined him, pronounced him 'tough and stout', although he still found tenderness in the kidney region. Writing to Robertson, William gave a full report on Henry and remarked, 'His constipation meanwhile has been reduced to very manageable limits and will probably give him no more serious trouble. He ... seems in every way a different being from what he used to be.'

For the moment Henry sought some point of re-attachment to the old scenes. He had a sense of lost time and of pressure to get back to his writing. A few days after his return, writing to Grace Norton, who was still abroad, he proceeded to Italianize Harvard.

Here I am – here I have been for the last ten days – the last ten years. It's very hot: the window is open before me: opposite thro' the thin trees I see the scarlet walls of the president's *palazzo*. Beyond, the noble grey mass – the lovely outlines, of the library : and above this the soaring *campanile* of the wooden church on the *piazza*. In the distance I hear the carpenters hammering at the great edifice in process of erection in the college yard – and in sweet accordance the tinkle of the horse-cars. Oh how the May-wind feels like August. But never mind : I am to go into town this p.m. and I shall get a charming breeze in the cars crossing the bridge ... Howells is lecturing very pleasantly on Italian literature. I go to the lecture room in Boylston hall; and sit with my eyes closed, listening to the sweet Italian names and allusions and trying to fancy that the window behind me opens out into Florence. But Florence is within and not without.

He goes on to ponder his course.

I wish I were able to tell you ... what, now that I have got America again, I am going to do with it. Like it enormously *sans doute* : they say there is nothing like beginning with a little aversion. My fear is that mine is too old to end in a grand passion. But America is American : that is incontestable, and consistency is a jewel. I wish I could tell you how characteristic every thing strikes me as being – everything from the vast white sky – to the stiff sparse individual blades of grass.

Two days later he went to lunch at Shady Hill. Cambridge was in the fullest beauty of the spring.

The grass was all golden with buttercups – the trees all silver with apple blossoms, the sky a glorious storm of light, the air a perfect hurricane of zephyrs. We sat (Miss C. Hooper, Miss Boott &c.) on a verandah a long time immensely enjoying the fun. But oh my dear Grace it was ghostly. For me the breeze was heavy with whispering spirits. Down in that glade to the right three women were wading thro' the long grass and a child picking the buttercups. One of them was you, the others Jane and Susan – the child Eliot. Mesdemoiselles Hooper and Boott talked of Boston, I thought of Florence. I wanted to go down to you in the glade and we should play it was the Villa Landor. Susan would enact Miss Landor. But the genius of my beloved country – in the person of Miss

Hooper – detained me. I don't know indeed whether I most wanted you to be there or to be myself in Florence. Or rather I do very well know and I am quite ashamed of my fancy of robbing that delightful scene of its simple American beauty. I wished you all there for an hour, enjoying your own.

The year in Europe had worked its spell: and Henry could announce to Grace Norton, 'When I next go to Italy it will be not for months but years.' In the meantime there were contrasts and comparisons to be made between the Old World and the New, tales to write out of his journeys, and the question of his career. He had tasted enough of Europe to want to see more of it: ill-health and the money anxieties of Quincy Street had interrupted his course. What was to follow now was a period of careful exploration of New England and then a renewed and longer experience of Europe. It was William James who in a letter to Robertson peered into Henry's future.

'I fear his taste of Europe will prevent his ever getting thoroughly reconciled to this country and I imagine that he will end, when he becomes self-supporting, by spending most of his time there. Certainly with his artistic temperament and literary occupations, I should not blame him for the choice.'

When he was writing the closing words of *Notes of a Son and Brother*, almost half a century later, Henry James said that he and William felt the death of Minny Temple to be 'the end of our youth'. He qualified this in the opening words of *The Middle Years*: 'We are never old, that is we never cease easily to be young, for *all* life at the same time.' And he went on to liken youth to a continuing 're-luctant march into the enemy country, and the country of the general lost freshness'.

If in 1870 one phase of his youth seemed at an end, another was about to begin; a great fund of freshness had not yet been lost. By trial, by error, by the happy accidents of nature and the long ordeal of endurance, the artist had been formed, a quiet, pondering, sovereign being, with a great, strange, passionate gift of expression wedded to gifts of observation and insight. 'Mysterious and incontrollable (even to oneself) is the growth of one's mind,' he wrote to William. 'Little by little, I trust, my abilities will catch up with my ambitions.'

They were catching up more rapidly than he knew. He was ready now to test to the full the literary resources of his country before he would again test those of Europe. The fledgling years, the untried years, were at an end. The long ordeal of the war, the struggle for health, Minny's death, 'the whole infinitude' of pain, 'door within door', had been experienced. 'I have in my own fashion learned the lesson that life is effort, unremittingly repeated.'

Now, before him, stretched the broad new decades, the years of saturation and maturity.

BOOK THREE:
THE YEARS OF SATURATION
1870–75

The great thing is to be *saturated* with something – that is, in one way or another, with life; and I chose the form of my saturation.

HENRY JAMES

Part One:

A Season in Cambridge
1870-72

36

The Precious Wound

IN the spring of 1870, when he had returned from his 'passionate pilgrimage' abroad, Henry James settled down in No. 20 Quincy Street in Cambridge, Massachusetts, with his elderly parents, his brother William and his sister Alice. He had spent fifteen months in the Old World. The worst of such an adventure, for a constituted cosmopolitan, was the coming back. It was a little like being born again. James looked anew at the Cambridge horizons – the Harvard elms, Mount Auburn and Brattle, the friendly verandahs of Kirkland Street, the horse-cars in Harvard Square, the large trough and pump for the horses, the cows grazing in the lot beyond the Common. To this he was reduced, after his journey – after the campaniles and cathedrals, the glimpses of pagan and papal Rome, the theatres of Paris, the studios of the Pre-Raphaelites. In Cambridge the scene remained rural, even rustic. The detached houses were set on their lawns or in small fields : the Harvard Yard was fenced with granite posts sunk at intervals, with three rails between, as if to keep animals from straying in; it possessed none of the mystery or the beauty of the Oxford colleges with their thick walls and cloistered privacy. A row of plain wooden houses inhabited by members of the Harvard faculty stood on the opposite side of Quincy Street; facing No. 20 was President Eliot's residence, in awkward red brick, with a close-fitting, top-heavy, slate mansard roof.

For a young cosmopolitan, whose only desire was to be 'literary', the parochialism of Cambridge and the sparseness of the New England scene represented intellectual and sensual starvation. He had little in common with his Cambridge coevals; they had had their grand tours and were happy to be starting their careers on American soil. His elder brother mingled with 'long-headed youths', who had founded a metaphysical club, in which they 'wrangle grimly and stick to the question'. It gave Henry a headache merely to know of it. 'I belong to no club myself and have not great choice of company either to wrangle or agree with,' he wrote to Charles Eliot Norton, who was still abroad. In the next sentence he alludes to his loneliness in Cambridge, as artist, as well as gregarious human being: 'If it didn't sound weakmindedly plaintive and fastidious, I would say I lacked society. I know no "nice men" – that is, passing few, to converse withal.' John Fiske was giving a long course in town on Positivism; Wendell Holmes, for whom Henry predicted (even then) a rise to eminence 'in a speciality, but to a high degree', was lecturing on jurisprudence. Henry Adams, whom he had recently met, was teaching history at Harvard and editing the *North American Review*. William Dean Howells and his old Newport friend T. S. Perry were his sole literary company; but Howells was now busy at the *Atlantic Monthly*, and could only occasionally resume his old walks and talks with his friends. Henry complained there was little to do, little for his eyes to rest upon – 'in a hundred places there are some charming bits of the picturesque – the Yankee picturesque of course I mean – which I devour as I go; but the more I go, the larger grows my appetite, and my sense aches at times for richer fare. When I go to Europe again, it will be, I think, from inanition of the eyes.'

The older generation offered him occasional distraction. Longfellow could be bland and mild and anecdotal; Lowell, who might have been a valuable resource in spite of their difference in years, he knew but slightly. Sometimes he would be bidden to feasts in honour of celebrities and find himself among the Cambridge and Boston worthies: as when Cambridge fêted Bret Harte, 'a clever writer,' Henry observed, 'but with a monstrous newspaper-made reputation which vulgarizes him in spite of himself'. For the rest, he spent certain hours at his writing-desk, and he gave himself over to the round of the seasons: autumns in which the crickets filled the nights, and yellow leaves announced the drifting snows; the spring with its deepening green in President Eliot's front yard; summers of idle wandering in the Waltham and Arlington Hills. 'I lie there, often, on the grass, with a book in my pocket,' Henry wrote to his friends in Europe,

thinking hungry eastward thoughts; but thinking too that we have very good things near us at home – witness these untrodden hills and woods – so utterly unhaunted that I can people them with what shapes I will, with this vast outlook into purple distances and nameless inland horizons fretted by superb undulations – which all simply means honest Massachusetts.

He could not wholly reconcile himself, however, to substituting honest unfurnished Massachusetts for the furnished scenes of

Europe. 'My year in Europe,' he writes to Grace Norton in the autumn of 1870,

is fading more and more into an incredible past. The continuity of life and routine and sensation has long since so effectually re-established it-self here, that I feel my European gains sinking gradually out of sight and sound and American experience closing *bunchily* over them as flesh over a bullet – the simile is apropos! But I have only to probe a little to hear the golden ring of that precious projectile.

He had received a lasting wound; and his ache was the ache of having been free on an old and picturesque continent. Now he was tethered in a little street, in a suburb of Boston, with only memories to feed on. Sometimes he called his wound a virus; sometimes it be-came a poison. In a later and more American image, the bullet was a buried arrow, 'one of those well-directed shafts from the European quiver to which, of old, tender American flesh was more helplessly and bleedingly exposed'. His most characteristic image was that he had been fed 'too prompt a mouthful' of the fruit of the Tree of Knowledge. Why, he was to ask himself, had it left 'so queer a taste' during all his early years of travel with his family on the Continent? In old age, when he looked back, he wondered at the 'infinitely greater queerness' which he had experienced on his return from his first adult journey abroad, between 'the summer of '70 and that of '72, when it set me again in motion'.

I

The 'queerness' was the stark contrast between his two worlds, and his dilemma : for however much he belonged to New York and Boston, his 'home' seemed even more now to be Europe. He passed many melancholy hours. When William, years later, after a term abroad, spoke of America's 'scraggy aspects', Henry told him :

I tasted of that intensity once and forever when I returned from Europe in May 1870 – and determined, in the deadly days, on my future life. I felt then, as I felt after subsequent returns, that the only way to live in America was to turn one's back on Europe; that the attempt to *mix* them is a terribly comfortless business.

The 'deadly days', the episodes of his Cambridge life, took on a certain humorous aspect as he described them in 1870 to Grace Norton.

Mr J. T. Fields lectured here on Cheerfulness lately (as who should say: I know I'm a humbug and a fountain of depression, but grin and bear it) and Mr Longfellow feasted him afterwards at supper. Apropos of which Mr Longfellow is just issuing a new poem *The Divine Tragedy*, on the Passion and Crucifixion. I don't suppose it will be quite as strong a picture as the San Cassano Tintoretto; but it will have its points. Lowell seems to write nothing. I believe he is given over to the study of Low French – I use the term in a historic and not a moral sense.

Howells, he told his friend, was making a good editor of the *Atlantic*; it was probably with him that James passed his most congenial Cambridge hours. The *Atlantic* editor was to remember the sort of things they talked about – 'how we might eliminate the everlasting young man and young woman' from fiction. 'I remember he had one very notable scheme for a novel whose interest should centre about a mother and a son.' But Howells could not meet the exigent standards of Henry James.

He has been writing a series of articles descriptive of a western tour he made last summer – which have greater finish and beauty than any thing he ever wrote. But there is to me a somewhat pathetic discordance in his talent – the need of applying really first-class handling to subjects belonging to *la petite littérature*. The more I think of it the more I deprecate the growing tendency – born of the very desperation of the writer – to transfer directly and bodily, without any intellectual transmutation, all the crude accidents of his life as they successively befall, into the subject-matter of literature. Before we are fairly launched here, we are being swamped by the dire vulgarity of it.

'We have over here the high natural light of chance and space and prosperity,' he tells Norton. Looking about for himself he had concluded that 'the face of nature and civilization in this our country is to a certain point a very sufficient literary field. But,' he added, 'it will yield its secrets only to a really *grasping* imagination. This I think Howells lacks. (Of course *I* don't!) To write well and worthily' of American things one needs even more than elsewhere to be a *master*. But unfortunately one is less!'

2

During his two years in Cambridge Henry James wrote not only a series of tales, but a short novel, eight travel-sketches, two dramatic sketches, seven book-reviews, and three art-notices – and counted himself 'wantonly idle'. Following the course of the Franco-Prussian war, he told Grace Norton that he was so busy reading newspapers 'that I largely manage to forget that I am doing no work of conse- quence'. He held a large part of his desire to return to Europe to be 'morbid'; he reasoned that 'I should be very much less subject to it, if I were engaged here in some regular and absorbing work'.

This was a further element of the 'queerness'. The literary life, in a busy and preoccupied America, seemed to Henry an idle life. His fellow-citizens were creating industry and building railroads, or were preoccupied with the law or even with metaphysics. In the Cambridge society, trying to live by his pen and earning his meagre supply of dollars, Henry seemed confined to his room with his blank sheets of paper, and largely to female society. The hero of *A Pas- sionate Pilgrim* remarks that in England 'my vulgar idleness would have been – don't laugh now! – would have been elegant leisure', and Rowland Mallet tells a young lady in *Roderick Hudson*, 'I have the misfortune to be a rather idle man, and in Europe the burden of idleness is less heavy than here.' This was his repeated refrain : the profession of literature seemed out of harmony with his Ameri- can environment.

3

'Cambridge society is a little arid,' Henry remarked to his friends in Europe. 'My dissipations have been in Boston chiefly.' The transla- tion from Cambridge to Boston could be accomplished almost at any time without undue effort. Henry had but to board a plodding horse-car in Harvard Square – let us say on some afternoon of the long winter – a huge, low omnibus, brightly painted, and decorated with dangling bells, dragged by small horses along grooves in the pavement. The journey took him over the long, low bridge that seemed to crawl on staggering posts across the Charles River. If he looked back, his view was of 'the desolate suburban horizon, peeled and made bald by the rigour of the season'. It was all 'hard, cold, void' – boards and tin and frozen earth, sheds and rotting piles and railway-lines across puddles. The picture was one of clutter – loose fences, vacant lots, mounds of refuse, yards bestrewn with iron pipes, telegraph-poles, and the bare wooden backs of places.

In the streets round Boston Common the scene was sufficiently animated : the shop-fronts glowed through frosty panes, the bells of the street-cars were heard in counterpoint with the cries of news-boys in the cold air; and behind large plate-glass windows the in-teriors of the hotels, with their marble-paved lobbies, revealed their life in the white gaslight glare. Western visitors sprawled on divans, stretching long legs in a particular kind of American angularity, while young bell-hops with old faces handed them periodicals and discussed the town's entertainments. The illuminated playhouses to which Henry resorted seemed seductive behind swinging doors of red leather or baize, flanked by posters and photographs of actresses. Or he might make his way to the central haven of culture, the Music Hall, where he was to set the final scene of *The Bostonians* – high, dim, dignified, with its great and sombre organ overhanging the bronze statue of Beethoven. Henry James had long ago ex-hausted the city's nocturnal life.

He reached out in his 'dissipations' for anything that might offer an evening's relief from ennui. He ventured into private meetings and seances, demonstrations of mesmerism, speeches by ardent young reformers or discourses by lady editors advocating new reli-gions, listening attentively to their flow of ready-made oratory de-rived from 'circus-tent' cultural evenings and lecture-halls, all reflecting Boston's spirit of good-doing which continued to animate the citizens in the wake of Abolition. Henry looked, as he rode through the streets, upon rows of red houses that seemed dusky in the lamplight, with 'protuberant fronts, approached by ladders of stone'; or he gazed into the interiors of tenements, in dark streets with their narrow halls and human misery, and wandered into areas where new detached houses gave a fine show of ornament – all in wood. Freshly-painted cupolas and belvederes, bow-windows, pil-lared piazzas and flourishes, scallops, brackets, cornices, presided over by silvered house-numbers painted in high letters over the door-way designed to be visible to the passing horse-cars and all testifying to exuberant and ephemeral carpentry. Years later Henry could still describe minutely his exploration of the down-at-heels South End. To a reader many years later who inquired about the particular Boston house in which he had sketched the rooms of Miss Birdseye in *The Bostonians*, James answered he was thinking of a street near the old Worcester station, 'and I *smell* the house, inside, even yet'.

37

The Exquisite Provincials

IDLE though he might seem, he did not allow himself to be crushed by his recurrent nostalgia for Europe, nor lulled into inaction by his melancholy. He was barely re-settled in Quincy Street in the early summer of 1870 when he persuaded the *Nation* to accept a series of travel-articles from his pen – pictures of Rhode Island, Vermont, New York: a strange enterprise, this writing of sketches of familiar American scenes. It was an opportunity to earn some ready money; it was also a way of convincing the *Nation* how lively a travel-writer he could be – especially if he were in Europe.

There was, however, a deeper prompting. He told Grace Norton he wanted time for his plans 'to mature and accumulate beneath this Western sky'. He would be 'haunted and wracked', he said, if he returned to Europe with a 'thankless ignorance and neglect' of America. If only in self-defence, it was necessary for him to make up 'a little list of accomplished devotions and emotions'. He would therefore 'see all I can of America and *rub it in* with unfaltering zeal'.

The words 'rub it in' somehow diminished the piety of his devotions. They suggested Henry would take his native land as if it were a stiff dose of medicine. Nevertheless he insisted that he enjoyed his homeland 'with a poignancy that perpetually surprises me'. His tour consisted of a month in Saratoga, where he drank the waters and 'cunningly noted many of the idiosyncrasies of American civilization'; a week at Lake George; a fortnight at Pomfret, where his parents were on holiday; and a fortnight at Newport 'where nature was perhaps more attractive, and man rather less so, than ever'. At the end of this summary he remarked: 'I spent lately a couple of days with Mr Emerson at Concord – pleasantly, but with slender profit.'

I

James's *Nation* articles offer us a good account of what he saw and how he travelled. His article on Newport explores the difficulty of the life of leisure in America. The question haunts him. His article on Saratoga is a witty appraisal of American manners. His view of

the American landscape in all its wild richness contains in it neither
Emerson's affection for nature nor the studied observation of Thoreau. It is that of a man who appreciates it best when it has been
tamed. To have seen the Italian hillsides from Perugia to Narni, with
their old walled towns, their vineyards, their domesticated landscapes, and then to be confronted with the undisciplined green mass
of upper New York State was indeed a contrast for Henry's eyes to
brood upon : not a little like trying to compare walled-in Oxford
with fenced-in Harvard. James spoke of the 'complete absence of
detail' as he crossed Lake George and explored Burlington and Ticon-
deroga, which Hawthorne had painted before him. Or the surroundings of Saratoga, 'no white villages gleaming in the distance, no
spires of churches. no salient details. It is all green, lonely, and
vacant.' Around him, as he journeyed and strolled in the great
American land, Henry felt 'the eloquent silence of undedicated
nature'.

Occasionally he would stumble on what he called 'the pure picturesque'; by this he meant 'the presentation of a picture, self-
informed and complete'. A little unpainted dwelling, on a grassy
slope, 'leaden-grey in the shade, silver-grey in the sun. Against the
darkness of the open doorway, from where I stood, I saw a white
butterfly soar and sink – I almost heard in the noonday stillness the
soundless whirr of his wings'. And he went on to give an idyllic
account of milk-pans glittering in the sun, hollyhocks lifting their
blooming stalks, the expanse of golden-rod, the crowded apples on
the crowded trees of the orchard all set in an 'emanation of reflected
composite light and colour, of leafed and bladed and fruited green'.
Nevertheless the foreground, more often than not, was bleak and
nondescript: a wooden building, a saw-mill, a high black chimney,
all 'as transient and accidental as the furniture of a dream'. There
spoke the traveller who had looked upon the stones of antiquity –
the *historical* picturesque.

The describer of scenery however was also an observer of
manners, and already in these articles the future novelist is absorbed
in the study of the American character. As he sits on the large
piazza of his hotel in Saratoga, he notices the overdressed mothers
and their young daughters idly circling in the broad noonday. In
Europe, he muses, young women might spend their time at needle-
work, or cultivate the art of conversation, but 'here at Saratoga, at
any hour of morning or evening, you may see a hundred rustling

beauties whose rustle is their sole occupation'. The men, lounging about the hotels, struck Henry as diagonals – tilted hats, tilted chairs, feet and cigars tilted up, 'they are not the mellow fruit of a society which has walked hand-in-hand with tradition and culture; they are hard nuts, which have grown and ripened as they could. When they talk among themselves, I seem to hear the cracking of the shells.' And the children, left asleep in the big leather chairs of the lobby at all hours of the night – Henry had had his glimpse of Daisy and Randolph Miller, in their home environment.

2

Henry James's visit to Emerson was a private matter, not chronicled in the *Nation*. He was invited because Emerson remembered his letters written during his European wanderings, which the elder James had brought to Concord and read to him. Howells had said of this correspondence that 'you're in great danger of having your private letters stolen and published'. Emerson had asked the elder Henry whether he mightn't keep some of them, so that he could study them. Paternal vanity was strong, however, and the father carried them away to show to others. Emerson 'does nothing but talk of your letters,' William had reported to his brother. Henry expressed uneasiness at this public display of his private musings.

Emerson's notebooks show no record of the visit: but then young Harry James came to him in all familiarity. We can, however, reconstitute elements of the scene. The near-by woods were showing their autumn colours; an aroma of apples hung over the sleepy town. There stood the familiar houses – Alcott's 'academy', the old Manse hard by the rude bridge, and there was Walden, under its New England sky, with the bird-sounds and the animal life Thoreau had made literary. Henry saw his father's friend in his homely surroundings. If the young writer had been looking at characteristic American landscape in recent weeks, he found himself here in the one town outside the beaten path of American material triumph where the 'landscape of the soul' had been contemplated always in close harmony with nature. Hawthorne was six years dead; Thoreau eight. It was as if they still lived, as if the great moment in the town's history had not yet passed – that moment when there resided at one end of Concord a sage whose utterances were 'the most poetical, the most beautiful productions of the American mind' while at the

other – with rows of tall New England elms between – there lived
an exquisite teller of tales.

Again and again James would use the word 'exquisite' in speaking
of Emerson and Hawthorne. They were both 'exquisite geniuses'. He
spoke of them also as 'exquisite provincials'. Provincial, to be sure,
was not used by Henry in a pejorative sense: the adjective 'exquisite' testified to this. James was simply stating a fact; the two
men remained foreign to city streets; the large cosmopolitan world
he possessed had not been theirs. He was to wander later with
Emerson in the Louvre and the Vatican. 'But his spirit, his moral
taste, as it were, abode always within the undecorated walls of his
youth.' So too, James remarked, Hawthorne had spent fifty of his
years in small American towns, Salem, parochial Boston of the early
nineteenth century, Concord, Lenox, West Newton; he had led what
might be called a 'village life'. He too had been 'exquisitely and consistently provincial'.

The meeting of Emerson and the young writer in that early
autumn was a meeting of past and future. James always remembered
Emerson's voice: it was 'irresistible' and he had a 'beautiful mild
modest authority'. He also had (and James was to remark on this
again and again) 'that ripe unconsciousness of evil which is one of
the most beautiful signs by which we know him'. The Emersonian
innocence, the exquisite provinciality of it, touched him deeply.
Life had never bribed Emerson to look at anything but the soul. And
the young realist, busy looking at the visible things of life and at
human behaviour around him, pondered this,: one might make up
poems about the soul, or write philosophical essays; one could
hardly write a novel about it. It gave the future novelist food for
thought – that Emerson had considered Hawthorne's novels 'not
worthy of him'. This was a judgement extremely odd: 'How strange
that he should not have been eager to read almost anything that
such a gifted being might have let fall.' Emerson's insensibility to
imaginative writers, from Shelley to Dickens, Dante to Jane Austen,
Aristophanes to Cervantes – Henry enumerated them – was 'a large
allowance to have to make for a man of letters'.

A day or two after James's visit, Emerson wrote to his transatlantic friend, Thomas Carlyle: 'A multitude of young men are growing
up here of high promise, and I compare gladly the social poverty of
my youth with the power on which these draw.'

3

In Cambridge, later, James read the newly-published French and Italian journals of Hawthorne. Reviewing them for the *Nation* early in 1872, he remarked that they 'show us one of the gentlest, lightest and most leisurely of observers, strolling at his ease among foreign sights in blessed intellectual irresponsibility, and weaving his chance impressions into a tissue as smooth as fireside gossip'. The words 'intellectual irresponsibility' might have escaped the eye of a reader at that time: but they express James's vision of Hawthorne in Europe. Hawthorne had been an idle Yankee loiterer with an ineffable charm, 'bending a puzzled, ineffective gaze at things, full of a mild genial desire to apprehend and penetrate'. The word 'ineffective' might also give us pause. The truth was that he looked at things 'as little as possible in that composite historic light which forms the atmosphere of many imaginations'. Hawthorne's observations betrayed 'a childlike evenness and clearness'. He assented to nothing he could not understand. He seemed wholly unreceptive to certain elements in the pictures and statues; he was 'unreconciled' to the nudity of the marbles. Such a sentiment could only come, Henry remarked, from someone to whom sculpture was a sealed book. But then much of Europe was a sealed book to Hawthorne. 'We seem to see him strolling through churches and galleries as the last pure American – attesting by his shy responses to dark canvas and cold marble his loyalty to a simpler and less encumbered civilization.'

Henry James would never be able to stroll through the churches and galleries of Europe with quite the same purity, the same air of innocence – or of ignorance.

4

During this time he had ample leisure in which to ponder his own ambiguous state. He could look at Europe with American eyes, and he knew that he looked at America often as if he were a European. He might speak with irony later of the 'baleful spirit of the cosmopolite' and the 'uncomfortable consequence of seeing many lands and feeling at home in none'. Cosmopolitanism was a civilized state of being; yet it was hardly the ideal state. The ideal, James believed, 'should be to be a concentrated patriot'. The international mind seemed to him an accident of nature. When it did happen, one had to make the best of it.

There comes a time when one set of customs, wherever it may be found, grows to seem to you about as provincial as another; and then I suppose it may be said of you that you have become a cosmopolite. You have formed the habit of comparing, of looking for points of difference and of resemblance, for present and absent advantages, for the virtues that go with certain defects and the defects that go with certain virtues. One became an initiate 'into the merits of all peoples'. National virtues were numerous. They could be very different. 'Downright preferences' were hard.

Such was the lesson of his summer's travels, of his Concord visit, of his hours in Quincy Street. Henry James came to see himself in the ironic light of the story of Eden. America was his lost paradise and his had been the 'fortunate fall'. 'Very special and very interesting,' he was to write, 'to catch in the fact the state of being of the American who has bitten deep into the apple of "Europe" and then been obliged to take his lips from the fruit.'

38

The Dispossessed

IN a passage of reminiscence set down when he was 55 Henry James spoke of his Cambridge period as a time of 'brooding exile'. He imagined himself as having been like 'dispossessed princes and wandering heirs' deprived alike of kingdom and of inheritance. The kingdom, he believed, was the Europe of his *Wanderjahr* – where he wanted to be; the inheritance was his matured vision of the transatlantic world, which he could contemplate now only from the ruralism of Quincy Street and the town-pump in Harvard Square. The princely palaces had shrunk to the life of the provinces, the domicile of his immaturity.

The passage of memory in which the middle-aged Henry James looked back on his 27-year-old self was prompted by his re-reading certain of his early stories, and his selection of two of them for inclusion in the definitive edition of his novels and tales. He chose *A Passionate Pilgrim* which he wrote at the beginning of his Cambridge 'exile', and *The Madonna of the Future* which he had written at the end, when he was once more in Europe. These tales marked two significant moments in his career. In resurrecting them he described himself as having been engaged in 'sneaking attempts to substitute the American romantic for the American real'. He had done more; he had used romantic fancy to probe the personal 'real'. Henry admitted that he found the stories 'in the highest degree documentary for myself'. They are so for us as well.

I

In using the phrase about dispossessed princes and wandering heirs in speaking of himself, James was echoing a remark dropped by his narrator in A Passionate Pilgrim. Speaking to the 'pilgrim' of the story, as they wander in the grounds of his ancestral home in England, the narrator says: 'Here you can wander all day like a proscribed and exiled prince, hovering about the dominion of the usurper.' And in The Madonna of the Future the hero speaks of Americans as being the 'disinherited' of art. Dispossession, disinheritance, exile, usurpation – James's heroes in these stories think of themselves as deprived of their birthright, turned into spiritual (and actual) wanderers, unable in their new strange state to enter into possession. James's tale of his American pilgrim in England is a sentimental and romantic rhapsody on this theme, amid English fields and country houses and the colleges of Oxford. The sensitive New Yorker, who makes the pilgrimage, has found himself out of place in America. 'I came into the world an aristocrat,' he says.

I was born with a soul for the picturesque. It condemns me, I confess; but in a measure, too, it absolves me. I found it nowhere. I found a world all hard lines and harsh lights, without shade, without composition, as they say of pictures, without the lovely mystery of colour. To furnish colour, I melted down the very substance of my own soul.

Sitting in a park in England he is 'on the misty verge of what might have been'.

The pilgrim's name is Clement Searle, and he is one of those old-time 'claimants', who believes he still has a right to his ancestral property in England, an Elizabethan manor house named Lockley Park. When the narrator and Clement arrive at the manor, they are received with cordiality by the pilgrim's remote English kin, until their host discovers Clement's design. They are then ordered from the great house. The pilgrim recognizes that he has had a vain dream;

he has wished to possess something that in reality belongs to others. He wanders into delusion; he even fancies that he has become his ancestor, living in an earlier time. And he dies at Oxford of a delirious fever. He has been killed by an excess of sensibility, of spiritual 'dispossession'.

In dying, Clement thinks of the homeland he has abandoned. He speaks of 'a certain heroic strain in those young imaginations of the West, which find nothing made to their hands, which have to concoct their own mysteries, and raise high into our morning air, with a ringing hammer and nails, the castles in which they dwell'. Clement's last act is to give his modest belongings to an impecunious Englishman who wants to emigrate to America. 'My friend, there is to be one American the less. Let there be one the more.' If he has replaced the present by a dream of the past, he makes this small concession to the future in America.

The future is in the title of James's second tale of an American, this time a painter, who has arrived in Florence and passed twenty years dreaming before a large canvas that his great work (as in Balzac's tale of an 'unknown masterpiece') would be the epitome of all the madonnas that ever were, the very ideal of the maternal, in its highest spiritual form. He is eloquent, this little artist, with his red untidy hair emerging from beneath his *beretto*, his wide eyes, his shabby velvet tunic. It is he who proclaims that 'we are the disinherited of Art', as he orates to the American stranger he has met in the moonlight beside the Palazzo Vecchio. 'We are condemned to be superficial!' he says; 'the soil of American perception is a poor little barren, artificial deposit', and he adds, 'we are wedded to imperfection. An American, to excel, has just ten times as much to learn as a European. We lack the deeper sense. We have neither taste, nor tact, nor force.' He continues: 'Our crude and garish climate, our silent past, our deafening present, the constant pressure about us of unlovely circumstance, are as void of all that nourishes and prompts and inspires the artist, as my sad heart is void of bitterness in saying so.'

This passage has often been quoted as revealing Henry James's misgivings about his own future as an artist in his homeland. Up to a point he seems indeed to be doing some private pleading. What has been overlooked, however, has been the reply made by the narrator: 'You seem fairly at home, in exile, and Florence seems to me a very pretty Siberia.' And he goes on to say that nothing is so idle as to talk about our want of a nutritive soil, of opportunity, of inspiration, and all the rest of it. The worthy part is to do something fine! There's no law in our glorious Constitution against that. Invent, create, achieve! No matter if you've to study fifty times as much as one of these. What else are you an artist for?

Theobald discloses his dream of a 'madonna of the future'. He has met the Italian madonna-type; he has sketched her, studied her, loved her. The narrator is told by a member of the American colony that 'the months passed by and the miracle hung fire : our master has never produced his masterpiece'. When the narrator remarks to Theobald, quite casually, that his model has lost her youth, it is as if he gives the painter a mortal blow. Serafina is, in truth, middle-aged, and fat. She 'had made twenty years pass as a twelvemonth'. The artist turns his face to the wall. Like Clement he dies in a raging fever. His masterpiece is 'a mere dead blank, cracked and discoloured by time'. In his last moments he mutters : 'While I fancied my creation was growing, it was dying.' He knows now that he has wasted his life in preparation. He has lived with an obsession – and has clung to a sterile past.

2

Beyond their vividness as stories, these tales of the Cambridge period are a mirror of James's deepest feelings at the time. On the surface they embody the novelist's debate between America and Europe, which was highly active at this time and seeking resolution. On a deeper level they picture Henry's double exile – his sense of being an outsider at home, his fear of being an outsider in Europe. He knew himself to be a prince who had taken possession of his domains in Europe, and tasted the joys of personal freedom. But by the familiar hearth he was once again the Henry James Jr of his past, the wide-eyed little Harry James, observed and observant, who had to defend his status within the family. We are reminded in these tales of earlier episodes – and earlier stories – in the lives of Henry and his brother, in which they had played Jacob and Esau to one another, believing that each was a usurper of the other's birthright. In the United States, in a word, Henry James was not fully in control of his destiny; there was a family past as unreachable – and as smothering – as Clement's in England. The prevailing anxiety in these tales resides in this state of 'dispossession'.

In a word, Henry James in Quincy Street knew that he had out-grown his past and needed to be freed from it; he knew that he had lingered too long at the family hearth, and that he must escape. The silver cords however were still strong. If the story of the painter in Florence, worshipping an eternal mother, and the pilgrim clinging to an unattainable family past were told on a fanciful and imaginative plane, there were other tales which are cruder and less imagined. These were not resurrected half a century later, and when we read them we can understand why. They take us close to the inner life of No. 20 Quincy Street and the world of the young artist who was curbing his restless soul, or giving it relief in the perorations of suffering heroes.

One of the tales was called *Master Eustace*. It was probably the story 'whose interest should centre about a mother and son' of which James had spoken to Howells. The mother in this tantrum-packed tale, a widow, has treated her only child as if he were a lover, and also as an 'heir-apparent'. She spoiled him in every way. She liked to lean her head on his shoulder, and 'resting in this delicious contact, with her arm round his neck and her cheek on his hair, she would close her eyes in a kind of tremor of ecstasy'. She also would stroll with him in the garden giving him occasionally a 'compulsive hug'. Small wonder that Master Eustace experiences ecstasy as well – a sense of complete possession. He leaves for his grand tour of Europe; and if he is not a passionate pilgrim, the passion is reserved for his homecoming. His mother has married an old and loyal friend, and his rage explodes in speeches such as James must have heard upon the New York stage during his childhood. 'I'm like Hamlet,' says Master Eustace; 'I don't approve of mothers consoling them-selves.' And he is indeed a small-town Hamlet of the New World with a wooden house for his Elsinore. While he was wandering in far-away places a stranger had occupied the domestic throne.

Did she hope to keep it a secret? Did she hope to hide away her hus-band in a cupboard? Her husband! And I – I – I – what has she done with me? Where am I in this devil's game? Standing here crying like a schoolboy for a cut finger – for the bitterest of disappointments! She has blighted my life – she has blasted my rights. She has insulted me – dis-honoured me. Am I a man to treat in that fashion? Am I a man to be made light of? Brought up as a flower and trampled as a weed! Bound in cotton and steeped in vitriol!

Eustace's outrage is that of a husband who has an unfaithful wife, rather than that of a son whose mother has sought happiness in a new marriage. From now on Eustace is only a pretender to a throne he believed to be his. The drama, like its speeches, is resolved in a pistol-flourish, and the mother's death of heart-failure. Dispossession is complete.

So Henry, returning from his grand tour, discovered distinct changes in the climate of Quincy Street. He might still be the preferred son of his mother, the old-time 'angel' of the family, but Mary James had settled into late middle age, serene, matronly, queenly, vaguely indifferent. Her children were grown; her domestic empire had been extended, for the younger brothers were in the west. Quincy Street was accustomed to Henry's absence. The elder brother had remained at home, in comfortable possession. Into a second tale Henry projected this pendant side of the familial situation, his old fraternal attachments and animosities. As *Master Eustace* is a story of mother and son, so *Guest's Confession* is a tale of two brothers, the elder a successful man who is also a hypochondriac with a vengeful disposition, and the younger a sensitive and artistic individual.

The terms on which we stood were a perpetual source of irritation. We were utterly unlike in temper and taste and opinions, and yet, having a number of common interests, we were obliged, after a fashion, to compromise with each other's idiosyncrasies. In fact the concessions were all on my side. He was altogether too much my superior in all that makes the man who counts in the world for me not to feel it, and it costs me less to let him take his way than to make a stand for my dignity ... He was a miserable invalid, and was perpetually concerned with his stomach, his lungs, and his liver, and as he was both doctor and patient in one, they kept him very busy.

When we recall Mary James's description of William James's multiple symptoms at this time, his 'morbid sympathy' with 'every form' of physical trouble, we are led to feel that Henry is writing at uncomfortably close quarters. William, much more literally than the fictitious Edgar, was both 'doctor and patient in one'.

The crucial scene in the story is one of the most painful and awkward ever written by James. The younger brother has been courting a young woman he has met at a summer resort. Edgar, the elder brother, arrives and discovers that the girl's father is a man who once defrauded him in a shady business deal. He seizes this moment for revenge : he forces the older man to kneel in public and confess his business sins. He gives no thought to the fact that he is ruining his brother's chances with the girl. In other words, the elder brother, by a crude revengeful impulse, limits his younger brother's freedom of action.

'Was I, after all, so excessively his younger brother?' the suitor muses. The story shows that he was. And while Edgar bears superficial resemblance to William James, the fraternal rivalry and fraternal animosity described in this tale offer vivid illustration of Henry's submerged feelings. William may have sensed some part of himself in the story, for he singled it out to emphasize certain of his chronic complaints against Henry : his use of French phrases, his 'note of literary reminiscence in the midst of what ought to be pure imagination'. The two phrases William focused on for attack were *les indifférents* and 'to whom I had dedicated a sentiment'. What he said about them was valid enough. The manner in which he criticized the story shows, however, an excess of feeling :

Of the people who experience a personal dislike so to speak of your stories, the most I think will be repelled by the element which gets expression in these two phrases, something cold, thin-blooded and priggish suddenly popping in and freezing the genial current. And I think that is the principal defect you have now to guard against. In flexibility, ease and light power of style you clearly continue to gain. *Guest's Confession* and this last letter in the *Nation* are proofs of it . . . I meanwhile say nothing of the great delight which all your pieces give me by their insight into the shades of being, and their exquisite diction and sense of beauty and expression in the sights of the world.

In effect, William, for all his praise, was calling Henry 'cold, thin-blooded and priggish'. Moreover, he added words hardly edifying to an imaginative writer : 'I still believe in your greatness as a critic.'

39

'The Great American Novel'

FOR Henry James, spending his days in Cambridge in what he deemed to be a state of sinful idleness, the logical solution seemed to be to write a novel which would establish his fame, earn him some money, make possible perhaps a return to Italy. Unmistakable hints had appeared in his *Nation* travel-sketches. Describing a group of houses in the Lake George region, he had written : 'One of them there was – but of it I shall say nothing. I reserve it for its proper immortality in the first chapter of the great American novel.' Arriving at Newport, which he found substantial and 'civilized' after Saratoga, he reflected : 'I can almost imagine a transient observer of the Newport spectacle dreaming momentarily of a great American novel.' Henry's dream apparently was not momentary. The innocent *Nation* reader would hardly be blamed for inferring that their anonymous author was planning – perhaps even embarked upon – a novel which he hoped would be both distinctively American and 'great'. Even Henry James, who in later years might have found the cliché intolerable, had this youthful dream of literary glory.

I

By the time the Saratoga and Newport seasons of 1870 were at an end, the writer had submitted three parts of a five-part work of fiction to Mr Fields, Howells's superior at the *Atlantic Monthly*. A surviving letter shows Henry adroitly pressing for early publication, or, in lieu of that, early payment. He was never to be modest in writing to editors and publishers. On this occasion he hoped Fields would content himself 'with my assurance that the story is one of the greatest works of "this or any age" '. This may have been his little joke : it is of a piece with his daydream of 'the great American novel'. To Norton he wrote in a less exuberant vein. The subject was 'something slight; but I have tried to make a work of art, and if you are good enough to read it I trust you will detect my intention. A certain form will be its chief merit.'

The modern reader may wonder what this certain form was, for *Watch and Ward* emerged demurely in the pages of the *Atlantic* as the story of an effete young Bostonian, who wears lavender gloves and consoles himself for failure in love by adopting a 12-year-old girl. His motive can hardly be said to be disinterested; he nourishes the private hope that Nora Lambert, on attaining womanhood, will marry him : he will have thus married, so to speak, his own carefully-raised daughter, without incurring the risk of incest. Moreover, by this Pygmalion act, he tries to remove himself from the competition of courtship. He is not wholly successful, for his cousin, the Rev. Hubert Lawrence, a worldly clergyman, shows unusual interest in the young lady; and Nora's own cousin, a penniless and rather shabby individual named Charles Fenton, also pursues her in the hope of a substantial dowry. We can see from this that Henry somehow has been unable to stray from picturing family relations: indeed everyone seems related to everyone in this novel. As Henry describes the two Lawrence cousins, we find ourselves listening to familiar words:

He and Roger had been much together in early life and had formed an intimacy strangely compounded of harmony and discord. Utterly unlike in temper and tone, they neither thought nor felt nor acted together on any single point. Roger was constantly differing, mutely and profoundly, and Hubert frankly and sarcastically; but each, nevertheless, seemed to find in the other a welcome counterpart and complement to his own personality.*

Thus the brothers of *Guest's Confession* are converted in this novel into Roger, the man of sentiment, and Hubert, the religious-worldly type. In the end Hubert's insincerity and Fenton's opportunism are unmasked. Roger wins his wife – after arousing her pity by a prolonged illness. Once again James has duplicated his old stories of a 'heroine of the scene' surrounded by suitors who possess traits of the significant figures in his childhood, with himself as the unassertive and self-doubting aspirant. But this time he gives himself the victory.

2

Conceived as a study of Boston manners, *Watch and Ward* deals rather with the *mœurs* of Quincy Street. Indeed there is no painting of the Boston scene: we are unaware that we are in that city until the middle of the book. At every turn we are aware, however, of the relationships among the characters. The book is of a piece with the tales of the 'dispossessed'; Henry James has moved into a further phase of dispossession. Where before he made tantrum-tales of it, he now writes a fairy-tale. The rejected Roger entertains James's dream of fair women: and the ideal woman, this time, will be secured from rivals by an act of previous possession. If in *Master Eustace* the Hamlet-theme showed strong sensual feeling between a mother and a son, the relationship between Roger and Nora has a more overt element of sexuality but how conscious James was of this is a moot point. It must have seemed harmless in its day, since it escaped Mr Field's watchful eye, and that of his assistant, Howells,

* This was revised in 1878 to read 'an irritating counterpart and complement'.

as well as the type-setters of the *Atlantic*. Both the serial and book versions – published eight years apart – contain a passage in which Roger wonders after adopting Nora whether at the worst a little precursory love-making would do any harm. 'The ground might be gently tickled to receive his own sowing; the petals of the young girl's nature, playfully forced apart, would leave the golden heart of the flower but the more accessible to his own vertical rays.' This is a curious passage to come from an inveterate reader of French novels. It may have been penned tongue-in-cheek; yet it may represent also a certain unconscious eroticism. Another and better-known passage describes Nora, in *déshabille* at bedtime, bringing her watch to be wound, with Roger's key proving a 'misfit' and Hubert Lawrence's rather more successful, even though 'some rather intimate fumbling was needed to adjust it to Nora's diminutive timepiece'. These passages survived the close revision of *Watch and Ward* in 1878, after William James had found in the manuscript of *The American* certain phrases which, he wrote Henry, were so 'shocking' as to make the 'reader's flesh creep'. William had no difficulty in inducing Howells to remove them from the copy, and when Henry was informed, he gave Howells *carte blanche* over any future 'infelicities' of this kind.

Watch and Ward found a public in the magazine, but long before it had run its course Henry must have realized that his claims for it had been rather large. He was to republish it in book form in 1878 only because of expediency and for purposes of copyright. Yet his original strong feeling for the work is understandable. It contained certain personal emotions which were to yield him at least three of his best-known novels: *The Portrait of a Lady*, which has better claim to be judged a 'great American novel'; its later and grandiose version, *The Wings of the Dove*, and the ever-popular story of a father, a daughter and a fortune-hunter, *Washington Square*. James's fault in this first novel was similar to that of most beginners: he tried to cram too much of his subject-matter into the single work; he achieved a fiction rich in potential material and overstuffed in performance. *Watch and Ward* is a harbinger of Henry's greatness, a glimpse into the beginning of his creative process. His verdict, when he finally brought it out as a book, was at the opposite pole to what he had said to Fields or to Norton. It was 'pretty enough' he remarked after revising it; still it was 'very thin and as "cold" as an icicle'.

40

Alice

HENRY JAMES had written a novel about a young man of his own age, a maturing girl and her suitors. The suitors seemed to resemble figures in his own family. The young heroine reflected, to a considerable degree, James's discovery on his return from Europe that his only sister Alice, some four years his junior, had arrived at charming – if nervous and high-strung – womanhood. She had figured first in his life as a young and romping presence. When she was a quiet and troubled adolescent, Henry was going through his own troubles of the Civil War years. Now, after his absence, he saw her with new eyes. At 23 she was gentle, almost sedate; her eyes were large and candid; she had a broad brow, a strong mouth, a straight nose. She was of medium height and combed her thick hair back tightly from her forehead. Photographs suggest a colleen of American growth, with a certain strong facial resemblance to her novelist-brother and her father.

I

Alice had grown up in a family circle wholly masculine, save for the presence of her mother and her aunt. Five men, four brothers and a father, loomed in her childhood and youth: the father and the two elder brothers had always bestowed upon her elaborate mocking gallantries. She was a much-teased child – that is a child exposed to more than a modicum of peculiar, and often aggressive, adult behaviour. Even the great Thackeray, paying a call on the family one day in Paris, raised a laugh at her expense. Bending friendly eyes on her frock, he lifted his voice in high and simulated shock: 'Crinoline – I was suspecting it? So young and so depraved!'

One gathers that life in the nursery was an endless battle. When her two younger brothers, those closer to her own age – Wilky and Bob – did not ignore her, they subjected her to the usual petty indignities which small boys heap on sisters. She remembered a trip in an open carriage to the outskirts of Boulogne-sur-Mer, when she had been 7 or 8, and 'the anguish, greater even than usual, of Wilky's and Bob's heels grinding into my shins'. The words 'greater even than usual' convey a world of juvenile history. Outside the nursery, life proved deceptive and ambiguous. Certain female figures – Aunt Kate, her mother, governesses – hovered over her. They were admonitory, critical, disciplinary. In the front parlour, however, the elder Henry smothered her with affection, while the older and more distant brothers, Willie and Harry, petted – and teased. Like her brothers, Alice lived with contradictions; in her youth she fought back, but as she grew older the fight became too much for her. She took refuge in the defences of Victorian spinsterhood.

The brotherly teasing seems harmless when we read it. William sends his love to the 'cherry-lipped, apricot-nosed, double-chinned Alice', and wishes she would sass him 'as of yore'. Alice 'sassed'. And then the mother refers to Alice's 'sweet, loving chaffing' of their father. It was difficult to be silent in the midst of brilliantly talkative brothers. Alice learned her share of wit and sarcasm and the aggressive disguises of humour. Imitation was protection. She cultivated the robust attitudes of mind of her male siblings. Her soprano chimed in with the deeper voices around her. But, as the brothers move out into the world, and she finds herself isolated, we begin to see the melancholy beneath the chaffing, the desperation in the 'sassing'. Adolescence brought crises. 'The ancient superstition as to spring and youth being the joyous periods is pretty well exploded,' Alice would write in her journal. 'As the one is the most depressing moment of the year, so is the other the most difficult of life.' Her solution – a nun-like withdrawal, an attempt to achieve emotional neutrality. She remembered 'absorbing into the bone that the better part is to clothe one's self in neutral tints, walk by still waters and possess one's soul in silence'. Alice's memories of Newport, when she should have been awakening to life, were of 'the low, grey Newport sky in that winter of 62–63, as I used to wander about over the cliffs my young soul struggling out of its swaddling-clothes'. She got out of her swaddling-clothes; but she donned a spiritual straitjacket.

The girl's attachment to her father was strong; and it was transferred to her brother Henry. Since he was the quiet one, among the children, he probably constituted less of a threat to her selfhood than the lively William, or the boisterous shin-kicking younger brothers. The remembered ride in the carriage in France frames a picture of childhood hierarchies in the James family. The occasion had been an outing to the home of their French governess at Boulogne. The American children were fed an enormous frosted cake, and then were turned into a sandy garden to play with their French friends. William did not accompany them. At 14 he had his own resources. Henry, 12 or 13, was senior-in-charge. The younger brothers 'disappeared, not to my grief', and she was left alone with Henry. He took possession of a swing. She stood near by. The dreary minutes passed. The sun slanted; Henry remained lost in thought. Then he remarked, 'This might certainly be called pleasure under difficulties.' Alice recorded 'the stir of my whole being in response to the exquisite substance and original form of this remark'. Her literary brother had put into words the essence of the afternoon's experience. This little passage of brother-and-sister history reveals the early bonds of understanding that existed between them.

2

'In our family group,' James was to write, 'girls seem scarcely to have had a chance.' Alice had no chance at all in this group of vigorous and competing masculine egos. In our time she might have learned to play tennis, to swim, to row, to ski, to drive a car – to leave home and find her own way in life, expend some of the great store of vitality of which she gave, at first, abundant proof. Instead, the time came when she sat with folded hands and cultivated a Victorian composure, the mask of modest dress and quiet demeanour concealing intensities of feeling. She sat and waited – waited as the young women of her time did – for the liberation matrimony might bring. She possessed the social graces and the intellectual vigour of her elder brothers; she watched the younger ones go off to war – they disappeared from the family as they did from her presence that day in Boulogne. William and Henry were absorbed by their ailments and their careers. She was committed to the company of the aging parents and, for a long time, to that of her beloved aunt. She went to parties, in hope; she gossiped with friends about engagements and marriages. However, no cavalier came for her and she lapsed progressively into the familiar invalidism of so many of her Victorian sisters. 'Her tragic health,' Henry was to write, 'was, in a manner, the only solution for her of the practical problem of life.'

Her brother discerned the truth. Alice's high spirits and her fund of energy could not be sufficiently discharged upon the world. In the end she discharged them upon herself. In 1868 – when she was 20 – she had a nervous prostration. For the next ten years she was recurrently ill, with periods of recovery. When she was well, she worked for charities, went to Cambridge 'tea-fights', attended weddings. For a while she tried horseback-riding and there were pleasant domestic summers at resorts. She was able during one period to travel abroad with Henry and her Aunt Kate. Her second nervous collapse occurred in 1878. After this was she frequently ill. When she had her relapses, doctors treated her for ailments that seemed to them emotional and neurasthenic. They prescribed massage, cold water treatment, ice and electric therapy, 'blistering', Turkish baths. This was the best that medicine could do for Alice James. Like Henry James, his sister had her 'obscure hurt'.

3

Her first illness is vividly recalled in her journal. She lets us see a person wishing to use to the full the energies of her body; however, 'violent turns of hysteria' are substituted. Then she finds her mind 'luminous and active and susceptible of the clearest, strongest impressions'. Relief came in this way. She envisaged her fight as 'simply between my body and my will'. The will was worn out, she saw, by 'the strains of its constabulary functions'. She wrote:

As I used to sit immovable reading in the library with waves of violent inclination suddenly invading my muscles, taking some one of their myriad forms such as throwing myself out of the window or knocking off the head of the benignant pater as he sat with his silver locks, writing at his table, it used to seem to me that the only difference between me and the insane was that I had not only all the horrors and suffering of insanity but the duties of doctor, nurse, and straitjacket imposed upon me too. Conceive of never being without the sense that if you let yourself go for a moment your mechanism will fall into pie and that at some given moment you must abandon it all, let the dykes break and the flood sweep in, acknowledging yourself abjectly impotent before the immutable laws. When all one's moral and natural stock-in-trade is a temperament forbidding the abandonment of an inch or the relaxation of a muscle, 'tis a never-ending fight.

The impulses recorded in these words, and the strong need for self-policing, could not be stated more clearly. Alice's desire to 'knock off the head of the benignant pater', even though she adored him, must have been but one of the crowning assaults she would have liked to discharge upon any inhibiting figure.

Her illness of a decade later was described as 'an exaggerated recurrence of her old troubles' and as 'a nervous breakdown of a very severe character'. Alice's own memory of it, was of 'that hideous summer of '78 when I went down to the deep sea, and its dark waters closed over me, and I knew neither hope nor peace'. She told her parents at one point 'I cannot hear anything that touches my feelings.'

When she was mending, her mother wrote that 'her periods of depression and feelings of inability to meet life are less frequent, and in the intervals she is quite cheerful and like herself'. She added: 'She is able now when driving to take the reins herself, and has done so for an hour and a half at a time. She always enjoyed this very much, and the country is so exquisitely lovely just now, that I am in hopes she will get great gain by being out in this way.' The detail may be a small one, but Alice's pleasure in holding the reins was perhaps more than a return of strength during convalescence: it suggests with some vividness how much she would have relished some kind of 'driver's seat' in her existence. This she was never to have. When she did become independent, she no longer had the power to use her freedom.

She frankly talked to her father of suicide. She was intelligent enough to know that this would deeply disturb him. Her father, however, was a match for his daughter. She put the question to him on religious ground. Was it a sin for her to feel 'very strongly tempted' to suicide? He replied that he did not think it was. It might be, he philosophically said, 'when a person from a mere love of pleasurable excitement indulged in drink or opium to the utter degradation of his faculties, and often to the ruin of the human form in him'. But, he added, it was absurd to believe it sinful, if she wished to escape from suffering. He gave Alice (as he wrote to his youngest son) his fatherly permission to 'end her life whenever she pleased', exhorting her only to 'do it in a perfectly gentle way in order not to distress her friends'.

The elder Henry James had in this simple fashion made his daughter aware that she was mistress of herself. Alice told him, after considering his answer, that 'now she could perceive it to be her *right* to dispose of her own body when life had become intolerable, she could never do it; that when she felt tempted to it, it was with a view to break bonds, or to assert her freedom'. After this talk, the elder Henry told his family he no longer felt she would do away with herself, 'though she often tells me she is strongly tempted still'. And indeed, although Alice was to undergo intolerable suffering, she never took the final step that would have brought her an earlier peace.

41

The Painter's Eye

WILLIAM JAMES had good reason to believe in his brother's 'greatness' as a critic. A reader of Henry's early melodramas with their rage-filled soliloquies, might understandably show a preference for his book-reviews and art-notices. These are the work of a cool, competent, witty appreciator of the arts. His touch is always light, and there is tidiness of formulation, orderliness of thought, quiet authority. He finds a 'deplorable levity' in Disraeli and a 'great deal of small clevernesses'. He muses on that novelist's sovereign opportunity for disenchantment, and how it is nullified by his 'infantine joy' in being initiated into 'the value and glory of dukes and ducal possessions'. The fictions of Gustave Droz, one of the last novelists of the Second Empire, delight Henry. They have French precision of thought and statement, the 'old Gallic salt of humour'. He is particularly struck by one which tells of the history of a watering-place. Its central character, a Frenchman who tries to build his fortune by promoting a mineral spring, reminds him of 'the Yankee type (not the best) self-made, sharp as a razor, "genial", ambitious, bent on finding an "operation" in all things'. For Taine's classic work on English literature he is all admiration. He would like to rename it *A Comparative Survey of the English Mind in the Leading Works of its Literature*. The book is pictorial and critical; he cannot accept its philosophy, nor its theory of 'the race, the milieu and the moment' – but it is a 'literary achievement'. Taine, however, is 'a stranger to what we may call the intellectual climate of our literature'.

A reader of these reviews, which included a notice of Hawthorne's French and Italian notebooks, is constantly aware of being in touch with a curious, ranging, logical mind. It is empirical; its interest lies in places and persons, in generalizations about peoples, not in abstract ideas. Henry James is concerned above all with things his eyes can rest upon. By this process he shows himself, at every turn, the novelist performing as critic.

I

Towards the end of 1871 Howells asked James to serve as an occasional art-reviewer for the *Atlantic Monthly*. He probably remembered how entertaining Henry's comments on pictures had been in his letters from abroad. He knew also that he possessed what John La Farge called 'the painter's eye', a rare virtue in a man of letters. Through a wedding of the visual sense and verbal power he dominated and used his other senses.

Painters, he wrote in a review of French art,

always have a great distrust of those who write about pictures. They have a strong sense of the difference between the literary point of view and the pictorial, and they inveterately suspect critics of confounding them. This suspicion may easily be carried too far. Painters, as a general thing, are much less able to take the literary point of view, when it is needed, than writers are to take the pictorial; and yet, we repeat, the suspicion is natural and not unhealthy.

It was no more than just, he said, that a writer who wants to talk about art 'should be required to prove his familiarity with the essential conditions of the production of such works'.

In accepting the task of art reviewing for the *Atlantic* James predicted his work would soon collapse for want of material. His articles appeared with agreeable consistency for three months – January to March 1872. They were unsigned. After a lapse of two months one further article appeared, this time dealing with an exhibition in New York. Thereafter he had all the Continental galleries to roam in, and he dispatched from London a detailed account of the showing of the Wallace Collection in Bethnal Green. He wrote a few more pieces of art-criticism for the *Atlantic* when he returned to Boston two years later, but he never made of this part of his critical endeavour a very prolonged or consistent effort. In all, there are extant about sixty papers on art and artists. Certain of these have been collected by John L. Sweeney in *The Painter's Eye*. Mr Sweeney, in his appraisal of their content, reaches the conclusion that the novelist was 'an amateur, rather than a strict connoisseur' of the pictorial arts, and this is undoubtedly true. He had had what John Ruskin considered a prerequisite to any art-criticism, the experience of holding a paintbrush in his hand. He had also carried a sketch-book with him during his European travels. He had studied the masters. James's essential art critic is the literary spectator.

2

E. M. Forster remarked that when Henry James served as reviewer for the *Atlantic* he possessed 'a background of culture and a foreground of information that have been denied me in my late seventies'. One marvels indeed at the assurance and ease of the young American looking at what was available in Boston, or later at the Metropolitan Museum in New York or the Royal Academy in London. James's precision and precocity in his art writings may be judged for example in the way he shows us Sir Noel Paton's *Christ the Great Shepherd* – in two sentences. 'Christ is walking through a rocky country with a radiance round his head, and a little lamb in his arms towards whom he gently bends his face. The little lamb is very good.' Or the realism of Meissonier's *Battle of Friedland* acquired by an American at a price James deemed 'prodigious'. (Its transport alone cost a fortune 'though it occupies less space than the most emaciated human being. And it eats nothing.') The best thing in this picture, the young art critic wrote, was 'a certain cuirassier, and in the cuirassier the best thing is his clothes, and in his clothes the best thing is his leather straps, and in his leather straps the best thing is the buckles'.

Of Leighton's nudes, he remarked that their texture 'is too often that of the glaze on the lid of a prune-box; his drawings too often that of the figures that smile at us from the covers of these receptacles'.

On Millais: 'Mr Millais always knows thoroughly well what he is about, and when he paints very badly he is certainly aware of it, and of just how it serves his turn; indeed, I may say that to paint so badly as Mr Millais occasionally does, a great deal of knowledge must be brought to bear.'

Or the directness of: 'When Sir Henry Raeburn has to render a hand, an arm, a leg he usually draws it far better than Gainsborough, or even Sir Joshua; but his manly and respectable work lacks a certain charm which one always finds in theirs. The touch of fancy is absent; it is all plain, nutritive prose.'

Or a Dutch painter:

A picture that need not fear juxtaposition with Rembrandt is an admirable specimen of a Dutch painter who is rarely encountered – John de Capella: a gray, moist harbor-scene; the edge of a pier near which a boat is unloading, and an expanse of a quiet water, with other boats vaguely

seen beyond it. This small picture is a masterpiece; the look of the monotonous sky, stuffed, as it were, with small rain clouds; of the warm,
damp, air, with softened muffled sounds passing through it, is a marvel
of quiet skill.

One wonders where James heard the 'softened muffled sounds' while
looking on the picture. Art at this moment became for him total
reality.

3

He was not, as modernity defines it, an 'art critic'. He wrote about
pictures in this literary and descriptive way. His 'painter's eye' never
carried him into technique or 'painterly' feeling. He was slow in
assimilating the impressionists, although he went to the first impressionist show at Durand-Ruel's in 1876; and he was inevitably
bewildered by the post-impressionists in his old age. It took him a
long time to appreciate Whistler of whom he first said 'his manner
of painting is to breathe upon canvas'.

Art-making, art-watching, art-collecting is to be found in twenty-
five of James's first thirty stories. This suggests that James's school of
the novelist was indeed the museum world quite as much as the
classics of literature. He maintained this relationship between the
pictorial arts and life in his novels. His famous 'portrait' of a lady
includes the most scathing characterization in literature of an art-
dilettante who is the lady's husband. He writes Portraits of Places,
Transatlantic Sketches: his pen seems to be also a brush.

The art criticism in Henry James belongs then not to the specialist,
but to that of the genius who uses pictures to feed his own art; his
was a visual sense that, in the end, came to regard pictures as life
itself, to feel that artifacts, whether the work of a goldsmith or a
master of the brush, spring from human resources and are intended
for human uses. In that sense his criticism of painting was never
detached from the paintings' surroundings. He was aware of the
wall on which the painting was hung, as well as the museum in
which he was seeing it; he was aware of what the painter was doing; that is, he was 'psychological', and he was aware that he was
bringing to bear on that painting the accumulated civilization of his
being. A total life experience faces the given picture, and James was
not prepared to narrow this vision or experience for specialized 'art
criticism'. The picture for him was not only canvas and paint; it was
feeling and memory, history, ambition, power, conquest.

In sum, James had certain qualities which better critics sometimes do not possess – the advantage above all of his way of looking
at everything. And he had his style. He could describe pictures with
such exactness and brilliance that we forget that the description is
often as critical as it is descriptive. The central fact remains that in
James's lifelong flirtation with the 'picture' he remained 'literary',
and only slowly accepted new forms and new experiments. He never
looked at a picture simply as a painting, as a painter looks at it.

42

Escape

LATE in the summer of 1871 Henry James visited Canada briefly,
from Niagara to Quebec, writing articles as before on his travels for
the *Nation*. His little tour began with a boat-trip – from Toronto
across Lake Ontario; in due course he studied Niagara and rhapso-
dized for his readers in the manner of one of his own untutored
Americans in his tales – 'it beats Michelangelo'. This he later modified into a more aesthetic judgement – 'in the matter of line it beats
Michelangelo'. His observations of Quebec were happier. Here at
least was evidence of an older culture, instead of nature in the raw.

The city seemed to snatch a past 'from our scanty annals' and he
wondered what its future might be. Quebec reminded him somewhat
of Boulogne-sur-Mer, where he had spent his 14th year. He grasped
quickly the nature of the French-Canadian society, 'locked up in its
small dead capital, isolated on a heedless continent, and gradually
consuming its principal, as one may say – its vital stock of memories,
traditions, and routine'. Evenings in Quebec, he thought, might be as
dull as Balzac's scenes of provincial life. Did they play *loto* and
arrange marriages between their sons and daughters, whose education was confided to abbés and abbesses? He encountered in the
streets little old Frenchmen who looked indeed as if they had stepped
out of Balzac. Quebec, he mused, must be a city of gossip, for he
saw no sign that it was a city of culture. He scanned the windows of
the booksellers: a few Catholic statuettes and prints, two or three
Catholic publications, 'a festoon or so of rosaries, a volume of
Lamartine, a supply of ink and matches'. James walked in the
market-place and listened to the *patois* of the farmers and noted

their 'evident good terms with the tin-spired parish church, standing there as bright and clean with ungrudged paint and varnish as a Nürnberg toy'. One of them spoke to him 'with righteous contempt of the French of France. "They are worth nothing; they are bad Catholics."' In these words, and with his searching scrutiny, Henry James caught the unchanged note of French Canada.

I

Early in 1872 he began to hint in his letters that he had some hope of getting to Europe : it was still 'absurdly vague', he told Elizabeth Boott, but he was determined to cross the ocean 'by hook or by crook in the late summer or early autumn'. If he did so, he said, he could hardly stop short of Florence or Rome. A month later he was still speaking of 'vague moonshiny dreams' of escape 'with what speed I may'. What is clear now is that sometime between the beginning of that year and May, when he sailed, he was able to convince the *Nation* that he could write a usable series of European travel-articles for the journal; and he obtained from his father an advance of money for the trip, which he hoped to pay back by literary earnings.

What aided him was the feeling in the James family that it was time for Alice to be given the advantage of foreign travel already enjoyed by William and Henry. This must have been debated for some time, because of Alice's precarious health. The devoted Aunt Kate offered to go as Alice's companion; and it was accordingly settled that Henry would act as escort to the womenfolk, looking after their travel-arrangements as well as being *cicerone* and protector. The plans were broad, and the itinerary would depend upon Alice's ability to support fatigue. Alice felt it would be wise not to plunge at once into London, but to reach it by easy stages. Henry acquiesced in this, since it would give him a chance to do a series of pieces on rural England. Switzerland seemed indicated as a place for a vacation in the midst of travel; and James hoped that if all went well they might, at the end of the summer, dip into Italy for a month. As far as he was concerned the experiment would show whether he could keep his pen profitably busy. He felt strongly that his literary material lay in Europe; moreover, he had solemnly vowed he would return to Rome. Since Alice's travel-plans had to be flexible, he made none himself. Time would take care of them.

2

One day that spring Henry walked to Shady Hill, the home of Charles Eliot Norton, where he had spent many happy hours in the past, to attend the funeral of Susan Norton, Charles's wife. She had died in February, in Dresden, and Norton, in Europe with his young children, had not been able to accompany the body home. Henry had been fond of Susan : he had many memories of their meetings abroad. It was with her that he had gone, one day in England, to lunch with the Darwins, and afterwards they had taken a memorable stroll through Holwood Park.

On 6 May 1872 James, writing to Norton and describing the burial, sought to comfort his correspondent. His thoughtful words showed the road he had himself travelled during his Cambridge months. He urged Norton to allow himself to experience to the fullest his loss and pain. One had to stand face to face with 'the hard reality of things'. Henry added that he presumed to speak to his friend in this fashion 'out of my own unshaken security'. The human soul was 'mighty, and it seems to me we hardly know what it may achieve (as well as suffer) until it has been plunged deep into trouble'. But James recognized that such words might be small comfort to one who had lost a wife and the mother of his children. At the end of the letter he mentioned casually that his departure for Europe was but five days off.

Henry James had had his season in Cambridge. His own spirit again and again had tested 'the hard reality of things'. Now his trunk was packed, and his own design was clear. He would stay abroad as long as he could, to show whether his pen could accomplish in Europe what it had failed to do in America – give him freedom and independence. This, he was now well aware in his 'unshaken security', he could not obtain in Quincy Street.

Part Two:

Transatlantic Sketches

43

Brother and Nephew

IT was as brother and nephew, rather than as writer for the *Nation*, that Henry James sailed for Europe in May 1872. Escorting Alice and his Aunt Kate seemed a modest price to pay for going abroad. It meant, for the time being, that he travelled with Quincy Street for company; he knew, however, that at the summer's end his companions would sail for home and he would then possess himself – and Europe. They crossed on the *Algeria*, a sturdy Cunarder which brought them to Liverpool in a little over eight days. The ladies experienced some seasickness; James did not miss a meal. On arrival in England he promptly booked an October return for his companions on the same ship.

I

They went first to Chester and its Roman ruins, favourite starting-place for many an American tour. Years later Henry would launch his 'ambassador', Lambert Strether, at the little hotel in Chester. Their itinerary took them to Lichfield and Warwick, North Devon and Salisbury; they passed through the rich farmland of the Shakespeare country – 'too ovine, too bovine, it is almost asinine,' quipped the *Nation* correspondent – and then, reaching Oxford, they wandered from college to college and garden to garden. In London they spent only a week, on the theory that cities would be exhausting for Alice; in Paris they lingered just long enough to spend a day with Norton and his children at St Germain-en-Laye and to see a play at the Théâtre Français. While the ladies rested, James visited the burnt-out ruins and barricades of the Commune. They took an overnight train to Geneva and presently were settled at Villeneuve, on Lake Leman, in the Hôtel Byron, near the Castle of Chillon. A few years later Daisy Miller, in her flirtatious finery, would make her appearance at nearby Vevey on her way to Rome. During this phase of their travels Alice withstood fatigue remarkably well. James and his aunt were determined, however, not to force their luck. The stay in Switzerland was designed as a breathing-spell from train and coach, a gain of coolness and quiet.

At the Hôtel Byron they met, by pre-arrangement, their loyal friends, the Italianate-American Bootts, Francis and his daughter Elizabeth, who was Alice's age. Assured of sociable companionship, Henry looked forward to several weeks of Swiss tranquillity. However, a period of torrid weather set in; and, after a week at Villeneuve, the Jameses and the Bootts moved by way of Berne and Interlaken to Grindelwald, at 3,400 feet, partly in the belief that Alice needed a more bracing climate. Here towards the end of July they seemed to have found the answer to their problem; but the tremendous Alpine sun drove them higher and higher. This time the Bootts did not join them. Francis was not fond of mountains, and Lizzie liked the sociability of urban hotels. In a letter from Grindelwald, the brother and nephew confessed that 'the romance of travel – of *tables d'hôtes*, strange figures and faces, and even of Alps – soon rubs off and the throb of admiration and surprise soon subsides into a tolerably jogtrot sort of pulsation'. Nevertheless he had been able to distil the romance of travel into four pieces for the *Nation*, the record of their sight-seeing in England. He had also distracted himself by climbing the Faulhorn, an eight-hours' trudge, and was pleased to discover that 'my old Swiss legs, such as they are, haven't lost their cunning'.

From Grindelwald the Jameses went by slow carriage to Meyringen, and finally to the Grisons, with Alice and Aunt Kate following on horseback. Here they put up at a hotel at Thusis, on the Splügen road. Now the air was too bracing for Alice, and Henry's letters spoke of her being made nervous by it. What this meant in reality was that she had taken to her bed in a state of nervous exhaustion. As soon as she could move, they went on to Chur, but Henry was ready to conclude that 'Alice has tested stiff mountain air to its condemnation'. She had need of the 'human picturesque'.

So long as she was kept busy in towns and cities she would manage her problems decently well; left alone to idleness and repose, in high mountain resorts, she sooner or later succumbed to her neurasthenia. He did not tell this to Quincy Street, and it is only in later letters that we learn what really happened during this part of their travels. There seem to have been three occasions on which Alice became ill and had to be nursed and comforted, for Henry was to speak of her 'performances at Thusis, Andermatt and Batzen', and during a later illness wrote to her, 'I am sorry I am not near you to heal you and comfort you as I then did – as you will vividly remember.' He performed his role as brother, guide and morale-builder with affectionate loyalty. But Switzerland proved a trial alike to him and his aunt. Long before their journeyings were over, he was eager to be free.

2

After Alice's breakdown at Thusis, Henry lost no time in moving his companions to Berne. They found the Bootts in an old-fashioned hotel amid 'a large entourage' of Bostonians. The writer, on his side, was glad enough to be in a city again. He confessed in one of his *Nation* articles that he relished 'a human flavour in his pleasures' and felt that there was a more equal intercourse between man and man than between man and mountains. He said he had found himself grumbling on occasion that the snow-peaks of the Oberland were not the marble pinnacles of a cathedral, and that the 'liquid sapphire and emerald of Leman and Lucerne are not firm palace-floors of lapis and verdantique'. The Jameses enjoyed their visit to Berne and while they feared they might be rushing matters to go to Italy in late summer they set out cheerfully on 26 August, limiting their tour to northern Lombardy and Venetia, with the promise of a return to coolness in the Austrian Tyrol.

James's letters to Quincy Street, placed beside his travel-sketches, give us a lively picture of their travels. On a warm August evening they are in Chambéry in lately-occupied Savoy; Alice and Aunt Kate are leaning out of their hotel windows watching a French military band in red leggings, serenading an inspector-general who is banqueting within. While the women rested, the indefatigable Henry had gone to Les Charmettes, where Jean-Jacques Rousseau had lived with Madame de Warens. The cracked yellow spinet still stood there and on the table lay Rousseau's turnip-shaped timepiece which had once ticked the hours in the great man's waistcoat pocket. After the opulence of Ferney and Coppet, the haunts of Voltaire and Madame de Staël, this seemed poverty-stricken indeed; and the hero and heroine of the place, James reflected, had been, after all, first-rate subjects for psychology rather than poetry.

Twenty-four hours later, they negotiated the Mont Cenis tunnel. Old sensations made him aware how intense had been his 1869 experience of Italy – the balcony, the Venetian blind, the cool floor, the speckled concrete; the Castello in Turin's square with its shabby rear and its pompous front; the brick campaniles in the mild, yellow light; the bright colours, the soft sounds – it was the eternal Italy and also his personal Italy. Under the arcades the human scene was unchanged: handsome officers, buxom females, civil dandies with religious faith in their moustachios; ladies in lace mantillas, with a little too much display 'in the region of the bodice'. In Milan they inspected the cathedral; they paused at Lake Como and devoted four dreamy days to Venice. The mosquitoes kept them awake at night, but in the daytime they lived in gondolas and found coolness on the lagoons and in the churches. They ate figs, went every night to Florian's for ices and ransacked the place for photographs of works of art. An afternoon at Torcello was memorable. Two strong-armed gondoliers helped them cut 'the wandering breezes of the lagoon, like a cargo of deities descending from Olympus. Such a bath of light and air – colour and general luxury, physical and intellectual.'

Austria-bound, they paused at Verona and broke the trip to Innsbruck at Batzen, where Alice had a brief collapse. Henry found Germany 'uglier than ever' by contrast with Italy. But, he confided to William, it was a relief to be turning toward Paris again. 'What colossal tastelessness!' Henry exclaimed after visiting the *Hofkirche* at Innsbruck. It was a shame to go into a *Hofkirche* to laugh – 'but I distinctly smiled'. Munich was 'a nightmare of pretentious vacuity: a city of chalky stucco – a Florence and Athens in canvas and planks'. Nuremberg was only a little better, and Henry was prepared to trade a thousand Nurembergs for 'one ray of Verona'. Toward the end of the German trip he was convinced – so he wrote from Heidelberg – that he should 'listen to the voice of the spirit – to cease hair-splitting and treat oneself to a good square antipathy'. He could never hope, he said, 'to become an unworthiest adoptive grandchild of the fatherland'. So much for William's continuing insistence that he should have a period of study in Germany.

Strasbourg was gloomy and battered; utterly conquered and fast being Germanized. They crossed the frontier and after a day's hard travel were in Paris again, at the Hôtel Rastadt, in the Rue Neuve St Augustin, where they found the old family friends, the Tweedys, Edmund and 'Aunt' Mary. They dined with them almost daily and helped relieve 'the mutual monotony of our by this time extremely familiar selves'. The Nortons were in Paris, and Henry, Alice and Grace had an evening together at the theatre. The sister and aunt were occupied with visits to dressmakers and milliners, dispatching parcels and trunk-packing, leaving Henry free to roam during long afternoons. 'Alice has just shewn me a ravishing bonnet,' the brother tells Quincy Street, 'which will certainly, next winter, be the wonder and envy of all Cambridge.' Aunt Kate is weary and eager to go home; 'she has had no heart evidently in our journey on her account, and yet her devotion to Alice has been immeasurable'. In retrospect James felt the tour had been of great value. 'We seem to have seen a vast deal and to have had innumerable delightful days and hours and sensations.' It appeared to have been 'absurdly easy'. What he does not say is that both for him and Aunt Kate a constant anxiety had undermined many of the days and hours of which he now spoke with pleasure.

The brother and nephew was loyal to the end. He crossed the Channel with his charges, paused briefly in London, escorted them to Liverpool and saw them aboard the *Algeria*. He could now begin his career abroad in earnest.

44

The Sentimental Tourist

QUINCY STREET had been carefully prepared for the news that Henry was remaining in Europe. Five of his travel-sketches had appeared in the *Nation*; *Guest's Confession*, which he had written before leaving, was published that autumn in the *Atlantic* – his father had read proofs for him – and during his brief stay in London he had taken Alice to see the Wallace Collection at the Bethnal Green Museum, to write another of his art-pieces for Howells. 'A decent little sum' was thus due to him from the magazines. 'You have learned, by my recent letters,' he informs William, 'that I mean to try my luck by remaining abroad. I have little doubt that I shall be able to pull through.' He wanted to spend a quiet winter, he said; he would read a good deal. 'I shall be able to write enough and well enough, I think: my only question is how to dispose of my wares. But in this, too, I shall not fail.' A few days later he told his parents: 'I suppose you are resigned to not seeing me this autumn. I can't say that I am to my prospects of exile, but I try to steel myself.

Seriously speaking, I expect this coming year or two, over here, to do a great deal for me. It will not be my own fault if it don't.'

The verbally fastidious Henry tended to indulge in the colloquial when he addressed his parents. His allusion to the 'coming year or two, over here' envisaged a greater expanse of time than he had hitherto mentioned. There remained the practical side. It would be economical to remain in Paris for a while; he had never lived there, had used it always as a way-station, and would try now to stay out the autumn. His destination, however, was Italy. One reason was that the *Nation* had a Paris correspondent, but none in Rome. Having explained this, he asked permission to draw on his father's letter of credit intended for his and Alice's tour, 'to help me on my way to Italy; for the clothes and the journey together would rather diminish my private fund'. £50, he felt, would 'start me in life and carry me ahead for a long time, as regards clothes'.

The elder Henry agreed. He proposed that the magazines send their payment for his son's articles directly to him. He would thus be Henry's banker as well as his literary agent. 'It is the best plan,' Henry replied, little realizing that he was thereby still tethered to Quincy Street. 'I shall do very well without ruining you.'

I

Henry James's travel-sketches in the *Nation* – his English notes, embodied in four long papers, his Swiss notes and later his record of his journey with Alice into Italy and Germany – readily won a public, for Howells presently was asking him for similar articles for the *Atlantic*; and the *Galaxy* in New York, which had printed some of Henry's tales, was quite prepared to publish his essays. He thus broadened his market at this crucial moment, and by this tolerably easy kind of journalism – easy at any rate for him — gave himself the material foundation for a continuing stay abroad. From Quincy Street his brother William kept up a running fire of praise and criticism. He complained of Henry's 'over-refinement and elaboration'. He offered advice : 'Recollect that for Newspaporial purposes, a broader treatment hits a broader mark; and keep bearing that way as much as you can with comfort. I suppose traits of human nature and character would also agreeably speckle the columns.' The elder brother's opinions were valued by Henry but viewed with objectivity and aloofness. The younger brother had the guidance of

Howells and the other editors for whom he was writing, but William tended to speak out of his long-assumed authority. He returned again and again to the charge: Henry had to cultivate directness of style. 'Delicacy, subtlety and ingenuity, will take care of themselves.' He confessed, however, that he had been surprised at the number of persons who were reading his brother and liking what he wrote. He himself thought 'the style ran a little more to *curliness* than suited the average mind'.

To such a running commentary Henry finally gave response. Doubtless with practice, he said, he would be able to be a little less refined: yet beyond a certain point he did not feel that this was desirable, 'for me at least, who must give up the ambition of ever being a free-going and light-paced enough writer to please the multitude'. The multitude, he said, had no taste 'that a thinking man is bound to defer to'. To write for the few who have taste was perhaps to lose money, but he was not afraid of starving. He preferred to work his material close, to try to cultivate a style. This was the only way, as an artist, that he would not feel himself risking 'intellectual bankruptcy'. He had 'a mortal horror of seeming to write thin'.

It was clear thus from the first that there was a fundamental difference between the two brothers. William, in reality, was pleading for that lucidity which he himself possessed, in so rare a fashion. He failed to appreciate the artist side of his younger brother. William was all for communication; Henry was all for artistic statement – and for style. William was to achieve a style of his own, apparently without taking sufficient stock of the artist within himself.

2

In writing his travel-sketches James proceeded from a very clear conception of what he wanted to do. The observations of an intelligent traveller were worth recording, he believed, even when the experience was confined to the beaten track. He praised Taine's Italian and English travel-writings because there was in them a constant effort 'to resolve his impression into a positive and definite statement'. He insisted that the prose of travel had to be a 'tissue of images and pictures', such as he found in Théophile Gautier. He was aware also that the travel-writer must keep the reader within a certain angle of vision. Although he designates himself in the *Nation*

as 'our old friend the sentimental tourist', he is above all 'an observant American'. His vision may be cosmopolitan, but he tries to
use his eyes on behalf of his domestic readers. It takes, he remarks
in England, 'a poor disinherited Yankee to appreciate the "points"
of this admirable country'. During his walks he seeks the 'fine differences in national manners' as well as the 'foreign tone of things'.
He remarks:

The tone of things is, somehow, heavier than with us; manners and
modes are more absolute and positive; they seem to swarm and thicken
the atmosphere about you. Morally and physically it is a denser air than
ours. We seem loosely hung together at home, compared with the English, every man of whom is a tight fit in his place.

There is considerable method in James the traveller. His attention
is divided between the works of nature and the works of man: his
concern is with the works of man – the flow of life into art, the flow
of art into life. Descriptive prose by now comes easy to him: he can
evoke Devon's flora and fauna with a few brushstrokes – the em-
bankments of moss and turf, the lace-work of trailing ground-ivy,
the solid walls of flowering thorn and glistening holly.

They are over-strewn with lovely little flowers with names as delicate
as their petals of gold and silver and azure – bird's-eye and king's-finger
and wandering-sailor – and their soil, a superb dark red, turns in spots
so nearly to crimson that you almost fancy it some fantastic compound
purchased at the chemist's and scattered there for ornament.

He tosses this off with a spontaneity that carries us with him: but
he also likes to get the reader out of the fields and into the towns
and cities. He is in Berne and has 'the vision of a long main street,
looking dark, somehow, in spite of its breadth, and bordered with
houses supported on deep arcades, whereof the short, thick pillars
resemble queerly a succession of bandy legs, and overshaded by
high-piled pagoda roofs'. And so to the shops, and the houses, and
the windows of the houses, and the human being framed by the
window, 'a Bernese fair enough, at least, to complete the not especially delicate harmony of the turkey-red cushion and the vividly
blooming plants'. His eye is always for the architecture, for the
buildings by which man has asserted himself. In Milan the cathedral
may have its shortcomings but 'it is grandly curious, superbly rich'.
Henry hopes he will never grow too fastidious to enjoy it; he reflects
that perhaps 'beauty in great architecture is almost a secondary

merit' beside the effect of mass – such mass as makes a building 'a supreme embodiment of sustained effort'. From this point of view a great building is 'the greatest conceivable work of art. More than any other it represents difficulties annulled, resources combined, labour, courage and patience'.

Within Milan's cathedral he has other reflections. He sees the altar-lamps twinkling through the incense-thickened air and thinks of fog-lights at sea; and the great columns rise to the roof with the girth and altitude of oaks; but they have little refinement of design, 'few of those felicities of proportion which the eye caresses, when it finds them'. The Jamesian eye is a caressing eye. Life is not immobile; it is all a human scene. In Turin he pauses before paintings but sees the people in them. In part of Van Dyck's portrait of the children of Charles I he thinks of the young ones not as images on canvas but as living babies; 'you might kiss their hands, but you certainly would think twice before pinching their cheeks'. He finds 'all the purity of childhood' in the picture and also 'all its soft solidity of structure, rounded tenderly beneath the spangled satin, and contrasted charmingly with its pompous rigidity'. In Venice, at Torcello, he meets a group of children not on canvas, 'the handsomest little brats in the world', clamouring for coppers; they are almost as naked as savages, with their little bellies protruding, and they show their handsome hungry teeth; yet they scamper and sprawl in the thick grass; they grin like cherubs and suggest 'that the best assurance of happiness in this world is to be found in the maximum of innocence and the minimum of wealth'. For an instant he combines art and life. One of the urchins has a smile 'to make Correggio sigh in his grave'.

His scenes are not always those of the lonely observer looking at children in pictures or children in life. He seems to have found it easy to spend time in 'starlight gossip at Florian's'. There are always compatriots. In Venice he greets a young American painter in the piazza on the evening of his arrival. The encounter foreshadows the opening scene of *The Madonna of the Future*, and he constructs with his eyes what should have been that painter's world, envying him his innocence – the fact that he is 'unperplexed by the mocking, elusive soul of things' –and his ability to be satisfied by surfaces, light-bathed, old things and old textures; his mornings in 'the clustered shadows of the Basilica'; afternoons in church, or campo, on canal or lagoon; evenings in the piazza feeling the languid sea-breeze throbbing 'between the two great pillars of the Piazzetta and over the low, black domes of the church'. Henry would have liked to spend all his days in the decaying city. 'The mere use of one's eyes, in Venice, is happiness enough.'

45

A Parisian Autumn

HENRY JAMES had returned to London after bidding farewell to his sister and aunt and he remained long enough to replenish his wardrobe as he had planned. 'Oh, the grimness of London! And, oh! the cookery of London!' He recrossed the Channel with relief. 'Even after all its tragedies, Paris has a certain natural wholesome gaiety which is a blessing of heaven.' At the Hôtel Rastadt he regained his old room and settled contentedly into it for the remainder of the autumn. Little larger than a ship's cabin, it was all the warmer for its smallness and its window framed a pleasant view of roof-tops. He wrote in the mornings, walked in the afternoons, and in the evenings dined out, usually in the Boulevard des Capucines on a *rosbif saignant* washed down by some prime English ale. Then he went to the theatre or simply returned to his room to read quietly by his fire. He was reading *Middlemarch*. Reviewing it later for the *Galaxy* he had at first qualified praise for it; nevertheless, he told Grace Norton that 'a marvellous *mind* throbs in every page'. He also wrote, during this time, two more travel-sketches and *The Madonna of the Future*.

I

He had led a 'madder and merrier' life in Cambridge, he remarked to his parents; as yet, the waiters in the restaurants were his chief society. However he found that the daily and hourly spectacle of human life in Paris was 'suggestive and remunerative'. If he was not meeting the French, he at least had no lack of native society. The Rue de la Paix and the Boulevard des Capucines looked to him like 'a perfect reproduction' of Broadway. And there were times when Cambridge seemed to have settled by the Seine. The Nortons had come and gone; the Tweedys had just left for Rome. Chauncey Wright, William's friend, had been at the Grand Hotel, 'trundling on tiptoes along the boulevard, as he did at home along Main Street' and as always 'serenity purpurine'. Samuel Rowse, the Boston artist, drifted in and out. The Lowells were in the Hôtel Lorraine, near the Quai Voltaire, in the company of John Holmes, brother of the autocrat of the breakfast table – 'the doctor *minus* versatility and *plus* modesty,' said Henry. He felt that Lowell, with all his reputation and advantages, was really indifferent to the world. Instead of moving in Parisian literary circles, 'here he is living in the heart of Paris, between his Cambridge wife and his Cambridge friend'. They made 'a little Cambridge together'.

The Seine was in flood. Swollen by heavy rains it looked like a 'civilized Mississippi'. Henry crossed it regularly to dine with Lowell, with whom he had had only a nodding acquaintance at home. Now they struck up a 'furious intimacy'. It had begun when Norton asked James to take a message to Lowell; the next day Lowell returned the call and 'we went out to walk and tramped over half Paris and into some queer places which he had discovered on his own walks'. In later years James was never to cross the Seine on rainy winter nights 'amid the wet flare of the myriad lamps', and note the 'varnished rush of the river or the way the Louvre grows superb in the darkness', without recalling his old sociable errands to the Left Bank. He would have preferred to meet French writers and to make French friends; failing this, Cambridge-by-the-Seine mitigated solitude.

At Lowell's hotel he would dine at the *table d'hôte*. The landlord sat with his guests and carved. Lowell's letters to Cambridge, as well as Henry's, give a picture of the dingy room, the food, and the voluble political arguments. 'Henry James, Jr, joins us now and then at dinner,' Lowell wrote, 'and, as luck would have it, the first day he came was a regular field day. A political discussion was got up for his special benefit, and such a row has not been heard since Babel.' It was, Henry reported to his father, 'stupidly expressed in epigrams', by four rather violent conservatives including the Marquis de Grammont, a French deputy, all with rosettes in their buttonholes. There was one republican. The conservatives tried to outdo one another in dreaming up ideas for repressive legislation. 'A page of Balzac, full of illustration for the humorist,' Henry recalled. 'Is this unhappy people booked for eternal chaos – or eternal puerility?' If France would not be a first-class power, Henry was certain that it 'can't fail to be a precious second-class one'.

2

One evening in mid-November 1872 James arrived at the Hôtel Lorraine to join the Lowells and found that Concord had joined the Parisian Cambridge. Ralph Waldo Emerson and his daughter Ellen were in Lowell's sitting-room; they were pausing briefly on their way to Italy and Egypt. Although Emerson had reached the years of his failing memory, he was still sufficiently alert and interested in the world. He seemed to remember Henry's art-letters, for he proposed that they visit the Louvre together. This they did on the morning of 19 November. Some weeks earlier Henry had paid a similar visit to the museum, accompanying the future professor of art history at Harvard, Charles Eliot Norton; he had written home that 'he takes art altogether too hard for me to follow him'. Emerson, he now found, did not take it hard enough. 'His perception of art is not, I think, naturally keen; and Concord can't have done much to quicken it.' Nevertheless, he was pleased that he appreciated the splendours of Paris and of the Louvre. Even when Emerson had nothing to say, 'his presence has a sovereign amenity'. He was 'peculiarly himself' on the morning during which they walked together through the galleries. To Concord, Ellen Emerson wrote: 'Father came home enchanted.'

Some years later Henry recalled that 'certain chords' could not vibrate in Emerson. He wrote in an essay:

I well remember my impression of this on walking with him in the autumn of 1872 through the galleries of the Louvre and, later that winter, through those of the Vatican: his perception of the objects contained in these collections was of the most general order. I was struck with the anomaly of a man so refined and intelligent being so little spoken to by works of art. It would be more exact to say that certain chords were wholly absent; the tune was played, the tune of life and literature, altogether on those that remained.

3

Emerson was unworldly; Norton was cold; Lowell touched James deeply – 'the oddest mixture,' as he was to say, 'of the lovable and the annoying, the infinitely clever and the unspeakably simple'. The lovable side in the end weighed much more heavily with Henry than the annoying. Lowell was 53 and Henry 29 when they met in Paris:

and their friendship was to extend and deepen during the remaining twenty years of Lowell's life. On the surface the two seemed hardly compatible. Lowell was a homespun Yankee, a lover of the American vernacular who also much preferred Cambridge to the Champs-Élysées. James remembered this when he spoke of him as having the 'simplicity as of childhood or of Brattle Street'. His weak point, he wrote to William would always be his opinions. His strong point was that he was the American of his time 'most saturated with literature and most directed to criticism'. James thought his poetry was that of the outraged citizen smiting a lyre, rather than the poetry of an artist; and he smiled gently at Lowell's pugnacious parochialism. 'I don't feel as if I should ever get anything very valuable out of him,' he remarked on meeting him a year or two after their walks in Paris. Nothing valuable for his work, but he got an extraordinary degree of acceptance of himself and the loyalty of a profound friendship.

In Lowell James found a kind of rugged yet gentle parent, who could point out slips of English and typographical errors in his work even while bestowing the fullest measure of affection. 'It is because you write so well that I care how you write,' Lowell would say. Or he would remark, on finding too many French words in a page of James's prose, 'You know French well enough to afford writing English.' He was proud of his accomplishments, almost as if Henry had been his son.

They took ten-mile walks together that autumn. They browsed endlessly in bookshops and along the quays, Lowell driving great bargains with the antiquarians. If Lowell was bookish, he was, in the Parisian streets, 'the least pale, the least passionless of scholars'. His Puritanism, deeply rooted, had in it 'the strong and simple vision, even in aesthetic things, of evil and of good, of wrong and of right', James was to remark that there was less of the 'peace of art' in Emerson and Hawthorne than in Lowell. This meant that Lowell was less of an artist; it made him a better companion. His company could be shared without experiencing overtones of moral ravage or inner conflict. A broad daylight cheerfulness surrounded the poet. When he couldn't find great pleasures, he was content with small ones. 'No situation could be dull for a man in whom all reflection, all reaction, was witty.'

Lowell's wit made Paris agreeable for James during a November and December otherwise rain-washed and dreary. 'Two whole *months* of uninterrupted rain,' he wrote to his sister; and yet he lingered while Rome beckoned. Christmas of 1872 was approaching when Henry began to uproot himself from his little room in the Hôtel Rastadt. He was still walking, play-going, Louvre-going, reading and writing. He had just been to the masked ball at the opera and found it stale and flat – and unventilated. The crowds in the street, the great pyramids of gaslight, the cabs laden with maskers, all seemed to him like some ancient revel in Babylon. At least this is what he told Quincy Street.

On 18 December James took his cab to the railway station. It was evening and the boulevards were filled with holiday-makers. Paris was mild and gay, and he wondered whether he wasn't making a mistake in leaving. The journey to Turin took twenty-four hours. He rested for a day, then went on to Florence. Here he found a letter from his 'Aunt' Mary Tweedy. Her husband was ill in Rome with gastric fever. A few hours later, during the evening of 23 December, Henry was once again – after three years' absence – in the Eternal City.

Part Three:
Roman Hours

46

A Roman Winter

HE noticed at once signs of change since his visit to papal Rome in 1869. The kiosks displayed secular newspapers; in the old papal Rome there had been only those of the Vatican. There were new gas-lamps round the spouting Triton in the Piazza Barberini. Putting up at the Hôtel de Rome, in the middle of the Corso, he went out immediately into the narrow, crooked streets. They were dark and empty. After the glittering boulevards of Paris, the Eternal City seemed a sleepy *ville de province*. He paused before the Spanish Steps; they had shrunk since his last visit. He climbed them and turned into the Via Gregoriana. All was silent and deserted. At No. 33 he knocked, and a few minutes later was being greeted affectionately by Mary and Edmund Tweedy in a charming little crimson drawing-room. Edmund had been ill but was mending. They wanted him to stay with them, but Henry declined. To accept their hospitality would have made him feel the world was a small place indeed.

He awoke next morning to perfect weather. The air glowed and throbbed under a sky of intense blue. Paris had offered him weeks of monotonous rain-washed asphalt. Rome glittered in the winter sun. He called on Lizzie and Francis Boott, and stayed with them for dinner on Christmas Eve. They fed him turkey and apple-sauce. On Christmas Day he dined with the Tweedys, and drove with Aunt Mary to St Peter's in her open carriage. James took great delight in the open-lipped caressing Roman speech of the coachman, Giuseppe, whom he had no difficulty in understanding. During the succeeding days, while Tweedy was convalescent, James became Mary's escort; when she wasn't driving to the butcher's and the baker's, they visited churches or drove out over the old and the new Appian ways. At the end of their sightseeing Aunt Mary made him comfortable in the crimson drawing-room, served him excellent dinners and launched him in Roman – that is expatriate American 'society'.

I

The new Rome seemed to Henry hostile to the picturesque. The *monsignori*, who had walked the streets in their purple hose followed by solemn servants, were gone. There were no more scarlet coaches of the cardinals, swinging with the weight of footmen. The Pope was no longer to be encountered, sitting in the shadow of his great coach with uplifted fingers. Instead, as James passed the Quirinal, there was King Victor Emmanuel in person, with a single attendant, receiving petitions from a group of men and women. Never had royalty been in such hand-to-hand relations with their subjects. Italy still had its full measure of beggars and children pleading for coppers with their fine eyes and intense smiles. Was Porta Pia bombarded three years before, Henry wondered, that Peppino should still whine for money?

He found it pleasant to sit coatless at the window of his large room in the hotel, while the January sun poured in. Flies buzzed round his nose; occasionally he annihilated a mosquito. Or he took his daily walk, often alone, but sometimes with Francis Boott, down back-streets from the Corso to the Capitol, past the low Capitoline hill and the meagre quadrangle – which made Roman history seem so small – to emerge on the other side at the Forum, where gradually he began to feel a certain sense of the picturesque. Nowhere in Rome was there more colour, more charm, more 'sport for the eye' – lounging sun-seekers along the slope, beggars, soldiers, monks, tourists; the legendary wolf accommodated in its artificial grotto; and on high the statue of Marcus Aurelius, its pagan arm extended as in a blessing. Then down to the Forum where the new régime had launched excavations. As yet only an immense stretch of pavement was laid bare, studded with broken pedestals. Henry liked to lean on the railing with the idlers. He found it odd 'to see the past, the ancient world, as one stands there, bodily turned up with the spade'.

And so on around to the Colosseum, to gaze on Rome present and past, Pagan and Christian, medieval and modern, and the contrast between bright light and mouldering cruel ruin. He took this particular walk one day when the Roman carnival had filled the Corso with hundreds of masked revellers. As the hubbub died away in the distance, he found himself strolling up a byway on the Palatine hill, from just behind the Arch of Titus. It was steep, but Henry was a stout walker and it led him between high walls and round a bend,

past a series of dusty little pictures of stations of the cross. At the
end of this path stood the little church of St Bonaventure with a
modest façade. Lifting the leather curtain, James found himself in a
small poor whitewashed interior; the candlesticks were tarnished,
the altar was decorated with muslin flowers. He would not have
remained had he not been struck by the attitude of a solitary priest
in the place – a young, pale, kneeling figure, who gave him a sidelong
glance as he entered. The figure was 'so charged with the languor of
devotion' that James remained. He watched the priest visit the altars
in turn and kiss the balustrade beneath each one. While the Carnival
was creating tumult in the streets, here was one figure kneeling for
religion. James was struck by his 'pious fatigue, his droning prayer,
and his isolation'.

It gave him, he wrote, a 'supreme vision of the religious passion –
its privations and resignations and exhaustions, and its terribly small
share of amusement'. The priest was young and strong, evidently not
too refined to have enjoyed the Carnival. Planted there, his face pale
with fasting, his knees stiff with praying, he seemed a stern satire on
the thousands in the streets.

Henry regarded religious passion as 'the strongest of man's heart'.
He accepted 'some application of the supernatural idea' as an essential part of life. However, among the 'churchiest churches' in Europe
– those of Rome – he reflected that the man-made houses of God had
been 'prayed in for several centuries by a singularly complicated and
feudal society', forming the constant background of a human drama.
Abroad, in the streets of Rome, Henry felt himself a part of this
continuing drama.

2

His first fears were that he was falling into a Cambridge-by-the-Tiber,
analogous to that which he had witnessed by the Seine. On his third
evening in Rome he went to a party given by a friend of the Nortons,
Mrs Henry Russell Cleveland. Its being in Rome made it no different
from a party in Cambridge. Here he met Sarah Butler Wister, of
Philadelphia, daughter of Fanny Kemble, the actress. Mrs Wister
promptly invited him to her 'at home', two nights later, and he was
introduced to 'the terrific Kemble herself, whose splendid hand-
someness of eye, nostril and mouth were the best things in the
room'. Sarah Wister, in Rome with her husband and son, took an

immediate fancy to Henry James. She was strikingly handsome and possessed a magnificent head of hair to which he made allusion in many letters. She was 'literary', a woman of ideas, and had much of her mother's energy and force. With a promptness that took James by surprise, she invited him to accompany her the next day to the French Academy in the Villa Medici.

They went instead to the Colonna gardens, 'where we wandered for nearly a couple of hours among mossy sarcophagi, mouldering along heaven-high vistas of ilex and orange and laurel, and lingered at the base of damp green statues'. He was surprised at Mrs Wister's informality; but he was also distinctly charmed. 'A beautiful woman who takes you to such a place and talks to you uninterruptedly, learnedly, and even cleverly for two whole hours is not to be disposed of in three lines,' he told his mother. But he hasn't time to tell her more. He must be off to the 'Cambridge Greenoughs, confound 'em. I have not come to Rome for Cambridge tea fights'. He added, 'The chapter of "society" here – that is American society – opens up before me.'

It did, more largely than he had imagined. The presence in Rome of an eligible and charming literary American bachelor, addicted to good manners and good conversation, became known almost immediately. The Terry household in the Odescalchi Palace had two marriageable daughters; the Storys, also with a marriageable daughter, were no less hospitable in their great apartment in the Barberini. Presently Henry is attending musical and theatrical evenings in 'the rival houses of Terry and Story'. At Mrs Wister's he meets a great beauty of Boston and Washington, Mrs Charles Sumner, separated from her political husband and awaiting a divorce. He encounters the lively and Amazonian Alice Bartlett and the haunting Elena Lowe; and there are the Bootts, with their circle of friends. He complains, but he surrenders himself wholly to this society and to the 'sovereign spirit' of the city – the Rome, as it was to become, of *Roderick Hudson* and *The Portrait of a Lady*. He passes long hours in the villas and their gardens, nearly always in the company of some young and attractive woman. Mrs Wister tends to monopolize him. He joins the ladies in gallops across the Campagna, where the lonely arches stand crowned with weeds and the footfall of his horse is muffled in flower-carpeted terrain : wild roses, honeysuckle, half-buried violets and pale anemones, the white narcissus and the cyclamen. High overhead he suddenly hears the disembodied song of the lark. He meets American artists in palaces and studios; he makes excursions to the Alban and Sabine hills; he visits scenes of antiquity and takes part in picnics, with hampers packed at Spillmann's; the food and wine are laid out on the warm stones of ruined temples. He spends days at Frascati and 'ineffable hours' at the Villas Mondragone and Aldobrandini, lying on the grass at the foot of ilexes. Returning from his rambles, he finds friendly doors opening wide to him on all sides.

3

Henry James knew that certain of these great doors, in villas and palaces, had opened wide fifteen years before to a distinguished American predecessor, and there were moments when he distinctly felt himself following the footsteps of Nathaniel Hawthorne. The writer from Salem had been 'the last of the old-fashioned Americans' in Rome. An American 'of equal value with Hawthorne, an American of equal genius, imagination and, as our forefathers said, sensibility', he observed, would now accommodate himself more easily to the ways of foreign lands. He added, 'An American as cultivated as Hawthorne is now almost inevitably more cultivated, and, as a matter of course, more Europeanized in advance, more cosmopolitan.' One could hardly be in doubt who this American might be. And the Roman Americans, whether they were the counterparts of Kenyon, of Hilda or of Miriam, presented to the newcomer an interest all the deeper for having been a part of an earlier novelist's experience. The little group of artists and amateurs of Hawthorne's day had grown in the intervening years. American painters and sculptors continued to come abroad. There were no art-schools to speak of in the United States, no expert stone-cutters, nor an 'atmosphere' in which they could create. In Rome young American sculptors found the Italian marble and qualified technicians to handle it: there was alabaster and malachite, lapis and porphyry and the centuries-old work in mosaic. And in Rome, too, as Hawthorne had shown, there were subjects for novelists as well.

With these artists came also the dabblers and the dilettantes. There always were amateurs beside hard workers; always dilettantes to read poems, admire pictures – and to imitate them. And then in the American colony there were men and women who simply enjoyed the soft climate of Rome, in preference to the harsher one they had abandoned, and who gave themselves over to the simple pleasures available in the ancient city.

James, from the first, was prepared to enjoy these pleasures. Like his character Rowland, he 'took to evening parties as a duck to water'. He liked nothing better than to find an agreeable corner, next to an agreeable and attractive woman; such women were not lacking in the Roman drawing-rooms. James always came at appointed hours and left his card. He might, like Rowland, do this with 'exaggerated gravity', but gravity did not diminish his enjoyment. He thrived more on people that on scenery. He tended, however, to emphasize the emptier side of this society to Quincy Street. Cambridge, after all, was expecting him to be industrious. And he always felt he was not working enough. He feared that his social relaxation might seem, if not sinful, at least wasteful to his mother and father. 'Every week I hope "society" is over – but it spurts up again,' he writes home. He confesses, however, that 'I have deliberately taken all that has come of it and been the gainer'. The words 'Forgive me!' intrude in his letters at odd moments – whenever he describes some particular pleasure he has had, as if that pleasure were a crime committed against William, or Alice, or the generosity of his parents. 'I mingle enough in society to give a flavour of magnificence to my life,' he says. But he also tells his mother that the American colony in Rome is 'a very poor affair indeed'. It is limited and isolated, 'without relations with the place, or much serious appreciation of it', and so tends to tumble back 'upon itself and finds itself of meagre substance'. Was this society as meagre as he claimed? Later he was to speak of 'the incomparable *entertainment*' of Rome in 'manners, customs, practices, processes, states of feeling', and all this over and above the museum side – objects and treasures and relics. He was referring to his compatriots, for he had little access to the Italians. 'Entertainment' of this kind was the very stuff of life for a novelist; and Henry was seeing how Cambridge and Boston moved against a grandiose background. Were they not all dancing to good music – and in the noblest ballroom in the world?

47

The Two Palaces

HENRY'S playful allusion to 'the rival houses of Terry and Story', as if they were Montague and Capulet, singled out in the American colony two artists who lived in old princely palaces and vied with one another in entertaining Americans. The Storys were housed in splendour, an apartment of more than forty rooms, in the Palazzo Barberini, on the slope of the Quirinal. The Terrys were in a lesser palace, in rooms on the second floor of the Odescalchi in the Piazza dei Santi Apostoli, opposite the Colonna Palace. With neither household can James be said to have become intimate; but he found it 'a kind of pretty spectacle to go to their houses'.

I

One might laugh at Italian palaces, Henry wrote in a travel-sketch – at their peeling paint, their general nudity, their dreariness – but they had the great quality of their design : an elevation and extent. Their doorways and arches seemed meant for cathedrals; their wide windows opened upon panoramas; they spoke of a proud indifference to the cost of materials or of labour. Both the Barberini and the Odescalchi had been built from designs by Bernini; and while the effect of grandeur went with an effect of gloom, the Barberini could rejoice in brightness of façade and an almost modern gaiety. It had embodied the grandiose dream of Urban VIII, who built it in the late Renaissance out of the 'quarry' of the Colosseum. It was 'greatness unadorned' – 'great lines, great spaces, great emphasis, great reserve'.

As Henry climbed the stairs leading to the small door of the right wing, he could hear the splash of the Barberini fountain, 'the most Roman note of all', as if by an incessant play of water the Romans would wash away the bloodstains of history. He passed, on one of the landings, the bas-relief of a Thorwaldsen lion. The modest doorway, with the name 'W. W. Story' inscribed on it, swung open into grandiose reception-rooms. He was led by servants in livery into the red drawing-room, or the theatre-room, tapestried and chandeliered, where since the middle of the century this American from Salem and Cambridge had been host to former American presidents, writers, painters, and Roman nobility, secular and ecclesiastical. Story's windows looked out upon 'iridescent horizons, accidental pictures, terraces, treasures of space'. On the morning after one of his receptions Henry wrote to his mother:

An apartment in a Roman palace is a very fine affair, and it certainly adds a picturesqueness to life to be led through a chain of dimly-lighted chambers, besprinkled with waiting servants, before you emerge, sonorously announced, into the light and elegance of a reception-room with a *roof*, not a ceiling.

The picture which Henry was to draw of the lawyer turned sculptor was accurate enough – so far as it went. Story was a genial host; 'talk was his joy and pleasantry his habit'. He was animated and gay, with a faculty for humour and mimicry: he was interested in ideas, in people – in everything. He was incisive and over-assertive, a kind of milder Gilbert Osmond, or even perhaps, in certain aspects, the Gloriani of *Roderick Hudson*, a clever man without artistic integrity. To spend an evening in the high-roofed theatre-room, with the play of taper on tapestry, listening to chamber music (say some of the amateur quartets of Francis Boott), or to watch the performance of some of Story's theatricals, meet celebrities, indulge in small talk, offered Henry a strange and fascinating picture of expatriate life. Story was never deficient in anecdote and his Roman memory was long. Severn, Landor, the Brownings, Thackeray, Tennyson, Hawthorne, General Grant, a row of Cardinals and British prime ministers, had paid homage to him in his palace. Pope Pius IX had been his greatest patron. It was he who, on seeing Story's statue of Cleopatra – the statue admired by Hawthorne and described in *The Marble Faun* – paid the cost of transporting it to the London Exhibition of 1862, where it captured the Victorian imagination and made Story famous. On visiting Story's studio in the Via San Nicolo di Tolentino – that studio which is Kenyon's in Hawthorne's novel – James told Grace Norton he found the sculptor 'in the midst of an army of marble heroines, which were not altogether unsuggestive of Mrs Jarley's waxworks'. To Charles Eliot Norton he wrote: 'So you're acquainted with Story's muse – that brazen hussy – to put it plainly. I have rarely seen such a case of *prosperous* pretension as Story. His cleverness is great, the world's good nature to him is greater.' Story's 'endless effigies' were 'almost fatally unsimple'. Mrs Henry Adams, visiting the same studio at this time, exclaimed: 'Oh! how he does spoil nice blocks of white marble. Nothing but Sibyls on all sides, sitting, standing, legs crossed, legs uncrossed, and all with the same expression as if they smelt something wrong.' Her husband's impression, years later, boiled down to the rather general statement in the *Education* : 'William Story could not touch the secret of Michael Angelo.' There were, indeed, many secrets Story could not touch, and Henry James, in his late biography of him, offered the ultimate verdict. Story's career, he said, was 'a sort of beautiful sacrifice to a noble mistake'.

2

In the more modest Odescalchi Palace life was pitched in a minor key, but still with pretensions to style. Luther Terry lived there with his wife, sister of Julia Ward Howe and widow of the sculptor Thomas Crawford. There were three Crawford children, the two marriageable daughters, Annie and Mimoli, and the son Marion, then at school, and destined to popular fame as a writer of romances. Terry had left his native Connecticut at twenty, and spent the rest of his life in Italy. A rough-bearded, lonely man, he was a comfortable expatriate whose work James scrutinized in his studio at 23 Via Margutta with an eye more critical than his host suspected. His studio pleased James : it was situated in a squalid house, in a squalid street, promising gloom within. On ascending the long stone staircase, however, Henry found himself in a pleasant first-floor court, a sort of hanging garden, open to the sky : straight out of this opened the large studio. Terry showed James a painting called *The Artist's Dream*, another *The Vision of St John* – 'the queerest old survivals of the American art of thirty years ago. It is an agreeable curiosity to see their author sit and look at them seriously and expound his intentions and yet be on the whole a sensible man of the world.' Another writer, perhaps with unintended irony, has described how Americans visiting Rome purchased pictures from Luther Terry as 'a grateful memorial' of pleasant sociabilities. This suggests that a certain charm of 'salesmanship', genial and without Story's flamboyance, animated his host. The charm was also one of background. The Odescalchi Palace, built of stone and brick round a colonnaded court, has high rooms with coffered ceilings. In the ante-room at the Terrys, sat liveried messengers. In the library the books were ensconced in elaborate carved bookcases; and the notable Magenta

Room, which is described in the various memoirs of the Crawfords and the Terrys, had panels of pink brocade with oleander and silver-grey flowers in their design; the ceiling was vaulted, and painted with a heavy grapevine trellis on a background of burnished gold. Bellerophon on Pegasus kills the Chimaera in blue-and-white pastel shades. The presiding genius of the Terry household was Annie Crawford, who, Henry wrote home, 'has every gift (including a face so mobile and expressive that it amounts almost to beauty), but she is as hard as flint and I am pretty sure she will never have an adorer. He will have to be a real lion-tamer'. The judgement was shrewder than he knew. Annie married Erich von Rabe, a Junker baron with a dominating will, an estate in Prussia and violent anti-English prejudices.

3

In addition to Story's pretentious statues and Terry's mediocre paintings, Henry saw the imitative art of other Americans who had come to Rome in the earlier years. He met Harriet Hosmer at the Storys', and looked at her with much interest; fifteen years before she had escorted Hawthorne to her studio and shown him her statue of Zenobia. He had described Miss Hosmer as 'bird-like' and wondered how so brisk a creature – she had made a popular statue of Puck – could create work 'so quietly impressive'. In middle-age she struck Henry as 'a remarkably ugly little grey-haired boy, adorned with a diamond necklace, but she seems both "vivacious" and discreet and is better, I imagine, than her statues'. He called at the studio of Eugene Benson, a few doors from Terry's in the Via Margutta; he was a friend of the elder Henry James, then a striving painter of landscapes, who never lost his devotion to the classical mode. Henry was to know him later in Venice. He pronounced his work 'careful, and conscientious, but very uninspired'. Edward Darley Boit and his teacher, Frederic Crowninshield, he also met, and he called on an elderly lady artist, Sarah Freeman Clarke, a friend of his father's and of Emerson's, who had once studied with Washington Allston. Since she was known to Quincy Street he described in detail the black staircase leading to her apartment and the series of drawings she had done after piously visiting all the spots in Italy 'reputed to have known the tread of Dante's wandering foot'. He found her drawings 'mild'; she had invented a delightful pastime for herself.

He was most at home in the studio of Lizzie Boott. She was a conscientious amateur and Quincy Street was interested in her progress. 'Lizzie is as sweet and good as ever. She has a little studio, where she paints little tatterdemalion Checcos and Ninas – with decidedly increasing ability.' To Alice : 'I had an errand this morning at the Piazza Barberini – (the Boott's) – and found Lizzie in her studio, *en tête-à-tête* with one of the very swell models – a wondrous youth in a sheepskin jacket and bandaged legs and flowing curls and the most pictorial complexion.' Again :

Going up early the other morning to make a riding appointment with her, I found her in her studio with a certain little Peppina – the most enchanting little nut-brown child model you can imagine : in structure, colour, costume, everything, the handsomest little miniature woman. There sat Lizzie happily painting this delicious object. Where will she get a Peppina in Cambridge?

There was one other artist on whose fate he meditated in later years. Indeed at one time James is said to have sat to him for his portrait, but the painting does not seem to have survived. This was J. Rollin Tilton of New Hampshire. Like Story he lived in the Barberini, but in a more modest corner. James remembered the apartment as 'a minor masterpiece of early eighteenth-century tarabiscotage, of contorted stucchi, mouldings, medallions, reliefs of every form, a small riot of old-world elements'. He described Tilton as 'a very queer genius. He is great on sunsets and does them (and all sorts of aerial luminosities etc.) very well'. But he was 'the most blatant humbug in his talk you ever heard – assuring you, every twenty minutes, that Emerson is the "lens of the Almighty"'. James scrutinized his paintings of Italian and Egyptian landscapes, in the manner of Claude, 'the stone-pine, the ruin, the sunset', and wondered at Tilton's one moment of fame in London, when his work was recognized by the Academy. Then he fell from sight, his 'reputation sadly, publicly, permanently unfinished'. He was still another type of an American artist-failure in Europe.

4

Although James's letters from Rome mention only these artists, it is clear that he encountered others and that he studied closely a series of artistic 'cases' which he incorporated into *Roderick Hudson*, the novel he wrote during the following year. What kind of artist could an American be in a foreign environment, he seems to have asked himself – an environment as congenial and as soft as Rome, which conspired to make him lazy or imitative; or pretentious, like Story; or mediocre, like Terry; or plodding, like Benson; or inspired but unprofessional, like Tilton. Charles Eliot Norton had written to James during his lonely months in Cambridge:

Born and bred in New England as we were, where the air we breathe is full of the northern chill, and no other philosophy but that of utilitarianism is possible – it is not easy to learn to be content with the usefulness of doing nothing. Italy is a good place, however, for deadening the overactive conscience, and for killing rank ambition.

There were examples on all sides, even to the dabblers and amateurs like Sarah Clarke or Lizzie Boott. They came from an as yet half-formed America; they seemed content with so little. What if an artist arrived in this environment with a vaulting ambition, such as Henry's, and felt within himself the stirring of greatness? What might happen to him?

The time was to come when Henry would seek to answer these questions. In *Roderick* there is a memorable scene in which Roderick Hudson's friends gather to admire his Roman statues, fruits of his labour abroad. Roderick is all impulse and fire. Gloriani, the clever but cynical opportunist, seems to be an Italian version of Story but with a greater future; Singleton is probably a combination of Benson and Tilton; and the amateur Augusta Blanchard, who lives alone and paints people with their backs turned (because she is 'a little weak in faces'), could be both Lizzie and Sarah Clarke. James places before us the inspired, the clever, the persistent and the plodding creators. Roderick's candle will burn out in one night. Singleton's goals are too modest: quiet industry satisfies him. Augusta is sincere, but unprofessional. Only Gloriani, the European, will outlive his superficiality. And it is when, in the fullness of time, he gains large insight into life, above 'the mere base maximum of cleverness', that he will be saluted as Master. In Rome, in 1873, that vision was not yet possible to Henry. He looked, however, with a critical eye upon the American artists. They worked and abandoned themselves to their momentary experiences while the novelist sought to read the lessons of their careers. They would serve both as example and warning to himself.

48

Roman Rides

ONE day toward the end of January 1873, when he had been in Rome a month, Henry James hired a horse and rode out of the Porta del Popolo to the Ponte Molle (Ponte Milvio), where the Tiber flowed between its four ecclesiastical statues. He rode over the crest of the hill and along the old post-road leading to Florence. He had never been much of a horseman, but he knew how to stay in the saddle. The day was mild, the air filled with a mellow purple glow. As he rode, the beauty of the landscape, the sense of movement, the feeling of power – and of control – took possession of him. After an hour he pulled up and stood for some time at the edge of a meadow. The country rolled away in slopes and dells, purple, blue, brown. In the Sabine mountains he watched a play of sapphire and amber. In the foreground a peasant jogged along on an ass; far off, a grey tower added a painter's touch to the landscape. It was bright, yet sad; alive, yet charged, 'to the supersensuous ear, with the murmur of an extinguished life'. The experience was altogether strange – deliciously strange. To ride once was to ride again; from that moment he gave to the Campagna a generous share of his Roman days. 'I can stick on a horse better than I supposed,' he wrote to Quincy Street.

I

Presently he was galloping in the grassy shadows of aqueducts and tombs and taking ditches as if he were a huntsman. Riding doubled his horizon; he could pass with ease from one Roman picture to another. He hired a horse by the month and justified the expense to his mother by explaining how good it was for his health. In March he engaged another 'nice little horse for a month. He has a charming little character and yet is sufficiently lively to assist me somewhat to learn to ride.' By the time this period was up he was boasting that he had taken 'four ditches with great serenity and was complimented'.

In Cambridge he had been a leisurely walker. It was a measure of his new-found freedom that he could now proceed at a gallop over the Roman countryside. 'The Campagna,' he was to remember thirty years later, 'was an education of the taste, a revelation of new sources of solitary and of social joy.' His solitary rides yielded him aesthetic adventure and ideas for stories. The 'social joy' is reflected in his letters to his parents. He boasts, 'I am now in the position of a creature with *five* women *offering* to ride with me.' There was a note of exultation in the words. Not a word about his old back-ache, the 'obscure hurt' of the Civil War, which might have kept him from the saddle.

The Campagna was at its best on mild winter days, 'when the brilliant air alone suffices to make the whole landscape smile'. When the sirocco blew, it was as if he rode in a world without hope. Detail and ornament varied from week to week. In Italy man lived more with nature than in New England, 'it does more work for him and gives him more holidays than in our short-summered clime'. He could sit in an arbour of twisted vines with his feet in the dirt and think that in February, on the other side of the Atlantic, his feet would be seeking the warmth of the parlour hearth-rug. Henry liked to gaze at sun-cracked plaster and indoor shadows. He stared into gateways of farms, with their moss-coated stairways climbing outside a wall. It was a comfort not to be in snow-blown Cambridge.

On the homeward stretch, in waning light, he would rein up by an old tavern and buy a bottle of their best; their worst and their best, with shifting price, was always ordinary *vino bianco* or *vino rosso*. There was a ragged bush over the door and within sat half a dozen peasants in indigo jackets and goat-skin breeches, their feet planted on crooked cobbles and their elbows on the table. These were primitive hostelries, with Garibaldi's portrait on the wall, or a picture of a lady in a low-necked dress opening a lattice. The taverns often had a yard, with a pine-wreathed arbour casting shadows on the benches, and the tables covered with white highway dust. But more often than not, Henry did not follow the highway. He liked to ride along the newly-disinterred walls of Rome. In Boston, a year before, he had looked at raw plank-fences advertising patent-medicines. Now he glanced with contemplative eyes on ancient stones 'in which a more learned sense may read portentous dates and signs – Servius, Aurelius, Honorius', the wall-builders, the architects of empire.

2

Servius, Aurelius, Honorius – Henry James on horseback caught from
the ancient stones, from the great arches and the towering aqueducts,
that emanation of grandeur and that echo of *imperium* which he had
known from the first. His earliest memory was of the Place Vendôme
in Paris. He had lived as a youth under an Empire, a late and
diminished one it is true – the Second Empire of France – but filled
with the sound of trumpets and showing bravely eagles and banners
of recent glories. Now, in his adult years, he was reading the signa-
tures of history written across Rome; the very names he plucked
from the chiselled stones were those of the great, the imperial time.
In Italy the *gloire* experienced as a boy in the Louvre existed on all
sides. He could identify himself with Servius the wall-builder; or
Aurelius the stoic conqueror; or Honorius seeking to shore up Rome
against decline; and reflect, with the irony of a poet and a dramatist,
upon the incongruous in these ancient stones in which pagan and
Christian elements were now mixed timelessly with those of a benevolent bourgeois monarchy. Unlike the romantic poets, he did not
gaze upon the past with melancholy or sadness; his pose might be
Byronic, but he was a cheerful Puritanical Byron. Nor did the great
symbols of stone speak to him as Ozymandias spoke to Shelley. For
him ancient stones meant grandeur rather than decay. As he wandered through the Forum, gazing upon the new excavations, the
marvel that filled him was not how much of the past had crumbled,
but how much endured. Before the tomb of the Valerii, to which he
rode one day, he could muse that it was 'strange enough to think
of these things – so many of them as there are – surviving their
immemorial eclipse in this perfect shape and coming up like long-
lost divers from the sea of time'. This had been his experience during
his earlier visit as well. He found a 'peculiar fascination' in things
recently excavated : an Augustus dug up some five years before or a
'ravishing' little bust of the same Emperor when he was a boy, 'as
clear and fresh in quality as if it had dated from yesterday'. All these
relics – the dying gladiator, the Lydian Apollo, the Amazon at the
Capitol – spoke to Henry 'of the breadth of human genius'. And
there were times when riding through ecclesiastical gateways, or
along the broad arches of the Claudian aqueduct, or skirting the
disinterred wall, Henry felt that he might have been 'a wandering
Tartar touching on the confines of the Celestial Empire'. A strange

image for a New World man in the presence of an imperial past. It established a kind of primitive distance from imperial power.

3

If Henry James relished the Roman relics as symbols of the endurance of art and of the nature of 'glory', he also experienced a profound uneasiness in their presence. Power was acceptable to him only in some attenuated or disguised form; seen in its nakedness, as in his dream of the Louvre, it had its nightmare side. Perhaps this was because he had always known it in disguise, behind the mask of resignation of his mother; and by the disguises he himself had assumed when he gave himself a motionless observer's role, and kept himself at a discreet distance from objects and people, while his eyes and mind took possession of them. 'I keep up a devil of an observing,' he wrote to his mother. It was the observing of one who could play omniscient author in the lives of his characters while finding many ingenious technical devices to conceal his omniscience. He was to become, as a consequence of this, one of the masters of the devious in modes of narration, and was to invent many new ways of concealing the storyteller from his readers. Unadulterated power had all the frightening qualities of open assault. Perhaps this is why we find so many allusions to the equestrian statue of Marcus Aurelius at the Capitol. The statue had been, when he looked at it in 1869, 'one of the things I have most enjoyed in Rome. It is totally admirable.' It spoke for power masked with kindness. He may have remembered that Matthew Arnold had seen in the pagan statue a 'portrait most suggestive of a Christian conscience' - in the very heart of Christendom. This softening of pagan imperial authority by something resembling Christian benignity, this mildness in an Emperor who had indeed shrunk from violence - while being committed to it - gave Henry pause.

His travel-essays and his letters to Cambridge show at every turn Henry's sense of power in his new-found freedom, allied with his relish for the strength and dominion reflected in his Roman surroundings. But his deepest anxieties created by this may be discerned in two tales written during these months. They sprang directly from his Roman rides and his exploration of ancient things. A visit to the tomb of the Valerii contributed to *The Last of the Valerii*; a glimpse of a shepherd asleep in the Campagna, 'with his naked legs stretched out on the turf and his soft peaked hat over his long hair', led to the writing of *Adina*. The tales were told in Henry's early manner. The speeches are often ranting monologues; in them we see the writer using his new materials and the new world of feeling into which he has entered.

4

In *The Last of the Valerii* a Roman Count, a kind of sleepy, dreamy, well-fed Donatello, marries a young American girl. In the grounds of the Valerio villa a statue is disinterred, much in the manner in which Hawthorne describes the digging up of a Venus, or as Merimée recounts a similar occurrence in the tale which James translated in his youth at Newport, *La Vénus d'Ille*. In Merimée's story the Venus comes marching into the bridal chamber to claim the hero for herself. The statue in James's story is a Juno, instead of a Venus; the sleepy-eyed Conte Valerio falls in love with the Juno, neglects his wife and ultimately abandons himself to worship and pagan blood-sacrifice. If the tale is an amalgam of Hawthorne and Merimée, its dénouement is pure James. 'When a beautiful woman is in stone, all he can do is to look at her,' the little Roman excavator remarks to the distraught American girl. She takes the hint. The past must not deprive her of the present. The Juno is quietly and secretly buried again. In this way the Contessa restores to her husband's arms her warm body – those arms which had been supplicating and sacrificing to stone. The young daughter of the Puritans has exorcised pagan evil – and triumphed.

The second tale, *Adina*, describes the shepherd, Angelo Beati, asleep in the Campagna; he is discovered by two Americans, an irritable and unpleasant classical scholar named Scrope and his friend, a proper Bostonian. Scrope notices that the shepherd clutches in his hand a discoloured object: he drags it from him, and when Angelo awakens, throws a few coins at him. The discoloured object appears to be some ancient jewel. Scrope spends days learning how to clean it. He works in solitude. One midnight, in high elation, he brings to his companion a beautiful golden topaz, carved with a laurel-crowned imperial figure and a frieze of warriors and chariots, bearing the words *Divus Tiberius Caesar Totius Orbis Imperator*.

Emperor of the whole world. The topaz was carved for Tiberius, the campaigner in Gaul, Armenia and Germany, the conqueror of the

Illyrians: also the Tiberius of the Gospel of St Luke and the murderer of his friend Sejanus. In a long oratorical speech Scrope boasts of his own conquest of the centuries in recovering the imperial symbol. He gives the stone to his fiancée, a young American woman named Adina Waddington. She, however, regards the stone as evil and refuses to wear it. 'I should feel most uncomfortable in carrying the Emperor Tiberius so near my heart,' she says. Moreover, Adina has been attracted to the young shepherd who, with his locks combed and in a suit purchased with Scrope's money, trails the American about Rome claiming he has been cheated. 'He has more than his share of good luck,' he says when he sees Adina. 'A topaz – and a pearl! both at once.' One evening Adina breaks off her engagement to Scrope; the next morning she climbs out of her window and runs off with Angelo. 'She's better than the topaz,' he says. The heavy-hearted Scrope, in due course, pauses on the bridge of St Angelo and commits the stone to the muddy Tiber. As with the Juno, the past is restored to the past – but in this instance Scrope's love is not restored to him.

Henry seems to be saying in these tales that the past can be dangerous to love and to life. Things buried for a millennium lose none of their baleful force when restored to the light of day. Much that lay uncovered in Rome fascinated James; he could speak of the 'breadth of genius' it revealed; yet clearly, by the testimony of his tales, he felt that the living – in order to go on living – consorted with it at their peril. The beautiful Juno-mother, the glistening topaz, contained within them a witchery of beauty – and a terrible destructive power. There was something morbid in disinterring them; they conveyed a feeling of mouldering, ancient decay. It was like an uncovering of the dead.

Henry James had arrived at his first clear statement of one of his major themes: the corruption to be found in Europe by a still innocent America. In both, innocence resists and defies evil. If James states his case in these clear-cut and even extreme terms, it is because his feeling for evil had in it all the mysterious awe and horror of his father's religious 'vastation'. The tales of the Juno and the topaz contain a sense of shock Henry experienced in discovering how close civilization can be to Paganism. On another level they suggest also his intuitive understanding that he would have to bury his personal past, the past of Quincy Street, and make his way in a disengaged present. The solution for him would become clearer as he mastered the lesson of his Roman days. The happy meeting-ground of puritan and pagan could be precisely the ground of art. An artist could be pagan in spirit and remain a puritan in fact. He could permissibly enjoy the pleasures of his senses – the very throb of Rome – and aspire to greatness without fear of punishment. Henry was engaged in a systematic and searching appraisal of old and new, the primitive and the civilized, corruption and innocence. And in this search he aspired to – and dreaded – the power of the artist. Courtesy and euphemism became his defence against dangerous ambition. In Quincy Street he had to be reticent. Abroad, on horseback, he could be resolute – and he could *feel* 'imperial'.

He would create indeed a kind of *imperium* of letters, annex Europe to his native America, achieve a transatlantic empire larger than that of other novelists. And like Marcus Aurelius he would offer the world the countenance of a conqueror who was, as Arnold said, tender and blameless – *tendentemque manus ripae ulterioris amore*.

49

Five Women – and a Sixth

'I AM now in the position of a creature with *five* women *offering* to ride with me.' There is a distinct swagger here, a suggestion to Quincy Street that its young writing son is a social success in Rome. There were indeed five ladies – two married, one about to be divorced, two eligible for marriage – who welcomed the company of Henry James Jr, of Cambridge, Mass. He bestowed it generously, yet with his customary caution. Let us look at these ladies, in the order in which Henry named them to his mother, look at them as they sit, on their steeds, smiling and responsive, admirably dressed for the Campagna – riding with him sometimes alone, sometimes in a group.

I

First there was Mrs Sumner. Before her brief marriage to Senator Charles Sumner, she had been the widow of William Sturgis Hooper of Boston, who had left her with one daughter. She was 35 – five years older than Henry – possessed of a slender, stately form, and what has been described as a 'high-bred manner and aristocratic reserve'. In Rome she was awaiting her divorce from Sumner. They had parted after a few months; both were ambitious, strong, not easily capable of the compromises of life. 'I have seen a good deal of late of Mrs Sumner and adore her,' Henry wrote to his father; and to Grace Norton, 'With her great beauty (which on horse-back is enormous), she has great honesty, frankness and naturalness.' When Henry announced that he 'adored' a woman, it was sufficient sign that he was in no danger of 'involvement'. He had long been a worshipper, at a distance, of idealized beauty. And he enjoyed being seen in the company of a woman who carried herself with queenly dignity. Some of Sumner's biographers have attributed to his wife a highly 'variable' temper and a certain moodiness; she was said to have married him in the belief that he would carry her to the White House. Mrs Sumner knew her mind; she also did not easily tolerate fools. She had a high social style, force and presence. After her divorce, as Mrs Alice Mason, she moved through the expatriate society of London, Paris and Rome in complete possession of her world. She entertained Emerson when he came to Rome; Henry Adams speaks of her with affection and respect; Sargent painted her; she remained a close friend of Henry James. During that winter he rode often with her and with her friend Alice Bartlett with whom Mrs Sumner shared an apartment in the Via della Croce.

I had one day a famous ride with Mrs Sumner and Miss Bartlett : both admirable horsewomen, especially Miss B., and both very handsome in the saddle. We went far away into the rolling meadows, where the shaggy-vested shepherds feed their flocks, and had a series of magnificent gallops, of which I acquitted myself *à mon honneur*. But for me and my infirmities, they ride at a rather tiring rate.

Thus the record for Quincy Street.

Second on James's list was Mrs Edward Boit, wife of the artist, and mother of the four little girls who figure in Sargent's large canvas in the Boston Museum. If she 'offered' to ride, it seems certain that the young man did not accept the offer. 'I shall fight shy of Mrs Boit who, I believe, is an equestrian terror.' As we gaze upon Sargent's portrait of Mrs Boit, seated floridly in her later and more matronly years, we may wonder that she could ever have been such a 'terror' on horseback, for she became heavy, with the fullness of middle age and of repeated motherhood. But the backward toss of the head, and the effect from a certain angle as if she were winking, suggests a personality with whom Henry may have feared involvement on other than equestrian grounds. He was extremely fond of her from the first – 'a decidedly likeable little woman – bating her giggling'. Later he remembered her as 'always social, always irresponsible, always expensive, always amused and amusing'. She became the affectionate 'Iza' of his later letters (her name was Louisa, and she was a Cushing, of Boston, who had married Boit in 1864). Henry spoke then of her as 'brilliantly friendly'· and also as 'eternally juvenile'. He liked her merry laugh and her light-heartedness: but this was fifteen years after that Roman spring, and Henry himself had advanced in life to the point where a woman who had the air of winking at him no longer disturbed him.

The third lady was Mrs Wister, and with her James rode often, sometimes alone and sometimes in the company of her husband. She inspired no 'terror', but she was not 'easy'. 'I went out the other day with Mrs Wister and her husband. They led me rather a dance, but I took four ditches with great serenity and was complimented for my close seat. But the merit was less mine than that of my delightful little horse.' There is ample evidence that Mrs Wister and Henry James were often seen together; not sufficiently often, perhaps, to set tongues wagging, for they were both discreet, but more often than one might have expected in a young writer not accustomed to the company of a married woman and carefully determined to keep a proper distance. Mrs Wister was eight years older than Henry. Her father had been Pierce Butler, the Southern gallant and slave-holder, who had married the fiery daughter of the Kembles, and taken her from the theatre to tame her to domesticity and a life on a Georgia plantation. He might have sought to tame a tempest. Sarah Butler had grown up separated from her mother, for Mrs Kemble abandoned her husband and the South and was in England during the Civil War. She married Dr Owen Jones Wister of Philadelphia and they lived in Germantown. This winter, reunited with her mother (Pierce Butler was by now dead), they both had their brief salon in Rome before returning to America.

Alice Bartlett, 'that mighty maiden', posed no romantic problems. 'I feel,' Henry wrote after a gallop in her company, 'very much as if she were a boy – an excellent fellow.' The fine thing about her was her spirit – her 'pluck, independence, energy'. During the spring James came every three or four days to the Via della Croce to improve his Italian by reading Tasso with her. Alice Bartlett was as much a friend of Lizzie Boott as of Mrs Sumner, and Henry was to see her often during the next five years in Europe as well as in Boston, and to salute her marriage with a Texan in these words written to Lizzie:

I think her Texan horizon much more natural to her than her Roman one. She was a European only by accident – not by natural sympathy, and she will become an ornament to the young civilization and the energetic society amid which she is to dwell. Yes, she will break in mustangs, and wear a lasso over her shoulder, and be the Diana of the Far West.

Last of the five was Lizzie Boott. She was the most Europeanized of his riding-companions and the one he knew best. Henry had met the Bootts in 1865, the year in which Francis brought his nineteen-year-old daughter back from abroad to her home-city of Boston. He had taken Lizzie to Europe in 1847, after the death of his wife, Elizabeth Lyman, member of an old Boston family and two years after the death of their infant son. Frank Boott seemed to clutch the baby girl to him in the fear death might claim her as well. With her nurse, who was to be with the Bootts for the next forty years, they had taken ship for Genoa. On this same voyage was William Wetmore Story, also bound for Italy, to make his career as a sculptor, after renouncing the law in Boston. In Italy Lizzie was reared by her father as if she were a hot-house flower, and indeed when Henry transposed her into *The Portrait of a Lady* he called her Pansy. She was given the upbringing of a European *jeune fille*. She had a sweet voice and took singing lessons; she learned to paint at an early age. Her father taught her to swim. Unlike her friend Alice James, Lizzie gave her energies, which were modestly creative, free play, and indulged them to the full. In the end she threw herself into her painting with an intensity that far exceeded her talents.

James had spoken of her on occasion as 'homely', but photographs and paintings show a chiselled, refined charm, a bland beauty. She was warmly American in spite of her markedly European manners. She had spent her adolescence in a large wing of the Villa Castellani, on the hill of Bellosguardo – one of those large Italian rural residences which afford space and coolness and a superb view of Florence. Here she had met the Anglo-Florentines, the Germans and the Americans, drawn to the city of art: the Brownings and Robert Browning's friend, Isa Blagden; the Trollopes; as well as the visiting

Americans – including Hawthorne, who had lived in the adjoining Villa Montauto.

Francis Boott, on his side, whiled away the eighteen years of his daughter's growing-up by a devotion to music. He took lessons in harmony, singing and piano, but felt rightly he had begun his training too late. His first string quartet was performed at Story's palace in Rome in the 1850s; and certain of his songs obtained a vogue in drawing-rooms on both sides of the Atlantic. There was something strange in this little man, with his prosaic and reasonable temperament, rigid in his habits, simple in his tastes, yet involved in the arts. Henry might be bored with him on occasion, but had an inescapable fondness for him and for his vigorous laughter. It was Lizzie however who became a cherished image in James's life, the 'Cara Lisa' of his letters, a link with Italy, an exquisite Italian memory, and the centre of a drama of which he would be a fascinated as well as a troubled spectator. She was one of the few women younger than himself for whom he acknowledged a 'great affection'. It was perhaps greater than he knew.

'As Lizzie depends upon me,' he wrote to his father, 'I shall be chiefly her companion.' And so they rode together often, joined sometimes by Miss Bartlett.

2

There was a sixth woman. She did not offer to ride with Henry; indeed she does not seem to have been particularly interested in him. This may have contributed to his interest in her. She attracted him by her beauty, her remoteness, her air of quiet intelligence – her mystery.

His allusions to her are fragmentary. Pieced together they suggest that Elena Lowe, daughter of a Bostonian named Francis Lowe, was a woman of exceptional appearance. She seemed to float in an air of melancholy, yet she carried herself with pride and distinction. Henry spoke of her as an 'intensely interesting personage'. But whether she really was, he could not make up his mind. She reminded him, he said, of the English Judge of whom it was said that 'no man was ever as wise as Lord so-and-so looked!' There are five allusions to her in Henry's letters, and they tell us very little. In March 1873 he writes to his father that he calls occasionally 'in the dusky half-hour before dinner' on a girl who is 'sweet and very clever', named Miss Lowe.

'She is very handsome, very lovely, very reserved and very mysterious, not to have many adorers. But I am not yet regularly enlisted
as one of them.' He adds : 'I've seen no one else in society here who
has caused a pulse of curiosity in the least to beat.'

In April he tells his brother that Henry Adams and his wife have
passed through Rome and that he dined with them. Present on this
occasion was Miss Lowe, 'beautiful and sad'. A few weeks later he
writes to Mrs Wister that he has been seeing few people in Rome;
however he has seen Miss Lowe once or twice, 'though I have tried
oftener'. In August Henry records that Miss Lowe is the subject of
wagging tongues. He informs Mrs Wister that he met the sad beauty
at Assisi, 'attended by the painter Bellay'. He adds that he heard
afterwards that 'it was a case for a more suggestive word' than
attended. A year later, on 29 July 1874, he writes to Mrs Wister that
he has read of Miss Lowe's marriage at Venice to a 'reputable British
gentleman', a consul. 'Happy man,' and Henry adds, 'So much for
Bellay.' Then Henry goes on to wonder whether the bridegroom is
really 'so ideally happy'. True, Miss Lowe was 'beautiful, mysterious,
melancholy, inscrutable'. Was this simply her 'way of seeming, or
had she unfathomable depths within?'

James went on to say to Mrs Wister that he thought Miss Lowe's
marrying a British consul 'a little of a prosy performance'. He qualified this by adding that she was 'certainly handsome enough to have
a right to be as prosy as she wished'. The performance, however, was
not as 'prosy' as Henry imagined. He had misread the announcement.
A paragraph in the 9 July 1874 issue of *Galignani's Messenger*, announced the marriage of Elena Lowe to Mr Gerald Perry, son of Sir
William Perry, retired British consul, and of the late Geraldine de
Courcy, sister of Lord Kingsale. Miss Lowe seems to have placed herself in good society. In Elena Lowe and her 'mysterious' qualities
Henry had found an image for the heroine of his first important
novel. When he came to create her he gave her a name which seems
to echo the original : Christina Light. Again and again in the novel
she is portrayed as an enigma and a 'riddle'. There are references
to her 'unfathomable' coquetry and to her nature as 'large and
mysterious'. Elena Lowe seems to have haunted Henry, for he was to
love Christina as he loved few of his heroines, and to find her sufficiently attractive and mysterious to revive her in a second novel.
Christina, Princess Casamassima, gave her name to a considerable
work of his middle period.

A Study in Mauve

HENRY JAMES's recurrent complaint to his family was that in Rome he lacked male companions. Neither Story nor Terry nor the younger artists could provide the stimulating literary talk of Lowell in Paris; or Howells in Cambridge; or his brother William in his own home. 'You feel altogether out of the current of modern civilization,' he wrote to his brother in April. 'I often hanker for the high culture and high finish of Paris – the theatres and newspapers and book-sellers and restaurants and boulevards.' And yet Rome had its com-pensations: there was something that 'forever stirs and feeds and fills the mind and makes a sentient being feel that on the whole he can lead as complete a life here as elsewhere'. Groping for words to render this more clearly, Henry ended by telling William that he was held by the 'unanalysable *loveableness* of Italy. This fills my spirit mightily.'

I

In these circumstances James looked to his women-friends for in-tellectual companionship. Mrs Boit certainly did not provide this, nor Lizzie Boott; Alice Bartlett and Mrs Sumner were 'both superior and very natural women, and Mrs Sumner a very charming one, but they are limited by a kind of characteristic American want of cul-ture'. And he added: 'Mrs Wister has much more of this – a good deal in fact, and a very literary mind, if not a powerful one.' Henry confided to Jane Norton that he had seen 'almost more of her than of anyone; and yet her beautiful hair is the thing to be praised about her. It's on the whole the handsomest I've ever seen.' To William, later, he also wrote that Mrs Wister was 'the one I saw most of'. From the first however he seems to have been of two minds about her. He tells his father that she has 'fierce energy in a slender frame', rides, walks, entertains, has musical rehearsals, and 'is very hand-some into the bargain' – but 'she isn't easy'. He reiterates that she has beautiful hair, but 'on the whole I don't at all regret that I'm not Dr Wister'. To William he writes that in a certain light, and at certain moments, with her hat on, she bears 'a startling likeness to Minny

Temple' – but the likeness, he adds, is all in the face. This suggests some of the appeal she had for him. From Henry's mother came warnings. 'Mrs Wister is too conscious of her own charms to be very dangerous I am told – but beware!'

Henry James had no need of such advice where handsome women were concerned. He replied 'Mrs Wister I see from time to time; she is a "superior" woman (but a beautiful bore. Tell it not in Philadelphia – where I don't believe they know it).' His father considered this remark unkind. Henry agreed it was rather 'brutal' and retracted it, expressing the hope that he had not been quoted. 'She is a fine person – not "easy," but perfectly natural.'

It is possible to read too much between the lines of such remarks, made for the entertainment of Quincy Street. Nevertheless, it is quite clear that Henry saw more of Mrs Wister than he even admitted. His use of the word 'adored' in describing Mrs Summer suggests no ambiguity; she was a woman frankly admired. No such feelings were expressed for Mrs Wister. She was charming, clever, lively – yet always not 'easy'. It was Henry who felt uneasy. He saw himself somehow 'involved' with a married woman. Sarah Wister seemed 'safe' – married, respectable, a mother, older than Henry. Yet she created a certain vague anxiety. She brought to the surface unknowingly that conflict which Henry would always experience and never quite resolve : his struggle between his need to be passive with women and to yet assert himself as a man. The artist in him told him to live dangerously, to invite passion, to feel and act. The reasonable self, the well-conditioned conscience, echoed his mother's 'beware'.

2

Henry James kept a note-book while he was in Rome. All that survives of it are certain pages which he edited and published as an article, 'From a Roman Note-book', in the *Galaxy* and reprinted in *Transatlantic Sketches*. In describing some of his Roman excursions he listed his companions by various initials, or the impersonal 'X'. But when he revised the book for Tauchnitz, as *Foreign Parts* in 1883, he substituted certain identifying letters. A.M. is Aunt Mary Tweedy; L.B. is Lizzie Boott; Mr E. is Emerson, and X becomes W., Mrs W. or S.W.* At the time Henry wrote to Mrs Wister saying that

* Many years later, revising the article again, for inclusion in *Italian Hours*, James forgot he had already substituted initials in *Foreign Parts* and intro-

she would 'recognize an allusion or so' in his Roman pieces. 'Enjoy them and forgive them according to need. You will see – I had to make up for small riding by big writing.'

December 30, [1872]. I went yesterday with Mrs W. to the Colonna Gardens – an adventure which would have reconverted me to Rome if the thing were not already done ... It's a very pleasant thing ... to stroll and talk there in the afternoon sunshine.

January 26th, [1873]. With Mrs W. to the Villa Medici ... What mornings and afternoons one might spend there, brush in hand, unpreoccupied, untormented, pensioned, satisfied, resolving the picturesque into pictures.

January 30th. – A drive the other day with Mrs W. to the Villa Madama, on the side of Monte Mario; a place like a page out of Browning, wonderful in its haunting melancholy.

February 12th. – Yesterday with Mrs W. to the Villa Albani. Overformal and (as my companion says) too much like a tea-garden; but with beautiful stairs and splendid geometrical lines of immense box-hedge ... The Alban mountains of an intenser broken purple than I have ever seen them ... Mrs W. suggested again the Roman villas as a 'subject'. Excellent, if one could find plenty of facts, à la Stendhal. A lot of vague picturesque talk would not at all pay.

Middle of March. – A ride with Mrs W. out of the Porta Pia to the meadows beyond the Ponte Nomentana – close to the site of Phaon's villa where Nero, in hiding, had himself stabbed. It was deeply delightful – more so than one can really know or say. For these are predestined memories and the stuff that regrets are made of; the mild divine efflorescence of spring, the wonderful landscape, the talk suspended for another gallop.

We wonder how often talk was suspended for another gallop. On this occasion :

Returning, we dismounted at the gate of the Villa Medici and walked through the twilight of the vaguely perfumed, bird-haunted alleys to H[ébert]'s studio, hidden in the wood like a cottage in a fairy tale. I spent there a charming half-hour in the fading light, looking at the pictures while my companion discoursed of her errand.

The visits to the Villa Medici were more frequent than the notes record. Mrs Wister had many friends there including the young

---

duced new ones. Most of the later initials tally with the earlier ones; the few differences may be attributed to lapses of memory. The Tauchnitz volume appeared a decade after his stay in Rome, when Henry was forty; his revisions of 1909 were made at 66.

artist-director, Ernest Hébert. They took occasional walks in the gardens. One day James spied Edmond About and looked at him with soft memories of his youthful reading of his romantic-pathetic tale of *Tolla*. Henry dined at the Storys' with the Wisters and Hébert, 'the Marchese Somebody, a mellifluous Italian master of ceremonies to the King', and Hattie Hosmer. Miss Story sings for them afterwards in her strange but pleasant tremolo. 'After the dinner – at 11 o'clock, while you were all virtuously snoozing,' he writes his sister, 'I repaired with Mrs Wister to the Villa Medici. Here, in a great saloon, hung all round with antique Gobelins – a most delicious apartment – were congregated the twenty students of the Academy, a knot of effete young *attachés*, and three or four formidably fine French ladies. A great deal of solemnity. A little music, and no introductions.' They leave at one a.m. 'through a tremendous tapestried library and wondrous portico, walking out on the gardens of the Villa, flooded with magical moonlight'.

Mrs Wister challenged James. She asked questions; she invited him to join her in appreciating art, experience, history; to have ideas on 100 subjects while being gallant, attentive, devoted, in a word 'involved' in her fancies and moods. The problem for Henry, however, was how to maintain a discreet distance. This may explain why praise of Mrs Wister in his letters is usually cancelled out by depreciation. The reticences expressed to Quincy Street are genuine; in a sense they are invitations to his mother to back him up. But the Roman notebook itself, if we read between its purple-splashed lines, suggests that the friendship had deepening roots and underlying intensities for Henry, heightened by a sense of the place and the 'divine efflorescence' of the spring. When the moment of parting came toward the end of March, and Dr and Mrs Wister and their son Owen (the future novelist) turned their faces toward Philadelphia, Henry told his father, 'I took her last ride with her away and away under the shadow of the aqueducts. She is most broken-hearted to exchange Rome for Germantown.' Henry may not have been as broken-hearted, yet a distinctly romantic moment in his life had come to an end.

3

Some months later, when he had left Italy and was living in an inn near the Taunus Mountains, at Bad Homburg, he wrote a story which embodied his experiences as a young unmarried man enjoying the friendship of a married woman. Perhaps it was his memory of the purple Campagna, the scarlets and lavenders and violets of Rome, the perpetual lavender satins and purple velvets worn by Mrs Kemble, or even the name Wister itself, with its evocation of lilac wistaria – at any rate he named the story *Madame de Mauves*. The tale embodies the earlier theme of old and new, corruption and inno-cence, but in more subtle and less morbid form. At the same time it is the first of a long series of stories written by James about idealis-tic Americans observing, in their innocence, complex international marriages.

Euphemia Cleve, a convent-bred American girl, has nourished from her early years those love-romances which stirred the blood of Emma Bovary. The difference between Euphemia and Emma is that Emma acts upon her dreams of an unattainable love by taking a series of lovers. Euphemia is doomed in quite another way: she clings to her illusions and to a dream of the past – of a chivalry un-related to life and transformed into puritanical self-righteous suffering. She has married the young, dissipated Baron de Mauves and when Longmore, the American hero, discovers her she is already an unhappy, rejected woman, deeply hurt by her husband's in-fidelities and aggressively determined to endure them. Longmore thinks he loves her. They walk along garden paths and shady woods at St Germain-en-Laye (like those of the Villa Medici). For a moment Longmore dreams of taking Euphemia away. What she needs, he tells her, is a husband 'of your own faith and race and spiritual sub-stance'. Euphemia is unmoved. 'I have nothing on earth but a con-science, nothing but a dogged, clinging, inexpugnable conscience.' The conscience will keep her from 'doing anything very base', she says. It will also 'effectually prevent me from doing anything very fine'. We might add that it prevents her from doing anything.

Longmore wavers. He is in conflict. 'To renounce – to renounce again – to renounce forever – was this all that youth and longing and resolve were meant for?' And again : 'Was a man to sit and de-liberately condemn his future to be the blank memory of a regret, rather than the long reverberation of a joy?' Longmore is unable to translate these hedonistic thoughts into action; he does not put his arms round Euphemia, as a young hero might, and bid her to flee from her wicked husband. Euphemia's defences are formidable; but they are never put to the test. In a dream which James contrives for Longmore, his hero is separated from Madame de Mauves by a stream in the forest. He thinks of plunging into it to cross over to her; but he does not act. Someone else turns up in a row-boat and conveys him to the other side. When he gets there, Madame de Mauves is by now on the opposite bank – eternally unreachable. And the oarsman turns out to have the visage of the Baron, her husband.

The Baron de Mauves, throughout the story, has been more than a complaisant husband. He has urged Longmore to make love to his wife; he sees no reason why she should not accept his own relaxed view of the marriage-tie; it would remove her from her high moral throne and her ascendancy over him. Of this Euphemia is aware. Her puritanism stands firm and her fidelity becomes her instrument of revenge. The Baron is overwhelmed by so much virtue and high-mindedness. When his wife closes her door to him, he cannot tolerate the frustration, and Henry James asks his readers to believe that in his despair the hedonist blows out his brains. Longmore, who is back in America, is moved at first to rush to her; but he has a second thought. Something holds him back. In the midst 'of all the ardent tenderness of his memory of Madame de Mauves, he has become conscious of a singular feeling, – a feeling for which awe would be hardly too strong a name'. These are the last words of the tale.

<h1 style="text-align:center">4</h1>

The two preceding tales – those of the recovered statue and the restored topaz – had treated evil and corruption as inexorable historical forces, in an atmosphere bordering on the supernatural and the morbid. In *Madame de Mauves* evil is embodied in the Baron de Mauves, the representative of 'Europe', but now as part of everyday life. And while Longmore faces corruption as a Puritan, he does not see it as a force emanating from the devil.

Evil is quite simply a part of life; a part of the bad that must be taken with the good. Experience hurts; it does not necessarily kill. The tension of *Madame de Mauves* is less the result of extremes and of shock than of human ambiguities. At the end of the story one feels that the Baron, whatever his moral laxities, had a decidedly rigid wife. On the other hand Longmore invokes our attention in much the same way. He too is 'difficult'. For what James seems to have converted into this tale, is not the person of Sarah Wister, who bore little resemblance to Euphemia Cleve, but his relationship with her in Rome: the young lover is of two minds; yet he is never convinced that he should make love to Madame de Mauves. He merely seems to feel that in this situation he should try. Yet he cannot bring himself to act. 'Women were indeed a measureless mystery,' Longmore ponders – even as his author had pondered, in looking upon Elena Lowe, or in praising and cancelling out his praise of Mrs Wister. In *Madame de Mauves* Henry expressed his ambivalence toward the opposite sex. Longmore wonders at one point whether 'it is better to cultivate an art than to cultivate a passion'. For Henry the answer was clear. One cultivated an art passionately.

Sarah Wister saved Henry James's letters. They are propriety itself. She remains to the end 'Dear Mrs Wister'. The letters are charged with friendship and memory. 'Never, never have I forgotten,' he wrote to her, 'how some of the most ineffaceable impressions of my life were gathered ... fifteen years ago in your society.' But he was to write in much the same way to Alice Mason after the turn of the century: 'May *your* way [to Rome] be blessed to you, again, this year – the golden air will bring back something at least of the gilt of the old feeling. I can't think of them (air, feeling, everything) without pangs, yearnings, memories, despairs, almost tears.'

We seem to catch the image of Mrs Wister in a tale written almost twenty years after their springtime in Rome, an elegant trifle called *The Solution* in James's high comic manner, dealing with a young man whose teasing friends tell him he has compromised a young lady. When the young man actually proposes to her, the friends realize they have carried a joke too far and must 'disengage' him. To this end the narrator seeks the aid of the charming Mrs Rushbrook. She accomplishes her task, and marries the young man herself. In the description of Mrs Rushbrook James seems to be setting down a sketch of Mrs Wister as he had known her: and writing out his old dormant fantasy of a love affair:

She was extravagant, careless, even slightly capricious. If the 'Bohemian' had been invented in those days she might possibly have been one – a very small, fresh, dainty one ... She had a lovely head, and her chestnut hair was of a shade I have never seen since ... She was natural and clever and kind, and though she was five years older than I she always struck me as an embodiment of youth – of the golden morning of life. We made such happy discoveries together when I first knew her: we liked the same things, we disliked the same people, we had the same favourite statues in the Vatican, the same secret preferences in regard to views on the Campagna. We loved Italy in the same way and in the same degree ... She painted, she studied Italian, she collected and noted the songs of the people, and she had the wit to pick up certain *bibelots* and curiosities – lucky woman – before other people had thought of them.

For James, Rome, Mrs Wister and the rides in the Campagna had been indeed 'the golden morning of life' – and it was tinted mauve.

51

A Monocle

ONE day toward the end of February 1873 Henry James entered the Caffè Spillmann on the Via Condotti, one of his Roman haunts, and observed an English family at lunch – a mother, a father, and a little girl. The father had characteristic Victorian side-whiskers, a large sensitive mouth, a broad-lined brow. The face was serious and captivating. James recognized it at once. Here was an idol of his youth. A decade earlier he had walked through the New Hampshire woods with his young cousins declaiming the verses of Matthew Arnold. Among the earliest of Henry's published reviews had been his notice of *Essays in Criticism*, read with intense emotion in the ink-besmirched proof supplied by J. T. Fields. In Matthew Arnold the young Henry James had found an intellectual kinsman, an Englishman with a continentalized intelligence like his own, an individual of 'natural sensibilities'. 'Hundreds of other critics have stronger heads,' he had written, 'few, in England at least, have more delicate perceptions.'

What James could not have known was that Matthew Arnold had discovered the unsigned review in 1865 and had written to his sister : 'The *North American Review* for July had an article on me which I like as well as anything I have seen.' He had proceeded to generalize on the 'intellectual liveliness and ardour' he found among Americans in Europe. One wonders what he would have thought had he known, on his side, that his transatlantic reviewer was a young man of 22 who had just begun his literary career.

On the evening after James's glimpse of Arnold at Spillman's, he found himself face to face with him in one of Story's tapestried rooms. There was no doubt about it : Arnold had a powerful visage, but James, looking into it, found it was not as 'delicately beautiful', as he might have hoped of an individual with 'delicate perceptions'. Arnold's manner was easy, mundane, even 'somewhat gushing'. What seems to have set James off particularly in this casual encounter was the 'little glass he screwed into one eye'.

The author of the Obermann verses with a monocle! Henry had never pictured this. He was prepared to avow to Mrs Wister that it was 'simply *my* want of imagination'. Nevertheless he did have to reconcile the emphatic verses, in which Arnold eulogized Étienne Pivert de Senacour, Obermann's creator, with this somewhat dapper worldly figure:

> Ah! Two desires toss about
> The poet's feverish blood.
> One drives him to the world without,
> And one to solitude.

Decidedly this chattering Englishman with a monocle was not the Arnold of solitude: this was a drawing-room individual exchanging lightweight talk with the lightweight Story. Arnold was now 51; James was 30 – but the Henry who waited that evening for precious words to fall from the lips of Matthew Arnold, was the young writer of 22, the brooding Henry of the Civil War. And so he wrote that he had 'first and last a little small talk with him'. The note was almost rueful. 'He did nothing to make it *big*, as my youthful dreams would have promised me. He's a good fellow, I should say, but he is decidedly a disappointment, in a superficial sense.' To William he wrote that Arnold 'said nothing momentous' – as if there were anything momentous to say during a casual social evening at the Barberini. To Norton he wrote: 'He is not as handsome as his photographs – or as his poetry. But no one looks handsome in Rome – beside the Romans.'

They met shortly after, at a dinner in the Villa Mattei, home of Baron Richard von Hoffmann and his American wife, Lydia Gray Ward. The villa stood on a hill above the wall of Servius. The Hoffmanns served a 'vast and ponderous' repast, 'all flowers and footmen and dreariness'. Matthew sat, amid this Romano-American extravagance, his glass screwed into his eye.

In Rome in 1873 Arnold had no way of knowing how much he and the young American had in common: their admiration for George Sand and for Sainte-Beuve, their strong ties with the Gallic mind. Matthew Arnold was as vocal in denouncing the English Philistine as James was in condemning American 'vulgarity'. Later, when James was famous, and Arnold had lectured in America, Henry wrote an article about him for the *English Illustrated Magazine*, defending him alike for his literary views and his entry into theological controversy. What he cherished was Arnold's cosmopolitanism. 'I like him – love him rather – as I do my old portfolio, my old shoehorn,' he wrote to T. S. Perry, 'with an affection that is proof against anything he may say or do today, and proof also against taking him too seriously.' Arnold, when he got to know James, reciprocated the affection.

Long after, James recorded his memory of the Roman meeting. He had so admired Matthew Arnold, he wrote, that 'nothing could have seemed in advance less doubtful than that to encounter him face to face, and under an influence so noble, would have made one fairly stagger with a sense of privilege'. The sense of privilege had to be postponed. In the Barberini it was 'as if, for all the world, we were *equally* great and happy, or still more, perhaps, equally nothing and nobody; we were related only to the enclosing fact of Rome, before which every one, it was easy to feel, bore himself with the same good manners'. The 'enclosing fact of Rome' concealed in it the memory of a monocle.

52

A Personal Timetable

'THE days follow each other in gentle variety, each one leaving me a little more *Roman* than before,' Henry James wrote home that spring. He abandoned himself wholly to the enjoyment of the new season; he rambled in the Borghese gardens, admired the white roses tumbling over the walls, plucked violets from the roots of high-stemmed pines, and rode with Mrs Sumner and Miss Bartlett who had three horses and placed one at his disposal. The Corso was emptying itself; the Pincio seemed deserted; he had the galleries to himself. One day he escorted Emerson – homeward bound from his Mediterranean journeyings – to see the Vatican sculptures, much as he had escorted him a few months earlier through the Louvre. He found him 'as lovely as ever, serene and urbane and rejuvenated by his adventures'. In early April the Henry Adamses arrived. Henry dined twice with them, once in the company of Miss Elena Lowe and once at Mrs Sumner's. He had known the historian during his Cambridge months. He found him 'improved', and Mrs Adams – the former Marian (Clover) Hooper seemed to have had her 'wit clipped a little' – but he supposed she had 'expanded in the affections'.

The warm weather made his hotel-room stuffy, and James moved into a little fourth-floor apartment in the Corso – No. 101 – where he had a *loggia* with a view of roof-tops and two comfortable rooms, vividly upholstered in cobalt and yellow, with magenta *portières*. His landlord sold Catholic images in a shop in the basement and lived with a large family in a curtained alcove down the hall from his tenant. Henry was closely neighboured and surrounded by good-natured Italian volubility. The little Italian maidservant was only too eager to please ('She would even satisfy mother,' Henry wrote) and rushed to nail his card to the door downstairs – upside down as he later noticed.

One evening, before the Wisters' departure, he found William Wetmore Story in their drawing-room, seated with a large manuscript, a five-act play on the life of Nero, which he was about to read to Fanny Kemble. Story got through three of the acts, and years later Henry remembered that 'though my ears ... were all for Story, my eyes were for our distinguished companion in whom the whole matter was mirrored, commented, silently represented'. At the time he saw this performance as a display of Storyesque vanity and 'restless ambition'. Henry was 'unavoidably' absent when the remaining two acts were read on a later evening.

He had hoped to settle down now to less desultory writing; however he complained of his lassitude. 'Lingering on here in these lovely languid days of deepening spring,' he wrote to Mrs Wister, 'I felt as if I were standing on some enchanted shore, sacred to idleness and irresponsibility of all kinds.' But not too irresponsible for he wrote to Quincy Street: 'The other day, I became THIRTY – solemn fact! – which I have been taking to heart.'

I

Henry was 30, and he could show only modest beginnings for one who had grandiose dreams. He had been writing for ten years and he had not yet published a book. He had written only scattered tales, reviews, sketches, and travel-impressions. His months in Rome however had shown him that he stood firmly planted in his career. There is a kind of serene confidence in his letters when he speaks of what he is doing and what he will do. He is a little unhappy that he has not written more; but when the time comes he knows that he will be able to write at will. 'Mine is a slow progression, but a progression I believe it is.' There were indications that his search was elsewhere : what he is really 'taking to heart' is the question of what *kind* of artist he is to be, and *how* he is to arrange his artist's life. The short things for the magazines come to him with tolerable ease; yet he feels that he is writing too slowly, because of his 'still unformed and childish habits of application'. For the rest, if Quincy Street still tugs at the silver cord, he is learning how to resist. He has been discovering the meaning of freedom : he is learning belatedly to feel comfortable in the world. And the world appreciates him. His father may offer unprofessional advice; his mother may talk in purely material terms, as she counts his literary dollars; his brother may carp at his prose, but only the other day Norton had written from London that Ruskin was delighted with Henry's comments on Tintoretto in the *Nation*. 'You may be pleased from your heart,' wrote Norton, 'to have given not merely pleasure, but stimulus, to a man of genius very solitary and with very few friends who care for what he cares for.' Ruskin wished Henry James Jr had been appointed Slade Professor of Fine Arts at Cambridge rather than Sidney Colvin. 'Nothing could have given me more substantial pleasure than your note about Ruskin,' Henry replied, 'the invidious comparison as to Mr Colvin included.'

He has misgivings as to the value of art-criticism – indeed of all criticism. He tells Grace Norton that he seriously believes that a moratorium on reviewing for half a century would represent a great stride for civilization. He speaks also at this time of writing *A History of Prose Fiction Since Cervantes*. But what he really wants to do is to write prose fiction, not its history. 'To produce some little exemplary works of art is my narrow and lowly dream,' he tells Miss Norton : 'They are to have less "brain" than

Middlemarch; but (I boldly proclaim it) they are to have more *form.'*

The sense of a personal schedule which he will follow, regardless of the schedules of Quincy Street, is strong in his letters. Both his father and William have easy advice for the son and brother: he thanks them – and follows his own counsel. His father had sounded out a Boston publisher and offered to pay for the printing of a volume of Henry's tales; Henry replied that he was not ready for this. He had little use for most of his published work. 'There is the impossibility of the things being printed as they stand, uncorrected. They are full of thin spots in the writing which I should deplore to have stereotyped, besides absolute errors to which I was always very subject.' He is prepared to wait until he has written some new stories. His answer shows, moreover, that at last he has his vision of a large theme. 'What I desire is this,' he tells his mother, 'to make a volume, a short time hence, of tales on the theme of American adventurers in Europe, leading off with the *Passionate Pilgrim*. I have three or four more to write.' This would indeed be his first book. He knows what his second book will be. William had written praising Henry's articles on French writers and urging him to make a book of them.

I may come to it, some day, but there are various things I want to do first. Just at present I shall write a few more notes of travel: for two reasons: 1° that a few more joined with those already published and written will make a decent little volume; and 2° that now or never (I think) is my time. The *keen* love and observation of the picturesque is ebbing away from me as I grow older, and I doubt whether, a year or two hence, I shall have it in me to describe houses and mountains, or even cathedrals and pictures.

These replies demonstrate the extent to which Henry James had taken the measure of himself and his opportunities. He was never one to rush into print heedlessly. He might be 30, and his apprenticeship might be long. But he had his own time-table. He would not be led astray by the well-meaning counsels of Quincy Street.

2

The question of money was quite another matter – a rather ticklish matter – for Henry James, perhaps because his father abandoned finances to his mother, and left it to her to discuss them in detail with her son. The accounts of Quincy Street had to be closely watched; there was a heavy drain on them. William and Alice lived at home; the younger sons had poorly-paid jobs in the West and often required help; and Henry drew regularly on his letter of credit. It was no less true, however, that Henry was now publishing more and being adequately paid, according to the standards of the time. Quincy Street vigorously protected the interests of its writing son; it also exerted a certain kind of pressure. This arose from Henry's arrangements to have the magazines pay his father rather than himself. Quincy Street became Henry's personal banker, and he was increasingly held accountable to his family for his expenditure – and, as it seemed, for his life – abroad.

There was an understandable maternal interest in the welfare of her son when Mary James wrote:

What are you living on, dear Harry? It seems to me you are living as the lilies, and feed like the sparrows. But I know too that you toil and spin and must conclude that you receive in some mysterious way the fruits of your labour. We have been all along under the impression that your publishers were to send your money to us, and as nothing has come, and nothing has been drawn by the Bankers since Nov. 1st, it is quite a mystery to me.

Henry reassures her. He isn't starving. He had drawn on his letter of credit before leaving Paris. There are inevitable delays in payment by magazines. Life in Rome is moderately expensive: at the hotel he paid seventy Italian francs ($14) a week for service, breakfast, beefsteak, potatoes, fires and light. His standard seems luxurious, perhaps, yet he could not get the same for the price at a poor Boston boarding house. His only 'serious expense' had been his riding. He pays $50 a month for a horse, or a little more than $2 for a single long ride. 'But this,' he explains, 'is so substantial a pleasure and profit that I can manage it.' It is true, he says, that he is not writing much. He is not reading or studying either; he has simply surrendered himself to 'seeing "life" here insofar as it offers itself'. He believes that 'with practice I shall learn to write more briskly and naturally'.

His mother's next letter announces that $250 had been received in Quincy Street for five pieces in the *Nation*, but two articles had been published since, and 'I presume they send directly to you.'

Henry replies, 'We must keep things regular,' and early in May

when he could look back to a certain amount of published work he
set down in two columns the balance sheet of his Roman sojourn:

Drawn by me since Dec. 18th		Paid and to be paid father on my account.		
Paris	£30	From	*Nation*	$250
Rome	20	,,	*Nation*	75
,,	20	,,	*Atlantic*	60
,,	40	,,	*Galaxy*	30
,,	20	,,	*N.A.R.*	75 (?)
	130	,,	*Galaxy* (for story I think	
= $650 *in gold* (I suppose			I asked $150)	
not more than) $575				150
at most in paper.		,,	*Atlantic* (for story forth-	
$575			coming)	100 *at least*
			$640	

He hoped to reach the stage where payments from the magazines
would come in 'like revenue'. Then as if to make certain, he verifies
his figures and discovers that his total should have been $740.
Maternal pressure, perhaps, was not conducive to good arithmetic.
At any rate the final balance is sufficiently reassuring. Henry may
not have written as much as he had hoped in Rome, but he had done
enough work to cover his expenses. He had paid his way according
to his own plan.

3

June was approaching. The heat was not yet intense; nevertheless
there was a 'peculiar quality' in the air. James needed something
more bracing. In the 'loving mood of one's last days in Rome' he
went to St John Lateran forty-eight hours before setting forth on his
travels. A sirocco was blowing. Rome for the moment had become
the mouth of a fiery furnace. Gone was the lovely winter aspect of
the region: where there had been soft yellow sun and purple
shadows there was now green and blue everywhere. The Campagna
rolled away in great grassy billows; they seemed to break high above
the aqueducts. The Alban hills were almost monotonously green.
Henry paced the twelfth-century cloister; the shrubs were blooming,
the old well was surrounded by dazzling light. He contemplated the
façade with its robed and mitred apostles, bleached and rain-washed
by the ages, rising in the air like strange snow-figures in the hot

wind. He crossed the square to the Scala Santa – the marble steps brought to Rome from the praeterium in Jerusalem – and studied them through a couple of gilded lattices. Impious thoughts crossed his mind: the steps seemed oriental or Mohammedan. On them, where they were to be ascended only on bended knee, his imagination seemed to place sultanas in silver veils, in silken trousers, sitting cross-legged on crimson carpets.

James said his farewells at the rival palaces. He dined with the Terrys *en famille* and his last evening in Rome he spent with Story, who, in his large cool Barberini rooms, usually remained until July. They parted almost affectionately, although he wrote home 'I don't care an inordinate number of straws [for him]. Story is too much occupied with himself.' As he packed his bags, he seemed to experience a reluctance not unlike that which he had felt half a year before when he was on the point of quitting Paris. 'One would like, after five months in Rome, to be able to make some general statement of one's experience, one's gains,' he wrote in the final paragraph of that portion of his Roman note-book which he published. 'It is not easy. One has the sense of a kind of passion for the place, and of a large number of gathered impressions.' Many of these, he said, were 'intense, momentous', but they had come in such profusion that he did not have the time to sort them out. 'They store themselves noiselessly away, I suppose, in the dim but safe places of memory, and we can live in an insistent faith that they will emerge into vivid relief if life or art should demand them. As for the *passion*, we needn't trouble ourselves about that. Sooner or later it will be sure to bring us back!'

Everything that had happened that winter now took on 'the most iridescent hues'. Rome had given him more impressions and more life – the kind of life he needed – than he might have gathered elsewhere in years. He was ready now to write more tales, ready to begin a novel. Years later he would wonder whether Rome hadn't been 'a rare state of the imagination', a Rome of words made by himself, 'which was no Rome of reality'. Enchanting things could doubtless also happen by the Thames, the Seine, the Hudson – even the Charles – but somehow he did not 'thrill at their touch'. The Roman touch had the ultimate fineness. 'No one who has ever loved Rome as Rome could be loved in youth wants to stop loving her,' he wrote – almost fifty years later.

Part Four:

The Choice

53

William

In Cambridge William James was settling into his career, slowly, and with difficulty. He was often ill and despondent. He still lived at home. He had had his period abroad, earlier, before taking his medical degree. Unlike his younger brother, he found little in Europe to please him save German psychology and German *Gemütlichkeit*. On his return to Cambridge he had relapsed into its quiet life, with a sense of dreary inertia. If there was a pronounced difference in temperament between the two gifted brothers, it stemmed, not only from the archetypal rivalry of older and younger brother but from the marked difference in their relation to the family group. William, first upon the scene, had learned to take the world in his own large stride: he was quick, active, often impulsive, nimble of mind, warming to experience. His brother, who had to include William among his elders, had learned in childhood to assert himself from behind a mask of deceptive serenity and secrecy. Submerged and silent, Henry found freedom from family pressures and rivalries by devious means; and there was, later, escape to his writing-desk. William was much more vulnerable. He possessed no defensive weapons, save the brilliant counter-attack of wit. Between the son who was active and rebellious, and the son who was peaceful and submissive, Mary James did not remain neutral. She showed a decided preference for the quiet one – he caused much less trouble. She also, unfortunately, showed a certain cold disapproval – crushing in its effect – toward her firstborn. William's defence was to poke fun at Henry who on his side assumed the role of adoring brother.

The record of William's early years is a series of sallies into achievement – and a series of retreats from each sally. The more daring he was, the more crushing seemed each subsequent 'defeat'. Every positive accomplishment gave him a feeling of increasing powerlessness. Success could not alter the sense of inadequacy engendered by maternal coldness and a paternal softness that seemed almost indifference. William himself was – perhaps on this account – to describe brilliantly how the human personality can be split by such conflicting emotions into the 'me' and the 'not-me'. And on one occasion he was to write that 'with no attempt there can be no failure; with no failure, no humiliation'. This expresses his personal problem. The trouble was that he could not resist making attempts, though to do so meant having his wings clipped.

His refuge, when pressures became too great, lay in symptoms – back-aches, headaches, eye-trouble, loss of appetite. These increased his melancholy. He found occasional relief from submerged anger in a lively baiting of his fellow-members in the family. This he accomplished adroitly, so that his teasing invariably provoked good-humour and laughter, but it contained within it certain animosities and deeper barbs. The family, for instance, might call Henry 'angel' – as Mary James invariably did. William scoffed back – 'angel, hero, martyr'. It was he, however, who felt himself the martyr.

The differences between the ultimate work of Henry and William James reflect the personalities thus formed. Behind the intensities and passions of his imaginative life, Henry could be patient, per-sistent, calculating, secretive. He had in him a touch of Mary James's fixity of purpose in dealing with practical matters, as well as his father's poetry. William's nature remained openly assertive. For all his years of morbid introspection, he was capable of reaching always the warm sunlight of human intercourse. William was to discover himself in teaching, in daily communication with young minds, in his relations with fellow philosophers and psychologists in many countries. Henry was always to remain solitary and subterranean, in spite of an outwardly strenuous social life. He was a recluse of the writing-desk and he harboured and built up his creative resources; the drive to power from his inner fortress was, from the first, com-pelling. William prodigally expended himself in immediate action and wide friendship. He married and had children. Henry remained celibate. William's style was direct and easy, bubbling spontane-ously into lucidity. Henry's had in it more art, much greater literary power – and also more indirection. William was all idea and intellect warmed by feeling; Henry was all feeling – often intellectualized.

In these hidden ways, each brother achieved his originality and his genius. Henry forged an inimitable style and created an *imperium* of letters; William became one of the rare philosophers of this world who could meditate on the conduct of life in the words of the human spirit. The process was long; and it was hard.

I

While Henry was in Rome tasting for the first time the happiness of self-possession and freedom, William remained in Quincy Street exposed to an imprisoning emotional climate. He had stayed beyond his youth in an obsolete environment. He enjoyed his father's talk up to a point; his mother was attentive and solicitous, but in a rather uncomfortable way. She was impatient with William's self-absorption. The family surroundings renewed the conditions which had from far back troubled him. Mary James reported to Henry that his brother complained too much. He had a 'morbid sympathy' with physical ailments. He was hypochondriacal; he worried and lost his temper; he had to express every fluctuation of feeling. For thirteen years – from his 23rd year to his 36th, when he finally left home – the life of William James was marked by recurrent lapses in health and spirit. He was like a mountain-climber who triumphantly scales a peak, only to be terrified by the height he has dared to ascend. He had tried first to be a painter, and had revealed a striking talent. He thereupon abruptly dropped his brushes and turned to scientific study at Harvard. Young and adventurous, he had gone with Agassiz to the Amazon. He returned in gloom and despair. His sojourn in Europe, the months of his studentship in Germany, seemed reasonably cheerful and profitable; he came back to further depression. He then threw himself into medical study and received his doctor's degree at the time of Henry's 'passionate pilgrimage' in 1869. This culmination of his studies ministered in no way to self-esteem. He seems to have had no thought of setting up in practice. It was at this time that William 'touched bottom'. He wondered whether he would ever bring himself into any harmonious relation 'with the total process' of the universe. What he needed was something less cosmic. He had to learn to achieve a harmonious relationship with himself.

We know that William was profoundly involved with his father as with his mother : and his later preoccupation with the emotions and memories of amputated persons may have been prompted by his sense that during these years he had been as emotionally crippled, as his father had been physically. Such a speculation arises from the record he set down in *The Varieties of Religious Experience* of his 'hallucination', which seemed almost a repetition of the 'vastation' recorded by the elder Henry James. William not only duplicated his father's experience, but felt a need to duplicate the manner of making it known to the world, that is by putting it into a book. The father had, in a moment of well-being, experienced a presence, an ugly horrible shape, in the same room as himself, and with this had come an intense anxiety and mental disequilibrium that lasted for weeks. William's account also included a horrible shape summoned, however, from actual memory, and therefore not hallucinatory. What he recalled was the image of an idiot youth seen in asylum during his medical studies:

I went one evening into a dressing-room in the twilight to procure some article that was there; when suddenly there fell upon me without any warning, just as if it came out of darkness, a horrible fear of my own existence. Simultaneously there arose in my mind the image of an epileptic patient whom I had seen in the asylum, a black-haired youth with greenish skin, entirely idiotic, who used to sit all day on one of the benches, or rather shelves against the wall, with his knees drawn up against his chin, and the coarse grey undershirt, which was his only garment, drawn over them, inclosing his entire figure ... The image and my fear entered into a species of combination with each other. *That shape am I*, I felt potentially. Nothing that I possess can defend me against that fate, if the hour for it should strike for me as it struck for him.

And William, late in life, went on to describe how the anxiety endured; how every morning he awoke with a 'horrible dread at the pit of my stomach, and with a sense of the insecurity of life that I never knew before, and that I have never felt since'.

An anxiety as prolonged and recurrent and as overpowering could stem only from a personal dilemma. The outer world had presented William with no real difficulties: he had always encountered it with vigour and geniality. His inner self was plagued by phantoms. Possessing a philosophical cast of mind, he translated his anxieties into metaphysical and rationalistic terms: however, his preoccupation with freedom of the will during the early period seemed to stem, from his own lack of inner freedom. His father, at the time of his vastation, had been able to find solace in the writings of Swedenborg. William, living in the age of Darwin, Huxley, Spencer, could not seek answers from visionaries. What he looked for was a cure for his soul-sickness (and his bodily ailments) for which his fellow medical doctors – as he well knew – had no remedy. William James 'required a philosophy to save him', his biographer tells us, but what he does not say is that William needed to be saved above all from Quincy Street. Ralph Barton Perry has described William James's moral dilemma :

To his essentially interested and ardent nature the counsel of resignation could never be more than a temporary anaesthetic, and he was too profoundly human to find consolation in heaven. He was too sensitive to ignore evil, too moral to tolerate it, and too ardent to accept it as inevitable. Optimism was as impossible for him as pessimism. No philosophy could possibly suit him that did not candidly recognize the dubious fortunes of mankind, and encourage him as a moral individual to buckle on his armour and go forth to battle. In other words, to cure him from his weakness he needed a strong man's medicine. He *was* a strong man, overtaken by weakness – a man of action cut off from action by bodily incapacity, a man to whom no teaching of acquiescence or evasion could be either palatable or nutritive.

Like his father he seems to have found a partial answer in a book. Reading the essays of the French philosopher Charles Renouvier, William was struck by his definition of free will – 'the sustaining of a thought *because I choose to* when I might have other thoughts'. This was not unlike the senior Henry's discovery of the meaning of Selfhood in Swedenborg. It was also like Alice's recognition that she did have a choice over the fate of her body. From this William was to write in his diary words, since much quoted : 'My first act of free will shall be to believe in free will.'

2

William might believe in free will; the ghosts that haunted him were not prepared to depart at the summoning of a belief. He found no solution for almost another decade; marriage and the creation of his own home proved in the end his salvation. He began his teaching at Harvard in 1872, and although he was appointed instructor in physiology, his mind was already at work upon the problems that would yield his *Principles of Psychology*. In the spring of 1873 the elder Henry James could report to his son in Rome that William was getting on 'swimmingly with his teaching'. What William had done at this stage, as the father put it, was to give up 'the notion that all mental disorder required to have a physical basis'. He added : 'This had become perfectly untrue to him. He saw that the mind did act irrespectively of material coercion, and could be dealt with therefore at first hand, and this was health to his bones.' This was the ground upon which Charcot in France, and William James and Freud – who both listened to Charcot's lectures – were to build certain of the basic tenets of modern psychology.

If William was doing 'swimmingly' in March at Harvard, this could only mean that he would probably have a sense of drowning shortly thereafter. His feelings at the end of the semester are described to Henry by his mother:

Will's vacation is fast approaching, only one week's work more. He was late to dinner just now, and came in with his hands full of primroses and cowslips from Grace Ashburner's garden – he had been sauntering in the Norton woods with Sara. He will be glad to get through; he has done his part well, I am sure, although, with his usual self-depreciation, he insists on pronouncing it a very superficial thing. He hears that the class next winter will be three times as large and feels much discouraged with the prospect.

President Eliot offered William a renewal of his appointment and asked him to teach anatomy, with the prospect of a permanent post. William's first impulse was to decline. 'I told him I had resolved to fight it out in the line of mental science,' he wrote to Henry. He finally changed his mind and accepted. Then he changed his mind again, for he resisted the teaching of anatomy. By the end of May he began to toy with the idea that he might take the year off, and escape to Europe. In a letter to his brother he broached the subject of joining him, and remarked: 'I don't know whether you still consider my ailments to be imagination and humbug or not, but I know myself that they are as real as any one's ailments ever were.' He wondered whether in Europe he might suffer from loneliness and *ennui*:

Here at home there are various modes of killing time, the ride to Boston and back destroys one hour, there are constantly visitors in the house to me or to the others who cheer one up, and one can lounge over meals and in the parlour or look in upon the Gurneys and Ashburners etc., in short escape being shut up face to face with one's impotence to do anything, that I should think a lonely invalid might find rather desperate in Europe.

Henry was in Switzerland when he replied. He suggested that William might find Rome interesting; the place, he said, offered more resources for recreation than elsewhere in Europe. He himself had found that it stole much of his time from his writing. Henry's letter answers all William's questions, but it is interesting to note that it contains no attempt to influence William in one direction or another. Henry merely added that he planned to spend the autumn and spring in Florence and the mid-winter in Naples; but if William decided to go to Rome he would be happy to join him there.

We must not exclude the possibility that the old 'Jacob and Esau' struggle between the brothers may have had its share in William's malaise. The younger brother was at large in Europe and popular in the magazines. William, restless and lonely in Cambridge, faced the dreary prospect of a college instructorship. He did not reach an immediate decision. For two months he debated, amid fits of despondency and languor, whether to keep his $600-a-year job at Harvard or to take leave in pursuit of health. 'Poor fellow,' wrote his mother to Henry on 1 July 1873,

I wish it was possible for him to learn to live by the day, and not have to bear today the burden of coming months and years. He says the question of being able to do the work that lies before him next winter, and indeed his whole future career, weighs so heavily upon him that it keeps him from rallying. After a very serious talk with him yesterday, Father's advice to him was to give up the idea of working next winter ... I fear unless his resignation is given in at once, and the whole subject dismissed from his mind, that his recreation will yield him neither pleasure nor profit. He is very desponding about himself, but says that Alice's recovery and yours, especially Alice's (for he considers her weak, nervous condition very like his own present one) give him hope ... He has such a morbid sympathy with every form of trouble or privation, that he is not strengthening where he most wishes to be. For instance, he broke out last evening on the piazza into a most pathetic lamentation over the servants who had only one armchair in the kitchen. I promised him at once that I would supply the want, and that there should be three.

There is little doubt that William was far from being an easy son to have under the family roof. In July he was still saying that to go abroad would be a 'desperate act'. He was particularly troubled by the fact that he would have to ask his father for money. By August Henry had decided what William's decision would be, for he asked him to bring to Europe certain of his books and some American toothpaste and candy. William solved his financial problem by borrowing $1,000 from the loyal Aunt Kate and agreeing to pay her $75 a year interest on this capital out of his future earnings. On 2 September he could announce to Henry that 'the die is cast! The six hundred dollars' salary falls into the pocket of another! And for a year I am adrift again and free. I feel the solemnity of the moment, and that I *must* get well now or give up.' If his experiment failed it would be 'that I am a failure and between one or another mode of failing there is little choice'. What could not have been clear to either brother, each living within his own emotional world, was that Henry's resolute and successful pursuit of his career contributed to William's sense of being a failure. His mother writing a few days later told Henry: 'You will find him very much improved in appearance, looking as well as he ever did I think, but still very morbid, and much more given than he used to be to talk about himself. If, dear Harry, you could only have imparted to him a few grains of your own blessed hopefulness he would have been well long ago.'

William sailed for Europe on 11 October 1873. He paused briefly in London, devoted two days to Paris, and then travelled for twenty-two hours from Paris to Turin, and eleven hours to Florence, the appointed meeting-place of the brothers. He arrived towards midnight and went to Henry's hotel – the Hôtel de la Ville. Henry was asleep. William did not awaken him. Instead he went to his room and before retiring wrote a brief letter to his sister: 'The Angel sleeps in number 39 hard by, all unwitting that I, the Demon (or perhaps you have already begun in your talks to distinguish me from him as Archangel), am here at last. I wouldn't for worlds disturb this his last independent slumber.' William was going to bed with a light heart – and 'the certainty of breakfasting tomorrow with the Angel'.

54

Angel and Brother

HENRY JAMES left Rome, late in May of 1873; he visited the hilltop towns from Perugia to Florence as he had promised himself. Then he fled the Italian summer to Switzerland. After a stay in Berne, he crossed into Germany and settled at Bad Homburg, in a quiet inn, and later in lodgings. Here he spent ten weeks. Homburg was 'German pretty', cool, shady, comfortable; the Kursaal, from which gambling had been banished, looked like a tomb. Henry strolled in the evenings and listened to fussy band-concerts. Forty years later he could recall 'a dampish, dusky, unsunned room, cool, however, to the relief of the fevered muse, during some very hot weather'. The place was so dark that he could see his way to and from his inkstand only by keeping the door open. In this retreat he was 'visited by the gentle Euphemia, artfully editing the confidences with which she honoured me'. In other words, it was here that he wrote his tale of *Madame de Mauves*, blending into older memories of St Germain-en-Laye the emotions of Rome. He wrote travel-pieces as well and read Turgenev in a new German translation. To his mother he wrote: 'I drink, I read and scribble, I stroll in the woods and gardens, I listen to the music at the Kursaal; think of the tremendously fine things I shall certainly do when I am better.' He was feeling better. 'I have for two years been so well,' he told William, 'and have now in spite of everything such a standing fund of vigour, that I am sure time will see me through.'

He returned to Italy early in October. The record of his trip through Switzerland and by coach over the St Gothard may be read in *Transatlantic Sketches*. By this time he knew that William was on his way to Europe. He found Florence oppressively hot and delivered over to mosquitoes. He accordingly went to Siena. This yielded him an article for the *Atlantic* in which we find him indulging in what was to become a characteristic mannerism of his travel-writings – that of imparting a voice to houses, palaces and monuments. 'We are very old and a trifle weary,' the houses in Siena say to him, 'but we were built strong and piled high, and we shall last for many a year. The present is cold and heedless, but we keep ourselves in heart by brooding over our treasure of memories and traditions. We are haunted houses, in every creaking timber and crumbling stone.'

Into the midst of these colloquies between Henry and the Old World his elder brother intruded, bringing his unsentimental wit to bear upon the sentimental traveller. He brought with him also old obscure childhood memories. William, the fresh observer, the quick analyst, the lively eye of Cambridge, was a welcome guest. William, the unconscious bearer of old family wounds, the idealized elder brother – and the ancient rival of the nursery – was an intruder in Henry's Italian paradise. For in a sense William had come to reassert his ancient role, and, as it were, put Henry in his place – as he had done during the years of their childhood. 'I, the Demon,' he had said – placing himself in direct opposition to the brother ... the 'Archangel'.

I

From Henry James Jr in Florence to Henry James Sr in Cambridge, 2 November 1873:

I wrote to you a week ago, telling you of Willy's being on his way to me – and I had hardly sent my letter when he arrived. He had travelled very fast, stopping only one day in Paris, in his impatience to reach me. A compliment to me! I have delayed writing, as I wished to be able to tell you how he seemed, after a few days' observation. He looks indeed in exuberant health, and I am immensely struck with his change in this respect since I last saw him. He is very much charmed with Florence and spends a great deal of time in going about the streets and to the galleries. He takes it all as easily as possible, of course, but he already manages to do a good deal and has made a beginning which augurs well for the future. He has fallen upon indifferent weather, but the air is happily still very mild. I find great pleasure in seeing him and have plied him with all imaginable questions about you all. I feel almost as if I had been spending a week in Quincy Street. Would to heaven I could!

From William James in Florence to Mr and Mrs Henry James in Cambridge, 9 November 1873:

First – of the angel. He is wholly unchanged. No balder than when he quit; his teeth of a yellowish tinge (from the waters of Homburg, he says); his beard very rich and glossy in consequence he says of the use of a substance called Brilliantine of which he always keeps a large bottle on the table among his papers. His clothes good; shoes ditto he having just cabbaged from me the best pair of garters Conol. & Pwr. ever had in their shop as Mr Power informed me. He seems wholly devoted to his literary work and very industrious. I doubt if I get him home in the spring. The 'little affectations' of which Mother spoke I have not noticed. He probably fears me and keeps them concealed, letting them out when foreigners are present. He speaks Italian with wonderful fluency and skill as it seems to me; accompanying his words with many stampings of the foot, shakings of the head and rollings of the eye sideways, terribly upon the awestruck native whom he addresses. His manner with the natives generally is very severe, whereas I feel like smiling upon them and fattening the foot to them all round.

2

This was William James's first journey to Italy and the first time the two brothers had been united on European soil since a far-away German summer of nearly fifteen years before. For both the reunion was bitter-sweet: a mingling of intellectual delight and hidden ache. Henry felt at times as if Quincy Street had descended into his private world. William fretted constantly. He felt the weight of his 31 years. He wanted to be 'settled and concentrated'; he experienced the need to cultivate a patch of ground which might be humble, but still his own. He looked upon the beauties of Florence and the past of Rome with a jaundiced eye, feeling 'like one still obliged to eat more and more grapes and pears and pineapples, when the state of the system imperiously demands a fat Irish stew, or something of that sort'.

And then Florence invited on the part of the physiology teacher from Harvard speculations that were artistic and historical rather than anatomical. In these old Italian cities, historical problems seemed most urgent to the mind. 'Even art comes before one here much more as a problem,' he wrote to his sister, 'how to account for its development and decline – than as a refreshment and an edification.' William apparently could not accept Italy as it was, and enjoy it with his senses. He told Henry he feared the 'fatal fascination' of the place. It seemed to be taking 'little stitches' in his soul. He was too impatient and restless to be completely refreshed. He had been eager to go abroad. He was just as eager, shortly after his arrival, to return home.

He had before him, moreover, the constant spectacle of his younger brother's industry. This was salt on the wounds of his own idleness. The submerged competition between the brothers had always been strong. Henry spent his mornings at his writing-table; William's presence in Florence was not allowed to change this daily schedule. Only when his work was done was Henry ready to lunch with his brother and explore the artistic and human resources of the city. There are repeated allusions in William's letters to Henry's work-habits. He describes how he goes for a stroll and then, tired of sightseeing, returns to sit by a pungent wood-fire in Henry's room. While he is waiting, he starts a letter to his sister, and Henry, 'just this moment rising from the table where his quill has been busily scratching away at the last pages of his Turgenev article, comes to warm his legs and puts on another log'.

The record of their Florentine rambles was written by Henry in eight papers which he published in the *Independent*. These were combined into 'Florentine Notes' in *Transatlantic Sketches*. Occasionally we capture glimpses of his companion, as he carries out his inspection of Fiesole, or visits the castle of Vincigliata, or ponders the pictures in the Pitti as they 'jostle each other in their splendour' and 'rather fatigue our admiration'. William is 'the inveterate companion' or 'my irrepressible companion' or, in one instance, 'W –', who names a Baptism of Christ, by Paul Veronese, as the picture he most enjoyed in Florence; or remarks on looking at Santa Croce: 'A trifle naked if you like but that's what I call architecture, just as I don't call bronze or marble clothes statuary.' Henry picks up these occasional comments where they will serve him best. For the rest, he observes the city and its treasures in his characteristic way – a thoughtful survey of its architecture, a view of its paintings, and, with light touches, his sense of the character of its people. The earlier Roman pieces are charged with intense emotion and colour; the Florentine sketches are more intellectual, more pondered, more 'homely'. Yet Henry is constantly aware of 'the deep stain of experience' in the city, and he discovers interesting paintings in the shadows of the Academy or behind church altars. One gains the impression that perhaps the happiest hours spent by the two brothers were during these rambles. They could commune on the common level of painting – that art in which William had first thought he had a vocation; and they could be again, briefly, the two young boys who had wandered, in their teens, along the quays of Paris and in the salons of the Louvre. It is difficult to say how many words Henry puts into William's mouth, in some of the passages, or how much he lifts from him.

It was not specially for the pictures that I went to the Corsini Palace, however; and certainly not for the pictures that I stayed. I was under the same spell as the inveterate companion with whom I walked the other day through the beautiful apartments of the Pitti Palace and who said: 'I suppose I care for nature, and I know there have been times when I have thought it the greatest pleasure in life to lie under a tree and gaze away at blue hills. But just now I had rather lie on that faded sea-green satin sofa and gaze down through the open door at that retreating vista of gilded, deserted, haunted chambers. In other words I prefer a good "interior" to a good landscape. The impression has a greater intensity – the thing itself a more complex animation. I like fine old rooms that have been occupied in a fine old way. I like the musty upholstery, the antiquated knick-knacks, the view of the tall deep-embrasured windows at garden cypresses rocking against a grey sky. If you don't know why I'm afraid I can't tell you.'

Henry James is probably ringing in personal variations on a theme by his brother; the passage, however, suggests to us the observant, earnest, thoughtful, discussing American sightseers – future novelist, future pragmatist.

3

The Apennine winter descended in full force. William complained of the cold and wanted to move to Rome. Henry was at this moment quite happy by his Tuscan fireside; nevertheless, he felt he should accompany his brother and guide him in the city he had made his own earlier that year. They took the day-long journey by a leisurely train; and, as they passed the Umbrian hillsides which Henry had lovingly admired and described in the *Atlantic Monthly*, William looked upon them and upon the Italian scene with quite other eyes. The ancient walls, the spires, the huddled houses, seemed to the elder brother from Cambridge 'wicked and venomous', and in the winter landscape they seemed to him to be 'showing their teeth as it were to the world, without a ray of anything externally but the search for shelter and security'.

The brothers arrived in Rome during an evening in early December. The air was mild; there was a moon. When they were settled in their hotel, Henry led William to the Colosseum and the Forum. The old stones cast strange shadows; they seemed to be in a remote world of ruin. They looked upon the clear, silent arena, half in shadow, half in moonlit dusk, with its great cross half-way round, where Henry would place Daisy Miller at such a moment several years later. Henry seems to have been, as usual, delighted with the sad beauty of the ruins. Writing to his father he reported that William 'appreciated it fully'. William, however, had not wanted to dampen Henry's romantic ardour. His version to Quincy Street expressed a deep revulsion which seized him on the site where Christians had shed their blood. It was like a nightmare. If Henry had not been with him, he said he would have fled 'howling' from the place.

Rome weighed heavily on William James. He felt the decay, the mouldering paganism, the atmosphere of 'churchiness'; it heightened his New World sense of justice and democracy to the point of belligerency. St Peter's 'reeks as it stands now with the negation of that gospel which it pretends to serve', he wrote his father. Henry reported however that the artist side of William finally confessed to Rome's 'sovereign influence'. He enjoyed 'under protest', however, the very melancholy of antiquity which charmed his brother. Henry, however, took William's asperities in his stride and liked his 'lively and original and sagacious' remarks, adding his old-time note of brotherly homage – 'my own more sluggish perceptions can hardly keep pace with it'.

The brothers had taken rooms at the Hôtel de Russie, a quiet, fashionable hostelry near the Piazza del Popolo. But Henry discovered that the little apartment in the Corso of his Roman spring-time was vacant and moved in, leaving William alone at the hotel, with access to Henry's sitting-room, fireside and balcony. This was a sensible solution – Henry seems to have felt they needed to be free of one another. As in Florence, William spent his mornings in solitary sightseeing, while Henry worked. At lunch-time he went to a café in the Corso, and there awaited Henry who 'comes in with the flush of successful literary effort fading off his cheek'. Continuing in his characteristic vein of caricature, William assures his sister that he is dining frugally, and saving his dollars, even to total abstinence from liquor, 'to which Harry, I regret to say, has become an utter slave, spending a large part of his earnings in Bass's Ale and wine, and trembling with anger if there is any delay in their being brought to him'. He went on :

After feeding, the Angel in his old and rather shabby striped overcoat, and I in my usual neat attire, proceed to walk together either to the big Pincian terrace which overhangs the city, and where on certain days everyone resorts, or to different churches and spots of note. I always dine at the *table d'hôte* here; Harry sometimes, his indisposition lately (better the past two days) having made him prefer a solitary gorge at the restaurant.

William invariably resorted to caricature.

From Cambridge Mary James wrote to Henry on 8 December 1873 :

Mrs Norton said to Alice, the other day, with quite a sympathetic but serious look, 'I hope your brothers are getting on harmoniously in Italy.' Alice, of course, quite astonished, replied, 'What do you mean, Mrs Norton?' 'Oh! you know your brother William does not like Europe, and especially Italy, and Henry is so captivated with everything abroad.' – You may imagine Alice's consternation and the warmth of her assurance that her brothers never quarrelled and that no mere difference of taste, even if they had any, which she disclaimed, could possibly produce a want of harmony between them.

At least one neighbour in Cambridge recognized the distinctly rival temperaments of her sons.

4

Rome had never seemed more delightful to Henry James. After the freezing temperatures of Florence, he basked in the sunshine on the Pincio; he had fraternal company in comfortable doses; he took afternoon walks and drives, dined with William at the von Hoffmanns' in the Villa Mattei, introduced him to the sociable drawing-rooms in the two palaces (the Storys, he reported, 'are to be "quiet" on account of Mrs Story's health : i.e., receive not on fixed days twice a week, but *every evening*, regular'). For Henry – so he told his father – there was the 'especial charm of seeing Willy thriving under it all as if he were being secretly plied with the elixir of life'. William seemed 'greatly contented', and felt constant improvement. 'He does in fact a great deal, and walks, climbs Roman staircases and sees sights in a way most satisfactory to behold.'

This idyllic life – Rome recaptured in such an auspicious fashion – did not last for Henry as it might have, into the soft spring. At Christmas William was seized with chills and fever. Fearing malaria, he promptly took train back to Florence. Henry reluctantly followed him there, a day or so later. He found his brother in good medical hands, dosing himself heavily with quinine, and already distinctly improved. Henry felt an intense frustration.

'I was very willing to abide quietly in Florence in the autumn and attempt no higher flight,' Henry wrote to Alice.

But to go to Rome and take root there, and have all the old satisfactions come crowding back on one and call oneself a drivelling fool to have pretended to exist without them – and then to brush away the magic vision and wake up and see the dirty ice floating down the prosy Arno and find life resolved into a sullen struggle to catch half an hour's sunshine a day on a little modern quay, half a mile long – this is a trial to test the most angelic philosophy. Willy, happily, has no regrets to speak of.

To Grace Norton he wrote in a similar vein. He had been 'jerked away from Rome, where I had been expecting to spend the winter, just as I was warming to the feast, and Florence, though very well in itself, doesn't go so far as it might as a substitute for Rome. It's like having a great plum-pudding set down on the table before you, and then seeing it whisked away and finding yourself served with whole-some tapioca.' Two days after writing this letter Henry suddenly fell ill. He had a splitting headache and a bronchial cough and fever. William brought in a nurse to attend him. The fever abated after three nights and only the headache remained. William could discern no special cause for the illness; he described it to Quincy Street as 'an abnormal brain fever'. It was not malaria; the headache seemed to be the most uncomfortable feature. Henry spoke of it as 'a strange and mysterious visitation, it would be hard to say just what it was'. William dispatched regular communiqués to Cambridge, and at the end of the second week he reported :

He advances steadily and went out driving yesterday. He has just taken a breakfast of poached eggs, chocolate and toast and is sitting now (11 a.m.) by the fire reading the Roman paper. The sun is just beginning to slant into our window, and the sky is as blue outside as it has been almost every day since the middle of November.

5

It seemed once again, as in the time of their youth, that the Angel and his brother could not long remain in each other's company without experiencing a certain amount of physical and moral dis-comfort. Henry's headache, we may speculate, had an emotional origin; it could have spoken for the vexation and frustration ex-pressed in the letter to Grace Norton, that unvoiced helplessness of rage of his early childhood, when he had to accommodate himself to his elder brother's active life. There was even a touch of the nursery in the picture; the plum-pudding snatched from the table, the tapioca substituted for the more substantial dish. Each brother brought to this meeting in Italy his old boyhood self. While they experienced their new relationship as grown men, they were in some degree re-experiencing an older relationship as well. Put into the crudest terms, William in Italy could be quite simply a headache for Henry; and the latter a chronic irritation to William.

The elder brother did not linger. He was impatient to be home and he cut short his stay as soon as Henry was on the way to re-covery. He went to Venice and then to Dresden to visit the Tweedys. Early in March he sailed from Bremen. Quincy Street had nourished a hope that William would bring the lingering literary son back with him, but Henry had no desire to quit Europe. His illness, he wrote, seemed to have 'cleared him up', he felt better than ever and he wanted to take 'a more contemplative and ceremonious leave' of the Old World. He wished to 'hang on' for three or four months longer. 'I don't know when I may come again; and when I do it will be in an older and colder mood, when I shan't relish it as I do now nor get what I can now out of it.' He urged William to 'drop me from your mind and decide your own course freely'. Henry had quite decided on *his*: spring was coming, and he would remain in Florence. He was writing his series of Florentine sketches, and another tale. 'I confess,' he informed Quincy Street, 'I shall leave Europe without alacrity.'

55

The Fork in the Path

WILLIAM JAMES returned to Quincy Street towards the end of March 1874. Cambridge seemed shrunken and small, and he now understood better what Henry meant when he spoke of the 'provinciality' of Boston. When he encountered Howells he told him that he had 'a newly-quickened sense of the aridity of American life'. Howells retorted that American life teemed with suggestions to his imagination. William went to a party at the Bootts' – they had wintered in Cambridge – and found it 'dreariness and countrifaction'. Henry wrote home amusedly : 'I tremble for future days when I learn from Willy that even he finds Cambridge mean and flimsy – he who used to hanker so for it here.'

Willy's mood was temporary. It was necessary for him to make peace with Cambridge, since it was here he wished to build his future. In due course he wrote a letter reflecting certain of his own misgivings, but designed to warn Henry of the dangers of repatriation. 'It is evident,' he wrote, 'that you will have to eat your bread in sorrow for a time here. It is equally evident that time (but it may take years) will prove a remedy for a great deal of trouble.' Henry would have to 'snatch a fearful joy' from little things – such as Cambridge's wooden fences – 'a joy the more thrilling for being so subtly extracted. Are you ready to make the heroic effort?' William asked.

It is a fork in the path of your life, and upon your decision hangs your whole future. This is your dilemma. The congeniality of Europe on the one hand plus the difficulty of making an entire living out of original writing and its abnormality as a matter of mental hygiene – the dreariness of American conditions of life plus a mechanical routine occupation possible to be obtained, which from day to day is *done* when 'tis done, mixed up with the writing into which you distil your essence.

I

There was a double edge to this statement which William may not have recognized when he wrote it, so close was he to his own problems, so blind, at this time, to Henry's. William was saying that Henry could not support himself by his writing and would be wise to take a job when he came home – something Henry had long ago determined not to do. If, in this, there was a degree of William's elder-brotherliness, there was also the general fact, recognized by Henry, that in America, more than elsewhere at the time, to be a writer was to accept the way of loneliness and isolation; and William said that writing was an 'abnormality' that is not quite an active, manly, healthy way of existence. The three massive novels of James's middle period were to carry within them this burden of an artist's relation to his society. 'The pencil – the brush? They are not the weapons of a gentleman,' says the old politician in *The Tragic Muse*. He was echoing, in another form, what William had said to Henry: the pen wasn't a normal instrument for an American. Summing up, William told Henry that if he were not prepared to face a three-year 'slough of despond' he would do well to remain abroad.

William's advice to Henry was a rather blunt urging that he modify his dream of a literary career and conform to Cambridge. There seems to have been in William – it remained throughout his life – a certain blindness to the laws of art that dictated his brother's life. He had seen Henry joyously engaged in the act of writing and doing this religiously every day, without understanding the meaning of such dedication. Far from 'abnormal', this seemed to Henry the most 'normal' thing he could do. He never felt better or stronger than when he had completed a morning's work. A good day's writing gave him a sense of strength, of control, a victory of order and clarity over the confused battle for existence. William never seems to have sufficiently appreciated that the writing son and brother nourished visions of fame, fortune, literary power – the dream of an artist which was wholly unrelated to everyday logic – and which possessed a logic of its own. Henry was always to refuse to be bound by the expediencies advocated by his elder brother. And he felt none of the urgency William expressed about his future.

2

He chose not to reply directly to William. 'Tell Willy,' he wrote to his mother, 'I thank him greatly for setting before me so vividly the question of my going home or staying. I feel equally with him the importance of the decision.' He was aware that he was reaching a crossroads in his life, but the alternatives did not seem to him quite as bare and as merciless as William pictured them. He shrank, he said, from William's apparent assumption that a return to America at this time was 'to pledge myself to stay forever'. He had now had, in all, three years in Europe – a year of wandering during 1869 and 1870, and the two years since 1872 spent largely in Italy. Henry considered this a 'very moderate allowance for one who gets so much out of it as I do'. He was quite prepared to find life at home not simpatico and he knew that 'as regards literary work' his life would be 'obstructively the reverse'. He was quite prepared to return 'on stern practical grounds'. He could find 'more abundant literary occupation by being on the premises', and in this way he would relieve his parents of their 'burdensome financial interposition'. He did not intend to bother too much about that future of which William spoke. 'The present bids me go home and try to get more things published.' He underlined, however, the fact that the American cost of living would use up his income twice as fast as in Europe.

The 'burdensome financial interposition' of which he spoke was hardly of his making. He himself was only in a limited way a burden to his father. He had earned $1,800 since he had gone abroad, and certain other sums were outstanding. The effect of the parental financial help, nevertheless, was that Henry seemed chronically in debt to Quincy Street. This was conducive neither to a sense of security nor to a complete feeling of freedom.

3

There was a 'fork in the path' before Henry James, but it was not the one envisaged by William. At the very moment when Quincy Street was offering its counsels and Henry was preparing reluctantly to go home, the magazines began to compete for his works. His travel-pieces in the *Nation* had created a demand for them in the *Atlantic* and the *Galaxy*. And his efforts to find more outlets for his stories now began to bear unexpected fruit. The first intimation of this was contained in a letter from Howells asking James not to send any of his short stories to *Scribner's Monthly*. They were trying to lure away the *Atlantic* contributors, Howells said, 'and my professional pride is touched'. He admitted that the *Atlantic* could hardly lay special claims on Henry, but it had up to the present published all the fiction he had offered it. He promised it would continue to do so.

James, however, had just sold a story for the first time to *Scribner's*. He told Howells the *Atlantic* would simply be unable to print all the stories he was capable of writing. 'I need more strings to my bow and more irons always on the fire.' He promised Howells, how-ever, that he would always give the *Atlantic* his best things; and as token of this he sent the first part of his tale *Eugene Pickering* which he had been about to mail to *Scribner's*.

Meanwhile the editor of *Scribner's*, Dr Josiah Holland, had writ-ten to the elder James in Quincy Street, proposing that Henry do a serial for his magazine. The father's reply to Holland, composed without consulting his son, reveals at what a pitch of paternal gar-rulity and amateurishness Henry's literary affairs were being con-ducted at home. Polonius-like, the elder Henry gave Holland a full account of his son's illness in Florence, went on to say that he was delighted that *Scribner's* so highly esteemed his work, added that Henry had 'no power to push himself into notice, but must await the spontaneous recognition of the world around him', and promised that he would do his best to persuade his son to write the novel. He also mentioned that it was his opinion that his son's gifts did not lie in the realm of fiction. 'His critical faculty is the dominant feature of his intellectual organization.' He hastened to add, however, that his son did not agree with this estimate. He was certain that Henry would ponder 'your flattering proposition very seriously'. He assured Holland, 'I incline to think he will answer you favourably.'

In the face of William's belief that Henry's writing life was 'abnormal' and his father's depreciation of him as a writer of fiction, Henry's reply showed how firmly his feet were planted in the market-place of letters. For an individual with 'no power to push himself into notice' he seemed singularly hard-headed and business-like. He saw at once, what his father had failed to recognize, that there was a singular value in having two magazines competing for his work.

I am pretty sure the *Atlantic* would like equally well with *Scribner* to have my story, and I should prefer to appear there. It must depend upon the money question, however, entirely, and whichever will pay best shall have the story, and if the *Atlantic* will pay as much as the other, I ought, properly, to take up with *it*.

Holland had proposed $1,000 for the serial. Henry decided he would ask $1,200 from the *Atlantic*, that is, twelve instalments yielding $100 a month. He added that if the *Atlantic* declined, he was ready to take the $1,000 from *Scribner's*. 'The writing and publishing of a novel is almost as desirable a thing for me as the getting a large sum for it. The money-making can come afterwards.' And he took the precaution of reminding his father that this new undertaking might involve some further delays in paying his debts to Quincy Street.

To Howells, James wrote that, 'Sentimentally I should prefer the *Atlantic*, but as things stand with me, I have no right to let it be anything but a pure money question.' Howells sent him a contract, giving him the option of terminating his serial before it had run to twelve numbers. James signed it; he said he wished above all 'to write close, and avoid padding and prolixity'. It was the first time that the *Atlantic* had taken a work of his, as yet unwritten.

'My story is to be on a theme I have had in my head a long time and once attempted to write something about,' he told Howells.

The theme is interesting, and if I do as I intend and hope, I think the tale must please. It shall, at any rate, have all my pains. The opening chapters take place in America and the people are of our glorious race; but they are soon transplanted to Rome, where things are to go on famously. *Ecco*. Particulars, including name (which, however, I'm inclined to have simply that of the hero), on a future occasion. Suffice it that I promise you some tall writing. I only fear that it may turn out taller than broad.

'I shall immortalize myself: *vous allez voir*,' he told his family. He also announced that he would delay his return to Cambridge. A summer in Europe would speed the writing of his novel. 'I perfectly perceive the propriety of getting home promptly to heat my literary irons and get myself financially and reputationally on my legs. I have long tacitly felt it; but the moment for action has come.'

56

The Palpable Present

HENRY JAMES'S course was now clear. He would remain in Florence until summer, then travel northward. He planned to sail late in August. This would give him margin for a few more travel-sketches as well as a running start on his serial. 'By the time this reaches you,' his mother wrote in April 1874, 'you will be mentally launched upon the largest enterprise you have ever undertaken.' Everyone in Cambridge, she told him, was delighted with *Madame de Mauves*, 'so you must be sure not to fall below that'. James replied : 'I am determined that it shall be a very good piece of work.'

During early April, while he awaited final word from Howells, he broke his Florentine stay for an excursion to Leghorn; then he went to Pisa, Lucca and Pistoia, incorporating his impressions in an article entitled *Tuscan Cities*. He could not face the idea of doing a large piece of work in a small hotel-room, and on his return moved into an apartment at 10 Piazza Santa Maria Novella, at the Via della Scala. It consisted of a sitting-room and balcony, two bedrooms, a scullery and a china-cupboard. He did not need so large a place, but it cost only $25 a month. 'Blessed Florence!' he exclaimed to Alice. 'My literary labours will certainly show the good effect of my having space to pace about and do a little fine frenzy. Tell William I find the French restaurant in Via Rondinelli, with the lobsters and the truffles in the window, an excellent place to dine, so that I am altogether most comfortable.'

Years later he was to remember the setting in which the first chapters of *Roderick Hudson* were written – the shabby, charming, high sitting-room with the glare of May and June piercing the shutters. Re-reading the opening part of the book, which he set in Northampton, Massachusetts, James recalled not New England but the Florentine house, and the view his rooms gave on the piazza; the sleepy cabstand next to the obelisk, the clatter of horse-pails, the voices of the coachmen, the siesta stillness – all seemed mixed with his prose.

When he was not writing, he took long walks, and paid calls. 'Nothing particular happens to me and my time is passed between sleeping and scribbling (both of which I do very well), lunching and dining, walking and conversing with my small circle of acquaintance,' he wrote to his mother. The circle consisted of Mrs Lombard and her daughter Fanny, of Cambridge, and Greenoughs, Perkinses and Huntingtons. He described himself as reduced to accepting the Lombard parlour gratefully for half an hour on occasions as the nearest approach to a domestic foyer. Mrs Lombard was a chronic invalid who was always admirably coiffed, a detail which Henry introduced into his tales in describing certain itinerant American ladies abroad. From Quincy Street came the usual warning voice of his mother: 'They are both, I imagine, great invalids, so avoid committing yourself farther than you can help with them.' Other acquaintances included Dr Gryzanowski ('manners formed in diplomacy, brain formed in Koenigsberg') and his English wife, in their Borgo Pinto apartment with its ballroom-living-room as spacious, said James, as a Russian steppe. Florence decidedly was not Rome. Henry missed the full sense of the Italian spring he had so richly experienced the previous year: there were fewer places to catch it – no Campagna, no Villa Borghese, no Colosseum, no long walls overtumbled with cataracts of roses. Against the rugged walls of the Strozzi Palace, however, flowers stood in sheaves, and he had pleasant strolls in the Cascine. James Russell Lowell turned up for a few days and they renewed their friendship of two years before. Henry had great pleasure listening to him read some of his poems. 'I feel as if I know Lowell now very well,' he wrote home.

One afternoon he went to a party in the Villa Castellani on Bellosguardo, a wing of which contained the Boott apartment, and he commemorated the occasion by writing a letter to Lizzie, then in America. 'It was an enchanting day, the views from the windows were lovely, the rooms were perfumed with a wealth of spring flowers – and the whole thing gave me a sense that it might yet be strangely pleasant to live in that grave, picturesque old house.' He added prophetic words: 'I have a vague foreboding that I shall, some day.'

I

The writer of 31, who sat in his large shabby room in the Piazza
Santa Maria Novella during the Florentine spring of 1874, working
on his first important novel, was quite different from the troubled
Henry James of four years before who had hurriedly written *Watch
and Ward* and hoped it would make his name in American literature.
He had passed through a long period of self-searching among his
kinsfolk and his fellow-Americans; he had returned to Europe to
recover the emotions of his original *Wanderjahr*, and he had sharpened his pen by constant exercise and publication not only of tales
but of articles based upon personal experience and observation. He
had always had a sense of his destiny; and now he worked with
confidence, drawing his material out of the past decade of his life –
the days he had spent in Northampton, just after the end of the Civil
War; the days he had spent in Rome a year before – and out of his
inner vision as artist. *Watch and Ward* had been a small story set
in a vague Bostonian frame. In *Roderick Hudson* he drew upon a
view of life and art which seemed greatly enlarged in recent months,
so that he felt he had in his grasp not merely certain precious
moments of existence but a sense of intense living and feeling – and
doing – that would carry him forward to future creation.

There had been suggestions of this in his travel-sketches and
literary reviews, certain remarks which revealed that in his slow
process of growth he had taken possession of a personal philosophy
that would forever guide him. It was not a particular philosophy, to
be found in works of the old thinkers, nor in his father's religious
optimism; it stemmed rather from a saturation with certain aspects
of life and of literature, and a happy synthesis of the two – and from
his constituted personality : the way in which he had learned to
look steadily at – and accept – whatever life might bring into his
orbit. In one of his travel-sketches he spoke of 'that perfectly honourable and legitimate instinct, the love of the *status quo* – the preference of contemplative and slow-moving minds for the visible, the
palpable, measurable present – touched here and there with the
warm lights and shadows of the past'. Hawthorne's experience had
been exactly the opposite. 'The Present, the Immediate, the Actual
has proved too potent for me,' he wrote, and spent his life in conflict
over his essential isolation from the society of his time, which he
sought to overcome. 'I don't pretend in the least to understand our

national destinies – or those of any portion of the world,' James had written a year earlier to Charles Eliot Norton. 'My philosophy is no match for them, and I regard the march of history very much as a man placed astride of a locomotive, without knowledge or help, would regard the progress of that vehicle. To stick on, somehow, and even enjoy the scenery as we pass, is the sum of my aspiration.'

James, on his locomotive of history, offers a vision of a comparatively happy observer and artist; and in his seemingly passive acceptance of life there spoke a writer who shunned movements, or theories (save those involving his art), or prophecies, or advocacy, or didacticism : who preferred the active contemplation of the reality in which he had been placed by fate, and which fascinated him to such a degree that the task of observing and recording it from various points of appreciation and ironic judgement proved sufficient for a lifetime.

The image of the train was to have its variations; James would use it effectively in Lambert Strether's outburst in *The Ambassadors*, in which he argues that if man is a creature determined and moulded and carried through life, he still possesses the *illusion* of freedom, and should live by that illusion. Such formulations, it might be said, would tend to arise in the consciousness of an individual with a nurtured aristocratic temperament, one who has known a comfortable childhood and faces his environment with a sense of profound security. Experience, for such an individual, is something he takes hold of and feels free to mould into any shape he wishes – as distinct from another type of artist who has to conquer his environment through trial and error and struggle; who, so to speak, creates with one hand while holding on with the other to the very train on whose locomotive James, highly perched, is riding. The view of a 'palpable, measurable present' could be taken only by one firmly anchored; for James's less fortunate colleagues the view was inevitably less measurable and was coloured by friction with the world, if not by outright war upon it.

In this light we can understand the models to whom James turned, writers like himself who had been able to arrive at a large view – Balzac, in his 'palpable, provable world', teeming with life as if it were a five-ring circus; Thackeray, most certainly, when he pictured his *Vanity Fair*, and showed his characters acting themselves out in it; George Eliot, with her strong intellectual grasp of experience. To these predecessors James could now add the name of a contemporary, Ivan Sergeyevich Turgenev, a novelist with whom he had great affinity, both in his psychological turn of mind and in the aristocracy of his temperament. In the article he had just written about him, he saluted Turgenev as 'the first novelist of the day'.

What strikes us as we read that article is the extent to which James, in describing Turgenev, seems to be describing himself. Turgenev was 'a story-teller who has taken notes'; his figures were all portraits; 'if his manner is that of a searching realist, his temper is that of an earnestly attentive observer'; he had 'a deeply intellectual impulse toward universal appreciation'. No matter how he shifted his point of view, his object was constantly 'that of finding an incident, a person, a situation, *morally* interesting'. James speaks also of Turgenev's 'minutely psychological attitude'. But it is when he characterizes him as a cosmopolitan and speaks of his relation to Russia, that he voices certain of his deepest feelings. 'M. Turgenev gives us a peculiar sense of being out of harmony with his native land – of his having what one may call a poet's quarrel with it.' Americans could appreciate Turgenev's state of mind, he said, and if they 'had a native novelist of a large pattern, it would probably be, in a degree, his own'. Also 'we gather from his writings that our author is much of a cosmopolitan, a dweller in many cities and a frequenter of many societies'. James spoke as well of the 'impalpable union of an aristocratic temperament with a democratic intellect', a remark he withdrew in a later essay describing it as 'inane'. He said instead that Turgenev understood 'the opposite sides of life'.

These observations show the extent to which James had responded to the Russian. There is in this essay, however, a passage perhaps more important still, revealing the view James had reached in his personal philosophy at the moment he began *Roderick Hudson*. In it James used the old image of life as a battle: a moral and spiritual struggle, a kind of Olympian acceptance of life as something not to be defied, or argued with, but to be coped with and mastered. Revolt, he implies, is futile; and his strongest reproach to Turgenev is that he is a pessimist, that his work is tinged with two kinds of melancholy, the 'spontaneous' and the 'wanton'. 'Life *is*, in fact, a battle,' he wrote. 'Evil is insolent and strong; beauty enchanting but rare; goodness very apt to be weak; folly very apt to be defiant; wickedness to carry the day; imbeciles to be in great places, people of sense in small, and mankind generally, unhappy.' He continued:

But the world as it stands is no illusion, no phantasm, no evil dream of a night; we wake up to it again for ever and ever; we can neither forget it nor deny it nor dispense with it. We can welcome experience as it comes, and give it what it demands, in exchange for something which it is idle to pause to call much or little so long as it contributes to swell the volume of consciousness. In this there is mingled pain and delight, but over the mysterious mixture there hovers a visible rule, that bids us learn to will and seek to understand.

In literary terms this could be taken as the manifesto of a novelist who was to consider himself, and to be considered, one of the new realists in American fiction. It implies also the explorer of spiritual values in human conduct. The battle he chose to observe was the struggle within society for values and standards, for devotion to greatness of mind in art and in the imagination, 'the things that, as a race, we like best – the fascination of faith, the acceptance of life, the respect for its mysteries, the endurance of its charges, the vitality of the will, the validity of character, the beauty of action, the sensuousness, above all, of the great human passion'. By his embrace and stoic acceptance, James lifted his work into the realm of psychological truth. For he was a solipsist; he believed, as Proust did after him, that each human consciousness carries its own 'reality', and that this is what art captures and preserves. For the rest, he would try to compensate – by technical ingenuity, skill of form, grandeur of style – for elements which he lacked in his own experience. This was at times to make him the historian of the rarefied and the particular; it would also enable him to render the delicate and the exquisite in the human mind.

2

The pen that now was tracing the history of the passionate and irresponsible Roderick Hudson among the artists of Rome was driven by the nerves and the temperament of an individual impervious on the whole to the great scientific strains of his century. He had not only read but had met Darwin in 1869; the new science, however, and the debates about determinism, was to take on particular meaning for James only later in its literary manifestations, in the *naturalisme* of Zola. He had met Ruskin, but it was Ruskin's aesthetic observations rather than his social ideas which interested him. So too with William Morris, who yielded him not early socialistic thought but rather a sense of a quaint absorption in personal craftsmanship. The word 'measurable' in James's view of his immediate world was to acquire in his creative life certain distinct accretions of meaning: he was to place that which was 'visible' and 'palpable' within the window of a given point of view – that is his characters' angles of vision by which they measured the world around them. For James metaphysics could have meaning only when translated into art. He had been freed by his father from orthodox theology and had been spared the religious conflict many New Englanders felt between their will to reason and freedom and the overpowering demands of Calvinism. It was possible for him to abstract his world into a secular drama of good and evil as it affected the life of the mind and the conduct of individuals. He shared with his brother an interest in the 'varieties' of religious experience. Religious symbols were part of the fabric of man's emotional experience. In the James household religious and philosophical discussion belonged to his father and his brother; this was perhaps reason enough for Henry to go in search of other – of aesthetic – ground. Intellectual though he was, he gave a primary place to feeling: 'Where there's anything to feel I try to be there,' Gabriel Nash remarks in *The Tragic Muse*, and he also says: 'Merely to be is such a *métier*; to live is such an art; to feel is such a career.' James is drawing upon Arnold, Ruskin and Pater, upon the men who in one form or another, in the Victorian world, urged that life and 'awareness' were linked. If he indulged neither in the discussions of the hedonists, the positivists nor the utilitarians, he cultivated a personal doctrine of a ripe and mature civilization in which man faces reality by recognizing and not suppressing feeling and insisted that he, as artist, could not involve himself in ephemeral issues and at the same time cultivate his own modest garden.

He wrote his novel with great care and he recognized that he was concerning himself more with the life of the intellect and of the emotions than with the life of action. In a letter that summer to Mrs Wister he told her that he was reliving some of his Roman experiences; at the same time he prophesied with complete accuracy what would be criticized in his book – in the precise terms, as a matter of fact, which critics would continue to apply to his later productions: 'The fault of the story, I am pretty sure,' he said, 'will be in its being too analytical and psychological, and not sufficiently dramatic and eventful; but I trust it will have some illusion for you, for all that. Vedremo.'

3

'I am still lingering on here in Florence – one of the few survivors of the winter colony,' James wrote to his mother in June 1874. The hot weather had come; the piazza glared white in the noonday sun and seemed to scorch the eye as he looked out upon the huddled cabmen asleep in their boxes while loungers took their siesta half-naked, flat on their faces, on the paving-stones. He darkened his rooms and stayed on; he had no desire to travel and to live in hotels. In the morning he took walks and sought the coolness of the churches; he lunched early in a beer-garden, in the shade of a trellis, and spent the long hot hours of the afternoon in his room, working when possible, or simply taking a siesta along with the rest of the city. His plan was to make for Homburg, as he had done the year before, as soon as the heat became unbearable. His novel was proceeding 'not very rapidly, but very regularly, which is the best way'.

Four days after describing to his mother his way of coping with the Florentine climate, James fled. A great heatwave had descended upon the city. He went to Ravenna for a day, long enough to study the tomb of Dante and visit the two-storeyed dwelling in which Byron had lived. James wondered how Byron – even granting the particular attraction of the Guiccioli – could have stood the place for two years; it must have been possible, he decided, 'only by the help of taking a great deal of disinterested pleasure in his own genius'. Pushing on to Milan he found that even the cavern-like cathedral offered inadequate coolness and he sought the higher altitude of Monte Generoso near Como, which he ascended in a thunderstorm. 'In spite of the temperature,' Henry wrote to William, 'I have been lacerated at leaving Italy.' A week here, in a room hardly larger than a cupboard, sufficed for Henry. He made for Switzerland, via the Splügen. The journey is recorded in *Transatlantic Sketches*; he spent a night at Chur and a night at Basle, where he devoted some hours to studying the Holbeins. The thought of renewing acquaintance with Homburg, as he approached it, made him 'deadly sick'. He had had his fill of it the previous summer. He stopped therefore in Baden-Baden, settling in the Hôtel Royal, near the Trinkhall and the Kurhaus. The place was 'coquettish' and 'embosomed in a labyrinth of beautiful hills and forest walks'. Besides, he wrote to his father, 'Turgenev lives here, and I mean to call on him. Many of his tales were probably written here – which proves that the place is favourable to literary labour.'

He did knock on Turgenev's door, only to discover that the Russian was at Carlsbad in Bohemia recovering from a bad attack of the gout. James had sent him his article some weeks earlier; and in June Henry's father had written a rather fulsome letter to the Russian informing him that

my son's high appreciation of your genius is shared by multitudes of very intelligent people here. Should you ever cross the ocean, you must not fail to come to Cambridge, and sit with us on the piazza in the evening, while you tell us between the fumes of your pipe what the most exercised and penetrating genius of the old world discerns, either of promise or menace for humanity in the civilization of the new.

Turgenev replied cordially and modestly; he said he considered himself in a second or even third place, when compared with Dickens, George Eliot or George Sand. As for smoking a pipe 'under the verandah', he was not a smoker, but he would enjoy 'a quiet and pleasant conversation with the intelligent men and women of your society'. He doubted, however, whether at his age he would ever cross the Atlantic.

Turgenev's letter to Henry, written from Carlsbad, expressed pleasure in his article as being' inspired by a fine sense of what is just and true; there is manliness in it and psychological sagacity and a clear literary taste'. Turgenev himself gave proof of his own psychological sagacity by telling James that he found it difficult to judge someone else's critical appraisal : that he felt the praise too great or the blame too weak, and this not through 'diffidence or modesty', but perhaps because this was 'one of the many disguises which self-love enjoys'.

'It would please me very much indeed to make your acquaintance as well as that of some of your compatriots,' Turgenev concluded, and he gave James his permanent address in Paris in the Rue de Douai.

4

His days in Europe were now numbered. He spent some five weeks in Baden-Baden and then announced to Quincy Street that he had booked his passage. 'Be sure about Sept. 4th to have on hand,' he wrote to his mother, 'a goodly store of tomatoes, ice-cream, corn,

melons, cranberries and other indigenous victuals.' Baden was a bore
– he had spent there 'the dullest weeks of my life', he told Mrs
Wister. With gambling forbidden, the resort was given over to band-
concerts and tourists, and James's greatest solace was in the walks
he took in the Black Forest. 'I converse with the waiter and the
chambermaid, the trees and the streams, a Russian or two, and a
compatriot or two, but with no one who has suggested any ideas
worthy of your attention,' he said in his letter to the companion of
his Roman rambles. He seemed to have made up his mind what he
would do once he was repatriated. He would spend the autumn in
Cambridge, completing *Roderick*. Then he would try his fortunes in
New York. 'I have no plans of liking or disliking, of being happy or
the reverse; I shall take what comes, make the best of it and dream
inveterately, I foresee, of going back for a term of years, as the
lawyers say, to Italy.'

James left Baden-Baden in early August, and then by a Rhine
journey entered Holland, where he spent some days paying tribute
to the 'undiluted accuracy of Dutch painters', and relishing that
country's 'harmonies of the minor key'. He contrasted Amsterdam
with Venice – 'the way in which the thrifty city imparts the prosaic
turn to things which in Venice seem the perfect essence of poetry'.
He admired the cleanliness and ceremonious thrift of the Dutch, but
expressed surprise that the canals of Amsterdam and Leyden, in
spite of their waterside trees, offered not 'a single bench for a lounge
and a half-hour's aesthetic relish of the situation'. In Belgium he
gave much attention to Rubens – a painter who, he said, painted by
improvisation rather than by reflection. 'He never approaches something really fine but to miss it; he never attempts a really interesting
effect but to vulgarize it.' The trouble with him was that 'he throws
away his oranges when he has given them but a single squeeze'.

He had paid what was to be his only visit to the Low Countries,
and with his articles on them his European journey – his book of
transatlantic sketches – could be ended. Of the fortnight in England
before sailing we have no record. He appears to have visited the
Tweedys, who had taken an English country house. He sailed on a
slow Boston Cunarder, the *Atlas*, encountering on board his old
friend Wendell Holmes who was newly married. Our next glimpse
of him is in a letter written by Mary James to her youngest son
Robertson, at Prairie du Chien :

Harry has come home to us very much improved in health and looks. When he came in upon us from his voyage in a loose rough English suit, very much burnt and browned by the sea, he looked like a robust young Briton. He seemed well pleased to be home at least as yet, and I trust he will feel more and more for himself, what I daily feel for him, that it is much better to live near his family and with his own countrymen, than to lead the recluse life he so strongly tended to live abroad.

To the same brother Henry gave testimony of his feelings a month later:

My arrival is now a month old, first impressions are losing their edge and Europe is fading away into a pleasant dream. But I confess I have become very much Europeanized in feeling, and I mean to keep a firm hold of the old world in some way or other. But home seems very pleasant after the lonely shiftless migratory life that I have been leading these two years. Cambridge has never looked so pretty as during the last month and I have seen nothing in Europe in the way of weather equal to the glory of an American autumn.

Gradually, he felt, he would get accustomed to the American scale of things. The only other letters of this time seem to be two undated little notes to Longfellow, testifying to an evening or two spent with him and to James's lending the poet some of Turgenev's tales, 'the best short stories ever written – to my knowledge'.

57

Roderick Hudson

I

Roderick Hudson was the longest and, as James later said, most 'complicated' subject he had yet undertaken: that of a promising young sculptor from Northampton, Massachusetts, who is befriended by an amateur of the arts and taken to Rome to pursue his studies. He shows ready proof of his genius. Pledged from the first to marry his American cousin, he nevertheless falls in love with a great and ultimately unattainable beauty in Rome, a woman of a high and capricious temperament, and is consumed by his passion. He ceases to create and his disintegration is rapid. The moral of the story seems to be that love and passion can be fatal to art.

James began by weaving the familiar situations of his earlier tales

into a larger drama and against a richer background. The opening
sequence in Northampton is a skilful variation on familiar Quincy
Street problems. Roderick is a second son, unsure of himself in the
world, but unlike his creator bereft of a father and elder brother.
He is given a new father-brother in the art-patron, Rowland Mallet.
Adopted by him he is taken abroad not only to fulfil himself but
also to fulfil Rowland's hopes for him. Before sailing, Roderick becomes engaged to Mary Garland. Rowland also is attracted to her,
although he is, as yet, but half-aware of this. The patron in this
fashion is made also a rival of the hero. What saves the Northampton part of the story from the clumsiness of the earlier tales is the
clarity with which James pictures the artist's dilemma in the small
American town. In a few scenes he makes us feel its limitations and
the dull future before the gifted young man, who works in a lawyer's
office. For the first time James allows himself the clearest expression
of the American artist's need for Europe.

In Rome, Rowland and Roderick wander about very much as
Henry and William had recently wandered. If Rowland is more
appreciative of ancient things than William, he is nevertheless
present as Roderick's puritan conscience and *alter ego*. Roderick's
constant riot of emotion is tempered by Rowland's stuffy sobriety.
The young sculptor embraces Europe with intensity. He places a
Venetian watch-chain round his neck and a magnificent Roman intaglio on the third finger of his right hand. He tries, both in garb
and manner, to shake off his parochialism, and project himself into
other and more dramatic centuries. Rowland sees him as a 'nervous
nineteenth-century Apollo'.

2

Roderick's first statues are paternal and maternal – Adam and Eve.
He also wants to do a Cain and nourishes the ambition of embodying
Beauty, Wisdom, Power, Genius, even Daring in marble – and a
magnificent statue of America to boot. However, his fear of failure
is intense, his feeling of helplessness at times overpowering. 'What if
the watch should run down and you should lose the key?' says
Roderick in one of his monologues. 'What if you should wake up
some morning and find it stopped – inexorably, appallingly stopped?
Such things have been, and the poor devils to whom they happened
have had to grin and bear it. The whole matter of genius is a

mystery.' Roderick, in the Villa Mondragone, talks not a little like James's earlier artist, Theobald, in front of the botched and blackened canvas of his unrealized *Madonna of the Future*.

Before we have ventured far into the book we meet a group of artists, and through them James pictures for us the various types he had encountered in Rome. They are embodied, as we have seen, in Gloriani, the professional opportunist, the modest and single-minded Singleton and the lady-amateur Augusta. Among them Roderick is distinctly the inspired genius. Next to him it is Gloriani who fascinates James; he has the 'impudence of his opinions' mixed with 'the mere base maximum of cleverness'. If he possesses some of Story's humbug he has much candour, intellectual liveliness and the courage of his convictions. In his statues the hideous 'grimaces out of the very bosom of loveliness'.

We do not know Gloriani's future, however, and we would say that the future lies with Roderick. He is the romantic artist of tradition, the artist who 'lives dangerously'; and the difference between him and Gloriani is, in part, his new-world freshness, his openness to experience. We have seen him in his Northampton surroundings, a frustrated dreamer; we watch him gradually substituting a life of excess for the placid horizons he has abandoned.

Rowland's observation of Roderick is that 'the poor fellow is incomplete'. This is true; and it is Rowland who, in a sense, completes him. He possesses the cool measuring mind, the dispassionate heart, which Roderick needs – but also rejects. There is something chilly in Rowland; and in contemplating the two men, so romantically named and so involved in a kind of emotional duel – Rowland the rational, with no real sense of what it means to be an artist, and Roderick the impulsive, with no sense of how to curb his artist's ego – it seems as if James has abstracted the incandescence of his genius and placed beside it his decorous, cautious, restrained self or his mother's warnings beside his own desires. The one is rendered ineffectual by the other : it is as if James were saying to himself that to be free, impulsive and wilful is to court disaster. Rowland Mallet is thus the watchdog of his own spirit. 'You are watching me,' says Roderick to Rowland. 'I don't want to be watched! I want to go my own way; to work when I choose and to loaf when I choose.' Rowland cannot go away. He is literally a watcher, for we see the greater part of the story through his eyes. But he is also Roderick's other self. In the novel James seems to be asking himself an unanswerable question :

how can the artist, the painter of life, the recorder, the observer,
stand on the outside of things and write about them, and throw
himself at the same time into the act of living. To fall in love with a
beautiful woman – say Elena Lowe – would this not be a disaster
for any artist? How become involved in life – and remain unin-
volved? James is writing out, in this novel, the brief hint of the
young American in *Madame de Mauves* – his puzzled interrogation
of himself, whether 'it is better to cultivate an art than to cultivate
a passion'. Any suggestion that the two might be cultivated simultaneously seems to have been excluded from Henry's reasoning. He
treats them as irreconcilable. And he was to debate, in his later
work, both humorously and tragically, this law of his being. It was
as if a wall of glass stood between Henry James and his desires. The
glass at least permitted him to look at life. This explains why contemporary critics of *Roderick* complained that there were sections
of the book which seemed cold and even 'inhuman'.

James was sufficiently a Rowland to realize that he could never
be a Roderick. Instead of acting out his passions he could invest his
characters with them. In this novel the *feeling* self had to die. It was
too great a threat to the rational self.

3

Into the life of Roderick Hudson, during his early days in Rome,
there walks Christina Light, with her poodle, her grand manner, her
shifting moods. She has the 'step and carriage of a tired princess'.
She is as much at the centre of the novel as Roderick; and she grows
upon the reader as the achieved woman of a corrupt society. The
daughter of an American adventuress with large social pretensions
and an Italian Cavaliere, she has been brought up unaware of her
illegitimacy and prepared for the great marriage she will some day
make – prepared for it as some royal princess is prepared for her
royal duties. In Christina, James seems to have set down the deep
fascination he had felt in the mysterious and unreachable young
Boston woman he glimpsed so briefly in Rome. 'Beautiful, mysterious, melancholy, inscrutable,' were the words he had used to describe Elena Lowe; for no other woman of his acquaintance had he
used such language.

Christina is a strong woman capable of cruelty, yet redeemed by
certain moments of honesty, and her awareness that she is the play-

thing of forces she cannot change. Her final act – her marriage to Prince Casamassima – is carried out under her mother's coercion. She is never wholly a free agent. In one of her moments of self-abasement she exclaims: 'I am fond of luxury, I am fond of a great society, I am fond of being looked at. I am corrupt, corrupting, corruption.' Corrupt she doubtless is, in the sense that she is a creature of her world. She carries with her the sadness of her grandeur and all its futility. Miss Blanchard sees this when she speaks of her as 'half like a Madonna and half like a ballerina'. She is a struggling, questioning fated female; in later transformations she will become Madame Merle and Kate Croy.

She was the great success of *Roderick Hudson*. Created as a foil for Mary Garland, representing corrupt Europe as Mary represents innocent New England, she testified in her success to the traditional fascination which evil exercises on the Puritan soul. It was inevitable that she should be all colour and vividness, while Mary is as prosaic as she is dull. If James thought Europe when he thought Christina, and New England when he thought Mary Garland, he could not do otherwise.

Years later he was to recognize this and other defects in the book. He had needed his contrast. Mary Garland had to be plain and Christina had to be varnished. But what remained in the work, even after he revised it, were certain chilly passages which its contemporary critics shrewdly discussed. One critic in particular gave as an example of this the extent to which James's aesthetic feelings were allowed to affect the death-scene, so that Roderick's body is found at the foot of a cliff, washed by the rain and altogether 'arranged' as a pleasing statue rather than as the mangled corpse of a young man who had died a violent death.

James's friend Mrs Wister wrote an anonymous notice of the novel in the pages of the *North American Review*. It gave full recognition to the maturity of the prose and the auspicious character of Henry James's emergence as a full-fledged novelist. Mrs Wister compared his use of language to 'the facility of a great pianist'. The personages were real and living, but 'we do not identify ourselves with them'. She added: 'We are intellectually interested, but as unmoved as one may suppose the medical class of a modern school of vivisection to be.' Her final words must have given Henry pause: 'All it lacks is to have been told with more human feeling.'

THE Roman novel began its course in the *Atlantic Monthly* in January 1875, and *A Passionate Pilgrim*, James's first volume of tales – the book he had described as being 'on the theme of American adventurers in Europe' – came out on 31 January. J. R. Osgood published it and paid him a royalty : it was not subsidized by his father, as the elder James had originally proposed. During this month of his début as a novelist and man of letters, James set out to 'try New York' and discover whether it might serve as a place in which to live and work. He was acutely aware of his 'irresistible longing' to be in Europe; and he left Cambridge for Manhattan with frank scepticism, but also, as he said, 'with very loyal intentions'. He felt it his 'duty to attempt to live at home before I should grow older, and not take for granted too much that Europe alone was possible'. Europe for him then meant Italy, and Italy had in some measure been a lotus-land : it did not 'lead to anything'. He wanted something more active, 'and I came back and sought it in New York'.

I

The history of his six busy months in the city of his birth clearly confirms the loyalty of his intentions. He seems almost literally to have sat at his work-table day and night and 'scribbled', as he put it, in a kind of rage of endeavour to see how much he could earn. He was receiving $100 a month from *Roderick*. He managed to earn another $100 each month from miscellaneous writing, largely for the *Nation*. He contributed one or more book-reviews to almost every issue of the weekly during his stay in Manhattan, and sometimes theatrical and art reviews as well. He was later to say that 'it was these two tasks that kept me alive' – his novel and his journalism. At the same time he saw his second book, *Transatlantic Sketches*, through the press, and made arrangements to publish *Roderick Hudson* in book-form at the end of the year. James allowed his father to cover the cost of the plates of the travel sketches, since Osgood apparently considered the book more of a risk than the tales; but it paid for itself rapidly. For the time being, however, once he had completed *Roderick*, he ceased wholly to write fiction. New York, in other words, turned him into a literary hack. What he seems to have proved was that by incessant drudgery he could earn an adequate livelihood for himself in America. He published only one tale during 1875, and it was doubtful whether, with this constant need to feed articles into the weeklies and monthlies, he would find time, or energy, to start another novel. The *Nation* had paid him anywhere from $10 to $35 for a review, depending upon its length. He had to read three or four books and write about them to earn as much as he could gain from a single travel-article. His New York stay proved that it was better economy for him to live in Europe. Manhattan, he wrote to Lizzie Boott, was 'a rattling big luxurious place, but I prefer F——. Excuse me I can't trust myself on that chapter.' And in the next sentence he was telling her that if he had been with her he might have 'fancied I was again in R——? It will out, you see.'

He invoked Florence and Rome; yet they were not in reality the alternatives he was seeking to New York. One of his problems in Italy had been his loneliness: his loneliness, that is, as a writer who would have liked to know colleagues and who wanted the company of men instead of the perpetual female society to which he had been exposed. He had lacked, he told his mother, 'a *régal* of intelligent and suggestive society, especially male'. Such society existed, he supposed, in Paris and London, but he was not sure how to find it. 'I chiefly desire it,' he said, 'because it would, I am sure, increase my powers of work.'

He did not find such society in New York. Manhattan seemed to confine him in the world 'uptown' while all its activities went on 'downtown' in the world of business. Henry was to remember his isolation during this time. He had discovered not only that 'the major key was "downtown" but that downtown was, all itself, the major key'. This reduced 'uptown' to being the minor, so that 'the field was meagre and the inspiration thin for any unfortunate practically banished from the true pasture'. Seated for several months 'at the very moderate altitude of Twenty-Fifth Street' Henry felt himself alone with the music-masters and the French pastry-cooks, the ladies and the children. There was 'an extraordinary absence of a serious male interest'.

2

On arriving in New York from Cambridge early in January, James found two rooms at 111 East 25th Street between Lexington and Fourth Avenues, the Rose Hill section of the city. In its up-island progress since James's Washington Square childhood, Manhattan had fixed the centre of its life in the Madison Square neighbourhood at 23rd Street and Fifth Avenue. This was within easy walking distance of his domicile. His sitting-room was small, but sufficiently comfortable, with a fireplace, and he apparently had next to it a hall-bedroom — if we assume that the rooms in which he placed Basil Ransom, in The Bostonians, were like his own. Ransom lived further along the street, in the semi-slum near Second Avenue, which Henry came to know during his sojourn. His picture of the area which James said in the novel he included 'for old acquaintance sake' – its unpaved rutted streets, its down-at-heel tenements – shows his familiarity with it : the Dutch grocery, with its fragrance of molasses, its odour of smoked fish and its panniers of vegetables on the sidewalk, the delivery-horse drawn up at the curb, giving the place a pastoral air in the midst of the city; the yawning cellar-doors; the drooping gas-lamps at the corners, the ash-barrels on the sidewalks (he had described these vividly in Watch and Ward). It was a sordid, uncivic New York, and on leaving his domicile Henry could see, eastward, the 'fantastic skeleton' of the elevated railway, which smothered the avenue 'with the immeasurable spinal column and myriad clutching paws of an antediluvian monster'.

Few letters of this period have survived. But there is abundant evidence of his industry, for the articles he carried to the Nation office at 5 Beekman Street show the range and variety of his book-reviewing. The journal's editor was still Edwin Lawrence Godkin, whom Henry had known from the first issue of the journal, to which he had contributed. The book-review department was in the hands of Wendell Phillips Garrison, son of William Lloyd Garrison, the abolitionist. The younger Garrison had been a printer and he was methodical in all things. Thanks to his careful record of payments made to James, it has been possible to reclaim the reviews from their anonymity in the Nation's pages. Godkin was now a power in American journalism. His flourishing weekly, with its 10,000 circulation – substantial for that era – was prepared to publish James alike on books, art exhibitions, theatres. Godkin's assistant was an old friend, Arthur G. Sedgwick, of the Cambridge family into which Norton had married. The novelist occasionally dined with him 'at theatrical chop houses', and boasted to Howells of being 'a naughty bohemian'. His later letters to Sedgwick allude to their sociable evenings and reveal a continuing curiosity about New York life 'a city for which I have retained a sneaking affection'. He speaks retrospectively of 'the halls of Delmonico – of Brunswick – of Jacques', apparently their favourite restaurants.

'I feel vastly at home here and really like it,' he wrote to Howells shortly after settling in Manhattan. He added, however, 'pourvu que ça dure'. Later he spoke of this winter as 'bright, cold, unremunerative, uninteresting'. His life was humdrum; he saw few people, and those, he told Lizzie Boott, were 'very stupid'. Of the seventy notices and articles James wrote during 1875, thirty-nine appeared in the Nation during his six-months' residence in New York, two in the Atlantic and one in the Galaxy. Garrison seems to have given him free choice of the books that came into the office, but Henry's selection was still circumscribed by what was available. He preferred travel, literary essays, biographies of New England worthies, anything relating to America and Europe. He eagerly took all French subjects. But he reviewed also such works as Nordhoff's The Communistic Societies of the United States; or Ismailia, a narrative of an expedition to Central Africa for the suppression of the slave trade. Many of the volumes were dull; and he wrote until all hours of the night by his smouldering fire. There is no fatigue evident, however, in the writing. His reviews are light and humorous; they have authority; some could be called scholarly, although the imagination of the literary creator frees them from any suggestion of pedantry. What Henry brought to them was his taste for the flavour as well as the substance of any work he read. Reviewing a volume of essays by Masson, he could speak of 'one of those familiar fine passages from Pope, in which the rhythm is that of the pendulum, and the philosophy so bent on keeping terms with the epigram, that one loses half one's faith in its consistency'. Reviewing a biography of Ezra Styles Gannett he sketches him rapidly as 'a man, we shall say, of an extreme simplicity of organization. He was a born minister; he stepped straight from his school days into the pulpit, and looked at the world, ever afterwards, from the pulpit alone.' Reviewing Greville's journal he is fascinated, as always, not only by the way in which the diarist portrayed his society, but by the portrait he left indirectly of himself. He has occasion to refer to Emerson's 'magnificent vagueness', and he had clearly been reading Mark Twain's Mississippi instalments in the *Atlantic*, for he on one occasion observes that 'in the day of Mark Twain there is no harm in being reminded that the absence of drollery may, at a stretch, be compensated by the presence of sublimity'. Speaking of French attitudes toward Fenimore Cooper he remarks that 'if we take his trappers and his Indians in good faith, Europeans could hardly do less, and the prairie and the virgin forest, as he portrayed them, had, when contemplated from the Boulevard, a prodigiously natural air'. Of Stopford Brooke's essays on theology in the English poets he remarks that 'he rather too readily forgives a poor verse on the plea of a fine thought'. And so his pen races along, cheerful, easy, carefree, imparting to the readers of the *Nation* accounts of Dr Livingstone's journals, the life of the Prince Consort, the story of a missionary bishop, the correspondence of William Ellery Channing with Lucy Aitken, Taine on Paris, Augustus Hare on Rome – and all with a spontaneity which did not reflect the sheer pressure of production in 25th Street.

His inspection of the New York theatres, as reflected in his *Nation* articles, was not edifying. 'The public evidently likes playgoing, and is willing to pay for it – to pay a good deal and to pay often,' he wrote. But with the exception of the Fifth Avenue Playhouse this public saw few American plays; it received rather 'an Irish image, a French image, an English image' in the tinkered dramas brought from overseas. This was not to say that the American plays at the Fifth Avenue Playhouse demanded much intellectual effort. A concoction called *Women of the Day* was 'as preposterous an attempt to portray as it was a dreary attempt to entertain'. If the theatre was a 'superficial institution' in America, it shared this peculiarity 'with other social phenomena'. Seeing this play, which he described as 'ghostly, monstrous, a positive nightmare', he regretted that audiences in America did not indulge in the old-fashioned freedom of hissing.

The five art-notices contributed to the *Nation* during this period are in his characteristic vein. One of them, *On Some Pictures Lately Exhibited*, contains a spirited defence of art-criticism. 'We frankly confess it to be our own belief,' Henry told the *Nation* readers,

that even an indifferent picture is generally worth more than a good criticism; but we approve of criticism nevertheless. It may be very superficial, very incompetent, very brutal, very pretentious, very preposterous; it may cause an infinite amount of needless chagrin and gratuitous error; it may even blast careers and break hearts; but we are inclined to think that if it were suppressed at a stroke, the painters of our day would sadly miss it, decide that on the whole it had its merits, and at last draw up a petition to have it resuscitated.

He proceeded – as he invariably did – to give a good example to the *Nation* readers of what a perceptive and schooled eye, supported by aesthetic feeling and strong verbal skill, could do in the observation of pictures. Notable particularly during this year was his praise for the work of Frank Duveneck, a painter who had trained himself in Munich and who was attracting attention in Boston and New York. James discovered certain Velasquez qualities in his portraits : their great merit was their 'extreme naturalness, their unmixed, un-redeemed reality'. They were brutal, hard, indelicate, but 'they contain the material of an excellent foundation'. He would 'take it hard', he said, if Duveneck failed to do something of the first importance.

3

The New York winter was cold but there was much brilliant sunshine; and the spring was a mixture of rain and snow. James would take the elevated train uptown and walk over to the long narrow tract of Central Park, and its periphery of mansions. There was a 'raw delicacy' in the April air; and in spite of the Park's rockwork grottoes and tunnels, its pavilions and statues, its 'too numerous' paths and pavements, 'lakes too big for the landscape and bridges too big for the lakes', he at least got some feeling of the vernal season. Spring brought back memories of Rome. His letters to Lizzie Boott lapsed into Italian. '*Mille grazie, cara Lisa, di vostra graziosa lettera, scritta nella vera lingua di Dante – Dio la benedica! Sapete che la vita di N.Y. é nemica di tutta occupazione seria e simpatica e potrete dunque perdonar al mio silenzio fin'ora.*' And he went on to remind Lizzie of her visit to Manhattan a month earlier (he was writing in March) and how they had lunched at Delmonico's. He had never had so much pleasure at such a low price. '*E per provari che non mi ha rovinato vi diro che vi prendo ancora la colazione ogni domenica nello stesso posto!*' His Italian might be a collection of traveller's clichés, but it was impregnated with memories of his transatlantic life. These had been revived a few weeks earlier by a visit to Butler Place in Philadelphia, the home of Mrs Wister, where the recollections of their Roman days two years earlier had seemed vivid amid the winter snows. Mrs Kemble was living at York Place, near her daughter, and James remembered calling on her one morning. The aging actress was induced to read certain passages from Edward FitzGerald's translation of a Calderón play. James remembered the sunny drawing-room, the morning fire, the 'Berlin wools' she was wearing, the way her spectacles were placed on her nose, and her rich English tones. She reminded him of a picture he had once seen of Mrs Siddons, Mrs Kemble's aunt, reading Milton in her mob-cap and spectacles. She read as only she could read, and 'the poetry of the passage being of the noblest, with such rising and visible, such extreme and increasing emotion, that I presently became aware of her having suddenly sought refuge from a disaster in a cry of resentment at the pass she had been brought to and in letting the book fly from her hand and hurtle across the room. All her "art" was in the incident.'

Mrs Wister introduced Henry to her New York friend, Florence Lockwood, descendant of an old Delaware family, the Bayards. Her Manhattan home provided him with excellent conversation; 'a remarkable woman,' he wrote to Mrs Wister, 'and a very exquisite creature,' perhaps too tense, and too intense, but 'so singularly lovely that a tête-à-tête with her is a great bliss'. Years later he was to speak of her as 'packed almost hard with thought' and 'thoroughly in the grand style'. He apotheosized her as 'one of the big figures of one's experience'.

Transatlantic Sketches was published on 29 April; in proof-reading it he relived all the stages of his European journeyings, from the time of his going abroad with his sister and aunt to his final departure from Belgium and Holland the previous autumn. By June, when the hot weather came, he felt that his experiment had given him the answers he needed. He might have tried to write fiction instead of book-reviews, and eventually earned an adequate living. But the New York scene offered him few themes compared with those which he found abroad; and to write fiction would mean placing himself once again on the Quincy Street budget. We have no way of determining how he weighed the alternatives between New York and the capitals abroad. But his choice had been really made from the first. A few words set down many years later by Logan Pearsall

Smith suggest his decision was a foregone conclusion. 'In speaking of New York he said that it was impossible to have a picturesque address there, and he told me that he had gone back to New York to live and be a good American citizen, but at the end of a year he had quietly packed up his few belongings and come away.'

4

The one piece of fiction written by Henry James during his winter in Manhattan was an allegory entitled *Benvolio*. It was to be his only venture into this form, since he considered allegorical writing unworthy of the realist in fiction. Allegory, he remarked later, is 'apt to spoil two good things – a story and a moral, a meaning and a form'. *Benvolio* however had neither story nor moral; it was a *jeu d'esprit*, a fairy-tale James set down one day in 25th Street, and its meaning is not difficult to discover, for its author underlines it several times. The tale was frankly like one of Hawthorne's allegories, and the old Philosopher and his daughter in it might have been Rappaccini and Beatrice; only there was no evil in the Jamesian garden and there is none in the tale.

Benvolio, a young-man-about-town, is 'more than twenty-five' but not yet 'thirty-five' and in the revised version he is actually just turning 30 – in other words he is of Henry James's age. He lives in two chambers in a city; one of them offers him a view of the great square and its teeming life; the other, his bedroom, resembles a monk's cell, and looks out on a quiet garden. He is a man of fashion; he sports an intaglio, or 'an antique Syracusan coin, by way of a pin, in his cravat'. He is equally capable of putting on a 'rusty scholar's coat' and braving the daylight without ornament. He is a man of peace, named for Romeo's friend who tried hard to keep the Montagues and Capulets from brawling with one another. What this Benvolio tries to do is to keep the two sides of his nature from brawling: not that they are really at war. On the contrary: Benvolio is very well satisfied, although he thinks he should make up his mind between the life offered him by a certain Countess, a life of great extravagance and much amusement, and the life he enjoys with a young woman named Scholastica, daughter of a Philosopher into whose garden he looks from his bedroom window. The Philosopher, like Henry James's father, or his brother William, thinks the young man altogether best fitted for philosophy, and spends his time discussing the Absolute and the Relative with him. But Benvolio, when he is with the Countess, is inclined to write brilliant comedies rather than philosophical disquisitions.

We do not have to look far to see what the Countess represents in this tale. Benvolio says to her: 'You represent the world and everything that the world can give, and you represent them at their best.' The Countess is the world, and the world is Europe – when indeed did America have Countesses? And Scholastica is the daughter and granddaughter of Hawthorne's New England – the good studious life seen in the modest unimaginative terms of Quincy Street. Or she might well be also that side of Henry James which could function as critic and drudge, as he was doing in New York, when his inner being craved the sensations of Italy, the freedom of Europe, the liberty to write as he pleased. In describing Benvolio James wrote that 'it was as if the souls of two very different men had been placed together to make the voyage of life in the same boat, and had agreed for convenience's sake to take the helm in alternation'. Here he was leading a divided life, the author of *Roderick Hudson* and at the same time of endless anonymous reviews of such books as someone's journey up the Nile, or travels in Tibet, or the book on communistic societies in America. America or Europe? The life of the teeming square, or the life of the monastic cell? The writing of plays for the Countess or the meditative life with Scholastica? – this is the general substance of Henry's little allegory.

There is no resolution. When Benvolio is away from the Countess, and when Scholastica, feeling rejected, flees to the Antipodes, Benvolio misses them both and leads 'an extremely fretful and unproductive life'. When he resumes his life with Scholastica, he is productive again, but his poems are 'dismally dull'. If the story arrives at no solution, it seems to imply one: for Benvolio seems to be both critic and creator. They occupy the same boat, and Benvolio is quite content to alternate between the two.

Benvolio's ultimate outburst to the Countess does contain a suggestion. When she has chided him for his infidelity, he tells her that she is destroying the very sense of 'contrast' by which he lives: 'Don't you see, can't you imagine, that I cared for you only by contrast? You took the trouble to kill the contrast, and with it you killed everything else. For a constancy I prefer *this*.' And Benvolio taps his 'poetic brow'.

It was precisely by contrast, by the vision of the two great worlds between which he shuttled, the Americans in Europe, the Europeans in America, the polarities of the parochial and the cosmopolitan, that Henry was to live. Contrast and comparison were to be the law of his life; and in the performance of this an act of critical judgement was necessary as well as an artistic function. He reconciled both; and he paid his price. He became at once the most intellectual of artists, and the most sentient of critics. And he led always that double life of Benvolio: he courted Europe, and he never forgot America.

5

What strikes the reader in this fantasy is the fact that the two personages dwelling within Benvolio, although quite different, nevertheless manage to enjoy peaceful co-existence. The spectacle of life is pleasing to both. Benvolio is happy when he looks out on the square and lives with the Countess; he is no less happy when he contemplates the garden and Scholastica. In his philosophy he can be faithful to two women at the same time. There is a frank egotism in the way Benvolio takes up with the Countess, for weeks on end, experiencing only the thinnest kind of guilt at leaving Scholastica; and then, on an impulse, a shadowy memory, a moment's longing, he returns to Scholastica, quite certain that he will find her patiently waiting for him. And now he is oblivious of the feelings of the Countess. This suggests that in certain fundamental areas James was an individual without conflict. He saw the world as it was and pursued his aims without hesitation. He could be single-minded in his dedication to literature; he could be 'social' and literary at the same time; and he never doubted his literary destiny. At the end of his stay in New York, he did not find himself in any particular dilemma. If there was a fork in his path, he simply had to decide which way to go. He had known from the first that he wanted to live in Europe. It was, as he had said of his *Atlantic* serial, purely a question of money. The writing of *Benvolio* was probably his way of settling the matter in his mind.

He returned to Cambridge in mid-July of 1875, knowing that his first two books were receiving good reviews and having an honourable sale. Howells had launched *A Passionate Pilgrim* with superlatives, causing Charles Dudley Warner to remark that if what he said was true 'all the rest of you might as well go to bed'. 'In richness of expression and splendour of literary performance,' wrote Howells, 'we may compare him with the greatest, and find none greater than he.' Henry possessed 'a style distinctly his own', and few had the 'abundance of felicity of his vocabulary'. Other critics did not go to such extremes; they recognized the qualities of the style, but found flaws in Henry's characters. The reviews of *Transatlantic Sketches* were more complimentary; here the critics did not have to contend with fictional method and their varying opinions of James's cosmopolitan bias. The *Nation* did remark however that Henry, as a traveller, imposed certain difficulties on his readers; he not only discussed the objective scenery but also put into his writing the 'scenery of his own mind'. The critics were unanimous that Henry James Jr was a sensitive, intelligent and cultivated writer and they were aware of the singular maturity of his techniques.

Particularly encouraging was the news that in three months Henry's travel-book had sold almost 1,000 copies and seemed launched on a long career in the bookshops. Henry had thus finally taken hold of a literary place in America : and he had the assurance that his third book would be published by the end of the year. The question to be resolved was how, and in what circumstances, he could now take his leave of Cambridge and re-cross the Atlantic. The best thing he could imagine was to go abroad and 'try Paris' as he had tried New York. This time he envisaged a thorough 'siege', not a mere visit as in 1872. In the French capital he would probably meet Turgenev. Moreover he had already discussed with the *Galaxy* an idea broached some time before by William James, that he should write a series of essays on the important French novelists. Paris would be the best place to do this.

At this moment, appropriately enough, when he was poised between his winter's grind in New York and the thought of Paris, Henry James wrote the first of these essays – his first major literary essay. The definitive edition of Balzac's works had recently appeared in twenty-three volumes; and re-reading the novels and tales he recaptured his fascination for the professional power and literary dedication of 'the first of the realists'. 'What is most interesting in Balzac,' James wrote, 'is not the achievement but the attempt' – the attempt to recreate the whole of France through the power of language. Even more he was fascinated by Balzac's persistence and labour, his productivity, his methods of revision, his financial embroilments and the range of his imagination; 'the things he invented were as real to him as the things he knew'. Through his entire career Henry was to feel strong affinities between himself and the writer he chose as his model. He would call him 'the father of us all'. There was a marked congruity between James's selection of Balzac as the first of the French novelists about whom he was to write for the *Galaxy* and this moment in his life. Having just published his first novel in his 32nd year, he alludes to the fact that Balzac had spent a decade trying to write novels before he had learned the world.

The wings of great poets generally sprout very early; the wings of great artists in prose, great explorers of the sources of prose, begin to spread themselves only after the man is tolerably formed. Good observers, I think, will confess to a general mistrust of novels written before thirty. Byron, Shelley, Keats, Lamartine, Victor Hugo, Alfred de Musset, were hardly in their twenties before they struck their fully resonant notes. Walter Scott, Thackeray, George Eliot, Mme Sand, waited till they were at least turned thirty, and then without prelude, or with brief prelude, produced a novel which was a masterpiece. If it was well for them to wait, it would have been infinitely better for Balzac.

Thus the American novelist who had also waited. The autobiographical overtones of this passage, and of the passages in which James describes Balzac's money-needs, suggest that Henry had thought of himself as a Balzacian scribbler during those weeks in 25th Street in which he had turned himself into a writing-machine: Balzac was always, as a writer, 'a man of business in debt'. 'We cannot say how much Balzac liked being in debt,' James remarked, 'but we are very sure he liked, for itself, the process of manufacture and sale, and that even when all his debts had been paid he would have continued to keep his shop.'

There was in Henry James, who had just 'manufactured' and sold three books in this single year of his début as a full-fledged novelist, a consistent reference back to Balzac in all that he was to do. Balzac was his touchstone for the novel; and years later he was to express astonishment that a writer schooled in things French, like George Meredith, seldom spoke of Balzac. Planning once again a transatlantic leap, what more natural than to test the land and city of Balzac, to be himself like one of Balzac's young men from the provinces – even if from the American provinces – arriving in the great metropolis, a metropolis of conquerors, like Balzac or Napoleon, there to conquer not with a sword but with a tireless pen? But how was he to do this? What he needed above all in Paris was some foothold, some regular means of writing that would furnish him his needed revenue, as the *Nation* had done in New York.

6

The answer, as he later recorded it in his journal, 'loomed before me one summer's day in Quincy Street'. He had met in New York John Hay, who had been an assistant secretary to Lincoln, and was now an editorial writer for Whitelaw Reid, publisher of the *New York Tribune*. To Hay, Henry wrote, on 21 July, that he had 'a tolerably definite plan of going in the autumn to Europe' to establish himself for a 'considerable period' in Paris. 'I should like, if I do so,' he said, 'to secure a regular correspondence with a newspaper.' It would be non-political, wholly concerned with manners, habits, people, books, pictures, the theatre, perhaps travel-sketches in rural France. He had noticed, he said, that the American readers were fond of this sort of thing and that 'it is as a general thing rather flimsily and vulgarly supplied'. He offered to supply it in a 'more intelligent and cultivated fashion'. In fact he had 'a dazzling vision of doing very good things'. He added: 'I think I know how to observe, and may claim that I should observe to good purpose and chronicle my observations agreeably.'

James recognized that the *Tribune* had a correspondent – the Frenchman Arsène Houssaye – who was writing the kind of sketches he envisaged, but he felt he could do these from an American point of view. If this correspondent's 'relations with the paper are destined within the coming couple of months to terminate – and let me not seem obtrusively to assume that they are – or if you are weighing the question of removing them – my proposition may have a certain timeliness'. Hay promptly sent a memorandum to the publisher urging that James be engaged – 'you know his wonderful style and keen observation of life and character'. Hay added something that the novelist had not suggested, that 'he has no hesitation in saying that he can beat Houssaye on his own ground, gossip and chronicle, and I agree with him'. James had not proposed to furnish 'gossip', and this was later to be an issue between him and the publisher. Hay proposed that Houssaye be dismissed at the time of James's going abroad with the explanation that the labour of translation created extra difficulties for the paper.

Whitelaw Reid saw the force of this argument. He was inclined to offer $20 a letter instead of the $25 James asked; this was what he paid his American correspondents. 'It is a smaller sum that I should myself have proposed,' Henry told Hay, but if it was 'good newspaper payment, I summon philosophy to my aid'. With $60 or $80 monthly from the *Tribune* he could live comfortably in Paris and augment his income by writing fiction. There would now also be royalties from the sales of his books. It seemed to him that he could go abroad on a sounder financial footing than ever before.

He began at once to gather together all available funds. He asked the *Atlantic* to advance the $400 due on the four remaining instalments of *Roderick Hudson*. He postponed his sailing till late October in order to see his novel through the press. He wrote a number of reviews for the *Nation*; he completed his Balzac essay. His father agreed once more to back his needs with a letter of credit. Thus armed, he bade farewell to his family, had a final breakfast with Howells, embraced the family dog Dido, and sailed on 20 October for Liverpool on the *Bothnia*.

'Harry James is gone abroad again not to return, I fancy, even for visits,' Howells wrote to John Hay. There were gale-winds and the Cunarder tumbled and tossed during its ten-day voyage. James discovered that Anthony Trollope was on board and had some talk with him. He was struck by his 'plain persistence' in writing every day, no matter how much the ship rocked. 'The season was unpropitious, the vessel overcrowded, the voyage detestable,' he later wrote, 'but Trollope shut himself up in his cabin every morning.' He had had the ship's carpenter rig up a rough writing-desk and 'he drove his pen as steadily on the tumbling ocean as in Montagu Square'. Trollope had 'a gross and repulsive face and manner, but appears *bon enfant* when you talk with him. But he is the dullest Briton of them all.' In the evenings the British novelist played cards with Mrs Arthur Bronson of Boston, a future friend of James.

On 31 October, a Sunday, James stepped off the boat-train in London and went to Story's Hotel in Dover Street, off Piccadilly. He sat down to a meal of cold roast beef, bread, cheese and ale. It had happened before – six years before – in Liverpool, when he had started his grand tour. On Monday morning, to get his land-legs; he walked up Piccadilly and into Hyde Park. He would once more patronize London tailors and take a wardrobe with him for his Paris winter. In the afternoon he sat down and wrote to Quincy Street, to the entire family, to 'Dear People All' – to his father and mother, William and Alice, and to Aunt Kate to whom the letter would be forwarded. The exclamatory opening sentence would do for all the ensuing decades: 'I take possession of the old world – I inhale it – I appropriate it!' He had made his choice: he had consummated his adventure. No conquistador, planting a flag of annexation, could have sounded a note more genuinely triumphant.

BOOK FOUR:
THE SIEGE OF PARIS
1875-6

59

Ivan Sergeyevich

IN New York one could not have a picturesque address. Henry James's now was 29 Rue de Luxembourg. The street has since been renamed Rue Cambon and has been overrun by commerce. Located in the very heart of Paris, it extends its narrow length from the Rue de Rivoli to the Boulevard des Capucines. In 1875 it was still composed of large residences, with old high garden-walls. James had a second-floor apartment consisting of a parlour, two bedrooms, an antechamber which could serve as a dining-room, and a kitchen filled with shining casseroles. The furniture was 'clean and pretty'. There were mirrors, clocks, curtains, lamps, picturesque candle-sticks; there was a woodpile in the kitchen.

From his windows he had a good view and he was to remember the particular light click of the passing cab-horses on the clear asphalt, 'with its sharpness of detonation between the high houses'. Re-reading some of his writings thirty years later, he recovered between the lines the sounds of Paris. Each morning a troop of cuirassiers charged down the street and filed through a portal into barracks leading to one of the ministries which fronted on the Place Vendôme. Henry had to force himself to remain at his work-table when he heard the hard music of the horses' hoofs. He lingered at the window's cross-bar enjoying the uniforms, the plumes, the splendid animals.

The porter at No. 29 took care of his needs for $6 a month, and his rent was $65 a month. 'When I reflect upon my last winter's disbursements in New York, it is remarkably cheap,' he wrote home. His woodpile cost him $5 and his linens less than $2 a month. He confessed to Quincy Street however that he had been rather extra-vagant in England. His new wardrobe had made inroads on the paternal letter of credit. He was certain that he would rapidly work off this debt. London had been cold, damp, foggy; he had sloshed through the mud and rain, yet had found the place 'enchanting' and he would probably have remained there had he not been committed to Paris. Leslie Stephen had been 'good and friendly as before'; and he had gone to see the acting of Henry Irving – 'clever, but by no means a genius'. If he belonged to a London club and were in English society London would make an excellent domicile; but 'if one can't be in London, this is next best'.

James had arrived in Paris on 11 November 1875. He was settled within the week and on 22 November he dispatched his first letter to the *Tribune*. Eight days later he was reminding the editor of the *Galaxy* of his proposal to write a serial for that magazine. 'I have got at work upon one sooner than I expected, and particularly desire it to come out without delay. The title of the thing is *The American*.' And in the 15 November issue of the *Revue des Deux Mondes* – the salmon-coloured journal that for years had represented to him the summit of French literature – he discovered a translation of his tale *The Last of the Valerii*. His permission had not been asked; literary piracy in pre-copyright days nevertheless could be a charming form of flattery. It was almost as if his arrival were being trumpeted in France.

I

On the day that he mailed to New York an article entitled *Paris Revisited*, destined for the *Tribune*, Henry James made his way to Montmartre. Climbing its hilly streets, he found the Rue de Douai, No. 50, a three-storey house, with a low wall between it and the pavement. He passed through an iron gate and a small front court-yard, and on entering was ushered into the presence of Ivan Sergeyevich Turgenev. He was to remember his meeting with the tall, white-haired Russian, the large sofa, in the green room on the second floor, built to accommodate Turgenev's sprawling figure; the walls draped in green, the *portières* of the same colour. He remembered the white light of the Parisian street, which came in through windows more or less blinded in their lower part, like those of a studio. There was a fine painting by Théodore Rousseau on one wall; a Corot on another, a bas-relief of Pauline Viardot, the singer in whose house Turgenev was living (and whom he had followed into the West, from Russia, as her lover, some said, certainly her intimate, ever since her famous concerts in Moscow and St Petersburg). Nothing seemed out of place. There were none of the odds and ends one expected in the rooms of a man of letters; no accumulation of papers; few books. Everything seemed put away. Henry James recalled however that Turgenev wrote little in Paris; that he did most of his work during long periods of withdrawal to his properties in Russia.

The American novelist was a short man; he seemed to feel himself dwarfed by Turgenev. The Russian was exceedingly tall; his frame was so large as to suggest brute strength. James called him a 'magnificent creature'. One could see in him the sportsman, the hunter, the man of the out-of-doors. He had a finely shaped head; his features were irregular, and yet there was much beauty in the face; it was distinctively Russian, almost everything in it was wide; his expression, James was to write, 'had a singular sweetness, with a touch of Slav languor, and his eye, the kindest of eyes, was deep and melancholy'. His hair was abundant and straight; and his beard, trimmed and short, was as white as his hair. James found he had an air of neglected strength, of singularly noble modesty.

Turgenev had asked James to come between 11 and 1. He arrived at 11, met the Viardots; then for the next two hours, speaking largely in English, the two writers discussed 'a variety of topics'. In a letter to his Aunt Kate he said he recalled nothing in particular that Turgenev said on this occasion. The novelist spoke English well, but rather 'stiffly', he had remarked that no language was comparable to the Russian. 'He seemed very simple and kind. His face and shoulders are hugely broad, his stature very high, and his whole aspect and temperament of a larger and manlier kind than I have ever yet encountered in a scribbler.'

With characteristic generosity, Turgenev offered to introduce his new friend to Gustave Flaubert, and if possible to George Sand, who, however, was now rarely in Paris. There was something benign and gentle in the Russian, 'a delightful, mild, masculine figure'. James had come prepared to like him for his novels. Instead he found a human being who was 'adorable'. He was 'so simple, so natural, so modest, so destitute of personal pretension', a singularly complete human being, interested in everything, and without a particle of vanity.

This was James's first vision of the novelist and there was in it a considerable measure of hero-worship. Later he was to discern flaws in the hero, particularly his 'softness' and his passivity. However he took him as he was. What Turgenev's view of James was we can only deduce: but it is distinctly wrong to say that 'the young man did not particularly impress' the Russian writer, as one of Turgenev's biographers remarks. He could no longer be called 'young', Turgenev received him as a mature *confrère* with courtesy, interest and respect. The evidence points to his finding the American charming. He liked him well enough to return his visits promptly, to sit with him for long hours in restaurants discussing the art of fiction and to describe to him his working methods. He came later to see him in England. In address his letters passed from 'My dear Mr James' to *'Mon cher ami'*, and Turgenev's characterization of Henry to his translator in England, W. R. S. Ralston, refers to him not only as 'amiable' and as 'having much ability', but as possessing also in his work *un certain penchant à la tristesse*. For a melancholy Russian to discern a *penchant* for melancholy in an American suggests a community of feeling, which Turgenev's letters to James clearly show. A friend of Turgenev's was to tell James later that the Russian spoke of him with an appreciation *qui alla jusqu'à l'attendrissment*, and a tenderness 'in a way that he had rarely spoken to him of anyone'. Even if we discount this as a possible attempt at flattery, the *attendrissement* matches the other evidence. For presently Henry was accepted as an intimate of the Turgenev-Viardot household and was invited to its 'at-homes'.

2

The meeting of American and Russian, divided by their years (James 32, Turgenev 57), by geography, language and background, took place on the wide ground of their cosmopolitanism; they had in common their craft, their artistic temperaments, their sense of the great sprawling land-mass which each had left for the alien yet friendly soil of France, of that Paris where neither was wholly at home and yet where both found a kinship of spirit and discovered their brothers in art. Large historical forces had been in motion behind them: they were, in a strange sense, both products of a powerful ferment in the 'provinces'. Turgenev had been an influence in the emancipation of the serfs; James had lived through the struggle by which America freed the serfs of the New World. If he had seen some union between aristocracy and democracy in the Russian, he himself spoke for a similar melting together of these elements, with emphasis on the aristocracy. Russian society, like that of America (as Henry observed), was in process of formation, and the Russian character was 'in solution' in a sea of change such as existed also in the United States. These were the analogous backgrounds from which they stemmed. Deeper similarities might be found in their family history. Turgenev had had to contend with a tyrannical mother; Henry with a mother who concealed an iron grip: both had emerged with a certain inner softness as well as an ability to 'tune in' to the feminine consciousness. What they had in common as artists came from their similar view of their fellow-humans, so that while James was influenced in certain respects by the older writer, there are distinct qualities, resembling Turgenev's, which the American possessed from the first. Both had the power of creating the atmosphere of place; both knew how to see into the essence of personality; both were 'tidy' to the point of finickiness in their portrayal of character; both were 'realists', that is their work has a certain historical and documentary as well as psychological value; both dealt with individuals involved in the problems of their inner life, and both – above all – took a certain melancholy pleasure in their belief in renunciation. If we recognize also that both conceded moral supremacy to certain types of women, while harbouring a sense of the feminine sex as a destructive force, and that both wrote from strong poetic impulse, although they were artists in prose, we can discern how much they could find in one another that was attractive and congenial. They were articulate spokesmen for all that was civilized in their two countries – and a civilization both nations had 'imported' from western Europe. Small wonder that James, in his first essay on Turgenev, singled out a series of themes which might have been his own. He found in all Turgenev's young girls 'a touch of the faintly acrid perfume of the New England temperament – a hint of puritan angularity'.

For all this, it would be difficult to make a New Englander out of Turgenev, or a Russian out of Henry James. In Paris they were both 'outsiders', possessing a vision wider than that of their French colleagues. In meeting Turgenev, James had discovered a man old enough to be his father and younger enough to be his friend; and a man of singular allure. He had the gentleness of the elder Henry James without his bristling qualities; and he accepted him as an artist, which his father never wholly did. A month after their encounter James wrote to Quincy Street: 'I have seen him again several times, with unabated regard. He seems rather older and drowsier than I first thought him, but he is the best of men. He has twice called on me.'

60

Four Meetings

In his later memoir of his Russian friend Henry James described the elation he used to experience after being with Turgenev. He always left him, he said, in a state of intimate excitement, 'with a feeling that all sorts of valuable things had been suggested to me'. This condition was like a man swinging a cane, leaping lightly over gutters, stopping for no reason at all, to look, with an air of being struck, into a shop window – where he actually saw nothing.

What was this enchantment of talk which made Henry behave like a young man in love and brought him such 'valuable things'? He recorded one such occasion in three different essays; and the others, after the years, came together into a kind of supreme sense of artistic feeling and artistic spontaneity, the example of a man of genius who was sentient, aware, capable of warm human relations, enjoying laughter – even at himself – and seeing life with detached irony and melancholy. Four meetings stood out, four scenes of vivid memory.

I

The first had its prelude in James's going to call on Turgenev towards the end of January 1876. The Russian had the gout. He was stretched out on his sofa and James sat with him for an hour; he came away feeling that he had listened to extremely gifted talk; everything Turgenev said had measure and *justesse*. Returning a few days later, he was told that Turgenev was too ill to see him; he had bronchitis. On 31 January Turgenev wrote : 'The last time you came I was ill and had gone to bed. I am not budging from home these days.' He invited James to return.

It was raining when the American arrived at the Rue de Douai. He was once again in the green room, and Turgenev sprawled on his sofa. If he has been ill, he shows little sign of it in his talk. He is animated, responsive, reflective. He begins to tell how stories come to him. He never thinks of a plot. The germ comes in the form of some figure he has known, hovering and soliciting him, or grouping itself with other figures. Before writing about this figure, Turgenev wants to know it intimately; he compiles its dossier, as if he were a police functionary; he writes out its biography. Only when he knows his character intimately does he become aware of what it will do and how it will act. How his people 'look and move and speak and behave, always in the setting I have found for them, is my account of them'. Critics observed *que cela manque souvent d'architecture.* Turgenev did not care. He would rather have too little architecture than too much. As James put it, Turgenev was trying to arrive at the 'intensity of suggestion that may reside in the stray figure, the unattached character', the *disponible* personage; starting with the figure, he invented, selected, pieced together 'the situations most useful and favourable to the sense of the creatures themselves'. And James could say, years later: 'I have not lost the sense of the value for me, at the time, of the admirable Russian's testimony.'

The testimony confirmed James in his own way of story-telling. He, too, began with his personages: the vision of Roderick had started him on his novel; the vision of an American in Paris was keeping him for long hours at his desk at this moment; a vision of an American girl affronting her destiny would lead him to *The Portrait of a Lady.* That winter in Paris he still had the feeling that in working in this fashion he was putting the cart before the horse; that plots, not people, were what he should be looking for. To have the man he regarded as 'the first novelist of the day' reassure him, gave new authority to his own methods. Turgenev's way had the 'immense recommendation that in relation to any human occurrence, it begins, as it were, further back. It lies in its power to tell us the most about men and women.' Certain readers would say 'We don't care a straw about men and women: we want a good story.' For those who did care, here was a way of work, essentially psychological, in which the author sought the truths of human behaviour.

And so the long rainy afternoon passed – a vivid unforgettable afternoon – and Henry wrote to his brother that Turgenev 'gave me a sort of definition of his own mental process, which was admirably intelligent and limpidly honest. This last is the whole man; and it is written in his face.' Turgenev was an *amour d'homme* – a 'beautiful genius'.

2

The second meeting. It occurred on another damp day in the rawness of the Paris winter. But the cafe in the Avenue de l'Opéra is new and bright, with large settees made for comfort and talk. Turgenev has come from Montmartre for *déjeuner*. They eat and they talk. The hours pass. The day wanes: the lamps are lit. The habitués take their places over their glass of absinthe, or ponder their games of dominoes. James and his Russian friend linger over their noonday meal. Turgenev talks about Russia: he tells of curious visits paid him by emigrés; he describes nihilists he has known, remarkable figures that have come to light among them; he dwells on the 'dark prospects of his native land', the great steppes and forests, the inarticulate Russian masses, the anguish of struggle and revolt. When he is in this vein (James later observed) he is powerful, the splendid story-teller, speaking to the imagination of his listener, 'extraordinarily vivifying and stimulating'.

The third meeting: Turgenev and the Viardots by now feel James to be a familiar of their entourage. He is invited to Madame Viardot's Thursday musicals, and to the family's Sunday evenings. The Sunday evenings are devoted to simple sociabilities, mainly charades. They remind James of Concord and of the 'historical games' of his childhood. Madame Viardot, past her prime as a singer but still a great personality fascinates the American. She is 'as ugly as eyes in the side of her head and an interminable upper lip can make her, and yet also very handsome'. There is something 'strange and sweet' in Turgenev – the same Turgenev of the serious talk and the meditative manner – prancing and crawling on the floor, wearing old shawls and masks, 'at his age and with his glories' as if he were a child. 'Fancy Longfellow, Lowell, or Charles Norton, doing the like, and every Sunday evening!' James writes to Quincy Street. He describes the evenings as 'dingy', remarks that Turgenev has 'not a gram of dramatic talent' and says that 'the whole entourage is much beneath him'. Nevertheless he recognizes that he is witnessing a certain type of European spontaneity – spontaneity and capacity for enjoying simple pleasures – in a gifted man. As he puts it to Charles Eliot Norton: 'It pays to see even only a little of a man of genuis.'

The fourth meeting: spring has come. It is April. James has met a young Russian, Paul, son of the famous poet and translator, Vassili Zhukovski, who had been a friend of Goethe and tutor of the Tsar.

Paul is a dilettante painter, a good conversationalist. He is also a
friend of Ivan Sergeyevich. Zhukovski invites Henry and Turgenev
to dine with him, and turns up with a dark-eyed and sympathetic
Russian woman, the Princess Ourousov. Turgenev says he has discovered an excellent place, a little restaurant in the square in front
of the Opéra Comique. They find themselves in a low entresol; the
food is hardly what they hoped, but Ivan Sergeyevich has never
been more charming. He is jovial, prattlesome, entertaining. Henry
delights in his mixture of wit and almost infantile naïveté. The
evening seems scarce begun, however, before Turgenev leaves. He
has faithfully promised Pauline Viardot he will be home by 9.30.
The party breaks up. The Princess invites Zhukovski and Henry to
her home; she too has her little salon – it is frequented by Turgenev,
and certain of the French writers; later Maupassant will be of their
number; still later André Gide. Here the American writer and the
Russian dilettante are joined by Prince Hohenlohe, the German
Ambassador to France; and so another memorable occasion comes to
an end.

3

There would be later meetings, reunions in London and again in
Paris, but these were the most precious of Henry's year in the French
capital. He had seen certain aspects of Turgenev that revealed him
as a lovable human being; James could not have enough of him. No
one in New England had attracted him as much. To be sure, Turgenev had his weaknesses. Did not Flaubert call him a *poire molle*,
a soft pear? Turgenev himself quoted this and laughed. He had an
'expansive softness, a comprehensive indecision', like so many of his
characters. Henry retailed to his parents the local gossip: Turgenev
was Pauline Viardot's 'slave', she guarded him as if he were a piece
of property, she was reputed to have had a child by him; the Viardots treated him as a *vache à lait* and made free and easy with his
money. And the 9.30 curfew! All this was told not so much in depreciation but in a tone of regret. Madame Viardot stood between
James and more frequent meetings with the beloved Ivan. He may
have cut the silver cord of Quincy Street but he had for the moment
fastened the dangling end to the Rue de Douai.

This perhaps illuminates a strange passage in James's memorial
essay in which he remarked, that Turgenev 'to the best of my belief'

ignored his writings, and 'was unable to read them'. He went on to say that the Russian

cared, more than anything else, for the air of reality, and my reality was not to the purpose. I do not think my stories struck him as quite meat for men. The manner was more apparent than the matter; they were too *tarabiscoté*, as I once heard him say of the style of a book – had on the surface too many little flowers and knots of ribbon.

This seems to be an honest avowal and most of James's readers have accepted it as a fact. Turgenev's letters do not suggest that he thought Henry's tales were not 'meat for men'. He praises the early part of *Roderick Hudson* as written with 'the hand of a master'; he tells him that the first volume of *Confidence* strikes him as 'finer and more simple' than Henry's earlier writings; he assures him that he will read *The American* and give an honest opinion 'as one must, where a person possessing an ability such as yours is concerned'. Earlier Turgenev had praised the 'manliness' and the 'psychological sagacity' of James's style. And we have the independent testimony of his letter to Ralston urging him to meet James and saying 'he has much ability'.

One possible reason for Henry's self-abasement suggests itself. William James had often reproached Henry for his 'fancy' writing – the 'knots of ribbon' – and the gallicisms sprinkled through his prose; his father praised his essays at the expense of his fiction. We may speculate that James may have unconsciously transferred to Turgenev the reservations of Quincy Street. Accustomed to some note of criticism in those dearest to him, holding Turgenev dear, and sensing in him paternal and fraternal qualities, he endowed the Russian with the familiar things of his own life. In assimilating the lessons of his master, he assimilated him also into his inner existence: in setting him up as an authoritative figure he grouped him with the candid critics of Quincy Street.

61

Councils of the Gods

TURGENEV kept his promise. Three weeks after their first meeting he took Henry James to one of Flaubert's Sunday afternoons (it was probably on 12 December 1875). In a letter a few days later to his friend Perry, written in French, James remarked with pride and irony – 'je suis lancé en plein Olympe'.

I

It seemed indeed as if Henry James had suddenly been transported to some Olympus – an Olympus, to be sure, where the gods were uncommonly talkative, and inclined to paunchiness: disputing the art of fiction, gossiping about the latest scandals of Paris, discussing censorship, royalties, publishers, sexual adventures, the theatre, politics. No subject was sacrosanct. All Paris seemed to pass in review. Some of the gods were mortals, younger men like himself, making their careers in literature; and the 'immortals', for all their allure, could have feet of clay. There were the young god-aspirants too: Guy de Maupassant, 25, a protégé of Flaubert's, who so far had published nothing.

On that memorable Sunday in December, when Henry and Ivan Sergeyevich climbed to the high end of the Faubourg St Honoré and then mounted five flights of stairs to Flaubert's Parisian perch, it seemed to the American that he was listening to genuine conversation for the first time. Flaubert was at home, when he was in Paris, on Sunday afternoons from one to seven: his servant had the day off; he always opened the door himself. He embraced Turgenev, as if he were receiving a beloved brother. The Frenchman was tall; the Russian was even taller; both towered over Henry. As Flaubert shook hands with his transatlantic visitor, he greeted him in a timid, friendly way and bothered himself over what he could do or say to his guest. The French novelist had a massive physical development. His face was serious and sober; his complexion was mottled and he wore long tawny moustaches; he had light-coloured salient eyes. James thought he looked like a weather-beaten old military man.

The guests were ushered into a high small room that seemed

'bare and provisional', save for a gilded and painted Buddha of considerable size on the chimney-piece. Flaubert wore what James described as 'a long colloquial dressing-gown', with trousers to match, a costume often affected by French men of letters, 'the uniform of freedom of talk'. Here before his cheerful fire the author of *Madame Bovary* dispensed his hospitality. '*C'est un naïf*,' Turgenev said of him. James agreed. He liked the man; he was not at all what his books had led him to suspect; and there were moments when he was to wonder whether he wasn't fonder of Flaubert than of Turgenev, though he greatly preferred Turgenev's work. On this first occasion James met Edmond de Goncourt, 53, a year younger than Flaubert, the busy survivor of the fraternal writing team: tall, slender, *type du gentilhomme français*, James said of him, unaware of the prodigious journal Goncourt had begun with his brother and was still keeping. James is not mentioned in the journal; his stay in Paris was to be too brief to involve him in the centres of literary gossip which constitute the journal's fascination. He was also introduced to Émile Zola, 35, author of *Thérèse Raquin* and the first volumes of his series of the Rougon-Macquart. 'A very common fellow,' was Henry's first impression. The only other persons mentioned as being present on the first occasion were Charpentier, the publisher, and the poet Catulle Mendès.

James met Alphonse Daudet on his second Sunday visit. This was in mid-January of 1876. Daudet was Zola's age; his hair hung over his eyes; he had a black wispy Bohemian beard and a visage that was – with his later physical sufferings – to be generally considered 'Christlike'. James's first impression of him was also negative. He described him as 'a little fellow (very little), with a refined and picturesque head, of a Jewish type' and a brilliant talker and raconteur, an extreme imitator of Dickens, 'but a *froid* without Dicken's real exuberance'. He had greatly liked *Lettres de Mon Moulin*, and *Fromont Jeune et Risler Aîné*, but *Jack*, was 'dreary and disagreeable, and in spite of cleverness intrinsically weak'.

2

They were charming talkers. James repeated with delight Flaubert's characterization of Turgenev's talk: the Russian always found '*l'expression à la fois étrange et juste*'. Daudet had said this reminded him of Sainte-Beuve. Goncourt's rejoinder was: '*Sainte-Beuve trou-*

vait bien l'expression juste mais – pas étrange.' 'As editor of the austere *Atlantic* it would startle you to hear some of their projected subjects', James told Howells. On one occasion Zola confided in a matter-of-fact way to the group that he was collecting all the *gros mots* of the language, the familiar talk of the working class, a veritable small dictionary of obscenities. Goncourt on his side said he was interested in an episode he was writing in a novel 'into which he was going far'. When Flaubert asked him to say what it was, he replied, 'A whore-house *de province.'* The remark may not have been Goncourt's, but that of the future author of *La Maison Tellier.* Flaubert was gathering, with characteristic compulsiveness, material for his 'dictionary of accepted ideas' out of which he wanted to fashion *Bouvard et Pécuchet.* James described the consequences of Zola's collection of the working-class *argot.* His new novel, *L'Assommoir,* was starting its run in a magazine; he was being well paid for it; but the journal had received protests from provincial subscribers against the serial's indecencies and it looked as if publication would be suspended. The *cénacle* was stirred up; its opinion was that while this was a bore, it could only do the book good. 'Among your tribulations as editor,' James told Howells, 'I take it that this particular one is not in store for you.' On his way down from Flaubert's on another occasion he encountered Zola climbing the long staircase, 'looking very pale and sombre', and James, who had been asked by Howells to run a serial a full year in the *Atlantic* instead of nine months as planned, saluted Zola 'with the flourish natural to a contributor who has just been invited to make his novel last longer yet'.

One afternoon Maupassant told a long involved story about Swinburne and a jealous monkey. 'Distinct to me,' James wrote many years later to Edmund Gosse,

the memory of a Sunday afternoon at Flaubert's in the winter of '75–'76, when Maupassant, still *inédit*, but always 'round', regaled me with a fantastic tale, irreproducible here, of the relations between the two Englishmen, each other, and their monkey! A picture the details of which have faded for me, but not the lurid impression.

Swinburne had been rescued from drowning at Etretat by Maupassant and had invited the Frenchman to the cottage where he was staying. Here Maupassant discovered the strange household. James recalled that it was a case of a 'resentful and impassioned beast' which had seen a young Englishman installed on the scene 'after he [the monkey] was more or less lord of it', and in the end somehow destroyed himself in an access of jealousy. 'The drama had essentially been,' James recalled, 'one of the affections, the passions, the last *cocasserie*, with each member of the quartette involved.' But what Henry recalled above all was Maupassant's 'intellectual, critical, vital experience of the subject-matter'.

James did not go every Sunday to the Faubourg St Honoré. He preferred to see Turgenev by himself; and he wanted intimate talk with Flaubert. He paid several private visits to him on week-days. He seems to have visited the *cénacle* about once a month during his stay in Paris. Perhaps he held back because so much of the talk was local and rather 'parochial'; no group of Boston Brahmins, discussing the gossip of 'the hub', could have been more local. With his real joy in the wit and intellectual power of the Flaubertians, he found them also distinctly insular. They were *'affreusement bornés'*, he told Perry : 'They are a queer lot, and intellectually very remote from my own sympathies,' he wrote his mother. 'They are extremely narrow and it makes me rather scorn them that not a mother's son of them can read English. But this hardly matters, for they couldn't really understand it if they did.' James was perhaps tailoring his impressions to the horizons of Quincy Street. Turgenev at any rate spoke English fluently; and Flaubert had mastered enough to read Shakespeare. Zola and Daudet, however, could not meet him on the ground of *his* language and literature, as he could on theirs; there was no doubt that the French men of letters were inclined to consider Paris as their all-sufficient country. This is the burden of Henry's complaints, even while he finds himself rejoicing at being in touch with men engaged in literary action, 'in a manner full of interest for one never previously privileged to see artistic conviction so systematic and so articulate'. He had lacked male company in Rome. Paris met this need in some measure.

3

James was astonished how little respect these men had for the *Revue des Deux Mondes* and with what ease they dismissed certain of the minor novelists he had enjoyed and reviewed : the novels of Victor Cherbuliez, the sentimental sketches of Gustave Droz, the romantic-sentimental of Octave Feuillet. Such writers, he was to say years afterwards, 'were not even conceivable' in that room. The matter troubled him a little; was this a failure in *his* literary taste, or simply the *brusqueries* of dogmatists? He alluded to the matter in one of his *Tribune* letters:

You ask a writer whose productions you admire some questions about any other writer, for whose works you have also a relish. 'Oh, he is of the School of This or That: he is of the *queue* of So and So,' he answers. 'We think nothing of him: you mustn't talk of him here; for us he doesn't exist.' And you turn away, meditative, and perhaps with a little private elation at being yourself an unconsolidated American and able to enjoy both Mr A. and Mr X. who enjoy each other so little. Of course subsequently you do them justice in their mutual aversions, and perceive that some of the qualities you admire in their writings are really owing to their being intrenched behind their passwords. A little school that dislikes every other school, but is extremely active and industrious within its own circle, is an excellent engine for the production of limited perfection . . . It is simply the old story that, either in politics or in literature, Frenchmen are ignorant of the precious art of compromise.

This was James's impression after his first visit to Flaubert. If he was being made welcome at the *cénacle* it was decidedly not on the strength of his tales which were appearing in the *Revue* during that winter (after the first, three more were published, in rather poor translations). On one occasion, when the name of Gustave Droz came up, Zola muttered an obscenity to Henry; he actually said Droz's books were '*morde à la vanille*'. But, said Henry, 'they generate poor stuff themselves' To his sister he spoke of 'the little rabble of Flaubert's satellites', who were not worthy to tie Turgenev's shoe-laces. It also made James 'sick' to hear Turgenev seriously discussing Daudet's *Jack* with Flaubert. He, on his side, had been enjoying George Eliot's new novel, *Daniel Deronda*, 'partly for reading it in this beastly Paris, and realizing the superiority of English culture and the English mind to the French'.

'I have seen almost nothing of the literary fraternity,' he was to write late that spring to Howells, 'and there are fifty reasons why I should not become intimate with them. I don't like their wares, and they don't like any others.' Turgenev, he said, was worth 'the whole heap of them, and yet he swallows them down in a manner that excites my extreme wonder'. We must make large allowance for these complaints – to Howells, to his mother, to Alice – complaints in reality to his own puritan side as well as that of Cambridge. The truth was that he greatly enjoyed himself among his young French peers and he saw more of them than he seemed to admit. As for Flaubert and Turgenev, he sought them out as often as was decently possible. He was to say that the talk of the *cénacle* had 'extreme intensity and variety'. For all their 'narrowness' he cherished their memory.

In the magisterial essays which he wrote in 1902 on Flaubert and in 1903 on Zola, his backward glance reflects old pleasures and an old warmth. His memories to be sure were fused with later ones, further meetings with Daudet, Zola and Maupassant in middle age; and by then the three were dead. He speaks of Flaubert's friends as constituting a 'rich and eager *cénacle*' made up almost wholly of 'the more finely distinguished' of Flaubert's contemporaries – philosophers, men of letters and men of affairs belonging to his generation and the next. And in the memorial essay on Turgenev he stresses the elements in the Rue du Faubourg St Honoré which were important to him. It was at Flaubert's, he said, that Turgenev's 'beautiful faculty of talk showed at its best'. Everything the Russian said was 'touched with the exquisite quality of his imagination'.

What was discussed in that little smoke-clouded room was chiefly questions of taste, questions of art and form; and the speakers, for the most part, were, in aesthetic matters, radicals of the deepest dye. It would have been late in the day to propose among them any discussion of the relation of art to morality, any question as to the degree in which a novel might or might not concern itself with the teaching of a lesson. They had settled these preliminaries long ago, and it would have been primitive and incongruous to recur to them.

The Victorian debate between art and morality did not concern them. 'The only duty of a novel was to be well written; that merit included every other of which it was capable.' This was the common ground on which James stood with these 'deep-dyed radicals' and he was never to shift to any other. And it was this that made him recognize, long after, that his year in Paris, 'was time by no means misspent'. It became 'all a golden blur of old-time Flaubertism and Goncourtism! How many more strange flowers one *might* have gathered up and preserved.'

62

Pastel

I

IN the little high room at the Faubourg's end Henry James heard always many voices: but one mid-week afternoon towards the end of March he found Gustave Flaubert alone. He sat with him a long time. They talked freely and James found himself greatly liking this prematurely old, sad, distinguished man. Their conversation turned to French writers, and Flaubert gave Henry certain reminiscences of Théophile Gautier, who had been his intimate, and whom Henry greatly admired. Not long before, James, in the pages of the *North American Review*, had spoken of Gautier as 'one of the first descriptive poets'; his verses were always 'pictorial and plastic', his sonnets pieces of 'self-amused imagery'. Flaubert said he preferred Gautier to Musset. '*Il était plus français,*' more generally French in the quality of his melancholy. Neither Goethe, nor Heine, nor Leopardi, neither Pushkin, nor Tennyson, nor, as he said, Byron, could at all have matched Gautier in *kind*: other nations had the equivalent of Musset; Gautier, in his 'extreme perfection', was unique. And reaching for Gautier's volumes he began to read a poem. It dealt with old and yellowing portraits in oval frames, lying along the quays of Paris, portraits of beauties faded and violated by time, by dust and specks of mud, yet clasping forever their withered century-old bouquets, a poem nostalgic and fragile in its artful sadness. *J'aime à vous voir en vos cadres ovales*, Flaubert read, slowly and in measured tones, *Portraits jaunis des belles du vieux temps* – a kind of distant echo of all the French poets who had written of vanished snows of yesteryear:

> J'aime à vous voir en vos cadres ovales,
> Portraits jaunis des belles du vieux temps,
> Tenant en main des roses un peu pâles,
> Comme il convient à des fleurs de cent ans.
>
> Le vent d'hiver, en vous touchant la joue,
> A fait mourir vos œillets et vos lis,
> Vous n'avez plus que des mouches de boue
> Et sur les quais vous gisez tout salis.

Il est passé, le doux règne des belles;
La Parabère avec la Pompadour
Ne trouveraient que des sujets rebelles,
Et sous leur tombe est enterré l'amour.

Vous, cependent, vieux portraits qu'on oublie,
Vous respirez vos bouquets sans parfums,
Et souriez avec mélancolie
Au souvenir de vos galants défunts.

Flaubert rather loudly declaimed these lines – he used to speak of his 'bellow' – but the moment was filled with deep emotion for James. There was something extraordinarily tender in the way Flaubert showed his affection for his friend's delicate verses. It may have been the deep sincerity of the massive Norman, and his strong literary feeling; it may have been also the quality of the poem itself, with its suggestion – to the author of *The Madonna of the Future* – of enshrined dead beauty, but it struck a strong chord of response in James. He always vividly remembered this moment, when the author of *Madame Bovary* had read to him – to him alone – in the quiet little room in the old Faubourg. He described the scene to his father a few days afterwards; he wrote it into his journal half a dozen years later; and in his essay on Flaubert he devoted an entire page to it. To the elder James he said that Flaubert deemed Gautier unique in his extreme perfection, 'and he recited some of his sonnets in a way to make them seem the most beautiful things in the world. Find in especial (in the volume I left at home,) one called *Les Portraits Ovales*.'

In his journel he gave another name to the poem, referring to it as *Les Vieux Portraits*. And in his final essay he somewhat ruefully confessed he couldn't recall the title. The poem had been new to him; and since that time, he said, he had never been able to discover it in Gautier's works, 'hunt as I will in every volume of its author'. This was perhaps a happy thing, he believed, since it caused

Flaubert's own full tone, which was the note of the occasion, to linger the more unquenched. But for the rhyme in fact I could have believed him to be spouting to me something strange and sonorous of his own. The thing really rare would have been to hear him do that – hear him *gueuler*, as he liked to call it.

Henry could not recover the poem because he looked for a title with the word *portraits* in it, whereas the poem is entitled *Pastel*.

What he had remembered were phrases from the first and last stanzas. The reader of James may be tempted to see in these verses some of the sentiment that invests the inspection of the 'faded pastels' in *The Sacred Fount*; or be reminded of Jeanne de Vionnet who seems to Lambert Strether 'a faint pastel in an oval frame', and to recall also the feelings of Milly Theale, standing before the portrait of the Bronzino in *The Wings of the Dove* – her sense of the lady in the picture, long dead, 'handsome in sadness' and 'fading with time' in her brocaded and wasted reds.

2

There were other weekday occasions at Flaubert's when they talked alone, and sometimes on Sunday James was the first to arrive and had the elderly writer to himself. He considered him 'the most interesting man and strongest artist of his circle'. Turgenev was involved in the Viardot household and not always available; Flaubert had 'an accessibility to human relations' as well as a conception of courtesy. As for the other writers he met at the house, they were distinctly 'not *acceuillants*', they made no overtures of hospitality. In part this was traditional French reserve; in part it was because the younger men were preoccupied with their careers; and like James they were among the 'received' rather than the receiving.

Of Flaubert's art James had already spoken in an essay written for the *Galaxy* before he met him, and he was never to modify his view of it. *Madame Bovary* was a masterpiece, this he recognized. His other works were failures. *Salammbô* was as hard as stone; *L'Éducation Sentimentale* was as cold as death; the *Tentation de St Antoine* seemed to be a patchwork covered with pieces of metal. As for *Bouvard et Pécuchet*, the posthumous novel, he would call it 'puerile' – there was 'extreme juvenility' in its main idea of trying to make a fiction out of a 'dictionary of accepted ideas'. *Madame Bovary* alone had enough emotion to take off the chill of the other works. There was 'something ungenerous' in Flaubert's genius, and James was to note that in all Flaubert's letters there was no mention of 'any beauty but verbal beauty'.

He talked of Flaubert one day with Turgenev. The Russian said that Flaubert's great trouble was that he had never known a decent woman. He had passed his life exclusively '*avec des courtisanes et des riens-du-tout*'. Neither of them apparently knew of Flaubert's affair with Louise Colet; that had been long ago; and indeed if Turgenev had known, from some old gossip, he would probably have considered her also a *rien-du-tout*. There is a genuine tone of surprise in James's later review of Flaubert's letters as he comes upon his correspondence with the energetic and opportunistic bluestocking. But in 1876, telling of his talk with the Russian, he writes to William: 'In poor old Flaubert there is something almost tragic; his big intellectual temperament, machinery, etc., and vainly colossal attempts to press out the least little drop of *passion*. So much talent, and so much naïveté and honesty, and yet so much dryness and coldness.'

Flaubert might have a 'big intellectual temperament', but James distinctly felt that he himself could 'easily – more than easily – see all round him intellectually'. This was hardly a boast. It reflected James's conviction that Flaubert's superiority lay in his being a 'painter of aspects and sensations'. As a painter of ideas and moral states he was 'insignificant'. There was however something human and even 'august in a strong man who has not been able completely to express himself'. Flaubert was 'cold – and he would have given everything to be able to glow'.

James's final verdict on him, set down in the intimacy of his journal, was that he was of 'a powerful, serious, melancholy, manly, deeply corrupted, yet not corrupting nature. He was head and shoulders above the others, the men I saw at his house on Sunday afternoons.' Exception made, of course, for Turgenev.

63

Parisian Life

THAT winter Henry James moved in a sort of cosmopolitan enclave within Paris – among Russians and Americans – but having only occasional glimpses of the French. He felt himself distinctly an outsider even though he had access, as artist, to the *cénacle*; indeed, this made him feel more of an outsider than ever. 'The half-dozen charming houses to which it would be pleasant to go of an evening do not open their doors to one,' he told his mother. No one appeared to receive in the evenings. The only time people were visible was during the afternoon. Six months later, when summer had come, he could announce to Howells that he was 'turning into an old, and very contented Parisian'. He felt he had struck roots into the Parisian soil and that they could even grow 'tangled and tenacious' there. But he added: 'Of pure Parisianism I see nothing.' The real Paris remained a painted background to his comings and goings among the Muscovites and the society of Boston and New York grouped in apartments around the Arc de Triomphe.

I

He was to say, years later, that the French are 'the people in the world one may have to go more of the way to meet than to meet any other'. This was partly because they stayed closer to home. Anglo-Americans travelled more. He recognized also that the people of England and America had more expensive accommodations for entertainment, and that hospitality in France was more national than international. Yet James did obtain limited entry into certain French houses and had brief glimpses – all the more tantalizing – of what he would have liked to know. He might have fancied himself a sort of Eugène de Rastignac, laying siege to Paris, enviously eyeing the great houses in the Faubourg St Germain, yet unable to penetrate their mysterious existence. For one as curious as James and as interested in manners, and one as saturated with Balzac, this must have been a chronic exasperation. Godkin had given him a letter of introduction to the political correspondent of the *Nation*, Auguste Laugel, who received him cordially. The Laugels tried very hard to launch their American acquaintance, and did provide a series of amusing evenings for him; nevertheless these led to no continuous relationships, and provided no opportunities for forming the kind of friendships to which James was accustomed in America. Laugel was a French mining engineer and writer on scientific subjects who regularly described for *Nation* readers the drama of French Republicanism in its struggle with Orléanists and Bonapartists. He had 'a deadly melancholy tone and manner which depress and distance one', but he invited James often to his home. He had been secretary to the Duc d'Aumale, and Madame Laugel obtained for James an invitation to a ducal reception, where he met members of the Orléans family. He was much amused by a corpulent Princess of Saxe-Coburg who was rather deaf and chatty, and who gave him 'a realizing sense of what princesses are trained to'. The experience was promptly written into *The American* in the scene between Christopher Newman and the fat duchess. The Laugels also arranged dinners at which James met Ernest Renan and Émile Montégut, who had acquired distinction as a French critic of American literature. He liked Renan : his talk was 'really exquisite for urbanity, fineness and wit – all quite without show-off'. Toward Montégut he developed an acute personal dislike, so strong that he could no longer read him: he was 'a Frenchman of the intense, unhumorous type', who was always 'spinning out his shallow ingeniosities with a complacency to make the angels howl'.

James complains constantly of being caught in concentric social circles, but he makes the most of them. Through an American friend he is invited to the salon of the old Marquise de Blocqueville, daughter of one of Napoleon's marshals. She is 'a literary dowager' and patroness of Émile Montégut, 'a very gracious and caressing woman', whose red house on the Seine opposite the Louvre he evoked years later. 'She is a great invalid, very corpulent, never leaves the house and has her head swathed in long veils and laces *à la sultane* – but with the remains of beauty.' The French have a habit of not introducing anyone to anyone else, and James complains that he wanders about among 'a lot of people'. He tells his brother he will go again to her Monday at-homes, and 'by keeping it up long enough shall perhaps get something out of it'.

The trouble with many of these salons is their addiction to music. Henry had an unmusical ear : and he finds 'music at Madame Viardot's, music at Madame de Blocqueville's, music at the Baronne de Hoffmann's, music a couple of nights since at Miss Reid's', and hears assorted divas, tenors, string quartets. At Madame Viardot's 'I stood the other night on my legs for three hours (from 11 to 2) in a suffocating room, listening to an interminable fiddling, with the only consolation that Gustave Doré, standing beside me, seemed as bored as myself.' When Pauline Viardot sang, however, as she now rarely did, it seemed to him 'superb'. Henry heard her do a scene from Gluck's *Alceste*, which was 'the finest piece of musical declamation, of a grandly tragic sort, that I can conceive'. Late in the year at Paul Zhukovski's he listens from 9 to 2 a.m. to a young pianist playing selections from Wagner's Bayreuth operas, then in their early French vogue, before a small Russian circle. 'I enjoyed the circle, but I had an overdose of Wagner, whom Zhukovski vastly admires.'

Henry manages to meet assorted figures in the Parisian world. He dines with the new Minister of Education, William Waddington, who has an American wife; he meets the Duc de Broglie one day at the Longchamps military review, whither he has been piloted by Madame Laugel. Becoming an intimate of the widow and children of the Russian emigré, Nikolai Turgenev, distant relatives of Ivan Sergeyevich, he again encounters Renan and they have a long talk after dinner. He is introduced to the grandson of Jérome Bonaparte, of the American branch of the family, a 'fine-looking stupid man'. He encounters John Lemoinne, 'a dwarfish man with a glittering eye', the writer for the *Débats*, just elected to the French Academy, and Louis de Loménée, the politician, who regales him with an analysis of the Biblical style of American anti-slavery orators. During another evening he is in a private house where the Minister of the Interior, Louis Buffet, is guest and decides that his 'physiognomy expresses the beau ideal of toughness'. It is all a parade, a kind of reception line in which James shakes hands with figures as they pass. There is French wit and French incisiveness in the air all about him. He remains nevertheless simply one of the audience.

Most remembered of all these ephemeral encounters will be his few visits to a certain house in the Rue de Bac. He has gone there with a letter from Fanny Kemble, and met the 83-year-old Madame Jules Mohl. Her memories go back to Madame Récamier, and to Chateaubriand who died in the very house in which she lives. Madame Mohl was actually Scottish; her maiden name had been Mary Clarke. She had conducted one of the last of the Romantic salons. 'Imagine a little old woman, with her grey hair in her eyes, precisely like a Skye terrier, a grotesque cap and a shabby black dress. It is hard to imagine her as the quondam rival of Madame Récamier and the intimate friend of the Queen of Holland and other potentates. She was very kind and friendly with me.' Out of the windows of her third and fourth floor apartments at 120 Rue du Bac James looked upon the formal garden of a school for missionary priests, and watched the young novitiates walking up and down, breviary in hand. Madame Mohl talked of Chateaubriand's death, and of how the 80-year-old Madame Récamier (at whose bedside she sat after her lover was dead) had said with adorable grace, 'I don't want to seem pedantic, but I wish for nothing now but virtue.' It is to this anecdote that Henry alludes in his 'project' of the novel which became *The Ambassadors*. There are subtle autobiographical overtones in the passage in the novel in which Lambert Strether, sitting in a garden next to what had been Madame Mohl's house, has the sense of 'names in the air, of ghosts at the windows, of signs and tokens'. One ghost at the window was perhaps Henry James himself.

2

Henry James saw little purpose in cultivating 'the American village encamped *en plein Paris*', but it cultivated him. He found Mrs Mason there when he arrived; she was on the point of leaving for Rome – 'a most comfortable creature, especially for so handsome a woman'. Mrs Wister's friend, Mrs Lockwood, passed through the capital and Henry saw much of her. He also renewed acquaintance with Mrs Charles Strong, of New York, the former Eleanor Fearing, who was to be an expatriate all her life. He had met her in Rome in 1869. Mrs Strong had 'a spark of the *feu sacré*, an ability to interest herself and *s'enthousiasmer* which is sincere and pleasing'. She was a Catholic convert and he was ultimately to see her as

agreeable, shallow, elaborately and unsympathetically dressed, at once very exacting (of attention) and very appreciative, restless, nervous, melancholy, frivolous, querulous, attractive, irritable, irritating and in spite of her fanatical and ludicrous (in its applications) little religion, quite unable to occupy herself. So she occupies her friends!

He went with her to the opera; he liked to have idle talk with her. Among the unmarried, James met that spring one woman at whom he looked very carefully. By now he seems to have made up his mind that he would never marry; however, it is interesting to capture, in one of his letters, his first glimpse of Henrietta Reubell, whom he was to claim as one of his most devoted friends in the French capital. He described her in April 1876 as being 27 or 28, 'extremely ugly, but with something very frank, intelligent and agreeable about her'. He went on : 'If I wanted to desire to marry an ugly Parisian-American, with money and *toutes les élégances*, and a very considerable capacity for development if transported into a favouring medium, Miss Reubell would be a very good objective. But I don't.' The cautious 'wanted to desire' indicates the extent of his fear. He had nevertheless entertained the fancy. Etta Reubell's home at 42 Avenue Gabriel was to be a cherished foyer in the coming decades; and he was to write to her some of his most entertaining social letters. She was for him the perfect example of the perpetually expatriated American woman.

James was most at home in the household of the Edward Lee Childes, friends of the Nortons, who sought him out and often entertained him. Mrs Childe was French, the former Blanche de Sartiges, and James found their intimate dinners pleasant and sophisticated. Childe, a nephew of General Robert E. Lee, did not interest him very much, but he liked Mrs Childe's alertness and vivacity. 'I call in the afternoon and find Mme Lee Childe in black velvet by her fire (she is a very graceful, elegant and clever Frenchwoman) with old decorated counts and generals leaning against the mantelpiece.' James would like to have a *tête-à-tête* with her, but her fireside is always pre-empted. On one occasion he dines at the Childes' and meets a Mrs Mansfield, an Englishwoman steeped in diplomacy, 'and the most extraordinary, clever and entertaining woman I ever met. I can't describe her, but some day I shall clap her into a novel. Trollope, with a finer genius, might have invented her.' The Childes themselves suggest, in a number of ways, the Franco-Americans of *The Reverberator*.

3

Perhaps the strangest of James's American friendships that winter was with Charles Sanders Peirce, the physicist, astronomer and logician, who ultimately laid the foundations upon which William James built his philosophy of pragmatism. An aggressive, 'difficult' individual, Peirce was swinging pendulums at the Observatory. He learned from William that Henry was in Paris, called upon him, took him to dinner; and the two presently fell into the habit of meeting at regular intervals. William was much amused, for their temperamental difference was great. He told James he must find Peirce an 'uncomfortable bedfellow, thorny and spinous'. He advised him to treat him like a nettle – grasp firmly, contradict, push hard, make fun of him. This was William's way of dealing with Peirce. Henry used his own methods. He recognized that Peirce, who was four years older than himself, was a brilliant man with a large exploratory mind. He confessed he did not find him of 'thrilling interest', but found him more gentle and urbane than he had known him to be in Cambridge. They helped each other through certain hours of loneliness.

Peirce described Henry to William as 'a splendid fellow', not as fond 'of turning over questions' as he was. This, he said, was a manly trait, 'but not a philosophic one'. Henry would have agreed. He was not interested in splitting logic with the philosopher; however, as a novelist he was much interested in Peirce's sense of dislocation in Paris; his feeling that French scientists treated him indifferently; his tendency to live luxuriously, wear extravagant clothes, employ a secretary, yet lead a life of 'insupportable loneliness and sterility'. Peirce saw in Paris 'not a soul but myself and his secretary'.

The scientist read *Roderick Hudson* and declared himself an 'extreme admirer' of the book. Apparently this was all he read of James's work, for many years later – in 1909 – he showed a belated curiosity and wrote to William that 'one winter, about forty years ago or less, I used almost every day to dine with your brother Harry and we used to talk a great deal about the novels he meant to write'. Had the books ever got themselves written? Would William send him – one at a time – 'a specimen of each kind that he writes?' William was not too helpful. He sent Henry's latest novel, *The Golden Bowl*, and told Peirce 'I hope you'll be able to finish it!' Henry's final verdict on Peirce had been recorded years before, when he was summarizing his Paris winter in his journal: 'I saw a good deal of Charles Peirce that winter – as to whom his being a man of genius reconciled me to much that was intolerable in him.'

4

The French were inaccessible; and James had hardly come abroad to pay calls on Americans. He was happiest, therefore, with the cosmopolitan Russians. In addition to being received in the Rue de Douai he became a familiar in the Faubourg St Germain home of Madame Nikolai Turgenev, widow of 'the William Lloyd Garrison of Russia', who had died in 1871. James found these Turgenevs, mother and grown children, 'an oasis of purity and goodness in the midst of this Parisian Babylon', and of 'literally more than Bostonian virtue', and 'a virtue worthy of Cambridge'. Ivan Sergeyevich and these remote relatives of his, and 'a young man whose acquaintance I have lately made, give me a high idea of the Russian nature – at least in some of its forms'. The young man was the dilettante Zhukovski, a bearded soft-eyed Russian of James's age with a great fondness for the music of Richard Wagner. They liked each other from the first.

Zhukovski had the manners of an aristocrat and the ardour of a romantic. Turgenev called him a 'naïve epicurean'. Orphaned early – he was the child of his poet-father's old age – he had been brought up at the Russian court, dandled by empresses and princesses. His mother was German and he had memorabilia of his father's friendship with Goethe, including some of the German poet's drawings ('awful', said Henry). In his young manhood Paul had lived in Venetian palaces. His large Parisian studio and apartment were filled with Italian treasures. James described Zhukovski as 'a most *attachant* creature', although he recognized that he was also 'a lightweight and a perfect failure'. An amateur painter, he was exhibiting two large canvases that spring in the Salon. James studied them and decided that if Paul Zhukovski was 'one of the flowers of civilization' he would also never be anything 'but a rather curious and delicate dilettante'. He appreciated his delicacy and enjoyed his company. 'He is much to my taste and we have sworn eternal friendship,' he told his sister. 'He asks nothing better than to make me acquainted with all sorts of interesting Russians.' It was Zhukovski who told James that Turgenev had spoken of him with an appreciation that went almost to the point of *attendrissement*, and in a way that he rarely spoke of anyone. James was pleased, and repeated this to Quincy Street 'at the risk of seeming fatuous'. Zhukovski gossiped freely about Turgenev and describing his 'want of will' said that he couldn't even choose a pair of trousers for himself. Zhukovski spoke also, however, of Turgenev's 'absolute goodness and tenderness'. This he said could not be exaggerated. There was a great want of will in Zhukovski also; but he was 'very sweet and *distingué*'. The two cosmopolitans – the American and the Russian – knocked about Paris a great deal together that spring.

James found the Princess Ourousov, Zhukovski's friend, attractive. A miniature in the possession of her descendants testifies to her youthful beauty. She had dark hair, flashing dark eyes, a rather characteristic broad Russian nose. Gide, who met her a decade later, described as being '*d'une beauté plantureuse*'. She was the daughter of the great Russian industrialist, the pottery czar, Maltzov, who had built himself a small private narrow-gauge railway on his vast estates. Marie Maltzov had always moved among aristocrats and she had ended by marrying a prince. The family fortune dwindled, however, and she was living 'without princely splendour'. In later years, in Russia, she was to know Tolstoy; during summers at

Berchtesgaden Brahms would play for her; in Paris Maupassant frequented her salon; the young André Gide brought Oscar Wilde to meet her. The spontaneity Gide found in her was there when Henry James knew her, for he spoke of her being 'as easy as an old glove'. He felt he had laid 'the foundations of an intimacy' with her, by which he probably meant nothing more intimate than quiet *tête-à-têtes*, of the kind he enjoyed with Mrs Wister or Mrs Mason. Her only fault, he told Quincy Street, was that 'she smokes too much'. Through the smoke-haze, however, James found a woman 'of such liberal understanding and culture that conversation with her is a real pleasure'. Nevertheless when the Princess introduced her sister, the Countess Panin, Henry felt that she had been eclipsed. The Countess was 'a ravishing young widow, and one of the sweetest, freest, charmingest women I have ever met'. James never achieved the 'intimacy' he sought with these women : they were too much out of Paris and he went to live in London. In later years, however, during his Paris visits, he used to call on Marie Ourousov. Turgenev remained a strong link between them.

His Russian friends, he told his father, 'are quite the most (to me) fascinating people one can see; with their personal ease and *désinvolture* and that atmosphere of general culture and curiosity which they owe to having (through their possession of many languages) windows open all round the horizon'. Moving among them, and among his compatriots, and gaining his glimpses of the French, the transatlantic visitor found himself abandoning certain Cambridge rigidities, taking life a little less hard, giving himself over to the simple pleasures of genial living.

64

Silk Purse and Sow's Ear

HENRY JAMES had told John Hay confidently that he would write entertaining letters from Paris for the *New York Tribune* and Hay had taken him at his word. He went to some pains in his first letter and, since he was fresh upon the scene, made it broad and general; his tone was easy, and he chatted about the obvious : the aspect of Paris to a revisiting American, the pre-Christmas atmosphere, the subjects in the daily headlines. The *Tribune* launched its new correspondent with a laudatory editorial, *Paris Through Fresh Eyes*, probably written by Hay. It promised an extended series of dispatches by James and spoke of him as 'one of the best-equipped Americans who have crossed the Atlantic'. 'No essayist of recent years,' said the *Tribune*, 'has shown such powers of delicate and intelligent observation, such refined and wholesome humour, such a felicitous command of pure and idiomatic English as Mr Henry James.'

When James read his first letter in print he recognized that it was too general and too long, pitched 'in too vague and diffuse a key'. He also confessed, when the time came to write a second letter, that 'I can think of nothing in life to put into the *Tribune*. It is quite appalling. But I suppose it will come.' He took refuge in an exhibition of animal statuary, the decorations of the new opera, the renovation of the Odéon. He knew, however, that this was hardly the intimate Paris-from-the-inside type of letter that was wanted. His letter was distinctly Paris-from-the-outside, and this describes the seventeen Parisian letters he wrote for the *Tribune*. Three others were published, one about George Sand and two describing Chartres, Etretat, Rouen and Le Havre, in James's familiar travel-style.

James had perhaps all-too-readily decided that it was as easy to write for the *Tribune* as it was for the *Nation*. He discovered soon enough the difference between everyday journalism and the literary journalism at which he was adept in the weeklies and monthlies. It was one thing to review a book, or describe foreign manners and foreign art; it was quite another to furnish incident, observation and criticism in a regular column. To be 'chatty' about Paris and the Parisians was more than he could do. And he had in reality a contempt for newspapers, which he was to express repeatedly in his correspondence and his fiction. Writing for the *Tribune* not only went against the grain; he was temperamentally unsuited for it.

'Subjects are woefully scarce,' he complained to his mother in January; and to his father, two or three months later, he spoke of 'a painful dearth of topics to write about'. We have thus the spectacle of a man of James's large imagination unable to imagine subjects for a newspaper – and in a city teeming with them. He could hardly make capital of his private encounters with Turgenev or the Flaubert group; and these were subjects that might have had interest for the *Tribune* readers at the time. There still remained all Paris to write about, and a strong resurgent France recovering from the

Franco-Prussian war and the Commune. James could and did exploit the theatres, the art-shows, occasional books of general interest, newspaper controversies and the human interest in the effervescent political scene – all of which was his province. The newspaper was not relying upon him for ordinary reportage: the seasoned William H. Huntington took care of that; for political stories it could call on its correspondent, John Paul. James was quite free to deal with whatever struck his fancy. And yet an acute helplessness pervades his *Tribune* letters. They are readable when he performs in his characteristic magazine vein; for the rest they are rather forced, and often on the dull side. 'I am glad my *Tribune* letters amuse you,' he wrote to Howells. 'They are most impudently light-weighted, but that was part of the bargain.' To his father he wrote: 'The vulgarity and repulsiveness of the *Tribune*, whenever I see it, strikes me so violently that I feel tempted to stop my letter.' He could not, however, yield to this temptation: he needed the money.

2

Try as he might, Henry James could never speak in the journalistic voice. The voice we hear in the *Tribune* letters is that of the artist. When all else failed him, and his *Tribune* pen lagged, he could fall back upon his aesthetic faculty. He could also fall back on his faithful eyes:

The huge towers of Notre Dame, rising with their blue-gray tone from the midst of the great mass round which the river divides, the great Arc de Triomphe answering them with equal majesty in the opposite distance, the splendid continuous line of the Louvre between, and over it all the charming colouring of Paris on certain days – the brightness, the pearly grays, the flicker of light, the good taste, as it were, of the atmosphere – all this is an entertainment which even custom does not stale.

'Entertainment' doubtless for the mind and imagination of Henry James, but what concern, we may wonder, did the average newspaper reader have with 'the good taste, as it were, of the atmosphere'? This is the painter-observer at work with blue-grey, pearl-grey and flickering light; it is distinctly not newspaper reportage; nor was the wandering sentence suitable for journalism. When we travel with him to Versailles, where the French Assembly is sitting, we find him abridging his attendance in that musty little red and gold playhouse in which the Assembly sits, for the sake of wandering about the terraces and avenues of the park. The day had that soft, humid mildness which, in spite of the inveteracy with which you are assured here that every biting blast is 'exceptional', and which consequently piles up your accumulated conviction that it is the rule – is really the keynote, the *fonds*, as they say, of the Paris winter weather.

We can indeed imagine the copyreader struggling with these clauses within clauses, the quoted 'exceptional', the *fonds* of the matter.

If a *Tribune* reader was willing to accept the literary tone, the unorthodox sentences, the substitution of colour and atmosphere for hard fact, he could find his rewards, over and above the descriptive felicities. He could tour the salon of 1876 with the patience and vigour required in visiting this annual French display of miles of painted canvas; he could encounter works by Taine, Rénan, Zola, Sainte-Beuve, carefully reviewed and analysed; he could catch Henry James Jr at a ball watching Johann Strauss conduct his waltzes; and on another occasion he would be present to hear Giuseppe Verdi lead his Requiem. In these articles we walk through the foyer of the new opera with James and examine the decorations and the gilt; we muse over the traceries and carvings at Chartres; or we travel down the Seine to Rouen looking at scenery and finally relax on the beach at Etretat, when summer takes us away from the capital. Had James been more of a journalist and less of a connoisseur, he might have found more to say when he made his pilgrimage to the Durand-Ruel gallery and examined an exhibition of the early Impressionists which was to pass into history. 'I have found it decidedly interesting,' he tells us.

> But the effect of it was to make me think better than ever of all the good old rules which decree that beauty is beauty and ugliness ugliness, and warn us off from the sophistications of satiety ... the 'Impressionist' doctrines strike me as incompatible, in an artist's mind, with the existence of first-rate talent. To embrace them you must be provided with a plentiful absence of imagination.

And he went on to say that Impressionists 'abjure virtue altogether, and declare that a subject which has been crudely chosen shall be loosely treated. They send detail to the dogs and concentrate themselves on general expression. Some of their generalizations of expression are in a high degree curious.'

Allowing for the ampler view which we have, and the triumph of Impressionism since that time, we can see in this account James's failure as a reporter. He might quarrel aesthetically with Impressionism, as all the committed 'representationalists' did; he nevertheless could have brought his power of description to let his American audience see with him exactly what the paintings looked like. The Impressionists may have failed, in this instance, to impress; what James failed to see was that they were 'good copy'. William James's comments reflected his awareness of his brother's problem: 'Your first letter was a very good beginning, though one sees that you are to a certain extent fishing for the proper tone and level.' Again: 'Keep watch and ward lest in your style you become too Parisian and lose your hold on the pulse of the great American public, to which after all you must pander for support.'

Had James ever obtained such a hold? His letters were passively received. The correspondence columns of the paper contain letters of praise for most of the *Tribune's* other correspondents, but no praise and little blame for James. A single letter may be found in the issue of 22 January 1876, complaining that James has harshly misjudged Barye's animal sculptures. When later Houssaye resumed his letters, a group of readers wrote to commend his work, and expressed the hope that he would be heard from often. And Whitelaw Reid was to comment that not only were the *Tribune's* readers silent, but other journals, which often quoted the newspaper, seemed oblivious of Henry's letters.

This explains James's summary of his *Tribune* experience in his journal six years later. 'I wrote letters to the New York *Tribune*, of which, though they were poor stuff, I may say that they were too good for the purpose (of course they didn't succeed).' A truer statement was embodied in a tale in which the heroine confesses she has agreed to write London letters for a provincial paper; 'I can't do them – I don't know how, and don't want to. I do them wrong, and the people want such trash. Of course they'll sack me.'

3

The *Tribune* did not 'sack' Henry; but ever after he was to speak as if it did. By midsummer, when he had written twenty letters and received the tidy sum of $400 – and knew that he had been as well paid for his work as for anything he had done for the *Nation* – he asked Whitelaw Reid for more money. What he suggested was that he receive half as much again, $30 per letter. He apparently felt that his trial-period with the paper was at an end; perhaps also he knew that Houssaye had been paid more. Certainly the effort he was obliged to put into any one of these letters must have been out of proportion to the amount he received. Reid's reply, at any rate, was unexpected. The publisher offered a compromise. He explained that James's subjects were 'too remote from popular interests' and that it was possible to over-estimate the 'literary culture' of the readers. He reminded James that newspaper-readers are people in a hurry who want brevity, variety and topics of sustained interest. He therefore proposed that James alter the character of his letters: make them shorter and 'newsier', and that he space them more widely – particularly since the United States was entering upon an election year. 'You must not imagine,' Reid wrote, 'that any of us have failed to appreciate the admirable work you have done for us.' He added, however, the forthright statement: 'The difficulty has sometimes been not that it was too good, but that it was magazine rather than newspaper work.'

Reid touched James's professional sensitivity; and his concluding sentence had a peculiar and painful force. James was left defenceless. He could hardly try to convince Reid that he had chosen topics of wide interest; he knew all too well how few topics he had been able to scrape up. He knew also that he could not lay claim to having written good journalism or argue that the *Tribune* should publish magazine-work. The terms also offered no ground for negotiation. If he was to receive the same amount for less work, this 'less' had also to undergo a qualitative change – be more 'newsy', informative, gossipy. A literary hack, a professional journalist, a man accustomed to 'tailoring' copy to a given medium, might be addressed in this manner and would not think twice about it. Reid however could take no other view. The pen which answered the publisher was more incisive than it had ever been in the columns of the *Tribune*.

James began mildly enough. He recognized that his letters were considered not 'the right sort of thing for a newspaper'; he had been expecting to hear as much from the publisher. He could readily imagine that the general reader would have little time for him during the excitement of an election. He was prepared to grant the magazine-quality of his writing. He thereupon selected the one point on which he might counter-attack. This was Reid's request that he incorporate more gossip. 'I know the sort of letter you mean,' he wrote; 'it is doubtless the proper sort of thing for the *Tribune* to have. But I can't produce it – I don't know how and I couldn't learn how.' He added 'it would be poor economy for me to try and become "newsy" and gossipy. I am too finical a writer and I should be constantly becoming more "literary" than is desirable.' The next sentence revealed his deeper feelings:

If my letters have been 'too good' I am honestly afraid that they are the poorest I can do, especially for the money! I had better, therefore, suspend them altogether. I have enjoyed writing them, however, and if the *Tribune* has not been the better for them I hope it hasn't been too much the worse.

To his father he wrote that Reid 'had stopped off my letters to the *Tribune* – practically at last – by demanding that they should be of a flimsier sort. I thought in all conscience they had been flimsy enough. I am a little sorry to stop, but much glad.' The episode was to haunt him for years. He was ultimately to make a short story of it, *The Next Time* – 'the idea of the poor man, the artist, the man of letters, who all his life is trying – if only to get a living – to do something *vulgar*, to take the measure of the huge, flat foot of the public … to make, as it were, a sow's ear out of a silk purse'.

What James forgot, when he came to make an artistic picture of the creator's dilemma, was that his own had not been comparable. He had simply ventured into an alien medium. The magazine world was quite prepared to accept him. He did say to Quincy Street shortly after resigning his journalistic chore: 'You needn't commiserate me for my *Tribune* cessation; I don't miss the *Tribune* at all; I can use my material to better advantage.' And he did.

65

The American

HENRY JAMES'S financial situation on reaching the French capital had been as follows: he had drawn upon his father's letter of credit in London to pay for new clothes and for his installation in the Rue de Luxembourg; he had certain miscellaneous sums outstanding from the *Nation* and the *Galaxy*, and had arranged to have them paid directly to himself, instead of to Quincy Street: royalties from the book-publication of *Roderick* (it was published in Boston on 20 November 1875) were to be sent to his father to reimburse him. He was committed to start another novel for Howells, but a certain delay was necessary following serialization of *Roderick*. He was, therefore, short of funds. His fortnightly letters to the *Tribune* did not cover his rent; his fugitive reviewing and other writings would barely feed him. He needed about $150 a month. The only practical course was to start a new serial, as quickly as possible, in some other magazine. He would explain to Howells that he could not afford to wait. Having already had tentative talks with the editors of the *Galaxy*, he wrote to them from Paris on 1 December 1875 that he would 'take for granted, as soon as I can, that you will be ready to publish, on receipt of them, the opening chapters of a novel'. He announced he had begun a work called *The American* sooner than expected. He planned to complete it in nine months; his price would be $150 an instalment. He would thus earn in three-quarters of a year more than *Roderick* had brought in during a twelvemonth.

Transatlantic Sketches had yielded a royalty balance of $200 at the end of the year, and this money had gone directly to Quincy Street. On 24 January he received a letter from his mother accusing him of extravagance, and informing him that his autumn draft on his father had been 'excessive and inconvenient'. James replied that her words had given him 'a wretched hour'. It was true, he said, that he had drawn more largely, and at shorter intervals 'than could be at all agreeable to you'. Nevertheless this had been a necessity of his situation. 'I have hardly had my expense off my mind an hour since I have been abroad, and I had arranged my life here, in Paris, well within my means.' Paris was not cheap; but it was not as dear as New York and 'once under way, as I am now, I am in for nothing that I cannot face'. He said he was certain that by the end of the year he would have a balance in his favour 'and I shall be able to refund and compensate inconveniences'. He added: 'Banish from your mind your visions of my extravagance. I am living simply as well as physical well-being and decent mental cheerfulness seem, in lonely life, to demand.'

The effect of his mother's letter was, for the moment, to undermine James's sense of security. He could draw no further on his father; and he had to find ways to keep his pen busy. This may explain his suddenly developing a ten-day headache, not as violent or feverish as the one he had had in Florence when William was with him, but sufficiently uncomfortable to keep him at home. He had to cancel his plans to attend a fancy-dress party at the Viardots', and Turgenev came the morning after, to comfort him and describe the fun he had missed.

The *Galaxy* did not reply, and James stopped writing *The American*. Instead he hastily wrote two tales in his old, pre-*Roderick Hudson* vein – *Crawford's Consistency* and *The Ghostly Rental*. He deemed them inferior and sold them to *Scribner's* for $300. Meanwhile Howells wrote to say he would take James's serial whenever he was ready to let him have it. Henry ruefully replied: 'I took for granted that the *Atlantic* would begin nothing till June or July, and it was the money question solely that had to determine me.' *The American*, he said, was the only subject 'mature enough in my mind to use immediately. It has in fact been used somewhat prematurely; and I hope you find enough faults in it to console you for not having it in the *Atlantic*.' He said, however, that if the *Galaxy* continued to ignore him, or if its editors were not satisfied, he would ask them to forward the first instalment to Howells. His price remained $150 a month for nine instalments.

Howells was determined to keep James in the *Atlantic*, and he lost no time in offering to take *The American* if the *Galaxy* did not want it. James, on his side, laid down an ultimatum to that journal: 'If you are unable to begin *The American* at the latest in the May *Galaxy*, I must forgo the pleasure of having the story appear in the magazine. I decided it should be plain that this and the price I fixed per number ($150) were the only terms on which I offered it.' He repeated: 'These then are my terms – $150 a number – to commence in *May* – and failing this to send the copy instantly to Cambridge.' The editors of the *Galaxy* obliged. Howells scheduled the serial to begin in the *Atlantic*'s June issue.

I

The American was a firm, rapid stride on the part of Henry James into full literary maturity. The endless debate on art in *Roderick Hudson* gave way now to determination and action. James had found it necessary in his first novel to create two characters to express his full intention. It took Rowland Mallet, playing God, to complete Roderick. Christopher Newman also wants to play God – to the whole world – but in the process he stands aggressively planted on his own two feet, in Paris, where James himself was now launched.

He told Howells he was writing the novel 'prematurely'. What he meant by this was that he was uncomfortably close to his materials; there was an almost excessive flow of daily incident from life into his book without prior assimilation and synthesis. The consequence was that this novel, of all James's works, is written, as might be said, 'off the top of his head'. Yet he had long nourished the image of Christopher Newman. He had thought of him, one day, while riding in an American horse-car, as the figure of a robust American confronting an aristocratic society. The point of his story would be that this American 'should suffer at the hands of persons pretending to represent the highest possible civilization and to be of an order in every way superior to his own'. The old idea could now be brought into James's new environment. He would write a novel about an American businessman and his siege of Paris, of Balzac's Faubourg St Germain, and of which he himself was having a passing glimpse. He speaks in the novel of 'those grey and silent streets of the Faubourg whose houses present to the outer world a face as impassive and as suggestive of the concentration of privacy as the blank walls of Eastern seraglios'. The streets he had in mind were the Rue de l'Université, where much of the novel's action takes place, the Rue de Lille and the Rue de Bellechasse. There was also the Rue du Faubourg St Germain, and the short Rues Monsieur and Madame. Other streets a little farther out of the 'old residential and noble parts of the city' were the Rue St Dominique, the Rue de Grenelle and the Rue de Varenne. In James's time there were a great many fine old hôtels in these streets, with their wide gates and coachyards. James had hoped that some of these gates would swing open for him. His American, Christopher Newman, however, has a much higher hope – that of marrying into one of the Faubourg's old aristocratic families. He reflects, in a measure, some of James's frustration at not achieving entrance into this world which Eugène de Rastignac had conquered and in which, through saturated reading of French novels, he felt himself, in his imagination, to be initiate. The result is that the Faubourg which Henry creates is in part the Faubourg of literature, rather than that of life; on it he superimposes the few shreds of fact and the glimpses he himself had had during the reception at the Duc d'Aumale's or his meeting with the Orléanist princess. These episodes would be converted into the great party in the house of the Bellegardes.

Newman is thus an image of James's Parisian life of action, while at the same time being a mordant portrait of an American – a portrait indeed so rich in national ambiguities that several generations of readers have seen him largely as an expansive generous warmhearted hero without sufficiently noticing that he embodies also everything that James disliked in the United States. Newman's qualities show the American character in all its forthrightness and innocence as well as in its predatory aspects. The Californian was in some respects 'quiet', and his author even claimed for him a certain 'shyness', which is nowhere present in the book. He was 'nice' in many ways. But there was in him a strong and vulgar streak of materialistic self-satisfaction which James had understood from the first and to which many American readers preferred to close their eyes. Constance Rourke long ago pointed James's synthesis of an American 'type' : his naïveté, his boastfulness, his impatience. There is also his failure to grasp deeper human values. Americans reading this book are often apt to overlook that side of Newman which Charles Dudley Warner noticed, when it was still appearing in the *Atlantic Monthly*, and about which he wrote to Julian Hawthorne : 'It seems to me the cleverest thing James ever did; perhaps it is too clever. He actually makes us believe it possible to marry a Californian boor to a Bellegarde, and then he cruelly breaks the match.'

'Boor' may be a strong word; the boorishness in Newman resides not in his pretensions – decidedly superficial – to art or architecture; it is the side of him which is at once pride in being 'self-made' and his belief that anything can be bought. Little phrases throughout the book tell us this. Henry James, however, has handled his character so adroitly and placed him so distinctly in the position of an individual wronged and thwarted, that they are not sufficiently noticed. The very description of his protagonist reveals this. Newman has 'an eye in which innocence and experience were singularly blended'. It is 'frigid and yet friendly, frank yet cautious, shrewd yet credulous, positive yet sceptical, confident yet shy, extremely intelligent and extremely good-humoured'. There is also 'something vaguely defiant in its concessions, and something profoundly reassuring in its reserve'. Newman would seem to be that future paradox in the civilized world : the American who is hospitable to life's chances, but who is 'committed to nothing in particular' save his own incredible self-assurance.

Christopher Newman begins with the belief that 'Europe was made for him, and not he for Europe'. He has for his standard 'the ideal of one's own good-humoured prosperity'. His 'specialty' has been 'to make the largest possible fortune in the shortest possible time'. When the Marquise de Bellegarde says that she is a 'proud and meddlesome old woman' his only answer can be 'Well, I am very rich'. He has made his pile of money, and what he dreams of is a wife; 'there must be a beautiful woman perched on the pile, like a statue on a monument'. She has, indeed, to be 'the best article on the market'. Newman is not often embarrassed, for 'his unconscious sang-froid was boundless'. He has 'not only a dislike, but a sort of moral mistrust, of uncomfortable thoughts'. If he avoids mental discomfort, however, he has no real sense of physical comfort. He may have 'a relish for luxury and splendour', yet he 'scarcely knew a hard chair from a soft'. He has as a prime conviction 'that a man's life should be easy' and it is the ease of one who has had a continent to conquer, who has lost and made fortunes in leather, wash-tubs, copper. At the same time he possesses that morbid fear of idleness which coloured James's days in Cambridge. 'Elegant leisure comes hard,' he says. He confesses also to never having had 'time to feel things'.

He does not wave the Stars and Stripes belligerently. However, with his wealth he carries the solid belief that his homeland is 'the greatest country in the world' and that Americans 'could put all Europe in their breeches pocket'. Americans, Newman remarks, (and it is one of James's slyest jokes), who speak ill of their country 'ought to be carried home in irons and compelled to live in Boston'. And he adds that 'this, for Newman, was putting it very vindictively'. When he is told that he has 'a sort of air' of being thoroughly at home in the world he ascribes this to the privilege of being an American citizen. 'That sets a man up.' And what lets a man down, he comes to discover, is being thwarted. Even though he is an American, he cannot arrange life entirely on his terms, or according to his values. 'He had a burning, tingling sense of personal outrage. He had never in his life received so absolute a check' – this when the aristocratic family changes its mind about him. It cannot swallow a commercial American as a son-in-law. Newman finds the sensation of defeat intolerable.

He is never more American than in his belief that 'energy and ingenuity can arrange everything', that a willing American can learn anything. When Newman remarks that the Bellegarde house in the Faubourg is 'curious', Valentin asks him whether he is interested in architecture. He replies with a typical statistic that he had visited 470 churches during his summer's travel. 'Perhaps,' Valentin responds, 'you are interested in theology.'

'You are the great Western Barbarian,' he is told, 'stepping forth in his innocence and might, gazing a while at this poor effete Old World and then swooping down on it.' This is one side of Newman, a side thoroughly dissimulated, however, behind the energy, geniality and 'drive' with which he moves through the book, impervious to all save his own anchored dollars and the sense they give him that he can do as he pleases.

2

This was the ice on which James skated – the thin ice of American national sensitivity – and his performance in the novel, in spite of all the fustian and melodrama, is brilliant. Even though he sketches an innocent Western Barbarian, he shows us also the candour of his innocence and the courage of his ignorance. The central irony of the book is that Newman has not been corrupted by his gold; he is still one of 'nature's noblemen' and, in the end, he is as moral and therefore as noble as the corrupt Europeans. The truth is that the Marquise de Bellegarde is simply a European version of Christopher Newman; she sits upon her aristocratic sanctity with the same tough possessiveness and assurance that Newman sits on his pile of dollars. In the struggle between the two, it is Newman who emerges the better Christian. The woman he loves, or rather prizes, and wishes to take possession of as if she were a railroad or a mine, has immured herself in a convent in the appropriately named Rue d'Enfer. In this street Newman once again stands before a wall that bars his way, a wall 'pale, dead, discoloured'. He goes to Notre-Dame; and sitting there he hears 'far-aways bells chiming off, at long intervals, to the rest of the world',* and decides that revenge isn't 'his game'. Critics have spoken of this splendid scene as an act of 'renunciation'. New-

* In his revision of this passage many years later Henry was more poetic, speaking of 'far-away bells chiming off into space at long intervals, the big bronze syllables of the Word'.

man simply recognizes the realities before him. He could take his revenge, but he will not regain Claire de Cintré. And because the Bellegardes have been cruel to him is no reason for him now to be cruel to them. A good American, a shrewd business man, does not indulge in waste effort.

It is a good ending to the story, and it does impart to Newman an aura of nobility. The original readers of the novel did not experience this. They felt as frustrated as Newman; they had hoped for a happy ending; they had read the *Atlantic* instalments from month to month, in the fond belief that their author would give Newman the prize. Howells pleaded with him to do so; Lizzie Boott, on behalf of herself and Alice Bartlett, asked for the happiness of seeing Newman married. On the other hand Fanny Kemble, in the serenity of her old age, and speaking out of her transatlantic experience, expressed a fear lest he should put the marriage through. '*Voyons,*' James wrote to Howells, 'they would have been an impossible couple'. And he went on to argue that they would have had no place to live: Claire de Cintré would have hated New York, and Newman could not dwell in France. Leaving out Asia and Africa, there would be 'nothing left but a farm out West'. Newman was confronted by an insuperable difficulty from which the only issue, as far as James could see, was forfeiture. The image he chose was singularly apropos. it described the determinist barriers of the Faubourg and the Rue d'Enfer:

We are each the product of circumstances and there are tall stone walls which fatally divide us. I have written the story from Newman's side of the wall, and I understand so well how Madame de Cintré couldn't really scramble over from *her* side! If I had represented her as doing so, I should have made a prettier ending, certainly; but I should have felt as if I were throwing a rather vulgar sop to readers who don't really know the world and who don't measure the merit of a novel by its correspondence to the same.

In replying to Lizzie Boott he also argued that Claire wasn't really in love with Newman and 'that in putting it into Newman's power to forgive and contemptuously "let off" the haughty Bellegardes, I was doing quite the most dramatic and inspiring thing'. He reminded Lizzie: 'I am a realist.'

This is the fundamental point. In telling Howells that his unhappy ending corresponded to life, and in insisting that he was a realist, Henry James overlooked the essential fact that he had written a romantic novel. His persons were real enough; their backgrounds were real; but the story of what happened to them moved across that borderland of the actual and the imaginary which Hawthorne liked to celebrate – although Hawthorne's 'imaginary' often went as far as the supernatural. James's resided simply in the melodrama of his plot, that element of the arbitrary in his situation which he endowed with plausibility, but which, on the whole, was quite as impossible as any melodrama can be when it is closely scrutinized. Having aroused the reader's sympathies on Newman's behalf, and having made the reader endure the death of the charming Valentin, James continued to turn the romantic sunshine of the book into depressing gloom by locking up Claire in a convent and crushing Newman in an ending no more 'real' than would have been a happy one. It was not so much a question of throwing a sop to his readers as making the book true to itself; given the book's initial character, its ending was false. James was to recognize this in later years; he substituted a happy ending when he dramatized the novel. In his late preface he made the romanticism of the book his greatest plea for the reader's acceptance of its improbabilities. He recognized that the Bellegardes 'would positively have jumped at my rich and easy American' and not have minded any drawbacks; moreover, there were 'few drawbacks to mind'.

This being the case, why did James insist on breaking off the marriage instead of seeking means to unite his lovers – as lovers usually are united in romantic novels. This was always to be one of his problems. We may speculate that having ruled out marriage for himself, he found it genuinely difficult to offer it to his heroes. James's tales of the artist-life invariably contain the admonition that marriage could only be a distraction, a form of servitude fatal to art. Identified with Newman as an active and independent individual, James shut up Claire de Cintré in the convent as he shut women away from himself. And in endowing Claire with weakness and inconstancy he underlined his sense of women's fickleness as well as his own fear of them. One of his pot-boilers at this time shows the extent to which James pondered this question. In *Crawford's Consistency*, the genial hero, like Newman, falls in love with a young woman, strongly in the clutches of her family, who at first accept him and then turn him down. Crawford, on the rebound, marries a common woman who ends by ruining his life and ill-treats him to the point of pushing him down some steps and crippling him. This crude story, based on an anecdote told by his father, reflected an old and tried theme in his tales. It embodies his two visions of woman: the young and the unattainable; or the cruel and the destructive.

Bernard Shaw was to say to James years later that an author can give victory to one side as easily as to another. Certainly this did not apply to tragedy. But in a comedy like *The American* Henry James did have the choice: his 'determinism' (and fear of marriage) nevertheless prevailed.

3

It is doubtful whether Henry James thought of *The American* as a comedy. He thought he was writing a Balzacian novel. Nor, apparently, was he aware for all his seriousness, that, he was writing a high comedy. 'I suspect it is the tragedies in life that arrest my attention, more than the other things, and say more to my imagination,' he wrote to Howells, even while he was writing his monthly instalment of the comic chapters of *The American*. For one who felt himself to have a penchant for the tragedies of life, James managed to write a large number of successful comedies during the next few years: upon them, indeed, he built his greatest fame. In *The American* James for the first time revealed to the full the two genuinely original elements in his work that were to constitute his claim to renown during the first half of his writing life: his grasp of the contrasts in manners between America and Europe, and his subtle vein of humour, as original as any in the nineteenth century. Certain critics recognized this as soon as they read his new novel. 'Among American story-writers,' said the reviewer of the *Globe*, a newspaper published in the city to which Newman would have confined recalcitrant Americans, 'Henry James stands alone – imitating no one, and, as yet, having no imitators.' This was completely true. Earlier writers had barely sketched his American-European theme; and none had seen the humour in it. Indeed James himself was not yet fully aware of the extent of his skills. To grasp his vividness and humour one must read the unrevised version, that version which readers of the *Atlantic* saw from month to month and which, with very little change, was issued in volume form in 1877. The later version, systematically and exhaustively revised in 1905 for the New York Edition, is almost another book – a better one, in terms of structure and style, but it lacks the freshness, the visual sharpness and the exuberance with which Henry wrote this tale in a Paris that kept him at arm's length.

The touch of comedy is present on almost every page – save those which James gives over to unutterable melodramatic gloom. Even when he is describing the death of Valentin, however, he is unable to resist the comic delineation of the aristocrats round the deathbed: and there is 'black' humour, for one of them hands Newman a volume of Faublas, which we may be certain was known to few of the *Atlantic* readers – *Les Amours du Chevalier de Faublas*, an ancient frivolous novel of seductions and *amours* that would have made the strait-laced American shudder. James himself felt the allusion recondite; in his revised version he substituted Choderlos de Laclos' *Les Liaisons Dangereuses*, which served his purpose equally well.

James's scenes between Newman and the aristocrats are nearly always on a plane of *double entendre*: the exchange of wit is constant, and quite often so is an element of mockery of which Newman is unaware. When Newman offers a recital of his life to the Bellegardes and tells them of his sisters' early marriages, he mentions that one of them had made a match with the owner of the largest indiarubber house in the west. 'Ah,' observes the Marquise, 'you make houses also of india rubber.' And young Madame de Bellegarde takes up the cue: 'You can stretch them as your family increases.' Newman finds this hilarious, wholly unaware that they are laughing at him. The fat duchess asks Newman whether it isn't true that he has founded an American city and would be richer still 'if you didn't grant lands and houses free of rent to all newcomers who'll pledge themselves never to smoke cigars'. This concept of the marriage of feudalism with puritanism is but one of the ironic ways in which James keeps the play of comedy constant. Or simply the casual remark of the Marquise de Bellegarde, when she first meets Newman: 'You're an American. I've seen several Americans.' To which Newman replies, 'There are several in Paris.' Not least there is the charming touch of old M. Rochefidèle, who has seen his American long ago, 'Almost the first person I ever saw – to notice him – was an American.' Newman learns it was 'the great Dr Franklin'.

This is the comedy which flows easily from the characters and from the situation in which Henry placed them. If Newman himself proves he can indulge in give and take, it is only to make himself more pleasing to the grand and the mighty of the Faubourg. The Marquis does concede he is polite, the Duchess finds him amusing. He is guilty of one serious error and it is his undoing – when at his engagement party he asks the Marquise to parade with him among the guests, as if to give him the *cachet* he lacks. She does up to a point, but she reaches a moment when she has to say to him 'This is enough, sir.' His failure in tact has been complete. Advertising and salesmanship, so to speak, have overcome shrewdness and caution. From this point Newman's good fortune goes into decline.

4

Roderick Hudson had represented James's final dialogue with Quincy Street, a last tug at the silver cord. He had made his choice, and his story of Christopher Newman was symbolic of his own stepping-forth into the world – as a new man. But the vivid personalities of Quincy Street, the conflict of its strong egos, remained. The rivalry with William emerges in *The American*, no longer in the complaining terms of the Cambridge time, but simply as a hard fact of life. The unpleasant Marquis de Bellegarde, who is fifteen years senior to his brother Valentin, represents one extreme of ancient family feeling; the other is the portrait of the American clergyman Newman encounters during his travels. Here, at last, William recognized himself. 'Your second instalment of *The American* is prime,' he wrote. 'The morbid little clergyman is worthy of Ivan Sergeyevich. I was not a little amused to find some of my own attributes in him – I think you found my "moral reaction" excessive when I was abroad.'

By the same token, the second son, Valentin, in this version of Henry's familial experience, is charming, ineffectual and doomed. He shows the benign side of William. Dominating the book is the matriarchal old Marquise, the archetypal mother-figure of James's work, in whose hands husbands are crushed or robbed of their manhood, or – as in this instance – murdered.

The book's reception in America was mixed. It was, however, read more attentively, and aroused more discussion, than anything James had done before. The character of Newman was generally liked, although some reviewers felt the novelist might have found a nicer American to oppose to the aristocrats; and James's friend

T. S. Perry was not even sure that Newman had made an honest fortune; he wondered 'which side of the market he operated upon'. The style, the technique, the narration were universally praised. The strongest fire of the critics was reserved for the plot: the failure to provide a happy ending, they argued, was inconsistent with what the story had prepared them for: and certain critics again significantly saw James's detached and 'cold-blooded' attitude towards his personages. This might be 'realism', yet it revealed a critic, an analyst, 'rather than the sharer of strong feeling'. The originality of James's international theme was recognized and nearly all the critics were prepared to consider the novel an important contribution to American literature. They were not yet prepared however – and this they said – to place James beside Hawthorne or Trollope or Dickens – or for that matter George Eliot.

66

In the Provinces

HOWELLS liked The American and decided that he would spread it through twelve monthly issues of the Atlantic instead of nine. James agreed to take the same price for the twelve as he had asked for the nine, since the amount of copy was unchanged. This would yield him $1,340. The novelist's livelihood was assured until the following year.

As James worked at his instalments of The American he had the feeling of 'the life of the splendid city playing up in it like a flashing fountain in a marble basin'. Everything in his environment could be grist to his mill. He heard a joke (repeated in his Tribune correspondence), that of the hard-working maidservant who saved up thirty crowns to give herself a dowry, and then was asked why she had married a hunchback. 'What sort of husband can one get for thirty crowns?' she replied. The joke emerges in the pages of The American when Noémie Nioche asks Newman: 'What sort of a husband can you get for 12,000 francs?' His warm friendship with Paul Zhukovski is reflected in the friendship between Newman and Valentin: it has the same kind of camaraderie. And one day a distraught American girl knocked at James's door to inform him that she had read Roderick Hudson, and to beseech his help. Would he intercede in a duel about to be fought over her between an American and an Englishman? Whatever vision James may have had of his pacific self trying to intervene in a flourish of pistols and swords was quickly dissipated. The rivals could not wait on romantic formalities. They slugged it out. And so probably the more fatal duel in *The American* had its relation to life as well as literature.

I

The time had come to say farewells. The Princess Ourousov left. Turgenev was leaving. He was returning to Russia for the summer, hoping to finish *Virgin Soil*. Wishing to see as much of him as possible before his departure, James joined the Viardot household for charades once again on a Sunday evening, and again watched the Russian novelist scampering about on hands and knees; and then he called on him one morning and found him 'more charming than I had ever seen him'. There was such 'an extreme sense of *justesse* in his great Cossack body' that James felt like embracing him. A day or two later Turgenev joined James and Zhukovski at dinner and 'was again adorable' – but once again he had to return to Madame Viardot at an early hour. Late in May, Henry went to Flaubert's last Sunday afternoon. He had an hour alone with the author of *Madame Bovary*, after which he said his summer goodbyes to the *cénacle*. He would never see Flaubert again. Eight years would elapse before he would renew his friendship with Goncourt, Zola, Daudet, Maupassant – in the full tide of 'naturalism'.

Zhukovski remained in the city for a while and James attended various musical evenings at his studio. A later tale called *Collaboration* describes one such evening. When the Bootts turned up in Paris, James arranged a dinner-party for them. Zhukovski found Boott 'extrêmement sympathique' and thought he looked like one of Titian's men; and Lizzie, to James's surprise, revealed great fluency in French. The Bootts established themselves near Paris, at Villiers-le-Bel, where Lizzie studied painting with the French master, Thomas Couture. James thought him 'a vulgar little fat and dirty old man'. Lizzie said he was an admirable teacher.

James was still in Paris in July. It was hot and he frequented the cafés, drinking beer, watching the crowds, dining in the Champs-Élysées under the trees, beside ivy-covered walls. He liked to pass evenings on the *terrasse* of the Café Riche 'with a little table and a bock'. This was pleasant enough, simply to watch the human spectacle 'in spite of the *cocottes*, the too too numerous *cocottes*'. Or he would take a penny steamer to Auteuil, eat fried fish at a *guinguette* on the river-bank, and return on top of a horse-car. For a change he would dine in the Bois de Boulogne and drive back through the woods at night in the cool air. 'Your last few letters,' William wrote to him, 'have breathed a tone of contentment and domestication in Paris which was very agreeable to get. I'm afraid though that your native snobbery will wax wanton on your intimacy with crowned heads and that you'll be more intolerably supercilious than ever if you do return home.' From Elmwood, Lowell wrote: 'Don't get to be too much of a Mounseer and come home as soon as you can.' James had no thought of return. 'The longer I live in France,' he wrote to William, 'the better I like the French personality, but the more convinced I am of their bottomless superficiality.'

2

One day in late July he packed his bags, reserved his apartment for the autumn, and took a boat down the Seine, to Rouen, to Honfleur, to Le Havre. He inspected the bourgeois streets of Rouen, which Flaubert knew so intimately, and wrote about them in one of his last letters for the *Tribune*; Honfleur had all the charm of an Old World fishing port; and in Le Havre he had a ship-board feeling. He finally settled at Etretat, taking lodgings near the beach and his meals at the Hôtel Blanquet. He bought himself a fishing cap and canvas shoes; he wore his old clothes; and for a month he wrote peacefully, giving over his spare time to explore fishing villages, taking long walks across the dunes, or lying on the beach watching the French bathers. He found the Boston-Roman Edward Boits living in an old house nearby, and went on excursions with them, once to the restaurant of *la belle Ernestine*, where they breakfasted in the orchard in front of the house and found some rather offensive American young men with a party of French actresses. James trudged ten miles to see the races at Fécamp, and admired the 'plastic' landscape of Normandy. At the Casino one day he studied Jacques Offenbach, sitting placidly over his drink; and on evenings he went to the light operas.

During one of his strolls he found a shepherd flat on his stomach, resting among his shorn sheep. He had been tending sheep for thirty-five years. When James remarked that it was pleasant to do so under such beautiful skies, the shepherd observed rather dryly that in thirty-five summers there were a certain number of rainy days. James looked at the closely-knit French families taking their summer holidays, and mused on the differences between French matrons and their American sisters.

I have never seen such richness of contour as among the mature *baigneuses* of Etretat. The lean and desiccated person into whom a dozen years of matrimony so often converts the blooming American girl is not emulated in France. A majestic plumpness flourished all around me – the plumpness of triple chins and deeply dimpled hands.

He went on to analyse the difference in manners between America and France and the institution of the *jeune fille*. He did not believe it was hardship for French girls to be tied to their mothers' apron-strings until they were wedded. 'Mademoiselle is married certainly, and married early, and she is sufficiently well informed to know, and to be sustained by the knowledge, that the sentimental expansion which may not take place at present will have an open field after her marriage.' The subject interested him during all the years to come. Ultimately it yielded him a complex dialogue-novel, *The Awkward Age*. Turned round, it was the essence of *Daisy Miller*.

3

He would have gladly lingered at Etretat but he had promised Edward Lee Childe and his French wife Blanche that he would visit them in their home at Amilly-Loiret, in the Gâtinais. He found himself in an enchanting part of France surrounded by the bounty of the land and the ancient traditions of country life. In the warm August evening his hosts drove him to the little castle in which they lived; – on an island just large enough to hold it, surrounded by three-foot thick walls and a moat. It looked operatic. They put him in the Blue Room, with a separate washroom in the turret and a valet to wait on him. He had not expected to experience the baronial style. There were garden flowers on the further bank of the moat and James took long walks before eating massive country breakfasts. He was taken to nearby Le Perthuis, the *maison de campagne* in which Blanche Childe's mother lived, the Baronne de Triqueti, a robust woman of 80. She had 'the strength of an ox' and took a great liking to the brown-bearded American, inviting him to stay with her. After a breakfast at the Baronne's, 'the most heroic and succulent *déjeuner de province*', James decided that 'under her roof I should have died in thirty-six hours of an indigestion of game and melons'. The landscapes were Lambinet, Troyon, Daubigny, Diaz, all silvery lights and vivid greens. He liked Le Perthuis with its grass plateau, bordered on one side by a short avenue of horse-chestnuts and on the other by a dusky wood. Beyond the trees were the steep russet-roofed yellow-walled farm buildings and a stretch of turf where he watched the farm-servants play at bowls on Sundays. From the windows of the drawing room he looked out at the *pigeonnier*, in a corner of the garden, the old stone dovecote, a corpulent building, as broad as the base of a lighthouse, with its roof shaped like an extinguisher, and a big hole in its upper portion in and out of which a dove was always fluttering.

James was fascinated by the relics of feudal life in the region. Blanche Childe took him to visit the peasantry in their cottages, as charming an affair as a chapter in one of George Sand's rural tales. 'We made a dozen visits, in a dozen queer little smoke-blackened big-bedded, big-clocked kitchens, and everywhere I was charmed with the nature of the people – with their good manners, quaintness and *bonhomie*, and the way they did the honours of their little huts.' This was a 'thrifty, grasping, saving, prospering France, where alone the commercial disasters of the day are not felt. Some of the "peasants" we saw are worth sixty and eighty thousand dollars made franc by franc.' They had 'the instinct of civility' and a talent for conversation. He liked the women in particular: they struck him as possessing 'a stronger expression of the qualities of the race' than the men. He called on the local curé whose drawing room reminded James of a Yankee parlour. It had a rude stone image of the virgin; and he listened to the curé talk about his parishioners, their morals, their piety. James was charmed by the local country street – he liked its name, the *Promenade des Belles Manières*.

In the Childe household was a handsome boy, with long eyelashes, an orphan nephew, the son of Édouard de Triqueti, a young painter of the family, who had died in a riding accident. Henry took a great liking to him, and was to know him later as Paul Harvey, diplomat and man of letters (still later the learned compiler of the *Oxford Companion to English Literature*). An attractive boy, a country house, a tower, a valet: there seems to be here an early coming together of elements which would figure in one of James's most famous tales, *The Turn of the Screw.*

4

At the end of August, James decided to visit south-western France. He went directly to Biarritz but found it crowded and unpleasant. He retreated to Bayonne and stayed a week. Unseasonal rains proved depressing and James decided to return to Paris. Before doing this he crossed to San Sebastian and enjoyed a brief glimpse of Spain. He studied a life-sized Virgin in a church with a flamboyant façade and felt that she was as solid as a character in Cervantes; in fact, he said in his travel-sketch,

I addressed her as Doña Maria of the Holy Office; whereupon she looked round the great dusky, perfumed church, to see whether we were alone, and then she dropped her fringed eyelids and held out her hand to be kissed. She was the sentiment of Spanish catholicism; gloomy, yet bedizened, emotional as a woman and mechanical as a doll. After a moment I grew afraid of her, and went slinking away.

In Bayonne he found the Childes, whom he had visited so recently. They were staying at a castle above the town, the Casa Caradoc, and James was invited to dine. 'I enjoyed the dinner,' he wrote to his father, 'in spite of my taking it hard to see a depressed English governess sitting in servitude to French people.' And then, with the Childes, their hosts, and a couple of young officers from the local garrison he went once again to San Sebastian to see a bull-fight. He liked the spectacle; the ladies who sat beside him often yawned, but never shuddered. He liked the toreadors as well, 'yet I thought the bull, in any case, a finer fellow than any of his tormentors, and I thought his tormentors finer fellows than the spectators'. James's summer had begun with an abortive duel; and it ended with a bull-fight. 'A bull-fight will, to a certain extent, bear looking at, but it will not bear thinking of.' He never visited Spain again.

67

A Channel Crossing

HENRY JAMES returned to Paris on 15 September 1876 and discovered that, despite his precautions, his apartment had been let. He was promised another, on the fourth floor, but would have to wait until it was vacated. He accordingly took a room in the Rue de Beaune, in Lowell's old hotel, and certain final pages of *The American* were written there. A few days later he moved outside the city, to St Germain-en-Laye, where he stayed at the Pavilion Louis XIV. He worked quietly here until he was able on 29 September to move into his rooms. He saw the Bootts off to Italy, and had a desire to go south himself. He had decided, however, that he would attempt a second winter in the French capital. In the high *salon* of his new quarters, at 29 Rue de Luxembourg, a room in which there was a black-framed Empire portrait-medallion suspended in the centre of each white panel, he worked on the last intalments of his novel. The Indian summer was beautiful: his casement windows were always open, and once more the 'thin, quick, quite feminine surface-breathing of Paris' provided the final accompaniment to the sad ending of Christopher Newman's romance. In the last pages Newman, on an impulse, crosses the Channel to visit England. The same impulse now came to James.

He had for some months, in his letters home, shown signs of impatience with France. Like Newman, he seems quite simply to have lost interest. A long letter to William, written from Etretat, gives the more extreme expression of his feelings: his satiety with the French mind, his belief that all he had got out of France was a great deal of the Boulevard and 'third rate Americanism'. He had gone so often to the Théâtre Français, he said, that he knew its repertoire by heart. He had done with the French, he told his brother, 'and am turning English all over'. A more moderate statement was written to his mother that autumn. He felt, he said, that another six months of Paris would suffice. 'Charming and supremely easy it is, on its material side, but (as I have found it) – most innutritive on its social. Still, anyone who has ever lived in Paris will always have a corner of affection for it in his heart and will often go back.'

By the time he had written the last words of his novel he had made up his mind. His recollection of this period of transition is recorded in his journal :

I settled myself again in Paris – or attempted to do so; I had no intention of giving it up. But there were difficulties in the Rue de Luxembourg – I couldn't get back my old apartment, which I had given up during the Summer. I don't remember what suddenly brought me to the point of saying – 'Go to; I will try London.' I think a letter from William had a good deal to do with it, in which he said, 'Why don't you? – That must be the place.' A single word from outside often moves one (moves *me* at least) more than the same word infinitely multiplied as a simple voice from within. I *did* try it.

Although his mind was made up early in November he remained for almost a month. He renewed his friendship with Zhukovski, the Princess Ourousov, and the Nikolai Turgenevs. He was delighted to see Mrs Mason again. But for his 'flimsy compatriots' he felt a complete indifference : the idea, indeed, of beginning to play at 'society' with them once more was intolerable. He no longer had his *Tribune* correspondence, which might have justified a continued sojourn. 'There is nothing else, for me personally, on the horizon,' he told Quincy Street, 'and it is rather ignoble to stay in Paris simply for the restaurants.'

He had written a long article on Balzac before taking up residence in the French capital. And now, on the eve of leaving, he wrote another. This time he reviewed Balzac's letters, lately published. They fired his imagination. For the first time the story of Balzac's fierce dedication, his methods of work, his stubborn professionalism, his grandiose sense of *métier*, was told in detail. Certain phrases from the letters were to be echoed again and again by James in his correspondence with his family during the coming years. He seems to have been fascinated by Balzac's Napoleonic promises to those nearest him : glory justified everything, glory would pay for everything. James saw in this a 'magnificent egotism' and an 'incomparable power'. As he prepared to cross the Channel he could say to himself that he had now fully mastered the lesson of Balzac. He too could possess, as artist, a kind of massive self-sufficiency; he too was not to be swayed from his course where his craft was concerned; and he too would try to fill Quincy Street with the reflected rays of the glory he was certain he would attain. Ambitious and resolute, James left Paris without regrets. This was but one more step in his advancing career. He had 'tried' New York. He had by now spent a full year in France. He was about to try London. In his journal a single sentence offers the best reason for his departure: 'I saw that I should be an eternal outsider.'

James crossed the Channel – Boulogne to Folkestone – on 10 December 1876.* The Parisian weather was beautiful to the last. It was hard to leave. He had retraced his steps to the now-familiar Rue de Douai and found Ivan Sergeyevich as he had often found him, stretched out on his green sofa, with his gouty foot. The Russian was as affectionate as ever. He talked in great detail of *Virgin Soil*. James asked him to give the English translation rights to his friend T. S. Perry. Turgenev willingly consented. He made James promise to write from London; he promised he would answer. '*Adieu, cher ami*,' the Russian said as they parted. The friendly words, the tone, went to James's heart. Ivan Sergeyevich had been 'adorable' to the end.

* In his journal Henry recalled that 'I went to London in November 1876.' This was, however, a slip of memory, as his correspondence reveals.

BOOK FIVE:
THE CONQUEST OF LONDON
1876–81

Part One:

A London Life

68

The Observant Stranger

'I took a lodging at 3 Bolton Street, Piccadilly,' Henry James was to write in his journal (some half-dozen years later), 'and there I have remained till today. I have *lived* much there, felt much, thought much, learned much, produced much; the little shabby furnished apartment ought to be sacred to me. I came to London as a complete stranger, and today I know much too many people. *J'y suis absolument comme chez moi.*'

He fell into London during the dark and sleety winter of 1876 as if he had lived there all his life. 'I took possession of it,' he said; and it took possession of him. Bolton Street was two streets from Half Moon Street, in the very heart of Mayfair, where he had stayed in 1869. It is a short street. One end looks out upon Green Park; the other opens into Curzon Street, where Becky Sharp lived. In his comings and goings he thought of it as her street, and Thackeray's, 'just as I was to find fifty other London neighbourhoods speak to me only with the voice, the thousand voices, of Dickens'.

He moved into his lodging on 12 December, and the next morning awoke to his first domestic breakfast – bacon, eggs, slices from an 'exquisite English loaf', cups of tea, served by a dark-faced maid with the voice of a duchess. 'You may imagine the voluptuous glow in which such a repast has left me,' he wrote to Alice. To his mother he wrote: 'I am very glad I wasted no more time in Paris. I shall work here much more and much better, and make an easier subsistence.'

Although his windows on the first floor looked on to the street and he had a balcony, it could scarcely be said that he had 'a view'; at best he could obtain a sideways glimpse of Green Park. He used to sit writing with a featureless, sooty, brown brick wall facing him across the way, the wall of a great house, Lord Ashburton's. James spoke of his 'dark back-bedroom' and 'dim front sitting room'. For him, however, the rooms had 'a vast convenient neutrality', like the curtain of a private theatre. When he went out into London, the curtain rose.

It rose on a city that endlessly delighted him. The season was dark and wet; the fog was 'glutinous', as if Thames mud had been spread in solution over the house-tops and chimney-pots. And yet James experienced a contentment he had never known in Paris. 'I like the place,' he told his mother; 'I like feeling in the midst of the English world, however lost in it I may be; I find it interesting, inspiring, even exhilarating.' He took long walks in the rain. He brought home armfuls of books from Mudie's Library and read them by his fire. Sometimes it was so dark that he had to light his candles at noon. Whatever mood the dark and the fog induced, he felt that London was 'on the whole the most possible form of life' – that is, for one who took it as he did. 'I take it,' he wrote, 'as an artist and a bachelor; as one who has the passion of observation and whose business is the study of human life.' New York's streets had been 'fatal to the imagination', and besides he had had to work too hard. Paris was bright and spacious, but he did not feel at home there. London, in spite of its 'agglomerated immensity', became 'home'. It was 'ugly, dusky, dreary, more destitute than any European city of graceful and decorative incident'. Brown brick house-walls stretched for miles in perpetual monotony, corroded with soot and fog, pierced with stiff straight slits that figured as windows. The light leaking and filtering from the cloud-ceiling turned harshness into softness, gave subtle tones to objects and buildings, created beautiful pictorial effects. London was certainly 'not agreeable, or cheerful, or easy, or exempt from reproach', and yet, James added, 'it is only magnificent'. It was 'the most complete compendium of the world'. The human race was better represented in it than anywhere else. It was a veritable kingdom for a novelist. A generation of French writers had had their Paris, and Balzac had made it his world. James would have his London world. He would assimilate its streets, its clubs, its society. It was the London of Defoe, of Dr Johnson, of Dickens, of Thackeray : there was no reason why it could not become, by a process of observation and absorption, the city of a transatlantic stranger, an American, born in New York, who as a boy in 14th Street had read *Punch* and the English novelists.

I

When James tried later to recall the beginnings of his London life, he noted that 'little by little I came to know people, to dine out, etc. I did, I was able to do, nothing at all to bring this state of things about; it came rather of itself.' This was true. But that cold December, when all London seemed like a great grey Babylon, he made certain initial overtures to mitigate possible loneliness. Shortly after his arrival he got into touch with a young Englishman named Benson, who had visited the James family in Quincy Street. Benson promptly invited him to lunch at the Oxford and Cambridge Club and introduced him to Andrew Lang who, 'though a Scotchman, seemed quite a delightful fellow'. Henry called also on G. W. Smalley, the London correspondent of the *New York Tribune* whom he had met in Paris. Smalley 'has a very pretty house and wife, and is very civil'. There was also a young Englishman whom James had met the previous summer at Etretat, Theodore Child, a graduate of Merton who wrote for the *Pall Mall Gazette*. Child invited Henry to lunch with him at the Arts Club on Christmas Eve 1876. He was Jewish, and James had hitherto known few Jews: he conceived of them as he had known them in certain plays and novels – outlandish, with beaked Shylockean noses and Fagin-like beards: Child did not fit the stereotype. He was lively, literary, aesthetic. Henry wrote to his mother that he was 'a Jew and has a nose', but he added that he was 'handsome and looks very much like Daniel Deronda'. They distinctly liked each other and this was the beginning of a rewarding friendship.

If these sociabilities promised well for London, that Christmas was perhaps the loneliest of Henry's life. The holiday fell on a weekend and he spent three solitary days in a tightly-shut city with blank streets and wet vistas of sooty bricks. His Yuletide letter to Quincy Street ended with 'your lone literary exile'. But as soon as the festivities were over, he found himself the object of traditional English hospitalities. A lady he had met at Smalley's (her name is not mentioned in his letters) invited him to a 'heavy London dinner, composed of fearful viands and people I didn't know'. Here he was introduced to Frank Hill, editor of the *Daily News*, his wife, who reviewed books, and Lady Hamilton Gordon, granddaughter of the astronomer Herschel. He was invited also to the home of Mrs Pollock, who had heard from the Smalleys that he was in London. She had read him in the *Atlantic Monthly*. 'Who she is I haven't any idea,' he wrote home; but he goes out of pure civility to discover himself in the home of the distinguished jurist and his wife, the future Sir Frederick and Lady Pollock, who would remain his friends during all his London years. At still another dinner he meets Sir

Charles Dilke, a rising political figure, and discovers their common interest in French literature. He dines in due course with the Andrew Langs, 'a very nice fellow with a pleasant graceful mind and a great facility and understanding'. He finds him the most gentlemanly of the London journalists, but Lang publishes too much, using 'his beautiful thin facility to write everything down to the lowest level of Philistine twaddle'. Dinner leads to dinner. Thus at the home of Sir William Power, K.C.B., 'a very polite and pleasant Irishman', son of Tyrone Power, the actor, he encounters the ubiquitous Mrs Cashel Hoey, cousin of the then unknown Bernard Shaw, 'a curious and interesting specimen of the wondrous type – the London female literary hack'.

'I am getting quite into the current of London life,' Henry wrote to Quincy Street. He had been in England barely six weeks.

2

As he began to see London interiors and the comfortable side of the Victorian world, he could not help contrasting them with the raw London through which he often walked late in the evening after dining out. He had had glimpses of it from carriages during his childhood, seen it then as Dickens's London : but now it seemed to him rather the London of Hogarth. There were too many gin-shops, 'too many miserable women at their doorsteps; too many, far too many, dirty-faced children, sprawling between one's legs'. Also the young ladies of these neighbourhoods were too ardent, 'too addicted to violent forms of coquetry'. And one dark night, against the dismal background of fog and sleet, James came upon 'a horrible old woman in a smoky bonnet, lying prone in a puddle of whisky'. The vision struck him as symbolic. 'She almost frightened me away,' he wrote.

He had seen poverty and squalor in many forms in France and Italy. But it had a certain out-of-door picturesqueness. In London it became 'the hard prose of misery'. Strolling at Easter into a crowded Westminster Abbey, he was driven away by an odour that 'was not that of incense'. Proceeding early one March morning to Barnes Bridge to watch the Oxford and Cambridge boat race, he stood in the midst of 'a dingy British mob, with coal smoke ground into its pores'. The landscape was sodden and dank; the view was of taverns, railway-bridges and Thames mud. In this setting the only aesthetic experience was the sudden view of the two crews – 'great white water-swimming birds, with eight feathered wings' caught in the morning light. Later, spending a day at Epsom and watching the Derby, James was struck by the general intoxication of the crowd. He found the women 'too stout, too hot, too red, too thirsty, too boisterous, too strongly accoutred'.

The crude state of poverty in London gave Henry pause. He was struck by 'the rigidly aristocratic constitution of society; the un-aesthetic temper of the people; the private character of most kinds of comfort and entertainment'. The Victorian world was carefully organized to preserve – to reinforce – respect for traditional insti-tutions. This was one way of maintaining national stability. To a member of America's upper middle class, where society was in a state of flux, England's codes and rules, and its stratified class-structure, proved a revelation. They gave Henry a standard by which he could greatly enlarge the process, begun long ago, of comparing peoples and manners. Church and State, Religion and Science, Pro-gress and Poverty, God, Duty, Immortality and British Domestic Virtue – all seemed to have their firm and hierarchic place in Vic-torian England :

In the sight of the English people getting up from its tea and toast of a Sunday morning and brushing its hat, and drawing on its gloves, and taking its wife on its arm, and making its offspring march before, and so, for decency's, respectability's, propriety's sake, taking its way to a place of worship appointed by the State, in which it repeats the formulas of a creed to which it attaches no positive sense, and listens to a sermon over the length of which it explicitly haggles and grumbles – in this exhibition there is something very striking to a stranger, something which he hardly knows whether to regard as a great force or a great infirmity.

Surely, James reflected, this was a conformity as starched as Prus-sian militarism.

The thought occurred to him that in a nation in which the explo-sive force of the British personality was repressed to this extent, there had to be some safety-valve. Where had the Britons placed the 'fermenting idiosyncrasies' that had been corked down? He did not find an immediate answer : but he was to see it in due course, in the Piccadilly riots, the Irish agitation, the Dilke scandal, the Parnell case, the trial of Oscar Wilde.

Now he stood in Trafalgar Square and watched the Queen – no longer the slim, small woman of his boyhood, but an ample widowed matron – ride in state to open the Parliament over which Disraeli presided and where in a matter of weeks she would be proclaimed Empress of India. He noted at the same time that, on the other side of the square, men marched with placards and banners expressing various forms of social unrest and focusing them through demands for the release from prison of the Tichborne claimant.

'The upper classes are too refined,' James was to write, 'and the lower classes are too miserable.' The judgement may have seemed to him in later years too summary, too unsubtle. His revising pen altered it to 'The better sort are too "genteel," and the inferior sort too base.' This might be the measure of the distance he was to travel from Bolton Street into the life of England's leisured class.

3

James would become the historian of 'the better sort'. But he was not to lose sight altogether of the Hogarthian London of this early time. He was to ask himself, during ensuing years, what life would be like to one who had not had his own singular good fortune: he had found in England 'freedom and ease, knowledge and power, money, opportunity and satiety'; he was to acknowledge in his late memoirs that he had had 'an excess of opportunities'. For him the doors of London opened 'into light and warmth and cheer, into good and charming relations'. Yet the place 'as a whole lay heavy on one's consciousness'. And this heaviness James tried to deal with and understand in the brooding novel of his middle years, *The Princess Casamassima*, which he described as having its origin in his habit of walking the streets 'during the first year of a long residence in London'. He had walked a good deal, 'for exercise, for amusement, for acquisition and above all I always walked home at the evening's end, when the evening had been spent elsewhere, as happened more often than not'. And he added: 'One walked of course with one's eyes greatly open.' His observation of poverty and high life in England was that of an intellectual and a humanitarian; it was not that of a reformer. He had called himself in his earlier English articles 'the sentimental tourist'. He called himself now 'the observant stranger'.

He insisted upon the 'stranger'. He had no desire to change his status of outsider, even though he was to become identified with much of English life. As he explained to Charles Eliot Norton, 'I am not at all Anglicized, but I am thoroughly Londonized – a very different thing.' As an 'observant stranger' he could describe without necessarily passing judgement; he could also compare; he could – as he was about to demonstrate – satirize Americans with the same ease as the English. But he had no desire to be a satirist. His forte was irony. Later when Lizzie Boott praised his English sketches, he said he had sought 'the happy medium of irony – to be ironical enough without being too much so'. To his friend Perry he wrote that when he would make a book of these essays it would be 'very complimentary and urbane', but it would also have 'many *sousentendus* and much reserve'. He confessed that he had withheld a great many impression. 'One can't say everything when one is settling down to enjoy the hospitality, as it were, of a country.'

One couldn't say everything; nevertheless James managed to say a great deal. His remarks contained nothing that had not been said in one form or another by Arnold, or Ruskin, or Morris, or by du Maurier in his caricatures, or by Gilbert in the verses Sullivan set to music. James could describe British philistinism as readily as Matthew Arnold. But what happened now was that he began to make certain comparisons; he could on the one hand compare London with Paris; even more, he was studying a social structure of such strength and depth that he was enabled to indulge in comparative study of Anglo-American manners. British responsibility, British leisure, British traditions, the longevity of British institutions, could be compared with American irresponsibility, American failure to enjoy leisure, the as yet comparative absence of tradition, and above all the absence of *standards* generally. On the other hand James's patience with the British upper classes often wore thin; and he rejoiced in American forthrightness. When William wrote to him that as an American he should be studying life in Washington rather than London, he replied that he would come to this in good time. 'I know what I am about,' he wrote, 'and I have always my eyes on my native land.'

To Grace Norton he was to write on 7 July 1878 :

In one sense I feel intimately at home here, and in another sense I feel – as an American may be on the whole very willing, at times, very glad, to feel – like a complete outsider. There are some English institutions and idiosyncrasies that it is certainly a great blessing to be outside of. But I suppose one may claim to feel at home in a place when it ceases to be a land of mystery and vagueness – when one's impressions have become continuous and mutually consistent. I have learned a good deal about British manners and the British mind (thinking on the whole finely of the latter and meanly of the former) – and they no longer have any terrors – or even perplexities – to me. There are times indeed when I seem to myself to carry all England in my breeches pocket.

Again and again he spoke of liking London as 'a big city and a regular basis of mundane existence', but he adds that he sometimes gets 'woefully tired of its people and their talk. There seems something awfully stale and stupid about the whole business.' To his mother he writes at another moment that he finds English society 'a collection of mediocrities, mounted upon the pedestal of their wealth, their family, their respectability, their consecrated habits etc.' To be sure, he adds, it could be said that 'the great stock of society is everywhere a set of mediocrities and that those who have pedestals are better than those who haven't'. And so complaining, he continued his London round; it might bore him, but it also fascinated; he found it difficult to stop being an observant stranger.

'It was, in fine, dear Charles,' he wrote to his friend Norton ultimately,

a very happy inspiration of mine, two years since, to come to London to live; so thoroughly have I attached myself to its mighty variety and immensity, so interesting do I find the spectacle of English life, so well do I get on, on the whole, with people and things, so successfully, on the whole, do I seem to myself to assimilate the total affair.

He had a real tenderness for the 'personal character of the people. It seems to me many times the strongest and richest race in the world – my dream is to arrive at the ability to be, in some degree, its moral portrait-painter'.

4

And this indeed he became, although he was to paint even more successfully the moral portrait of Anglo-American manners and relations : to paint them once and for all, so that his pictures were as prophetic as they were real. The man who dissected the nature of the international marriage and pictured the young American beauties trailing through Europe to become duchesses and princesses did not explicitly foresee the time when a cinema star might occupy a small European throne; but he in effect predicted it, for it is as implicit in his stories as the ultimate marriage of a British king to a Baltimore woman. 'For a Bostonian nymph to reject an English duke is an adventure only less stirring, I should say, than for an English duke to reject a Bostonian nymph,' he wrote in his essay on the art of fiction.

The tales James wrote during the first year of his residence in England, no less than his essays, testify to his accuracy of observation. Only a man who had 'successfully' assimilated the total affair could write stories which foreshadowed as well as depicted the manners and customs of international society. And it was with the same accuracy that James, at the end of his first year in Bolton Street, wrote a prophetic letter to his brother William. The passage begins with his discussion of the continuing fear of England's involvement in the Russo-Turkish war. He had been dining out, and had listened to army men indulging in 'the densest war talk'. In the light of his close attention to the talk, he went on to tell William that he wasn't sure he could accept the arguments of peace at any price :

At any rate I believe that England will keep out of war for the reason that up to this stage of her relation to events in the East, her going to war would be simply for the sake of her 'prestige', and that the nation as a whole, looking at the matter deliberately, have decided that mere prestige is not sufficient ground for a huge amount of bloodshed. This seems to me to indicate a high pitch of civilization – a pitch which England alone, of all the European nations, has reached. It has been curious to see that all the French republican papers have lately been denouncing her fiercely for not pitching into Russia – the defence of prestige being a perfectly valid *casus belli* to the French mind.

And then came the prophecy :

It certainly remains to be seen whether in material respects England can afford to abdicate even such a privilege as that. I have a sort of feeling that if we are to see the *déchéance* of England it is inevitable, and will come to pass somewhat in this way. She will push further and further her non-fighting and keeping-out-of-scrapes-policy, until contemptuous Europe, growing audacious with impunity, shall put upon her some supreme and unendurable affront. Then – too late – she will rise ferociously and plunge clumsily and unpreparedly into war. She will be worsted and laid on her back – and when she is laid on her back will exhibit – in her colossal wealth and pluck – an unprecedented power of resistance. But she will never really recover as a European power.

This, said James, was 'the vision I sometimes entertain, and which events, doubtless, will consummately bring to naught'. By the time 1914 came he had probably forgotten his prediction: and in our own time we can look back at the Battle of Britain and see how Henry James, more than half a century before, understood and spoke – almost in Churchillian cadences – of the deepest nature of the people in whose midst he made his home. Where James erred was in a further remark in this letter that Britain's 'stubbornly aristocratic social arrangements' made compulsory military service in England difficult against a Europe armed to the teeth: gentlemen would not stand in the same ranks with peasants, servants, town boys – cads in short. Perhaps from the moment in the Victorian era in which he was speaking he was right. He could not foresee the levelling that was to occur in the twentieth century, or perhaps he misread here the unifying power of an enemy. The passage testifies however to James's saturation and his uncanny ability to see reality and to read its meaning. This was possible in all matters in which his deepest personal emotions were not touched – where he could be distant, detached, surgically analytical.

69

London Clubs

JOHN LOTHROP MOTLEY, nearing the end of a busy life as historian and diplomat, called on his fellow-countryman in Bolton Street early in February 1877 to tell him that he had put him on the honorary list of The Athenaeum. This meant that James had temporary access to a club in England which gathered under its substantial roof in Pall Mall the nation's eminent men of letters, philosophers and churchmen. He had hitherto had little experience of clubs. Elected to the Century in New York two years before, he had never had occasion to take his place in that association of artists and amateurs. On his arrival in London he had briefly used the Savile, thanks to Smalley of the *Tribune*, as he was later to have temporary access to the Travellers' and the St James's. At the Athenaeum he could not only dine sociably at the end of a long day's writing, but he had the use as well of a fine library and occasion to meet certain of his transatlantic peers. He had complained to T. S. Perry that London was less convenient than Paris for a 'lonely celibate'. The club admirably extended his sense of home; it was, so to speak, a luxurious annexe to his lodgings. 'Such lounges and easy chairs!' he exclaimed to Quincy Street. As he settled down into one of them he pronounced the Athenaeum 'the last word of a high civilization'.

'I am writing this in the beautiful great library,' he told his father in a letter on the club's stationery of 13 February 1877.

On the other side of the room sits Herbert Spencer, asleep in a chair (he always is, whenever I come here) and a little way off is the portly Archbishop of York with his nose in a little book. It is 9.30 p.m. and I have been dining here. An old gentleman put himself at the table next to me and soon began to talk about the 'autumn tints' in America – knowing, heaven knows how, that I came thence. Presently he informed me that he was the son of Sir Richard Westmacott, the sculptor; and that the old gentleman on the other side of him was a nephew of Lord Nelson etc. etc. I give you this for local colour (it is a great blessing, by the way, to be able to dine here, where the dinner is good and cheap. I was seeing arrive the day when London restaurants, whose badness is literally fabulous, would become impossible, and the feeding question a problem so grave as to drive me from the land. I am not sure that some day it won't).

There were to be other intimate glimpses in his early club life. Remembering his Thackeray, Henry relished describing to his sister the dignitaries sprawling or reading their papers – 'all the great chairs and lounges and sofas filled with men having afternoon tea – lolling back with their laps filled with magazines, journals, and fresh Mudie books, while amiable flunkies in knee-breeches present them the divinest salvers of tea and buttered toast'. And seeing certain of Alice's favourite authors at the club he proceeded to satirize them :

Lecky the historian, and Green ditto (author of Alice's favourite work – the fat volume which she gave me) have just come and seated themselves in front of me : two such grotesque specimens of the rickety, intellectual Oxford cad that I can't forbear mentioning them. Only du Maurier, in *Punch*, could do them justice; and if Alice could see in the flesh her little wizened, crawling Green, with eyes like ill-made button-holes, she would take to her bed for a month and renounce her 'historic-reveries'. The delights of London are only equalled by its disillusionments.

The London club was to become for the bachelor of Bolton Street a necessity, a means by which he gave himself a more spacious existence. He could meet and make friends; he could entertain fellow-writers and reciprocate certain hospitalities; it was a place as fundamental to his existence as the old coffee-houses had been to an earlier London. Unfortunately his access to the Athenaeum had its term. For some time he went to the Travellers', thanks to Charles Milnes Gaskell and Frederick Locker; and for a good while to the St James's, haunt of young diplomats. In all he was guest in seven London clubs before his election to one he could call his own. This happened much more promptly than he anticipated. Before he had been six months in England he was put up for the Reform Club by Frank Hill of the *Daily News* and C. H. Robarts. The Reform was the Athenaeum's neighbour in Pall Mall, the club of the country's liberals in the political and literary walks of life. It could not boast as many celebrities as the Athenaeum, but it was one of the best clubs in the capital, and materially 'the most comfortable corner of the world'. He was elected in May 1878, with the help of Sir Charles Dilke, 'who, poor man, appears to have found time (up to his neck in the House of Commons as he is) to read and be "struck" by my French essays'.

'*J'y suis, j'y reste* – forever and a day,' he announced triumphantly to his father and drew £42 on his letter of credit to pay his entrance-fee. He told his sister that his election had 'doubled my "selfhood", as Father would say', and added, 'bookless and houseless as I am, it is a great blessing, and since my election I have done nothing but sit there and read Jowett's Plato and Beaumont and Fletcher'.

70

The Bird of Paradox

HENRY ADAMS had sent James a letter of introduction to Richard Monckton Milnes, Lord Houghton. Characteristically enough, the English peer invited him to one of his familiar breakfasts before James had a chance to use the letter. Lord Houghton's breakfasts were legendary. The 'bird of paradox' was a great collector of cele-brities. Henry Adams considered him 'the first wit in London, and a maker of men – of a great many men', and he would write in the *Education* : 'A word from him went far. An invitation to his breakfast-table went farther.' Monckton Milnes had written verses as a young man and had been Keats's first champion. In Parliament his speeches had been too literary. He had, said Adams, an 'almost Falstaffian mask and laugh of Silenus'. But Adams had known him during the earlier decades. In 1877 Lord Houghton was 68, a little rusty but still as eager a collector of celebrities for his breakfasts as he was of rare volumes and erotica. He had cultivated the art of being a man of the world, almost as if this were a profession. Disraeli, disguising him as Mr Vavasour in *Tancred*, had written : 'Mr Vavasour's breakfasts were renowned. Whatever your creed, class or country – one might almost add your character – you were a welcome guest at his matutinal meal, provided you were celebrated. That qualification was rigidly enforced.'

We may judge then that by Lord Houghton's standard Henry James could consider himself a celebrity – or certainly on his way to becoming one. The breakfast-groups could hardly be said to resemble Flaubert's *cénacle*; fame rather than dedication to art seemed the fundamental criterion. However, they were occasions for pleasant talk, high gossip and a kind of extended fellowship among 'personalities'. Henry never compared it with the Saturday Club to which his father belonged in Boston; and yet one might have seen an analogy – with the distinction that in Boston the faces were nearly always the same, while at Lord Houghton's there was endless rotation and variety. We have no record of the men James met at the first breakfast he attended. He seems by that time – a bare twelve weeks after settling in London – to have become sufficiently blasé about such occasions. He had been discovering that most of the Englishmen he met were, as he told Quincy Street, 'of the "useful-information" prosaic sort'. There is a note of world-weariness in his speaking of the first breakfast to William as composed of half a dozen men 'all terribly "useful-informationish," and whose names and faces I have forgotten'. But he is bidden again by Lord Houghton to another gathering, the Cosmopolitan, a kind of 'talking club, extremely select', and here he encounters, amid a little knot of parliamentary folk, his fellow-passenger of two years before, Anthony Trollope.

James found Lord Houghton to be 'very kind and paternal' and

a battered and world-wrinkled old mortal, with a restless and fidgety vanity, but with an immense fund of real kindness and humane feeling. He is not personally fascinating, though as a general thing he talks very well, but I like his sociable, democratic, sympathetic, inquisitive old temperament. Half the human race, certainly everyone that one has ever heard of, appears sooner or later to have stayed at Fryston Hall. This represents an immense expenditure of hospitality and curiosity, trouble and general benevolence.

By the time James wrote this he had passed from being a breakfast-guest to a dinner-guest and to visiting Lord Houghton in the country. At one dinner he encountered Tennyson, Gladstone, and the excavator of Troy, Dr Heinrich Schliemann, James sat next but one to Tennyson. He described the Bard as swarthy and scraggy and less handsome than he appeared in his photograph. He talked exclusively of port wine and tobacco; 'he seems to know much about them, and can drink a whole bottle of port at a sitting with no incommodity'. He had a strange simplicity, 'and seemed altogether like a creature of some primordial English stock, a thousand miles away from American manufacture'. James continued:

Behold me after dinner conversing affably with Mr Gladstone – not by my own seeking, but by the almost importunate affection of Lord Houghton. But I was glad of a chance to feel the 'personality' of a great political leader – or as G. is now thought here even, I think, by his partisans, an ex-leader. That of Gladstone is very fascinating – his urbanity extreme – his eye that of a man of genius – and his apparent self-surrender to what he is talking of, without a flaw. He made a great impression on me – greater than anyone I have seen here though 'tis perhaps owing to my naïveté, and unfamiliarity with statesmen.

In very little time Henry James found himself considered not merely an 'item' in Lord Houghton's celebrity-collection, but a personal friend. The 'collector' asked James for an introduction to Turgenev and Flaubert. The American suggested Turgenev might introduce Lord Houghton to Flaubert. He also wrote to Flaubert; it is the only letter extant from James to the French novelist. He speaks of his memories of Flaubert's Sundays and 'les causeries auxquelles j'assistais un peu en étranger mais bien en admirateur'. He asks Flaubert to introduce Houghton to Zola, whom he wanted particularly to meet. To Lord Houghton he explained that Flaubert was 'the only one of ces messieurs with whom I established personal relations', adding he was certain 'the others won't do me the honour to remember me'.

He also pointedly told Houghton he was leaving the letters of introduction open 'according to the rules of American civility – which has more rules than are commonly supposed'.

71

An Autumn Journey

HENRY JAMES firmly established himself in the London world between the time of his first solitary Christmas in 1876 and the Easter of 1877. Since he was unable to place a serial while *The American* was appearing, he continued to support himself by fugitive writing and he sold ten articles during that year to the *Galaxy*, for which he received $1,200. Four of them completed his French series begun in 1875 with the essay on Balzac; one dealt with his previous summer in France; five were devoted to his discovery of England. He was also able to place three articles for the first time in *Lippincott's*, and these, with his usual writings for the *Nation* (which yielded him about $400), brought his earnings for 1877 to about $2,500. With the prospect of a serial for the *Atlantic* in 1878, James felt at ease financially and was able to plan a trip to the Continent. He wanted above all to re-visit Italy.

He remained in London until midsummer and then discovered the pleasures of country visits. Henry Adams had urged him to stay with his friend Charles Milnes Gaskell, and when he received the invitation he gladly went to Wenlock Abbey, a ruin in Shropshire, partly restored and modernized, where he spent several pleasant days. 'You feast on the pictorial, you inhale the historic,' James wrote. 'It is not too much to say that after spending 24 hours in a house that is 600 years old, you seem yourself to have lived in it for 600 years.' He enjoyed the sensation of stepping from the medieval stone gallery – where the monks used to pace – into a modern drawing-room. Another invitation to visit friends in Warwickshire was gladly accepted, and James found himself in a great house, in an immense park, where there were grazing deer and massive ancient oaks. He mingled with some fifteen friendly guests, and 'the combination of the spacious, lounging, talking-all-day life, the beautiful place, the dinner-party each night, the walk to church across such ideal meadow paths with such a lovely young Miss Bouverie (the product of similar agréments in Devonshire) – all this was excellent of its kind'.

Still in Warwickshire, he stayed with the Carters (Mrs Carter being a sister of James's Parisian friend Eleanor Strong) at 'The Spring', near Kenilworth. Mr Carter was an ardent Liberal, 'extremely intelligent and high-toned, devoted to workingmen's clubs, snubbing the parson, buying out taverns etc.' (We catch a glimpse of him later in *Lady Barberina*.) The place was small and charming, and across the lawn, from the drawing-room window, James looked straight at the world of Sir Walter Scott, the romantic mass of Kenilworth Castle. He began his visit by going to a party at the old rectory and dancing all evening with shy, rosy Warwickshire maidens. 'The women dance ill,' he told Lizzie Boott, 'but they are soft and clinging.' Another day the party went to Stratford to visit Mrs Kemble's second daughter, Mrs James Leigh, who lived 'in a divine old rambling, wainscotted, brown-chambered manor house' on the Avon. Mrs Leigh, wife of a clergyman, talked much to James of Philadelphia and her nostalgia for the Georgia rice-fields.

I

Before crossing to the Continent the novelist gathered together his French essays – as William had long ago urged him to do – and sent the manuscript to the firm of Macmillan, which had expressed an interest in publishing him in England. He had not thus far brought out a book or published an article in the country now his home, although certain of his volumes had been imported into England and in a few instances reviewed in a temperate if condescending way. The reviews had noted his advent upon the American literary scene, praised his accuracy of observation and felicities of style, criticized his characterizations and measured him in general by the standards of Victorian fiction. They found plot and story wanting, and an excess of character-analysis instead of incident. However, only about eight notices of any length had appeared in England since the publication of James's first volume of tales. He was, in other words, largely unknown. In the United States he had built up a reputation by a long process of periodical publication, and during the past two years by the appearance of two novels, his tales and his travel-book. There existed thus for James a serious problem : what sort of début should he make in England, where he would, so to speak, come before the reading public 'cold'. In the United States he could hold his own among his fellow-writers; but in the land of Dickens, Trollope, Thackeray, George Eliot he seemed to have felt his way with care. He had remarked some months earlier to T. S. Perry that if the British 'want a novelist, they want also a critic'. He could offer them both, but it probably seemed to him that the most cautious thing he could do would be to publish this modest volume of essays. He no longer considered *Roderick Hudson* suitable; he felt he could do much better. He apparently was not sure that *The American*, just out in Boston and New York in book-form, was good enough; it had been written too hastily. A volume of essays could not injure his reputation as a writer of fiction – and he could then prepare a proper and bold entry into English literature. In other words we have the interesting spectacle of Henry James deciding with characteristic deliberation to appear in England not as a novelist but as a critic of novelists, and not as a writer of tales or of travel but as an authority on French literature, especially on French realism. Indeed, he seemed to think the book particularly suited for the English, since he never published it in the United States. He accordingly deposited a manuscript titled *French Poets and Novelists* at the offices of the Macmillans, and left for the Continent.

2

First there was Paris. The city glistened in the September sun. The Parisians had cut a wide boulevard from the ornate Opéra to the chastely-columned Théâtre Français – the Avénue de l'Opéra – knocking out many old streets familiar to James from his earlier years. The avenue was imperial, yet it substituted for things old and cherished a kind of blank, pompous, featureless sameness – and the smell of asphalt! It achieved, to be sure, one splendid thing; it linked the great temple of French music at one end with the great temple of French comedy at the other.

James looked at the French people with new pleasure. They were alert, bright, vivacious. From the moment he saw the porters in their blouses on the quay at Boulogne, he felt himself rediscovering agreeable sensations. It was a pleasure to have lunch at the railway buffet; to be offered soup without having to ask for it; to find a pint of Bordeaux at his plate, to be given a napkin, to take up a long stick of French bread and break off a crisp, crusty morsel. In Paris he returned to the Café Riche on the boulevard for his breakfasts. The *garçon* remarked that *monsieur* had been away a long time, led him to his favourite table and brought him his usual newspaper. James noticed the familiar faces of certain habitués, sitting over their drinks or their dominoes. He was prompted to compare them with

the gentlemen he saw in the London clubs. In London he could discern a majestic social order massed behind the clubmen. What was
behind these Frenchmen was probably not adapted for exhibition.
Behind the English – whatever their personalities or even their
irregularities – there was reared an immense body of private proprieties and comforts, domestic conventions, theological observances.

He was in no hurry to reach Italy. He found a couple of shabby
rooms off the Champs-Elysées, above the Palais de l'Industrie, in the
Avénue d'Antin, with a view of tree-tops tinted by early autumn.
Here, in spite of his holiday, he did his daily writing. The rest of his
time was devoted to Paris and to his friends. His first act was to
inform Ivan Sergeyevich of his arrival. Turgenev had kept his word;
he had corresponded with James. His warm and affectionate letters
were filled with melancholy over the Russo-Turkish war. 'We have
missed you here,' he wrote when the younger man described his
London life, 'but I suppose we mustn't complain since you are, after
all, satisfied with your stay – and are able to work.' It was a question
of adaptation, 'but we would have all been so happy if you had come
back to *adapt* yourself to Paris'. *Virgin Soil* had not only been a
failure in Russia; one had even heard the word *fiasco* mentioned.
Turgenev, who usually wrote to James in French, added : '*La fortune
n'aime pas les vieillards – même en littérature.*' He had lately read
Zola's new novel, *L'Assommoir*. It wasn't immoral – it was simply
'devilishly dirty!' If he were a cartoonist for *Punch*, he would amuse
himself by drawing a cartoon captioned: 'Queen Victoria reading
L'Assommoir.'

James had reviewed *Virgin Soil* in the *Nation*, and praised the
book while recognizing that it was not the best of Turgenev. The
Russian wrote to him : 'Something was lacking in this last work
which a spirit of such fine perceptions as yours must have discerned :
a sense of freedom. I wrote always under a cloud.' James had sent
him *The American*, which Turgenev acknowledged from his country
house at Bougival, near Paris. He was despondent; things had not
gone well; his affairs were in confusion; the war preyed on his mind.
'I am so distant from all literary activity that I ask myself whether
I have ever been active – and whether it was really I who wrote
books which had a beginning, a middle and an end.' He told James
'I count on seeing you.' When he learned of his arrival he sent a note
in his rather stiff English : 'I am very glad that you are in Paris and

very desirous to see you. In my present state of mind I rather avoid to see human faces – but you are naturally an exception.' The Russian came into the city and they breakfasted at Bignou's, in the Boulevard des Italiens. Turgenev talked incessantly of the Turkish war. He expected total collapse on the part of the Russians; the badness of the generals, the viciousness of the system of having ignorant Grand-Dukes as commanders-in-chief, could produce no other result. He doubted whether such failures would result in an uprising of the Russian people. The Tsar could with impunity 'do absolutely what he chooses with them'. All this gave Ivan Sergeyevich sleepless nights and dreadful visions.

James saw Turgenev several times, visiting him in his spacious chalet at Bougival on the Seine, next to the summer home of the Viardots. On one occasion the two novelists lunched with the Nikolai Turgenevs, who were Bonapartists, and it pleased the American writer to hear the Russian novelist come up 'with a larger republican and generally liberal profession of faith than I have heard him utter before. He was magnificent.' On the whole, however, 'Russians, just now, are depressed and depressing company,' James told Quincy Street.

Elsewhere in Paris he renewed certain friendships. He dined with Theodore Child, now Paris correspondent of the *Daily Telegraph*; he saw Mrs Kemble on her way to London from her usual Swiss summer; and during this visit he became a closer friend of Henrietta Reubell, whom he had liked from their first meeting in 1876. 'Not the least poignant' of his Paris memories, he wrote when back in London, were those of the hours spent in her 'admirable little salon'.

He went as always to the theatre. One evening he saw *Le Demi-Monde* by Dumas *fils*, at the Théâtre Français, and came away with a feeling of 'lively irritation'. He had seen the play several times before. On this occasion it had been brilliantly acted by Delaunay and Mademoiselle Croizette. James found it very difficult to swallow the morality of the piece. It was one of those characteristic nineteenth-century dramas exploring the fate of a 'woman with a past' of which *La Dame aux Camélias* was the prototype. The heroine of *Le Demi-Monde* seeks to marry a respectable young man who loves her. The young man's friend, whose mistress she has been, is determined to prevent the match, and is quite prepared to tell a lie so as to make the woman compromise herself. James, walking the lamp-lit streets after the theatre, found himself wondering whether an English audience would consider this kind of conduct gentlemanly and fair. 'Madame d'Ange has blots in her life, and it is doubtless not at all proper that such ladies should be led to the altar by honourable young men.' Nevertheless an English audience, even while not condoning her irregularities, would also dislike the ungentlemanly behaviour of the former lover. He would be judged a 'meddlesome' individual, and his victim would certainly not be considered 'fair game'.

Later James found himself wondering whether he might not give another turn to the situation. What if an American lady – say with a long list of divorces – tried to crash her way into British society? What if a British matron sought to uncover the American woman's past? Would an American gentleman tell? He did not know it that September in Paris, but he had found the plot for one of his most amusing 'international' comedies, *The Siege of London*.

3

Early in October James went to Rheims to inspect the cathedral and the champagne country. Then he took the train to Turin, lingered briefly, and proceeded to Florence. He made his way to Bellosguardo, to see Francis and Lizzie Boott in their apartment at the Villa Castellani. Frank Boott showed his age; Lizzie remained charming, busy, artistic. They were 'a most friendly, lovable, pure-minded, even touching couple', and Lizzie was the same 'noiseless little active and productive force as ever'. Boott's devotion to his daughter was 'more intense and absorbing than ever and his unremitting attention to every stroke that she draws or paints, half-touching, half-amusing'.

He had had an earlier glimpse of the Villa, had even used it in *Roderick*. But this was the first time that James had had an opportunity to see the quiet life of the father and daughter on Bellosguardo, its limited nature and their constant industry, Lizzie with her painting and Frank with his music. During the week James stayed in Florence, he left his hotel by the Arno daily, passed over the Ponte Vecchio, walked to the Roman Gate, then climbed the steep and winding way to the villa along a narrow road bounded by mottled, mossy garden walls. He spent long afternoons on the sunny terrace, or sauntered along it by a moon that threw shadows on the buildings below in the softly-scooped hollow of the hills.

He knew the Bootts well enough to describe what he saw in the columns of the *Atlantic* without seeming to invade their privacy. In an article entitled *Recent Florence*, he spoke of the 'row of high-waisted cypresses', the grassy courtyard, the long serene horizontal lines of the other villas, flanked by their trees, disposed on the neighbouring hills; beyond the city the changing colours of the mountains, the shifting shadows. 'What a tranquil, contented life it seemed, with exquisite beauty as a part of its daily texture!' And he went on:

When such a life presents itself in a dull or ugly place, we esteem it, we admire it, but we do not feel it to be the ideal of good fortune. When, however, the people who lead it move as figures in an ancient, noble landscape, and their walks and contemplations are like a turning of the leaves of history, we seem to be witnessing an admirable case of virtue made easy; meaning here by virtue, contentment and concentration, the love of privacy and of study. One need not be exacting if one lives among local conditions that are of themselves constantly suggestive.

It was charming entertainment for a week: to walk about and look at the villas: Montauto with its tower, where Hawthorne had lived; the Brichieri, associated with Mrs Browning; other ample houses built with thickness of wall and depth of embrasure; to wonder at the height of the cypresses and the depth of the loggias; to walk home in the fading light noting on westward-looking walls the glow of the opposite sunset. In imagination James found himself renting each villa. And yet there seemed to be something melancholy in the place. The fanciful stranger could only murmur to himself: 'Lovely, lovely, but oh, how sad!'

The terms of this passage, the picture of the elderly man and the daughter he had reared in Italy, in the continental manner, the setting – all this appealed to Henry's mind and imagination. In writing this travel-sketch he little knew that he was recording a setting for Gilbert Osmond and his daughter Pansy. Perhaps we may discern also in the article the germ of a much later subject: for in the observed relationship of a father and a daughter he had at this early date the central personages for the ultimate *Golden Bowl*.

4

In Rome he found a little apartment in Via Capo le Case, No. 45, the 'rather ragged and besmirched establishment' of a Cavaliere Avvocato Spinetti. His rent was modest and the rooms were flooded with sunlight. On his first evening he made his pilgrimage to the Colosseum. The place seemed shrunken and prosaic. 'When even picturesqueness intermits, then fallen Empires are fallen indeed'. Rome seemed 'very modern'. As for the American circle of three years before, Story was in Boston and the Terrys had had financial reverses. James spent some hours with Mrs Tilton in the Pantaleone apartment in the Barberini, she defending the charms of Rome and he lamenting the changes. 'Rome has changed and I have changed,' he told Quincy Street. A few days later, however, he was writing to Grace Norton: 'The old enchantment, taking its own good time, steals over you and possesses you, till it becomes really a nuisance and an importunity.' He had hoped to get some work done; the sunshine and the atmosphere drew him constantly out of doors. He saw Alice Bartlett and met a Mrs Hawker, who lived in the Palazzo Bonaparte. The Bootts arrived from Florence to spend the winter in the Holy City, and five weeks slipped by. Macmillan by this time had accepted *French Poets and Novelists* and sent it to the printer; proofs would be forthcoming shortly. He reluctantly took train for the French capital.

Before leaving he recaptured the old pleasure of riding in the Campagna – the golden atmosphere, the violet mountains, the flower-strewn grass, the lonely arches crowned with wild weeds and crumbling in the sunshine. All the lost sensations were there: the cool yellow wine handed him at some suburban *osteria* as he sat in his saddle, the peasants lounging in their leather leggings, the shepherds and their flocks. His previous rides had been in the springtime. Riding now in the autumn he found certain differences: there were other kinds of flowers – the faded fields were made rosy, for instance, by 'little pink autumnal daisies'.

It may have been while they were galloping over the daisies of the Campagna, or one evening while they were together with the Bootts. At some point Alice Bartlett had occasion to mention an episode which had occurred in Rome during the previous winter. Her anecdote concerned a simple and uninformed American woman who had been trailing through the hotels of Europe with a young daughter, 'a child of nature and freedom'. The girl picked up, with the best conscience in the world, a good-looking Roman 'of a rather vague identity'. The Italian seemed astonished at his luck. He was serenely exhibited, and introduced, in the Victorian-Roman-American society, where 'dating' was much less relaxed than it is today. Miss Bartlett seems to have furnished few details. There had been some social setback, some snub administered to the innocent girl. Henry's pencil made a brief record of this seemingly trivial anecdote.

5

One of the first things that confronted him on his return to England, on all the railway book-stalls, was a pirated edition of *The American* with a dramatic picture on the cover showing tall Christopher Newman, flanked by Valentin de Bellegarde carrying a candle and Claire de Cintré, rather more blonde and less dignified than she was ever intended to be. These were the days of piratical publishing, and if James felt pleased at being so widely displayed – prematurely – in England, he also knew he would receive not a penny from the sale of this popular edition. His feelings moreover were not assuaged when he opened the volume. It was 'vilely printed' and carelessly edited; whole paragraphs were omitted. Nor was he happy to receive proof from Germany of his growing fame – a pirated translation of the same novel, with a happy ending substituted for his own. Quite clearly it was time for him to take hold of his affairs not only in England but on the Continent.

What James did not see was the confidential report which John Morley had written for the Macmillans on *French Poets and Novelists*. The document reads rather quaintly today and shows Morley's blindness to James's essential qualities – a blindness that would persist to the end. He reported the essays were sensible and refined, free from narrowness and prejudice, and that they served their turn as fugitive criticism. 'Of charm, delicacy, finesse,' he said, 'they have none. They are prosaic to the last degree, and *as criticism* not at all interesting.' He had compared them with Sainte-Beuve and 'Mr James, by such a test, must be called mediocre'. The book might have some slight sale; nevertheless, Morley did not believe it would make a deep literary mark. 'The style wants *cachet* and distinction, and the method wants depth and subtlety.' He called it 'honest scribble work and no more'. As a reader, Morley erred in seeking a French parallel to essays written for an English-speaking audience. What was much more important was that there had been no book on the new French writers in English as important as this one. The real question was whether these essays, written originally for American magazine audiences unfamiliar with France's mid-century writers, could serve a similar function in England. Morley failed to recognize, and perhaps could not have done at the time, that James had singled out with critical prescience the very writers who were ultimately to be influential in the English-speaking world. A reader today would quarrel with very few of James's subjects. And the dry, high-minded Morley was insensitive to style. When the book came out early in 1878 certain of the Victorian journals dismissed the essays as dealing with the 'indecent' novelists of France. A qualified reviewer such as George Saintsbury, however, pronounced the papers on George Sand and Balzac 'admirable' and astutely pointed to resemblances between Turgenev's work and James's. The only essay in the collection which was a distinct failure was the one devoted to Baudelaire. James lagged in his understanding of symbolism, as he lagged in his grasp of impressionism. He was never a good critic of poetry. His method in general was to seek the personality of the writer in his work. This caused Saintsbury to argue that the book was too biographical, and not sufficiently critical. James believed, however, with Sainte-Beuve, that a critic could not but read a writer's works as the expression of the man. The critic had to remember that the artist 'is present in every page of every book from which he sought so assiduously to eliminate himself'.

The Macmillans decided to bring out the book in spite of Morley's adverse report. They recognized that James was a productive writer, and they wanted to handle his work in England. If *French Poets and Novelists* would not make money, it would nevertheless place him under their wing. Bundles of proofs awaited James in Paris and he spent ten days reading them – and paying visits. He had an opportunity to see Turgenev several times – 'very bad with the gout'. He felt himself 'better friends with him than ever'.

He re-crossed the Channel just before Christmas 1877. Fanny Kemble had asked him to join her at Alverston Manor House, Stratford-on-Avon, at the home of her daughter. He arrived on Christmas Eve and we glimpse him, in a letter of Mrs Kemble's, as 'our dark-bearded, handsome American friend', helping to trim the tree in the large nursery with its open arch roof, oak rafters and huge chimney. 'Our American friend seemed very well pleased with all the ceremonies of the day, including church service in Shakespeare's church.' The weather was brilliant. The picturesque house, with its big fires and its hangings of holly and mistletoe, provided a distinctive final setting to a remarkable year in James's life – the happiest and most 'lived' year yet. He had found an anchorage in London. *The American* was in its second edition in the United States, and Tauchnitz had just bought it for a Continental edition. He had profited by its success to revise minutely his old novel *Watch and Ward*, of six years before. *French Poets and Novelists* would be out in February and Macmillan was already asking for simultaneous serialization, in *Macmillan's Magazine*, of his next *Atlantic* novel. He faced the coming year with confidence.

72

Daisy

'MY London life flows evenly along, making, I think in various ways, more and more a Londoner of me,' Henry James wrote to William at the end of January 1878.

If I keep along here patiently for a certain time I rather think I shall become a (sufficiently) great man. I have got back to work with great zest after my autumnal loafings, and mean to do some this year which will make a mark. I am, as you suppose, weary of writing articles about places, and mere potboilers of all kinds; but shall probably, after the next six months, be able to forswear it altogether, and give myself up seriously to 'creative' writing. Then, and not till then, my real career will begin. After that, *gare à vous*.

The passage reads as if Henry were proceeding according to a deliberate time-table. He must be patient for a 'certain time'; he will make his mark 'this year'; he will, after the next six months, be ready to begin to write in earnest. There was strange insight here into the calendar of his life. For what came to pass was that James wrote *Daisy Miller* during that winter. It was accepted by mid-April for the *Cornhill Magazine* – the journal of Thackeray and Trollope – and was published within six months. After that Henry James was to be considered by the world 'a (sufficiently) great man'.

I

Almost the first thing he had done after returning from the Continent to his fireside in Bolton Street was to write the tale suggested by Miss Bartlett's anecdote of the American girl who was snubbed in Rome. The story reads today – has always read – as if it had flowed spontaneously out of the tip of his pen; it has a fine lucidity and a vividness of detail; ironic laughter echoes between its lines until it reaches its final, gently-sketched scene of pathos. The circumstantial detail of *Daisy* lives with extraordinary authenticity, for it was transposed directly from James's half-dozen years of Continental journeyings. The little crimson drawing-room in the Via Gregoriana, where Mrs Walker turns her back on Daisy – we have seen James there, in January 1873, visiting the Tweedys; Vevey and the Castle of Chillon – this was where Henry and Alice joined the Bootts during their long-ago summer of Swiss travel; the Colosseum by moonlight, William's touch of the Roman fever, Giovanelli as a *cavaliere avvocato*, the Protestant cemetery – all spill over into fiction from felt backgrounds and Roman springtimes to give the tale its air of freshness and reality. There is no lingering, no explaining; the story moves objectively with quiet incident to its conclusion.

Its logic resides above all in the image of Daisy Miller. Miss Bartlett had no need to describe the young lady of her anecdote – James had seen her in her multitude, stepping confidently ashore from the transatlantic liners, in fine dresses with flounces and ribbons, carrying her head high, possessed of the *tournure* of a princess. Young Daisy is pure nineteenth-century Schenectady or Utica, exposed to the bright summer-sun on Lake Geneva and the turquoise skies of Rome. For all her brilliant array of dresses and her air of sophistication, she is garbed in the innocence of Eve. She has never tasted of the apple.

James first submitted the tale to the editor of *Lippincott's* in Philadelphia, who returned it without comment. He was not certain why, and he found the absence of comment grim. He accordingly asked a friend (perhaps Leslie Stephen) to read the story; the opinion he got was that the editor had probably rejected it because he considered it 'an outrage on American womanhood'. James himself was not convinced; he thought that perhaps the story was simply too long. At any rate he submitted it to Stephen of the *Cornhill*, who accepted it 'with effusion'. In fact it was sent to the printer at once, and James made his bow for the first time in an English magazine in the June and July 1878 issues. His failure to assure himself of American publication lost him the valuable magazine market in the United States. The story was pirated immediately both in New York and Boston, and when Harper's brought it out in their Half-Hour Series as a pamphlet it sold 20,000 copies in a matter of weeks. James's royalties were negligible. 'I have made $200 by the whole American career of Daisy Miller,' he told Howells. The tale was destined, however, to be 'the most prosperous child' of Henry's invention. All unaware, he had written a small masterpiece.

2

Daisy Miller had a sub-title; James called it *A Study*, to suggest that he had written the equivalent of a pencil-sketch on an artist's pad, rather than a rounded work. Later he said it was because of 'a certain flatness' suggested in the very name of his heroine. And indeed the slightness of the story has made a later generation wonder why it should have proved so attractive. A modern reader, unrehearsed in the history of manners, might wonder at the social fuss which occurs merely because an American girl 'dates' an Italian. The informality of the twentieth century can little understand the formality of the nineteenth.

The story of Daisy's short-lived adventure in Europe begins in Vevey at the Trois Couronnes, where the Europeanized American, Winterbourne, meets in the garden of the hotel the little American boy Randolph, who is boastful, unhappy, full of misplaced energy and a quite justifiable sense of being dragged about Europe when he would rather be at home. While the unbending Winterbourne – through whose eyes we see Daisy – chats with the boy, his sister joins them, and presently they are talking quite familiarly to one another, even if they have not been properly introduced. Her name is Annie P. Miller but everyone calls her Daisy. She is a pleasing flirt. 'Did you ever hear of a nice girl that was not?' She expects young men to give her their undivided attention, and she arranges to go, unchaperoned, with her new acquaintance to visit the Castle of Chillon. Winterbourne's aunt, who knows all the proprieties, sniffs her disapproval, between migraine headaches; the best she will allow Daisy is that 'she dresses in perfection – no, you don't know how well she dresses'. For the rest, Winterbourne admits that the girl is rather 'uncultivated'. 'She is very common,' says his aunt.

Daisy is described to us, more often than not, in negatives; she is not insipid, and she is not exactly expressive; there is no mockery in her, and distinctly no irony. She has a bright, sweet, superficial little visage; her features are eminently delicate. 'There isn't any society,' she claims in describing her experiences in Europe and she adds 'I have always had a great deal of gentlemen's society.' Her misfortune is that she does not know the European definition of a gentleman.

Later that year, in Rome, Winterbourne meets her again. We continue to see her through his eyes. As in the anecdote, she has acquired a charming Italian; his name is Giovanelli. He has a moustache, is attentive, and if he does not understand her flirtatious nature, he 'must wonder at his luck'. Winterbourne perceives quite clearly that Daisy is not interested in marrying him and that the Italian does not hope to marry her; but he enjoys her company, and she is pleased to have a 'gentleman' dance attendance on her, as her boy-friends did in Schenectady. It never occurs for a moment to Daisy that she is the subject of gossip, and that her behaviour violates European codes; that young girls simply do not go about without a chaperon. Mrs Walker overtakes her and Giovanelli in the Pincian gardens and points out to her that what she is doing 'is not the custom here'. Daisy replies ingenuously enough : 'Well, it ought to be, then!' The girl has no standards; she has never been given any; she does not even know what 'standard' means. And even when she is snubbed in Mrs Walker's drawing-room, she does not comprehend the meaning of the gesture. She cannot accept the notion – it is fundamental to her nature – that behaviour is different anywhere from what she has known in Schenectady.

Winterbourne wonders whether this bright, young, admirably turned-out example of the new American generation is 'honest' or frivolous, whether she is innocent or depraved. A true Jamesian male, he never quite makes up his mind. When he encounters Daisy and Giovanelli rambling late in the evening in the Colosseum he thinks his worst suspicions may be right. The story moves swiftly to its end. Daisy catches the Roman fever and dies of it; and 'by the raw protuberance among the April daisies' in the Protestant cemetery Winterbourne and Giovanelli exchange the remarks which are, so to speak, her epitaph. 'She was the most beautiful young lady I ever saw, and the most amiable,' says Giovanelli – whose name expresses youth and irresponsibility – and he adds 'she was the most innocent'. Winterbourne, whose name expresses the chill Daisy complained of in him, can only stare at the grave and decide that Miss Miller would have 'appreciated one's esteem'.

3

If the tale of the girl from Schenectady is now a piece of superseded social history, one aspect of it has assumed a new importance : this is the unerring vision which James always had of the total abdication, by the mass of American parents, of authority over their children. The entire discussion of 'permissiveness' and the re-evaluation of progressive education makes James's picture of the two Miller children singularly documentary. Daisy is allowed to wander about Rome with Giovanelli at all hours of the night; it is she, not her mother, who exercises authority over the travelling group; both in turn abdicate authority to Eugenio, the courier, who is treated as if he were a member of the family. Nine-year-old Randolph does as he pleases.

'Did you get Randolph to go to bed?' asked the young girl.
'No; I couldn't induce him,' said Mrs Miller, very gently.
'He wants to talk to the waiter. He likes to talk to that waiter.'

Daisy recalls that 'it isn't so bad as it was at Dover'.

'And what occurred at Dover?' Winterbourne asked.
'He wouldn't go to bed at all. I guess he sat up all night – in the public parlour. He wasn't in bed at twelve o'clock : I know that.'
'It was half-past twelve,' declared Mrs Miller, with mild emphasis.

The logic of this is that 9-year-olds apparently must be talked into going to bed, instead of being simply put there; and Randolph's rugged individualism is but the pioneer version of a generation of spoiled young allowed to dominate the American scene. James had remembered well his glimpses of children asleep in leather chairs in Saratoga hotel lobbies at late hours. He was to continue, in his tales, to portray the consequences for a civilization of an absence of standards and codes, of a society knowing no rules, and of a 'freedom' which consisted in a kind of meaningless pampering of the young – offering the future citizens of his country neither a sense of history nor a charted course in life and civilization.

He gave forcible utterance shortly after *Daisy* to this picture of the new American generation in *The Point of View*, in which a re-patriated American woman at Newport writes:

The country is made for the rising generation; life is arranged for them; they are the destruction of society. People talk of them, consider them, defer to them, bow down to them. They are always present, and when-ever they are present there is an end to everything else. They are often very pretty; and physically they are wonderfully looked after; they are scoured and brushed, they wear hygienic clothes, they go every week to the dentist's. But the little boys kick your shins, and the little girls offer to slap your face! There is an immense literature entirely addressed to them, in which the kicking of shins and the slapping of faces is much recommended. As a woman of fifty, I protest. I insist on being judged by my peers. It's too late, however, for several millions of little feet are actively engaged in stamping out conversation, and I don't see how they can long fail to keep it under. The future is theirs; maturity will evidently be at an increasing discount. Longfellow wrote a charming little poem called *The Children's Hour*, but he ought to have called it *The Children's Century*.

Daisy Miller remains a remarkable story even if the manners it por-trays are outmoded; it has a spare economy, a quick painting of background and a chaste narrative, a summary sketching of Ameri-can ignorance confronting American rigidity in Europe. It remains also the prototype of the 'international' story. Henry was to write more important and more brilliant tales, but *Daisy Miller*, like its name, still blooms among his works, 'the little tragedy', as he ex-plained to a lady who wrote to him, 'of a light, thin, natural, unsus-pecting creature being sacrificed as it were to a social rumpus that went on quite over her head and to which she stood in no measur-able relation'. The delicate pathos of this predicament softens Daisy's hardness of surface, and makes her a victim not only of parental and national ignorance, but of her own innocence. Winterbourne, at the end, can only wonder whether he hasn't lingered too long in Europe, whether a civilization – or absence of it – was developing in his native land which he did not know or understand.

4

The story, as literary history knows, was an extraordinary success, but not the *succès de scandale* which legend attributed to it. There was nothing in the public reaction to warrant any suggestion of 'outrage'. On the contrary, Daisy was distinctly liked by many American readers. She was a girl of spirit and from the American point of view, as Edmund Wilson observed, that spirit went marching on. She resisted the inflexibility of the Europeanized Americans and stood her ground as a 'child of nature and of freedom'. Only one reviewer seemed to feel that she was unreal; the others, in general, complimented James on his portrayal of certain types of Americans travelling abroad – types, they said, perhaps too often found in Europe. The vogue set off by Daisy continued for a long time afterwards: she became a perennial figure – and 'a Daisy Miller' was to be a much-used descriptive phrase whenever some particularly charming, forward young lady from America showed up in Continental surroundings. For a time there were *Daisy Miller* hats in the millinery shops, and presently another book appeared titled *An English Daisy Miller*, by a magazine-writer named Virginia W. Johnson. The little book was 'Dedicated to American Women' and its general theme followed James, substituting an English girl for the American. James's story was widely translated.

He had discovered 'the American girl' – as a social phenomenon, a fact, a type. She had figured in novels before, in Trollope, for example, but never had she stood in fiction so pertly and bravely, smoothing her dress and asking the world to pay court to her. Hawthorne's American girl in Rome, Howells's American girl in Venice, had not been contrasted with Europe; and those Europeans who were reading Louisa May Alcott had a picture of the American girl largely in her domestic surroundings. The rustling young ladies on the verandahs at Saratoga, the busy beauties of uptown New York, the graceful, idle females of Newport, suddenly became James's large subject; and all by the simple turn of exhibiting them in their finery as in all the stages of their timidity or insolence, their doubt or their triumph – at the moment of their encounter with Europe and their refusal to yield their heritage of American innocence and ignorance. The magazines clamoured for his tales and he addressed himself to making the most of his new-found fame. In fast succession there came from his little sitting-room in Bolton Street *An Inter-*

national Episode, The Pension Beaurepas, the short novel Confidence, and in due course such tales as A Bundle of Letters. Henry James made himself the acknowledged master of the 'international' and he was to use it on a large stage, with substantial characters, in novels yet to be written. 'The Americano–European legend,' he was to call it in the end. And it was his creation, his peopled world. He was to deal with the American girl and the American woman – exhibit them for almost half a century in their march through foreign countries and their exposure to foreign societies. A critic in the Edinburgh Review was prompted early to reflect on the strange new types which James had brought upon the horizon of English literature. American men who corresponded not at all to the popular notion of travelling Americans, and certainly less Philistine than Englishmen abroad, looking at churches, admiring works of art, indulging in civilized conversation, and contemplating their fellow-Americans – Winterbourne, for instance; Daisy Millers who availed themselves in Europe of the liberality and licence permitted to young unmarried women in the United States. Their unconventional behaviour and their seeming indiscretions might scandalize Europeans, the reviewer felt; but he noticed that even when their passing flirtations were tinged by romance, they usually married for satisfactory settlements. American women in all their variety passed before James: the timid, the adventurous, the self-made, the divorcée in search of respectability, the heiress in search of a princedom, the demure maiden in the European pension engaged in an earnest quest for 'culture' and self-betterment – and always there was the chase for the husband. These were all but a series of sketches from which he would paint his larger, full-length portraits. In a late preface he would define the various states which he depicted, the predicaments of these fresh, positive, beguiling ladies. They were innocent and they were democratic; they were woefully ignorant of any concept of society – any sense of the old hierarchies and standards; they suffered from an acute state of 'queenship', being the spoiled darlings of American men who in the 'young roaring and money-getting democracy' were busy with their own affairs, possessing none of the leisure upper-class European males enjoyed in courtship. American men wooed strenuously and when they married spent their days creating fortunes for the use of the womenfolk. 'An American woman who respects herself,' says one of James's married ladies, 'must buy something every day of her life. If she cannot do it herself, she must send out some member of her family for the purpose.' Thus she explains one of her functions; and in a country of absentee husbands, women, in their reinforced egotism, assume supremacy; they take over education; they exercise control over the young. It is either excessive or excessively relaxed. James's concern for some years was to be with 'the practical, positive, passionless young thing as we let her loose on the world'.

Much that James wrote was true of any newly-rich society; and the absentee husband existed in Europe as well – indulging in his adulteries while his wife indulged in hers. What was new for the Europeans was the general freshness and innocence of these products of the new society, their spirit of conquest, their belief in themselves and their ability for self-improvement: above all the strange new egalitarianism, which nourished the legend that an American could do anything. These newcomers to the ancient civilization came from an order of wealth rather than of aristocracy; and James's picture of them contained a large measure of affection even while he satirized and criticized.

James was to tell an anecdote many years later: how in Venice one day a lady-friend observing two young American girls had spoken of them as 'Daisy Millers'. This was to lead to a remonstrance from a second lady in the gondola. She remarked that these crude creatures were the real Daisies, about whom James had *not* written, and that the one he had created was a distortion, because he endowed her with form and prettiness and pathos and bathed her in the beautiful light of his own imagination. James was prepared to agree. 'My supposedly typical little figure was of course pure poetry, and had never been anything else; since this is what helpful imagination, in however slight a dose, ever directly makes for.' She was, as we say today, 'archetypal'.

5

By the time *Daisy Miller* appeared in the *Cornhill* during midsummer of 1878, Henry James, writing with speed and assurance, had posted to Howells all four instalments of the serial he had promised him a year earlier – a short novel narrated in 100 pages of the *Atlantic Monthly*. In writing it he kept two promises made to his friend: he remained within the space allotted to him (the novel actually fills 91 pages), and he made up for his unhappy ending of *The American* by giving the reader no less than three marriages. *The Europeans* reversed the 'international situation', to which James was, for the time, committed; instead of taking Americans to the Continent, he transferred two Europeans to America, to the Boston of 1840, even as in his next tale he placed a British peer and his friend in midsummer Manhattan and Newport.

The Europeans began its four-month run in the *Atlantic* in July 1878, the very month in which *Daisy Miller* was beginning its long vogue, in both legitimate and pirated form. The new work further increased James's popularity. Written in the same clear ironic prose, the short novel possessed the compact beauty of *Daisy*; it was a light and humorous satire. Its characters were without development, almost stock personages. What sustained them was the beauty of the writing. In this novel Henry was saying with a touch of carica-ture that the puritans of New England's 'silvery prime' possessed no *joie de vivre*. They are described as 'of a pensive cast; they take things hard'. Mr Wentworth, the head of his clan, looks 'as if he were undergoing martyrdom, not by fire but by freezing', and he welcomes his European relatives not through any human sense of hospitality but solely as an 'extension of duty'. When the European–American, Felix, wants to paint his portrait, he solemnly replies: 'The Lord made it. I don't think it is for us to make it over again.'

'What a pleasant house!' observes Felix on entering the New England dwelling. 'It's lighter inside than it is out.' He expatiates on its features: 'It's very clean! No splendours, no gilding, no troops of servants; rather straight-backed chairs. But you might eat off the floors, and you can sit down on the stairs.' The inhabitants of this bright establishment are sad; they 'take a painful view of life'. 'Nothing makes them happy. No one is happy here.' The Baroness observes, 'You Americans have such odd ways. You never ask any-thing outright; there seem to be so many things you can't talk about.' James's epigrams are emphatic in their comic truths. 'Noth-ing exceeds the license occasionally taken by the imagination of very rigid people.' 'Curiosity, pushed to a given point, might become romantic passion.' 'You are all so afraid here of being selfish.' 'I am told they [Bostonians] are very sincere; they don't tell fibs.'

There are fine atmospheric touches in *The Europeans*: the horse-cars, the sunsets, the Boston streets, the steel-engravings of religious mottoes on the walls – all painted as in clear water-colours. James gave Howells more marriages than he had asked for, but he remained true to himself : the important marriage of the story does not take place. Mr Acton, the congenial New Englander who has travelled in the East and is not altogether parochial, cannot bring himself to propose to the interesting and glamorous Eugenia; like Winterbourne he is not sure she is an 'honest' woman; he is quite sure that she does occasionally tell a fib. Eugenia accordingly returns to her little European duchy and her morganatic marriage, while her younger brother, an easy bohemian, marries the uninspired though romantic Gertrude Wentworth. James did not take *The Europeans* very seriously, nor did he intend it to be anything more than the light comedy he made of it. Nevertheless it has all the quiet tenderness of a Jane Austen novel; and when it came out as a book in the autumn of 1878 it found a large public both in London and in Boston. Certain Boston reviewers, among them T. W. Higginson, murmured very much like James's characters in the novel, at his imputation of parochialism in the Boston way of life. But posterity judges it as showing the same sureness and mastery as *Daisy Miller*.

In Madrid the new American minister to Spain, James Russell Lowell, chuckled over the novel. He had grown up with Mr Wentworth's generation, and he wrote to James, 'You revived in me the feeling of *cold furniture* which New England life has often *goosefleshed* me with [so] that I laughed and shivered at once.' Before going to Spain, Lowell had asked the State Department to appoint James as secretary of legation. He now congratulated himself that it had refused his request. The department had taken the view that one senior inexperienced diplomat in a legation was enough. Lowell had not even consulted Henry James, who, on learning of his proposal, had been worried lest he should be given the appointment. He felt that it would have been difficult to decline. He had no desire to assume a position at the very moment when he was achieving the greatest measure of personal freedom and success he had yet known.

6

As 1878 drew to a close James wrote one more tale. This was his story of Lord Lambeth on Broadway and in Newport, his offer of marriage to a young American bluestocking and her rejection of him. James placed great store by his idea of having a young girl from Massachusetts reject a British peer. In *An International Episode* Bessie Alden constantly admonishes Lord Lambeth for taking no interest in his responsibilities as one of his nation's aristocrats. The story begins with the two Englishmen dawdling in a hot New York filled with mosquitoes; but it wanes a little once the Englishmen reach Newport, although the comedy is sustained. The characters are mere sketches and the tale underlines the bad manners of certain members of the British aristocracy and the democratic feeling of the American girl. There had been, perhaps, a little too much laughter at Daisy Miller's expense in England, and James did not want to appear in the invidious role of a satirist to the English world of Americans abroad. His suspicions were borne out by a review of *An International Episode* written by Mrs F. H. Hill whom James had met socially in London. She accused James of caricaturing the British nobility, and of putting language into its mouth which it would never utter. James, on this occasion, replied, since he knew the lady, and his letter is a magisterial defence of his work and his art.

In it he denies that he made his Englishmen repeat 'I say' too often. He had studied English colloquialisms at the St James's Club, and had heard 'more "I says" than I had ever done before'. And then he defended himself against Mrs Hill's charge that in describing the manners of the two rude English noblewomen he was expressing a view of English manners in general.

A man in my position, and writing the sort of things I do, feels the need of protesting against this extension of his idea in which, in many cases, many readers are certain to indulge. One may make figures and figures without intending generalizations – generalizations of which I have a horror. I make a couple of English ladies doing a disagreeable thing – *cela c'est vu:* excuse me! – and forthwith I find myself responsible for a representation of English manners! Nothing is my *last word* about anything – I am interminably supersubtle and analytic – and, with the blessing of heaven, I shall live to make all sorts of representations of all sorts of things. It will take a much cleverer person than myself to discover my last impression – among all these things – of anything. And then, in such a matter, the bother of being an American! Trollope, Thackeray, Dickens, even with their big authoritative talents, were free to draw all sorts of unflattering English pictures, by the thousand. But if I make a single one, I am forthwith in danger of being confronted with a criminal conclusion – and sinister rumours reach me as to what I think of English society. I think more things than I can undertake to tell in 40 pages of the *Cornhill*. Perhaps some day I shall take more pages, and attempt to tell some of these things; in that case, I hope, there will be a little, of every sort, for every one! Meanwhile I shall draw plenty of pictures of disagreeable Americans, as I have done already, and the friendly Briton will see no harm in that! – it will seem to him a part of the natural fitness!

To his mother he wrote:

It seems to me myself that I have been very delicate; but I shall keep off dangerous ground in future. It is an entirely new sensation for them (the people here) to be (at all delicately) *ironized* or satirized, from the American point of view, and they don't at all relish it. Their conception of the normal in such a relation is that the satire should be all on their side against the Americans; and I suspect that if one were to push this a little further one would find that they are extremely sensitive. But I like them too much and feel too kindly to them to go into the satire-business or even the light-ironical in any case in which it would wound them – even if in such a case I should see my way to it very clearly.

Whatever the sensitiveness of his readers, whether in London or in Boston or New York, Mrs Hill's review was more than a straw in the wind. James had the sense at last of the power of the writer whose image of society becomes the mirror in which society looks at itself. He had come to England two years before comparatively unknown and had moved with the silence of an observer through the English scene. Now he was a literary lion, an authoritative voice, a recognized artist. His had been a swift and remarkable success – a conquest of an alien society and an alien audience, accomplished by his pen alone, the force of his imagination, his genius.

His third Christmas in England was a far cry from the first in Bolton Street, or even the second with Mrs Kemble. This time he went into Yorkshire to be the guest of Charles Milnes Gaskell; and to greet the new year at Lord Houghton's. It was 'a hideous part of England – the Yorkshire manufacturing country, which is blighted and darkened by smoke and cinders, and the presence of a dreary population'. The population formed 'a not very attractive element in that great total of labour and poverty on whose enormous base all the luxury and leisure of English country-houses are built up'. Gaskell drove him in a sledge through the deep snow to Bretton to call on Lady Margaret Beaumont, grand-daughter of Mr Canning, 'a drawling, lisping fine lady enclosed in her great wintry park and her immense, dusky, pictured, luxurious house – with her tea-table at one elbow and a table-full of novels at the other'. Lord Houghton took Henry to visit the old Duchess of Somerset, a one-time 'Queen of Beauty', and now 'a dropsical, garrulous old woman'. The 'Bird of Paradox' was charming as usual.

Lord Houghton has just come into my room [Henry remarks in the midst of writing a letter to his sister Alice] to know why I haven't come to afternoon tea, and plumping himself into my armchair, is apparently lapsing into social slumber. He is a very odd old fellow – extremely fidgety and eccentric; but full of sociable and friendly instinct, and with a strong streak of humanity and democratic feeling. He has begun to snore violently and I must finish my letter as I can.

The letter is not finished. Henry goes down to dinner and listens with delight to endless anecdotes told by Mrs Procter – intimate pictures of Carlyle, arriving at Basil Montagu's, her father's, earlier in the century and leaving with a bundle of borrowed books carefully wrapped up in a big blue calico handkerchief '– but I must check my frivolous gossip, dearest sister,' James writes late in the evening, 'in which I have indulged in the hope of affording you a little innocent amusement.'

The new year is coming in over the frosty land. 'It is just 12 o'clock – 1879. My blessing on it for all of you. I hope you are having a reasonable winter – here it is a very different affair from the two last and the Yorkshire climate has given me back the chilblains of infancy. Love to dear parents, from your *devotissimo*. H. James jr.'

73

The Two Secretaries

I

THEIR names were Hoppin and Nadal. William Jones Hoppin was First Secretary of the American Legation in London and Ehrman Syme Nadal was Second Secretary. Mr Hoppin was 63, perhaps a little too old to be starting a career in diplomacy. A successful lawyer and a man of means, he had been nominated to the post by the new administration of President Hayes and had arrived in the British capital a few weeks before Henry James. The First Secretary had practised at the bar in New York for many years. He was a gregarious individual with an interest in the arts. A bachelor who had written verses, translated plays from the French and was conversant with the latest art criticism, he had felt that he must accept this call to national duty; moreover the idea of descending upon London, in the Indian summer of his life, appealed to him. If his post was not that of a full-fledged Minister, it was the next best thing to it – and indeed for a period between the ministry of Mr Welsh and that of Mr Lowell he did act as *chargé d'affaires*.

Mr Nadal, the Second Secretary, was a Virginian, twenty years younger than Mr Hoppin. He had served in the London Legation at the beginning of the seventies and then returned to New York to be a journalist. He had written his impressions of London social life and sundry articles for the magazines. Now he was resuming his diplomatist's career. The two Secretaries had distinctly different temperaments; they belonged to different generations and different sides of the once-divided nation. Mr Hoppin was a strenuous Yankee, Mr Nadal a relaxed southerner. The only thing they shared in common, over and above their responsibility to their position, was an ambition to succeed in British society.

Mr Hoppin, in all that he did, showed the signs of his Puritanism and his New England sense of duty. Although a man of wealth, he had carefully resigned from all his financial posts before coming abroad; and while he could have afforded a large establishment he took a modest place and engaged only a housekeeper. Having a long legal experience, he performed his duties punctiliously. Feeling also that this was to be the largest experience of his life, he began to keep a *Journal of a Residence in London*. Since he remained in London for a decade, the journal is of some amplitude : it runs to twelve large bound volumes in which Hoppin's regular entries, written in a neat and flowing hand, are embroidered by all the mementoes of his London life : theatre-programmes, newspaper-clippings, restaurant-menus, and other ephemera. The journal itself, never published and preserved in the Houghton Library at Harvard, provides an interesting record of the comings and goings of Americans in London and the official activities of the ministries of Pierrepont, Welsh and James Russell Lowell. It records also Mr Hoppin's mild pleasures, largely cultural and social, in the capital. In New York Mr Hoppin had moved in the very best circles. He was a member of the Union League Club and a founder of the Century Association. He wanted to discover good society in London, to meet amiable ladies and to frequent celebrities. Henry Adams, writing to Lowell when the latter was named Minister to England, told him that 'Hoppin is rather sensitive, and you will perhaps need to be a little careful to humour him.' Hoppin was indeed inclined to be fussy and compulsive; but he had great respect for Lowell and served him faithfully and well. Nadal later described his elderly colleague as 'a cultivated and very agreeable man, about as good a type of American gentleman as it would be possible to find'.

Mr Hoppin would not have been flattered, since he considered Mr Nadal a lightweight; his journal abounds in his irritated sense of his colleague's laxities. It was true that Nadal contented himself with doing as little work as possible, dawdling about London and cultivating the English and whatever literary folk came his way. His *Impressions of London Social Life*, published in 1875, and his later volume of reminiscences, reflect his superficial and amiable view of life. Henry James had reviewed the first book during his winter of work in Manhattan; he described it as a 'gentlemanly book', in good taste and free of indiscretions. But Nadal's observations seemed to James 'vague and ineffectual'. Mr Nadal was a little more assertive than Mr Hoppin, but not disagreeably so. Mr Hoppin, on his side, felt that his years, his social and diplomatic position, could always speak for him. He seemed, therefore, a trifle shy. At least twice during his London residence he was the subject of particular comment in the press. The first was when, during a Guildhall dinner, he announced his rank so indistinctly (and insisted on calling himself *chargé d'affaires*, when he was, in effect, American Plenipotentiary for the occasion) that the heralds' voices stumbled over the French and sank to a whisper. Mr Smalley, reporting to the *Tribune* that the German Ambassador was cheered, added that the 'American diplomatist would not have been less warmly greeted had his presence been made known with equal distinctness'. The other occasion involved questions of dress. Edmund Yates, who had been the subject of an historic quarrel between Dickens and Thackeray, inserted a paragraph in his gossip-column in the *World* which read : 'Mr Hoppin, the American *chargé d'affaires*, has taken to attending courts and drawing-rooms in a nondescript uniform, which includes "breeches". Will he be censured by his Government?' The *Daily Telegraph* apparently scoffed at this, by referring in an article on the opening of Parliament to 'the defiant simplicity of the white tie and swallow coat of the American representative'. Mr Hoppin noted apropos of the 'breeches' that it was the same dress he had always worn; it had been worn by all members of the Legation since Reverdy Johnson advanced the matter with Lord Clarendon in February 1879. A journal-entry of a few days later records a dinner at which Henry James, the Henry Adamses, Lady Hamilton Gordon and Mrs Duncan Stewart were present and there was 'a great deal of joking about my "breeches" '.

2

Early in 1877, when Mr Hoppin had been in London but a few months, he met Lord Houghton. So far as we know he was not invited to his breakfasts. But the literary peer had always liked Americans, and he gave Mr Hoppin a card to the discussion club, the Cosmopolitan, to which Henry James had also been invited. On a Sunday evening in March Mr Hoppin directed his footsteps to 30 Charles Street, Berkeley Square, at about eleven – for the discussions were usually held informally and at the evening's end. He surveyed the large gloomy house which seemed deserted save that its skylight, covering the topmost storey, was illuminated. The building had served as a studio for the painter George Frederick Watts. Mr Hoppin entered, found that Lord Houghton was not yet there, and was persuaded by the doorman to take off his coat and hat and mount the stairs. Here he discovered a large barnlike studio with an immense mythological picture on the side-wall. There were tables with tea-cups, three bottles of spirits, and a provision of soda. Six or seven gentlemen were seated round the fire. None rose; no one noticed Mr Hoppin. 'This was characteristically English,' he wrote in his journal. He marched about, looked at some of the pictures, and when Lord Houghton did not show up descended the stairs.

Another gentleman was just arriving. He was rather short and stocky, and wore a dark beard. He spoke to the doorman and then turning to Mr Hoppin introduced himself as Henry James, an American; he said he too was waiting for Lord Houghton, and the two mounted the stairs again. Mr James knew one of the men, Mr Edward Dicey, and introduced Hoppin. Presently Lord Houghton arrived and 'everything thenceforth was smooth and easy'.

The incident was banal enough, save that Mr Hoppin recorded the circumstances without giving any indication of the talk. This is one of the exasperations of his journal. It retails facts, but it seldom describes; it has the true flavour of a dry diplomatic report. After this evening the name of Mr Henry James begins to appear with a certain frequency in the journal. Thus it records that they met at the St James's Club on 6 January 1878. Mr Hoppin's account of that occasion reads:

I dined there last evening for the first time. Henry James, the author, was there, who had been introduced by Nadal, and I joined table with him. Nothing remarkable in the talk – I think that men [who] live by writing for the magazines on current topics seldom ventilate their choice ideas. They keep them to be fresh in the market. The dinner was not so good as I had expected.

Perhaps Mr James did not care to ventilate his 'choice ideas' to Mr Hoppin; for a later account of James's talk, set down by Nadal, says that 'James talked incessantly and with the originality and somewhat of the authority of those who read aloud to you their thoughts out of their own mind. His talk was very alert and eager.'

Nadal and James had met at the American Legation during the Fourth of July reception of 1877, four months after the novelist's first encounter with Hoppin. Nadal too has left us a record of the occasion: 'A rather dark and decidedly handsome young man of medium height, with a full beard, stood in the doorway and bowed rather stiffly, as if he were not to be confused with the rank and file of his compatriots. I was at once struck by his appearance.' He is introduced and when he discovers that James lives in Bolton Street mentions that he had had rooms there when he first came to London, at No. 6. Henry invites him to come and see him. 'Mine are No. 3, the half of your old number; you can remember it by that.' Nadal in due course comes. He remembers that the door was opened by a slender dark young woman. James explains she is not a servant but a relative of the landlady. 'She's an English character,' he explains. 'She isn't a lady and she isn't a woman; she's a person.' He was always discussing English class-distinctions, and Nadal noted that he made a point constantly of saying he was a foreigner. He resented, he told Nadal, the remark made by a lady of the middle class he had visited when she said: 'That is true of the aristocracy, but in one's own class it is different,' meaning, said James, 'her class and mine'. The American novelist did not wish to be 'adjudged a place in English society in accordance with English standards'.

Nadal's memories of James are also recorded in a factual manner, but with more perception; they seem circumstantial, and reasonably authentic. Nevertheless Henry James, like Mr Hoppin, would have considered Mr Nadal a superficial reporter. To his sister Alice he described 'the little second secretary of legation' as 'a most amiable nature but the feeblest and vaguest mind, and socially speaking, a perfect failure here – though he is not aware of it and it doesn't seem at all to have embittered him. He is a wonderful specimen of American innocence.' And to Norton he wrote after Lowell became Minister, 'I wish he had a pair of secretaries that ministered a little more to the idea of American brilliancy. Lowell has to do *that* quite by himself.'

3

If Henry James had been able to read over Mr Hoppin's shoulder as he wrote in his steady straight-line hand the record of his London doings he would have discovered that, unlike Nadal, Hoppin knew that he was a failure in London society and it made him bitter. In the second year of their acquaintance, after the 1878–9 Season, Mr Hoppin was prompted to write an essay in his journal, *The Position of a Stranger in London Society*. This little essay stemmed from James's remarking, on meeting Mr Hoppin, that he had dined out that winter no less than 140 times, a figure somewhat higher than that which he had given Grace Norton two months before, when he had said he had dined out 107 times. In the intervening period he had apparently eaten thirty-three additional dinners. Mr Hoppin had been crushed.

This great success of James leads me to inquire how it is that some people succeed so well here while others constantly fail. I class myself decidedly among the failures. I make new acquaintances but they never lead to friendships. I meet a woman at a dinner, I talk to her as pleasantly as I can – I hear afterwards that she speaks of me as agreeable. But she never asks me to her receptions or dinners. There was Mrs Douglas Salters, for instance, whom I took in to dinner at Mr Washington Jackson's. She enjoyed my talk, I know – but she never asked me to visit her. I am satisfied that youth and personal appearance have a good deal to do with such matters. An old fellow like myself with an unprepossessing exterior has but a small chance. I don't write this by way of complaint. I merely state the facts. I amuse myself sufficiently without these attentions.

Nevertheless Mr Hoppin was determined to understand the Jamesian success and to explain it to himself. He felt that society in London was so immense that a man could attract attention only by having high rank or personal attractiveness – or the art of enlisting attention and regard. In London one had no time to '*grow* into favour. You must strike for it at once.' He returns to the novelist:

Henry James is good looking, has good manners, but more than all, he is a popular author. People read his books and their curiosity is piqued to know him. I don't think he talks remarkably well. I believe he keeps his most piquant ideas for his novels – but he has that dash of cynicism which is in fashion. There is nothing that pleases a woman so much as to hear some spicy ill-natured *Wort* about her best friends. A kind-hearted man who is naturally disposed to like people – to admire beauty – to find out who is becomingly dressed – has no chance at all in companion with an ill-natured growler who growls in an original tone.

Mr Hoppin then speculated on how he might have achieved success. If he had allowed the word to spread that he had an income, and if he had entertained more and had a larger establishment, 'this would have brought all the angular old maids and widows with their projecting teeth and big feet to term and I should have been enormously in request'. There was one comfort. 'Such kindness as I do receive is for myself and not for my money.'

In their talk about society and social success in London, Nadal gained the impression that Henry James did not want to be 'in smart English society because he really preferred the company of smart people. It was rather that he did not like to feel that he was shut out from that or any other kind of company.' He told Nadal that he wanted 'to be taken seriously' by the English. This was a phrase he often used. He particularly detested 'that excluded feeling'. Nadal added: 'I dare say also that he wanted to be enough in smart company to know what it was like. He wished to be an international novelist, and desired to know that as well as other parts of English life.' Lafcadio Hearn, who had undergone a more difficult expatriation than James's, also remarked on this. 'There are very few men strong enough to stand the life of society and to write,' he observed. 'I can think of but one of importance – that is Henry James – but his special study is society.'

One day Nadal spoke critically of certain Americans who had pursued social success in London and had been snubbed. Nadal had disapproved of their attempt: he saw no reason why they should have exposed themselves to rudeness at the hands of London's social leaders. Henry James's reply was perhaps the most significant of all that Nadal set down:

'I don't agree with you. I think a position in society is a legitimate object of ambition.'

74

A Position in Society

IN his late years Henry James was to look back on the old Victorian society in London, which he had known intimately, as a strange other-world. 'Nowhere so much as in England was it fortunate to *be* fortunate.' He had said as much in the early days of his English domicile; he reaffirmed it in the grandeur of his final style. 'I confess without scruple to have found again and again at that time an attaching charm in the general exhibition.' He was writing when the guns of the First World War had already opened up across the Channel, obliterating decades of memory and of 'progress'. That world had been, he could see, 'the fool's paradise really rounded and preserved, before one's eyes, for those who were so good as to animate it'.

And thus he could speak of 'the extinct societies that once were so sure of themselves', of the 'thousand dimmed illusions' and 'certain complacencies of faith and taste'. It had been the day of the 'blandly idle and the supposedly accomplished', of 'amiabilities and absurdities, harmless serenities and vanities, pretensions and undertakings, unashamed'. This was the backward-vision. In 1878 and 1879 – the two years of Henry James's descent upon and conquest of London – it had all been a swiftly moving adventure, this return of an American to the past of his culture and his race, and his deep plunge into a society comparatively small and comparatively unquestioned. A society, as W. H. Mallock wrote,

mainly founded on the hereditary possession of the land, its nucleus being the heads of more or less ancient families whose rent rolls enabled them to occupy London houses and play an agreeable and ornamental part in the business of entertaining and being entertained for the few months called the Season. It was part of the order of Nature.

Hyde Park, at certain hours of the day, had the aspect of a garden-party; Piccadilly 'was a vision of open carriages brilliant with flower-like parasols, high-stepping horses and coachmen, many of whom still wore wigs'. For the American from Cambridge this London, which he could observe both as 'insider' and 'stranger' – and en-counter with much greater freedom than if he had been an English-man – provided an endless opportunity for exploration and discovery. He took it in a large American stride. Yet he had no illusions. 'Heaven knows one is an outsider here,' he wrote to Henry Adams, 'but the outsider that one must be in Europe one is here in the least degree.'

1

If in France Henry James had but walked the periphery of society, in London he was presently swept into its centre. It was a gradual and almost imperceptible process: one call led to another, one dinner to another, until he was constantly dining out. At first he accepted invitations to luncheon; very soon, however, he had to take precautions against being drawn into the morning and afternoon leisure of the upper classes. Only his evenings were dedicated to the pursuit of his 'legitimate ambition'. It was he who in reality was pursued – pursued to the point that, after a year or two, he tended to flee London or to frequent it during the 'dead season'. For the time, however, he gave himself over to the social process with the same systematic care he had exercised in the planning of his pro-fessional career. During his first winter he was the observer and explorer; by the time the second came round he had achieved literary fame and was in continual demand. During the winter of 1878–9 – by the count of his engagement-book and Hoppin's record – he dined out 140 times. One may suppose this to represent an almost unparalleled account-keeping of sociability and gregarious-ness. To have had the stamina to face so many evenings of talk – not all of them good talk, by any means – so many heavily-loaded tables, so much 'stuffy' Victorian formality, was some kind of test of en-durance. James thrived on it. It enabled him to complete his 'Lon-donizing process'.

He would write 'when one starts in the London world it goes with constantly increasing velocity'. He was in a sense launched by G. W. Smalley, whom he had met during his *Tribune* association in Paris. Smalley, a New Englander, had known little of 'society' during his Puritan youth and now went in for it strenuously. As the principal American newspaperman in London, he was able to make his home into an Anglo-American meeting ground. Here James sat down to dinner with Mr Froude, the historian and biographer, Mr Kinglake, whose book of eastern travels had enchanted him during his adolescence, his fellow-American Mr Motley, and with Mr Browning. Henry's attention focused first of all on the poet, also one of the heroes of his youth; and on Kinglake, who, sitting beside him, was 'a most delicious, sweet, old man, as urbane and deferential as Emerson'. Browning, however, was a bit of a shock. He was 'no more like to Paracelsus than I to Hercules', and to Howells he said he was 'a great chatterer, but no Sordello at all'. At 65 Robert Browning was a hardened diner-out. The young novelist and the old poet were to find themselves often at the same lamplit Victorian tables.

'Robert B. I am sorry to say,' he writes to Alice,

does not make on me a purely agreeable impression. His transparent eagerness to hold the *di de la conversation* and a sort of shrill interruptingness which distinguishes him have in them a kind of vulgarity. Beside which, strange to say, his talk doesn't strike me as very good. It is altogether gossip and personality and is not very beautifully worded. But evidently there are two Brownings – an esoteric and an exoteric. The former never peeps out in society, and the latter has not a ray of suggestion of *Men and Women*.

He was to continue to find Browning an idle gossip; but he was to say of him also that he was 'the writer of our time of whom, in the face of the rest of the world, the English tongue may be most proud – for he has touched *every*thing, and with a breadth!'

2

And so Henry James was launched. His personal charm and wit opened doors for him and as his work began to be published in England he found himself much in demand, not only for dinners but as a country house guest. The new life is reflected step by step in the correspondence with Quincy Street; to his mother and sister he enumerates the various dinners and sketches certain of his table-companions; to his father he mentions the personalities which would interest him; with William he is inclined to be a little more cautious and he generalizes. William is critical, and Henry is always flexible in his epistolary skills. 'I suppose William will call me a "fat snob" for mentioning these names,' he writes to his mother after enumerating certain dinners, 'but if they amuse Alice and you, I don't care for William.'

(In England three years later William was to write to Quincy Street: 'The way he worked at paying visits and going to dinners and parties was surprising to me, especially as he was all the time cursing them for so frustrating his work. It shows the perfect fascination of the whirlpool of a capital when once you are in it.' It was more than fascination. It was all part of the writer's daily work.) To Henry Adams he said that 'in writing to my relatives I ransack my memory for every adventure that has befallen me and turn my pockets inside out; so that they receive, and possibly propagate, an exaggerated impression of my social career'. But the career speaks for itself. During these early London years James came to see many walks of English life. There was first of all the fascination of meeting writers whom he already knew intimately through their works. Browning was but one instance. He meets Walter Pater at the home of the Hertz's, German Jews living in a pleasant house in Harley Street. They 'are insatiate lion-hunters and most naif in their pursuit of notabilities'. Pater is 'far from being as beautiful as his own prose', and though James chats with him he does not tell Quincy Street what they chatted about. George Meredith he encounters at a dinner in the home of the Positivist, J. Cotter Morison; he finds Meredith 'a singular but decidedly brilliant fellow, full of talk, paradoxes, affectations, etc. but interesting and witty, and of whom, if he didn't live in the country, I should see more. He hates the English, whom he speaks of as "they".'

'Their conversation is dreary,' said Meredith on this occasion to Henry, 'their food is heavy, their women are dull.'

At the home of Madame du Quaire he meets Matthew Arnold for the first time since their encounters at the Barberini. 'I cannot get over a feeling of pleasure that he writes just as he does; even his limitations have a practical excellence.' Later at W. E. Forster's he meets Arnold's entire family and sits next to the eldest daughter, 'as pretty as an American girl and chattering as freely'.

Then there is the Thackeray-Stephen-Ritchie circle. He had met Leslie Stephen in London long before, and the editor of the *Cornhill* had been kind and hospitable. He encounters him now after the death of his wife, the former Miss Thackeray, and finds him 'rendered more inarticulate than ever'. Later he meets his new wife and is charmed by her beauty. He finds himself fond of the surviving Thackeray daughter, recently married to a man much younger than herself, Richmond Ritchie. He takes her in to dinner on one occasion, 'further advanced toward confinement than I have ever seen a lady at a dinner party'. She is 'lovable and even touching' in her 'extreme good nature and erratic spontaneity'. He tells Grace Norton that she has 'the minimum of common sense, but quite the maximum of good feeling'. He is invited to the home of the famous Victorian dilettante, Charles Hamilton Aïdé, 'an aesthetic bachelor of a certain age and a certain fortune, moving apparently in the best society and living in sumptuous apartments'. Here he meets George du Maurier, 'a delightful little fellow'. They will become close friends. Early in his dining out he re-encounters Trollope, 'a very good genial ordinary fellow – much better than he seemed on the steamer when I crossed with him'. At Sir Robert Cunliffe's, a friend of Henry Adams, he meets the talkative poetaster and civil servant F. T. Palgrave, who will ultimately be remembered for that substantial symbol of his era, *The Golden Treasury*. Palgrave takes a great liking to James, and frequently visits him in Bolton Street in the morning on his way to his office in Whitehall, thus breaking into the novelist's working hours. 'Palgrave is the biggest talker in England or the world – it's a current there's no standing against – and he is frightfully abusive of everyone and everything save a very small number of perversely-chosen idols. But his bark is worse than his bite.' And again : 'He is, I imagine, the most disappointed man in England. He was the great man of his day at college and was expected to set the world on fire. But here he is at middle-age only an inspector of schools and an editor of little books of verse. He feels it much and it has soured him.'

He meets the well-known Positivist, Frederic Harrison, 'who in spite of his aspect, complexion, hair-brushing etc. as of a provincial second-rate dandy, is very good company. The contrast between Harrison's Comtism, communism etc. and his highly ornate and conventional appearance, is most singular.' There is also W. H. Mallock, then the talk of London because his *New Republic* had just been published, 'a most disagreeable and unsympathetic youth, with natural bad manners increased by the odious London affectation of none. He strikes me as "awfully clever"; but I opine that he will produce no other spontaneous or fruitful thing.' The judgement was accurate.

3

Not all the dinners are pleasant. 'I dined last night,' he writes to William,

> at the New University Club with Ernest Myers and four or five *çi-devant* Oxford men who are supposed to be choice spirits – Andrew Lang – a leader writer for *The Times* etc. I suppose this strikes you as an attractive occasion and in the stillness of Harvard Street excites your envy and speculation. But it failed to give me a sense of rare privilege – owing, partly, I think, to the ungemütlich *associations* I have, humanly, with Oxford – dreary, ill-favoured men, with local conversation and dirty hands. (All men in London, however, have dirty hands.)

He writes in the same vein of a dinner at the Albert Diceys', 'who are good, but decidedly too ugly, useful-informationish, grotesque-Oxfordish, poor-dinnerish etc., too surrounded with emulous types of the same not to make one feel that one can do better'.

A dinner at Frederick Locker's – the writer of light verse and bibliophile – proves deadly dull, Lord and Lady Thurlow, General Hamley etc. Thurlows speechless; Hamley disagreeable; James listless with a horrible cold, the Lockers trivial, and the room freezing. But if this can happen on one evening, there can be others when a pleasant incident colours the stuffiness of the diners and the dinners. In one of the great houses he finds himself sitting next to an ugly little wizened old woman who is very entertaining and reminiscent. She is the great dancer Taglioni. She has run through her various fortunes and in the evening of her days gives lessons to the daughters of the aristocracy. She tells Henry that she is well-received *dans le monde*. '*J'ai ma position de femme mariée et puis j'ai ma position de – Taglioni!*'

He meets the British scientist in the person of T. H. Huxley, 'a delightful sympathetic man' to whose home he is invited, a 'pleasant, easy, no dress-coat sort of house' in St John's Wood, in Marlborough Place, where James had lived as a boy.

> Huxley is a very genial, comfortable being – yet with none of the noisy and windy geniality of some folks here, whom you find with their backs turned when you are responding to the remarks that they have very offensively made you. But of course my talk with him is mere amiable generalities. These, however, he likes to cultivate, for recreation's sake, of a Sunday evening.

He meets the British soldier, embodied in the personality of Sir Garnet Wolseley – in a great house in Portman Square, filled with Queen Anne bric-à-brac 'to a degree that quite flattens one out'. Here he finds 'plain women, gentlemanly men etc. Sir Garnet is a very handsome, well-mannered and fascinating little man – with rosy dimples and an eye of steel : an excellent specimen of the *cultivated* British soldier.' In the ensuing years they will become friends.

He meets editors and publishers as a matter of course; and in certain houses, less rigidly Victorian, the stagefolk are beginning to be received. There are cosy dinners at the home of Mrs Rogerson – Christina Stewart Rogerson – one of London's more informal hostesses, who compensates for her homeliness by her dark skirt and white shirts of the finest linen with stiff cuffs and links, and Highland shoes with large silver buckles. He describes her as 'a clever liberal woman, who invites me every four or five days'. It will be chronicled that he said of her : 'If she had been beautiful and sane, she would have been one of the world's great wicked women.' At her table the novelist meets his fellow-countryman, James McNeill Whistler, 'a queer but entertaining creature', whom he has sharply criticized in certain of his anonymous accounts of the London galleries published in the *Nation*. 'They may be good studio-jokes, or even useful studio-experiments,' he had written of Whister's nocturnes and arrangements, 'but they illustrate only what one may call the self-complacency of technicality.' And he had echoed his own remark about the Paris Impressionists : 'It may be good to be an impressionist; but I should say on this evidence that it were vastly better to be an expressionist.' Whistler invites James to one of his Sunday breakfasts in Chelsea. 'He is a queer little Londonized Southerner and paints abominably,' Henry writes home. 'But his breakfasts are easy and pleasant, and he has tomatoes and buck-wheat cakes. I found there Sir Coutts and Lady Lindsay (the Grosvenor Gallery people) – who are very sociable (and Sir Coutts the handsomest man in England).' He would later revise his opinion of Whistler.

Elsewhere he meets Frederic Leighton, the Holman Hunts, Thomas Woolner the sculptor, 'good plain conceited fellow', and Samuel Lawrence, 'the artist who did your bad portrait in the dining-room,' he tells his father, 'a very kind, soft little man : who, when I told him he had done my father's portrait, said that was what every American told him'.

4

Henry James looks with curiosity at certain Englishmen, fortunate in all the circumstances of their life, and yet limited by their fortune to a kind of passive elegance, and the superior forms of amateurism and conformity. Thus he has close observation of Henry Adam's friend Charles Milnes Gaskell, 'an originally good fellow, depraved by snobbishness, over-many possessions and a position giving him all sorts of opportunities for taking himself and his luxuriant appurtenances with praeternatural seriousness'. Or 'nice young Sydney Holland', whom he sees in Scotland, the grandson of Sir Henry Holland, 'one of those manly, candid, good-looking young Englishmen who only need a touch of genius, or of something they haven't got, to make one think that they are the flower of the human race. As it is, they come near being it.'

There are the historical-political figures, for example James Bryce, whom James was to know during all his London years. The author of the famous work on the Holy Roman Empire calls on the novelist in Bolton Street and takes him to Oxford as his guest during Commemoration, where James watches the conferring of honorary degrees. Bryce always talks well and is 'distinctly able'. However he possesses three conflicting dispositions – literature, law and politics – 'and he has not made a complete thing of any of them'. James sees him as belonging to the class of 'young doctrinaire radicals (they are all growing old in it) who don't take the "popular heart" and seem booked to remain out of affairs. They are all tainted with priggishness – though Bryce less so than some of the others.'

Bryce later takes James to Cambridge, to Trinity, to dine with a kind of Oxford and Cambridge co-existence club, composed of half and half, and half in residence and half non-resident, meeting alternately at each university. The dinner is dullish. He has Henry Sidgwick on his right, and the others include Dicey, Godfrey Lushington, Leslie Stephen, Vernon Harcourt and Dilke. Dilke takes him fraternally by the arm and walks James over Cambridge and shows him 'all its lovely picturesqueness'. James decides that 'in detail, I think, it beats Oxford; though inferior in *ensemble*'.

He studies Dilke closely. 'The man who is shooting ahead much faster than anyone else is Charles Dilke. His ability is not at all rare, but he is very skilful and very ambitious, and though he is only thirty-five years old, he would almost certainly, if the Liberals should come into power tomorrow, be a cabinet minister.' And again :

Dilke is a very good fellow, and a specimen of a fortunate Englishman : born, without exceptional talents, to a big property, a place in the world, and a political ambition which – resolute industry and the force of social circumstances aiding – he is steadily *en train* to realize. And withal, not a grain of genius or inspiration. But he is only now emerging – much less radical than he began – from his early cloud – his having attacked the Queen and *cremated* his (deceased) wife.

Pure political ability such as Dilke's did not appear to James to be a 'very elevated form of genius'. His assessment of Dilke was shrewd, as history would show.

This was James's vision of London dinner-tables; and it is possible, in the memoirs of the period, to discover how he was seen by others. When Justin McCarthy, the journalist and Member of Parliament, came to write his reminiscences, towards the end of the century, he devoted the following paragraph to the novelist, it casts an interesting light on James's 'position' in society :

Henry James is an American who may be said to have thoroughly domesticated himself in London Society ... No man is more popular in London dining-rooms and drawing-rooms than Henry James, and a first night at a theatrical performance would seem incomplete if his familiar figure were not to be seen in the stalls or in one of the boxes. Henry James, too, has an interest in political life, and dines with leading public men in the London clubs which represent the one side of politics and the other. He is a delightful talker, and in his talk can develop views and ideas about every passing subject which can clothe even the trivial topics of the day with intellectual grace and meaning. Every now and then some vivid saying or some sparkling epigram comes in, and indeed, there is only, so far as I know, one thing which Henry James never could do in any conversation – he never could be commonplace.

This can be taken as a large verdict in which many other volumes of Victorian reminiscence concur.

5

There came a time when he wrote to his sister Alice (it was in May 1879) that his dinners were falling 'into a sort of shimmering muddle' in his memory, and in fact he was rarely tempted to keep them very distinct. There was one he had given himself, at the Reform Club, to a small and select circle, John Cross, Edward Piggott, Andrew Lang and Mowbray Morris : 'the thing was pleasant and the dinner was good'. He went on :

I am trying to think over my other dinners, but for the life of me I can't remember half of 'em. There was one at the Bishop of Gloucester's; I sat between the Bishopess and one of her daughters – a curious location, and not a lively one; the Bishopess being a regular Mrs Proudie and the daughter very deaf, I was sustained only by watching the fine sincere gallant-looking old face of Sir Henry Rawlinson (the orientalist), who sat opposite to me. Then there was one at the Stansfelds' at which I took in to [dinner] Mrs Jacob Bright, the essence of Birmingham and the flower – a rather faded one – of the middle class. Then there was one at Lady Holland's where I took in a large, plain, buxom Miss Lowther, a young woman of high fashion, and had on the other side of me Lady Carnarvon, who, though 'nice' and pretty, has not the genius of conversation.

The passage has in it certain foreshadowings : there is a dinner in *The Wings of the Dove*, in the home of a woman whose name is but a slight variant on the name Lowther, in which a Bishop figures among the guests; and the reader wonders what function this church-man fulfils in the novel, where he is never again mentioned although he has been pointedly described. It is almost as if, in writing the passage, Henry was recalling one or another of his old London dinners, and bringing in all the characters he remembered round the table. The dinners of his fiction were to be in the end composites of old dinners eaten during the Victorian decades. 'If you dine out a good deal in London,' he wrote to William, 'you forget your dinner the next morning – or rather, if you walk home, as I always do, you forget it by the time you have turned the corner of the street. My impressions evaporate with the fumes of the champagne.' The moment of surfeit had come. 'The genius of conversation in the great upper middle class is not a dazzling muse; it is a plain-faced, portly matron, well covered up in warm, woollen garments and fond of an after-dinner nap.' And again : 'I am tired of the "common run" of the London world and of the British upper middle class. I can meet them and get on with them; but I can't expatiate upon them.' Writing thus to his mother he adds : 'Such is the penalty of having a nature so tiresomely framed as that of the "artist" H. J. Jr.'

At the beginning of his life in London he had told Lizzie Boott,

'My personal life is much less *thin* than on the Continent.' Now he spoke of his 'excess of opportunities' – 'I have too much material – in the way of observation I lay it in at the rate of a ton a day, and already am much embarrassed for storage room.' Writing to Grace Norton he expresses the wish for some American to talk to, like herself, or her brother, to unburden himself of his many impressions. 'Everything is corked up, the feelings, impressions, judgements, emotions, of every kind, that are being perpetually generated, and that I can't utter to a single Briton of them all with the smallest chance of being understood.'

He had reached the point where he might still be a foreigner, but he no longer felt he was a stranger. 'I am living here too long to be an observer,' he writes to Grace Norton on 8 June 1879 :

I am losing my sense of peculiarities and differences – I am sinking into dull British acceptance and conformity. The other day I was talking to a very clever foreigner – a German (if you can admit the 'clever') – who had lived a long time in England and of whom I had asked some opinion. 'Oh, I know nothing of the English,' he said, 'I have lived here too long – twenty years. The first year I really knew a great deal. But I have lost it!' That is getting to be my state of mind, and I am sometimes really appalled at the matter of course way of looking at the indigenous life and manners into which I am gradually dropping! I am losing my standard – my charming little standard that I used to think so high; my standard of wit, of grace, of good manners, of vivacity, of urbanity, of intelligence, of what makes an easy and natural style of intercourse!

He quickly adds however that his words about his 'standard' must be taken with a grain of salt, and he apologizes to Miss Norton for treating her as if she also were 'a dull-eyed Briton'.

The truth is that I am so fond of London that I can afford to abuse it – and London is on the whole such a fine thing that it can afford to be abused! It has all sorts of superior qualities, but it has also, and English life generally and the English character have, a certain number of great plump flourishing uglinesses and drearinesses which offer themselves irresistibly as *pin-cushions* to criticism and irony. The British mind is so totally un-ironical in relation to itself that this is a perpetual temptation.

He continued to abuse London, to abuse the Season, to complain about the social pressures – and went on dining and visiting and observing.

Part Two:

A Reasonable Show of Fame

75

The Objective Genius

THE year 1878 had been Henry James's *annus mirabilis*. The new year, whose arrival he welcomed amid the snows of Yorkshire, saw the establishment of his fame on both sides of the Atlantic. He had created a vogue. He himself made allusion to it in a story in which a French Academician, writing from America, says: 'They have a novelist with pretensions to literature, who writes about the chase for the husband and the adventures of the rich Americans in our corrupt old Europe, where their primaeval candour puts the Europeans to shame. *C'est proprement écrit*: but it's terribly pale.' Some of it was pale; and James sometimes stretched his material thin. But he knew that his style, his charm, his observation, could stand him in good stead even when he had only an anecdote to relate. Magazines wanted his stories. He could spin conversations out of thin air; and then there were many kinds of magazines: he could afford to write 'thin' for some of them. He did not like the illustrated journals. Therefore *Scribner's*, which later became the *Century*, continued to receive what he regarded as his poorer efforts. His best was reserved for the *Atlantic*.

He lost no time, now that his name was known in England, in bringing out those novels which had already appeared in America. These he carefully revised. It became his established procedure to revise from magazine to book, from edition to edition. The rapid production of his works in England made him seem a prodigy of letters: in the history of authorship few novelists have seen through the press so many books in a single year. *An International Episode* came out in America, in the Harper Half-Hour pamphlet series, at the end of January 1879. In England in February James brought out three tales in two volumes, *Daisy Miller*, *An International Episode* and *Four Meetings*. In March the English edition of *The American* appeared; in May a completely revised version of *Roderick Hudson*. In August he began a six-part serial in *Scribner's*, entitled *Confidence*, which came out in book-form in December on both sides of the Atlantic. Meanwhile he had assembled some of his earlier stories for the British public, and these appeared as *The Madonna of the Future and Other Tales* in October (he included *Madame de Mauves, Eugene Pickering, Longstaff's Marriage, Benvolio* and *The Diary of a Man of Fifty* – a new tale). Finally, at the end of the year, he completed his brilliant study of *Hawthorne* for the English Men of Letters Series. It was published in December.

This was not all. He managed, in the midst of this activity, to write the tale of *The Pension Beaurepas* for the *Atlantic, The Diary of a Man of Fifty* for *Harper's,* and *A Bundle of Letters* – a tale written in a single long sitting, in Paris, which he was persuaded by his friend Theodore Child to print in Child's small English-language newspaper, the *Parisian.* James was happy to please him; but he once more forgot the risk he incurred – that of being pirated in America. Pirated he was, within a matter of weeks, by a friend of the James family, who produced the tale in a pretty paperback form in Boston. When James's parents spoke with pleasure of this publication, they received an angry answer : the 'friend' was, in effect, boldly robbing him. In the absence of copyright he had no legal redress.

He was showing in his daily life a Balzacian fertility; and with it something Balzac did not possess; a perfection of style and of form, a precision of prose that seemed to belie the rapidity of his writing. When Quincy Street became worried lest he be exhausting his physical powers, he replied (to William): 'I am as broad as I am long, as fat as a butter-tub and as red as a British *materfamilias.* On the other hand, as a compensation, I am excellently well! I am working along very quietly and steadily, and consider no reasonable show of fame and no decent literary competence out of my reach.' He added, for William's benefit, that he was decidedly not bloated morally : 'I am philosophic to leanness – to stringiness. Physically it's another affair.'

Later, to his mother, who also expressed uneasiness at his perpetual social life and seeming over-work, he wrote :

Perturb yourself not, sweet mother, on the subject of my headaches, of my exhausting life, of my burning the candle at both ends, of being nipped in the prime of my powers – or of any other nefarious tendency or catstrophe. I never was better, more at leisure, more workable, or less likely to trifle in any manner with my vitality, physical or intellectual. I wish you could see me in the flesh. I think a glance would set your mind at rest.

In spite of daily long walks, fencing, weight-lifting, he did indeed put on considerable weight during this period. 'I am in superb health,' he wrote home, 'and so fat that my flesh hangs over my waistband in huge bags. My appearance attracts general attention.'

It was not his plumpness which attracted attention. On London staircases people turned to look at the American with the trimmed, silky beard which gave him the appearance of an Elizabethan sea-captain. He was a much-discussed author, a literary lion. What disturbed him was that his financial returns were not keeping pace with his reputation. 'I have got a good deal of fame and hope some day to get a little money,' he wrote to his friend Perry. 'I have had, I think, more success with the dull British public in a few months than with that of my native land in all these long years that I have been scribbling to it. This fact, of course, helps me to be comfortable and contented here.' To Howells he wrote in the same vein : 'My fame indeed seems to do very well everywhere – the proportions it has acquired here are a constant surprise to me; it is only my fortune that leaves to be desired.' To his brother he wrote :

My reputation in England seems (considering what it is based on) ludicrously larger than any cash payment that I have yet received for it. The Macmillans are everything that's friendly – caressing – old Macmillan physically *hugs* me; but the delicious ring of the sovereign is conspicuous in our intercourse by its absence. However I am sure of the future – that is the great thing.

His royalties were small; but he commanded larger sums from the magazines. He had sufficient money to live at ease and to travel; he was no longer tied to the Quincy Street letter of credit. And he possessed a great serenity. When his parents expressed concern lest he be embittered by the British criticism of *An International Episode* his reply was :

I honestly believe that it would be impossible to be less at the mercy of common criticism than I. I know too perfectly well what I intend, desire and attempt, and am capable of following it in absolute absence of perturbation. Never was a genius – if genius there is – more healthy, objective, and (I honestly believe) less susceptible of superficial irritations and reactionary impulses. I know what I want – it stares one in the face, as big and round and bright as the full moon; I *can't* be diverted or deflected by the sense of judgments that are most of the time no judgments at all.

This was to be his attitude towards criticism during all his years of success. Although at first he was interested in what critics said, he ultimately became indifferent. He went his way with all the assurance of his craft and all the power of his imagination.

76

The Bachelor of Bolton Street

HE had long ago made up his mind he would not marry. It was not so much a matter of making up his mind, as of following his inclination : given his difficulties with younger women, and his comfortable relationship with elderly widows and old ladies, he saw no reason why he should change his pleasant celibate status for one that might prove a threat to his art and his personal sovereignty. In his tales dealing with writers and painters he is always clear about this. The most famous of this group, *The Lesson of the Master*, turns the question of matrimony into a joke : the great writer advises the dedicated novice against marriage – against what he calls the 'idols of the marketplace' – among which he includes 'placing one's children and dressing one's wife'. 'One's children interfere with perfection. One's wife interferes. Marriage interferes.' The young writer, who has shown an interest in a young lady, takes his advice and goes abroad only to learn later that the Master – widowed – has married his young lady. The story ends in an irony; its lesson is as clear as the Master's, and it is repeated in such tales as *The Next Time*, in which the gifted writer is forced to resort to journalism in order to support his family; or it is stated in violent terms, in *The Author of Beltraffio*, where the writer's wife considers his books so horrible that she allows their boy to die during an illness rather than have him live to read them. This is one of James's terrible tales – a Medea-story – which reveals his deepest fear of woman : she can rob him of his creative power. In *The Lesson of the Master* the writer is forced by marriage into the market place. 'My wife makes all my bargains with my publishers for me, and she had done so for twenty years. She does it consummately well; that's why I'm really pretty well off.' And all this is obtained at the price of shoddy work : 'I've led the life of the world, with my wife and my progeny; the clumsy, expensive, materialized, brutalized, Philistine, snobbish, life of London.' James names him St George and the presumption is that his

wife must be a dragon. The Master talks in this vein, even to confessing that his wife had made him burn one of his books. Wives
not only harnessed their writing husbands to a treadmill; they were
censors as well.

I

'I am too good a bachelor to spoil,' Henry James wrote to Grace
Norton. 'That sounds conceited – but one may be conceited in self-
defence, about a position with which the rest of the world associates
a certain idea of the ridiculous.' And in a letter to Lizzie Boott, four
or five years later, when she returned to the question – as his lady-
friends did – he wrote :

What strikes me most in the *affaire* is the want of application on the part
of society of the useful, beneficent, and civilizing part played in it by the
occasional unmarried man of a certain age. He keeps up the tone of
humanity – he stands for a thousand agreeable and delightful things.
People ought really to be ashamed not to feel better than that *what* one
is doing for it. *Dunque, cara Lisa, non mi sposero mai – mai!*

By remaining a bachelor James could live modestly; instead of
having to find a house, or a large apartment, he could for the present
remain in his little rooms in Bolton Street. He was in the heart of
London. His routine of life was as simple as his establishment. His
hours of writing and reading – he always had some pile of proofs
to read when he wasn't reading books – were also the hours during
which he seems to have built up rather than depleted his reserves
of energy for the other – the strenuous complicated social – side of
his existence. He rose usually after a sound sleep, having taken a
long walk before going to bed. He began work without breakfast. He
would eat a substantial mid-morning *déjeuner*; and he would write
sometimes for five or six hours after that. Only in the late afternoon
was he ready to cultivate his leisure with the same elegance as the
members of the British upper classes. At the end of his work-day
he paid calls, went to tea, or during free evenings turned to his club
to read the newspapers before his solitary meal. It was a pleasure
to eat in peace, when there was no need 'of swallowing inscrutable
entrées and tugging at the relaxed bell-rope of one's brain for a
feeble tinkle of conversation'. After dinner he would chat with
fellow-clubmen, or read in the library, or write letters. He dealt
with a voluminous correspondence – there was Quincy Street, and

his continental friends, and the usual social 'twaddle' in answer to invitations. There was also his business correspondence, for he took care of all his publishing arrangements. Thousands of his rapidly-scrawled letters survive; everyone kept them, even his relatives who were admonished to burn them. There was too much style in them, too much charm. The recipient could not bring himself to destroy so much liveliness, warmth – and life.

2

London was particularly delightful to the bachelor when he could be solitary; after so much social intercourse he enjoyed the 'dead season', during which Society moved to its country houses and estates. James liked the quiet that descended on the city. At night he could hear the creaking boots of the lonely policeman passing along Bolton Street; and in the morning the sharp double-tap of the postman bringing the usual deluge of mail. He enjoyed the routine irruptions of the domestics into his rooms bringing him his tea and bread-and-butter, or his chop and potatoes. On occasion he would record the talk for Quincy Street:

H. J. (to the maid): Can't you do anything in the world with potatoes but thus drearily boil them?
The Maid: Oh dear yes, sir, certingly, we can *mash* them!
H. J.: That comes to the same thing. No other way?
The Maid: I don't think we have heard of any other way, sir.
H. J.: You can't fry them?
The Maid: I don't think we could do that, sir. Isn't that French cookery, sir?

Whereupon James remembered Turgenev's remark, a reminiscence of the Russian's winter in England during the Franco-Prussian war, '*Que voulez-vous? Un pays où on ne sait tirer parti ni des œufs, ni des pommes de terre!*'

On another occasion he described a new domestic, hired to replace the maid 'who had grown grimy in my service, and who went away to marry a deformed cobbler, dwelling in a little mews, out of Curzon Street'. When the new maid arrived James said: 'You had better tell me your name, please.'

She: Well, sir, it might be Maria.
H. J.: It *might* be?

She: Well, sir, they calls me Maria.
H. J.: Isn't it your name?
She: My name's Annie, sir, but Missus says that's too familiar.

'So I have compromised,' James told Quincy Street, 'and call her Annie-Maria.' And he went on to explain that 'it is part of the British code that you call a servant any name you like, and many people have a fixed name for their butler, which all the successive occupants of the place are obliged to assume, so that the family needn't change its habits'. He was to make use of this, in *A Bundle of Letters*, where the English girl writes: 'Lady Battledown makes all her governesses take the same name; she gives £5 a year for the purpose. I forget what it is she calls them – I think it's Thompson.' The English girl adds: 'Governesses shouldn't have too pretty a name – they shouldn't have a nicer name than the family.'

3

Life was never dull for a bachelor absorbed in his work and in his world as James was. If he felt lonely he walked in the park; there was always something to look at and to study; and by this time he seems to have had enough friends at whose door he could knock of an evening. We get glimpses of him even knocking, on occasion, at Mr Hoppin's door, and the First Secretary makes a literal record of the talk of two bachelors about their common acquaintances.

Last night while I was dining *Henry James* called and I asked him to take a part of my soup and braised mutton. He was pleasant in his talk. I don't think he appreciates the *high tone of domestic life* at home while he attaches an undue importance to *society* in Europe. To be sure, as he says, there's no such thing as *society* in America. It is an auxiliary – an accident – an occasional diversion there. Here it is a paramount occupation. – We spoke of the circle of which we see a good deal – Mrs Rogerson, Lady Gordon, Mrs Hughes, etc. These women appear to have no other idea than to divert themselves. Every evening is pre-engaged for theatres or dinners. It is the business of life. At home the business of life is to make the family fireside happy. *Gallantry* takes up a good deal of the time and thoughts of the women here.

Mr Hoppin's observations were on the prosy side, and his examples were the reverse of felicitous. Mrs Rogerson's children were full-grown and her husband was a drunkard. There was no fireside to make happy. Lady Hamilton Gordon was a woman of a 'certain age'. Mr Hoppin and James discussed, what it was like to bring 'an imaginative sentimental New England wife into such surroundings'. The elderly diplomatic bachelor and 37-year-old literary bachelor thus made their tour of the London social horizon and dwelt on the dangers of scandal. At the end of the entry Mr Hoppin generalizes: 'Scandal spares nobody in this society. A beautiful Countess, one of the professional beauties, is supposed to have had an *amour* with her groom before she was married, and the most dreadful stories of a similar character have been circulated about the noble Duchess — !'

77

Three Old Women

THERE were three old women in London society, full of the world and its ways, who took their special places in Henry James's life: places more important than those of the younger women he constantly met. Their longevity and experience – he once said that their combined ages amounted to about 250 years – made them objects of the deepest interest to him. They were creatures of an older order; they offered him a relation with the past. This alone would not perhaps have sufficed. They were also high-spirited, witty, full of old stories; and they were imperious and demanding. Some hidden appeal brought him into close touch with them and made them important to him in a round of days already crowded with people and action. Writing at the time of George Eliot's marriage to John Cross, a man much younger than herself, James told his mother: 'Old women are marrying young men, by the way, all over the place. If you hear next that Mrs Kemble, or Mrs Procter, or Mrs Duncan Stewart is to marry *me*, you may know we have simply conformed to the fashion. But I will ask your consent first.' When he wrote this Mrs Kemble was 71, Mrs Procter 82 and Mrs Duncan Stewart 83.

I

For James, Fanny Kemble was 'the first woman in London'. She was also 'one of the consolations of my life!' Thirty-two years older than the novelist – and in fact one year older than his mother – Fanny

Kemble became one of his great attachments. What had begun as a nodding acquaintance in Rome in 1873, and had been followed by a brief and friendly meeting in Philadelphia in 1875, blossomed into a valued intimacy by her fireside in Cavendish Square. In the 1870s Fanny Kemble was still sufficiently active to accompany James to art-exhibitions and on occasions to the theatre – where she was often unrestrainedly demonstrative, weeping profusely or exclaiming violently, over memories of her own stage career. She possessed great strength of character and of will; and a blazing artistic temperament. The images Henry found for her were nearly always fiery ones – when they were not symbols designed to express subterranean qualities. She was a volcano in eruption : or she gave him 'a positive sense of having a deep, rich human nature and having cast off all vulgarities'. Mrs Kemble, he wrote, 'has no organized surface at all; she is like a straight deep cistern without a cover, or even, sometimes, a bucket, into which, as a mode of intercourse, one must tumble with a splash'. Sometimes he compared her to the Alps.

Such a temperament made for constant surprise; more often than not it gave rise to the dramatic. There was, too, a rather unpleasant side to Mrs Kemble, which James seems to have been incapable of perceiving : she possessed a kind of hard aggressivity. She was capable, for instance, of saying that G. H. Lewes looked as if 'he had been gnawed by the rats – and left' James, who would have shuddered at such a violent image on someone else's lips, laughed when Mrs Kemble uttered it – and repeated it to Quincy Street.

Fanny Kemble was a link with the early part of the century, with the great figures of the London stage and London drawing-rooms. As a rule James did not like actresses and the 'mountebank' side of their art. Mrs Kemble however was an actress with a strong aversion to the stage; and who had, in spite of this, mastered it; she brought to her art an intelligent competence as well as a remarkable personality. And she remained, until she was a frail old lady, a powerful presence, a great histrionic voice possessed of a beautiful utterance. She always had anecdotes to tell, and certain of her stories were transformed by James into novels and tales; the original anecdote of *Washington Square* stemmed from her. Even her casual remarks furnished ideas for stories. Proud of spirit, she gave James a vision of female grandeur that surpassed all others in his experience. 'My sublime Fanny,' he said of her. He responded to her 'human largeness' and she brought out in him all that was most filial and charming. 'Oh, friend of many lonely hours,' Mrs Kemble wrote in a sonnet which she sent to him; and in turn he could speak of the 'grand line and mass of her personality'. Long after she was dead, James carried, so to speak, the beat of her heart with him : her legacy to him was her travelling clock. 'I think of you almost as if you belonged to me,' she had written to him.

2

Mrs Procter – Anne Benson Procter – had known almost everyone of importance during the nineteenth century. She had stories of Shelley and Keats, Byron, Coleridge, Wordsworth, Southey, Landor. She once made a list of her famous friends and it filled two closely covered sheets of note-paper in double column. James considered her 'the best talker I have met in England'. Fanny Kemble called her 'the queen of newsmongers', but James wrote to the actress, 'What a capacity for *caring* – taking sides, resenting etc ! I don't see why, when one *minds* as much as that, one shouldn't live forever.' On the New Year week-end, when James was visiting Lord Houghton at Fryston Hall, and found Mrs Procter among his fellow-guests, he wrote that 'considering she is eighty years old, she is, at breakfast, lunch and dinner, a marvel. She abounds so in reminiscences and in *esprit* that one of her speeches chases another from one's mind. She has known literally every one.' And to his sister Alice he retailed an anecdote told by Mrs Procter about herself which incidentally helps to characterize her :

Mrs Procter (*to Sydney Smith, at the end of a dinner*) : Who is that at the end of the table?
Sydney Smith : Macaulay.
Mrs Procter : What? *The* Macaulay? I haven't heard him speak a word all dinner.
Sydney Smith : I gave him several opportunities, but *you* always took advantage of them.

Long after she was dead James was to write : 'It was her tone that was her value and her identity, and that kept her from being feebly modern.' He said also that she testified to a stouter and harder world than that of the Victorian era : her memory went back to the time of Napoleon and to personalities who belonged to the eighteenth century. His final tribute to her was : 'She was a kind of window in the past – now it's closed there is so much less air.'

But the profile of her which G. W. Smalley sent to the *Tribune* at the same time suggests other aspects of her personality. 'She had regal notions of what was due to her, and there was occasionally something imperious in her way of expressing her wishes.' He said also her idea of human nature was 'perhaps a little cynical'. Kinglake had called her 'Our Lady of Bitterness'. Smalley added that she uttered her bitter sayings in a felicitous manner : nevertheless 'her skill in the use of the knife was surgical'. He concluded by observing that she had masculine qualities – energy, decision, abruptness, 'clear ideas of what she wanted and how to get it'. Like Mrs Kemble she possessed an overbearing side to her nature.

She was nearly 80 when Henry met her, and it got to be a little joke between them that he would some day marry her. Thomas Hardy, calling on her in 1879, saw a photograph of Henry James on her table and made this note in his diary : 'She says he has made an offer of marriage. Can it be so?' 'I expect soon,' James wrote at this time to his mother, 'to hear that I am engaged to Mrs Procter *aetat* 82. I have indeed proposed to her several times, but she seems to think she can do better. As poor old William Hoppin, the American Secretary of Legation here, age 67 or so, was lately reported to be about to espouse Mrs Duncan Stewart, who is 83 or so, you will see to what an advanced period people here are assumed to keep up their interest in life.'

3

Mrs Duncan Stewart wore voluminous capotes and capes of old lace and black velvet. She was said to have been the natural daughter of an earl; she had been brought up in a convent in France and was distinctly Gallicized. At 24 she had married Duncan Stewart, a merchant, and had lived for years in Liverpool, bringing up several sons and a daughter. The daughter was the Mrs James Rogerson to whose home James was frequently invited. The mother, widowed in 1869, settled in London and became a fixture of its society. She had limited means and lived in small rooms at 101 Sloane Street, where she gave pleasant luncheon parties. She had known Washington Irving and Leigh Hunt and counted Disraeli among her friends. On 29 February 1884 James wrote to his sister : 'We are having the first cold of the winter and Mrs Duncan Stewart is dead. But the cold is bright and wholesome and Mrs Stewart had become a kind of talking melancholy ghost. She was a charming old being, however, and I shall miss her much. Some day I shall put her into a book.' In the same letter he said : 'I have seen Mrs Kemble and find her constantly a little more and a little more broken and, as it were, indented. I shall never put *her* into a book.'

In his notebooks, three years after Mrs Stewart's death, in sketching the tale which became *A London Life* he wrote : 'There must be an old lady – like Mrs Duncan S. – only of rank – a genial, clever, worldly, old-fashioned, half comforting, half shocking old lady, whom she [the heroine] goes to see and talk with.' He describes the forthright Lady Davenant who, in the tale, tries to comfort the hapless American girl, Laura Wing, very much as Mrs Stewart must have appeared to him – 'full of life, old as she was, and had been made, finer, sharper and more delicate, by nearly eighty years of it'. She expects a great deal of attention; the witty expression of her face shines 'like a lamp through the ground glass of her good breeding'. In the tale, as in life, Mrs Stewart has firm opinions and is capable of strong quick sympathies. He endows her also with Mrs Procter's friendships.

Mrs Stewart also possessed a certain hardness and sharpness; and this emerges when one reads her letters to Mr Hoppin which he preserved in his scrapbook-journal. They are brief, amusing, flirtatious – at 80. She chides him for neglecting her; she points out that Mr James does not neglect her. One gains a sense of a demanding woman with a rough fund of witty attack and a sharpness of tongue, when the occasion warranted.

4

'I constantly hear,' the novelist wrote to his mother in 1880, 'that I have been "very attentive" to numerous spinsters and widows, and also that many of my well-wishers think that I should be "so much happier" if I would only marry.' He was writing in reply to rumours that he was engaged. His sentence might have been amended to read 'elderly widows and spinsters of a certain age'. That he was attracted to older women because they offered him the polished surface of London wit and cultivation and their long social histories, is understandable in an insatiable student of manners. What is less understandable is his inveterate choice of women who were strong and domineering and had in them a streak of hardness, sometimes even of cruelty. These women probably appealed to him because such qualities were distinctly familiar: Mary James and his Aunt Kate had been quite as hard, firm and sovereign. Indeed during all the years of his childhood he had learned how to make himself agreeable to such women.

His various writings suggest that he looked for the same qualities in younger women. A gentle passive feminine creature like Lizzie Boott pleased him, but she was an open book: he would never have thought of marrying her. She had no mystery, life with her would have been rather dull. A 'beautiful, mysterious melancholy, inscrutable' woman like Elena Lowe intrigued him so much that he sought for years to understand her.

James created in his novels a race of formidable and sometimes terrifying female power-figures: the Mrs Gereths, Madame Merles, Kate Croys, or the child-destroyers, Rose Armiger of *The Other House* and the governess of *The Turn of the Screw* – 'bad heroines', women seen ambivalently as destructive and yet admirable. He could create them without recognizing wholly that they embodied certain accurate traits of the older women in his life. His experience of the manipulating, manoeuvring, meddling woman had been always with the elderly female. When he encountered certain spinsters closer to his own age, spinsters still possibly marriageable, he tended to subject them to the play of his often-irresistible charm; and then was astonished to discover that they were not merely as receptive as the older ladies – they also expected an offer of marriage.

Finally, when he came to younger women, the full contradiction asserted itself: they were charming, they were sometimes beautiful, soft, clinging, intense, and James could only ask himself, as he asked of his image of Elena Lowe – could they really be trusted? Even so simple and *insouciante* a creature as Daisy Miller is a puzzle. Is she a flirt, or is she virtuous? Is she simply heartless or a hard and cynical young woman assuming a mask of innocence? A tale he wrote immediately after Daisy, *The Diary of a Man of Fifty*, expresses his original bafflement. The diary-entries in the tale are dated as of the time of the writing of the first chapters of Roderick, and in the city where he wrote them. It is the story of a middle-aged man, returning to Florence; here, a quarter of a century before, he had turned his back on a difficult woman, whom he had decided he could no longer trust. Now he meets a young man in love with this woman's daughter, and thinks his old experience is being re-enacted.

562   THE CONQUEST OF LONDON 1876-81

He tells the ardent young lover, whom he regards as his youthful self: 'You admire her – you adore her, and yet secretly you mistrust her.' The young man tries in vain to persuade him that the circumstances are different. 'You can't rid yourself of the suspicion that at the bottom of all things she is hard and cruel, and you would be immensely relieved if some one should persuade you that your suspicion is right.' James could never rid himself of this suspicion: but in this tale the marriage does take place – and the narrator ends by wondering whether he had really been right or whether his old suspicions had been ill-founded.

During this time, when he could easily laugh at the possibility of his marrying the Mrs Kembles and Mrs Procters of the London world, he wrote to Grace Norton (who, in Cambridge, was another version of this sort of woman): 'I am unlikely ever to marry.' His reason was hardly convincing: 'I should pretend to think just a little better of life than I really do.' Besides, he said, he had become used to his unmarried state, and 'an amiable bachelor here and there doesn't strike me as at all amiss, and I think he too may forward the cause of civilization'.

There was to be no doubt that the bachelor of Bolton Street was to forward the cause of civilization: his experience of the overriding female had created a permanent damage to his relations with women: and in that marvellous way in which nature insists on compensations and solutions, his constant effort to repair the damage, to understand what had gone wrong, gave him the necessary distance and aloofness – even while creating momentary blindnesses – that enabled him, of all novelists, to undertake the writing of *The Portrait of a Lady*, and to create a whole generation of American girls.

Strangely enough the Second Secretary of Legation, the light-weight Mr Nadal, had a perception of this. Trying on his side to do what Mr Hoppin had done, that is analyse James's success in London, he remarked in a reminiscence written years later, that James proved attractive to women of all ages because he was genuinely distinguished 'in a marked degree, both as a young man and an old one'. Secondly he 'possessed an inscrutability which piqued their interest and curiosity'. More important still, women liked him, said Nadal, for his sympathetic and delicate discernment of their own qualities. 'He seemed to look at women rather as women looked at them. Women looked at women as persons; men look at them as women.

The quality of sex in women, which is their first and chief attraction to most men, was not their chief attraction to James.' This was an accurate observation. It enabled him to draw them in his fiction with both detachment and intimacy.

78

Visits

THERE was no way of getting to know the English better, James felt, than by seeing them 'through their great invention of country-house life'. The letters of the novelist to his family and friends in Cambridge are filled with his accounts of great as well as simple homes in England and Scotland: the life led there, the large parties, the hunts, the open-air scenes and the company, interesting or dull. The upper classes in England depended on country visits in order to 'get at each other', an indispensable complement to the fugitive contacts of London. 'It is certainly a thing they have brought to great perfection,' he told Grace Norton, 'and if one can stand the occasional dullness and the superabundance of poor unanimated talk, one can get much that is entertaining and interesting out of it.'

Periodically James embarked on a round of visits; during his first years he enjoyed their novelty and their variety; he welcomed the break they offered in the rhythm of his London days. With time, he became discriminating; but this was only after he had been surfeited, and had, in the process, seen many corners of England. His visit to Charles Milnes Gaskell at Wenlock Abbey during his first summer in England had been but a foretaste. After *Daisy Miller* the visits multiplied, and in the autumn of 1878 he made his first trip to Scotland, to stay with Sir John Clark, an 'amiable, demonstrative, appreciative' friend and his 'rather satirical invalid gentlewoman of a wife'. The weather was splendid, the hospitality generous, the company 'inoffensive', and James wrote with rapture of the breezy moors, the brown and purple hills, the rich mixture of autumn mist and sunshine. There were highland sports, long rambles over the sun-warmed heather: James had never before been on the moors and for three days he had a feast of them. Even though he was not a sportsman, he enjoyed watching the frightened grouse starting up across the blue. He made a trip to a ruined castle on horseback and returned stiff and sore from his hours in the saddle, only to go to a ball and dance polkas half the night. Lily Langtry, the great beauty, was present and James watched her in a highland reel (which she had been practising for three days) with young Lord Huntly, a very handsome fellow in a kilt who leaped, hooted, romped and reminded Henry that ancient Caledonian 'barbarism' still lurked among the Scots.

There was a visit of a different order, 'not a very interesting episode'. At Wenlock Abbey he met Lady Portsmouth and in due course visited Eggesford Manor, in North Devon.

The place and country are of course very beautiful and Lady P. 'most kind'; but though there are several peopl⁻ in the house (local gentlefolk, of no distinctive qualities) the whole thing is dull. This is a large family, chiefly of infantine sons and daughters (there are 12!) who live in some mysterious part of the house and are never seen. Lord P. is simply a great hunting and racing magnate, who keeps the hounds in this part of the country and is absent all day with them. Ther is nothing in the house but pictures of horses – and awfully bad ones at that. Yesterday, before lunch, I walked in the grounds with Lady Rosamund, who is not 'out' and doesn't dine at table, though she is a very pretty little pink and white creature of 17; and in the p.m. Lady P. showed me her boudoir, which she is 'doing up' with old china etc.

Lady Portsmouth takes Henry for a drive in her phaeton through lovely Devonshire lanes. In the evening the nursery *corps de ballet* comes into the gallery with governesses, and dances cachuchas and minuets 'with the sweetest docility and modesty'. The next day the weather turns bad, and Henry sits alone 'in a big cold library of totally unread books, waiting for Lord Portsmouth, who has offered to take me out and show me his stable and kennels (famous ones)'. Writing home, James says he will try to get away the next day. 'I don't think I could stick out a Sunday here.' Though there are innumerable flunkeys about the house, he tries in vain to get the fire refreshed. Two or three come in and look at it, but it doesn't appear to be their business to bring in coal.

The visit to the stables is deferred until after lunch. It finally takes place and Henry goes the rounds with Lord P. and a couple of the other visitors – forty horses, mostly hunters, and a wonderful pack of foxhounds 'lodged like superior mechanics'.

Then there was Lord Rosebery, his Rothschild wife and their vast estates, Mentmore, the Durdans, Dalmeny House. Rosebery was destined to be one of the last of Victoria's prime ministers. He possessed great conversational gifts; he was an active racing man; and he was vigorous in politics, capable of rousing large audiences by his oratory. His enemies called him an opportunist; his friends recognized him as a hard-working Liberal, possessing strong intellectual qualities and an unyielding nature. Henry James enjoyed his hospitality on a number of occasions, watching his political career and his rise to power with unabated interest. Late in the autumn of 1880 he was invited by Lady Rosebery to Mentmore, the great house built by Mayer Amschel Rothschild in 1851. His fellow-guests included John Bright, the idol of Birmingham and champion for many years of the middle class in Parliament, and Lord Northbrook, the last Liberal Viceroy of India. Sir John Everett Millais, the painter, one of the originators of the Pre-Raphaelite movement, was there part of the time, and James took a walk with him to the stables where three winners of the Derby were trotted out in succession for them. Lord Rosebery, 'with youth, cleverness, a delightful face, a happy character, a Rothschild wife of numberless millions to distinguish and demoralize him, wears them with such tact and bonhomie, that you almost forgive him'. Lady Rosebery Henry found 'large, fat, ugly, good-natured, sensible and kind'. He continues:

I have spent a good part of the time in listening to the conversation of John Bright, whom, though I constantly see him at the Reform Club, I had never met before. He has the repute of being often 'grumpy;' but on this occasion he has been in extremely good form and has discoursed uninterruptedly and pleasantly. He gives one an impression of sturdy, honest, vigorous, English middle-class liberalism, accompanied by a certain infusion of genius, which helps one to understand how his name has become the great rallying-point of that sentiment.

He reminded Henry a good deal of 'a superior New Englander — with a fatter, damper nature, however'.

As he wrote this letter, the guests were at tea in a vast hall 'where an upper gallery looks down like the colonnade in Paul Veronese's pictures and the chairs are all golden thrones belonging to the ancient Doges of Venice'. James had withdrawn from the glittering scene 'to commune with my mammy', and his letter had in it those thoughts which he knew would be found agreeable in Quincy Street.

He is meditating by his fire 'on the fleeting character of earthly possessions'. The footman arrives and lays out his things.

You may be interested, by the way, to know that Lord Rosebery said this morning at lunch that his ideal of the happy life was that of Cambridge, Mass., 'living like Longfellow.' You may imagine that at this the company looked awfully vague, and I thought of proposing to him to exchange Mentmore for 20 Quincy Street.

Lord Rosebery's diary of 29 November 1880 offers its summary record. It quotes James as saying 'I mean to write a great novel before I die, Lord Rosebery, but I do not mean to be in a hurry.' And Rosebery adds 'he tells me he is thirty-five and has made up his mind not to marry'.

James was to have a later view of John Bright, during a week-end at Oxford, as guest of George Brodrick, the Warden of Merton. He had sent him some of Longfellow's poems which Bright now described to him, and he went on to tell of 'a splendid novel by General Lew Wallace – of which he related the plot at extraordinary length'. No doubt *Ben Hur*. 'His "culture",' wrote James to Grace Norton,

is so narrow, his taste so bad, and what remains of his intellect so weak, that I wondered greatly that a 'great statesman' should have coexisted with such limitations. It made me think that great statesmen may sometimes be very measurable creatures. However John Bright was never, and never pretended to be that : he was simply a great orator, with a special gift of speaking which, having died out, has left him childlike and bland, and rather bare.

The word *bare* was apropos. For Bright wrote in his diary, after he had told Henry about Lew Wallace : 'Sat up late for two nights with Mr James. Conversation on America interesting.'

From Mr Hoppin's unpublished journal, Sunday, 12 December 1880 :

I had a pleasant call from Henry James a few evenings ago. He had been staying with the Henry Hollands and with the Roseberys. He described the luxury and elegance at Mentmore as something fabulous. James thinks there is a great drawback in making a country visit. Although we hear a great deal to the contrary, a guest must give up much of his personal independence. To be obliged to be agreeable morning, noon and night for several days is a great task upon one's spirits – if not one's intellect. It is better that we should never go into society excepting when we are in a mood for it and when we can show ourselves at the best.

Another Christmas (1880), and this time James is the guest of the commanding officer in the Government House at Devonport, the official residence of General Pakenham, who commands one of the big military districts into which England is divided. General Pakenham is nephew by marriage of the old Duke of Wellington. The house stands on the edge of Plymouth Sound, looking straight across the narrow channel at Mount Edgcumbe, the most beautiful 'nobleman's seat' Henry has seen in England. Mrs Pakenham, a former American belle, is now intensely Anglicized. There are two sons home from Eton and destined, like their ancestors, to go into the Army. The day after Christmas James is taken by a young Captain Brand, son of the Speaker of the House of Commons, aboard his ship, to be present while he reads the service, the Chaplain being absent. James breakfasts with the officers in the wardroom, and is conducted over the man-of-war, one of the old-fashioned big line-of-battleships. Mrs Pakenham urges James to stay for the big New Year's ball. Henry begs off. He would be lost, he feels, in a wilderness of redcoats. He goes instead to the Clarks', who have come down from Scotland to Cornwall in the winter, and is driven by Sir John far away to Penzance and then to Land's End. The morning is soft and moist. He stands meditatively watching the winter Atlantic heaving gently round the outermost point of old England. After that he is happy to recover his fireside in Bolton Street.

79

A Dinner at the Reform

THE occasion was modest enough and yet one of those evenings that Henry James was later to remember with deep pleasure. This time it was he who was the host. In June 1879 there came from Paris a brief note from Ivan Sergeyevich written in his elegant and quaint English. He was leaving Paris for Oxford; the university 'does me the unexpected honour of making me a D.C.L.' The 'promotion' he said would take place on 18 June: in a week. On his way back he had 'the greatest desire of seeing you, myself'. He proposed 'a quiet dinner'.

A year and half – a momentous year and a half – had elapsed since James had sat beside Ivan Sergeyevich's gouty bedside. He was over-

joyed at the prospect of seeing his Russian friend again, and this
time it seemed to him that he should forgo the pleasure of the intimate dinner. Instead he would share the great Russian with certain
of his London friends. He accordingly proposed to dine him at the
Reform to fête the honorary degree, the first ever given by Oxford
to a novelist. James would greet Turgenev from his own more elevated station in the literary and social world.

The dinner was arranged, and at the last moment James was able
to add a familiar from Cambridge. 'The other night, John Fiske rose,
moon-like, above my horizon, apparently very well and happy,'
Henry wrote to William,

and I immediately invited him to dine with me to meet Turgenev next
week – the latter coming over by invitation to receive the D.C.L. degree
at Oxford – a very pretty attention to pay him – (to which I imagine
James Bryce chiefly put them up). He has promised very solemnly (by
letter from Paris) to dine with me on the 20th; and it is quite on the
cards that he should play me false; but I trust he won't. I wish you were
here to adorn the feast. Fiske on his return will tell you about it.

James remembered the diverse occasions on which Turgenev had,
at the last minute, cancelled appointments in Paris: the sudden
attacks of gout, his complicated involvements with the Viardots, the
demands made upon him by his fellow-Russians. His visits to London
were always brief.

The group that gathered round the table at the Reform Club was a
curious one: it seemed more philosophical and political than literary
– but then Turgenev had given James very little notice. He invited
W. R. S. Ralston, Turgenev's translator; J. Cotter Morison, the Positivist; John Cross (who was to marry George Eliot a few months
later) and Mowbray Morris, of *Macmillan's Magazine*. Bryce and
young Hugh Arnold-Forster (ultimately Secretary for War under
Balfour) joined the party later in the evening.

'Dinner at 8 o'clock at the Reform Club with Henry James,' wrote
Fiske exuberantly to his wife. 'Turgenev was the hero of the oc-
casion, and he is splendid – not unlike Longfellow in appearance.
James Bryce, the great historian, was also there, and my ever-
delightful Ralston. Magnificent dinner, and brilliant conversation.
Ralston walked home with me at midnight.'

'It was all extremely pleasant, dear Ivan Sergeyevich being at his
best and most charming, which is not saying little,' James wrote to
his mother. 'His simplicity and sweetness are as great as his wit and

intelligence, and his conversational powers are flavoured (excuse the culinary expression) by the most captivating *bonhomie*.'

At Oxford, Bryce, as Regius Professor of Civil Law, had extolled Turgenev's influence in the emancipation of the serfs. The novelist received his honour in the company of John Ruskin and Sir Frederick Leighton. Turgenev was delighted with the gift made to him of the gown he had worn at the ceremony. It would serve admirably for Sunday charades at Madame Viardot's.

80

Carthorse and Racer

TURGENEV was Henry James's touchstone for the English novel. Writing to W. E. Henley, he pointed out that the Russian was the exact opposite of Meredith. Turgenev didn't care a straw for an epigram or a phrase; Meredith cared enormously. Turgenev wasn't a whit literary, but simply human and moral. Meredith was a mannerist, a coquette – like 'that pitiful prostitute Cherbuliez'. (He was now being as harsh about him as Zola.) So too, in thinking of George Eliot, he observed that she was a philosopher, while Turgenev was a poet. One could call Turgenev a 'magician' – a word he would never apply to George Eliot. The Russian cared for the aspect of things; she for the reason of things.

James nevertheless looked with high affection upon George Eliot. He hoped that he would meet her again. There had been one brief occasion, in 1869, during his grand tour, when Grace Norton had taken him into the presence of the overpowering lady – brief because a son of G. H. Lewes was writhing on the floor in the next room in a fit of pain and Lewes himself had gone to the apothecary for morphine. Now a Londoner, no longer a tourist, James embraced the first possible occasion to pay his respects to the author of *Middlemarch*. Early in April 1878 John Cross invited him to a dinner at the Devonshire Club at which Lewes was present. 'Capital talk and stories,' Lewes wrote in his diary at the evening's end. James's version was different :

I sat next to Lewes, who is personally repulsive, but most clever and entertaining. He is rather too much of a professional *raconteur* – he told lots of stories; but he recounts very well – chiefly in French. He remembered, as soon as I was introduced to him, my queer visit to George Eliot in 1869, with Grace Norton, and asked me to come back, which I shall do.

He did – probably on 21 April 1878 – and reported to William:

The Leweses were very urbane and friendly, and I think that I shall have the right *dorénavant* to consider myself a Sunday *habitué*. The great G. E. herself is both sweet and superior, and has a delightful expression in her large, long, pale, equine face. I had my turn at sitting beside her and being conversed with in a low, but most harmonious tone; and bating a tendency to *aborder* only the highest themes I have no fault to find with her. Lewes told some of his usual stories, chiefly French.

In a later memory of the Priory – as George Eliot's house was called – he spoke of 'a kind of sanctity in the place, an atmosphere of stillness and concentration, something that suggested a literary temple'. Even a 'superficial acquaintance' with the novelist assured him that her rich and complicated mind was both benignant and receptive. It was also a 'deeply reserved' mind and very far from being egotistical, so that 'the creations which brought her renown were of the incalculable kind', that is, they had been shaped 'in mystery, in some intellectual backshop or secret crucible, and were as little as possible implied in the aspect of her life'.

He was destined to meet the Leweses once more under strange circumstances. The story of that encounter has become a celebrated anecdote; for Henry James fashioned it himself in the fragmentary pages of what would have been the third volume of his autobiographies: how, being taken by a hostess, Mrs Greville, with whom he was staying in Surrey, to visit the Leweses in their house nearby, he realized on arrival that they were not altogether welcome guests. It was a drenching afternoon; the bland and benign George Eliot stood beside a fire in a chill desert of a room with the master of the house guarding an opposite hearthstone, and both conveying to James's keen observation that if they greeted them with a show of warmth they 'should more devoutly like it when we departed'. In his reminiscence he relates, with a sense of the high comedy of it how they left shortly after, and Lewes, seeing them to their waiting carriage, suddenly rushed back into the house and brought out a couple of blue volumes Mrs Greville had lent to the household. 'Ah, those books – take them away, please, away, away!' And Henry recognized ruefully that the two blue volumes were *The Europeans* – and that neither George Eliot nor Lewes apparently had in the least 'connected book with author'.

Lewes was to die shortly afterwards; and George Eliot married John Cross. She was 60; he was twenty years younger. When word reached James, who was then in Florence, he wrote to Cross on 14 May 1880: 'I have congratulated friends before on their approaching and accomplished nuptials; but I have never had the privilege of doing so in a case in which I felt (as today) all the cordiality of mankind mingling with my individual voice. Don't let this mighty murmur drown my feeble note.' George Eliot, writing to a friend a few days later, said 'Johnnie had a graceful letter of congratulation from Mr Henry James, who is still at Florence.'

She lived but a few months longer. To his mother Henry wrote that her death was all the sadder in that 'she, poor woman, had begun a new (personal) life: a more healthy, objective one than she had ever known before. I doubt whether she would have written, but she would have lived – and after all, at 60, and with a great desire to live, she was still young.'

A few days later he paid his respects to Cross. He was received in the novelist's 'beautiful little study they had just made perfect' and sat in the chair George Eliot used to occupy.

She was surely an extraordinary woman – her intellectual force and activity have, I suspect, never been equalled in any woman. If, with these powers, she had only been able to see and know more of life, she would have done greater things. As for the head itself, it was evidently of the first order – capable of almost *any* responsibilities. She led a wonderfully *large* intellectual life – and Cross said that her memory and her absolute exemption from the sense of fatigue, were more amazing the more he knew her. He, poor fellow, is left very much lamenting; but my private impression is that if she had not died, she would have killed him. He couldn't keep up the intellectual pace – all Dante and Goethe, Cervantes and the Greek tragedians. As he said himself, it was a carthorse yoked to a racer: several hours a day spent in reading aloud the most immortal of works.

To James's vision there had been two elements in George Eliot – the 'spontaneous and the artificial'. It was almost as if within her there were also the carthorse and the racer: the carthorse wrote *Romola*, so to speak, and the racer *Middlemarch*. Her spontaneous side enabled her to observe life and to feel it. But she had fallen into a high-minded circle which had compelled her to give an exaggerated attention to lofty generalizations. In the process spontaneity was tethered to the intellect; when she felt life in her works she was at her best; when she tried to feel 'views' upon life, she became a burden to her story-telling. To her genius, at its best, he paid and continued to pay homage – and his greatest tribute was his writing of *The Portrait of a Lady*, a 'George Eliot novel' written (or re-written) in the way he would have wanted her to write.

81

The Bard and Mr Browning

ON the day after Henry James's visit in the downpour to George Eliot and Lewes, when his two blue volumes had, in a manner, been hurled after him, the 'friend of the super-eminent', the loquacious and eccentric Mrs Greville, took him to still another celebrity living near her Surrey cottage. This time James was an invited guest; they were expected at Aldworth, and Alfred Tennyson suffered from no lapse of memory about the identity of his visitor. He had met James at Lord Houghton's, and had talked to him with much warmth about one of his tales. James never revealed which tale it was; but he did feel this was some kind of compensation for the rebuff at the Leweses'.

On that autumn day, Mrs Greville (whom James described as a large, elegant, 'extremely near-sighted and extremely demonstrative lady' with a genius for 'friendship, admiration, declamation and expenditure', brought James to Tennyson's house, and when they had lunched the Poet Laureate was urged to read a poem. They went upstairs to his study. One of the great poems of Henry's youth had been *Locksley Hall* and this was the poem he asked for. Tennyson growled it from its noble cadenced beginning through its full length : it wasn't Flaubert's *gueuler*, but it was a continual monotonous vocalization.

James sat at one of the windows that windy watery autumn day; sometimes the glass was sheeted with rain. He asked himself whether this were really he, and whether this was the Laureate; he wanted to pinch himself when he remembered the emotions this poem had aroused in him in his youth; he wondered why he did not swoon for very ecstasy, It was all the reverse : he felt none of the vibrations of those long-ago days at Newport, or the effect upon him of the volume of Tennyson's poems, which his father had given him when he was a boy. 'Why in the name of poetic justice had one anciently heaved and flushed with one's own recital of the splendid stuff if one was now only to sigh in secret "Oh dear, oh dear"?' The author lowered the whole pitch. He took 'even more out of his verse than he had put in'. Tennyson, in a word, wasn't Tennysonian.

On this same occasion there was a certain humour in the way in which Victoria's Poet Laureate pricked up his ears when the chattering Mrs Greville mentioned a French relative whose name was Laure de Sade. Tennyson promptly launched into a discussion of the works of the Marquis de Sade, enumerating titles, and saying many things, with only James, among those present, aware that he was speaking of an author one did not mention in polite Victorian society. Tennyson didn't know – unless he was teasing his guests; had he really read the Marquis or was he merely reciting 'useful information'? Mrs Greville listened with 'the blankest grace' to her friend's enumeration of his [Sade's]

titles to infamy, among which that of his most notorious work was pronounced. It was the homeliest, frankest, most domestic passage, as who should say, and most remarkable for leaving none of us save myself, by my impression, in the least embarrassed or bewildered; largely, I think, because of the failure – a failure the most charmingly flat – of all measure on the part of auditors and speaker alike of what might be intended or understood, of what, in fine, the latter was talking about.

James pondered this phenomenon : the Laureate who had become a mere growling voice; who spoke words – his own – without feeling and facts without knowledge.

'I went to lunch with Tennyson,' Henry wrote to Charles Eliot Norton.

I was staying near him, with an amiable and clever, but fantastic and ridiculous Mrs Greville, and he took me up into his study and read aloud – not very well – 'Locksley Hall,' from beginning to end! I don't know whether you saw anything of this author, who personally is less agreeable than his works – having a manner that is rather bad than good. But when I feel disposed to reflect that Tennyson is not personally Tennysonian, I summon up the image of Browning, and this has the effect of making me check my complaints.

James held Browning in high esteem; and if at moments he was depreciatory, he was to recognize, when he recalled the contrasting figure of the Laureate, that there was a distinct difference of temperament – that the scales weighted in favour of Browning. Whatever Tennyson had been, he was, as a 'Bard', a growler of his own lines. Browning on the other hand – but we have Henry's exact impression : 'One of my latest sensations was going one day to Lady Airlie's to hear Browning read his own poems – with the comfort of finding that, at least, if you don't understand them, he himself apparently understands them even less. He read them as if he hated them and would like to bite them to pieces.'

There was at least emotion. Browning might be 'loud, sound, normal, hearty', a presence 'bustling with prompt responses and expected opinions and usual views'. He possessed an intellectual eagerness to put himself in the place of other people; and there was in him 'a restlessness of psychological research'. In his personal delivery of the fruits of his genius he tended to harshness, however, 'the result was that what he read showed extraordinary life'. The mistake was James's : he had made, in his mind, quite another image of Tennyson. He had supposed him to possess all the fine flush of his own youth. That day James learned 'what a Bard consisted of' – as he learned earlier in Browning something of the nature of 'involvement' – in life and in poetry.

82

Voltaire in Petticoats

HENRY ADAMS and his wife arrived in England during the early summer of 1879, and sought out Henry in Bolton Street. James had seen very little of them since their meetings in Rome six years before. They were fresh from their voyage, rather tired and bedraggled, and his first impression – for he looked at them with the new eyes of distance and time – was that Adams could never 'in the nature of things be a very gracious or sympathetic companion'. Marian Adams (the Clover Hooper of his youth, Minny Temple's friend) struck him as 'toned down and bedimmed from her ancient brilliance'. The Adamses settled in furnished rooms, two streets away, in Half Moon Street, and Henry James got into the habit of dropping in to see them. He took them to a Sunday afternoon at the Grosvenor Gallery and introduced Clover to Mrs Duncan Stewart – 'delighted my dear in Americans,' the veteran lady told Clover, 'they are all so charming.' The generalization was rather wide, but James came to agree where it concerned his old-new friends, formerly of Cambridge, now of Washington. Later that autumn, when they met in Paris and spent evenings together in restaurants and theatres, he wrote to Quincy Street, 'I have become very fond of them – they are very excellent people.'

There was, however, a fundamental opposition of temperament between the two Henrys. The historian was interested in large generalizations; the novelist was concerned with the particular. Henry Adams's relationship to the past, to history, was a means by which he attempted to unravel the riddles of man and the personal New England riddle of himself. Henry James's relationship to the past was that it was part of a continuum of man's imagination. He was willing to deal with it only as a vast accumulation of creative awareness applicable to a palpable present. Adams was trussed up in the rigidities of ancestry and upbringing and was always struggling to be free. James accepted the world as it presented itself, and constantly moved to larger freedom. In his later letters to Adams he gently chides him, holding up the delights of spontaneity and the blessing of occasional obedience to impulse. For James life was an act of joyful and imaginative curiosity; for Adams it was a gloomy questioning of personal experience that he could not reconcile to the eternal flux of history. They had a patch of common ground. Henry James sought to create laws for novels; Henry Adams was seeking the laws of history. Yet even here there was a marked difference – that between a man who establishes order in his own world, as James could do, and a man who interrogates the entire world to extract a meaning from it. When Henry James read Adams's anonymous novel *Democracy*, he found it clever, although the satire seemed to him 'a good deal too coarse'. 'Who is it by, or attributed to?' he asked his friend Perry. 'A man or a woman? It is good enough to make it a pity it isn't better.' At the end the novelist was to speak of Adams's 'rich and ingenious mind', his 'great resources of contemplation, speculation, resignation'.

'Henry is very sensible, though a trifle dry,' was his comment during this period in London and Paris. He added: 'Clover has a touch of genius.'

James had always liked Clover Adams. Long ago he had spoken

of her 'moral spontaneity'. Now he had occasion to see how sharp, how cutting she could be; how she subjected everything that came under her view to a mordant and often highly humorous aggressivity. She had an abundance of wit: and an intense Americanism. Europeans were people to be judged, appraised and usually condemned. We know her in a great measure from her letters, and they – like Henry's to Quincy Street – were often written as family entertainment. Nevertheless the form they take, in their ever-present astringency, tells us much about this lively and yet self-doomed creature. 'Mrs Adams,' Henry wrote to Grace Norton, 'in comparison with the usual British female, is a perfect Voltaire in petticoats.'

The Adamses, after their trip to France and Spain, returned to London for the winter of 1879–80 and we catch glimpses of them in various great houses, often in the company of Henry James. They entertained in their own pretty house, which they took for the season, at 22 Queen Anne's Gate. Mr Hoppin notes in his diary after dining there that Henry James, the Matthew Arnolds, Lady Strangford and Mrs Duncan Stewart were among the guests. 'The talk,' he tells us, 'was very good. Arnold was particularly genial and loquacious.' Lady Strangford he describes as a rank Tory 'with unreasonable prejudices against Americans'.

James saw much of the Adamses. We can glimpse him on a Sunday afternoon, 22 February 1880; Adams, writing at this moment to Henry Cabot, records: 'Harry James is standing on the hearthrug, with his hands under his coat-tails, talking with my wife exactly as though we were in Marlborough Street.' What the Adamses offered James was the American companionship for which he longed in London: they were the kind of Americans he had wished for when he had written to Shady Hill that there were things he could never say to an Englishman. 'The Henry Adamses are here,' he told Lizzie Boott, 'very pleasant, friendly, conversational, critical, ironical.' He had sat up with them till one o'clock that morning 'abusing the Britons. The dear Britons are invaluable for that'. To Quincy Street he observed: 'It is agreeable to have in London a couple of good American confidants.'

The Adamses were 'not at all crazy about London'. Long before they left they were frankly homesick for Washington. When in the autumn of 1880 the time came for their departure James, again to Grace Norton, summed up what their presence in England had meant to him:

I go in an hour to bid farewell to my friends the Henry Adamses, who after a year of London life are returning to their beloved Washington. One sees so many 'cultivated Americans' who prefer living abroad that it is a great refreshment to encounter two specimens of this class who find the charms of their native land so much greater than those of Europe. In England they appear to have suffered more than enjoyed, and their experience is not unedifying, for they have seen and known a good deal of English life. But they are rather too critical and invidious. I shall miss them much, though – we have had such inveterate discussions and comparing of notes. They have been much liked here.

James was to observe them in due course in their native sur-roundings and the time was to come when 'Voltaire in petticoats' would make her appearance in one of his American tales.

Even as these *confidants* were leaving, a turn of the wheel brought to London the charming elderly Yankee who had made bright James's autumn in Paris eight years before. Lowell had been shifted from Madrid to the Court of St James's, and it was a little like the changing of the guard – for Mr Hoppin recorded in his journal that when Mr Lowell arrived in London Mr and Mrs Adams were at Vic-toria Station to greet him. Glad as James was that his old friend was assuming these onerous responsibilities in the British capital, he wondered whether he would be very happy – or successful – in his task. For once his doubts proved groundless.

During Lowell's London years his friendship with James deepened into an affectionate and enduring intimacy, built upon their com-mon Americanism and their common foundation of literary allusion. Thus was constituted a strange little American corner for the ex-patriate novelist; Lowell and his two secretaries, Hoppin and Nadal.

83

C'est Mon Plaisir ...

THE joys of the 'dead season' in London were short-lived for Henry James. He discovered soon enough that if the importunities of En-glish society ceased at certain times of the year, there arrived at such times on Britain's shore – and on his doorstep – many of his strenuous compatriots. There were days when he gave himself over entirely to entertaining old American friends, acquaintances of his brothers, Albany and New York relatives, and a continuing procession of literary pilgrims. American friends from the Continent would seek him out also, and while he enjoyed seeing some of them, they made great inroads into his working hours. If he had said to William that he always had his eyes on his native land, his native land, more often than not, had its eye on him.

Among the earliest of his visitors after fame had come to him was a Boston lady who thought herself descended from Scottish royalty – from Robert Bruce – and believed Mary Stuart to be an ancestor: and who, accordingly, conducted herself as if she were a Queen. Her motto, on the seal she ultimately designed, was *C'est mon plaisir* ... and being fortunately endowed, she could suit her life to her motto and her motto to her life. Whether Isabella Stewart Gardner had met Henry James in Boston earlier we do not know; but it is from this time that we have his letters to her. They are playful and filled with coquetry. She came abroad early in 1879 with her husband, and presently Henry James was telling her how to find her way to Burne-Jones's studio and hoping 'to see you often – if you will allow me'. He was a busy man, however, and probably was not available as often as the regal Mrs Gardner would have liked. The novelist's relationship to Isabella was handled with the same firmness and ingenuity that governed all his dealings with exalted – and self-exalted – personages. He quite fell in with Mrs Gardner's wish to be treated as if she were royalty. He was prepared always to be the most humble of her courtiers – but his tone was that of *noblesse oblige*. His letters were written as if he were flourishing a plumed hat before her and making formal obeisance. And yet he very carefully maintained a kind of distance designed to show Queen Isabella that it was he who was bestowing favours. For Henry understood her very well, and she greatly amused him. 'Look out for my next big novel,' Henry wrote in one of his earliest letters to her. 'It will immortalize me. After that, some day, I will immortalize you.'

Henry James's letters to Isabella Stewart Gardner – almost 100 of them preserved in the Venetian palace she ultimately built in Boston's Fenway – are masterpieces of epistolary persiflage. He indulged constantly in the mock-ironic and Isabella was flattered. If he suggested that she shed tears for the failure of one of his plays, it was to add that her tears were, of course, pearls. There is more flattery than meets the eye: Mrs Jack was an ardent collector of pearls. Or he could begin with an endearing compliment: 'Why are you so perverse? – Why do you come to London when I am away, and [go] away from it just when I come back?' Having made his flourish he could quietly add : 'Even your bright presence there does not make me repent having fled this year from the Savage Season.' And then the forcible conclusion : 'You wouldn't have made it tame – so what good should I have got? I hope you have found it as wild as you like things.'

Isabella found this exhilarating, and James had his fun. Such letters could have been written only by someone who, at bottom, really liked the self-inflated, wilful, and driven Mrs Gardner. James could rail at her in the privacy of his notebooks, see her as one of the tide of transatlantic 'barbarians' over-running Europe, carrying off shiploads of spoils – while at the same time he penetrated the façade and understood that Isabella's acute queenship concealed a certain strange shyness and timidity, a certain unsureness that no real Queen would have. Bernard Berenson was to call his patroness 'the serpent of the Charles'. James saw in her qualities that belonged to Eve rather than to the serpent. 'I think she is too amiable to become *really* fashionable,' he wrote to Mrs Daniel S. Curtis, who lived in a real Venetian palace on the Grand Canal and who, if she wasn't treated as a Queen, was saluted as a female Doge. 'I see her succeeding better at Grand Hotels than at grand manners. She tries too hard and listens too sympathetically – bless her innocent (after all) heart.' There were times when he was less patient. 'Mrs Jack returns to Paris tomorrow,' he wrote to Henrietta Reubell. 'She is not a woman, she is a locomotive – with a Pullman car attached.'

During the summer and autumn of 1879 James went sightseeing with Mrs Gardner on both sides of the Channel. On one occasion in Paris the Boston Gardners and the Washington Adamses, accompanied by the novelist, dined at a *café chantant* in the open air and they went to the *Cirque*, after which they ate ices at a wayside café. The experience could not have been lost on James : an imperious 'Queen' juxtaposed with a 'Voltaire in petticoats' in a setting such as Manet painted. 'I remember those agreeable days last summer in London and Paris,' he wrote, 'those talks and walks and drives and dinners.' Isabella took her place in the pattern of Henry James's days and years, and fixed her image in his work : for if one of his great themes was the chase of the American girl for the husband, another was the chase of the wealthy American for the artefacts of Europe.

Part Three:
Portrait of a Lady

84

A Storm in the Provinces

WILLIAM JAMES was married in July 1878 to Alice Howe Gibbens, a Boston schoolteacher and a woman of considerable charm and refinement. She came from Weymouth, Massachusetts, of an old New England family, and had lived abroad for several years with her mother. The marriage took place in the very month of *Daisy Miller*, and William, in the first flush of his honeymoon and of his release from the paternal hearth where he had lingered to his 37th year, resumed his vigorous criticism of his younger brother's work. We shall never know exactly what he wrote, for Henry destroyed William's letters of this period. William, however, kept Henry's and from these we can deduce some of his strictures. The elder brother attacked the slightness of *The Europeans* and objected to the ending of *Daisy*, which seemed to him frivolous. He asked for greater 'fatness and bigness' in Henry's stories. To the author of these works, flushed with his considerable success, William's observations seemed as ill-founded as they were ill-timed. His reply is sufficiently documentary: 'I was depressed on reading your letter by your painful reflections on *The Europeans*. But now, an hour having elapsed, I am beginning to hold up my head a little.' He felt that William tended to take such works 'too rigidly and unimaginatively'. He seemed to think that 'an artistic experiment was a piece of conduct, to which one's life were somehow committed'. Henry added: 'I don't trust your judgment altogether (if you will permit me to say so) about *details*; but I think you are altogether right in returning to the importance of subject. I hold to this very strongly.' He found William's criticism of *Daisy* 'queer and narrow', and any creative artist would so judge it. (William had felt that Henry's remark about Winterbourne's attachment to a lady in Geneva was out of place immediately after the scene in the cemetery.) Concluding, Henry explained to his brother that being 'very artistic' he had a constant impulse to try experiments of form, on which he had no intention of wasting 'big' situations. 'It is something,' he said, 'to have learned how to write, and when I look round me and see how few people (doing my sort of work) know how, I don't regret my step by step evolution.'

I

There was in reality nothing new in William's criticisms of Henry; the writing son of Quincy Street had had long experience of them and never without a certain pain. The new elements in the family situation were Henry's international success and William's marriage. William was still an unknown professor at Harvard who had published a few articles in learned journals and was engaged belatedly in setting up a household. Henry James Jr had become a name on two continents, his work translated into French and German, and appearing also in Tauchnitz. If the novelist's increasing fame was difficult for William to swallow – and he had to put his sibling in his place with a new barrage of disparaging criticism – his marriage was quite as profound a blow to his younger brother. It brought into sharp focus the whole early drama of 'brother and angel'. The marriage represented the first break in their primal relationship. A third person had stepped between them – between their ancient alliance of competition and affection and joint discovery of the world, first in the nursery and then during lonely weeks as 'hotel children' in Europe – always under William's leadership. Their rivalry was strong; yet Henry's fraternal devotion to William (never fully reciprocated) was stronger. He could be active and masculine in meeting the world and creating his career; he shrank into passivity and softness the moment he was in William's presence, almost as if some invisible marriage bond existed between them. The language in which Henry congratulated William is indeed highly suggestive. 'I have just heard from Mother that you have decided to be married on the 10th ult. [he was writing after that date] and as I was divorced from you by an untimely fate on this occasion, let me at least repair the injury by giving you, in the most earnest words that my clumsy pen can shape, a tender bridal benediction.' If this was a clumsy attempt at affectionate humour, we must recognize nevertheless that the pen raised in blessing set down the words 'I was divorced from you by an untimely fate on this occasion'. The deeper feelings implicit in the word 'divorce' were written at this moment into a novel called *Confidence* which Henry produced during the ensuing weeks. It is his poorest novel, perhaps because of its heavily-charged autobiographical content. It begins with a friendship between two young men, the familiar masculine friendships of James's stories. In this instance Gordon Wright works in Germany on scientific projects and has 'a firmly treading rather than a winged intellect'. So much for the critic of Henry's works! The friend, Bernard Longueville is a lover of art, a traveller; he sketches, charms young ladies, is clever, aesthetic, free in his way of life, and acutely analytical.

These two young men had formed an alliance of old, in college days, and the bond between them had been strengthened by the simple fact of its having survived the sentimental revolutions of early life. Its strongest link was a sort of mutual respect. Their tastes, their pursuits, were different; but each of them had a high esteem for the other's character.

Wright, the scientific young man, falls in love with a young woman named Angela. For the one and only time the 'Angel' is included in Henry's fiction as a name – but feminized. Wright asks his aesthetic and analytical friend to give him his opinion of Angela, for he has fallen deeply in love with her. Bernard, after much thought, tells him she is not his sort. Gordon takes his advice seriously; he marries on the rebound a flighty chattering female. In the fantasy Henry James not only appoints himself adviser to his brother on his marriage, but has him finally make a marriage from which Henry must rescue him. And then, within this fantasy, Henry recognizes the reality that his brother is married and that he must accept the 'divorce'. William is no longer linked to the aesthetic, yielding and also subjugated 'angel' of the family. Henry endows Angela with all of his artistic-aesthetic qualities; she is a woman of refinement, and later Bernard falls in love with her – that is, Henry falls in love or finally accepts the disparaged artist-side of himself. And now, in Henry's fantasy-fiction, Gordon, feeling he has made a wrong marriage, gives way to rage and jealousy. Angela steps in and untangles the emotionally-charged situation, as Henry was doing in writing *Confidence*.

James thus split himself into two characters and made William and himself into accepting and rejecting figures. In giving the William character the name of 'Wright' Henry revealed his long-seated fraternal acceptance of his elder brother as always in the 'right'. But he also manipulates his own hurt feelings in this strange story. He recognizes that the only marriage possible to him is to accept his artist self, even if William does not: and *Confidence* is perhaps important in Henry's life not as an expression of hurt at William's 'rejection', but as the beginning of his acceptance of the two sides of his own nature. The unusual title of the novel tells us what Henry was seeking. He needed confidence in the Benvolio sides of his nature; and in the puppet correlatives of this novel he rides through self-consolation, jealousy, rejection, assertion, in an attempt to rectify the disturbed familial emotions. Henry re-asserts his self-confidence, dealt a double-blow by William at the very moment of his life's triumph. And from this moment, as we shall see, he gives the lead to heroines instead of heroes in his novels; 'angel' is turned into 'Angela'.

2

Henry James's sense of having been set aside – with critical violence – in his brother's life would probably have had little consequences beyond this minor novel that ran through six instalments in *Scribner's* and yielded him $1,500, had there not been another occurrence of a larger public nature. He had completed his book on Hawthorne for the 'English Men of Letters Series'. Macmillan set it up rapidly and published it in the midst of Henry's fictional successes. In writing it, he had made no pretence of original research; he used standard materials, relied mainly on Hawthorne's own works, and, largely for courtesy's sake, had a few conversations with Hawthorne's son, Julian, then resident in England. The book proved extremely popular among his British readers. They liked its quiet tone, its wit, the authority and brilliance of Henry James's pictures of the New England of Hawthorne's time. In fact Macmillans were so pleased that they invited James at once to do a study of Dickens for the same series, and offered a large advance to tempt him.

The *Hawthorne* had not been out long before James realized that he had profoundly irritated his American reviewers. The first intimation came from Quincy Street. His mother spoke of the book as having taken some courage to do. James wondered why. 'Mother thinks me very "bold",' he wrote to his father, 'to have braved the probable wrath of the Boston critics; but I am not conscious of any great audacity.' His mother, however, was right. Not only the Boston reviewers but those of New York attacked James for adopting a 'foreign' attitude toward Hawthorne, and for his emphasis on the parochial quality of New England life in Hawthorne's day. For the first time American critics began to suggest that James was losing his native point of view by his continued residence abroad. The reviewers felt that he treated Hawthorne with too much condescension. Others were angry at the repeated use of the word 'provincial'. A careful reading of what James said shows nothing truly offensive, but the tone of the book, and certain of his formulations, evoked a sharp, if characteristic, outburst of chauvinism. James's argument ran as follows: America had been bare of society and history when Hawthorne came upon the scene. Finding no rich social fabric, such as English novelists could draw upon, the romancer tissued his work out of haunted Puritan memories of New England. In depicting the America of the earlier part of the century, and in describing the elements 'absent' from American life, James distinctly touched certain sensitivities in a nation that had tended to be self-adulatory rather than self-critical. 'In the United States, in those days,' James had written, 'there were no great things to look out at (save forests and rivers); life was not in the least spectacular; society was not brilliant; the country was given up to a great material prosperity, a homely *bourgeois* activity, a diffusion of primary education and the common luxuries.' Such sentences, while accurate enough, seemed depreciatory. His saying 'in the light, fresh American air, unthickened and undarkened by customs and institutions' invited challenge. It little mattered that James had taken his cue from Hawthorne himself. Indeed the most celebrated – and condemned – passage in the book was nothing more than a series of variations on a theme from Hawthorne's preface to *The Marble Faun*. Hawthorne had written: 'No author, without a trial, can conceive of the difficulty of writing a romance about a country where there is no shadow, no antiquity, no mystery, no picturesque and gloomy wrong, nor anything but a commonplace prosperity, in broad and simple daylight, as is happily the case with my dear native land.' In the light of this passage James went on to make the famous enumeration of the things 'absent' from American life in Hawthorne's time which existed for British novelists. The passage is often quoted, but seldom in context, so that it does make James sound as if he were advocating adoption by the United States of those very British institutions which America had abjured. This was the offending passage:

The negative side of the spectacle on which Hawthorne looked out, in his contemplative saunterings and reveries, might, indeed, with a little ingenuity, be made almost ludicrous; one might enumerate the items of high civilization, as it exists in other countries, which are absent from the texture of American life, until it should become a wonder to know what was left. No State, in the European sense of the word, and indeed barely a specific national name. No sovereign, no court, no personal loyalty, no aristocracy, no church, no clergy, no army, no diplomatic service, no country gentlemen, no palaces, no castles, nor manors, nor old country-houses, nor parsonages, nor thatched cottages, nor ivied ruins; no cathedrals, nor abbeys, nor little Norman churches; no great Universities, nor public schools – no Oxford, nor Eton, nor Harrow; no literature, no novels, no museums, no pictures, no political society, no sporting class – no Epsom nor Ascot! Some such list as that might be drawn up of the absent things in American life – especially in the American life of forty years ago, the effect of which, upon an English or a French imagination, would probably as a general thing be appalling.

James went on to say that 'the American knows that a good deal remains; what it is that remains – that is his secret, his joke, as one may say'. In this variation on Hawthorne's theme James was also echoing the cadences of still another of his predecessors, James Fenimore Cooper, who had written in his *Notions of Americans* that there was 'no costume for the peasant (there is scarcely a peasant at all), no wig for the judge, no baton for the general, no diadem for the chief magistrate'. Cooper had further said : 'In short, it is not possible to conceive a state of society in which more of the attributes of plain good sense, or fewer of the artificial absurdities of life, are to be found than here.' For these reasons, and the fact that men found with ease other avenues to wealth and honour than the strenuous avenue of authorship, Cooper had considered the outlook for American literature in his time lacking in promise.

Even James's friend Howells was critical. The effect of the book upon him is reflected in the anonymous review he contributed to the February 1880 issue of the *Atlantic*. 'We foresee, without any powerful prophetic lens, that Mr James will be in some quarters promptly attainted of high treason.' James had over-insisted on American provincialism. 'If it is not provincial for an Englishman to be English, or a Frenchman French, then it is not so for an American to be American; and if Hawthorne was "exquisitely provincial", one had better take one's chance of universality with him than with almost any Londoner or Parisian of his time.'

Howells expressed delight in certain of the chapters, but to James's enumeration of the things absent from American life, he rejoined, 'we have the whole human life remaining, and a social structure presenting the only fresh and novel opportunities left to fiction, opportunities manifold and inexhaustible'.

3

James judged Howell's review 'handsome and friendly'; and in a long letter told him that the *Hawthorne* had been 'a tolerably meditated performance'. He admitted that he had used the word provincial too many times and also pleaded guilty to over-working the word 'dusky'. But on the question of provincialism he insisted 'I think it extremely provincial for a Russian to be very Russian, a Portuguese to be very Portuguese; for the simple reason that certain national types are essentially and intrinsically provincial.' As for his enumeration of 'absent' things, and his argument that the novel of manners required an old civilization, this seemed to James to be a truism. 'It is on manners, customs, usages, habits, forms, upon all these things matured and established, that a novelist lives – they are the very stuff his work is made of.' In saying 'we have the whole of human life remaining' Howells was begging the question. There was that much less of life when there were fewer institutions and fewer works of civilization. 'I shall feel refuted,' James said, 'only when we have produced (setting the present high company – yourself and me – for obvious reasons apart) a gentleman who strikes me as a novelist – as belonging to the company of Balzac and Thackeray.' James said he did agree with Howells that it was necessary to feel as he did about the possibilities of America as a scene for fiction; only in this way would the country ultimately produce such geniuses of the novel as had flourished in the older civilizations. But he doubted whether a Balzac or a Thackeray would agree with Howells. When he did, he, James, was prepared to 'lie flat on my stomach and do him homage', even in the centre of the *Atlantic Monthly*'s column 'The Contributors' Club', or on the threshold of the magazine or in any public place.

James was first bewildered and then hurt by the storm he had raised in America. He shrugged it off as 'a very big tempest in a very small teapot', nevertheless it made a deep impression on him. 'The hubbub produced by my poor little *Hawthorne* is most ridiculous,' he wrote to Perry.

My father has sent me a great many notices, each one more abusive and more abject than the others. The vulgarity, ignorance, rabid vanity and general idiocy of them all is truly incredible. But I hold it a great piece of good luck to have stirred up such a clatter. The whole episode projects a lurid light upon the state of American 'culture,' and furnishes me with a hundred wonderful examples, where, before, I had only more or less vague impressions. Whatever might have been my own evidence for calling American taste 'provincial,' my successors at least will have no excuse for not doing it.

He expressed this forcefully to his mother: 'It is like turning up the underside of a stone in the country – full of interesting revelations concerning the states of mind of the too numerous race of the literary animalculae.' And thanking his friend Perry for a favourable review, James wrote in April 1880: 'What a public to write for! – what an inspiration in addressing them! But let us hope they are not the real American public. If I thought they were, I would give up the country.'

In the end he shrugged the matter off as 'the clucking of a brood of prairie hens'. However, he was hurt, and puzzled. America, like his brother, had suddenly made him feel cast aside. His work had been spurned and abused at the very moment when he seemed to be harmoniously attaining all his aims. The tempest blew itself out; but the weight of fraternal and national disapproval, in which his friendly editor had joined, left a certain amount of wreckage in its wake. Superimposed upon the wounds of his boyhood – the endless times when he had been pushed aside and relegated to a quiet corner – the reception of his *Hawthorne* brought James to a turning-point in his development which was reflected immediately in his work.

85

The Frail Vessels

THE change which occurred – and which led James to write certain of his masterpieces – had been quietly symbolized by the fact that the 'Angel' was Angela in *Confidence*. From this moment James began to write novels about heroines instead of about heroes. Hitherto, in his larger works, he had recorded the adventures of the Rowland-Rodericks, or the Christopher Newmans; and even when he seemed to be studying American flirts abroad, like Daisy, it was through masculine eyes, such as Winterbourne's. Now, however, he found it necessary to create – and to show – how American women, 'heiresses of all the ages', responded to their destinies in a world that jilted, denied, betrayed – that made them, for all their fine will to freedom and independence, into second-class citizens in the very society that bestowed its heritage upon them. There were, to be sure, certain later exceptions: as with Hyacinth Robinson in *The Princess Casamassima* or Lambert Strether in *The Ambassadors*; but from now on the female protagonist took possession of the Jamesian scene, and she was to range from the juvenile Maisie, through the adolescent Nanda, to the mature Milly and Maggie of the later novels, not to speak of the Miriam Rooths, Fleda Vetches, Rose Armigers and Isabel Archers of other works along the way.

In a sense, what this may be said to have reflected, was Henry James's deepest personal feelings. Conquering London and its literary world, he could be as assertive and as powerful as Christopher Newman; but, rejected like Newman – or pushed to the wall by his elder brother and the critics of his *Hawthorne* – told that he wasn't fit to play with rough boys, or that his writing was full of knots and bows and ribbons, he found himself reminded forcibly that he was a perpetual 'mere junior', that he seemed to have been doomed from the cradle to abasements and inferiorities. One has but to mention the titles of his succeeding works to recognize the force of these emotions. They were expressed in a short and remarkable novel about a jilted heiress, and an even more remarkable novel about an American girl attempting to assert herself in the world. That these works should have been followed by a novel dedicated to the actual debate on feminism would seem, in these conditions, the most logical thing in the world. The circumstances of his emotional life had led James to his significant protagonists during the first great period of his writing life. He was ready (as *Confidence* showed) to accept the feminine side of his nature, and this led him to paint the 'portrait' of a lady. Years afterwards he was to ponder this and to attempt to explain what he had done. Contemplating his shelf of fiction, he asked himself why he had chosen to give the centre of his stage to his young heroines, rather than write stories of adventure and action, as other novelists did. 'By what process of logical accretion,' he wondered.

was this slight 'personality,' the mere slim shade of an intelligent but presumptuous girl, to find itself endowed with the high attributes of a Subject? – and indeed by what thinness, at the best, would such a subject not be vitiated? Millions of presumptuous girls, intelligent or not intelligent, daily affront their destiny, and what is it open to their destiny to *be*, at the most, that we should make an ado about it? The novel is of its very nature an 'ado,' an ado about something, and the larger the form it takes, the greater of course the ado.

It is significant that James used the word 'affront' and not 'confront'. Reasoning in this way, James was led to quote George Eliot's words, 'In these frail vessels is borne onward through the ages the treasure of human affection.' Eliot had had her heroines: Dickens, Walter Scott and even the subtle Robert Louis Stevenson had preferred to leave the task unattempted. Musing on this, James proceeded to justify his major studies of the female sensibility, his insistence, at the heart of his own work, upon the heroine rather than the hero.

'Frail vessel', however, was hardly applicable to James's strong and egotistical young women. They possess not a little of his own power, will and strength in imposing themselves upon the world. James, at any rate, argued that a novelist – a novelist like himself – did not necessarily have to deal with the life of action. He could, through characters such as Isabel, or Milly, record the fascination of mental and emotional experience – mild adventures, perhaps, certainly independent 'of flood and field, of the moving accident, of battle and murder and sudden death'. Isabel Archer could sit quietly by her fire during the long and remarkable sequence of her thoughts in the *Portrait* while she reviewed in subtle detail the history of her life. 'It is a representation,' James was to say, 'simply of her motionlessly *seeing*.' The challenge for him as novelist and narrator was to make of this act a matter as exciting 'as the surprise of a caravan or the identification of a pirate'.

I

Confidence was completed during the summer of 1879. Everyone seemed interested in what Henry James would do next. He had promised that he would write a 'big' novel, and Quincy Street was constantly curious about it. Compared to his lighter works, he told his parents, this work would be 'as wine unto water', and from this point the novel, destined to become *The Portrait of a Lady*, is spoken of in the family letters as the 'wine-and-water novel'. It was with the intention of starting this work in earnest that James had gone to Paris in the early autumn of 1879, on his way to Italy. On the eve of his departure from London he received a letter from his old Roman acquaintance, Matthew Arnold, congratulating him on *Roderick Hudson*, which had recently appeared for the first time in England. 'When will your Hawthorne be out?' Arnold queried genially. 'That is a man I don't much care for, but I am sure to like what you say of him.'

The study of Hawthorne had been completed that September at 42 Rue de Luxembourg, a few doors from the house in which he had passed his memorable winter, three years before. On the day the last sentences were written he had gone out to celebrate the occasion with Mrs Gardner. This was the time when the Henry Adamses were also in Paris on their way to Spain and James saw them almost daily. 'It is the same old Paris,' he wrote to T. S. Perry, 'seeming transcendently civilized, after the grimy Babylon by the Thames, but a million times less interesting.' Nevertheless James had a lively and enjoyable autumn. The English summer had been dreary and wet; the French capital was filled with sunshine. Certain of his English friends turned up and James acted as their cicerone. He found them quite as provincial as his American friends – the Andrew Langs for instance, who assumed they could post letters in Paris with English stamps. Hamilton Aïdé, the amiable dilettante, arrived, and James took him to Bougival to see Turgenev. The Russian was 'delectable as ever, though a little gouty'. Later in the autumn Ivan Sergeyevich joined him in town for what had become their traditional *déjeuner*. Of his old Russian friends James re-encountered the Princess Ourousov and had some enjoyable meetings with her. Zhukovski was in Naples, and Henry planned to see him there. However, early in December, as he was about to leave for Florence, a raging blizzard covered all Europe. The tunnels to Italy were blocked; the drifts were waist-high in Paris. At the height of the storm Henry sat snugly in his hotel, in the Rue Neuve St Augustin, whither he had moved with the advent of the cold, and wrote in a single sitting his light tale of American and European manners, *A Bundle of Letters*. This was the story, later pirated, which he gave to Theodore Child to publish in the *Parisian*.

For Child, the novelist also reviewed the newly published *Nana*, and while in the French capital he seems also to have written the long reviews of the recently published correspondence of Sainte-Beuve and of Delacroix. This return to the writing of criticism was confined to these reviews, and they show how much authority he had gained in the three years since his Paris residence. They are not only vigorous in their close analysis of the qualities of the writers; they demonstrate how much more receptive he was to their nature as artists. With Sainte-Beuve, and with Delacroix, he is much more sensitive than hitherto to the admixture of the masculine and feminine in their make-up. 'There is something feminine,' he writes of the French critic, 'in his tact, his penetration, his subtility and pliability, his rapidity of transition, his magical divinations, his sympathies and antipathies, his marvellous art of insinuation, of expressing himself by fine touches and of adding touch to touch.' He then goes on to enumerate the faculties 'of the masculine stamp' in Sainte-Beuve, 'the completeness, the solid sense, the constant reason, the moderation, the copious knowledge, the passion for exactitude and for general considerations'. He adds however that in any appreciation of the French critic 'it is impossible to keep these things apart; they melt into each other like the elements of the atmosphere; there is scarcely a stroke of his pen that does not contain a little of each of them'.

James had long mastered the art of generalization. There is now however a greater use of aphorism, of sharpened epigram. 'In the arts,' he writes, 'feeling is always meaning.' Or again, 'Art is but a point of view and genius but a way of looking at things.' If on the one hand James seems to toss these profundities at the reader with a light gesture, he seems to invite him on the other to give close attention to his seeded paragraphs. How accurate James's touch had become may be judged by a single sentence in which he summarizes Sainte-Beuve's idea of criticism. 'The critic, in his conception, was not the narrow law-giver or the rigid censor that he is often assumed to be; he was the student, the inquirer, the observer, the interpreter, the active, indefatigable commentator, whose constant aim was to arrive at justness of characterization.' And he speaks of Sainte-Beuve's search in his biographical studies for 'the seam as it were between the talent and the soul'.

The review of *Nana* remained buried for years in the *Parisian*; James never reprinted it. He complained, in the best Victorian manner, that the novel was simply 'unclean', and he did not have as yet the interest he was to show later in *le naturalisme*. Nevertheless he has much praise for the solidity and the strength of Zola himself. He is prepared to allow him his subject: indeed his complaint is that

Nana is not quite human and that there is an absence of humour in the book. Humour, he suggests, might have served as a disinfectant. 'It is not his choice of subject that has shocked us; it is the melancholy dryness of his execution, which gives us all the bad taste of a disagreeable dish and none of the nourishment.'

The cold winter and the heavy snows caused James to postpone his trip to Italy and the beginning of his wine-and-water novel until spring. He recrossed the Channel amid heaving wintry seas, and was happy to find himself again by his Bolton Street fire. Moreover he was writing a new short novel, and was deeply absorbed by it. He called it *Washington Square*. It was while he worked on this that his *Hawthorne*, as we have seen, created its storm in the American press.

86

Fathers and Daughters

HE had apparently begun *Washington Square* while he was on the Continent, intending it to be a short story, and hoping to send it to the *Atlantic*. Early in 1880 he wrote to Howells that 'I tried to squeeze it down for you, but it was no use'. At first he offered it to *Scribner's*, judging it to be a rather thin tale; however, that magazine had just finished the serial of *Confidence*. On an accurate estimate of its length, *Washington Square* turned out to be even longer than James supposed, requiring six instalments. He sold it finally to the *Cornhill*. *Harper's New Monthly Magazine* took it in America and both journals used illustrations by George du Maurier. This was the first time Henry had achieved simultaneous serialization on both sides of the ocean; it enabled him to lay plans for an even longer stretch of leisure for the writing of his promised novel.

I

Washington Square was based on an anecdote told him by Mrs Kemble, a small item of her family history. Her brother had jilted an heiress when he discovered that her father would disinherit the girl. This simple story James transferred to a mansion in New York. In

England, when it was published, the book began with a sale double its predecessor's, and it has always been one of the most popular of James's works, even though its author felt it was too simple and unvarnished a narrative. He had, indeed, told it without varnish, and with an unsparing economy, in a structure wholly scenic; and while James began by focusing the story on the jilting of the girl, he ended up with a brilliant picture of a father's clumsiness in dealing with his daughter's love and his crude failure to spare her feelings. The father understandably wants to protect his daughter, a rather plain and unpretentious girl. He is a successful medical man and also a martinet, and his skills in diagnosis and doctoring seem to have ill-equipped him for the simple task of attending to his daughter's heart. He prevents the marriage, but he also alienates the girl. She is left in the end alone, in the great house fronting on the Square, middle-aged, an heiress, her life blighted by parental want of imagination. The tale could claim as its ancestor *Eugénie Grandet*. It is a perfect piece of psychological realism, and with its four characters, the father, the daughter, the lover and a romantic foolish meddlesome aunt, named Lavinia Penniman, achieves a considerable degree of intensity and pathos. Although he has made her rather simple and plain, James's sympathies are clearly with the daughter, Catherine Sloper. And in terms of his recent life she is an image of himself as victim of his brother's – and America's – failure to understand either his feelings or his career. Dr Sloper would appear to be still another of James's fictional recreations of his brother: the William who had a medical degree and treated him and his work with sarcasm and contempt – the William who could love him and also spurn him. He seems to be embodied in the personages of both the father and the jilting suitor. Striking indeed is the way in which Catherine tries to deal with her predicament: she duplicates James's well-known manœuvre of resistance.

She was simply patient ... there was a great excitement in trying to be a good daughter ... It was as if this other person, who was both herself and not herself, had suddenly sprung into being ... She only had an idea that if she should be very good, the situation would in some mysterious manner improve. To be good, she must be patient, respectful, abstain from judging her father too harshly, and from committing any act of open defiance.

This was the young Henry in his familiar 'angel' disguise, trying to bide his time, avoiding all overt action and hoping, by a kind of dogged persistence, to triumph.

Catherine Sloper has her modest, if negative and painful, triumph. She does not yield an inch to her father; in the end it is she who can spurn her lover, when he returns years after, still possessed of a faint glimmer of hope that he can acquire the benefits of her fortune. She, however, can neither forget nor forgive. Among the endings of James's novels there is none more poignant than when Catherine, her interview with the middle-aged Morris Townsend over, picks up her morsel of fancy-work and seats herself with it, 'for life, as it were'. In the intensity of the narrative, the short scenes, the heightened dialogue, the clash of wills, Henry James showed the mastery he had now attained.

Washington Square is often criticized for having little to do with the Square and for reflecting almost nothing of the background of old New York. Yet this narrative, within its small compass, contains all the touches that are needed to evoke the old tight world of the city. If there is little direct scene-painting, we nevertheless experience the sense of Manhattan, half-provincial, half-metropolis, and the doings of its genteel upper class – their parties, their marriages, their Sunday dinners, their rigid manners. We are reminded of a New York that was – in brief allusions to the 'grassy waysides of Canal Street', the striking detail of Mrs Montgomery's home in Second Avenue, or the picture of the Square itself with its ailanthus trees and the summer heat hanging over its mansions. To a New Yorker the location of Townsend's office in Duane Street, and the oyster-saloon on Seventh Avenue are touches as precise as they are atmospheric. Above all, however, the novel is concerned with a struggle for power, a will to freedom, and the refusal of a simple soul to bow before the domineering spirit of another. This is the very heart of James's subject. He was to treat again and again of the relationship between fathers and daughters, but *Washington Square* was to remain at once the simplest and most dramatic – and most American – handling of the subject, framing an eternal drama of a certain kind of family life in a Square that was both a personal and an historical symbol of American upper-class life. The novel testified also to the destructive power of a materialism untouched by the imagination.

2

Washington Square was completed between James's visit to Paris, during that rude winter, and his departure for Italy in the spring of 1880. In the same interval Henry gave himself up to London's social life. He dined out strenuously, visited friends, and laid his plans for the large novel which he had been wanting to write for the past three years. His negotiations for its serialization had begun long before, when *The American* was still appearing in the *Atlantic*. He had then outlined for Howells his plan to do 'the portrait of the character and recital of the adventures of a woman – a great swell, psychologically a *grande nature* – accompanied with many "developments"'. But Howells could not take a large novel on the heels of *The American*. He had preferred the shorter work, *The Europeans*. This had been followed by the increased demand for James's stories and he had been side-tracked into writing certain of his international tales. He had made a beginning of his novel, however, and he described it as an 'aching fragment'. The delay enabled him to conclude better arrangements for publication; by the middle of 1879 it was agreed that he would start his *Atlantic* serial during 1880 and run it simultaneously in England in *Macmillan's Magazine*. The contracts must have been signed, for James felt free to tell G. W. Smalley of his plans, with the result that the London correspondent of the *New York Tribune* announced the forthcoming production in his newspaper on 5 August 1879. It was to be, he said, what the French called 'a *serious* work'. This did not imply that it had a religious character, but that 'Mr James will devote his powers seriously to the completion of a novel which shall represent him at his best'. Smalley went on to say that the English edition of *Roderick Hudson* in the conventional three-volume circulating library form was proving a success, and that 'the main objection to it is that it was written too long ago; in other words that Mr James has done nothing since which shows a sufficient advance in power upon that very original story'.

This paragraph had been published before the appearance of *Hawthorne* and *Washington Square*. In essence it reflected James's own feelings. The time had come for him to write a substantial work. 'I must try and seek a larger success than I have yet obtained, doing something on a larger scale than I have yet done,' he told Howells. 'I am greatly in need of it – the larger success.' He realized this acutely during his stay in Paris when his current royalty statement arrived from the Macmillans. He had had substantial advances against his royalties; nevertheless Macmillan now had six of his books in print, and the sum (which he did not mention) seemed pitifully small. On the day that he received the statement he wrote to Chatto & Windus offering them *Confidence*. If Macmillan could not do better, he would publish elsewhere. Chatto promptly accepted and paid him a good sum down for the rights to the novel during a three-year period. To Alexander Macmillan James wrote that it was a pity his novels were not doing better; they had been favourably noticed on the whole 'and apparently a good deal talked about'. The Macmillans, fearing they might lose their author, and disturbed by his move toward Chatto, sent an advance against future royalties. For the moment this mollified him.

Since he was negotiating from a position of strength, he made stiff terms for his big novel. The *Atlantic* was to pay him $2,500 and *Macmillan's* £250. He estimated that he would receive in all $5,000 by the end of the serialization. *Confidence*, *Hawthorne* and *Washington Square* had yielded him about $4,000. Early in 1880, when T. S. Perry offered to write an article on James's works to date, he told him to wait for the novel he would do that year. 'It is from that I myself shall pretend to date – on that I shall take my stand.' To Howells he announced that he had found his title – *The Portrait of a Lady*.

3

With the old fragment of his work in progress in his writing portfolio, and provided with ample funds, James left London for Italy on 17 March 1880. The memory of his winter crossing of the Channel the previous December was fresh in his mind. He cautiously waited at Folkestone for five days and took ship on a calm sea on 22 March, spent two or three days in Paris, and then, in a straight run *via* Turin and Bologna, arrived in Florence on the 28th. He put up at the Hôtel de l'Arno, in a room with a window on the river yellow in the spring sun; he spread his writing materials on his work-table – but he was not yet ready to start. He needed a holiday.

He lost no time in calling on the 'gentle and pure-minded' Bootts. They had wintered in Florence proper but were in the process of re-installing themselves in the thick-walled Castellani; they had possession of the big rambling apartment on the ground floor, where

Lizzie had her studio beside the rough terrace that led to a low parapet and a view of the towers of Florence, glittering in the Val d'Arno. Lizzie had been ill but was better. She now appeared to James rather elderly and plain, but happy in her indefatigable industry. 'She seems to spend her life in learning, or rather in studying without learning. and in commencing afresh, to paint in someone's manner,' wrote James, who had tried to place certain of her panels in London. His largest interest was reserved now for her newest painting-master, the burly Frank Duveneck, whom Lizzie had persuaded to move from Munich to Florence. To James, who had just written a novel about a stern father and a plain daughter, this image of the trio – Francis Boott, with his 'indefatigable devotion' to Lizzie and her simple-hearted and simple-minded painting-master – struck James as strange. Duveneck was a son of the frontier, a rough-and-ready 'child of nature and of freedom' from Kentucky, who had learned his craft decorating altars in Catholic churches all the way to Canada. He had been living in Munich, had studied at the Academy and carried off prize after prize. James considered his work strong and brilliant, 'the most highly-developed phenomenon in the way of a painter that the U.S.A. has given birth to'. It had about it a 'completeness' he would not have suspected from some of his things he had seen earlier in Boston and New York.

Aside from his painting he seemed the strangest person in the world to be in the constant company of Lizzie Boott. Lizzie, in her thirties, was a product of a careful education and a sheltered life. Duveneck had what Henry termed an 'almost *slovenly* modesty and want of pretension'. He was uncouth, vigorous and good-natured. Lizzie seemed to James to stand to him in 'a sort of double relation of pupil and adoptive mother – or at least adoptive sister. I hope,' he wrote to his Aunt Kate, 'she won't ever become his adoptive anything else, as, though an excellent fellow, he is terribly earthy and unlicked.' They were a curious group, the father, the daughter and the painter, and James was to watch the evolution of Lizzie's love-affair with her Bohemian teacher with the interested eyes of a friend – who was also a novelist.

87

A Neapolitan Episode

HENRY JAMES was restless and he decided, a few days after arriving in Florence, to take a ten days' run to Rome and Naples and fulfil his promise to Paul Zhukovski. They had sworn eternal brotherhood in their long walks in Paris in 1876 after intimate dinners with Turgenev and the Princess Ourousov. On his way to Naples James paused for a few days in Rome and found the city much changed – new streets, horse-cars, a hideous iron bridge over the Tiber – all 'so many death blows to the picturesque'. He had an enjoyable dinner however with the Storys, welcomed no longer as an aspirant in letters, but as one of the celebrities Story liked to receive in the Barberini.

What happened at Posilippo, in the Naples environs, we can only guess. Zhukovski had appeared to the novelist as a charming and romantic dilettante in Paris; now he saw him as a rather weak and dissolute hero-worshipper and perhaps became aware he was homosexual. His latest hero was Richard Wagner. He had met the composer at the Villa Ungri, where he was spending that year – at a short distance from Zhukovski's villa. The Russian was all for James's meeting Wagner at once. The American, however, had had his fill of Wagner operas, played on the pianoforte in Parisian studios during the spring of 1876, and he demurred. He frankly told Zhukovski he had no desire to meet 'the musician of the future'. He believed such a meeting would be futile – he spoke too little German, and Wagner spoke neither English nor French. James described Zhukovski as the 'same impracticable and indeed ridiculous mixture of Nihilism and bric-à-brac as before'. The Russian spoke almost simple-mindedly of Wagner – the 'greatest and wisest of men', and confided to Henry that it was his ambition to go and live at Bayreuth so as 'to take part in the great work'. James doubted whether Zhukovski would do this, since he seemed such an eternal dabbler. To his sister Alice he wrote that the Russian was

always under somebody's influence, first (since I have known him) under Turgenev's, then under the Princess Ourousov's, whom he now detests, and who despises him, then under H. J. Jr (!!) then under that of a certain disagreeable Onegin (the original of Turgenev's Neshdanov in

Virgin Soil), now under that of Wagner, and apparently in the near future under that of Madame Wagner.

James left Posilippo after three days and drove from Castellammare to Sorrento. There, in a hotel on the edge of the sea, looking out on to the Bay of Naples, with Vesuvius 'smoking his morning pipe', with fishermen under his window in red caps sending up a murmur of lazy sounds, he felt himself again in tune with the world. The gentle-looking flanks of Vesuvius were covered with patches of pale purple; there were bunches of oranges in the trees that looked like small Chinese lanterns, and their colour mingled with the silvery dusk of the olives. Writing to Grace Norton with this scene under his eyes, he told her he had just been observing 'the manners and customs of a little group of Russians'. These, he said, 'were about as opposed to those of Cambridge as anything could well be – but to describe them would carry me too far'. He did go on to tell her of Wagner and of Madame Wagner, the daughter of Liszt and Madame d'Agoult, and the divorced wife of von Bülow – 'a curious collection of attributes'. He has found the Naples museum more interesting than the 'vileness' of the humanity of Posilippo. In his letter to Alice he contrasted a day spent with English friends at Frascati near Rome and their 'admirable, honest, reasonable, wholesome English nature' with the 'fantastic immorality and aesthetics of the circle I had left in Naples'.

The group of Russo-German sensualists in the Wagner entourage had shocked James. There are no records of later meetings with Zhukovski. The Russian carried out his plan. He followed Wagner to Bayreuth and became a member of his inner circle. The composer was so attached to him that he spoke of him as his 'son by his first marriage' – thus avoiding making Cosima into Zhukovski's mother. The friendship lasted only three years, for Wagner died in 1883, but Zhukovski achieved his ambition. He painted the sets for *Parsifal*. A photograph of 1881 shows him on Wagner's right, with a fine curly beard, a high forehead, deep-set eyes and a balding dome. He contributed to the Wagner legend by painting the picture of the 'Holy Family' at Wahnfried, into which he incorporated Wagner's daughters as angels, and the face of the author of *The Ring*, with himself as a figure in the background.

Late in life he and James established touch again and one of his letters remained among James's papers. It is long, effusive, affectionate. He had been, for his brief moment, one of those with whom the novelist had thought he might have founded a lifetime friendship, so happy had been their Parisian encounters. James had to recognize that he had been mistaken. He had misjudged Zhukovski. The Russian had proved unworthy of his affection.

88

Fenimore

DURING the stormy winter of 1879–80 there had come to Europe an American authoress who had published many sketches in the magazines, a narrative poem entitled *Two Women* and a volume of tales, *Castle Nowhere*. Her name was Constance Fenimore Woolson. Her middle name proclaimed her ancestral relationship to American literature : she was a grand-niece of James Fenimore Cooper. She had crossed the rough Atlantic during late November on the *Gallia*, preparing a volume of tales of the South, *Rodman the Keeper*, for the press, and arriving in London had taken rooms in Clarges Street, adjoining Bolton Street. She was a trim and dainty lady of 39, with a clear complexion, an alert manner and the bearing of a gentlewoman. One of her treasured possessions was a letter of introduction to Henry James Jr which she promptly presented at No. 3 Bolton Street. 'Henry James is in Paris,' she wrote to a relative after she had been in London less than a week, 'and will not be here before Christmas, so we shall not see him after all.' The cold and damp made her seek the warmer climate to which she was accustomed. She had been living for some years in Florida. Miss Woolson crossed to the Continent at about the time that James was returning to London, after the big snow in Paris.

The letter of introduction had been given to Miss Woolson by James's cousin, Minny Temple's sister, Henrietta Pell-Clark who lived in Cooperstown, New York. The authoress wanted to meet James because she had read him, admired him, studied him, and enthusiastically reviewed him in the anonymous 'Contributors' Club' of the *Atlantic*. Miss Woolson had strong opinions, and a strong sense of her vocation. She had dedicated herself to literature before she had gone to her finishing-school in New York. New England-born, the sixth of nine children (eight of them daughters), she had grown up in the Lake Country on the shores of Erie and she knew the flora and fauna of America; she had caught, in the lands of *The Pathfinder*, some distant emanation of her great-uncle's genius. She had travelled in her father's buggy to outlying areas, walked Indian trails, visited islands and the marshes of the lake-shore, experienced the deep fogs, the prairie silence, and met the early settlers. Distinctly 'regional', her northern sketches imbibed both the tradition of her great-uncle and the spirit of Bret Harte and they had proved generally popular. Then circumstances had taken her to the South of the reconstruction. Her father had died and she had sought a mild climate for her mother. This marked the second phase of her still young career. Her imagination was captured by the society reconstituting itself after the fratricidal war, the garrison life, the run-down plantations, the wretched houses. She went to the war-cemeteries. 'I used to go out of my way to visit them,' she wrote to Thomas Bailey Aldrich. 'I have stood in many of these southern cemeteries – "National" they call them – poor lonely unvisited spots, the very perfection of their order only increasing their solitariness.' She was a solitary herself. She talked to negroes and made notes on their dialect. She took lonely walks at the end of hot days on the edge of rice-fields, skirting swamp-lands and observing the death-in-life of the South. She made the South hers as she had done the Lake Country, and the tiny brush-strokes with which she wrote the opening lines of one of her most celebrated sketches, *Rodman the Keeper*, show her talent for precision and neatness, as well as her banalities.

The small town, a mile distant, stood turning its back on the cemetery; but the keeper could see the pleasant rambling old mansions, each with its rose-garden and neglected outlying fields, the empty Negro quarters falling into ruin, and everything just as it stood when on that April morning the first gun was fired on Sumter; apparently not a nail added, not a brushful of paint applied, not a fallen brick replaced, or latch or lock repaired ... magnificence went hand in hand with neglect.

She had perceived, as Henry James was to say, 'that no social revolution of equal magnitude had ever reflected itself so little in literature, remained so unrecorded, so unpainted and unsung'.

She was starting a new life. Miss Woolson had discovered the works and the style of Henry James; she had come to know Europe through his writings. As she neared her forties she was in the typical predicament of devoted Victorian daughters – she had given her best years to her mother, who had recently died. She faced the world unmarried and alone. She had sisters, nieces, nephews – but these were other lives and others' children. She had her power of lonely sustained work, and a sufficient income from her writings. She would go to Henry James's Europe. Her friends John Hay and William Dean Howells encouraged her.

Europe, that winter, was as snowbound as her Lake Country. The cold drove her to the Riviera. Here in the bright sunshine she was happy. She settled into the Hôtel des Anglais at Mentone, a quarter of a mile from the Italian frontier. It wasn't as warm as Florida, but the scenery was more beautiful. The grandees of Europe were there, new facial types, new modes of life, the leisure class of England, France, Russia. The daughter of New England, and of the West and South, lingered until spring. She spent her mornings in her room writing a novel, *Anne*, that was to bring her a wider public still, and the afternoons in sightseeing and local excursions. She also wrote poems. She wrote a poem called *Mentone* –

> Upon this sunny shore
> A little space for rest. The care and sorrow,
> Sad memory's haunting pain that would not cease,
> Are left behind. It is not yet tomorrow.
> Today there falls the dear surprise of peace.

In the second stanza she spoke of 'a little space for love'.

I

Henry James returned to Florence at the end of April 1880 and re-installed himself in the Hôtel de l'Arno. There, 'in a room in that deep recess, in the front', he began *The Portrait of a Lady*, or rather worked over the 'aching fragment'. He was late in getting started on his book and rather than crowd himself wrote to Howells and to George Grove of *Macmillan*'s asking permission to begin the serial in October instead of in August as had been arranged. He argued that with *Washington Square* appearing in England and the United States until November, it would not be wise to have the two stories overlap. But he confessed also that the loveliness of Italy was causing him to look too much out of his window instead of remaining at his writing-desk. To his sister Alice he wrote that he was at last leading a quiet life, although Florence was 'a place where one is liable to tea-parties'. He added: 'I have to call, for instance, on Constance Fenimore Woolson, who has been pursuing me through Europe with a letter of introduction from (of all people in the world!) Henrietta Pell-Clark.'

Miss Woolson was living at the *pension* of Madame Barbensi on the Lung' Arno. When James finally paid his respects he seems to have been pleasantly surprised. Instead of the dowdy literary females he had often encountered in London, he saw a trim woman, her hair carefully braided and piled in rings at the back of her head, leaving a pair of delicate ears to the view. A fringe of hair concealed a high forehead. Miss Woolson had an oval face, questioning eyes, a straight nose and a wide mouth. She was obviously impressed. James represented for her a certain summit in American literature. She listened intently, and he noted that she seemed to be hard of hearing. 'Constance is amiable,' he wrote to Quincy Street, 'but deaf, and asks me questions about my works to which she can't hear the answers.' Actually he discovered that her deafness was confined to one ear, and it was a matter of being on the good side. Little that he said was lost upon her.

In ordinary circumstances Henry James would have limited his amenities to his countrywoman. However, her charm, her interest in his work, her bearing, and her sense of her own literary position quite disarmed him. Perhaps, too, he was still feeling his disillusion with Zhukovski and it was pleasant to find a new admirer. Miss Woolson had in her something of the flirt, a very cautious one of 40; and a competitive sense. She could be ironic in the manner of the members of the James family. She tended to pay high, if barbed, compliments. And then other forces were at work as well : Lizzie Boott, who always devoted much time to James when he was in Florence, was preoccupied with Duveneck. This combination of circumstances may have made him more attentive to Miss Woolson than he usually allowed himself to be to strange women. There seemed, after all, small danger of his becoming too interested in an earnest provincial, middle-aged, deaf woman who was trying very hard to learn the meaning of art and was clearly discomposed by the nudity of the statues. James quite forgot his usual reserve : he turned on the full power of his charm for Miss Woolson. She tended to exalt herself, and her Americanism, at the expense of his cosmopolitanism; this however touched familiar ground; James was accustomed to rougher mockery from Quincy Street, and he had had recently a rather large dose of it from the American press.

They did much sightseeing in the mornings. In the afternoons, during the warm part of the day, James liked to remain in his room and write. At the end of the day he went to his usual tea-parties and dinners with friends, including visits to the Villa Castellani.

The novelist did not reckon with Miss Woolson's loneliness and her craving to be loved. If she had given up hope of marriage, she must have now begun to wonder a little about the prompt and kind attentions of the aloof bachelor, three years her junior. James was all decorum and distance : nevertheless he showed endless patience; and he seemed delighted to be her cicerone and escort. Their interest in one another seems to have served as a kind of mutual flattery. The record of this, we must recognize, stems largely from Miss Woolson : in letters to friends and relatives she speaks of James's kindnesses – and frequently enough to show that they were far from perfunctory. Thus in the ancient city of the Medici, against a background of old palaces and the glories of renaissance art, this son of New York whose adopted home had been New England, and this daughter of New England whose adopted home had been the frontier, formed one of the strangest friendships in American literary history, and one of the most secretive. A long chain of evidence shows that Constance Fenimore Woolson – Fenimore as he was to call her – became one of those friends in his life whom he considered 'a private resource', and to whom he was always loyal, in his distant way. And she, as the years advanced, clung to him in a kind of pathetic dependency as the one man who gave her a 'disinterested' yet welcome attention. Gradually she would be absorbed into the little group on Bellosguardo and into the Italian experience of Henry James.

2

At first it was almost as if Fenimore were a kind of intellectual Daisy Miller in whom James, in the role of Winterbourne, was interested, without showing any willingness to let himself go. 'Florence,' Fenimore wrote to a friend shortly after meeting him,

is all that I have dreamed and more; here I have attained the old-world feeling I used to dream about, a sort of enthusiasm made up of history, mythology, old churches, pictures, statues, vineyards, the Italian sky, dark-eyed peasants, opera-music, Raphael and old Michael, and ever so many more ingredients – the whole having, I think, taken me pretty well off my feet! Perhaps I ought to add Henry James. He has been perfectly charming to me for the last three weeks.

The meaning is fairly clear: she had been swept 'pretty well off my feet' by all this – and by Henry James! She described him. He was rather taller than John Hay and with a larger frame. He had a 'beautiful regular profile', a brown beard and hair, and large light-grey eyes, from which, she wrote, 'he banishes all expression'. His manner was 'very quiet, almost cold'. His 'style' was unpretending and unobtrusive. 'Yet,' said Fenimore, 'I wouldn't like to be the person who should think from his unpretending quietness that he could not be incisive when he chose!' She had read her man well. 'He has many acquaintances in Florence,' she went on 'and he was constantly invited out to lunch and dinner parties; yet with all this, he found time to come in the mornings and take me out; sometimes to the galleries or churches, and sometimes just for a walk in the beautiful green Cascine.'

His criticsms were lively for a woman from the provinces new to Europe. From this time on, in certain of Miss Woolson's tales a Henry James character makes his appearance, with Henry's style of beard and his build, and always with grey *expressionless* eyes – eyes that refuse to commit themselves, one might say. By the end of that summer Miss Woolson had written and published a tale called *A Florentine Experiment*, in which she incorporated a certain number of James's observations on Florentine art, and her sense also of his aloofness, as well as what she seems to have considered his self-assurance and conceit.

From her letters:

'At present, I confess, Giotto remains beyond me. And H. J. says calmly, "Some day, you will see it." May be.'

'The Duomo is too vast and cold. I went there one rainy afternoon alone, and had the weirdest time! It was almost dark inside, and I was the only person in all the great gloomy space. I went there again with H. J. who admires it, and tried to make me admire it too.'

'The statue of Lorenzo in the new Sacristy of San Lorenzo is the finest statue, a thousand times over, I have ever seen. But I confess frankly that it is going to take some time for me to appreciate "the nude". I have no objections to it, I look at it calmly, but I am not sufficiently acquainted with torsos, flanks, and the lines of anatomy, to know when they are "supremely beautiful" and when not. Now "Lorenzo" is clothed and therefore comes within my comprehension and oh! he is superb.'

She goes on to say that the reclining statues by Michelangelo of Day, Night, Evening and Dawn 'are rather beyond me'. And she continues:

'In speaking of these statues, Henry James said – "Of course you admired those grand reclining figures?" "No," I replied honestly, "I did not. They looked so distracted." "Ah yes," he said, "*distracted*. But *then*!" Here words failed him and he walked off to look at a fresco, to recover from my horrible ignorance.'

'Yesterday Mr James came to take me to one of the galleries, and, as he is a delightful companion, because he knows all about pictures, I went, although I knew we were going in the afternoon to Fiesole.'

'I enjoyed being very much with Henry James ... he knows the pictures as well as I know Florida. He is a very quiet fellow; and very (though in an unobtrusive way) English.'

These fragments from the letters may be sketchy, but they suggest familiarity and friendliness; they suggest also that the artist in James overcame the usually discreet and cautious male who kept his distance from women. Something in Fenimore must have put him at his ease. It was almost as if he were entertaining Quincy Street – his mother or Alice – rather than speaking to a woman he had recently met for the first time. 'He delivered quite an epic upon Giotto's two little frescoes in the second cloister of Santa Maria Novella,' Miss Woolson wrote in her Florentine tale,

and he openly preferred the third there – the little Virgin going up the impossible steps – to Titian's splendid picture of the same subject, in Venice. He grew didactic and mystic over the round Botticelli of the Uffizi and the one in the Prometheus room at the Pitti; he invented as he went along, and amused himself not a little with his own unusual flow of language.

James was an easy improviser. He lost sight of something of which he was only too well aware in his tales; that an eligible bachelor could be generous and kind to a lady 'of a certain age' up to a point; and that beyond it she might feel that he should declare his intentions. He did have a certain awareness of Fenimore's feelings, for he wrote to his Aunt Kate on 3 May 1880 – that is, early in his newly-formed friendship – 'This morning I took an American authoress

[on] a drive – Constance Fenimore Woolson, whose productions you may know, though I don't, and who was presented to me (by letter) by Henrietta Temple. Constance is old-maidish, deaf and "intense", but a good little woman and a perfect lady.' He added to his aunt: 'I hope your spring is genial, without being (like Miss Woolson) intense.'

At another time James might have been more wary of such intensity. It is abundantly present in *A Florentine Experiment* in which a young American heiress, believing the Henry James character (whom she named Trafford Morgan) to be in love with another woman, trifles with his affections. The 'experiment' is hers; it stems from her belief in his masculine arrogance and conceit, which she is quite prepared to deflate. What the tale overlooks, understandably, is the heroine's own large measure of conceit as well. The James character, however, is rejected by the woman he loves, and comes back to conduct his 'experiment' in turn, and finally to win the heroine. In the tale, at least, Miss Woolson provided a happy ending.

There is another tale which is perhaps more significant in disclosing the deep literary ambition Miss Woolson nourished, and her feelings about an author like Henry James. It was written just before the two met, for it appeared in *Lippincott's* in the May 1880 issue, that is, during the very month of their sightseeing in Florence. The tale is set in Rome, which Miss Woolson had not yet visited. Titled *Miss Grief* it reflects a close reading of James's work. It is told in the first person by a man, a writer, who mentions that he models himself on Balzac, and there is an allusion to a tale of a buried god which would resemble *The Last of the Valerii*. *Miss Grief* is the author's nickname for a literary lady named Aarona Montcrief, which she has shortened to Crief. She is 43, and she tells the great author, 'I have read every word that you have written,' and then recites his favourite scene by heart. 'She had understood me – understood me almost better than I had understood myself.' She gives him the manuscript of her play to read. After he praises it, she tells him that his adverse criticism would have led to her suicide. The author however feels that one character in it is wrong. He tries to edit it. The character is so closely woven into every part of the play that 'to take him out was like taking out one especial figure in a carpet; that is impossible unless you unravel the whole'.

Miss Woolson, taking James's own tapestry imagery, had in this early story used a phrase that was to become the title of one of his celebrated tales – *The Figure in the Carpet*. In *Miss Grief*, however, it is not the phrase which is revelatory, so much as the literary lady's final declaration to the great author: 'You had success – but I had the greater power.' This he acknowledges after she is dead: 'She, with the greater power, failed – I, with the less, succeeded.' There is enough evidence to show, in what she was to write to Henry James, that Fenimore had a certain exalted notion of her own literary powers. She aspired to the style, the manner, the mastery of Henry James. In truth she could pretend to mastery only in such wish-fulfilling tales. As a story *Miss Grief* is better written than most of her discursive work. She was to try, during the ensuing decade – her final 'phase' – to write international stories, after the manner of the man to whom she became attached, and with whom she now felt herself, on some strange deep level, to be competing. Henry must have sensed this. It would have given her, in that case, something of the status of his brother. It is to some such appeal to his constituted nature that we may attribute his long and persistent friendship with Fenimore, an attachment that was to lead to secret meetings and a 'liaison' in Henry's life never suspected by his friends. The inevitable question may be asked at this point in the terminology of James's own novels: was it a 'virtuous attachment?' There is no reason for believing that it wasn't. And there are significant later tales among the greatest of James's stories – which offer us certain clues to one of the few relationships in Henry's life in which his eyes may be said to have been partially sealed. Insight was to come only in the long aftertime.

89

A Band of Egotists

WHEN Henry James bade farewell to Florence – and to Fenimore – late in May or early in June 1880, he had in his portfolio the first instalments of *The Portrait of a Lady*. This time his copyright would be safeguarded: the serial was to begin in October in England and a month later in America. Moreover, he now had the advantage of working from proofs supplied by Macmillan, and would not be dispatching raw manuscript to Howells. At this stage James was still writing in longhand and sending usually a first draft; in the *Portrait*, nevertheless, he worked over each chapter, 'every part being written twice', he later said.

In his journal-summary of his period he wrote:

I returned to London to meet William who came out in the early part of June, and spent a month with me in Bolton Street, before going to the Continent. That summer and autumn I worked, *tant bien que mal*, at my novel which began to appear in *Macmillan* in October (1880). I got away from London more or less – to Brighton, detestable in August, to Folkestone, Dover, St Leonard's, etc. I tried to work hard, and I paid very few visits. I had a plan of coming to America for the winter and even took my passage; but I gave it up. William came back from abroad and was with me again for a few days, before sailing for home. I spent November and December quietly in London, getting on with the *Portrait*, which went steadily, but very slowly.

I

James had had short notice of William's sudden trip. He engaged rooms for him under his own in Bolton Street and sought to offer him the amenities of London. William did not respond to Henry's hospitalities, arguing there was no point in meeting a great many persons whom he would never see again. The purpose of this trip abroad had been to obtain a change and a rest. He was still prone to nervous fatigue and eye-trouble, and after a while Henry left him pretty much to his own resources, since he was himself deeply preoccupied with his novel. William did not remain long, and he spent the rest of the summer on the Continent.

The brothers had not seen each other since James had come abroad in 1875. In the interval the novelist had found his place in life, and William had become a husband and a father. Henry reported to Quincy Street that he found him little changed, 'with the same tendency to descant on his sensations – but with all his vivacity and brilliancy of mind undimmed'. There remained in him, Henry felt, 'more of nervousness and disability' than he had supposed, 'and I can't get rid of the feeling that he takes himself, and his nerves, and his physical condition too hard and too consciously. As he takes himself however, so one must take him; but,' Henry added, in a letter to his mother, 'I wish he had a little more of this quiet British stoutness.' The 'angel, hero, martyr' associated himself with the maternal view of William.

Henry did, however, give a small dinner for his brother at the Reform Club. Otherwise his efforts to draw William into his own social habit failed; even an evening he arranged at the home of T. H. Huxley, feeling his brother should meet the scientist, was cancelled when William suddenly decided to leave London. He found England, he said, 'oppressively social'. On reaching the Continent the elder brother wrote a letter to Quincy Street which shows that he was still using the problems of his own career as a measure for his brother's. 'I think as he grows older,' William wrote, 'that he is better suited by superficial contact with things at a great many points than by a deeper one at a few points.' This was quite accurate in describing his own focused interests, psychological and philosophical, as against Henry's wide-ranging absorption in the ways of the world. But no one reading the fruits of Henry's contact with 'things at many points' would today use the word 'superficial'. And then there was in William's letter the need to find grace in parental eyes as Henry had found it. It took the form of his saying that during his stay in London he had often thought of his parents and their early visits to England and their burdens of travel with their children and the sacrifices they had made. And then, William said,

when I went into St John's Wood and its monotony, and contrasted the life you led there with that which Harry is now leading in Bolton Street, it made me feel how few things you laid claim to, and how entirely at that time your lives were given up to us. There is a strange inability on the part of children to project themselves out of their egoistic standpoint, so far as their parents are concerned.

William was sentimentalizing the past, for the elder James and his wife had led a highly gregarious life abroad confiding their children to tutors and governesses. Read in the light of the fraternal power-play, we might say that Henry had never been called an egotist with greater subtlety.

His brother's visit this time was but a ripple in James's generally contented life and work in London. Nevertheless William had barely left for the Continent when Henry was reporting to his mother that he was recovering from 'one of those wretched sieges of pain in my head which I have had so often and which are so unprofitable'. He also informed Quincy Street that he would not be returning to America that autumn as he had planned. It seemed to him the wiser course to remain abroad until his novel should be complete, and then give himself a total holiday at home. He was to get a great deal of money for *The Portrait*, 'and therefore I wish to carry it on quietly and comfortably – the more so as I have just been correcting the opening proofs and that they seem to me very good'. He might also decide, he said, to do the study of Dickens, and this could better be written in London than in Cambridge. He added: 'On this then I take your blessing and your embrace and assume that for the present you will philosophically cease to expect me.' In a later letter he thanked his parents for 'not reviling me for having disappointed you', and remarked that 'for the present, William will take you plenty of news'.

During his concentrated work on his novel James dined out less, but allowed himself certain country visits, including one to the American banker Russell Sturgis and his wife, in their luxurious country house – a type of expatriate he incorporated in the Touchetts in his novel; and he also allowed himself many week-ends away from Bolton Street. At the end of 1880 he paid a round of Christmas and New Year visits, and in February he turned once again to Italy, to complete his novel.

2

The Portrait of a Lady was the third of Henry James's large studies of the American abroad and twice as long as either of its predecessors. In *Roderick Hudson* he had posed the case of the artist, the limitations of his American background, and the frustration of his creative energy from the moment it was confronted by passion. In *The American* he had pictured an ambitious business man, bent on civilizing himself, proud enough to know his worth, and arrogant enough to think that the best of Europe was none too good for him. *The Portrait* was envisaged as a kind of feminine version of *The American*, and James began with the thought that his Isabel Archer would be a female Christopher Newman. Indeed this may be why he named her Isabel; there is a certain logic in moving from Christopher to the Queen who sent him faring across the ocean. And Isabel Archer deems herself good enough to be a Queen; she embodies a notion not unlike that of Isabella of Boston, whose motto was *C'est mon plaisir*.

In Isabel Archer the novelist wished to draw 'the character and aspect of a particular engaging young woman', and to show her in the act of 'affronting her destiny'. Like her male predecessors she goes abroad a thorough provincial, with her 'meagre knowledge, her inflated ideals, her confidence at once innocent and dogmatic, her temper at once exacting and indulgent'. A person who is dogmatic and exacting on the strength of meagre knowledge can only be characterized as presumptuous; and there is presumption in Isabel, for all the delicacy of her feeling: presumption suggests also a strong measure of egotism. James presents her to us as a young romantic with high notions of what life will bring her; and also as one who tends to see herself in a strong dramatic light. She pays the penalty of giving 'undue encouragement to the faculty of seeing without judging'; she takes things for granted on scanty evidence. The author confesses that she was 'probably very liable to the sin of self-esteem; she often surveyed with complacency the field of her own nature'. He speaks of her 'mixture of curiosity and fastidiousness, of vivacity and indifference, her determination to see, to try, to know, her combination of the desultory flame-like spirit and the eager and personal creature of her conditions'. And he adds: 'She treated herself to occasions of homage.'

The allusion to her 'flame-like spirit' suggests that Isabel is an image of James's long-dead cousin Minny Temple, for he would describe her in the same way. He confessed that he had thought of Minny, in creating the eager imagination and the intellectual shortcomings of his heroine. But Minny, as he pointed out to Grace Norton, had been 'incomplete'. Death had deprived her of the trials – and the joys – of maturity. James, as artist, could imagine and 'complete' that which had been left undone. Nevertheless, if Isabel has something of Minny in her make-up, she has much of Henry himself. He endows her with the background of his own Albany childhood and, as in *Washington Square*, he interpolates a section wholly autobiographical, depicting his grandmother's house, the Dutch school from which he himself had fled in rebellion (as Isabel does), the 'capital peach trees', which he had always sampled and always remembered. The scene is recalled years later in the autobiographies.

The most Jamesian of Henry's heroines is closely linked by her background and early life to her creator. And when he sends Isabel to Europe and makes her into an heiress, he places her in a predicament similar to his own. James was hardly an 'heir'; but his pen had won him a measure of the freedom which others possess through wealth. In posing the questions: what would Isabel do with her new-found privileges? where would she turn? how behave? he was seeking answers for himself as well as for her. The questions are asked in the novel by Ralph Touchett, Isabel's cousin, a sensitive invalid who has silently transferred his inheritance to her. He knows he has not long to live, and he wishes to see how Isabel's large nature will profit by endowment. If this is a sign of his love for her, and the sole way in which he can be symbolically united to her, it is also Ralph's way of living vicariously in Isabel's life and participating in whatever fate her temperament may reserve for her. He, too, has a substantial fund of egotism – and his author's wish for omniscience.

Like her early predecessor in *Watch and Ward*, Isabel presently finds herself with a series of suitors. The first is a young man of very respectable fortune and family from the United States who has pursued her abroad. His name is Caspar Goodwood. He is an individual who has a 'disagreeably strong push, a kind of hardness of presence, in his way of rising before her'. He insists 'with his whole weight and force'. He is in short monotonously masculine; and if Isabel finds his sheer sexual force attractive it is also terrifying. Passion, or sex, as with *Roderick*, is not freedom. She rejects Goodwood several times during the novel and flees from him at the end when she finds his kiss to be like 'white lightning'. When 'darkness returned she was free'.

The second suitor is less dull and much less terrifying. He is a British Lord named Warburton, someone like Bryce or Charles Milnes-Gaskell, a fine upstanding liberal, without too much imagination, one of the types Henry has met at his club or in country houses, fortunate heir of a position in a hierarchical society and the means by which to sustain it. He inspires a different kind of fear in Isabel.

What she felt was that a territorial, a political, a social magnate had conceived the design of drawing her into the system in which he rather invidiously lived and moved. A certain instinct, not imperious, but persuasive, told her to resist – murmured to her that virtually she had a system and an orbit of her own.

Social position in a word was also not freedom; moreover, social position in a hierarchical society represented a strong threat to a woman powerful enough and egotistical enough to believe that she had 'an orbit of her own'.

Isabel is romantic, and young. 'I'm very fond of my liberty,' she says early in the book, and she says also 'I wish to choose my fate,' quite as if the ultimate choice were hers. If we see this as containing a measure of the egotism of youth, we must recognize that in her it has its ingenuous charm. Nevertheless Henrietta Stackpole, an energetic and rather meddlesome newspaperwoman, recognizes it for what it is – for she is endowed with not a little egotism herself. She reminds Isabel : 'You can't always please yourself; you must sometimes please other people.'

At this stage James's heroine is still full of her hopes and dreams. Asked to define success – a matter of some interest to her author – she replies that it is to see 'some dream of one's youth come true'. And asked to define her idea of happiness she offers a vision of a journey into the unknown – 'A swift carriage, of a dark night, rattling with four horses over roads that one can't see.' The concept is largely that of a girl who reads novels. However, the young lady from America does not really mean what she says. She tries very hard to see, at every turn, the roads before her – and in broad daylight. She is supremely cautious in action, for one so daring in her fancy. And what she discovers is that even in daylight on a clear highway it is possible to take a wrong turning.

3

Isabel's wrong turning occurs without her knowledge, when she meets a woman of a certain age, worldly-wise and accomplished, the last word in refinement, an American expatriate of long standing, who has absorbed Europe into her being and bestrides the Continent with that appearance of freedom and insouciance to which Isabel aspires. The charm she exhibits, the deep attraction Isabel feels for her, are founded in part on the girl's inexperience of people and her inability to recognize the treacheries of life. The woman's name is Madame Merle. The *merle* is a blackbird. Serena Merle introduces Isabel to another American expatriate, who lives in a thick-walled villa in Florence on Bellosguardo, with his young daughter. At this point James places in his novel his early vision of Francis Boott and Lizzie recorded in his travel-sketch of 1877, when he had mused on the 'tranquil, contented life' of the father and daughter, and the beauty that was a part of their daily existence. He had spoken of Frank and Lizzie as 'figures in an ancient, noble landscape', and Gilbert Osmond and his daughter Pansy are such figures. Pansy, though pictured at a younger age than James had ever known Lizzie, is re-imagined as having the cultivated qualities of the *jeune fille*, the *achieved* manners of an old civilization. Osmond, however, bears no resemblance to Boott, who was an open, generous, naïve and easy-laughing amateur of life. Osmond's sinister character derives from other sources, and in all critical speculation as to who was his 'original' the principal original has been overlooked. To discover him we must compare him first with Catherine Sloper's father in *Washington Square*. He has the same intelligence and the same piercing sarcasm. As a father Osmond is capable of the same coldness to his daughter's feelings. But he is an infinitely more malign father, and his will to power is infinitely greater than Dr Sloper's self-aggrandizement in the Square.

'There were two or three people in the world I envied,' Osmond tells Isabel shortly after meeting her '– the Emperor of Russia, for instance, and the Sultan of Turkey! There were even moments when I envied the Pope of Rome – for the consideration he enjoys.' Nothing less than the Tsar of all the Russias, and the man who could claim to be holier than all others. We grant Osmond his fine irony, as he says this, but we must nevertheless recognize what it expresses. Since he cannot be Tsar or Sultan or Pope, Osmond has consoled himself with being 'simply the most fastidious young gentleman living'. By now he is no longer young; he is confirmed, however, in his own private domain of power, as the perfect collector of bric-à-brac and *objets d'art*, and a subtle manipulator of persons as well as things. Pansy has been made into one of these objects: and Isabel is to be added to the collection. Strange as it may seem, Osmond clearly expresses one side of Henry James – the hidden side – not as malignant as that of his creation, but nevertheless that of the individual who abjures power by clothing it in meekness and deceptive docility. In this sense James is the 'original' of his villain. Osmond is what he might under some circumstances have become on those occasions when snobbery prevailed over humanity, and arrogance and egotism over urbanity and his benign view of the human comedy. Perhaps the most accurate way of describing this identification with Osmond would be to say that in creating him James put into him his highest ambition and drive to power – the grandiose way in which he confronted his own destiny – while at the same time recognizing in his villain the dangers to which such inner absolutism might expose him. In the hands of a limited being, like

Osmond, the drive to power ended in dilettantism and petty rages. In James's hands the same drive had given him unbounded creativity.

Isabel and Osmond are then, for all their differences, two sides of the same coin, two studies in egotism – and a kind of egotism which belonged to their author. For Isabel, generous high-minded creature though she is, in pursuit of an abstraction she calls 'freedom', insists self-centredly (in spite of grim warnings from all her friends) that she has found it in Osmond. She sees 'a quiet, clever, sensitive, distinguished man ... a lovely studious life in a lovely land ... a care for beauty and perfection'. He is the 'elegant complicated medal struck off for a special occasion' and she feels it to be her occasion. Has she not always felt she was rather 'the special thing' herself – a subject of her personal homage? And now, possessed of her wealth, it is as if she could combine her own power with the quiet existence of this individual and his exquisite flower-like daughter. When she marries him she believes that it is she who brings powerful elements into the union; 'she would launch his boat for him; she would be his providence'. This is indeed an exalted notion of her role, and it suggests the role she assigned to Osmond. Thinking back on this later, she wonders at the 'kind of maternal strain' she had possessed in her passion : she believes that her money had been her burden. But this is rationalized after the fact. Isabel and Osmond had been attracted to one another because each saw in the other a mirror-image of self. The two had experienced an irresistible need for each other and in the end they cannot suffer each other. Power may be attracted to power, but cannot endure it. Each insists on supremacy. Osmond tries to bend Isabel to his will. She cannot be bent. Her kind of power refuses to be subjugated : it exerts its own kind of subjugation. His, more devious, returns perpetually to the assault. The impasse is complete.

James had written into this work two aspects of himself : there was his legitimate aspiration to freedom, and his covert drive to power hidden behind his compliance, docility and industry. In the largest sense, egotism and power are the real subjects of *The Portrait of a Lady*, concealed behind a mask of free will and determinism. How was one to possess the power and arrogance of one's genius and still be on good terms with oneself and the world? How was one to establish relationships with people when one felt – and knew – one was superior to them? Yet how avoid loneliness and isolation? Above all, how enjoy one's freedom and not make mistakes in the exercise of it? Ralph watches Isabel make her mistakes: and it is he who in the end delivers the uncomfortable verdict that she has been 'ground in the very mill of the conventional'. Ralph thereby accepts Isabel at her own evaluation; he believes, as she did, that she was worthy of something more than the conventional. And beyond the unhappiness of Isabel's marriage lies the revelation that she has been the victim of a carefully-laid plot: that Madame Merle had been the mistress of Osmond; Pansy is their child; and the marriage had been arranged by the wily blackbird to endow Pansy with Isabel's fortune.

It is possible in this light to see that Isabel's rejection of Goodwood and Warburton went beyond the mere sense that they threatened her freedom. They would have inhibited her freedom to exercise her power; but also she would be diminished by an aristocratic order; and she refuses to be a chattel-wife. Goodwood would have imposed his masculinity and the power of his passion; Warburton would have involved Isabel in a society where the determinants of power had been fixed long before. Isabel speaks for an egalitarian society in which a woman might claim full equality; she speaks also for a kind of Emersonian ignorance of evil. She had looked upon one aspect of herself in Osmond and had fallen in love with it. He had done the same in looking at her. The other image, that of Osmond's selfishness, and his 'demonic imagination', belong in all probability to James's 'buried life', some part of which he concealed even from himself, but which emerged in the writing of this character.

In *The Portrait of a Lady* there is a kind of continuous endowment of the characters with aspects of their author and the questions arising in his life even as he was writing the book – as if he were putting on different hats and different neckties and looking at himself in a series of mirrors. Curiously enough this observation was made long before the biographical knowledge we possess today enable us to identify this process of character-infiltration. James Herbert Morse, writing in the *Century Magazine* during the novel's serialization, observed that there was in nearly every personage of *The Portrait* 'an observable infusion of the author's personality'. He went on:

The men and women are almost equally quick-witted, curt and sharp. While each has a certain amount of individuality, the sharpness is one of the elements in common, preventing a complete differentiation. It is not wit alone, and repartee, but a sub-acid quality which sets the persons to criticizing each other. One does not like to call it snarling. Mr James is too much of a gentleman to admit snarling among ladies and gentlemen; and yet every leading person in the book does, in a polite way, enter frequently into a form of personal criticism of somebody else.

Since Morse wrote these lines we have come to understand the technique by which James sought to cover up what he was doing; his method of using shifting angles of vision so as to make us feel the way in which people see one another. We see Osmond through the eyes of all the principal characters, and this dramatizes even more Isabel's blindness to his faults during the period when she is debating whether she will marry him. Morse was right, however, in feeling that in a certain sense the various speakers in the novel were 'engaged in the business of helping the author develop his characters'. On the level of technique, this was one of James's brilliant devices: and later he was even to boast that he created artificial characters for this purpose and managed to endow them with the attributes of life. For biography, however, this method has the unusual effect of throwing a personal shadow behind the impersonal puppets. 'We cannot escape the conviction,' said Morse, 'that he has at least so far written himself into his books that a shrewd critic could reconstruct him from them.' And he went on to be the shrewd critic: 'The person thus fashioned would be one of fine intellectual powers, incapable of meannesses, of fastidious tastes, and of limited sympathies; a man, in short, of passions refined away by the intellect.'

In the end one feels that Isabel's disillusionment, the damage to her self-esteem and the crushing effect of her experience, resides in the shock she receives that so large a nature should have been capable of so great a mistake; and in her realization that instead of being unable to manœuvre her environment, as her freedom allowed, she had been manœuvred by it. Christopher Newman had had a similar shock, in the Faubourg St Germain. But he could write it off as the corruption and deceit of the French nobility. The deeper illusion here resides in the fact that Serena Merle and Gilbert Osmond are Americans, and the implications are that as expatriates, long divorced from their native soil, they also have been corrupted: they conceal a world of evil unknown to Isabel. America had ill-prepared her for this. The American and the Americana in Henry's two novels represented – in the larger picture – the New World's concept of its own liberties, the admixture of freedom and of power contained in America's emerging philosophy, and in the doctrines of pragmatism of which Henry's brother William was to be a founder. Thus are woven into the novel certain fundamental elements of a national myth: an ideal of freedom and equality hedged with historical blindness and pride; a self-interest which often takes a form of generosity; a sense of hurt when this generosity is discerned by others as a form of wielding power.

4

When he had sent off his early instalments, James received worried letters from Howells. The editor suggested that Isabel was being over-analysed; and that the figure of the American newspaper-woman, Henrietta Stockpole, was over-drawn. 'In defence of the former fault,' James replied, 'I will say that I intended to make a young woman about whom there should be a great deal to tell and as to whom such telling should be interesting; and also that I think she is analysed once for all in the early part of the book and doesn't turn herself inside out quite so much afterwards.' This in the end was not to be true; Henry was to consider the book's finest passage to be Isabel's self-analysis after she perceives the relationship between Madame Merle and Gilbert Osmond. As for Miss Stackpole, Henry told Howells that she was not 'I think really exaggerated – but 99 readers out of a 100 will think her so: which amounts to the same thing. She is the result of an impression made upon me by a variety of encounters and acquaintances made during the last few years; an impression which I had often said to myself would not be exaggerated.' James however added 'It is over here that it offers itself in its utmost relief.'

It is possible to discover one 'original' for Miss Stackpole in James's letters. Shortly after he had moved to London, William sent to him a young woman from Cambridge, a Miss Hillard (probably the Katherine Hillard who edited her mother's journal and later an abridgement of Madame Blavatsky's writings). Writing to William on 28 June 1877 he says:

I have got to go and see your – excuse me I must say – accursed friend Miss Hillard, who has turned up here and writes me a note every three days, appointing an interview. I do what I can; but she will cer-tainly tell you that I neglect her horribly. Do you admire her, particularly? She is, I suppose, a very honourable specimen of her type; but the type – the literary spinster, sailing-into-your-intimacy-American-hotel-piazza type – doesn't bear somehow the mellow light of the old world. Miss H. announced her arrival here to me by writing to ask me to take her to the Grosvenor Gallery and Rembrandt etchings and then go out and dine with her – at Hammersmith, miles away! – at the Conways'! And this a maid whom I had never seen!

On the back of this letter, in William's hand, are the following words: 'Do you notice the demoniac way in which he speaks of the sweet Miss Hillard?' Miss H. had impressed the brothers quite differently. In a letter a few days later James added 'She is a good girl: her faults are that she is herself too adhesive, too interrogative and too epistolary.'

Henrietta Stackpole, her forthrightness, good humour, meddlesomeness, and 100-per-cent Americanism, in *The Portrait* was to be but the first of a number of characterizations of the gossipy American journalist abroad. Miss Stackpole is able to say all the things Goodwood, in his supreme inarticulateness, does not utter. She is completely characterized in an interchange between Isabel and Ralph. 'She's a kind of emanation of the great democracy – of the continent, the country, the nation,' Isabel says. And Ralph replies: 'She does smell of the Future – it almost knocks one down.'

5

A great deal has been made of the resemblance of *The Portrait of a Lady* to *Daniel Deronda*. As *Roderick* had been James's conception of the novel Hawthorne might have written about Rome, so *The Portrait* was his way of making Isabel Archer the personality he felt George Eliot should have made of Gwendolen Harleth. His description of Gwendolen, in his paper on the Eliot novel, can be applied to Isabel: 'The universe forcing itself with a slow, inexorable pressure into a narrow, complacent, and yet after all extremely sensitive mind, and making it ache with the pain of the process – that is Gwendolen's story.' It is Isabel's as well. She is indeed the victim of her own complacent temperament, and the real determinism of the novel is psychological determinism. If *The Portrait of a Lady* can be related to George Eliot's novel (and the character of Grandcourt related to Osmond) – the work Henry wrote is still pure James, and the distillation of his own experience: his fierce will to freedom as an artist, his hidden fear of his drive to power, his awareness that, no matter how careful one may be, one can still be betrayed by one's egotism.

Over and above its substance *The Portrait of a Lady* established itself, by degrees, as one of the best-written novels of its age. In a prose of high style, with a narrative unsurpassed for its rhythmic development, with a mastery of character and of all the threads of his complicated story, Henry had created a novel that could be placed among the supreme works of the century. It introduced into a Europe that was reading Turgenev and Flaubert, and would soon be reading Tolstoy, a distinctly American heroine.

Her portrait hangs in the great gallery of the world's fiction. We can see Isabel as we saw her when she first stepped into the garden of the Touchetts, at Gardencourt; her clasped hands are in repose; they rest in the lap of her black dress. She looks at us with those light grey eyes of hers, and her face, framed by its black hair, possesses a distinctive American beauty. She holds her head high; she possesses a great pride, and there is a fierce shyness in her steady gaze. The gallery in which Henry placed her was remarkable. On its walls were the paintings of many other women who, like Isabel, had never literally 'lived'. All of them were tissued out of the minds of their authors, mere figments of literary imagination, creatures of the printed word. And yet all had taken on a life of their own – Becky Sharp, or Dorothea Brooke, the Lady of the Camellias or Jane Eyre, Anna Karenina or Emma Bovary. It was as if they had really lived. And Isabel Archer, who partakes of this reality, and who actually seems to have resided in Albany, and ultimately in a palace in Rome, retains her uniqueness among her European sisters. Theirs had been largely dramas of love, often of physical passion. Isabel's had been a drama of suppressed passion, passion converted into intellectual ideals and driven by a need for power that reckoned little with the world's harsh realities.

The painting is exquisite. Every touch of the artist's brush has been lovingly applied to his subject who, though not a daughter of the Puritans, has something of their rigidity in her bearing, and not a little of their hardness of surface. She looks down at us out of American 'transcendentalism', in the freshness of her youth – and the strength of her innocence and her egotism.

90

Venice

EARLY in 1881, with *The Portrait* scheduled to run through the magazines until autumn, Henry James found his novel so far advanced that he could seek once again the light and air of Italy. 'I wished to get away from the London crowd, the London hubbub, all the entanglements and interruptions of London life; and to quietly bring my novel to a close,' he said in his journal. This time he fixed his eye on Venice. He had often visited the water city, but he had never stayed there as long as in Florence or Rome. He waited only a day for a calm sea at Folkestone, and crossed on 10 February. As usual he gave up a few days to the Paris way-station – paying three longish calls, in particular, besides Turgenev's gouty couch. 'He seemed and looked a good deal older than when I saw him last; but he was as pleasant and *human* as ever. On the other hand, I can't get over the sense that the people he was with (the Viardot circle) are a rather poor lot and that to live with them is not living like a gentleman.'

Aside from Turgenev, he saw Henrietta Reubell, now firmly fixed in the circle of Parisian friendship, the Laugels, the other Turgenevs. The Edward Lee Childes gave a dinner in James's honour, and he was always to remember a remark made on this occasion by Guillaume Guizot, who had read his study of *Hawthorne*: '*Il sortait de toute espèce de petits trous – de Boston, de – comment appelez-vous cela? – de Salem?*' Once again James was struck by the 'lightness and brightness of the French conversational tone'. He greatly enjoyed his room at the Hôtel Continental, with his windows looking out on the Tuileries. Twelve days sufficed. 'In Paris, I suspect, it is always the little Parisian horizon,' he wrote home, and took his train southward.

I

He made a leisurely progress. He was in Marseilles on 24 February eating a big bowl of *bouillabaisse*, 'a formidable dish, demanding a French digestion', in a restaurant opposite the Château d'If. The carnival flourished in Nice, so he moved on to San Remo. Here he found the Lombards of Cambridge and spent three congenial weeks, working at his novel and using Miss Fanny and her mother as a social resource. 'I worked there capitally,' he was to remember, 'and it made me very happy. I used in the morning to take a walk among the olives, over the hills behind the queer little black, steep town.' The paved roads behind and above San Remo were of 'an extraordinary sweetness', with the sea glittering through the grey foliage. Between a big yellow sun and the bright blue Mediterranean, he enjoyed his morning strolls, often with Miss Lombard, after which he would return to his inn, eat his *déjeuner* and settle down to three or four hours of writing. In the fading light he would take another walk, dine, go to bed early and read until late. One day he went on an excursion with the Lombards to the mountain town of Ceriana –

the grand clear hills, among which we wound higher and higher; the long valley swimming seaward, far away beneath; the bright Mediterranean growing paler and paler as we rose above it; the splendid stillness, the infinite light, the clumps of olive, the brown villages, pierced by the carriage road, where the vehicle bumped against opposite doorposts.

On 16 March he was in Genoa for a day. In Milan he spent ten days. He worked industriously. The place was cold and he knew no one. He speaks of going to La Scala to see *Der Freischütz* and an 'interminable ballet'. Arriving in Venice he finds it cold and dreary and after a few days he leaves for Rome. On the way he stops in Florence for his customary visit to the Bootts. Lizzie was in Spain, travelling with a group of artists; she wrote urging him to join them. He was tempted. He had fallen into the habit of travelling a beaten path to Italy. It would have been 'more original and enterprising'. However he allowed the question to be settled by his work: he had no time for new adventures: *The Portrait* had to be finished; and he had arranged to write an article on Venice for the new *Century* magazine, into which *Scribner's* was being merged.

In Rome he stops at the Hôtel de Russie. It is wet and cold, and he has a violent attack of lumbago and a bad headache. Here, after a year, he sees Fenimore again. She has settled in the Holy City for the time being. We know this through one of her letters which accidentally survived and in which she speaks, at a later date, of 'a tea-table, with the same spluttering little kettle you saw in my sky-parlour at Rome'. Fenimore was living in a fourth-floor apartment, and we have no record of how often they saw each other during this time.

In his journal his account of his stay in Rome is sketchy and he seems to have been interested in another lady.

Toward the last part of April I went down to Rome and spent a fortnight – during part of which I was laid up with one of those terrible attacks in my head. But Rome was very lovely; I saw a great deal of Mrs V. R. : had (with her) several beautiful drives. One in particular I remember; out beyond the Ponte Nomentano, a splendid Sunday. We left the carriage and wandered in the fields, where we sat down for some time. The exquisite stillness, the divine horizon, brought back to me out of the buried past all that ineffable, incomparable impression of Rome (1869, 1873).

Mrs V. R. is never identified in Henry's letters and is always alluded to by her initials, or as the 'Rensallina' in his correspondence with the Bootts. This suggests that she was probably Mrs Philip Livingstone Van Rensselaer, who lived for many years abroad. A short, dumpy woman – a 'pincushion of a woman' in her old age, with three double chins – she seems first to have charmed Henry by her energy and liveliness; and then for a period in London, when she moved much in English society, she bored him; and eventually she became one of his London friends to whose home, on occasion, he could come for tea and talk over old days and old friends. She seems to have been widowed early, and during her Italian years James believed her to be searching for a husband. James's Roman headache may have been a consequence of finding himself caught in a cross-fire between two demanding women, Fenimore and Mrs V. R.

From Rome he returned to Venice, by way of Ancona, visiting Leopardi's birthplace at Racanati. 'Every day I lost was a misery, and I hurried back to my manuscript.' This too might have contributed to his headache, which seemed invariably to be the consequence of some personal frustration.

2

His stay on the Riviera and in Rome was the prelude to a memorable visit to Italy. As he had taken possession early of Rome, later of Paris and finally of London, so now he took possession of the city of the Doges – and for all his life – in its grandeur and decay. 'You desire to embrace it, to caress it, to possess it; and, finally, a soft sense of

possession grows up and your visit becomes a perpetual love-affair.'
Venice was one of the greatest topographical love-affairs of Henry's
life; it was a city to be visited, haunted and re-visited, for the sake
of piling memory upon memory. A dead city on the Adriatic, it was
yet alive with every change of weather. As he was to say,

the place is as changeable as a nervous woman, and you know it only
when you know all the aspects of its beauty. It has high spirits or low, it
is pale, or red, grey or pink, cold or warm, fresh or wan, according to
the weather or the hour. It is always interesting and almost always sad;
but it has a thousand occasional graces and is always liable to happy
accidents.

The city was not without its inconveniences. That spring there
were hordes of Germans encamped in the Piazza; they filled the
Ducal Palace and the Academy with their uproar. Later came the
English and the Americans; and there were a great many French
tourists too, but the latter were discreet enough to make very long
repasts at the Caffè Quadri, during which they were out of the way.
St Mark's, with its beggars and vendors, seemed like a booth in a
bazaar. And yet for James all Venice had an endless charm – there
was so much for his eyes to explore and study. He found rooms,
'dirty apartments with a lovely view', on a fourth floor at 4161 Riva
degli Schiavoni, near the passage leading off to San Zaccaria. He recalled that the niece of the landlady was a dancer at the Fenice
theatre and that she hovered about the premises in a velvet jacket
and a pair of black kid gloves with one little white button. Her
face, a charming oval, was always smeared with powder. His rooms
looked out on the lagoon. Straight across, before his windows, rose
the great pink mass of San Giorgio Maggiore, which, for an ugly
Palladian church, had a success beyond all reason. It was 'a success
of position, of colour, of the immense detached Campanile, tipped
with a tall, gold angel'. It stood suffused with its rosiness, 'a faint,
shimmering, airy, watery pink; the bright sea-light seems to flush
with it, and the pale whiteish green of lagoon and canal to drink
it in'.

In his journal his account of his stay in Venice, written a few
months afterwards, is the most lyrical passage in an otherwise long
enumeration of English dinners and country visits. 'I seemed to myself to grow young again,' he wrote. He passed his 38th birthday
there. 'The lovely Venetian spring came and went, and brought

with it an infinitude of impressions, of delightful hours. I became passionately fond of the place, of the life, of the people, of the habits.' He asked himself then, and was to ask himself every time he came to Venice, whether he should not have a permanent *pied-à-terre* in the city.

During the early part of his sojourn he stood at the windows of his room, with an opera-glass studying the gondolas and ships. No ballet was more beautiful than the rhythmical movement of arm and oar on every side. There was always the same silhouette – the long black slender skiff, moving yet seeming not to move, with the grotesquely-graceful figure on the poop. It stood like a dancing-master, but from the waist up it had a freedom of movement that did not belong to dancing, That mixture of grace and awkwardness was 'the boldness of a plunging bird and the regularity of a pendulum'. There was nothing elusive or reluctant about the gondoliers. For the most part they were excellent fellows, the very children of Venice, associated 'with its idiosyncrasy, with its essence, with its silence, with its melancholy'. And also with its sounds. The sounds were constantly in his ears. 'The view from my windows was *una belleza*: the far-shining lagoon, the pink walls of San Giorgio, the downward curve of the Riva, the distant islands, the movement of the quay, the gondolas in profile. Here I wrote diligently every day and finished, or virtually finished, my novel.'

3

He would rise in the morning and have an early breakfast at Florian's. Then he would go to the Stabilimento Chitarin for his bath. Refreshed, he would stroll in the coolness looking at pictures, watching the street-life, idling away the hours until it was time for his real *déjeuner*, which he would take at the Caffè Quadri. After this he would return to his rooms and work – sometimes till five and sometimes until six o'clock. A quarter of a century later he was to remember how again and again in the 'fruitless fidget of composition' he would respond to the human chatter coming up to his windows from the Riva, and would wander over to see whether 'out in the blue channel, the ship of some right suggestion, of some better phrase, of the next happy twist of my subject, the next true touch for my canvas, mightn't come into sight'. There were pages of *The Portrait*, when he re-read them, which recalled the colour-spots of the balconied houses, the undulation of the hunch-backed bridges, and the clicking pedestrians – 'the Venetian footfall and the Venetian cry – all talk there, wherever uttered, having the pitch of a call across the water'. Venice was an invitation, constant and repeated, to idleness – and yet he worked.

His writing done, he would go out on the water in a gondola for a couple of hours. In the evenings he would stroll about, stop at Florian's, listening to the music in the Piazza; and two or three nights a week he would visit Mrs Bronson and sit on the balcony of Ca'Alvisi smoking cigarettes with her and watching the traffic of the Grand Canal. For he had renewed his acquaintance with Katherine De Kay Bronson, his fellow-passenger during the memorable crossing of the Atlantic when he had sailed to embrace the Old World. Mrs Bronson, her husband and her daughter had gone out then, and she had fixed herself in this old Venetian house, as if America had never existed. She had a waterside salon, whose most distinguished members were Robert Browning and Henry James. 'She sat,' he was to write, 'for twenty years at the wide mouth, as it were, of the Grand Canal, holding out her hand, with endless good-nature, patience, charity, to all decently accredited petitioners, the incessant troop of those either bewilderedly making or fondly renewing acquaintance with the dazzling city.' Casa Alvisi was directly opposite the Baroque church of Santa Maria della Salute. In a city of palaces, it was a small house indeed: this is what Mrs Bronson liked about it. She made it 'the friendliest house in all the wide world'. James became attached to the stately balcony and its crimson cushions; he made friends with her big brown gondoliers; he was fond of her little yellow dogs. Everything seemed in the right proportion. She would have traded a Tintoretto or two, James said, for a cabinet of tiny gilded glasses, or a dinner-service of the right old silver. Katherine De Kay of New York had a vivid and lively personality. Less ambitious than Isabella of Boston, she preferred her quiet corner, her friends, her far-flung Venetian charities, and the life of Venice itself. 'The old bright tradition, the wonderful Venetian legend had appealed to her from the first, closing round her house and her well-plashed water-steps, where the waiting gondolas were thick.' Her affectionate portrait is sketched, one seems to see, as Mrs Prest in *The Aspern Papers*. Mrs Bronson was to have only one set of rivals in Venice for James's affection, the Daniel Curtises, who in greater opulence forsook Boston once and for all and acquired an apartment in the Palazzo Barbaro a short distance from Mrs Bronson's and diagonally opposite the Accadémia. Between this Palazzo, commemorated in *The Wings of the Dove*, and the Casa Alvisi, celebrated in *Italian Hours*, James had in later years his *pied-à-terre* in Venice – a very substantial one in each case.

The novelist complained during these early weeks that Mrs Bronson's *milieu* was too American for his taste. Nevertheless his testimony to its geniality is to be found in the closing sentences of his Venetian essay :

If you are happy you will find yourself, after a June day in Venice (about ten o'clock), on a balcony that overhangs the Grand Canal, with your elbows on the broad ledge, a cigarette in your teeth and a little good company beside you. The gondolas pass beneath, the watery surface gleams here and there from their lamps, some of which are coloured lanterns that move mysteriously in the darkness.

And if the serenading is overdone, he adds, 'you needn't suffer from it, for in the apartment behind you – an accessible refuge – there is more good company, there are more cigarettes'.

4

Late in May James came upon an unexpected companion. He encountered an old Cambridge friend. William used to bring him to Quincy Street where he greatly amused Mary James with his pleasant talk, his songs and his guitar. Apparently a man of some means, he had wandered far and wide, and he was to continue to do so during a long life. 'Tell William,' Henry wrote to his father, 'his old friend Herbert Pratt has turned up here, and I have seen a good deal of him. He is a queer, but almost delightful, creature and entertaining through all the strange eastern lands he has seen. He is romantic, sentimental and naïf, and is redolent of Persia. He seems to think always of William.'

If James was cosmopolitan in the sense that he could alternately be a western European and an American, or both at the same time, Pratt was the embodiment of the graceful American wanderer, the perpetual poetic hobo. He was at ease in all lands and he seems to have carried his good nature and his guitar wherever he went. He had in him a loitering soul, superimposed upon the refinements of Cambridge. There was in him that part of New England that lived perpetually in whaling ships and sought distant horizons. William had met him at medical school, where Pratt was completing his studies interrupted by the Civil War, in which he had served as an 'acting assistant surgeon'. He had done a little postgraduate study in Vienna and Berlin, and had set up in practice at Denver. From 1874, and for the next forty years, he was a wanderer upon the face of the earth, travelling in remote corners, always with an eye for manners and customs, scenery and architecture. James would have liked to be as foot-loose, without responsibility, and taking life as it came. He achieved this dream rarely. But the forces that made him a disciplined writer militated against his ever being able to emulate Herbert Pratt. There was always another instalment to be written, always some deadline to shatter his dreams.

'Herbert Pratt was there for a month, and I saw him tolerably often,' James wrote in his journal.

He used to talk to me about Spain, about the East, about Tripoli, Persia, Damascus; till it seemed to me that life would be *manquée* altogether if one shouldn't have some of that knowledge. He was a most singular, most interesting type, and I shall certainly put him into a novel. I shall even make the portrait close and he won't mind. Seeing picturesque lands for their own sake, and without making any use of it – that, with him, is a passion – a passion of which if one lives with him a little (a little, I say; not too much) one feels the contagion.

And James added : 'He gave me the nostalgia of the sun, of the south, of colour, of freedom, of being one's own master, and doing absolutely what one pleases.'

Pratt used to say : 'I know such a sunny corner, under the south wall of old Toledo. There's a wild fig tree growing there; I have lain on the grass, with my guitar. There was a musical muleteer, etc.' These words were put by James into the mouth of Gabriel Nash in *The Tragic Muse*, eight years later. The likeness is considerable, save that James endowed the fictional Pratt with a considerable degree of artistic aestheticism. But the easy, drifting quality of his 'original' is in the book.

They drifted in Venice when James was free. One evening Pratt took him to a queer little wineshop, frequented largely by gondoliers and *facchini*, and located in an out-of-the-way corner. They drank some excellent muscat wine. Pratt had discovered the place and made himself at home in it. On another evening he took James to his rooms, far down the Grand Canal, overlooking the Rialto. The night was hot. The cry of the gondoliers came up from the Canal. Pratt took out some Persian books and read extracts from Firdusi and Saadi.

'A good deal might be done with Herbert Pratt,' the novelist said to himself in his journal.

5

Mrs V. R. came out from Rome, and James went with her one day to Torcello and Burano; they carried their lunch with them and ate it on the edge of a canal. At Burano the children assailed him for coppers and pursued the gondola into the sea. Henry took away an impression of bright-coloured hovels, stagnant canals, young girls with splendid heads of hair and complexions smeared with powder, fishermen mending their nets. It was altogether a happy time and James recaptured his old faculty for experiencing and enjoying the picturesque which had faded during his long months in Bolton Street. In June he took a brief recess for five days and wandered in Vicenza, Bassano, Padua. Three of these days were spent at Vicenza, and a letter to Grace Norton records his impressions. 'It is a bright hot Sunday morning; I have closed the shutters of my smartly-frescoed apartment and only a stray sunbeam rests on the cool scagliola floor. I wish this rapid scrawl to carry a breath of the Italian summer, and of sweet Vicenza, into your New England hills.' James had sat the previous evening in the city's square. The place was flooded with moonlight. He had been recalling his 1869 visit and 'was pleased to find that on the whole I have not quite lost my "sensibility"'. The Vicentini strolled on the big smooth slabs of the piazza, and the tall slim campanile seemed to lose itself in the brightness of the night. Sitting at the café he found himself in conversation with an Italian officer, a captain of cavalry with a salary of $400 a year. He treated Henry to all the gossip of the place – and to generous complaints about the hardness of his life.

To Grace James confessed that he had 'fallen deeply and desperately in love' with Venice, in spite of the fact that they had begun to run steamboats up and down the Canal. He added:

I have enjoyed extremely this year being away from London during the spring. I receive every now and then, forwarded from Bolton Street, a memento of lost opportunities chiefly in the shape of invitations to dinner a month ahead; but they do nothing to turn my heart against

Venice. The rest, the leisure, the beauty, the sunsets, the pictures, are more than compensation. I go back to England, however, direct after July 1st, and it is PROBABLE that I go home in September.

He added that he was expecting his sister in London but this would not seriously change his plans.

Before he left the Adriatic city the heat had become intense. The days and the nights were now impossible. 'I left it at last and,' Henry wrote in his journal, 'closed a singularly happy episode – but I took much away with me.' From London he wrote to Mrs Bronson: 'I can't tell you with what affection I think of Venice, and how at this distance my whole stay there takes on the semblance of a beautiful dream. Happy you to spend your life in such a dream.'

When he consulted his memories he had, as Proust was to have after him, colours before his eyes, iridescence, little corners rather than images of the great Square. 'I simply see a narrow canal in the heart of the city – a patch of green water and a surface of pink wall. The gondola moves slowly; it gives a great smooth swerve, passes under a bridge, and the gondolier's cry, carried over the quiet water, makes a kind of splash in the stillness.' The old pink wall seemed to sink into the opaque water. Behind the wall was a garden, out of which the long arm of a June rose, one of the splendid roses of Venice, flung itself as a spontaneous ornament. On the other side of the small waterway was a great shabby façade of Gothic windows and balconies – on which dirty clothes were hanging – and there was a cavernous door opening from a low flight of slimy steps. It was hot and still. That garden, the rose, the gondola, the general Venetian colour and imagery – the memory of a girl crossing a bridge with an old shawl on her head seen against the sky as he floated beneath – were to melt together into *The Aspern Papers*. Almost a decade would elapse, however, before he would be ready to write this story.

BOOK SIX:
TERMINATIONS
1881-3

Part Nine:
Homecomings

91

Re-discoveries

IN his room in the Brunswick Hotel in Boston, late in November of 1881, Henry James found himself seated one day in front of a rather pretentious little marble-topped table, writing with an indelible pencil, in a fat scribbler he had purchased some months before in London. The walls of his room were white and bare; they shone at night in the flaring gaslight from a chandelier of imitation bronze, which hung from the middle of the ceiling and emitted a hissing brightness, flinging a patch of shadow across his page. When he extinguished the lights, illumination poured in through the transom over the double doors, flooded his bed, beat at his closed eyelids. There was too much glare, too much scorching air from the heating-system, too much ice-water in the perpetual pitchers carried by waiters and bellhops. Boylston Street decidedly was not Bolton Street. James had learned to accommodate himself to a fireplace and to candlelight; to adjust temperature and illumination to his needs. Nothing seemed adjustable in his hotel-room. He was lonely and homesick. Cambridge and Boston had enclosed him, as always, in a possessive embrace. This act of writing in the fat scribbler was a way of transporting himself out of his immediate American environment back to London – or to Venice. For what James was indelibly setting down was a statement unique among his surviving papers. It was a long retrospective summary of his six years abroad; a survey of his travelled cities and country visits, his new friendships and his Continental resources. He wrote in his light, rapid, characterizing manner, mainly a catalogue of sociabilities and impressions, as if to remind himself of all that he had seen and done, all that had been precious to him on the other side of the Atlantic.

He had returned to the old horizons, the house in Quincy Street, the Harvard Yard, with big square fresh buildings and slender elms reduced to spindles by the winter. Cambridge stretched away from the horizontal collegiate fence, low and flat, with vague featureless spaces. It looked like a clean encampment; the small wooden houses had a tent-like impermanence. There had been first a blaze of autumn; now the trees were profiles against high winter skies; the

piled snow had come with Thanksgiving. In his two-sided Atlantic
world there were these contrasts – the horse-car and the gondola,
the cultivated parks of London and Boston Common, the hierarchic
world of England and the 'tepid bath of democracy' in America.
Henry James was now an expatriate in his own land – and his
land was (he wrote Lord Rosebery) 'not so much a country as a
world'.

I

'Here I am back in America after six years of absence,' he wrote at
his marble-topped table, 'and likely while here to see and learn a
great deal that ought not to become mere waste material. Here I am,
da vero, and here I am likely to be for the next five months.' He was
glad that he had returned. He had needed to see his family, to revive
the 'sense of the consequences that these relations entail. Such relations, such consequences, are a part of one's life, and the best life,
the most complete, is the one that takes full account of such things.
One can only do this by seeing one's people from time to time.' In
this way James assured himself that his journey had not been in vain.
He added however: 'Apart from this I hold it was not necessary I
should come to this country.'

What follows is a passage in which James reflects upon the choice
he had made and its consequences. 'My choice,' he wrote,

is the old world – my choice, my need, my life. There is no need for me
today to argue about this; it is an inestimable blessing to me, and a rare
good fortune, that the problem was settled long ago, and that I have now
nothing to do but to act on the settlement. – My impressions here are
exactly what I expected they would be, and I scarcely see the place, and
feel the manners, the race, the tone of things, now that I am on the spot,
more vividly than I did while I was still in Europe. My work lies there –
and with this vast new world, *je n'ai que faire*. One can't do both – one
must choose. No European writer is called upon to assume that terrible
burden, and it seems hard that I should be. The burden is necessarily
greater for an American – for he *must* deal, more or less, even if only by
implication, with Europe; whereas no European is obliged to deal in the
least with America. No one dreams of calling him less complete for not
doing so. (I speak of course of people who do the sort of work that I do;
not of economists, of social science people.) The painter of manners who
neglects America is not thereby incomplete as yet; but a hundred years
hence – fifty years hence perhaps – he will doubtless be accounted so.

The statement is prophetic. Few Americans at the time would have understood it if they had been allowed to read it over Henry's shoulder. It would remain unpublished for more than sixty years and was to be read in that future foreseen by the novelist. When it was written, most Americans were as oblivious of Europe as Europe was of them: the people on the great continent were preoccupied with their relations to their own land and each other, not their relations with the world. And James's statement was, as he himself saw, the statement of a novelist in search of subjects larger than those offered him by the sparse American scene. 'My impressions of America I shall, after all, not write here. I don't need to write them (at least not à propos of Boston); I know too well what they are. In many ways they are extremely pleasant; but,' he added, 'Heaven forgive me! I feel as if my time were terribly wasted here!'

2

When James had left Venice five months earlier, he could not have foreseen that he would be sitting, homesick, in a Boston hotel, indulging in a long reminiscence, offering himself the solace of the past for the inconveniences and nostalgia of the present. He had gone to Lake Como and then to Switzerland. He had felt a great relief as the coach mounted the Splügen into the Alpine air, out of the stifling cauldron of Italy. He remembered a certain glass of fresh milk which he drank that evening far up in the gloaming – a woman at a wayside inn fetched it from the cow. It was 'the most heavenly draft that ever passed my lips'. He went to Lucerne to visit Mrs Kemble, but she had gone to Engelberg: he followed her to that 'grim, ragged, rather vacuous, but by no means absolutely unbeautiful valley'. One day he climbed the Trübsee toward the Joch pass. 'The whole place was a wilderness of the alpine rose – and the alpine stillness'; the beauty of the high cool valley, whose 'great silver-gleaming snows overhang it and light it up', revived for Henry his memories of his old Swiss days. 'I hadn't believed they could revive even to that point.'

After Switzerland he had returned to London to meet his sister. She had come abroad frail and convalescent from her long illness, accompanied by a Boston friend, Katharine Loring, a hearty woman who seemed to derive a genuine satisfaction in using her own vitality and strength to make life easier for her sickly friend. James recognized that Alice had become deeply attached to Miss Loring and seemed happy in her company and even dependent on her. The novelist spent a few days with his sister at Richmond, saw her afterwards at Kew and still later in Mayfair. It was clear to him that she was adequately companioned. She had her own itinerary and was scheduled to sail for Boston before Henry would be ready to leave. He accordingly departed to pay a series of visits while the final chapters of *The Portrait* were at the printer's. He visited the Anglicized Russell Sturgises at Leatherhead, he twice visited the Roseberys at Mentmore and on one of these occasions had Gladstone as a fellow guest. He went to his publisher's, Frederick Macmillan, at Walton-on-Thames and spent a week in Somerset at Midelney Place, the Lady Trevilian's. 'I think I have never been more *penetrated* – I have never more loved the land.' He found a mellow and ancient feeling in the country and above all its houses – Montacute, Barrington, Ford Abbey and others.

These delicious old houses, in the long August days, in the south of England air, on the soil over which so much has passed and out of which so much has come, rose before me like a series of visions. I thought of a thousand things; what becomes of the things one thinks of at these times? They are not lost, we must hope; they drop back into the mind again, and they enrich and embellish it.

Then, as his sailing-date approached, he had gone to Scotland to Tillypronie, Cortachy, Dalmeny, Laidlawstiel. He remembered the drive from Kirriemuir to Cortachy – a commonplace road by daylight, as he later discovered, but in the twilight it was romantic to ford the river at the entrance to Cortachy and to drive through the dim avenues up to the great lighted pile of the castle, where Lady Airlie, hearing the wheels of the vehicle on the gravel, 'put her handsome head from a window in the clock-tower'. She asked if this were indeed Henry James and wished him a bonny good-evening. James was in a Waverley novel.

3

Now, sitting in the uncomfortable hotel-room, writing and remembering, James was confronted by things far removed from Sir Walter Scott. He had crossed the October Atlantic on the steamer *Paris* by the St Lawrence route, so anxious yet resisting home that he dis-

embarked with the mails at Rimouski and then spent two days getting connections to Boston. He had gone directly to Quincy Street.
His mother struck him as tired and shrunken: she had passed into
old age during his six-year absence; his father was infirm and more
lost than ever in his self-composed world. His Aunt Kate had come
from New York to greet him. She found him 'the same dear Harry
who left us six years ago', but she also noted that he had become 'a
large, stout, vigorous looking man'. James made friends at once with
William's wife – the second Alice in Quincy Street – and saw his
sister again: she had arrived but a few days ahead of him. There
was also William's little boy, sufficiently articulate to boast shortly
after Henry's arrival that he was 'Uncle Harry's fascinating little
nephew'. He too had been named Henry – 'the little Henri-trois' his
uncle dubbed him. In the midst of so much 'family' Henry passed
almost a month before moving to the Boston hotel. He saw Howells
immediately; his friend had just resigned the *Atlantic* editorship, and
had been succeeded by the bland, sociable, gracefully-verbal Thomas
Bailey Aldrich. He saw his old friend T. S. Perry. He began to pay
calls on Mrs Gardner. He spent evenings with Grace Norton. He
journeyed to Newport to see the Tweedys. Newport was charming:
there were large light luxurious houses, planted with Dutch definiteness on the green of the cliff; the lawns touched each other without
benefit of English hedge or fence; the ladies were brilliantly dressed
and carried pretty parasols. The long lines of the far shore were soft
and pure. All in all the effect was quite delicate, 'and anything that
is delicate counts immensely over here'.

But he was restless. His removal from Quincy Street to a Boston
hotel had been designed to give him a feeling of his Bolton Street privacy; he wanted to resume his work. But he found the hotel hostile
to literature. Early in December he went to New York to see what
threads he could pick up there after his absence. He stayed at 115
East 25th Street with Edwin Godkin, in the same neighbourhood in
which he had passed his long book-reviewing months of 1875. Manhattan was hospitable to its literary son – *The Portrait of a Lady* had
just come out and had proved immediately popular. 'I have been
three weeks in New York,' James recorded in his journal, 'and all my
time has slipped away in mere movement. I try as usual to console
myself with the reflection that I am getting impressions. This is
very true; I have got a great many.' To Grace Norton in Cambridge
he wrote: 'I have seen many persons – but no personages; have

heard much talk – but no conversation. Nevertheless the sense one gets here of the increase of the various arts of life is – almost oppressive; especially as one is so often reminded of it. The arts of life flourish – but the art of living, simply, isn't among them.'

James went back to Quincy Street for Christmas. His younger brother, Wilky, increasingly an invalid, came from Wisconsin to be with the family, and with the exception of Robertson, the youngest son, the James family was briefly reunited. One gets a sense of sadness in the way in which, on the day after Christmas, in the old back sitting-room, James gave himself over once again to his journal and to his memories.

The freshness of impression and desire, the hope, the curiosity, the vivacity, the sense of the richness and mystery of the world that lies before us – there is an enchantment in all that which it takes a heavy dose of pain to quench and which in later hours, even if *success* have come to us, touches us less nearly. Some of my doses of pain were very heavy; very weary were some of my months and years. But all that is sacred; it is idle to write of it today.

In this passage he spoke of recovering 'the vision of those untried years'. Never, he wrote, was

an ingenuous youth more passionately and yet more patiently eager for what life might bring. Now that life has brought something, brought a measurable part of what I dreamed of then, it is touching enough to look back. I knew at least what I wanted then – to see something of the world. I have seen a good deal of it, and I look at the past in the light of this knowledge. What strikes me is the definiteness, the unerringness of those longings. I wanted to do very much what I have done, and success, if I may say so, now stretches back a tender hand to its younger brother, desire.

When Christmas was over James did not linger in Cambridge. He returned to New York to attend 'a gorgeous flowery banquet' given by Whitelaw Reid, whose Paris correspondent he had been. Here he met the just-retired Secretary of State, James G. Blaine. From New York he went to Philadelphia to pay a visit to Mrs Wister and her husband. From Germantown he went on to Washington. He had never been there. In *The Bostonians* he was to make one of his ladies ask whether anyone had heard of 'that little place', and to add that 'they invented it' while she had been abroad. James seems to have had this feeling as he stepped from the train one morning early in January, in streets filled with slushy snow, and looked at the single Dome of the Capitol and the single Shaft which then dominated the scene.

92

The Dome and the Shaft

HENRY JAMES found the streets of Washington 'enormous'. They were lined with little red houses. Nothing seemed to pass save the tramway. Two sun-filled rooms were waiting for him at 720 Fifteenth Street; Henry Adams had reserved them; and in the same street the novelist had access to the Metropolitan Club. The first thing he did was to take a solitary walk to the Capitol. With the critical eye that had many times studied St Peter's and the Florentine Duomo, surveyed the Invalides and the dome of St Paul's, he now appraised this great American dome, in the great democratic vista of a city that seemed to him still 'too much of a village'. False classic, white marble, iron, stucco. And yet it had a grand air He went into the rotunda. It was a little like entering a railway station. There were no functionaries, no officers, no uniforms, no door-keepers – not the least spot of colour such as one found in the European seats of government. What was missing was some incarnation of the national conscience and the national dignity. He was to make a character remark that 'this isn't government by livery'; however it is quite clear that James would have liked some livery in the vast expanse of marble, some relief from the ubiquity of spittoons.

He was to have later views of Washington, and to see the emergence of the designs over which Dome and Shaft preside. His was the Washington which had just buried President Garfield and was trying the assassin, Guiteau; in which the new President, Chester A. Arthur, moved in an easy intimacy, almost as a private citizen. The spittoons would recede, works of art would take over; but this was not, in effect, to change the artistic complexion of the place; Henry was to feel simply that the rotunda resembled 'a stonecutter's collection of priced sorts and sizes'. His first feeling, which he concealed, was that the Capitol was 'repulsive'. Later he was willing to concede that it embodied a kind of New World concept of space and air, of dominion and of power created *de chic*. His final picture was built on analogy – 'the Washington dome is indeed capable, in the Washington air, of admirable, of sublime, effects; and there are cases in which, seen at a distance above its yellow Potomac, it varies but by a shade from the sense – yes, absolutely the divine campagna-sense – of St Peter's and the like-coloured Tiber'. Looking at it a quarter of a century after his first vision of it, he was to speak of the Capitol

as a compendium of all the national ideals, a museum, crammed full, even to overflowing, of all the national terms and standards, weights and measures and emblems of greatness and glory, and indeed as a builded record of half the collective vibrations of a people; their conscious spirit, their public faith, their bewildered taste, their ceaseless curiosity, their arduous and interrupted education.

This was a neat mixture of the flattering and the derogatory; for Henry had to reckon with American complacency. What he felt in 1882, and was to express no less succinctly in 1907, was that there wasn't in Washington 'enough native history, recorded or current, to go round'. He was also to echo Oscar Wilde's quip that 'Washington has too many bronze generals'. Describing the perspectives and converging avenues, the circles and crossways, the sense of great wide gardens, he was to have the feelings that given such ample measurements 'the bronze generals and admirals, on their named pedestals, should have been great garden-gods, mossy mythological marble'. The long vistas yearned for something more than the mere brief military or naval commemoration – they 'waited for some bending nymph or some armless Hermes'. Washington was an oddly scattered city; he got a general impression of high granite steps, light grey corniced colonnades, harmoniously low, contending for effect with slaty mansard roofs and iron excrescences. It was all 'a loose congregation of values'. Much of the background seemed provisional, as if it could be unhooked and rolled up like canvas scenery.

The city had two faces for James. There was official Washington, 'the democratic substitute for a court city', and there was social Washington, harbouring a society well organized, with its own codes and standards, that seemed to have little to do with politics. Henry marvelled at this; for in London he met parliamentarians and lords everywhere; while in Washington he encountered chance legislators in a society that seemed bent on excluding senators and congressmen from its houses rather than admitting them. There seemed to be passages of national life in which 'the President himself was scarce thought to be in society'.

Society seemed to operate in the foreground, and it used official Washington as a backdrop. Elsewhere in America women were in control, and absentee husbands spent their days beside their ticker-tapes; but in Washington there was a 're-committal to masculine hands of some share at least in the interests of civilization, some part of the social property and social office'. James wondered how the foreign diplomats, facing the phenomena of a capital that differed from, rather than resembled, other capitals and other societies, could cope with their task of 'penetration and discretion'. One supposes that James found it difficult to be discreet. He was hardly an 'observant stranger' in his own capital. And the story which he began at this time and completed months later, *The Point of View*, is indeed the most sharply critical of any which he ever wrote about his homeland. He may have concealed his opinions in it behind those of foreign visitors to New York and Washington, whose letters he created with craft and cunning, but his own 'point of view' is unmistakable. One had to recognize, however, that much of his vision of Washington was influenced by the spacious drawing-room of 1607 H Street, in the tart reflections of his friend, the 'Voltaire in petticoats'.

I

'Thursday, Henry James put in an appearance; that young emigrant has much to learn here,' wrote Clover Adams to her father on 8 January 1882.

He is surprised to find that he can go to the Capitol and listen to debates without taking out a licence, as in London. He may in time get into the 'swim' here, but I doubt it. I think the real, live, vulgar, quick-paced world in America will fret him and that he prefers a quiet corner with a pen where he can create men and women who say neat things and have refined tastes and are not nasal or eccentric.

'I shouldn't wonder if the place were the most agreeable of our cities,' James wrote to Grace Norton.

The Henry Adamses, who are my principal friends here, have a commodious and genial house and have been very kind to me. The pleasant thing here is the absence of business – the economy-empty streets, most of them rather pretty, with nothing going on in them. I am making the best of everything – so much so that I feel at moments as if I were rather holding my nose to the grindstone. It goes very well – but I will confide to you in strict privacy that in my heart of hearts I am woefully and wickedly *bored!* I am horribly homesick for the ancient world. *There* we needn't be always making the best of things. One may make the worst of them and they are still pretty good.

To Henrietta Reubell he wrote: 'Enormous spaces, hundreds of miles of asphalt, a charming climate and the most entertaining society in America.' And to Godkin: 'I have seen a good many people, chiefly under the influence of the Adamses, and find the social arrangements, and the tone of conversation, very easy and genial.'

The Adamses constituted themselves James's guides and evaluators of all he reported from his social rounds. Mrs Adams paraphrased scripture to her father to describe the novelist's predicament – 'And a certain man came down to Jerusalem and fell among thieves ... and they sprang up and choked him.'* To which she added 'Henry James passed Sunday evening at Robeson's and dines tomorrow with Blaine.' On his side James wrote to Godkin that the Adamses disapproved of the company he was keeping, 'though I notice that they are eagerly anxious to hear what I have seen and heard at places which they decline to frequent. After I had been to Mrs Robeson's they mobbed me for revelations; and after I had dined with Blaine, to meet the president, they fairly hung upon my lips.' In the Adams house he was a constant visitor; Mrs Adams seemed to have a perpetual tea-party under way and frequent dinners at a little round table. Here Henry dined, early in his stay, with the new British Minister, Sir Lionel Sackville-West, fresh from his post in Spain where he had contracted his since-more-publicized alliance with Pepita, commemorated both by his descendant and by Virginia Woolf. 'A rather dull (though amiable) personage,' was Henry's verdict; however, he liked his 'delightful little foreign daughter, who is the most perfect *ingénue* ever seen in America'.

The Robeson of whom the Adamses disapproved was Congressman George Maxwell Robeson of New Jersey, whose wife of fifty Henry thought a 'personage' although 'fundamentally coarse'. The Robesons were about to attain much notoriety, sponsoring Oscar

* Mrs Adams was quoting from memory Luke 10: 30: 'A certain man went down from Jerusalem to Jericho, and fell among thieves, which stripped him of his raiment ...'

Wilde during his visit to the capital. Newly-arrived from England, trading on his Gilbert and Sullivan reputation, Oscar had brought his aestheticism to New York and Philadephia and now to Washington. The press talked largely of Bunthorne-Wilde. 'The newspapers haven't got scent of Henry James yet,' Mrs Adams observed, and he managed to keep out of their way. However he called on Wilde as a matter of courtesy. 'Oscar Wilde is here – an unclean beast,' he wrote to Godkin. He told Mrs Adams he found him a 'a fatuous cad'. But then James had admitted to Oscar he was homesick for London, and Oscar adroitly implied that this was rather provincial of him. 'Really! You care for *places?* The world is my home.'

The Adamses approved of James's seeing Senator Thomas F. Bayard, member of an old Delaware family and brother of Mrs Lockwood. Senator Bayard promptly sent him two invitations to dinner and offered him the use of a private room at the Capitol in which to entertain his friends. At Bayard's he met Horace Gray, a new associate Justice of the Supreme Court. He goes to a ball at the British legation; he dines with the Swedish Secretary; he chats with the Republican leader, Wayne MacVeagh, and pleases him by remembering that Matthew Arnold considered him quite the pleasantest American he had ever met. To Mrs Gardner James wrote that what he liked best in Washington society were certain girls, 'very charming with a *désinvolture* rather rare *chez nous*'. These included Miss Bayard and Miss Frelinghuysen, daughter of the new Secretary of State, 'happy specimens of the *finished* American girl – the American girl who has profited by the sort of social education that Washington gives'. The Bayard girls were (he told his mother) 'such as one ought to marry, if one were marrying'. For the rest he was seeing 'plenty of men, more than elsewhere, and a good many energetic types; but few "accomplished gentlemen" '.

2

James G. Blaine, after meeting James in New York, invited him to his home to meet the twenty-first President of the United States, Chester A. Arthur. It was an elaborate dinner attended also by the British Minister, the Governor of California, Generals Sherman and Hancock, Senator Hale, Murat Halstead, Andrew Carnegie, Hon. S. B. Elkins, and Allen Thorndyke Rice. The press called it 'a small and noted company', and Henry James Jr was described as 'that eminent novelist and anglicized American'. He observed the President's 'well-made coat and well-cut whiskers', and enjoyed an intimate chat with him after dinner. President Arthur had known various members of the James family in Albany; he had even been present at the suicidal deathbed of a distant relative, Johnny James; and he had known Smith Van Buren, son of President Martin Van Buren, who had married one of James's aunts. James wrote to his mother that he 'evidently believed me to be the son of Uncle William [the Rev. William James, elder brother of Henry's father] and wouldn't be disillusioned. This illusion was indeed apparently so dear to him, that I felt that if I had any smartness in me, I ought, striking while the iron was hot, to apply for a foreign mission, which I should doubtless promptly get.' To Mrs Gardner James wrote that he thought the President 'a good fellow – even attractive. He is a gentleman and evidently has that amiable quality, a desire to please.'

At the end of January the novelist was enjoying himself sufficiently to plan to remain another month, and he had thoughts of visiting the South. He was finding the capital 'genial and amusing'. On 27 January, however, his brother Robertson wrote that their mother had suffered an attack of bronchial asthma. On Sunday morning the 29th James wrote to her saying that it was 'impossible almost for me to think of you in this condition, as I have only seen you hovering about the bed of pain, on which others were stretched'. Late that evening, while he was dressing to go to a party, he received a telegram from William's Alice: 'Your mother exceedingly ill. Come at once.' There was no train until the next morning. Distraught and anxious, James rang the bell of the Adamses at 11 p.m. to inform them of his impending departure. He took the morning train to New York, and by that time Clover Adams had received an answer to a telegram she had sent to Boston. She knew – what he did not – that his mother was no longer alive.

93

Mary James

IN a driving snowstorm Henry James made his way from the Boston depot to Quincy Street. Thirty-six hours had elapsed since he had been summoned home. He had arrived in New York at five the previous evening; at his cousin's, Alice's telegram was explained to him: Mary James had died quite suddenly the previous evening, as she sat in the closing dusk with her husband and her sister – Aunt Kate – in the Quincy Street house. She had been recovering from the asthma. Her heart had simply stopped in her 71st year.

James went to the Hoffman House to rest until he could take the night train to Boston. 'I shall never pass that place in future,' he wrote in his journal, 'without thinking of the wretched hours I spent there.' Now, in the early snow-reflected light, with the flakes swirling in the wind, James entered the north room of the house where his mother lay in her shroud. He found her 'as sweet and tranquil and noble as in life'. She seemed unchanged by death; there was much life – unendurably much – in her lifeless face. He later said he had never known how tenderly he loved her till he saw her lying there that morning. His death-vigil was lonely – and triumphant: lonely, in that he had always felt a special tie between himself and his mother, as her favourite son; triumphant, in that he seemed to feel that with her death he came into full possession of her. In life he had had to share her with his father, with William, with his younger brothers and sister. Now, in the depths of his memory and imagination, she belonged to him. He had felt this long ago when his cousin Minny died – felt the way in which she had been translated from 'this changing realm of fact to the steady realm of thought'. And this was why, when he wrote the long elegiac passage in his journal, commemorating all that his mother meant to him, he spoke of these 'hours of exquisite pain'. He was ready to thank Heaven that 'this particular pang comes to us but once'.

His father and Alice, by the time he talked with them, had begun to reconcile themselves to this break in their lives. Alice, frail as she was, seemed to have sufficient strength and courage at this moment; and the elder Henry, infirm and tired, had his own philosophical way of taking the sorrows of life. Both were 'almost happy'. His mother still seemed to be there, in the house in which she had lived so long, 'so beautiful, so full of all that we loved in her, she looked in death'. Wilky arrived the next morning a matter of hours before the funeral, from Wisconsin. Robertson had been in Quincy Street while Henry was in Washington. For the first time in fifteen years – and for the last – the four sons and the daughter of Mary James were together under the family roof.

Wednesday dawned clear and cold. The storm had spent itself during the night. The sky was blue, the snow-shroud was deep, the air brilliant and still. In the bright frosty sunshine the sons of Mary and the elder Henry carried their mother to her temporary resting-place in a vault in the Cambridge cemetery. In the spring a site would be chosen for the grave.

'She was the perfection of a mother – the sweetest, gentlest, most beneficent human being I have ever known,' Henry James wrote to his friends. 'I was passionately attached to her,' he told Mrs Gardner. 'She was sweet, gentle, wise, patient, precious – a pure and exquisite soul. But now she is a memory as beneficent as her presence.'

94

An Exquisite Stillness

A FEW days after his mother's funeral Henry James moved from Quincy Street into Boston. 'I wish to remain near my father,' he wrote to a friend. 'I do not wish however to be in Cambridge.' He found rooms at 102 Mount Vernon Street on Beacon Hill. They were bare and ugly, but comfortable. Here he reconstructed, as best as he could, the conditions of Bolton Street. At first he felt that he should prolong his stay in America; his father was not well and Alice was not strong. William had his own family and his work. Of the sons of Mary James he alone was available. But as the weeks passed it became clear that Alice had for the time being found new strength in taking over her mother's role. She ministered to her father and ran the Quincy Street house without difficulty. The elder Henry insisted that his son return to his London tasks and to his own life. The novelist decided to maintain his original sailing-date in May.

I

On the day after he moved into his rooms – 9 February 1882 – he wrote a long passage in his journal on his mother's death, describing her as the 'keystone' of the James family arch. The passage is eloquent in its self-conscious grief, and it reflects Henry's complete idealization of his mother. There is nothing comparable to it in the available writings of his brother; William, in all that he set down, said very little about Mary James, with whom he had had so often been at odds. Henry's worship of her contains within it no suggestion that he ever imagined his mother as other than a creature of angelic tissue.

She held us all together, and without her we are scattered reeds. She was patience, she was wisdom, she was exquisite maternity. Her sweetness, her mildness, her great natural beneficence were unspeakable, and it is infinitely touching to me to write about her here as one that *was*. When I think of all that she had been, for years – when I think of her hourly devotion to each and all of us – and that when I went to Washington the last of December I gave her my last kiss, I heard her voice for the last time – there seems not to be enough tenderness in my being to register the extinction of such a life.

There were consolations. His mother's work was after all done; the 'weariness of age had come upon her'. He preferred losing her forever to seeing her begin to suffer. He thought 'with a kind of holy joy of her being lifted now above all our pains and anxieties'. Her death had given him 'a passionate belief in certain transcendent things – the immanence of being as nobly created as hers – the immortality of such virtue as that – the reunion of spirits in better conditions than these. She is no more of an angel today than she had always been.'

He felt as if an 'eternal stillness' had settled around him. It was 'but a form of her love. One can hear her voice in it – one can feel, forever, the inextinguishable vibration of her devotion.' He rebuked himself for not having been tender enough with her at the end; he had been too blind to her sweetness and beneficence. He wished he had known what was coming 'so that one might have enveloped her with the softest affection'. And he went on to speak of her continued restlessness, her preoccupation with her children, her loyalty to her husband. 'Summer after summer she never left Cambridge,' he noted. His father was responsible for this – 'it was impossible that Father should leave his own house'. The passage is worth mentioning; under the guise of praising his mother's self-sacrifice he seems to criticize the elder Henry.

The country, the sea, the change of air and scene, were an exquisite enjoyment to her; but she bore with the deepest gentleness and patience the constant loss of such opportunities. She passed her nights and her days in that dry, flat, hot, stale and odious Cambridge, and had never a thought while she did so but for father and Alice. It was a perfect mother's life – the life of a perfect wife.

One wonders why Henry, in his sorrow, made this point; there had been many summers spent away from Cambridge – in New England coastal resorts and Canada. James also seemed to glide over the fact that Alice had been seriously ill in recent years, and this, as much as the father's increasing infirmities, had kept his parents in Cambridge. In death as in life he made himself his mother's champion against a kind of family oppression. His peroration has in it a note of triumph:

To bring her children into the world – to expend herself, for years, for their happiness and welfare – then, when they had reached a full maturity and were absorbed in the world and in their own interests – to lay herself down in her ebbing strength and yield up her pure soul to the celestial power that had given her this divine commission. Thank God one knows this loss but once.

It was inevitable that James should give to these words all the resonance of a funeral oration. In a touching manner he sought to pay his lifelong debt in the most precious coin he possessed: in the power of language, the strength of imagery, the emotion carried by his pen. Mary James had been the central figure of all his years, and so she would remain. The strange thing was that on a deeper level of feeling, which he inevitably concealed from himself, he must have seen his mother as she was, not as he imagined and wanted her to be. She is incarnated in all his fiction, not the fragile self-effacing and self-denying woman he pictured in his filial piety, spending her last strength for her children. The mothers of Henry James, for all their maternal sweetness, are strong, determined, demanding, grasping women – Mrs Touchett or Mrs Gereth, Mrs Hudson or Mrs Newsome. Sometimes these mothers have great charm and strength; sometimes they become the frightening figures of the governess or of Mark Ambient's wife. It is perhaps strange to juxtapose the mothers of Henry James's novels and tales beside the ideal mother of the commemorative tribute. Only in life was Henry prepared to create such a mother; in his fiction she is neither ideal nor ethereal.

Mary James had reared a family of five children. The younger brothers and the daughter had been crushed by the irrationalities and contradictions of the familial environment over which Mary had presided. The elder sons had surmounted them. Out of these tensions and emotions generated by the mother, which played against the easy compliance of the father, there had emerged a novelist and a philosopher capable of expressing the very contradictions that had produced them – the one in brilliant fiction, the other in the lucid prose of rational thought.

2

'All those weeks after Mother's death,' wrote James, 'had an exquisite stillness and solemnity.' He kept his London hours. In the mid-morning he would walk across the Common and have his breakfast at Parker's. Then he would return to his rooms and write until four or five o'clock. In the gathering winter twilight he would walk to Cambridge, 'over that dreary bridge whose length I had measured so often in the past', a mile of wooden piles, supporting a brick pavement with its rough timber fence from which he looked at the frozen bay, the backs of many new houses and a big brown marsh. He had the horse-cars for company. Four or five times a week he would dine in Quincy Street with his father and sister. Then he would return to Boston in the clear American starlight. 'It was a simple, serious, wholesome time. Mother's death appeared to have left behind it a soft beneficent hush in which we lived for weeks, for months, and which was full of rest and sweetness.' James thought of her constantly as he walked to Boston 'along those dark, vacant roads, where, in the winter air, one met nothing but the coloured lamps and the far-heard jingle of the Cambridge horse-cars'.

His work interested him. He chose, during this period, to write not the fiction to which he was addicted, but a play, the harbinger of his later siege of the theatre. He had written, in his youth, three little skits or playlets, and published them; they had however relied neither on action nor on any particular characterization – had been simply little comediettas or farces sustained by a certain conversational charm. Now, however, he set to work to make a play of the least theatrical of his stories – *Daisy Miller*. It seemed to him that its success in the magazines and as a book could be duplicated on the stage. In New York he had had some preliminary negotiations with the Mallory brothers, who owned the new Madison Square Theatre. They had encouraged James and it was for them that he converted his celebrated tale into the concreteness of a dramatic action. To do this he had to invent new 'business'. In the first place Daisy had to survive; he could not kill her off; and she would marry Winter-bourne. A villain was needed. Eugenio, the courier, was given this role, and the foreign lady in Geneva, whom we never meet in the tale, now emerged as an *intrigante* such as James had witnessed often on the stage of the Théâtre Français. Daisy recovers from her malaria, while the Roman carnival is in full swing. The manager found it 'beautifully written' but distinctly too literary. 'It had too much talk and not enough action,' he said. In his journal James speaks of the Mallorys as behaving 'like asses and sharpers'. To Howells he wrote: 'When we meet, I will tell you how those gifted brothers led me on protesting over the same path you trod to the same flowery pitfall, and with another play.' Thus ended his first struggle – the first of a series – with theatre-managers. James seems to have been naïve enough to think that in the world of the theatre managers were like magazine-editors. He had his play privately printed; then he made an effort to get it accepted by the Boston Museum Theatre, and offered it to London managers. The verdict was always the same, and James finally sold it to the *Atlantic*, for $1,000. During this period he also roughed out a first act for a drama founded on *The American*, planning also to substitute a happy end-ing for Newman and Claire. The collapse of the 'Daisy' negotiations led him to put it aside.

The story he had begun in Washington lay unfinished in his port-folio, and play-writing filled in the time very well. It was like work-ing out an elaborate puzzle. 'My work interested me even more than the importance of it would explain – or than the success of it has justified,' he noted. He felt he had learned, vividly, that 'in the theatre one must be prepared for *disgust*, deep and unspeakable disgust'.

The dramatic form seemed to him 'the most beautiful thing pos-sible', but 'the misery of the thing is that the baseness of the English-speaking stage affords no setting for it'. When his play was written he carried his script to Mrs Gardner and read it to her, during two long evenings. She was a sympathetic listener. James had long ago imagined Benvolio reading his plays to an irresistible Countess. He had, so to speak, his private performance at the Court of Isabella.

3

Between bouts of homesickness for London and small Boston sociabilities James managed to decrease the distance to his May sailing-date. How desperate he must have been we may gather from his writing a letter to William J. Hoppin, asking for 'a little parcel of London items'. How was Mrs Duncan Stewart? What was the latest news of her daughter, Mrs Rogerson? He missed London, 'the full extent of my devotion to which I didn't know until I had put the ocean between us. My country pleases, in many ways, but it doesn't satisfy, and I sometimes wrap my head in my toga, to stifle (stoically) my groans.' He told the First Secretary of Legation that when he next arrived at Euston Station, 'I shall fall down and kiss the platform.'

Mr Hoppin dutifully pasted the letter into his diary; it is the only letter of any length he ever received from the novelist. On the same day James also wrote to Henrietta Reubell 'your little whiff of the great Parisian hubbub seems to me the carnival of dissipation'. To Mrs Kemble he wrote that he smiled with derision at her suggestion that he might be 'weaned' from 'my London loves and longings by remaining over here'. He was within a month of sailing. 'My father is much better than he was a month ago, and will not listen to my making any "sacrifices" for his sake.' He had heard from Mrs Wister; he had had a letter from Mrs Procter, 'who writes as neatly as she talks, and from whose firm and brilliant surface the buffets of fate glance off'.

Some time before he sailed his father and Alice took a small house in Mount Vernon Street. This represented the final breaking-up of the house in Quincy Street, which had been the seat of the James family since the end of the Civil War. The house was too large for William's needs; and the elder Henry and Alice wanted something smaller and more intimate. James saw them comfortably installed and was ready to sail with an easy conscience. Almost the last thing he did before his departure was to attend another funeral. On 27 April the bells of Concord tolled the death of Ralph Waldo Emerson, and James made the familiar journey three days later to pay his respects to the old family friend, the benign figure of his childhood.

The older generation was passing. Longfellow had died little more than a month before. It was a cool day in Concord and there was a threat of rain in the air. Regular and special trains brought a large congregation; others came in wagons and on foot to pay tribute to 'the principal gentleman in the place'. As a public funeral James found it 'curious, sociable, cheerful', a popular manifestation, the most striking he had ever seen provoked by the death of a man of letters. He cherished this memory of an almost rustic occasion, beside the new grave, near the grave of Hawthorne.

On the day before he sailed, his father wrote a long letter to him, to speed him on his journey :

My darling boy, I must bid you farewell. How loving a farewell it is, I can't say, but only that it is most loving. I can't help feeling that you are the one that has cost us the least trouble, and given us always the most delight. Especially do I mind Mother's perfect joy in you the last few months of her life, and your perfect sweetness to her. I think in fact it is this which endears you so much to me now. I feel that I have fallen heir to all dear Mother's fondness for you, as well as my proper own, and bid you accordingly a distinctly widowed farewell.

Henry was now his father's 'angel' as he had been his mother's. 'Goodbye then again, my precious Harry. We shall each rejoice in you in our several ways as you plough through the ocean and attain to your old rooms, where it will be charming to think of you as once more settled and at work.' And he repeated : 'A lingering goodbye, then, dearest Harry, from all of us! and above all from your loving Father.'

95

A Little Tour in France

HENRY JAMES crossed the Atlantic on the *Gallia* in eight days. He left the ship at Cork. Eager as he was to return to Bolton Street, he wanted a glimpse of the land of his father's father. He spent a week in Ireland and found the cities filled with constables and soldiers; otherwise he saw little but green fields and dirty cabins. He had no desire to become a sentimental tourist again, and if he had had any idea of turning his Irish visit into copy he abandoned it. On 22 May he was back in Bolton Street. Reclining on the sofa and awaiting him was an unexpected guest, his youngest brother Robertson. On his desk was a pile of invitations. The city seemed oppressive, big, black and, actual'. It was 'a brutal sort of a place', he wrote to Godkin, and while he reverted to it with 'a kind of filial fondness' everything somehow seemed changed. He was restless, he was bored. The death of his mother had, for the moment, drained life of all interest. The American episode was already fading away, and while he looked back at it with 'a great deal of tenderness', he knew that Boston meant 'absolutely nothing to me – I don't even dislike it', he wrote in his journal. He added : 'I like it, on the contrary; I only dislike to live there.' Much of his visit to his homeland seemed like a dream – 'a very painful dream'.

His nostalgia for London seemed to have evaporated as well. He went through the motions of participating in the Season, yet the London social world, into which he had plunged with such eagerness three years before, seemed to him 'a poor world, this time; I saw and did very little that was interesting'. And at the end of a brief journal-note, he remarked : 'I have gone in too much for society.' To make matters worse he found himself invaded by editors and friends. At various times that summer Howells and his family, Osgood, Aldrich, Charles Dudley Warner, John Hay, Clarence King, whom he met at this time, were all in London, not to speak of certain ladies to whom he was indebted in various ways for hospitality, and whom he liked well enough in their own surroundings. Henrietta Reubell crossed from Paris; Mrs Boit and her 'merry laugh' reappeared; Mrs V. R. arrived and took rooms a few doors away from James's lodgings; Mrs Wister came from Philadelphia to visit Fanny Kemble. In this 'bewilderment of conflicting duties and pleasures' James was fretful. 'All summer I had been trying to work,' he wrote in his journal, 'but my interruptions had been so numerous that it was only during the last weeks that I succeeded, even moderately, in doing something.' This was when the Season abated and the visiting Americans crossed to the Continent. He also notes : 'Shall I confess, however, that the evenings had become dull.' Even his election as an honorary member of the Athenaeum, where he had been proposed by Leslie Stephen, seemed now routine. He possessed two clubs in Pall Mall, side by side, and was on an equal footing as it were with England's political, literary and religious worlds; but a process of disenchantment had begun. Indeed he found his evenings so dull that he sought out William J. Hoppin for company. Hoppin's journal of Sunday, 25 August 1882, records:

I had a long visit from Henry James last Sunday evening. He spoke of the neglect he had experienced in Boston when he was there last winter. One would have thought with the literary taste attributed to these people they would have fêted him. But he got the privilege of the Union Club with some difficulty and was invited once to dinner. He spoke of all this without bitterness. Perhaps one should remember that he had just lost his mother and the Bostonians may have thought he did not care to be invited to parties. But they might have given him the chance of refusing.

I

To make James's restless summer complete, William suddenly decided to apply for a year's leave from Harvard with the double purpose of having a vacation and meeting some of his fellow-psychologists in Europe. Early in September the novelist found himself on his way to Euston Station to meet his brother's boat-train. The strange thing was that William chose to take this leave a few months after the birth of his second son (who had been named William after his father and great-grandfather). At this moment of renewed paternity he was planning to be away from his wife and infant for a year. He had done the same thing two years before after his firstborn had arrived – he had rushed abroad for a summer's vacation, as if the presence of infancy in his house was more than he could bear. To be sure, his house, in which his mother-in-law and his wife's sister also lived, must at times have been a bedlam, and William could hardly have found peace there for the pursuit of his work. Perhaps the new child, like the firstborn, may have also touched some chord of early memory in William and awakened an old anguish, that of little rivals invading *his* nursery – as Henry had done long ago. Shortly after arriving in Europe he wrote a letter to his wife which might have given her pause, were she not so preoccupied: he described the German peasant-women he had seen

striding like men through the streets, dragging their carts or lugging their baskets, minding their business, seeming to notice nothing in the stream of luxury and vice, but belonging far away, to something better and purer ... All the mystery of womanhood seems incarcerated in their ugly being – the Mothers! the Mothers! Ye are all one! Yes, Alice dear, what I love in you is only what these blessed creatures have.

That sentence about 'ugly being' and 'ye are all one', if whimsical, nevertheless betrayed a singular state of feeling. And perhaps this was why William had, for the moment, put an ocean between himself and Cambridge. To his brother it seemed that William's timing was unfortunate. He used the word 'abandoned' twice in writing to his sister-in-law. 'With your husband in Venice and your eldest brother-in-law in these strange French cities [he was writing from Bordeaux] you must feel rather bewildered and abandoned.' But clearly he did not think of himself as the abandoner. 'Your situation seems to me most unnatural, but I hope you bear up under it, and that you derive some assistance in doing so from your little Harry and William.' And he returned to the charge : 'Abandoned by your husband, you seem to me, dear Alice, very greatly to be pitied, and I assure you that I think of you with tender sympathy.'

As William descended from the train at Euston Station he gave high proof of his temper to his brother. It was a vigorous monologue :

My! – how cramped and inferior England seems! After all, it's poor old Europe, just as it used to be in our dreary boyhood! America may be raw and shrill, but I could never live with this as you do! I'm going to hurry down to Switzerland and then home again as soon as may be. It was a mistake to come over! I thought it would do me good. Hereafter I'll stay at home. You'll have to come to America if you want to see the family.

His eldest son, recording this many years later, remarked that William was always under the spell of Europe when he was in America – and was 'most ardently American when on European soil'. The account continues : 'The effect on Henry can better be imagined than described. Time never accustomed him to these collisions, even though he learned to expect them.' Henry usually ended by rushing William off to his continental destination – which was what he did this time, two days later – and, his nephew added, 'he remained alone to ejaculate, to exclaim and to expatiate for weeks on the rude and exciting cyclone that had burst upon him and passed him by'.

2

His season of malaise was reflected in Henry James's fiction. In Bolton Street he completed the tale he had begun in Washington – *The
Point of View* – and its picture of American life comes to us as in a
series of folding mirrors, capturing in a critical light the glittering
weaknesses of the American democracy. What he found was a country in which egalitarianism was diluting individuality; in which a
thinness of history and a smallness of national experience had to
be reconciled with a continental grandeur and a national sense of
space and freedom. The repatriated American gentlewoman, who
has spent years in European *pensions*, complains that 'there is no
respect for one's privacy, for one's preferences, for one's reserves'.
The lady at Newport remarks on the liberties given – and taken –
by American youth and their deformation of the English language.

Of course, a people of fifty millions, who have invented a new civilization, have a right to a language of their own; that's what they tell me,
and I can't quarrel with it. But I wish they had made it as pretty as the
mother-tongue, from which, after all, it is more or less derived. We
ought to have invented something as noble as our country.

She finds the men 'better than the women, who are very subtle, but
rather hard'. The men are simply professional and commercial,
'there are very few gentlemen pure and simple'.

The girls are not shy, but I don't know why they should be, for there
is really nothing here to be afraid of. Manners are very gentle, very
humane; the democratic system deprives people of weapons that everyone doesn't equally possess. No one is formidable ... I think there is not
much wickedness, and there is certainly less cruelty than with you.
Everyone can sit; no one is kept standing ... The general good nature, the
social equality, deprives them of triumphs on the one hand, and of
grievances on the other ... You will say I am describing a terrible society,
– a society without great figures or great social prizes. You have hit it,
my dear; there are no great figures ... There are no brilliant types; the
most important people seem to lack dignity. They are very *bourgeois*.

The emerging picture is of an easy democracy that breeds an easy
mediocrity, in an atmosphere of advancing material civilization and
chattering women,

The women listen very little – not enough. They interrupt; they talk
too much; one feels their presence too much as sound. American women

make too many vague exclamations – say too many indefinite things. In short, they have a great deal of nature. On the whole, I find very little affectation, though we shall probably have more as we improve.

This is one appraisal which America receives. Another is through the eyes of a British M.P. who surveys the same civilization good-naturedly, comments on the luxurious trains, and on the people, visits the schools and finds it extraordinary how many persons 'are being educated in this country; and yet, at the same time, the tone of the people is less scholarly than one might expect'. His impression is that children are better educated than adults. 'The position of a child is, on the whole, one of great distinction.'

Improved cooking-stoves, rosewood pianos, gas and hot water, aesthetic furniture, and complete sets of the British Essayists. A tramway through every street; every block of equal length; blocks and houses scientifically lettered and numbered. There is absolutely no loss of time, and no need of looking for anything, or, indeed, *at* anything.

The expatriated American aesthete complains at the absence of variety – 'Everyone is Mr Jones, Mr Brown; and every one looks like Mr Jones and Mr Brown. They lack completeness of identity; they are quite without modelling.' The French academician sees the women as engaged in a chase for a husband, and American literature contains 'no form, no matter, no style, no general ideas'. The books seem written for children and young ladies. The newspapers contain no news, only stories about marriages and divorces, 'not in six lines, discreetly veiled, with an art of insinuation, as with us, but with all the facts (or the fictions), the letters, the dates, the places, the hours'. His conclusion is that America is 'the last word of democracy, and that word is – *flatness*'. But James gives the last word to the Americans and largely to Marcellus Cockerell, who has had his fill of Europe. It is from his letter that Clover Adams culled the epigram most pleasing to herself, as it was to most Americans. 'We are more analytic, more discriminating, more familiar with realities. As for manners, there are bad manners everywhere, but an aristocracy is bad manners organized.'

The tale was published late in the year in the *Century* magazine. James had predicted to his father that it would 'probably call down execration on my head', and it did. The reviews were peevish: Henry's readers liked neither the sharpness of his observation nor the pointedness of his criticism. He was accused of being too severe in his treatment of the American national character. The tale tended to confirm the public image of the novelist: he was a chronic critic of the land of the brave and the free. James knew how 'to play the harp of fiction', said one reviewer, but, he added, his harp didn't have enough strings. These remarks inevitably made him feel that Americans were thin-skinned. In the fullness of time it is possible to observe that Henry James was saying nothing more to Americans about their land than what his fellow-novelists in France or in Russia or in England were doing to their countrymen, that is functioning as artists, and by this process functioning as critics.

His disenchantment with English Society emerged in a tale originally designed as a contrast between Anglo-American and French morality. It will be recalled that during his journey of 1877 he had seen Dumas's *Le Demi-Monde* and had found it impossible to swallow the denunciation of the heroine 'with a past' by a very moral young man who had been her lover. To 'tell' on a woman, even if she were not the most moral creature in the world, seemed to James ungentlemanly; and he could not accept the high virtue made of this in the French play. In *The Siege of London*, which he gave to Leslie Stephen for the *Cornhill*, he described the attempt of an American adventuress to obtain admission into London society. Nancy Headway wants to elbow her way to respectability in spite of her multiple divorces. She sets her cap at a stolid English baronet, Sir Arthur Demesne, under the observing eyes of a Secretary of Legation – a composite figure of Nadal and Hoppin, though somewhat more suave than either – as well as of a sophisticated American, rather like James himself. The society to which Mrs Headway aspires is certainly 'bad manners organized', and the lengths to which the mother of the baronet, Lady Demesne, goes to find out about Nancy's past embarrasses and finally irritates the sophisticated American. The tale is written in a vein of high comedy and its morality is the reverse of the French. Nancy gets her nobleman; and the American 'tells' only when he knows it is too late to change anything. But in reality this tale is James's farewell to London Society. He seemed to feel now that it was not much of an achievement to get into it – 'poor world' that it was – indeed that anyone could do so with a little honest effort, as witness the case of Mrs Headway. Even New York would find her acceptable, once she became Lady Demesne.

The matter is put with some force by the Jamesian observer; his remarks shows the road James had travelled since his talks with

Nadal three years earlier. 'I hate that phrase, "getting into society."
I don't think one ought to attribute to one's self that sort of ambition. One ought to assume that one is in society – that one *is* society
– and to hold that if one has good manners, one has, from the social
point of view, achieved the great thing.'

Perhaps James also felt the English had taken him up not because
he had good manners and was a gentleman, but simply because they
found him 'entertaining'. Nancy Headway proves to be a roaring
success on the strength of her quaint Americanisms and her bold
manner. 'When she saw her audience in convulsions, she said to
herself that this was success, and believed that, if she had only come
to London five years sooner, she might have married a duke.' This
reaction to London Society may have had some part in Henry's writing, at this time, his essay on *Du Maurier and London Society* which
he published a few months later in the *Century*. He praised du
Maurier for holding up 'a singularly polished and lucid mirror to the
drama of English society'. He showed with what closeness he had
studied du Maurier's cartoons in *Punch* ever since his boyhood. And
in a final passage he wondered whether the conquest of London had
been really worth while after all. Philistines were philistines, on
either side of the Atlantic; the artist was doomed always to be an
outsider anywhere in the world. Pondering du Maurier's Mrs Cima-
bue Brown and his satire of aesthetes, James concludes that no
revolution has occurred The English were simply not an aesthetic
people :

They have not a spontaneous artistic life; their taste is a matter of conscience, reflection, duty, and the writer who in our time has appealed to
them most eloquently on behalf of art has rested his plea on moral standards – has talked exclusively of right and wrong. It is impossible to live
much among them, to be a spectator of their habits, their manners, their
arrangements, without perceiving that the artistic point of view is the
last that they naturally take. The sense of manner is not part of their
constitution. They arrive at it, as they have arrived at so many things,
because they are ambitious, resolute, enlightened, fond of difficulties; but
there is always a strange element either of undue apology or of exaggerated defiance in their attempts at the cultivation of beauty. They
carry on their huge broad back a nameless mountain of conventions and
prejudices, a dusky cloud of inaptitudes and fears, which casts a shadow
upon the frank and confident practice of art. The consequence of all this
is that their revivals of taste are even stranger than the abuses they are

meant to correct. They are violent, voluntary, mechanical; wanting in grace, in tact, in the sense of humour and of proportion.

Art seemed to have no place, either in an industrially expanding America bent on equalizing everything, or in an England where the 'conventions and prejudices', not to speak of 'inaptitudes and fears', made James feel as if he were a freak of nature, or some curiosity, to be wined and dined and patted on the back without ever being truly appreciated or understood.

3

After he got William off to the Continent Henry James paid a few country visits – this was one way of escaping from the London crowd and his fellow-countrymen – and crossed the Channel in mid-September to do a specific chore. A Harper editor had suggested to him that he write a travel-book about France. This seemed to him a profitable thing to do. In spite of his large professional experience by this time, he did it without obtaining a definite commitment and Harper later backed out. But Henry James sold the book to Osgood and, as *A Little Tour in France*, it was to serve successive generations in the château country and the Midi. Before starting his tour he paid his customary visit to Turgenev at Bougival. This time he found him seriously ill. They had some good talk nevertheless, and Turgenev wrote to Ralston : 'Henry James has paid me a visit. He is as amiable as ever. But he has grown enormously fat.'

James devoted all October 1882 to his 'little tour'. He began at Tours, the birthplace of Balzac. Here he spent a week, joining Mrs Kemble and Mrs Wister who were holidaying there. Neither had the energy for much sight-seeing however. Mrs Wister had her young son Owen with her, later to be celebrated as the pioneer of the 'western' novel. James found him 'attractive and amiable', but felt he was 'light and slight, both in character and in talent'. Mrs Kemble was always her tragedienne self – 'neither light nor slight', and Mrs Wister was now 'a tragic nature, so much worn, physically, that I am sorry for her'.

He admired the châteaux and the country around Tours was 'as charming as the essential meagreness of the French landscape will allow it to be'. Leaving Tours and the Kemble-Wisters on 8 October, he first travelled a small circle – Angers, Nantes, La Rochelle and

Poitiers; then he went to Bordeaux, Toulouse, Carcassone, Narbonne, and Montpellier, and finally into the heart of Daudet's Midi – Nîmes, Tarascon, Arles, Avignon; after which he curved northward to Orange, Mâcon, Beaune and Dijon. By mid-October, when he was in the Midi, he wrote to William, who was in Venice : 'I pursue my pilgrimage through these rather dull French towns and through a good deal of bad weather, and all my desire now is to bring it to a prompt conclusion. It is rather dreary work, for most of the places, I am sorry to say, are much less rich in the picturesque than I had supposed they would be.' Decidedly the French provinces were not Italy. To Howells he wrote : 'There is no more to my purpose at Bordeaux than there would be at Fitchburg, and I am not even consoled by good claret, as what I am given here is very much what you would get at F.' He felt that France had preserved the physiognomy of the past less than England or Italy. Napoleon had erased much of the pictorial and the 'quaint'. He experienced a revival of interest, however, when he came to the Roman towns; and certain of the cathedrals, as always, deeply absorbed him. In Avignon the Rhône was in flood, and he was pleased to get out of its watery streets and make a straight line for Paris. He had kept a journal during his little tour (apparently later destroyed) and from it he wrote his book. It is much less personal than his other travel-writings, much more strictly a guide book, and while it abounds in accurate and vivid descriptive passages it leans a great deal on mere historic recital. The material was too architectural, and too historical; it lacked what he called the 'human picturesque', and the book suffered accordingly. But it suffered too, one might add, from the lack of his former freshness and from his general mood of fatigue and depression.

96

November Parting

NOVEMBER had come when Henry James travelled from Dijon to Paris, his little tour accomplished. He had seen more of France than ever before, and 'on the whole' liked it better. The autumn was uncommonly wet. He put up at the Grand Hotel and recognized once again that Paris had 'a little corner of my complicated organism'. He found the 'same rather threadbare little circle of our sweet compatriots, who dine with each other in every possible combination of the alphabet – though none of their combinations spell the word satisfaction. That, however,' he added to Mrs Gardner, 'is the most difficult word in the language – even *I* am not sure I get it right.'

The pleasantest coincidence was to find John Hay at the Grand Hotel. James had never known well the man who had been Lincoln's assistant secretary and who combined a love of letters with national duty in a way that was rare in Washington. But he respected him highly. With Hay was his friend Clarence King, author of the major governmental survey of the mineral resources of the United States, and friend of Henry Adams. Like Adams, James admired King's wit, his energy, his capacity for good talk, his ceaseless interest in the world around him. The three breakfasted together, roamed the boulevards, prowled in shops. 'He is a delightful creature, and is selling silver mines and buying water-colours and old stuff by the millions,' James wrote to Mrs Gardner. And to Howells he said: 'King is a charmer. He charmed all the bric-à-brac out of the shops.' After his solitary journey in the Midi it was a delight to come upon such congenial fellow-Americans in the French capital.

He had exchanged notes with Ivan Sergeyevich, who continued to be ill, and on 17 November went to see him again at Bougival, where the Russian had remained much later than usual, attended by doctors, among them J. M. Charcot, who could not diagnose what was wrong with him. More recently they had recommended a milk diet, and when James found him he was astonished at the change in his friend. His towering figure was stooped. His great frame was shrunken. But he was as *accueillant* as ever. 'He had been ill, with strange, intolerable symptoms, but he was better,' James later wrote, 'and he had good hopes.' Neither knew, that day in November, when the trees at Bougival were bare and the Seine was grey, what cruel months lay ahead. Ivan Sergeyevich had cancer of the spine.

After a period of complete immobility the Russian had begun to go out again, and on that afternoon he had to go into Paris. He did not want to take the suburban train because he feared he would find it uncomfortable. Ordering a carriage, he asked James to ride with him into the city. It was just eight years since they had met, when Turgenev used to mount with firm and powerful tread the endless stairs that led to Flaubert's perch. They rode through the thickening dusk and for an hour and a half James had his beloved friend to him-self. Turgenev talked constantly, and never better. He talked in English and James was to quote from this occasion a certain sentence to illustrate the peculiar literary quality of Turgenev's use of that tongue – remembered phrases encountered in books. This gave a charming quaintness and an unexpected turn to what he said. 'In Russia, in spring, if you enter a beechen grove' – these were the words that came back to him from their carriage-ride. What subjects they touched upon he never recorded; but it was the same spon-taneous talk which he had always cherished in the Russian.

When they reached the city James left the carriage at an exterior boulevard. There was a little French fair going on in the chill Novem-ber air, under the denuded trees. The nasal sound of a Punch and Judy show somehow became mixed with his farewell at the window of the carriage. Then the vehicle rolled away.

97

A Winter Summons

HENRY JAMES had hardly returned to London when word came from his sister and aunt that his father was rapidly declining and had not long to live. Although he had left the United States barely six months before, he made immediate plans to return. William was in Paris attending Charcot's clinics at the Salpêtrière. They agreed that Henry should sail, and William would come to London and stay in Bolton Street while awaiting further news. Henry ob-tained passage on the *Werra*, from Liverpool, leaving on 12 Decem-ber. The voyage was rapid. The ship reached New York on 21 December, and waiting for Henry at the dock was a letter from Alice written the day before, a Wednesday.

Darling Father's weary longings were all happily ended on Monday at 3 p.m. The last words on his lips were 'There is my Mary!' For the last two hours he had said perpetually 'My Mary.' He had no suffering but we were devotedly thankful when the rest came to him, he so longed to go, the last thing he said before he lost consciousness was 'I am going with great joy!'

The funeral would be on Thursday morning. 'There seemed no use in waiting for you, the uncertainty was so great.'

His father, then, had been buried that very morning while his steamer was pulling into New York harbour. James reached Boston at eleven that night and was met at the station by his brother Robertson, who had come from Milwaukee for the funeral, and was leaving in the morning. In Mount Vernon Street Alice was resting. Aunt Kate, however, was up and they talked into the morning.

The elder Henry had died as he had lived, with an unflagging moral optimism; although his physical strength had failed him, he had turned his sickroom into a place of joy. He announced that he had entered upon the 'spiritual life' and thereafter refused all food. The doctors spoke of 'softening of the brain', but all the evidence indicates that until his last hours he was in possession of his faculties. Francis Boott, who was in America, came to see him a day or two before the end and they had a long talk. He lay facing the windows and refused to have them darkened. He slept a great deal. He was told that Henry was on his way. The news gave him pleasure, but he showed no signs of impatience – save to die. Toward the end Aunt Kate heard him say 'Oh I have such good boys – *such* good boys!' Asked about funeral arrangements he said (Aunt Kate wrote this down):

That here is a man who has always believed in the only true spiritual life, a direct intercourse with God – and who leaves it as his dying wish that men should know and understand that all the ceremonies usually observed in births, marriages and funerals are nonsense and untrue. The only true life is the spiritual one and this is only interfered with by these foolish words and doings that man has invented. [He further said] that he did not believe in individual salvation, but in the free personal intercourse of all men with God.

In long letters to William, conveying to him all the details as he gathered them, Henry said the father's passing had been 'most strange, most characteristic above all, and as full of beauty as it was void of suffering. There was none of what we feared – no paralysis, no dementia, no violence.' He had simply felt a great weakness; had swooned repeatedly; and after that had taken to his bed. Only the nurse and the loyal aunt were with him when he died. Alice had been increasingly ill and was being ministered to by Miss Loring. Thus ended the life of one of the most 'original' of the earlier Americans, a strange, voluble, gifted man, who had led an unworldly life, out of the current of Transcendental thought. To an extraordinary degree he had given to his sons the vigorous qualities of his language, something of the bellicose Irishness of his nature, and the picturesqueness of his mind. 'A little fat, rosy, Swedenborgian amateur,' Ellery Channing had called him, 'with the look of a broker, and the brains and heart of a Pascal.' He had been, as Ralph Barton Perry said, a man with a mission dogged by a sense of futility – a frustrated writer who never quite conveyed his message in spite of his lively prose. In the fullest way in which any man may hope to be represented by his progeny, William and Henry James accomplished what their father had failed to do. If the world had not listened to him, with all the life and intensity of his being and his own idiosyncrasies of style and speech, it was to listen to them. They were to write themselves – and him – into the memory of the civilized world.

In the house in Mount Vernon Street, so recently animated by the presence of the elder Henry, a great silence reigned. Alice, in a state of collapse, had been taken by Katharine Loring to the Loring home at Beverly. Henry, deprived of his last glimpse of his father, developed one of his debilitating migraines and was ill for four days. Aunt Kate, sole survivor of the paternal group, who had dedicated her life to her sister, and her sister's husband and children, sat in silent meditation in the parlour, 'not only without a Christmas dinner but without any dinner, as she doesn't eat, according to her wont'.

The suddenness of James's jump from London to Boston left him dazed. 'The house is so *empty*,' he wrote to William. He had been down to the parlour to chat with Kate. She repeated again and again that the father had 'yearned unspeakably' to die. 'I am too tired to write more, and my head is beginning to ache.' He added: 'All our wish here is that you should remain abroad the next six months.'

98

A Blessed Farewell

ON the last day of the year 1882 Henry James walked through the deep snow of the Cambridge cemetery where the previous spring a family plot had been selected on a small rise in the land. Here the mother had been committed to the earth. Now, in the silence of the Sunday morning, he looked at the new grave, cut in the cold ground ten days before. The elder Henry lay very close to his wife. At some point during this visit the son took a letter from his pocket and began to read it aloud into the wintry air, addressing it to the graves. There was no eyewitness, so far as we know, no one to record the quality of Henry's voice, or the way in which he stood in the performance of this unusual act. But its very nature suggests a depth of feeling, a passion of tenderness. He stood there alone, under a blue winter sky, in the piled snow, within view of the distant field beyond the Charles.

What Henry read was a letter written by William to his father on 14 December, just after the elder son had arrived in Bolton Street. It had reached Cambridge the day before, too late by a fortnight for the man for whom it was destined. Substituting his own voice and presence for that of his brother, Henry now communicated it to the dead.

'Darling old Father,' Henry read,

We have been so long accustomed to the hypothesis of your being taken away from us, that the thought that this may be your last illness conveys no very sudden shock. You are old enough, you've given your message to the world in many ways and will not be forgotten; you are here left alone, and on the other side, let us hope and pray, dear, dear old Mother is waiting for you to join her. If you go, it will not be an inharmonious thing. Only, if you are still in possession of your normal consciousness, I should like to see you once again before we part. I stayed here only in obedience to the last telegram, and am waiting now for Harry – who knows the exact state of my mind, and who will know yours – to telegraph again what I shall do.

Henry read on:

Meanwhile, my blessed old Father, I scribble this line (which may reach you though I should come too late), just to tell you how full of the tenderest memories and feelings about you my heart has for the last few days been filled. In that mysterious gulf of the past into which the present soon will fall and go back and back, yours is still for me the central figure. All my intellectual life I derive from you; and though we have often seemed at odds in the expression thereof, I'm sure there's a harmony somewhere, and that our strivings will combine. What my debt to you is goes beyond all my power of estimating, – so early, so penetrating and so constant has been the influence. You need be in no anxiety about your literary remains. I will see them well taken care of, and that your words shall not suffer for being concealed.

William promised his father that he would compile a volume of extracts from the elder Henry's writings, after the manner of the extracts from Carlyle, Ruskin and others. 'I have long thought such a volume would be the best monument to you.'

As for us [Henry continued to read]; we shall live on each in his way, – feeling somewhat unprotected, old as we are, for the absence of the parental bosoms as a refuge, but holding fast together in that common sacred memory. We will stand by each other and by Alice, try to transmit the torch in our offspring as you did in us.

And so, after recognizing that he had at various times given his father trouble, and expressing the belief that in his own paternal role he would learn to understand his father's paternity, William ended:

As for the other side, and Mother, and our all possibly meeting, I *can't* say anything. More than ever at this moment do I feel that if that *were* true, all would be solved and justified. And it comes strangely over me in bidding you good-bye how a life is but a day and expresses mainly but a single note. It is so much like the act of bidding an ordinary good-night. Good-night, my sacred old Father. If I don't see you again – Farewell! a blessed farewell!

Henry had finished. He replaced the letter in his pocket. He had remained with his parents, in this solemn visit, a long time. He was certain, he told his brother, that the elder Henry had heard him 'somewhere out of the depths of the still, bright winter air'. And he also said: 'As I stood there and looked at this last expression of so many years of mortal union, it was difficult not to believe that they were not united again in some consciousness of my belief.'

The son and brother had performed his strange deeply-felt mystical act beside the two graves. Now he could turn from the dead to the living. As he walked back, he stopped at William's house and sat with his brother's wife and her two children, admiring the infant William, 'a most loving little mortal'. Then he called on Francis J. Child, professor of English at Harvard, whom he had known from his own student days, and who had appeared to feel the elder Henry's death more than anyone outside the family. He received the condolences of Wendell Holmes, recently made a Judge of the State Supreme Court, and in writing all this to William he enjoined him not to come rushing home. Everything was being taken care of; moreover there was nothing William could do, since the elder Henry's last will and testament had named his second son to be the executor. For the time at least Henry, the quiet 'angel', assumed legally the administration of the James family affairs. Jacob had indeed supplanted Esau – and Esau at this moment was in a far-away land.

99

Son and Brother

WILLIAM JAMES kept his word to his father. Within two years – in 1884 – he brought out *The Literary Remains of the Late Henry James*, a substantial miscellany of his father's writings with a long introduction by himself. His father's last book was William's first. Henry, receiving it, wrote to his brother that it gave him 'great filial and fraternal joy'. He spoke of the 'extraordinarily individual (some of them magnificent)' utterances in the volume. His father's religious system seemed intensely original and personal.

I can't enter into it (much) myself – I can't be so theological, nor grant his extraordinary premises, nor throw myself into conceptions of heavens and hells, nor be sure that the keynote of nature is humanity, etc. But I can enjoy greatly the spirit, the feeling and the manner of the whole thing, (full as this is of things that *dis*please me too,) and feel really that poor Father, struggling so alone all his life, and so destitute of every worldly or literary ambition, was yet a great writer.

Henry did his utmost to get the book noticed in England. Few seemed interested. And when the *Nation* did inadequate justice to it, Henry scolded Godkin.

I have a tenderness for my poor Father's memory which is in direct proportion to the smallness of the recognition his work was destined to obtain here below and which fills me with a kind of pious melancholy in presence of the fact that so ardent an activity of thought, such a living, original, expression of spirit may have passed into darkness and silence forever.

The volume, with his brother's introduction, he told Godkin, seemed to him to have 'a real literary importance'.

I

Henry James the elder left an estate valued at $95,000. It consisted of more than $80,000 worth of land, houses and stores, in Syracuse, New York, yielding seven per cent after taxes and maintenance, or about $5,000 a year. The remainder, largely money derived from the sale of the Quincy Street house, had been invested in prosperous railway stocks and bonds, with a yield per annum of $3,500. These latter were willed to Alice and provided adequately for an invalid spinster of that time. The estate was to be divided among the three brothers, William, Henry and Robertson. Garth Wilkinson James, the improvident and happy-go-lucky son, was omitted from the will because he had received his inheritance in advance. For some years he had been a constant drain on his father. Only a short time before, on declaring himself bankrupt, he had been given $5,000.

Wilky however was seriously ill; he had a rheumatic heart and other complications. He was crushed by his debts, and he had a wife and children in Milwaukee. Henry, from the outset, took the position that the will was 'unfortunate', and proposed a re-division into four equal parts. Robertson, who had ample means, agreed; Alice, insofar as she was a party to the testament, also voted with Henry. William, thinking of his two sons, wrote from abroad that he was not at all certain a re-division would be equitable, given the large sums Wilky had squandered. He reminded Henry of the difference between the bachelor state and the responsibilities of paternity, and proposed re-division into fifths. He also worked out an elaborate breakdown into sixteenths, according to the population of the James family groups. Henry opposed this, and as a matter of fact had already moved for equal division, assuming William would agree. William's first impulse was to book passage for home early in February. What ensued was a strange and lively correspondence in which Henry threw all his weight into convincing William he must stay abroad – as if his very life depended on keeping his elder brother in Europe. In a 2,000-word letter he pointed out that William would have no place to stay in Cambridge, since part of his house had been sublet, and to live away from his family would engender gossip. He insisted that if William returned before his appointed time it would be 'a melancholy confession of failure', a 'sort of proclamation of want of continuity of purpose'. William had made a point of going abroad because he needed rest and had work to do, and 'you were surely not altogether wrong'. Cambridge itself was 'barren' after London and Paris, Henry wrote, forgetting that this was his, not William's, feeling about the local scene. He peevishly said that William could be accommodated in Boston at the Mount Vernon Street house in the small guest-room, where Aunt Kate had stayed, but 'I won't offer to give up Father's room, because I lately made you a present of my rooms in London'. And he argued there would be 'a painful want of *form*' in William's returning to Cambridge 'prematurely' – especially after having remained away during his father's illness and death.

William replied that Henry was meddling in his affairs; that Cambridge was not 'barren' for him. His brother was treating him 'as if he were a baby'. However William cancelled his passage, and after further negotiation certain adjustments were made. A portion of the estate was set aside for Wilky's family, in a trust fund, with the net consequence that William and Henry would each receive about $1,300 a year.

Henry travelled to Milwaukee in a temperature of twenty below zero and a blinding blizzard for direct talks with the younger brothers, and later visited Syracuse to inspect the properties, which were located on James Street – the street named after the immigrant grandfather. William came home in March and Henry made over to him the general handling of the estate. His own income, he announced, was to go entirely to Alice – 'this I desire always to be its regular destination. She assures me that she will have no occasion to use it – will save it and invest it for my benefit etc. But I wish her to have it, to cover all the contingencies of her new existence.' Later, when William thought it his duty to keep Henry informed, he re-replied: 'Never, I again beg you, take the trouble to tell *me* twice anything at all about my Syracuse dividend. I have made my income entirely over to Alice and take no further interest in it.' Henry James would continue to live by his pen.

2

He drove his pen on Beacon Hill during these months, and ventured forth for walks in the snowy streets. He was to evoke, in a charming tale, *A New England Winter*, written some months later, the familiar aspect of the long straight avenue airing its newness in the frosty day, with its individual façades, and their neat sharp ornaments, the large clear windows of the curved fronts facing each other 'like candid, inevitable eyes'. The picture of Beacon Street revives an earlier age of plate glass.

There was something almost terrible in the windows ... how vast and clean they were, and how, in their sculptured frames, the New England air seemed, like a zealous housewife, to polish and preserve them. A great many ladies were looking out, and groups of children, in the drawing-rooms, were flattening their noses against the transparent plate. Here and there, behind it, the back of a statuette or the symmetry of a painted vase, erect on a pedestal, presented itself to the street and enabled the passer to construct, more or less, the room within – its frescoed ceilings, its new silk sofas, its untarnished fixtures. This continuity of glass constituted a kind of exposure, within and without, and gave the street the appearance of an enormous corridor, in which the public and the private were familiar and intermingled. But it was all very cheerful and commodious, and seemed to speak of diffused wealth, of intimate family life, of comfort constantly renewed.

James became thoroughly familiar with the Boston winter-scene –

the denuded bushes, the solid pond, the plank-covered walks, the exaggerated bridge, the patriotic statues, the dry, hard texture of the Public Garden for its foreground, and for its middle distance the pale, frozen twigs, stiff in the windy sky that whistled over the Common, the domestic dome of the State House, familiar in the untinted air, and the competitive spires of a liberal faith.

In Washington Street, on a winter's afternoon, he trod the slushy thoroughfare, past the crawling horse-cars, the thronging pedestrians, the 'sisterhood of shoppers' laden with satchels and parcels, the snow which thudded to the street from the sloping house-tops, the mounds of pulverized, mud-coloured ice on the pavements. The houses offered a jagged line of tall and short buildings, and there were staring signs, labels, pictures, familiar advertisements, a tangle of telegraph-wires in the air. Every fifty yards there was a candy-store. Behind the plate-glass, behind counters, were pale, delicate, tired faces of women, with polished hair and glazed complexions. In Bolton Street, months later, James could recall it as vividly as if he had just seen it. He was struck by the 'numerosity' of the women-folk; there was a 'deluge of petticoats'. Henry felt he was in a city of women, a country of women, and it was this that determined him in the selection of the subject for his next novel. The talk, the social life – everything – seemed so completely in the hands of the opposite sex that he wondered whether he were not in a country stricken by war, with the men away on the battlefields.

'I feel strangely settled here for the present,' he wrote to his publisher in London, 'and shall probably remain for the summer. But after that – open thy bosom, London of my soul!' It was clear to him that he would not return again to America for a long time; there was no further reason for doing so. 'My sister and I make an harmonious little ménage,' he wrote, 'and I feel a good deal as if I were married.' He told Mrs Kemble he had suggested to Alice that she come to England with him to set up a common household in London. His sister had, however, 'shrewdly declined', he said, 'for we are really both much too fond of our individual independence, and she has a dread of exchanging the comfortable *known* of Boston for the vast unknown of London'. It was true that he and Alice, during this period, seemed to derive pleasure from their brother-and-sister household; it was the last holding-together of the family, and Henry, in his father's room, and Alice, presiding over the house, must have felt a great deal as if they were re-embodying their parents. But if he spoke of Alice's 'independence', he nevertheless noted the extent to which she leaned upon her powerful friend, Katharine Loring. Miss Loring had quite taken over the foreground of Alice's life and entered into her daily well-being and her nervous prostrations. Alice had described Miss Loring shortly after meeting her in terms that leave little doubt as to her role in their relationship: 'She has all the mere brute superiority which distinguishes man from woman, combined with all the distinctively feminine virtues. There is nothing she cannot do from hewing wood and drawing water to driving runaway horses and educating all the women in North America.' James was to observe this relationship closely. One might say that the figure of Olive Chancellor in *The Bostonians* had appeared upon the novelist's very doorstep.

3

Henry James's productivity during the months he spent in America – in spite of family preoccupations – was impressive. But, as after his mother's death, he did not do much new work. He saw through the press the dramatized *Daily Miller* and he put together for J. R. Osgood a volume containing three tales, *The Siege of London*, *The Pension Beaurepas* and *The Point of View*. He assembled a volume of miscellaneous travel-papers to which he gave the title *Portraits of Places*, carefully editing those on England, so as not to offend his transatlantic readers, and reminding them, in a special prefatory note, that the papers had been written primarily for Americans. He included in this volume also his old papers on Saratoga, Newport and Quebec, and here he reminded both his American and English readers that these had 'only the value of history'. Thirteen years had brought many changes. He planned at this time to issue a volume of essays as well, to be titled *Studies and Sketches* or perhaps *Impressions of Art and Life*. However he abandoned this plan, feeling that he did not have a sufficient number of good essays. Four years later, when the volume came out as *Partial Portraits*, it contained an almost new table of contents. James reviewed all his American publishing arrangements and pledged himself to produce a novel and a series of tales, giving Osgood not only the serial and American book-rights but the English rights as well. This could only mean that he would receive more money from Osgood than he could realize by direct sale to Macmillan. The English publishing house, on its side, at this time proposed to Henry the issue of a small inexpensive pocket edition of his principal novels and tales. James welcomed the idea. Over and above the pleasure of having a collective edition on the market, he felt that this would give him an opportunity to establish his new identity on his title-page – to get rid of the Henry James 'Jun. or Jr' – the 'mere junior' – now that his father was dead.

The Macmillan edition was published late that year, in a series of attractive blue-bound volumes in small format. There were fourteen volumes in all. They sold for one and six apiece, and the full set for a guinea. James had written to Macmillan, 'I should like them to be *charming*, and beg you to spare no effort to make them so.' The first three volumes were devoted to *The Portrait of a Lady*; then followed *Roderick Hudson* and *The American* in two volumes each, after which came *Washington Square*, *The Europeans* and *Confidence*, one volume each; leaving four volumes for the miscellaneous tales. These consisted of *The Siege of London* and *Madame de Mauves* in the volume devoted to international marriages; *An International Episode*, *The Pension Beaurepas* and *The Point of View* – tales contrasting American and European manners; *Daisy Miller*, *Four Meetings*, *Longstaff's Marriage*, and *Benvolio* – representing a subtle mixture, stories in which the heroine is frustrated or dies, save for *Benvolio* which portrays the ambivalent hero of these tales; and finally *The Madonna of the Future*, *A Bundle of Letters*, *The Diary of a Man of Fifty*, and *Eugene Pickering*. The groupings were as close as James could come to achieving congruity of theme; he could not altogether carry out his plan, because some stories were shifted in the interest of uniform volume-size.

In addition to seeing this edition through the press, James completed the greater part of his French travel-sketches for Aldrich, and wrote the first of the series of tales he had promised Osgood. This was *The Impressions of a Cousin*, a story set in New York. The 'impressions' are recorded by the cousin in her diary, which contains her account of the way in which an executor defrauds a young heiress, who will not prosecute him since she loves him – and how justice is quietly done. James thus drew on his recent responsibilities in the family affairs. The tale is but half-heartedly written, a throwing together of miscellaneous observations of his American stay.

He was much more in the public eye during this winter than the previous year. This was due, in some measure, to a laudatory article about him which Howells had published the previous autumn in the *Century Magazine*, asserting that it was James who was 'shaping and directing American fiction'. Not many critics were prepared to accept this statement. With the article had appeared a neat engraving of James by Timothy Cole which suggests his fine head, his clear-eyed gaze, and his general well-groomed and pleasant appearance. His lips are parted as if he is in the act of speaking, and beneath the picture is his large signature, full size, with the flourish that suggests but does not quite convey the about-to-be-withdrawn 'Jr.' James called it 'a horrible effigy of my countenance'. Howells's article was part reminiscence and part criticism. Now that he was no longer James's editor he could allow himself the liberty of expressing in public all the praise he had been obliged hitherto to bestow in private. He rightly recognized that the art – the technique – of fiction was becoming much more subtle than it had been in the era of Dickens and Thackeray, and he discussed in some detail James's gift for creating character. 'Evidently it is the character, not the fate, of his people, which occupies him.' Howells also said that a reader could find in Henry James's writings 'a perpetual delight' in his way of saying things.

The effect of Howells's shrewd critical observations was not altogether what he expected. To some critics it seemed as if he were 'puffing' the work of his friend; and in England certain journalists

accused Howells and James of constituting an 'American Mutual
Admiration Society' – this in spite of the fact that James had never
written about Howells save an anonymous review of an early novel.
In a letter to Smalley, James referred to Howells's 'ill-starred amiabilities to me'. To Howells he remarked, a little ironically, that
'articles about you and me are as thick as blackberries – we are
daily immolated on the altar of Thackeray and Dickens'.

He had been approached three times to give a reading in public,
and finally he yielded. This was before a woman's 'Saturday Morning Club', where he read from a section of his little tour in France.
The newsapapers of the time reported that the rooms were crowded
'by people of taste and fashion'. James was introduced as the
'Thackeray of America', and (said the reporter) his 'English er-er-er-'
marred his utterance. He read in a monotonous manner, but the
matter 'more than made amends'. At the conclusion of the reading
he was given a bouquet of white daisies surrounded by leaves of the
homely seaboard plant known as 'dusty miller'. 'I have hundreds of
Daisy Millers here,' said Henry, in a statement the ambiguity of
which must have been lost on his preponderantly young female
audience.

He made one other appearance at a meeting of the American
Copyright League in New York. James had good reason to be interested in the work of the League; he had been pirated all too often.
At a given moment he asked for the floor. 'For ten or fifteen minutes,'
wrote Lawrence Hutton,

the speaker, known to every man present by his work, unknown in a
personal way to most of his hearers, talked of things à propos of the
matter in hand, in a manner absolutely to the point and carrying much
weight. He made as great an impression as a speaker as he had ever made
as a writer; and for the first time, after a long residence abroad, he was
brought into intimate contact with the men of his own guild in his own
country.

4

He was in New York on 15 April 1883, in the city of his birth – and
it was his 40th birthday. Ten years before, when he became 30 in
Rome, he had felt how short a distance he had travelled in his
career; and if, during the decade that had elapsed, he had achieved
his ambition, he was still dissatisfied. If anyone had told him that

he could cease writing at this moment and remain a major figure in American fiction, he would have scorned the suggestion. Contemplating the advent of his 40th year, he had written in his journal the previous autumn – on one of the days when he was in the Grand Hotel in Paris:

I have hours of unspeakable reaction against my smallness of production; my wretched habits of work – or of unwork; my levity, my vagueness of mind, my perpetual failure to focus my attention, to absorb myself, to look things in the face, to invent, to produce, in a word. I shall be forty years old in April next: it's a horrible fact.

The horrible fact had occurred. Having distinctly underestimated all his capacities, he had proceeded to offer himself some solace:

I believe however that I have learned how to work and that it is in moments of forced idleness, almost alone, that these melancholy reflections seize me. When I am really at work, I'm happy, I feel strong, I see many opportunities ahead. It is the only thing that makes life endurable. I must make some great efforts during the next few years, however, if I wish not to have been on the whole a failure. I shall have been a failure unless I do something *great*!

These sentences may be taken as an accurate measure by Henry James of himself. His first goal – success and a place in the world – had been achieved. He had made himself into an author and a figure known on both sides of the Atlantic. The next step was to do more – 'greatness' was a large word. In the meantime there remained almost half a year before he could see his way to returning to England, since he wanted to remain for a while longer with Alice. The record of these months is filled with small detail. He visited Washington and was pleased by its aspect in the spring. He saw his friends the Adamses again. In New York he met and befriended the young Jewish poet, Emma Lazarus, whose verses were to be inscribed two years later on the Statue of Liberty. She was about to go to London and he gave her an introduction to Mrs Procter and to the Smalleys. He was much preoccupied with Wilky, whom he met in Washington on his return from Florida, and escorted back to Cambridge. His brother's health had taken a turn for the worse, and in Mount Vernon Street Henry sat up nights with him, giving him what aid he could during his heart attacks. He paid calls as usual on Mrs Gardner, and he saw much of his old friend Grace Norton.

To this period belongs the forging of those links of emotional intimacy and attachment which were to make this one of the most valued of all his friendships. It did not resemble his friendship with Fenimore; Miss Norton was, after all, ten years older, and she was a woman who asked for the kind of philosophical comforting which Henry could give to her to the full, as he might have given to his mother. She was going through a bad phase at this time, a certain strain with her brother, a sense of isolation in the separate home she had fashioned for herself in Kirkland Street away from Shady Hill, and James wrote to her always with great gentleness, good humour and much feeling. Since he could no longer write the letters of a son to his mother, he had found in Cambridge someone to whom he could offer filial feeling – someone closer to him intellectually than his mother had been. Some of his fullest and certainly his wisest letters were addressed to Grace Norton, with a richness of detail and with large pictures of himself in the great world which he had of old given to Quincy Street. To her he wrote a letter which embodies within it the very heart of his philosophy and his attachment to reality – a kind of simple stoicism based on looking neither backward nor forward:

I don't know *why* we live – the gift of life comes to us from I don't know what source or for what purpose; but I believe we can go on living for the reason that ... life is the most valuable thing we know anything about and it is therefore presumptively a great mistake to surrender it while there is any yet left in the cup. In other words consciousness is an illimitable power, and though at times it may seem to be all consciousness of misery, yet in the way it propagates itself from wave to wave, so that we never cease to feel, though at moments we appear to, try to, pray to, there is something that holds one in one's place, makes it a standpoint in the Universe which it is probably good not to forsake.

And then, recurring to his frequent warning to his correspondent not to give herself too much to the world's woes and to the grief of others, he tells her:

Don't, I beseech you, *generalize* too much in these sympathies and tendernesses – remember that every life is a special problem which is not yours but another's and content yourself with the terrible algebra of your own. Don't melt too much into the universe, but be as solid and dense and fixed as you can.

And with this, his admonition was that Miss Norton adopt his own kind of doggedness: 'Don't think, don't feel, any more than you can help, don't conclude or decide – don't do anything but *wait*.'

We all live together, and those of us who love and know, live so most. We help each other – even unconsciously, each in our own effort ... Sorrow comes in great waves – no one can know that better than you – but it rolls over us, and though it may almost smother us it leaves us on the spot and we know that if it is strong we are stronger, inasmuch as it passes and we remain. It wears us, uses us, but we wear it and use it in return; and it is blind, whereas we after a manner see.

A darkness, such as she was passing through, he said, was *only* a darkness – not an end, not *the* end. And so, arguing for acceptance of feeling, for opening oneself to it, James embodied here the concept of 'living through' emotion until one has survived it. He argued equally for a certain kind of personal sovereignty in a world unfriendly to individualism.

James wrote this letter to Miss Norton within a month of his return to England. He took passage on the *Servia*, leaving Boston on 22 August; he filled in the intervening hot days by padding about in a state of undress in the Mount Vernon Street house and confining himself to lemonade and ice-cream. He kept reasonably cool, and he kept up his work. Wilky had left for Milwaukee to rejoin his family. Henry must have known that this was their final parting. Alice spent the summer in a rest-home, the Adams Nervous Asylum in Jamaica Plain, where her brother occasionally visited her. He saw little of William, who went off to the mountains with his family.

Some weeks before his departure he spent a friendly week-end at Marion near Cape Cod, visiting Richard Watson Gilder, of the *Century*, and his wife, who was a sister of Mrs Bronson's. His impressions are incorporated in *The Bostonians*, where Marion is renamed Marmion. In a later story, *The Patagonia*, he describes what must have been his general feelings on the empty summery Beacon Hill. Like its narrator, James had gone shortly before for a brief visit to Mount Desert – escaped to coolness and greenness – but he found it 'as beautiful as a place can be in which the details are mainly ugly', adding 'I liked the whole thing extremely – and wish never to see it again.' The Boston houses on the eve of his sailing were dark in the August night; Beacon Street seemed a desert. The club on the hill alone emitted light from its cylindrical front, and the sound of billiard-balls clicking within suggested the servants were passing the time in the empty place. The heat was insufferable. He thought with joy of the freshening breeze he would have on board ship. The crossing was uneventful, and on 29 August he arrived in Liverpool, where he stayed until 1 September. He had been but forty-eight hours in Bolton Street when word reached him that Ivan Turgenev had come to the end of his sufferings at Bougival.

5

This loss, now but one of the series Henry James had experienced, plunged him into renewed grief for his dead. One by one the fixed landmarks of his life were vanishing. 'I am greatly touched by his extinction – I wanted him to live – mainly, I am afraid, because I wanted to see him again : for he had done his work,' he wrote to the editor of the *Atlantic*, promising an article on the Russian. He followed with intense emotion the newspaper accounts of the final rites : the ceremonial at the station in Paris when the Russia-bound coffin was placed on the train, and the farewell orations of Ernest Renan and Edmond About on behalf of the writers of France. It was with Renan's noble words that James began his own tribute, written little more than a month later, words which he himself rendered with great felicity from the French :

Turgenev received by the mysterious decree which marks out human vocations the gift which is noble beyond all others : he was born essentially impersonal. His conscience was not that of an individual to whom nature had been more or less generous; it was in some sort the conscience of a people. Before he was born he had lived for thousands of years; infinite successions of reveries had amassed themselves in the depths of his heart. No man has been as much as he the incarnation of a whole race : generations of ancestors, lost in the sleep of centuries, speechless, came through him to life and utterance.

But if Renan spoke of Turgenev as impersonal, and if now it seemed in Russia the grief of the nation and the funeral pomp lifted Ivan Sergeyevich out of the range of familiar recollection, James set down, for the *Atlantic*, the 'personal' Turgenev : a simple record of his meetings with the Russian writer, his many recollections of him, his whole-hearted devotion to his work. The paper reads as if it had been written at a single sitting and as if Henry had poured out all that he could remember, clinging to certain moments as to personal treasures – the Sundays at Flaubert's, the little breakfast-lunches on the boulevards, the aspect of Bougival, Turgenev's manner of speech, the last ride in the carriage, when they had parted on the exterior boulevard in front of a Punch and Judy show. 'Intolerable pain had been his portion for many months before he died,' Henry wrote. 'His end was not serene and propitious, but dark and almost violent. But of brightness, of the faculty of enjoyment, he had also the large allowance usually made to first-rate men, and he was a singularly complete human being.' He brought his long and deeply-felt account to an end with these words – they were almost an epitaph : 'He was the most generous, the most tender, the most delightful, of men; his large nature overflowed with the love of justice; but he was also a rare genius.' *

At the request of the *Century* he translated for it Daudet's reminiscences of Turgenev: this he did anonymously and only the survival of the two manuscripts, Daudet's and his own, testifies to this silent act on behalf of his friend and his old acquaintance of the *cénacle*. Daudet's article appeared in the November 1883 issue titled *Turgenev in Paris*. Thus in two leading monthlies of America the passing of the Russian genius was eulogized through the agency of Henry James.

6

He had barely posted his tribute to the *Atlantic* when he found himself writing a private tribute of quite another sort to his father's old friend, the English Swedenborgian, Dr J. J. Garth Wilkinson. Wilky had been named after the doctor, and Wilky was now dead in Milwaukee at 38, the third member of the James family to die in two years, and the first of the children. He had been Henry's immediate junior; and if he had squandered his patrimony, it could be said that fate had squandered him. He had never had good health after his precocious service in the Civil War. When Henry got word that William had left for Milwaukee, summoned to Wilky's deathbed, he drew from among his possessions a little pencil-drawing William had made many years before, after Wilky had been carried home from the battlefield, wounded in the assault on Fort Wagner. It is one of the early vivid sketches made by Henry's elder brother, the head alone of the wounded, rough-bearded soldier. Sitting in Bolton Street Henry looked at this drawing a long time. The time of the war came back to him. 'It was taken,' he wrote to Lizzie Boott, 'at a moment when he looked as if everything was over, and is a most

---

* James altered this, in revising the essay for *Partial Portraits*, to read 'but he was also of the stuff of which glories are made'.

touching, little vivid picture. I say to myself as I look at it that it probably represents the dear boy now.' With the aid of the past Henry sought to visualize the present. He was to publish the drawing years later in his autobiographies. 'Peace be to his spirit,' he wrote to Lizzie, 'one of the gentlest and kindest I have ever known.'

And so Henry James buried his dead. Now he was once more in his lodgings in London at his large work-table by the Bolton Street window, looking out on Lord Ashburton's big house across the way. He had lived through a period of great grief; but as he had written to Grace Norton, one could not continue to be engulfed by sorrow. He had said good-bye to his parents in their graves on the Cambridge hillock, to his younger brother, dead before his time, and to the great Turgenev. The house on Quincy Street was no longer fixed in the orbit of his days. His return to Europe was almost like a new beginning of the career he had begun almost a decade before.

BOOK SEVEN:
A LONDON LIFE
1883-9

Part One:

The Art of the Novel

100

The Lost Freshness

HENRY JAMES'S first impulse on his return to London from America was to search for a house. His old lodgings at No. 3 Bolton Street now seemed to him small, dingy, impermanent. He had reached a point in life when a modest dwelling, in a secluded part of the city, would better fit his role as artist and man of letters. His perch in Piccadilly had seemed at best temporary. He had fallen into it in the winter of 1876 and lived there for the better part of a decade. Behind his quest for a home of his own in London, at this moment, we can discern, however, James's feeling of being adrift: the Quincy Street house had passed into memory. His short stay at his sister's on Beacon Hill had given him a feeling of greater space and comfort. He needed such a mooring in the England, in which he was now more fixed than he had ever been in Cambridge. He started his search in St John's Wood. Many of London's artists and writers lived there, above the rim of Regent's Park; in the 1850s his father had brought the James family to this part of London and James had played ball with his tutor in Marlborough Place. Presently he found a house in Elm Tree Road that seemed ideal; it had architectural distinction; a painter had lived in it. The studio was now converted into a noble dining room; the place was commodious; the garden was charming. James discussed his plans for domestication with various London ladies, and corresponded about them with Grace Norton and Lizzie Boott. They assumed at once that he was planning to marry. 'Sooner or later,' he wrote to Lizzie, 'I shall take a house, but there is no hurry, and when I do a conjugal Mrs H. is not among the articles of furniture that I shall put into it. I find life quite interesting enough as it is, without such complicated and complicating appendages.' To Grace Norton he wrote:

I shall never marry; I regard that now as an established fact, and on the whole a very respectable one; I am both happy enough and miserable enough, as it is, and don't wish to add to either side of the account. Singleness consorts much better with my whole view of existence (of my own and of that of the human race), my habits, my occupations, prospects,

tastes, means, situation 'in Europe', and absence of desire to have children
– fond as I am of the infant race.

And reflecting on his bachelor state, and the blessings of living in
a section of London within walking distance of his clubs and the
theatres, James had a 'sudden sense of being very well off where I
am'. He told himself he would spend half his time on the roads
riding the length of Regent's Park – and he broke off negotiations
for the house. His Bolton Street rooms might be shabby but he had
called them home for a long time.

I

This brief flurry of house-hunting, which occurred within a month
after James's return, was symptomatic. A change had occurred
during his two crossings of the Atlantic; old roots had been torn up.
He was now 40 and had made a further march into the country of
'the lost freshness'. England was now his true home; he was no
longer an 'observant stranger'. His republication of his English
sketches at this moment in *Portraits of Places* was clearly a sign of
this. What he felt distinctly, as he wrote to his American friends,
was that there was for him in London in any quarter of an hour
more *life* – he underlined the word – than he could experience in
America in six months. And much as he 'raged' against London
Philistinism and often felt the oppressive largeness of the city, he
believed it to be the right place for him to live. It was a matter of
'learning to live there differently from what I have done hitherto'.

One of the ways would be to restore the sense of 'permanency'
Quincy Street had given him, to find ultimately a more comfortable
and spacious home. The other was to break away from London
'society', and to go into it only at moments of his greatest ease. In
the same way he would bring to an end indiscriminate country-visits.
That 'gilded bondage' he had long outgrown. And so instead of
superficial contacts with the British upper classes, Henry James
began to form friendships of a more significant kind – with members
of his own class, the writers and artists of London; bereft of his own
sense of 'family', he involved himself with their family life, became
godfather to their children and a genial visitor at their board. This
period marks the beginning of his intimacy with the du Maurier
household in Hampstead, the Edmund Gosses in Delamere Terrace;

the Humphry Wards in Russell Square; the George Lewises in Portland Place. The list of his English friends and acquaintances was to
grow and remain largely in this easy stratum of society where he
felt most at home, and where he could consort with men whose
accomplishments were analogous to his own. His friendship with
George du Maurier was a deeply attaching one. He found 'something
in him singularly intelligent and sympathetic and satisfactory'. He
liked walking to Hampstead from Piccadilly on a Sunday evening
and sitting on a particular bench on the heath with du Maurier
where their conversation could roam over Anglo-French subjects
with an ease and affection that never diminished. The bench became
a symbol of something precious in his life. The marriages of the du
Maurier sons and daughters and the career of Gerald du Maurier
on the stage commanded his interest and loyalty. Some of his most
charming non-literary letters are addressed to his du Maurier god-
son. 'I'm an awful muff at games,' he wrote, sending him an Association football and inviting his visit, offering 'lots of breakfast and
dinner and tea' and promising no questions about studies, 'but if you
think that is because I can't – because I don't know enough – I
might get up subjects on purpose'.

He liked Mrs Humphry Ward and her husband, who was an editor
on *The Times*. She was high-minded and a blue-stocking, and her
novels were filled with intellectual ideas; they had in them no sense
of art, but James always wrote to her about them and lectured her
on the craft of fiction. He was at home in the Ward house in Russell
Square and on easy terms with the Ward children. It was the same
at the Lewises – Lewis being one of the great Victorian solicitors
whose home was open to the arts. A bundle of letters attests to
James's participation in social evenings, Christmas parties and
family feast days.

His friendship with Edmund Gosse, at first casual (Henry thought
him amiable but second-rate), became one of the most literary-
gossipy friendships in Victorian annals. Gosse was gifted: he had
great facility as a writer, he was an assiduous and critical reader;
but also a great busybody of letters. He had rebelled against a sternly
religious father, and had made his way by charm and ability from a
lowly post in the British Museum to become translator to the Board
of Trade. Later he would be Librarian of the House of Lords. A
writer of romantic lyrics, he was an indefatigable bookworm; he
wrote easy and pleasant literary essays, and critical and biographical

studies of some importance. Sir Osbert Sitwell characterized his studies of minor Elizabethans as 'impeccable in feeling, if not always, it appears, in fact'. If Gosse was indeed guilty of scholarly slips, he nevertheless had a way of cutting through to essence, and in the end he became not only an important practitioner of the art of biography, but author of a classic autobiography, his study of his relationship with his religious-absolutist father. James found Gosse an endlessly amusing companion. He helped to break the solitude of some of his dinners at the Reform or the Athenaeum. Gosse had from the first cultivated literary men and painters. He had his finger in almost every literary pie in London. He wrote to literary friends on subjects out of the daily press, provoked answers and built up an enormous literary archive; he was an eternal bee buzzing about friendly bookshelves; but with this he had grace of mind, a flair for gossip in a library. He knew the secrets of the literary generation; he was an artful exchanger of confidences. If James praised a certain book he quietly passed the praise along to the author; if an author praised James, Gosse discreetly communicated the praise. Such procedures can be risky and yet Gosse seems to have handled them with high diplomacy. He made an art of flattery and a political craft of gossip. Posthumous publication has betrayed him; as for example his telling Thomas Hardy that James admired *Tess*, even while James was denouncing the novel as 'vile' to Stevenson. We are left with the interesting question whether the duplicity was James's or Gosse's.

The friendship, at any rate, was genuine; and in the bourgeois sociabilities of Delamere Terrace, as well as in the later confraternity of the Royal Society of Literature, the two were faithful companions for the better part of four decades.

2

Thus by degrees Henry James began to find substitutes for the lost anchorage of Cambridge. The process was slow and much of it hidden from himself – an intuitive search for footholds, attachments, dependencies, which had vanished in America. He might have more speedily achieved some form of contentment had not the life of the entire decade in England undergone a marked change. The serenity of his own life, the triumphant time of *Daisy Miller*, had coincided with the greatest years of Victoria's *imperium*. Now the Victorian calm was being shattered by Irish dynamiters, anarchist violence, and the deep unrest of England's workers, in their starving despair of the early 1880s. 'Nothing *lives* in England today but politics,' James wrote. 'They are all-devouring, and their mental uproar crowds everything out.' England, he felt, was 'on the edge of an enormous political cycle, which will last heaven knows how long'. He added that he should 'hate it more if I didn't also find it interesting. The air is full of events, of changes, of movement (some people would say of revolution, but I don't think that).' His interest in English politics and public affairs attached him 'to this country and, on the whole, to its sometimes exasperating people'. During the phase of his re-settlement in the British capital there were moments when he felt distinctly as if he were upon a heaving and boundless sea, without a rudder to steer him into a friendly port.

The ministry is still in office but hanging only by a hair, Gladstone is ill and bewildered, the mess in the Sudan unspeakable, London full of wailing widows and weeping mothers, the hostility to Bismarck extreme, the danger of complications with Russia imminent, the Irish in the House of Commons more disageeable than ever, the dynamiters more active, the income tax threatening to rise to its maximum, the general muddle, in short, of the densest and darkest.

If this was one of the most condensed sentences of current history ever penned by a man of letters, it was also James's way of describing the density and the darkness that had come into his life. He would have an intimate glimpse of Gladstone a year or two later at Lord Rosebery's: 'the sublime old man' talked about bookbinding after dinner and next day after lunch discoursed on the new version of the Scriptures and the need for both a lay and clerical professor of Hebrew at Oxford. His mind seemed to have no preferences; he cared equally for all subjects.

What was clear to James now was that the day of his little 'international' tales was virtually at an end. He could still write them, but he believed he had worked that vein to exhaustion. He was moreover bored: and if *Pandora* and *Lady Barberina* of this time still have the old power, the undimmed perception of international manners, they represent a terminal point. *Lady Barberina*, as a study of an international marriage and a variant on the theme of *The Siege of London*, is one of James's most successful Anglo-American tales: his picture of the transported English lady married to a New York doctor, living in splendour in Fifth Avenue, and of the Americans around her who cannot understand her boredom with the society of Manhattan, is brilliantly written. The essence of the tale lies not in its criticism of the two societies, but in James's grasp of the true incompatibilities between an aristocracy of blood and its inflexibilities and an aristocracy of wealth and its pretensions. In effect James was saying that he, too, would be bored if he had to live in New York; and that he, too, would flee to London, never to return.

Henry James turned in this way to new subjects, only occasionally venturing back into the old 'international' in his shorter pieces. His novel of Boston, promised to Osgood, delayed for more than a year, had to be written; and after that he harboured in his imagination a long novel on London – actual London – that would mark his total removal to the Old World.

101

Castle Nowhere

IF Henry's artistic and mental life had their complications in this period of private – as well as public – depression, his personal life seemed no less embroiled. He had not seen Constance Fenimore Woolson since the spring of 1881, when he had visited her apartment in Rome; she had remained on the Continent during his absence in America and had written him long – very long – letters. Now, however, in the autumn of 1883, and in spite of her protests that the English climate disagreed with her, she arrived in the British capital, a bare month after James unpacked his bags in Bolton Street. Certain sentences of an importunate nature, in one of her letters to Henry, show how far her state of feeling had gone. 'You are never in Italy, but always in America, just going; or there, or just returned. How many times have I seen you, in the long months that make up three long years? I don't complain, for there is no reason in the world why I should expect to see you.' Fenimore complained in the very act of not complaining. Her appearance in London so soon after James's arrival seems to have been more than a coincidence. In her letters she had spoken of spending the winter in Algiers. She always said that she needed warmth and sunlight. Nevertheless James reports to Lizzie on 14 October 1883 that 'Costanza has just arrived in South Kensington', and in another letter to his Florentine friend he says that 'the *Littératrice* is here and is really an angel of quiet virtue'. Six months later he reports that 'the Costanza is handy, in Sloane Street, and is to remain, I believe, until August. But she is a most excellent, reasonable woman, absorbed in her work, upon whom I have not a single reflection to make. I like and esteem her exceedingly.' These veiled allusions fit no other lady writer of James's acquaintance. What we do know is that Fenimore did not go to Algiers; she braved English cold that winter, for she recorded in a letter of October 1884 that she had been in England for a full year.

I

In later years Miss Woolson and Henry James agreed to destroy each other's letters; and still later he recovered those she had not had a chance to destroy. However, when the James papers were given to Harvard, four letters from Miss Woolson to the novelist were among them. They belong to the period of his two trips to America and it seems quite likely that they were left behind in Cambridge, and became mixed with William's papers. When they were first placed in the Houghton Library they were recorded as from Miss Woolson to William James, whom she met, so far as we know, only once.

Fenimore's letters belong to the earlier stages of the friendship. Their inordinate length – the four which accidentally survived total approximately fifteen thousand words – reveals her propensity from the first to pour herself out to James. They contain a mixture of adulation and criticism; they exalt him – and they deflate him; they are filled with a kind of mocking and competitive challenge; she plays the woman scorned and the woman pleading; full of self-pity at her foot-loose state, she at the same time reminds him of her own rooted Americanism. Their tone, above all else, however, is one of depression and of a touching loneliness – a middle-aged woman reaching out to a man younger than herself for a friendliness which she had glimpsed during those long-ago weeks in Florence, and which absence threatened to efface. What he wrote in reply we can only guess; it is clear that he cautiously measured the intervals of correspondence – for among her complaints is that of his long silences.

She had written an early volume of tales called *Castle Nowhere*;

for this itinerant *littératrice*, wandering among the continental cities to places far removed from the Western Reserve and the American South, felt herself alien and solitary. She was constantly trying to make temporary homes out of impossible rooms in hotels and *pensions*; she likened herself to an encaged bird seeking to build a nest out of two wisps of straw; or a beaver she saw in a zoological garden in Dresden, far from his American haunts, constructing a pathetic little dam out of fragments of old boughs. Fenimore told herself the beaver was as American and as homeless as she was. Did Henry understand this? Surely he knew only beaver hats! He could know nothing of beavers or prairies – he only knew people like Madame de Katkoff, the Russian adventuress in his play-version of *Daisy Miller*.

The role in which Fenimore cast herself always in these letters is that of a rejected woman – for in the play of Daisy, as in the story, Winterbourne can never make up his mind; and he does have a European lady in Geneva in whom he is interested. Again and again in her letters, under the guise of discussing and criticizing James's writings, Miss Woolson seems to be saying to him that he is cold, disinterested, does not understand women – does not understand how a woman – say Miss Woolson – feels.

I have been thinking about all this work you have undertaken; [she is writing from Venice in May 1883] and I have wished that I could send you a message across the ocean – a spoken one. I will write it instead; you will believe, I hope, that it is said with the utmost sincerity, though you may not care for it in itself. – In one of the three novels, – or if that is impossible, in one of the shorter stories – why not give us a woman for whom we can feel a real love? There are such surely in the world. I am certain you have known some, for you bear the traces – among thicker traces of another sort. – I do not plead that she should be happy; or even fortunate; but let her be distinctly loveable; perhaps, let some one love her very much; but, at any rate, let *her* love very much, and let us see that she does; let us care for her, and even greatly. If you will only care for her yourself, as you describe her, the thing is done.

If you will only care for her yourself. And Fenimore ticked off on her fingers the love-affairs of Newman and Claire de Cintré, Daisy and Winterbourne, Isabel Archer and her suitors. None expressed real love. 'Take the one further step, and use your perfect art in delineating a real love as it really is. For you will never deny that it exists, though it may be rare.'

This was the deepest argument of her letters. And in long para-graphs, circling again and again to the same question, she would retail all the gossip and all her conversations about Henry James with his friends – always in a vein highly flattering to the writer but expressive also of her own affection. She had met Mrs Bronson in Venice. They had not been interested in each other until the name of James was mentioned. 'Mr James is one of my dearest friends,' said Mrs Bronson. 'He is also a friend of mine,' murmured Fenimore. And the Friends of the Friend thereupon 'began to smile and be con-tent'. Mrs Bronson told Miss Woolson that it was to her balcony James alluded in his article on Venice, when he spoke of smoking a cigarette at the end of the day and watching the traffic on the Grand Canal. Fenimore has a little spasm of jealousy. She ends the letter: 'The lagoons, the Piazzetta, the little canals all send their love to you. They wish you were here. And so do I. I could go in a gondola, you know, and see you on Mrs B's balcony. That would – be something. Goodbye.'

2

There was also the strong competitive feeling written into her letters. Fenimore was a dedicated writer; and she aspired to some of the greatness of her friend. On the one hand she proclaimed her inability to do the kind of writing he did; on the other she conveyed to him the helplessness to which this reduced her. She remembered well, she told him, how she had talked to him in Florence, in the Cascine, of her difficulties and the problem of making a clean copy of her stories; and how he had answered, 'Oh, I never copy.' On a mute gesture from Fenimore he had added: 'Do you think, then, that my work has the air of having been copied, and perhaps more than once?' She wrote: 'I think I made no direct reply, then. But I will, now. The gesture was despair – despair, that, added to your other perfections, was the gift of writing as you do, at the first draft!'

Again:

I don't think you appreciated, over there, among the chimney pots, the laudation your books received in America as they came out one by one. (We little fish did! We little fish became worn to skeletons owing to the constant admonitions we received to regard the beauty, the grace, the incomparable perfection of all sorts and kinds of the proud salmon of the pond; we ended by hating that salmon.)

And again :

How did you ever dare write a portrait of a lady? Fancy any woman attempting the portrait of a gentleman! Wouldn't there be a storm of ridicule! Every clerk on the Maumee river would know more about it than a George Eliot. For my own part, in my small writings, I never dare put down what men are thinking, but confine myself simply to what they do and say. For long experience has taught me that whatever I suppose them to be thinking at any especial time, that is sure to be exactly what they are *not* thinking. What they *are* thinking, however, nobody but a ghost could know.

That allusion to the Maumee river, by which Fenimore displayed her American geography to James, had occurred before. 'If you had never left the banks of the Maumee,' she had written to him, 'you would still have been dumbly an "alienated American" (I suppose you have no idea where the Maumee is!)' Miss Woolson was alluding to one of the rivers important to her in her childhood in the Lake Country. It runs from Fort Wayne, north-east to Lake Erie near Toledo.

In one of her letters she suddenly fears she is not being a very literary correspondent, and in the process gives us a hint of the way in which he wrote to her :

I am writing on in the most inconsequent inartistic way. But you know I never wrote to you half so much for your entertainment as for my own. At present it rests me to write to you. But the letter itself won't be, can't be, good. – If I were clever, I should always bear in mind the fact, that when I have written to you many sheets, I have received a short note in reply, beginning with some such sentence as this : 'Dear Miss Woolson. One doesn't answer your letters; one can't. One only reads them and is grateful;' and this followed up by three very small pages (in a very big hand) in which no allusion is made to anything I have said, the 'faithfully' of the signature occupying the room of several of my sentences. Then, when I have written you a short note myself, I have received from you a charming letter in reply, eight pages long, and not such a very big hand either, and the 'faithfully' even put across the top or side of the first page instead of being relied upon to fill the half of the last! But I am not clever. And then I am always thinking that perhaps you will improve. I hope right in the face of facts. It doesn't do any harm; and it amuses me. My idea is that we shall make a George Washington of you yet.

This is an accurate picture of Henry's epistolary strategy. On the other hand she tells him : 'Your letters are better than you are.' And then the praise: 'The best part of you is your incorruptible and dignified and reasonable modesty and your perfectly balanced common sense. It is such a comfort that you have them.' Yet she feels that he does not value her work as much as she would like him to, and she is not certain how much he values her. She knows that he has been rather contemptuous of 'literary women'. She remarks:

I have recently listened to a rather intimate description of the Miss Howard ('One Summer') of whom you spoke in Rome as the writer-ess who wished to make your acquaintance; I am sure you would not like her. However, I had better be careful; you liked that Miss Fletcher [Constance Fletcher, the author of Kismet]. But you do not want to know the little literary women. Only the great ones – like George Eliot. I am barring myself out here, because I do not come in as a literary woman at all, but as a sort of – of admiring aunt. I think that expresses it.

(In a tale she had made her heroine say: 'You dislike literary women very much.' The hero's reply was: 'Hardly, I pity them.')

3

If she could not give full expression to her feelings for her correspondent, she could do so freely for his work. When her enthusiasm led her to the man – and she felt that she might overstep the bounds of reticence – she promptly took refuge in praise of his writing, or in recording for him praise spoken by other persons. The affection is thinly masked however:

You could not possibly have pleased me more than by telling me – as you do in this letter – of your plans for work. I have often thought of the motif you told me about, in Rome; now I shall see it completed. You have undertaken a great deal. But I am very glad you have undertaken it. You will do it all; and superbly. There is no one like you; and pretty much everyone – (who amounts to anything) – knows it now. Turgenev is dying, I hear. You are now our Turgenev. (I don't mean that you are like him; but that you have his importance.)

Then, after describing her rooms in Venice she has a fantasy of James's coming to tea:

There is a very nice sofa here, placed just at the angle that commands the beautiful eastern view. And there is a tea-table, with the same sputtering little kettle you saw in my sky-parlour at Rome. If you could come in now, and rest a while (till time to go to the next dinner-party), I would make you some of the water which you consider 'tea'. And you would find at least the atmosphere of a very perfect kindness. You say you 'fall back' upon my 'charity', feeling that it is 'infinite'. You can safely fall back; for infinite it is. Only charity is not precisely the word. Call it, rather, gratitude. This isn't for you, personally – though of course you have to be included: it is for your books. You may be what you please, so long as you write as you do.

'Your books,' she says, 'are one of the entertainments of my life and I cannot give up talking about them just to please the author.' In another paragraph she speaks of his essay on Venice, 'those exquisite pages I love so much myself – whose every word I know, almost by heart'. From this, in a sudden burst of emotion, she tells him that 'the deepest charm' of his writings is that 'they voice for me – as nothing else ever has – my own feelings; those that are so deep – so a part of me, that I cannot express them, and do not try to; never think of trying to'. She concludes by telling him – she who had written of 'Castle Nowhere' – that his writings 'are my true country, my real home. And nothing else ever is fully – try as I may to think so. Do you think this is quite an assumption, or presumption?'

This identification of her feelings with his, her home with the very heart of his created work, cannot have been lost upon James. In the same letter she offered him a gift; certain ancient Greek coins she had had mounted as tie-pins. She remembered that Benvolio had worn a Syracusian coin; and that she had seen James wearing 'six rings on one hand'. Would he accept the gift? She was quite prepared to keep it a secret. 'Nobody knows of my coins – the ones destined for you.' If he didn't wear tie-pins he would have to wait, she said, recalling the tale of the Emperor's topaz, 'until I can dig up an antique intaglio for you on the Campagna'. She offers to send the gift to America, or to his London lodgings – 'should you ever arrive there during this life'. He could choose any one of three – a coin bearing an owl, one with the head of Bacchus and one with the shield of Boeotia. Apparently James chose the Bacchus. At any rate a photograph, front-face, of his later years shows a coin-pin in his cravat.

There is only one moment in these long and pleading missives where Fenimore seems to be on the verge of an outburst, some break in her self-control. She had spoken of returning to America. 'It is all very well to hold out the prospect of "talking it over" against an Italian church-wall,' she writes. 'As to a "church-wall", there has never been but that one short time (three years ago – in Florence) when you seemed disposed for that sort of thing.' And voicing her complaint about his long absences she remarks, 'Don't put in those decorative sentences about "Italian church" walls.'

4

And so Fenimore took up her residence in England (it seems clear) to be near the man whose writings were her 'real home'. In the letter in which she speaks of having been in England a year she mentions that she has seen only Dover, Canterbury, Salisbury and London itself; and during that year we know that her visit to Dover coincided with James's stay there, and that from Salisbury they went together to Stonehenge, on 7 September 1884, for she left a record of this excursion. We also know that one evening he encountered her in a theatre to which he had escorted Mrs Kemble; and since he had a better seat he introduced her to Mrs Kemble and gave Fenimore his place.

'The literary one' seems to have been self-effacing, and as might be expected James rarely alluded to her in letters to other friends. Only the Bootts knew of her existence in his life, or of the cautious intimacy that had grown between them. However there is one distinct allusion in a letter to Howells – since the Howellses during the previous year had seen something of Miss Woolson in Florence. Writing from Paris in February 1884 to his former editor, James said: 'Miss Fenimore Woolson is spending the winter there [in London]. I see her at discreet intervals and we talk of you and Mrs you. She is a very intelligent woman, and understands when she is spoken to; a peculiarity I prize, as I find it more and more rare.' There is one further remark: 'I wish you could send me anything you have in the way of advance-sheets. It is rather hard that as you are the only English novelist I read (except Miss Woolson), I should not have more comfort with you.'

For the moment he seemed to have arrived at a quiet and regular way of friendship with Fenimore – a friendship of 'discreet intervals'.

102

The Besotted Mandarins

DURING the nine years that had elapsed since his visits to Flaubert's *cénacle* Henry James had made no attempt to revive his friendship with Daudet, Zola or the elderly Edmond de Goncourt. He had, however, been reading their works. In mid-winter 1884–85 – on 2 February – James crossed the Channel for a brief holiday, long promised to himself. It was his first visit to Paris since his final glimpse of Turgenev; and his Russian friend seemed achingly absent. Yet there was another purpose in this journey – a strange, almost intuitive, reaching backward, out of the depths of his London gloom, for the early days of his European life, the talk and companionship, the memory of Turgenev's warmth and Flaubert's shy geniality. One of the first things James did after putting up at the fashionable Hôtel de Hollande, in the Rue de la Paix, was to search out his French colleagues. He did not try to reach them directly; he seems indeed to have thought that they would not remember him. If he had read them, he was quite certain they had not read him. But they had been young together, and now he – and they – had had a certain measure of success. In Gallic fashion James resorted to an intermediary : his friend Theodore Child was by now a well-established journalist and editor, thoroughly at ease in the Parisian world of letters. James asked him to arrange a meeting.

Child acted promptly. On the third day of James's stay Child sent a note to Edmond de Goncourt inquiring whether he could bring the American novelist to his home in Auteuil. Goncourt received them the next morning, not yet in the *Grenier*, which he was to establish later in the upper reaches of the house, where he and his brother had lived together for so many years and practised their esoteric art of self-conscious observation, notation and creation. We know very little of this visit, and our evidence is simply the note written by Child, preserved among the voluminous Goncourt papers, and James's report to various persons that they had had a talk. He offered a single reminiscence, a remark made by the survivor of the fraternal team, that there had been a 'great deal of crawling into bed and playing the truant' in the daily life of Flaubert. *'If faut vous dire,'* Goncourt said, *'que dans sa journée il y avait énormément de coucheries et d'école buissonnière.'* James quoted this amusedly to Edmund Gosse, and later used it as a footnote in his essay on Flaubert. An inscribed copy of *Germinie Lacerteux* in James's library may have dated also from this meeting. The remark about Flaubert suggests, however, that the saturnine Goncourt was sufficiently expansive and anecdotal. James found 'something indefinitely disagreeable' in Goncourt's writings 'something hard and irritated, and not sympathetic'. A few evenings later he saw Goncourt again, this time at Daudet's, where he was once more conducted by the loyal Child.

I

Daudet had responded cordially to Theodore Child's note that Henry James was in Paris. He invited the two and promised a cup of tea and 'a dozen persons – Goncourt, Zola, Coppée, Loti the sailor – *la haute gomme litteraire'*, that is, the 'swells' of current French literature. When James and Child were ushered into Daudet's modest bandbox-like apartment, on a fourth floor overlooking the Luxembourg Gardens, Goncourt, Zola and Daudet at once recognized the American. 'Why,' Daudet exclaimed, 'I have known you 150 years!' James proceeded to compliment Daudet. 'What happiness,' he said, 'what joy you must feel in writing, in composing your works, in all those *trouvailles* of phrases and epithets.' From Child's account we know that Daudet, twirling the two points of his silky beard, his eyes sparkling behind his glasses, launched into a discussion of the burden of writing, the need always to say things in a new way. Child described him as listening attentively to James; he was struck by Daudet's 'worn, fine delicate features, much drawn and yellowed and ravaged by incessant intellectual work'. In reality Daudet was already suffering from the illness that ultimately would incapacitate him. But he showed much alertness on this occasion. We can extract some of their conversation, as Child set it down, from his anonymous account later in the *Atlantic Monthly* in which he alluded to James as 'Mr X'. There need be no doubt that X was James: for he himself gave a full account of the evening in subsequent letters.

DAUDET (to JAMES): My dear sir, you are mistaken. I work with pain and misery, and I always feel that I have left the best in the inkstand. Beware of the literary fools who are always satisfied; the men who come up to you, rubbing their hands, and saying, 'Ah, my dear fellow, I am happy : I have just written a chapter, – the best thing I have done!' and then go and dine, happy. It is not the idea of a book, it is not the plan, the conception, that troubles me. I observe, I study, I brood over every detail of the proposed work. But when I come to put down my book on paper, then begin the tortures, the torments of style. I don't know whether it is so in your language or not.

JAMES: Yes I know what you mean. We take less pains with our style than the French writers. We are less observant; our observation is less fine, less rich in shades and refinements and delicacies.

DAUDET: Really? Ah, but if you only knew how unobservant most Frenchmen are! A man will travel with you, or take a walk with you, and afterwards, when you begin to talk with him about what you have seen, you will suddenly find him looking at you with a smile that betrays him: he has seen nothing! He thinks that you are a humbug. The other day an old acquaintance of mine returned from Australia, after five years' sojourn there. I asked him to tell me all about what he had seen : how people lived there; what the country was like, and the trees, and the towns, and the houses. All I could get out of him was this : 'Guess how much a pound of potatoes costs!' The poor devil had seen absolutely nothing, and the only thing that had struck him was the extreme dearness of potatoes.

JAMES: I have frequently remarked that in the English, who are constantly travelling and running about, and who rarely see anything in the course of their travels, and can talk about nothing but comparative hotel accommodation. Nevertheless, it seems to me that the average Frenchman is infinitely sharper in his observation than the average English-lishman or American: he takes in more details; he is more appreciative of *nuances* and shades; he is finer, more delicate; and, for me, the proof lies in the wonderful richness of the French language in epithets expressive of the greatest variety and minuteness of variation.

DAUDET: The material is so worn out, everything has been said again and again; every theme has been exploited. There are quantities of subjects and situations and psychological states that we can no longer touch upon : we can no longer touch upon love and sentiment enveloped in nature; we can no longer talk about the influence of flowers, of landscape, of sea and sky. The public finds that kind of thing worn out, threadbare, done for. 'We dare not sing more of roses,' Sully-Prudhomme has said, in one of his poems; and I assure you the poet's cry is one that has profoundly touched us. Then when we have found something new, some fresh combination, we arrive at the expression of it with infinite torment and suffering, and always with that horrible consciousness of having left the best part unwritten. And that combination having been treated, we can never return to it again. The public may forget, but the artist cannot repeat himself, and hash up the same thing again. Every sentence in our books is wrought with pain and torment. There is no happiness, no joy, in it. The torture of style kills all that. Is it not so, Zola.

ZOLA: Yes. It is a sad trade, – *C'est un triste métier.* The only happiness is when you are beginning, when you are planning. But when you have attained your object, when success comes, there is an end of happiness. Torture and misery all the time!

DAUDET: Ah how I used to envy the calm serenity of Turgenev, working in a field and in a language the white snow of which had so few footprints! He had only to walk ahead; every step left a footprint that you could see! With us, it is like walking over a shingle strand : we have to move boulders and rocks and cliffs in order to leave our mark.

Later James quoted Daudet as having said French writers were 'perishing' in the flood of books – 'they are suffocating us, they are killing us'. *'Nous périssons par des livres. Ils nous débordent, ils nous étouffent, ils nous tuent.'* Something of the old magic of the *cénacle* seems to have been recovered by James that night, for they had discussed indeed Flaubert's favourite subject – the 'torment of style', the search for the *mot juste*, the attempt to use prose as a plastic medium. On the next day (13 February 1884), Henry James described his evening to T. B. Aldrich, editor of the *Atlantic*. 'Paris is charming, bright, mild and a little dull, and "naturalism" is in possession *sur toute la ligne*,' James told Aldrich.

I spent last evening at Alphonse Daudet's and was much impressed with the intense seriousness of that little group – himself, Zola, Goncourt, etc. About Daudet's intensity of effort there is something tragical and his wasted, worn extraordinarily beautiful and refined little face expresses it in a way which almost brings tears to my eyes. The torment of style, the high standard of it, the effort to say something perfectly in a language in which everything has been said, and re-said – so that there are certain things, certain cases, which can never again be attempted – all this seems to me to be wearing them all out, so that they have the look of galley-slaves tied to a ball and chain, rather than of happy producers. Daudet tells me that the act of production, and execution, for him is nothing but effort and suffering – the only joy (and that he admits is great) is that of conception, of planning and arranging. This all proves, what one always feels that (in their narrow circle) terrible are the subtleties they attempt. Daudet spoke of his envy and admiration of the 'serenity of production' of Turgenev – working in a field and a language where the white snow had as yet so few footprints. In French, he said, it is all one trampled slosh – one has to look, forever, to see where one can put down his step. And he wished to know how it was in English.

The evening at Daudet's had profoundly impressed James. We gain a picture of his impressions in a long passage by Child which follows his account of the conversation; this contains the comments of 'Mr X' after the two walked away from Daudet's flat. The novelist said that the French were without equal in achieving 'an absolute accordance of the expression with the idea'; and it was this which gave to their prose 'a sensation of harmony, of secret beauty'. They were engaged in a search for the 'soul of words', and they were all too acutely aware of how late in time and literature they had come. It seemed, indeed, as if all the books had been written. In the Anglo-Saxon world the public made no distinction between writers who were artists and writers who were competent hacks. The French writers, by their very devotion to their task, were artists.

Still James held that the French writers were extremely narrow in their vision of the world. 'They see very little beyond their art; their observation, delicate and complete as it is in a sense, is not very wide, and by no means coextensive with modern French life.' To illustrate this, Henry expressed the belief that they neglected provincial life, and focused on the corrupt and ignoble aspects of life in Paris. He admitted that this was an extreme way of putting it. He explained the phenomenon as follows: Zola and Daudet were of humble origin. They had come to Paris to make their way by sheer force of talent. They led a café-bohemian life, or were students in the Latin Quarter. In neither case had they been in contact with a society that offered them social refinement and a polishing influence. Even though they had attained fame, French society itself did not welcome them. To be sure there were literary salons, where they were appreciated, but their bohemianism deprived them of 'the polish and tact necessary to secure [them] an agreeable position in society'. These writers felt ill at ease in talking to society women. They ended, through embarrassment, by ignoring society and so excluded themselves, and were excluded, from a large field of observation. Henry made exception for Edmond de Goncourt, who was an aristocrat before he became a novelist. Zola lived like a hermit, a slave to his great ambition, 'sulky, lumpy, and uncommunicative', and when he came to Paris he visited none but his literary friends. Daudet was never encountered save in 'purely literary gatherings'. And in the few houses he frequented – Pailleron's, Dr Charcot's, Madame Adam's, his publisher Charpentier's – he saw only authors and artists.

James expatiated upon this. In effect, he told Child, there was a 'Chinese quality' to the existence of his French contemporaries. It was 'mandarin'. They lived in an enclosed world, and studied 'warts rather than the beauties of man' and his creations. 'French novelists are not getting hold of that larger humanity which is alone eternally interesting.' To be sure, they achieved certain incomparable things – 'but incomparable in a very narrow way'.

To Howells the novelist wrote:

I have been seeing something of Daudet, Goncourt and Zola; and there is nothing more interesting to me now than the effort and experiment of this little group, with its truly infernal intelligency of art, form, manner – its intense artistic life. They do the only kind of work, today, that I respect; and in spite of their ferocious pessimism and their handling of unclean things, they are at least serious and honest. The floods of tepid soap and water which under the name of novels are being vomited forth in England, seem to me, by contrast, to do little honour to our race ... Read Zola's last thing: *La Joie de Vivre*. This title of course has a desperate irony: but the work is admirably solid and serious.

The essence of his impression, however, was set down by James in a letter to his brother five years later, after another visit to Paris in which he listened to his French friends and their talk. 'Chinese, Chinese, Chinese!' he exclaimed. 'They are finished, besotted mandarins and Paris is their celestial Empire.'

There was a postscript to this evening. Child's article, though anonymous, was read by Daudet; probably Child himself sent it to him. And it was, understandably, resented.

The article [wrote Edmond de Goncourt in his journal on 19 June 1884], while rendering justice to Daudet's talent, represents him as working in a study the size of a bandbox, and makes out the French novelists, with the exception of myself, to be people with no sense of custom, no education, unable to carry on a conversation with a woman, etc., etc. And he [Daudet] sees this article as inspired by the enmity of Nittis. And this supposition, while it is probably ill-founded, exasperates, irritates and makes him nervous.

The intrigue-suspecting Daudet seems never to have regarded the comments as coming from Henry James. He attributed them to a French artist, Giuseppe de Nittis, a friend of Child's.

3

'They are the children of decadence, I think,' James wrote to Grace Norton, 'a brilliant one – unlike ours: that is the English; and they are strangely corrupt and prodigiously ignorant. In spite of all this they represent a great deal of truth.' While in Paris he read widely in their works. He could not swallow 'naturalism' whole. '*Ces messieurs,*' he wrote to Child, 'seem to me to have lost the perception of anything in nature but the genital organs.' The Goncourts had been addicts of note-taking and documentation; Zola had introduced the element of *reportage* – the actual seeking out of scenes, local colour, and the 'doing' of a given scene in 'scientific' fashion. They had extended Balzac's realism to a minute painting of environment; and with this Zola had adopted also the popularized ideas of Darwin with a pseudo-scientific glibness gathered from his readings in Claude Bernard's works on scientific method. By nature James found Daudet more sympathetic; and they became warm friends. For Zola he acquired an ever-increasing respect. In his prefaces Zola is constantly mentioned along with Scott, Thackeray, Trollope, Dumas and Balzac – 'even the coarse, comprehensive, prodigious Zola'. Henry would write, 'Zola is awfully *sound* – I have a tenderness for Zola. Not a pennyworth of distinction, but a shopful of *stuff*. What he says is good for you – put on blinders – and jog on the straight road.' To his friend T. S. Perry, James wrote: 'Zola's naturalism is ugly and dirty, but he seems to me to be *doing something* – which surely (in the imaginative line) no one in England or the United States is, and no one else here.' And again: 'Zola has his faults and his merits, and it doesn't seem to me important to talk of the faults. The merits are rare, valuable, extremely solid.' 'I have read a good deal of naturalism,' James wrote to Mrs Humphry Ward as his visit neared its end. To his brother he said that 'seeing these people does me a world of good, and this intellectual vivacity and *raffinement* makes the English mind seem like a sort of glue-pot'. And to Howells: 'I regard you as the great American naturalist, I don't think you go far enough, and you are haunted with romantic phantoms and a tendency to factitious glosses; but you are in the right path.' As for himself: 'It isn't for me to reproach you with that, however, the said gloss being a constant defect of *my characters*; they have too much of it – too damnably much. But I am a failure – comparatively.'

He always considered himself a failure when he was writing to Howells, who enjoyed so much prosperity in America. But his mind was now working on the lessons of the naturalists even as he had long ago studied the lesson of Balzac. He was abandoning the 'international' theme. His new novels would 'do' Boston and London as Zola had done his Paris, and was to do the coal-mines – by descending into the very heart of his subject. James's fortnight in Paris – extended into a month – proved much richer than he had anticipated. It had brought him back to the fundamentals of his career, after the long American interval and the unsettled London return. The ferment set up in him continued all that summer, when he began to write *The Bostonians*, and in the autumn it was to emerge in a single splendid manifesto, his one great leap into the arena of controversy and debate on the art which he practised. He was ready to write his essay on *The Art of Fiction*.

103

An Insolence of Talent

THERE was another side to Henry's visit to Paris. He called on the Princess Marie Ourousov and had an intimate talk with her about Turgenev's last days. He visited Mrs Charles Strong, 'flitting with weary eagerness from one exhausted little Paris pastime to another'. He saw the Auguste Laugels, who were friends also of Henrietta Reubell. Laugel had been reading him. '*Vous êtes un moraliste*,' he told James; '*des hommes tels que vous font du bien à leur pays.*' Above all James spent many hours in Miss Reubell's salon at 42 Avenue Gabriel, and saw much of her friend Mrs Boit, now living in Paris. Henrietta Reubell remained the same genial, shrewd spinster, a striking figure with her bright red hair crowning (as one artist saw her) 'an expressive but unbeautiful face'. There was a touch of Queen Elizabeth in her physiognomy; something bird-like in it and in her voice. James liked her high laugh, her lorgnette, her original mind. In street attire he saw her as a 'lady with great plumes, great heels, great festoons, a great parasol and a great stir' – small wonder that he addressed her as *La Grande Mademoiselle* and talked of her as 'the tall Etta, who has so much *cachet*'. She moved in a world of writers, painters, pictures, studios. She numbered Whistler and Oscar Wilde among her friends, and was loyal to both. The young Will Rothenstein remembered the turquoise stones loaded on her fingers and her 'adventurous conversation'. She permitted, in her drawing-room, 'anything but dullness and ill-manners'. She delighted in wit and paradox.

James had many sentimental memories of her little parlour, and often alluded to a particular alcove, where on a particular sofa, under a golden canopy, he and Miss Reubell would have their intimate gossipy *tête-à-têtes* in a perpetual cloud of smoke. Like Mrs Bronson she was addicted to cigarettes in an age when tobacco was reserved for men. Later Henry nostalgically spoke of the 'dear little *lambris dorées*', and the 'delightful breakfasts, dinners, evenings, talks'. There always seemed to linger in this alcove 'the fragrance of all the cigarettes that have been smoked out in discussion of the pleasant things of Paris'. As he was about to leave the French capital he scribbled a farewell note to her:

For me you are much of Paris – and to take leave of Paris is, as it were, to take leave in person of you, the graceful incarnation. Au revoir, Mademoiselle. Continue to shine on Sundays and weekdays, not with a cold light. Look after *votre petit monde*, and, in alternation with Mrs Boit, be the shepherdess of the studios. I think that you and she, in this capacity, ought to mount little ribboned crooks.

I

It was in the entourage of this 'shepherdess' and of her friend Mrs Boit that James met the young American prodigy of painting, John Singer Sargent. He already knew his work and had stood in admiration before the striking picture of the young Boit daughters, which Sargent had done a year before, and certain other precocities. Sargent was now a mere 27. The American art-world had been waiting for a master. Whistler was famous but idiosyncratic; Duveneck had shown a powerful but limited talent. Sargent stepped into the full light of prominence and controversy from the start. James encountered a tall, athletic, ruddy-complexioned, dark-haired and dark-bearded man with vivid grey-blue eyes. Quiet, even sedate, cultivated, he formed a marked contrast to the rough-and-tumble bohemians of art, or the dilettantes. The novelist was promptly and powerfully attracted to him. Had Sargent been a little less self-contained, a little less poised and less centred on his painting, James probably would have found him as appealing as he had found the amateur Zhukovski, with whom he had been so taken eight years before. He told Grace Norton :

The only Franco-American product of importance here strikes me as young John Sargent the painter, who has high talent, a charming nature, artistic and personal, and is civilized to his finger-tips. He is perhaps spoilable – though I don't think he is spoiled. But I hope not, for I like him extremely; and the best of his work seems to me to have in it something exquisite.

They had so much in common that they must have seemed to each other, in certain respects, mirror-images. Continentalized from their earliest years – Sargent even more than James – innate aristocrats with a penchant for society and the *beau-monde* (and taking many of their subjects from it), possessing a dignity and distinction that commanded respect wherever they went, dedicated to their art, capable of extraordinary assiduity, they were counterparts in their different mediums. If James had a more subtle mind, and Sargent a greater naïveté, this resided in the differences often to be found between a writer and a painter. A musician also, Sargent at the pianoforte had the subtlety in his finger-tips which James had in his psychology. James was much more strongly intellectual than Sargent; and both had in them a vestigial stiffness of the American Puritan. James's New England conscience was to relax and change much more than Sargent's. It was no accident that the author of *The Portrait of a Lady* and this painter of portraits of great ladies should have found common bonds between them.

Sargent took James to his studio at 41 Boulevard Berthier and showed him his large painting of Madame X. The novelist described it to Lizzie Boott, 'a full length of a so-called French beauty (*femme du monde*), half-stripped and covered with paint – blue, green, white, black'. This was the portrait of Madame Gautereau which was to have a *succès de scandale* in the Paris salon a few weeks later. James only 'half-liked it'. But he was impressed by the talent that had produced it. And he was worried by this excess of skill in one so young. Success was coming easily to Sargent. James, who had won his fame with much greater difficulty, knew the dangers of too great a facility and too dazzling a virtuosity. 'His talent is brilliant,' he wrote to Lizzie Boott, 'but there is a certain incompleteness in it, in his extremely attaching, interesting nature a certain want of serious-

ness.' He wondered whether it was an advantage to an artist 'to
obtain early in life such possession of his means that the struggle
with them, discipline, *tâtonnement*, cease to exist for him'. Was
there not a danger of a certain 'larkiness', a skill that, for all its brilliance, would be lifeless? 'He knows so much about the art of painting that he perhaps does not fear emergencies quite enough.'
'Observers encumbered with a nervous temperament may at any
moment have been anxious about his future,' and he added that 'his
future is the most valuable thing he has to show'. James was to see
that future, and it was to be for him 'a knock-down insolence of
talent and truth of characterization, a wonderful rendering of life,
of manners, of aspects, of types, of textures, of everything. It is the
old story; he expresses himself as no one else scarce begins to do in
the language of the art he practises.'

2

Within a month after he said good-bye to Sargent in Paris, James
welcomed him to London. Sargent's reputation at that time was
almost wholly French, and James argued the time had come for him
to cross the Channel permanently – as he himself had done. 'I want
him to come here and live and work – there being such a field in
London for a *real* painter of women, and such magnificent subjects
of both sexes.' Since Sargent was a stranger to the British capital
James gave him 'a push to the best of my ability'. It was a strenuous
push indeed but both men were up to it. On Saturday, 28 March
1884, Henry took him to an exhibition of the works of Sir Joshua
Reynolds and then to the National Gallery; in the evening they dined
and went to the theatre. On the next day, Sunday, Sargent came to
lunch at 1.30 and during the afternoon the novelist conducted him
through ten artists' studios to see pictures just going into the spring
exhibition; and that evening he entertained him at dinner at the
Reform Club to which he invited half a dozen friends, including
Edward Burne-Jones.

   Among the studios he visited were those of John Millais and Sir
Frederick Leighton, President of the Royal Academy. To the old
guard of the Pre-Raphaelite movement and to the flossy erudite
Leighton, James was introducing a young man who had styled himself an 'impressionist'. The novelist was immensely struck by the
wealth and power of Millais and Leighton, 'the gorgeous effect of

worldly prosperity and success' they revealed. 'I suppose,' he wrote to Grace Norton,

it is the demon of envy – but I can't help contrasting the great rewards of a successful painter, here, and his glory and honour generally, with the so much more modest emoluments of the men of letters. And the painters who wallow in gold are – some of them! – so shockingly bad! Leighton in particular overwhelms me – his sumptuosity, his personal beauty, his cleverness, his gorgeous house, his universal attainments, his portraits of duchesses, his universal parties, his perfect French and Italian – and German – his general air of being above all human dangers and difficulties!

Burne-Jones invited James and Sargent to see his new painting of *King Cophetua and the Beggar Maid*, a characteristic – and since celebrated – 'literary' piece of art, then about to be shown at the Grosvenor Gallery. 'Burne-Jones was adorable,' Henry reported to his friends, and 'we had a charming hour'. Sargent enjoyed and appreciated the works of the older man, 'but I am afraid poor dear, lovely, but slightly narrow B. J. suffers from a constitutional incapacity to enjoy Sargent's – finding in them "such a want of finish" '.

The English art-critics at first felt Sargent to be crude and too startling in some of his effects. James admitted that there was 'a certain *excess* of cleverness : too much *chic* and not enough naïveté'. It was Sargent's character which he felt was 'charmingly naïf, but not his talent'. Within a year the American painter had settled in England, in Whistler's old house in Tite Street, Chelsea – as it proved, for life.

104

Matrons and Disciples

THE spring and summer of 1884 was filled with 'interruptions and distractions', easy sociabilities and the Season, amid the pressure of James's heavy writing commitments. He seems to have worked steadily from March until August. The record of his social activities during this time may best be suggested by the fact that nearly all his American friends seemed to be in London; and a cholera epidemic along the Mediterranean brought Continental friends as well. The result was that James declined invitations right and left but he was himself an almost constant host. At one moment during that summer his publisher, J. R. Osgood, and his friends Charles Eliot Norton, John Hay, and Clarence King were all in London. At another he had Mrs Strong from Paris, Mrs Gardner, freshly arrived from a world-tour, and Mrs Mason – all demanding his company.

Mrs Gardner heralded her arrival from far away. She wrote asking for an introduction to Mrs Bronson in Venice. This seemed almost a joke: James sent the note, but told Mrs Gardner to throw it overboard, Mrs Bronson was 'so absurdly easy to know' on her Venetian balcony. In the note he introduced Mrs Gardner as 'a forlorn, bereft, emaciated lady just returned from the Indies'. Later that summer he reported to Grace Norton:

Mrs Jack Gardner has just passed through London, at the close of her universal tour, and on me *her* hand too was laid: but very discreetly. She is worn and tired by her travels, but full of strange reminiscences, and in despair at going back to Boston, where she has neither friends, nor lovers, nor entertainment, nor resources of any kind left. She was exceedingly *nice*, while here, and I pity her. Mrs Mason, Mrs Strong and she consorted much together, and the group, as a representative American-woman one, was sufficiently edifying.

James added, 'Please burn this odious sheet.'

I

Henry James formed two new friendships during these weeks with members of the younger literary generation of France and England – two writers who promptly dedicated their books to him. To his rooms in July Sargent brought a rather flabby-looking Frenchman, with an unstable glass in one eye, and a shy manner. His name was Paul Bourget, James remembered having read his *Essais de psychologie contemporaine*, which he had judged 'almost brilliant'. Bourget was 32 but he looked 28, not a little like an average student whose visage expresses all the cares of a precocious wisdom. A small, rather sturdy man, for all his softness, he wore drooping, trimmed moustaches and parted his hair imperfectly on one side. He had long tapering hands and searching eyes. He was on obviously good terms with his tailor. He conveyed a mixture of careless elegance and deep melancholy; but he had a tone and style in conversation which gave James pause. 'I have an interesting – that is, rather – little Frenchman on my hands,' he reported to Miss Norton, 'bequeathed to me by Sargent, one Paul Bourget, literary, clever, a gentleman and an Anglomane, but rather affected. I take him next week to spend a day or two at Ferdinand de Rothschild's.' Bourget wrote *Cruelle Énigme* that summer. It made him famous in France; and he attached himself to James as a disciple. If the American novelist had been influenced by the French, he was to have now an influence on one of their writers, and one who would very speedily rise to considerable fame. But it is doubtful whether James, if he was aware of his influence, would have taken pleasure in it, for he cared little for what Bourget wrote, and some of his most interesting letters to his Continental friends are those criticizing Bourget's novels. It was Bourget the conversationalist that he found interesting. James dined Bourget at the Reform, introduced him to Gosse, made him his guest at the Athenaeum. Later that summer Bourget journeyed to Dover to be with him. James judged him 'too much of a dilettante', but found him a sympathetic and attractive being with a 'brilliant little intelligence', and 'one of the most charming and ingenious talkers I ever met'. Perhaps it was the sense of having in a Frenchman a certain kind of camp-follower that prompted James to save all Bourget's letters. They contain interesting glimpses of literary life in Paris and their preservation in the hands of one who did not spare most of his other papers underlines a deep irony : for Bourget too shared James's hostility to the leaving of fugitive writings to posterity. Yet he on his side saved James's letters to him. This is one of the rare instances in which both sides of James's correspondence survive.

'*Bourget est tragique*,' James wrote to a mutual friend, '*mais est-il sérieux?*' What they had in common was their interest in human motives, in a certain kind of psychological morality. James regarded Bourget's plots as factitious and felt his 'psychology' to be increasing superficial. *Cruelle Énigme* bore a rather flowery dedicatory epistle, which suggests what their friendship meant to the French writer. It was inscribed to the

memory of the time when I was beginning to write it and which was also the time when we became acquainted. In our conversations in England last summer, protracted sometimes at one of the tables in the hospitable Athenaeum Club, sometimes beneath the shade of the trees in some vast park, sometimes on the Dover esplanade while it echoed to the tumult of the waves, we often discussed the art of novel-writing, an art which is the most modern of all because it is the most flexible, and the most capable of adaption to the varied requirements of every temperament. We agreed that the laws imposed upon novelists by aesthetics resolve themselves into this : to give a personal impression of life.

James had talked to Bourget out of his already-written, but not yet published essay, *The Art of Fiction*. He was not flattered, however, by Bourget's words. 'I am greatly compromised here by the dedication of Bourget's novel,' he told Child, 'the story being so *malpropre*. But I admire much – not the story, but the ability of it.'

2

The second friendship, less intimate and personal was with Violet Paget, an Englishwoman of 27, who had lived most of her life in Italy and who had lately published, under the name of Vernon Lee, volumes entitled, *Euphorion* and *Belcaro*. They met in various London homes and James described her as 'a most astounding young female'. *Euphorion* was 'most fascinating and suggestive, as well as monstrous clever. She has a prodigious cerebration.' Tall, angular, with slightly protruding teeth and peering near-sightedly through her glasses, she seemed the traditional man-like blue-stocking. Perhaps it was on this account that Edith Wharton, later in life, made a point of saying that while she had been 'fortunate in knowing intimately some great talkers among men', she had met only three women who had that gift and one of them was Vernon Lee. The young woman, then known as Miss Paget, had lived largely in Florence.

From Miss Paget's privately printed letters to her mother and half-brother we recover the impression made on the young woman by Henry James. He paid her marked attention, and tended to be unaware of the effect he was having on her.

24 June 1884. To the Wards' *soirée*, where, despite the presence of Matthew Arnold and Mr Forster I found no one to amuse me except Henry James.

26 June 1884. Then Henry James came, 'who is most devotedly civil to me.' They go on to a party where 'I talked half the time with Henry James'.

4 July 1884. At a party for Sargent. 'Pater limping with gout and Henry James wrinkling his forehead as usual for tight boots and a lot of artists buzzing about.'

11 July 1884. The Watts are charming, 'but Henry James was even nicer : he takes the most paternal interest in me as a novelist, says that *Miss Brown* is a very good title, and that he will do all in his power to push it'.

25 July 1885. 'He came to see me again yesterday afternoon. He says his plan through life has never been to lose an opportunity of seeing anything of any kind; he urges me to do the same. He says that chance may enable me to see more of English life, if I keep my wits about me. He is really very kind and wise, I think.'

Henry James was helpful, curious, encouraging. He little realized how closely Miss Paget listened and to what extent he was involving the young writer in the emotions of a friendship that was on his side wholly 'objective'. The first warning sign came when Miss Paget decided that she would dedicate her novel to him. He could hardly refuse. He made a gallant flourish of acceptance. But he was cautious.

Reading her works James must have had second thoughts. There was something too sharp, too penetrating, in this inexhaustible young woman's mind. He wrote to her with delicate irony, saying it frightened him to have 'the honour of an invocation however casual', and proposed that perhaps 'dedication should come *to* you not *from* you'. He added : 'Please hint that you offer me *Miss Brown* only to encourage me!' The irony escaped Miss Paget. Her inscription was literal : 'To Henry James I dedicate, for good luck, my first attempt at a novel.' Even before he received the book he had written to T. S. Perry, that her novel would be inferior to what she had written critically; in her criticism he had found a certain amount of 'tangled talk'. When the novel reached him, James realized the danger of a too ardent admiration. He felt it was hardly the sort of book that should have his name on the dedicatory page. It was raw and violent; there were too many recognizable persons. This embarrassed him. He postponed thanking Vernon Lee; and the pressure of writing his serial, plus other pressures, resulted in his putting off acknowledgement from the autumn until the following May. When he finally sat down to write a letter, he was abjectly apologetic, feeling he returned admiration with discourtesy. What he wrote was such a statement as might be given to most young novelists.

You have proposed to yourself too little to make a firm, compact work – and you have been too much in a moral passion ! That has put certain exaggerations, overstatements, *grossissements*, insistences wanting in tact, into your head. Cool first – write afterwards. Morality is hot – but art is icy! Excuse my dogmatic and dictatorial tone, and believe it is only an extreme indication of interest and sympathy in what you do.

Speaking of her characters, James told her that there was a want of proportion and perspective; she was 'too savage' with her poets and painters and dilettanti –

life is less criminal, less obnoxious, less objectionable, less crude, more *bon enfant*, more mixed and casual, and even in its most offensive manifestations, more *pardonable*, than the unholy circle with which you have surrounded your heroine. And then you have impregnated all those people too much with the sexual, the basely erotic preoccupation : your hand was over-violent, the touch of life is lighter.

Miss Paget seems to have paid attention to James's criticisms, and to have recognized their value and authority. She shrewdly saw the difference between James the serious artist and James the social animal addicted to an excess of flourish; this she characterized with complete accuracy to her mother as his 'absolute social and personal insincerity and extreme intellectual justice and plain-spokenness'. This closed the first incident in one of the more curious friendships of James's life.

Already there was foreshadowed, however, in the friends James was forming during 1884, the future 'Master' – the idol of younger writers of the *fin de siècle* and the new century, the giver of counsel and of doctrine. Henry James was to be until late in life on the side of youth and of experiment in art. He had during this year met three of the younger generation – Sargent, Bourget and Vernon Lee. A still more important friendship was to be formed during the coming months under circumstances he would not have predicted during the crowded weeks after his return from Paris.

105

Atmosphere of the Mind

THE summer came and James was still in London – hot, tired, restless, uneasy. 'Infinitely oppressed and depressed,' he wrote in his notebook on 6 August 1884, 'by the sense of being behindhand with the novel – that is with the *start* of it, that I have engaged, through Osgood, to write for the *Century*.' He had two social engagements, he noted, one at Waddesdon, where he was going with Bourget. He would get these out of the way. 'Then I shall possess my soul, my faculties, my imagination again, then I shall feel that life is worth living, and shall (I trust) be tolerably calm and happy. *A mighty will*, there is nothing but that! The integrity of one's will, purpose, faith. To wait, when one *must* wait, and act when one can act!' He had not yet found a name for his novel. It was known for the moment only as *Verena*. Osgood was to pay a flat fee of $5,000 for the book-rights, for a specified period. James knew what his own earnings would be if he himself serialized and then controlled the book-rights – he had driven a good bargain. Moreover he had come to terms with the *Atlantic* for a second novel, for 1885–6. He had asked $500 an instalment, but had settled for $15 a page, or about $350 a month.

I

He remained in London that summer to write two tales for the New York *Sunday Sun* and its syndicate, and received for these, he told his correspondents, 'thousands', but did not name the amount. 'It is a case of gold pure and simple,' he wrote to Perry, and he explained that he had no objection to appearing in a newspaper – it would actually give him a wider public. The first of these tales was *Georgina's Reasons*, a strange unmotivated sensational story, written in the belief that this was what newspaper-readers wanted. He based it on an anecdote Mrs Kemble had told him – of some woman in society who married a naval officer in secret, and when she was to have a baby gave birth secretly, as if the child were illegitimate, and disposed of it to foster-parents. James's heroine accomplishes this in Italy; then she returns to New York, and remarries. When her husband, back from a long voyage, discovers what has occurred, he is faced with the dilemma of either denouncing her, or accepting the possibility of bigamy for himself, as she had done. He does neither; yet his freedom has been restricted by the bizarre conduct of his wife. The naval officer, during his travels, had become interested in two young women, sisters, in Naples, whose names are Kate and Mildred Theory. Mildred is dying of consumption – and here, in an early form, are the figures who will return to James's imagination later: Kate and Milly and the naval man, here named Benyon, later named Densher, will enact the drama of *The Wings of the Dove.* That *Georgina's Reasons* was regarded as sufficiently sensational may be judged from the headlines in one of the western journals:

GEORGINA'S REASONS!

HENRY JAMES'S LATEST STORY

A woman who commits bigamy and enforces silence on her husband! Two other lives made miserable by her heartless action!

The second tale written for the *Sun, Pandora,* was in James's best international vein. Told with great charm through the eyes of a literal-minded but not insensitive young German diplomat bound for his country's Embassy in America, the tale drew on James's Washington visits of the previous two years. The diplomat first meets Pandora Day on board ship. He has been reading *Daisy Miller,* and he wonders whether she is the flirtatious type depicted by the author of that tale. Presently he discovers that she dominates her parents; that she has a fiancé; and under the roof of a splendid Washington home, very much like that of the Henry Adamses, he learns that Pandora is really what is known as the 'self-made' American girl. Her parents have totally abdicated. The climax occurs when the President of the United States, attending a party at the home of the Adams characters – they are named here Bonnycastle – has a chat with Pandora and she obtains from him a post in the diplomatic service for her fiancé. The amazed German diplomat feels he now has full documentation on the resilience and daring of American young women. James by now possessed a fluent mastery of this type of story – the arrival in New York, the Washington interiors, the social rise of Pandora, every step seen through the Germanism of Count Vogelstein is told with a concreteness of data, and the lightest kind of irony. Adroit though James was, he could never deceive his readers, who still regarded the Teutonic-eye view of the American girl as really James's. The tale was as critical of 'permissiveness' and American institutions as James's other international stories. What many of James's readers could not appreciate was his technique and his boundless good humour; they experienced the humour as depreciatory.

When these tales were sent off and his visits were paid, James settled himself in Dover, in the Marine Parade. He had almost an entire lodging-house to himself. The Channel twinkled under his windows and he felt that he was hanging over the French coast, so near did it seem on the horizon. 'I have gone in for privacy, *recueil-lement* and literary labour,' he told Miss Reubell. He had never allowed himself so slim a margin before starting a serial. He was true to his self-admonition – to 'act when one can act'. By 1 October he had sent Richard Watson Gilder the first instalment of *The Bostonians* for the *Century*. Bourget came from London, and they sat on Henry's little balcony smoking cigarettes and looking across the Channel. James spent six or seven productive weeks here, put himself back into tune with his work, and returned to Bolton Street in late September with his novel well-launched.

2

Before leaving London Henry James had written a comparatively short but substantial essay, to which he gave the title *The Art of Fiction*, and sent it to *Longman's Magazine*. He had come upon a pamphlet containing a lecture delivered the previous April at the Royal Institution by Walter Besant, a busy Victorian who boasted that he had written eighteen novels in eighteen years. Besant's subject had been 'Fiction as One of the Fine Arts'. The burden of his argument was that novel-writing should be classed with the arts of poetry, painting and music, and taught as the laws of harmony are taught in music or perspective in painting. Besant also asked that the practitioners of the fictional art be given honours and prizes such as were reserved for the other arts. With much of this James had no argument, but when Besant undertook to say what a novel should be, and how it should be taught, James demurred. He could not accept Besant's dictum that a novel should possess 'a conscious moral purpose'. Nor could he agree with his remark that a lady novelist who lived in a quiet village might not write fiction about garrison life. She had only to be an observant damsel, he replied, to be able to write on any subject of her choice. By the same token James found it 'rather chilling' that Besant should have advised young novelists from the lower classes to refrain from launching their characters in high society. The truly imaginative novelist, he said, knew how to guess the unseen from the seen, 'to trace the implication of things, to judge the whole piece by the pattern'.

For the rest, James's main argument was that the novel, far from being 'make-believe', actually competes with life, since it records the stuff of history. Comparing fiction to painting, he said that 'as the picture is reality, so the novel is history'. He criticized the factitious novel with its spurious happy ending, the 'distribution at the last of prizes, pensions, husbands, wives, babies, millions, appended paragraphs, and cheerful remarks'. The core of his essay contained a defence of the novel as a free and elastic form, which made it difficult to prescribe 'what sort of an affair the good novel will be'. The novel would always be a personal impression of life; and its value would be greater or less 'according to the intensity of the impression'. Humanity was immense and 'reality has a myriad forms'. It was all very well for Besant to say one should write from 'experience'.

What kind of experience is intended, and where does it begin and end? Experience is never limited, and it is never complete; it is an immense sensibility, a kind of huge spider-web of the finest silken threads suspended in the chamber of consciousness, catching every air-borne particle in its tissue. It is the very atmosphere of the mind; and when the mind is imaginative – much more when it happens to be that of a man of genius – it takes to itself the faintest hints of life, it converts the very pulses of the air into revelations.

The best help to give to the fictional novice was not to lecture him on novel of character and novel of incident, but to say to him simply: 'Try to be one of the people on whom nothing is lost.'

The rest of James's paper was devoted to his argument that the novel is a living organism and that 'in each of the parts there is something of each of the other parts'.

What is character but the determination of incident? What is incident but the illustration of character? What is either a picture or a novel that is *not* of character? ... It is an incident for a woman to stand up with her hand resting on a table and look out at you in a certain way; or if it be not an incident I think it will be hard to say what it is. At the same time it is an expression of character.

James denied a *conscious* moral purpose to the novel. The province of art was 'all life, all feeling, all observation, all vision', and the critic should not prescribe which subjects were valid and which were not. The critic's concern was solely with what the novelist did with his material. What was wrong with the English novel, James argued, was that there existed a conspiracy, 'a traditional difference between that which people know and that which they agree to admit that they know'. Far from having a purpose, moral or otherwise, the

English novel had a 'diffidence'. Recalling his talks with his French *confrères*, James reached the conclusion that a novel invariably conveyed 'the quality of the mind of the producer' and that 'no good novel will ever proceed from a superficial mind'. This was the essence of his argument. *The Art of Fiction* remains a brilliant individual manifesto, written with elegance and grace, and with the finesse of Matthew Arnold, that of standing his ground firmly and stating his truths with high seriousness. Many novelists had discussed one or another of James's points before, but never had the case for realism in fiction, and for the novel as social history, been put in the English world with such force, nor 'experience' defined with such psychological understanding.

3

One remark in this essay caught the eye of an invalid at Bournemouth, a novelist who had been having severe lung-haemorrhages and who did most of his writing in bed. Discussing reality in fiction, James had alluded to *Treasure Island* and compared it with Edmond de Goncourt's *Chérie*. He pronounced the Goncourt novel a failure and Stevenson's novel a success, remarking: 'I have been a child, but I have never been on a quest for buried treasure.' Robert Louis Stevenson promptly wrote still another essay on the subject, titled it *A Humble Remonstrance*, and sent it also to *Longman's* where it appeared two months after James's paper. To the particular remark about *Treasure Island* Stevenson rejoined that if James had 'never been on a quest for buried treasure, it can be demonstrated that he has never been a child'. The burden of his argument was that a novel could not compete with life. It had to be 'make-believe'. Fiction, Stevenson said, simplified some 'side or point of life', and stood or fell by its 'significant simplicity'. He reasoned that life was 'monstrous, infinite, illogical, abrupt, and poignant', whereas a work of art was, in comparison 'neat, finite, self-contained, rational, flowing, and emasculate. Life imposes by brute energy, like inarticulate thunder; art catches the ear, among the far louder noises of experience, like an air artificially made by a discreet musician.'

Thus had been stated in public, during this year, three distinct views of the novel: Besant's had been that of the efficient and good-natured hack, the 'maker' of popular fiction; James had argued for the novel as a work of art which creates an illusion of reality; and

Stevenson spoke for make-believe. James had met Stevenson during the *Daisy Miller* period. On 14 September 1879 he had written to Perry: 'I have seen R. L. Stevenson but once – met him at lunch (and Edmund Gosse) with Lang. He is a pleasant fellow, but a shirt-collarless Bohemian and a great deal (in an inoffensive way) of a *poseur*. But his little *Inland Voyage* was, I thought, charming.'

They had never had occasion to develop this acquaintance, Stevenson being much out of England. But when his article appeared, James told him of his enjoyment 'of everything you write. It's a luxury, in this immoral age, to encounter some one who *does* write – who is really acquainted with that lovely art.' He thanked him for many of the things he had said – 'the current of your admirable style floats pearls and diamonds'. His own pages in *Longman's*, he explained, had been mainly a plea for liberty for the novelist: they represented only half of what he had to say. 'Some day I shall try and express the remainder. The native *gaiety* of all that you write is delightful to me,' and all the more so, he added, since he was aware how ill Stevenson was.

Stevenson replied that his own efforts were modest indeed beside James's, and he spoke of 'the despair with which a writer like myself considers (say) the park scene in "Lady Barberina". Every touch surprises me by its intangible precision.' As for their differences, 'Each man among us prefers his own aim, and I prefer mine; but when we come to speak of performance, I recognize myself, compared with you, to be a lout and slouch of the first water.' He remarked that, being sick, he liked visitors; and he invited James to come to Bournemouth, where he would put him up and offer him 'a fair bottle of claret'. These were the overtures to what was to become – other circumstances intervening – a strong and enduring friendship..

106

The Two Invalids

WHEN Henry James returned to London from Dover, he knew that his sister would be joining him shortly. The correspondence announcing her plans does not appear to have survived; however, a letter from Henry to William of 5 October 1884 mentions that

Alice's advent here is by this time (in prospect) a familiar idea, though I feel naturally a good deal of solicitude about it. It is certainly a good thing for me to do; and if she can adjust herself to a long rhythm, as it were, of improvement, instead of a short one, I have no doubt solid results will come to her. But she ought to be prepared to spend *three* years. I don't know what she will do, and don't exactly see how *I* can (when she is alone) be either with her or without her – that is, away from her. But this will doubtless settle itself; and if she learns to become more sociable with the world at large (as I think she will have to, in self-preservation), the problem will be solved.

Her sailing-date had not yet been set. What we do know is that Alice James, with both her parents dead and with Katharine Loring available only at certain times, had been leading a lonely life in Mount Vernon Street. Miss Loring had a sister Louisa with weak lungs; she could not therefore give undivided attention to Alice. But she was bringing Louisa abroad, and Alice, rather than remain alone in Cambridge, had decided to journey with her friends.

The ill-health and consequent dependency of Alice posed serious problems for James. They had talked of some sort of joint domestic arrangement; but with her invalidism this seemed out of the question. He was her one bachelor brother; they had been close to one another during their earlier years; and he felt the responsibility was his. He had implied this from the moment he had turned over to Alice the income from his inheritance. Grace Norton, as an old friend of the Jameses, felt free to write to Henry, warning him of the dangers he was incurring. Her letter has not been preserved, but James's reply suggests its contents: 'I have quite escaped, as yet, being alarmed by Alice's now impending advent. I *may* be wrong, and it *may* wreck and blight my existence, but it will have to exert itself tremendously to do so.' She was not even coming to visit him, he said; she was simply coming to Europe and

there is no question of her living with me. She is unspeakably un-dependent and independent, she *clings* no more than a bowsprit, has her own plans, purposes, preferences, practises, pursuits, more than anyone I know, has also amply sufficient means, etc. and, in short, even putting her possible failure to improve in health at the worst, will be very un-likely to tinge or modify my existence in any uncomfortable way.

It was quite true that Alice did not 'cling'. Nevertheless her illness, by its very nature, had its clinging side.

I

At Liverpool, where he met Alice's ship, James found his sister in a deplorable state. The voyage had not been rough; but she was in one of her fits of nervous prostration. She had to be carried off on a stretcher. Miss Loring had nursed her faithfully. Louisa, Katharine's sister, seemed in much better health than Alice, who was 'more infirm than I expected', Henry told his Aunt Kate. He had however 'perfect belief that she will not seem so after she has been on shore a week. But for the present I must rather give myself up to her.'

James discovered after some observation that his sister was markedly jealous of Louisa. She wanted Miss Loring for herself. And James, who had already noticed the attachment between the two – and who was now writing a novel about such an attachment – began to see the extent to which Miss Loring dominated his sister's existence. After Alice had been disembarked at Liverpool, James left her in the hands of a maid he had especially brought with him. Katharine Loring was taking Louisa to Bournemouth on the very next day. James had first thought Alice would be taken there as well, but Miss Loring's sister was, on her side, in a high state of nerves. Miss Loring tactfully suggested that Alice's arrival at the health-resort be postponed. After the better part of a week, which they spent in Liverpool, James took Alice to London and installed her with her maid at 40 Clarges Street, near his own lodgings. Later he moved her to No. 7 Bolton Row. By this time the drama of Katharine Loring and her two invalids was sufficiently clear. Louisa Loring and Alice James were engaged in a fierce subterranean competition for the nursing and attention of the stalwart Katharine. Alice would probably have been the last to admit that she was in a jealous rage whenever Katharine had to be with Louisa. The consequences, nevertheless, were that she sooner or later developed alarming symptoms. James would send an anxious telegram, and when Miss Loring dashed to the rescue, Alice's symptoms would subside. At the same time James observed another queer element in the situation. This was that even when the crisis was over, Alice insisted on remaining in bed so long as Miss Loring was available to care for her. 'I may be wrong in the matter,' he wrote to William,

but it rather strikes me as an effect that Katharine Loring has upon her – that as soon as they get together, Alice takes to her bed. This was the case as soon as Katharine came to London to see her (she had been up before) and she has now been recumbent (as a consequence of her little four-hour journey) ever since she reached Bournemouth.

James had finally taken her to that seaside resort when it became clear that Louisa was acquiring a considerable interest in English life and was on her way to recovery. The British doctors had given Alice a thorough examination: their verdict coincided with that of their American colleagues. They could find nothing organically wrong and they ended by treating her as neurasthenic. The move to Bournemouth was made in January 1885. His sister would have brighter and larger quarters than those available in Mayfair, and James commuted at fixed intervals to see her. So long as Miss Loring was with her, Alice had no particular need for Henry. But he promised her he would spend the spring in Bournemouth: it would be a good place to work and to avoid the London 'Season'. He took rooms there late in April, when the greater part of *The Bostonians* had been written. By that time he had called on still another Bournemouth invalid, Robert Louis Stevenson.

2

Before leaving London, Henry James had occasion to perform certain rites of friendship and loyalty for James Russell Lowell. Ever since his return to England, James had felt a certain solicitude for his old friend: he knew that his term of office would sooner or later end, and when it became clear that Cleveland would be the next American President, the novelist began to conjure up painful images. To Mrs Godkin, James wrote:

He [Lowell] has been living in social and material clover, the pet of countesses, the habitué of palaces, the intimate of dukes; and he will have to give it all up, in order to live again in the suburb of a suburb, look after his furnace, and see that his plank walk is laid down. I regard him as the sport of fortune, his situation preoccupies me much, and I lie awake at night thinking of it.

With all the reservations he had about Lowell's rusticity, his inability to be a 'real man of the world', James dearly loved him; and when in February 1885, Mrs Lowell died suddenly, the novelist felt his friend to be the sport of fortune indeed. For some days he remained with him, consoled him, gave him the companionship he needed. 'He is very quiet and simple – but I am very, *very* sorry for him,' James wrote to Lizzie Boott. 'The death of his wife leaves him much better conditions for remaining here, but there is no prospect whatever of his being left, and the idea of his returning, after these European years, to live alone in Cambridge, is too horrible.' James was reading his own ancient horror of Cambridge into Lowell's state. Nevertheless, Lowell too had now before him the vision of a lonely life in Elmwood, even though his relations with his wife had been perfunctory during the last few years, and he had been very much in the company of Mrs Smalley, wife of the *Tribune*'s London correspondent.

In due course Lowell left for America. The letter which James wrote to him, as he stepped down from the post he had brilliantly filled, was a kind of apotheosis to a whole phase of their London life; and it reflected the deep affection that had existed between them since they had become friends long ago in Paris :

As I look back upon the years of your mission my heart swells and almost breaks again (as it did when I heard you were superseded) at the thought that anything so perfect should be gratuitously destroyed. But there is a part of your function which can go on again, indefinitely, whenever you take it up – and that, I repeat, I hope you will do soon rather than late. I think with the tenderest pleasure of the many fireside talks I have had with you, from the first – and with a pleasure dimmed with sadness of so many of our more recent ones. You are tied to London now by innumerable cords and fibres, and I should be glad to think that you ever felt me, ever so lightly, pulling at one of them ... Don't forget that you have produced a relation between England and the United States which is really a gain to civilization and that you must come back to look after your work. You can't look after it there : that is the function of an Englishman – and if *you* do it there they will call you one. The only way you can be a good American is to return to our dear old stupid, satisfactory London, and to yours ever affectionately and faithfully, Henry James.

3

The novelist moved to Bournemouth in late April of 1885, when Miss Loring went to London with her sister. He was clearing the ground for the writing of *The Princess Casamassima*. It seemed to him that he could profit by his stay, minister to his sister's social needs, enjoy the sea air, and quietly pursue his novel. He took rooms on the ocean side, three minutes' walk from where Alice was staying. He did not much care for his lodgings, but they were adequate. Bournemouth he found wholly uninteresting, 'of an almost American newness and ugliness'. He enjoyed the view, however, especially of the Isle of Wight, which looked to him like a pretty marble toy on an ultramarine horizon. Alice had a nurse and a maid; and once or twice a day he would drop in for a twenty-minute visit. He did not stay longer because Alice was easily fatigued. In the afternoon, and sometimes in the evening, he became a regular caller at Skerryvore, where his favourite armchair was reserved for him and where he spent hours in happy talk with the euphoric Stevenson.

'An old acquaintance of mine is ripening into a new friend,' he told Miss Norton. Stevenson was 35, seven years younger than James; he had all the activity and make-believe of a boy in constant search of adventure. Certain of his letters to James, and the quality of his humour, greatly resemble the alertness and the liveliness of William James in his youth. Henry, on his side, seems to have embodied some image of benign authority for the ailing Scot. Disabled physically, as Stevenson was, he was extraordinarily prolific. He suffered little pain, and he seemed to have a rare capacity of pulling himself back, again and again, from the brink of death. Stevenson wrote verses to James, and received him with boundless affection and much ceremonial. Mrs Stevenson, who was American and older than her husband, treated her fellow-countryman with a certain awe and respect: the two transformed what might have been for James a lugubrious stay in Bournemouth into a pleasant literary and social way of life. So long as Alice had no crises, James fell into a happy routine of writing and visits to the two invalids.

The Stevensons lived in a house on the brink of the Alum Chine or gulley, a two-storey structure of yellow brick with a blue slate roof, overgrown with ivy. Its front faced away from the road to a garden sloping almost to the bottom of the Chine. They had renamed the place Skerryvore, after the great lighthouse built by the novelist's ancestor. Here, in the blue room, where hung a Venetian mirror which James had given to the Stevensons, they often received him and gave him a meal. Stevenson would sit at the end of the table rolling cigarettes in his long fingers. He had wide-set eyes, a straight nose, and long blonde moustaches over his thin lips. He wore bohemian velvet jackets; sometimes when it was cold he would drape himself in a maroon-coloured shawl, like a Mexican poncho. A passionate energy possessed his slight frame.

Stevenson's verses dedicated to Henry amused him. But when his friend published them he felt, with embarrassment, that privacy had been violated. The two best-known poems lead, in their moment of climax, to the entry of Henry James into Skerryvore – suggesting perhaps how much his daily coming was awaited. In a Shakespearean sonnet, in which Stevenson enumerated certain of Henry's female characters

> Lo, how these fair immaculate women walk
> Behind their jocund maker

(Madame de Mauves, Daisy, Laby Barb, Olive Chancellor), he ended with

> But he, attended by these shining names,
> Comes (best of all) himself – our welcome James.

The choice of characters was perhaps not too carefully pondered. No reader of *The Bostonians*, then or now, would regard Olive Chancellor as a 'fair immaculate woman'. The verses, however, were spontaneous and occasional, and must not be scrutinized too critically. The second poem celebrated the gift of the Venetian mirror; its last verse equally foreshadows an entrance. The mirror is speaking:

> Now with an outlandish grace,
> To the sparkling fire I face
> In the blue room at Skerryvore;
> Where I wait until the door
> Open, and the Prince of Men,
> Henry James, shall come again.

They had in common their devotion to style, their love of words and wit, their ranging imagination. Stevenson appreciated to the full the deliberate artistry of James; the latter enjoyed Stevenson's flair for vivid story-telling. In the first of the three essays he devoted to him, Henry speaks of his 'jauntiness'; he observes that heroines are wholly absent from his works and that 'the idea of making believe appeals to him much more than the idea of making love'. He characterized his work as 'the romance of boyhood' – which Stevenson had given to the world as other novelists deal with the peerage, or the police, or the medical profession. 'Though he takes such an interest in childish life, he takes no interest in the fireside,' James wrote. 'To his view the normal child is the child who absents himself from the family-circle.' This sense of his eternal boyishness endeared him to James.

'My only social resource,' he wrote to Howells,

is Robert Louis Stevenson, who is more or less dying here and who (in case that event should take place) gave me the other day a message of a friendly – very friendly – character to give to you when I should next see you. I shall wait till then – it is too long for a short letter. He is an interesting, charming creature, but I fear at the end of his tether; though indeed less apparently near death than he has been at other times.

Perhaps it was the fact that Stevenson seemed to consort on such amiable terms with the constant presence of death that gave an additional measure of intensity to this friendship. These were to be the days when they knew each other best. Stevenson was to live for another decade; and when he departed for the South Seas their correspondence took on the charm and spontaneity of their personal meetings. The letters can be read in the volume edited by Janet Adam Smith; the tone of communication on both sides continued to be one of deep affection, of unending friendship. It was at Skerryvore in 1886 that Stevenson gave James a copy of Kidnapped, inscribing it 'And I wish I had a better work to give as good a man.' The copy is scrawled with James's notes made during his reading.

4

James's closeness to Alice during these weeks gave him a clearer picture of certain of her problems. Whatever her physical ailments, if any, which medicine could not then diagnose, it was clear that she was involved in an inextricable human relationship. Early in May there was 'a cataclysm'. The companion-nurse he had engaged for his sister was something of a martinet and insisted on treating her as if she were 'a morbid and hysterical patient'. She 'proved a very high-tempered, decided, bridling little body,' James told Aunt Kate. But she was merely a small part of the episode. The point was that Miss Loring's presence was required, 'and Louisa is turning out so much better, that she could easily come'. An ordinary trained nurse was substituted for the spirited companion: and Katharine announced that she would, in a month or two, return to Alice, and release Henry. Louisa's weak lungs seemed cured, and, said James,

Katharine comes back to Alice for a permanency. Her being with her may be interrupted by absences, but evidently it is the beginning of a living-together, for the rest of such time as Alice's life may last. I think that a conviction on K's part *at bottom*, beneath her superficial optimism, that it *may not* last long, has something to do with these arrangements – for evidently it is a kind of definite understanding between them.

James felt that there was no alternative but to accept gratefully Miss Loring's willingness and generosity. He was not convinced that the relationship was a good one. There was something profoundly symbiotic in it. Alice took too much joy in being cared for by her friend. But there was nothing anyone else could do. 'There is about as much possibility of Alice's giving Katharine up,' he told his aunt,

as of her giving her legs to be sawed off. She said to me a few days ago that she believed if she could have Katharine *quietly* and *uninterruptedly*, for a year, 'to relieve her of all responsibility' she would get well. Amen! She will get well, or she won't, but, either way, it lies between them-selves. I shall devote my best energies to taking the whole situation less hard in the future than I have hitherto.

In a second letter to his aunt, a few days later, James directly attributed Alice's decline to her having had to share Miss Loring with Louisa. 'If Katharine is able to stay with A. with some *continuity*, which is her evident intention, allowing for short interrup-tions, Alice may go on, I don't say to recovery, but to no more certain or rapid decline, as she would if she were separated from her and constantly yearning and telegraphing for her.' And James went on to say that whenever Miss Loring would return,

I shall assent with a good grace, for the simple reason that it is the only thing I can do unless I take Alice completely on my own shoulders – which is obviously impossible, from every point of view. And if you were here you wouldn't make that any easier. Alice, too, would then have *five* people under contribution, really, to take care of her, and she has quite enough now.

A solution had been found for a deeply complicated situation. Louisa Loring did make a complete recovery and her elder sister increasingly confined herself to Alice. The novelist was liberated to pursue his work. But he was to continue to have Alice on his mind, and he frequently hesitated to take trips away from England on her account. She held him by her invalidism in a delicate moral bondage; but he too, at a later stage, derived an enormous gratification from seeing her frequently and bringing to her bedside the wide world in which he moved. Alice rarely left her bed after her arrival in England. She refused to risk a return voyage to America, and during the seven years that remained to her she lived largely in London and in Leamington. In her journal she recorded her gratitude to her brother's devotion, one day in March 1890:

Henry came on the 10th to spend the day; Henry the Patient, I should call him. Five years ago in November I crossed the water, and suspended myself like an old woman of the sea around his neck, where to all appearances I shall remain for all time. I have given him endless care and anxiety but notwithstanding this and the fantastic nature of my troubles I have never seen an impatient look upon his face or heard an unsympathetic or misunderstanding sound cross his lips. He comes at my slightest sign and hangs on to whatever organ may be in eruption, and gives me balm and solace by assuring me that my nerves are his nerves and my stomach his stomach – this last pitch of brotherly devotion never before approached by the race. He has never remotely hinted that he expected me to be well at any given moment, that burden which fond friend and relative so inevitably impose upon the cherished invalid.

She likened James's personal 'susceptibility' to her father's. The elder Henry James had spent many hours beside her bed long ago. To the end Alice wrested from the hovering Miss Loring and the loyal brother a full amount of attention and love which, in some large way, she felt had been denied her during an earlier period of her existence.

107

A Very American Tale

IN *The Bostonians* Henry James wrote the most considerable American novel of its decade. For all its compulsive detail, there is no other novel of such value and distinction to place on the bookshelf of the late nineteenth century: *Huckleberry Finn* might form an incongruous companion, but it belongs to a wholly different genre – as Mark Twain doubtless would have insisted, for he said he would rather be damned to John Bunyan's Heaven than read *The Bostonians*. Most Americans of the time shared Mark Twain's feeling; and the editors of the *Century*, where the ill-fated book ran through thirteen months, said they had never published a serial which had encountered such an awesome silence.

The first notation for the book was made on 8 April 1883 when James was in Boston, and in setting it down he spoke of it in the past tense – as if the novel were already written. 'I wished to write a very *American* tale, a tale very characteristic of our social conditions, and I asked myself what was the most salient and peculiar point in our social life. The answer was: the situation of women, the decline of the sentiment of sex, the agitation on their behalf.' Another notation, however, also exists. It is a single word, scrawled across the flyleaf of the *Correspondence of Thomas Carlyle and Ralph Waldo Emerson*, which James read and reviewed just after his father's and Emerson's death. The word is 'Reformers', and the page-number attached to it refers us to a passage in a letter of Emerson's: 'We are all a little wild here with numberless projects of social reform.' The novel which he finally began more than a year later brought together the two subjects – Boston reformers and the 'situation of women'.

Later, as his book took shape, James was to discover that the subject was 'less interesting and repaying than I had assumed it to be'. Perhaps he knew Boston too well; and the theme was clearly uncongenial. A kind of nagging hand seemed to tug at his pen; the fluid stylist of the international tales was replaced by Balzacian detail. Each scene was described with an exhaustive minuteness. If he was playing the French 'naturalist', he seemed almost hypnotized by his material. The first evening of the novel is spread through nine chapters; the next day occupies three more. Almost a quarter of the book is used to describe the opening hours of the tale – to be sure with a great deal of earlier history and retrospective analysis thrown in. We meet the hero in these chapters, and then he disappears until the middle of the book; the novel sprawls in a manner wholly alien to the author of *Washington Square* and *The Portrait of a Lady*. It has many fine pages, and much fine writing; and yet a kind of uncontrollable prolixity is everywhere. He had intended to tell his story as a six-part serial, of the length of *Washington Square*. And he was not paid for the seven additional instalments which he wrote. Having sold the novel outright for a given period to Osgood, he had nothing to gain by more than doubling its length save the dubious satisfaction of bringing into being a weighty 950-page manuscript.

The Bostonians is a strange instance of a writer of power so possessed by his material that he loses his mastery of it. What happened may be likened to a lecturer who cannot bring himself to stop at the end of his allotted time. Something in the very nature of the story, the deep animus James felt for certain aspects of Boston life, took possession. In the end James recognized this. He excluded the novel from the New York Edition. He admitted that it was 'too diffuse and insistent – far too describing and explaining and expatiating'. He confessed to William, 'I should have been more rapid and had a lighter hand.' His readers of that time agreed. The modern reader may also squirm over some of the *longueurs*: yet today the book's social documentation has an historical interest, and the writing is never without vividness. Moreover the 'women's liberation' movements of our century have given the novel a new actuality.

I

The drama of *The Bostonians* resides in a struggle for possession not unlike the drama of Katharine Loring, her sister, and Alice James. Olive Chancellor, a wealthy, chill, unyielding Boston intellectual, simmers in chronic anger over the subservience of women to men. She is capable indeed of no other passion. The usual things of her life fill her with 'silent rage'. Encountering a young and inexperienced girl named Verena Tarrant, who possesses a strange histrionic oratorical gift, she recognizes in her the instrument she lacks. Verena's wondrous gift of speech is carefully documented: her 'conditioning' began as a baby – in the era before baby-sitters – when she was taken by her parents to the inspirational lectures common in early New England. Verena is a product of the Puritan preacher, and the old travelling-tent institution known as the Chatauqua which brought 'culture' to outlying areas of America. She is schooled in primitive American grandiloquence. As a child in modern times may babble the 'commercials' heard on television, Verena develops into a finished Boston parrot, with all the orotundities and inflections of the old-time speech-makers in her voice. Her father, by a kind of laying on of hands, turns on this flood of 'built-in' verbiage. And Verena, although she does not have an idea in her rather pretty little head, can assemble fragments and phrases of remembered sentences into a meaningless semblance of unity. It occurs to Olive that she should adopt this girl; she would impart noble thoughts and noble aims to her; make her the sounding-box of the American feminist movement. Verena's parents readily accept; it seems natural to them that their girl-prodigy should acquire a patroness. And many pages of *The Bostonians* are devoted to the domestic evenings spent by the two women at Olive's fireside, reading great authors and planning a major assault on the citadels of masculinity.

James intended the story to be 'a study of one of those friendships between women which are so common in New England'. Modern critics have tended accordingly to regard the novel as portraying a 'lesbian' attachment; and doubtless Olive's masculinity, her hatred of men and her passion for Verena bespeak what would today be called a 'latent homosexuality'. But in terms of James's time, and Boston morality, it is more accurate to see the relationship in its overt nature: had Olive obtained physical possession of Verena, her need of her as an instrument of power probably would have diminished considerably. The focus of the story is on Olive's fierce possessiveness; the drama is her struggle to keep Verena from marrying Basil Ransom, a weak, easy but also powerfully possessive Southerner, a remote relative of hers. An 'outsider' in Boston and New York, all but recently an 'enemy' in the Confederate army, he has come north as a struggling lawyer because his father's plantations were ruined by the war. Ransom has pretensions to high social ideas; but an editor to whom he submits an article informs him his 'doctrines were about three hundred years behind the age; doubtless some magazine of the sixteenth century would have been very happy to print them'. While Ransom is sometimes a vehicle for Jamesian opinions – particularly his fear of the feminization of American life – he is in general presented as a shallow, egotistical individual. James himself told John Hay he was made up 'of wandering airs and chance impressions' and was 'rather vague and artificial, quite *fait de chic*'. Hay told James that Lucius Q. C. Lamar, a popular senator from Mississippi, whom James had met in Washington, seemed to recognize something of himself in the character. James confessed that he was 'in it a little ... one of the very few Mississipians with whom I have had the pleasure of conversing'.

The struggle between Olive, all rectitude and flaming feminine politics, and Ransom, determined to place Verena in the kitchen and the nursery, has in it elements of strong drama and high comedy. James, however, became so interested in the clashing egos that he did little with Verena herself. The reader seldom feels that the girl's conflict is serious: at best she will be a kind of oratorical actress or a submissive wife. James invests the situation with many interesting developments, but the tug-of-war is too protracted; moreover the subsidiary characters, which illuminate his study of American life, do not sufficiently advance the action. Had *The Bostonians* been written with James's usual economy and the same wit as *The Europeans*, he would have created something close to 'the great American novel' of which he had dreamed in his youth. What he created instead was a series of vignettes; and certain pages valuably critical of American institutions – the invasion of privacy by the press, the meddlesome character of Boston reformers, the general tawdriness and banality of certain aspects of American life of the time.

The reader is made to believe that in the struggle between Olive and Ransom he is watching a struggle between good and evil; James had represented an analogous struggle in *The Portrait of a Lady* between Isabel and Osmond. But it is again a struggle between mirror-images. Ransom and Olive are both egotists. Neither loves Verena for herself; she is an object to be acquired and used as the instrument of a personal idea. Ransom, one feels, is almost as dedicated to defeating Olive as marrying Verena. And Olive is too morbid and hysterical and jealous to make us believe she has Verena's good at heart. Here again those who have read the novel as 'lesbian' tend to see Ransom in a better light than James represents him – for they read him in the belief that he is rescuing Verena from Olive's depravity. James has little respect for either of his contending personages. It is their struggle for power which he finds fascinating; they are ruthless, self-seeking, blind to the feelings of others, aware only of their own needs. Olive wants to make Verena a projection of herself; Ransom is sufficiently of the post-war South still to believe that some persons should be enslaved by others. A cardboard Southerner, he is never less convincing than when he is trying to woo Verena. The ending of the novel defies the great tradition of romantic fiction. As Ransom leads Verena from the large hall in which she was to have made her most brilliant speech, he discovers she is in tears. 'It is to be feared,' says the unreconciled narrator, 'that with the union, so far from brilliant, into which she was about to enter, these were not the last she was destined to shed.'

2

The print in the *Century* was hardly dry on the early chapters of this novel when Henry James received word from his Aunt Kate, from James Russell Lowell and from his brother William that he had lampooned a much respected Boston reformer, Miss Elizabeth Peabody, the elderly sister-in-law of Hawthorne, whose good works and crusading zeal were famous. 'It is a pretty bad business,' William wrote, and Henry showed some perturbation over this remark. He pleaded not guilty. At best he had thought of Miss Peabody's spectacles on the bridge of her nose when he had described his character Miss Birdseye – 'the whole moral history of Boston was reflected in her displaced spectacles'. Doubtless certain passages in the three full pages devoted to her could fit all reformers. 'She belonged to the Short-Skirts league, as a matter of course; for she belonged to any and every league that had been founded for almost any purpose whatever.' The next sentence was an example of the way in which James tended to editorialize in this novel.

This did not prevent her from being a confused, entangled, inconsequent old woman, whose charity began at home and ended nowhere, whose credulity kept pace with it, and who knew less about her fellow-creatures, if possible, after fifty years of humanity zeal than on the day she had gone into the field to testify against the iniquity of most arrangements.

This sounds almost as if he were scolding. When she shakes hands with the hero it is to give him 'a delicate, dirty, democratic little hand'.

Henry replied to William that he had not seen Miss Peabody for twenty-five years, and that he had always had the most casual observation of her. 'Miss Birdseye,' he said, 'was evolved entirely from my moral consciousness like every person I have ever drawn.' He had wanted to describe 'an old, weary, battered and simple-minded woman', so as not to be left open to the charge of treating all the reformers 'in a contemptuous manner'. In subsequent instalments he enlarged Miss Peabody's heroism and her death-scene at the end of the novel, on Cape Cod, is one of the most charmingly narrated parts of the book. William, when he read the volume entire, withdrew his criticisms and praised it, but felt that it was overdone. Neither he nor anyone at the time noticed the close relationship between the names of the real-life character and the fictional lady. A 'bird's eye' is indeed a 'pea-body'. Henry James had perhaps imitated life more than he himself allowed.

3

A few weeks before he had begun the writing of this novel James composed a short story, *The Author of 'Beltraffio'*, published in the spring of 1884 in the *English Illustrated Magazine*. It is generally listed among his tales of the literary life. The tale is not concerned so much with literature as with a difficult marital situation, and a Medea-like dénouement. It had its origin in James's hearing from Edmund Gosse that the wife of John Addington Symonds intensely disliked his writings. James did not know at that time that Symond's homosexuality was the real issue. But he clearly had some divination of it and made it a subtle and poisonous narrative of Mark Ambient's struggle with his wife for possession – body and soul – of their exquisite little boy Dolcino. The mother's morbid fear that Dolcino will be contaminated by what she sees as evil in his father's art causes her to perform the act of Medea. She fails to summon medical help when the child falls ill, and Dolcino dies. The horror of the story is mitigated by the 'distance' James gives it through the eyes of an American spectator, an admirer of Ambient's, and his blandness of observation. The story is complex, subtle, unpleasant, throwing a delicate veil over the mother's ferocity and Ambient's helplessness. Mrs Ambient is the baleful female of many of James's tales, capable of doing away with husband or child, whether we meet her in her insouciant cruelty and selfishness in *The Pupil*, in her calculated perversity in *The Other House*, or in her courageous anxiety and madness in *The Turn of the Screw*. In these tales the bright piping voice of innocence is extinguished and the male is deprived of issue by a castrating female.

This tale of a struggle for possession heralded the struggle in *The Bostonians*. It seemed as if Henry James were back in some dim passage of childhood or youth in which he had felt himself identified with a powerful mother, whose strength is so often represented in the stories, and at the same time with the image of his maimed father. The picture of the American female in this novel is that of her pushing, ruling, dominating mastery of men and children, and her threat to American life. The disappearance of the home in

Quincy Street, the now permanent absence of a Cambridge hearth, is probably the single deepest emotion out of which *The Bostonians* sprang. There are moments, in Ransom's pleading for the *status quo*, against *all* change, when he seems to be only a degree less hysterical than Olive. The paradox of *The Bostonians* was that while James intellectually was holding up a satirical mirror to the city of his youth, another and younger self within him seemed to plead almost tearfully that nothing be altered, that he could not face the severed cable of his old anchorage. In the final scene in which Ransom insists that at this crucial moment Verena must make her choice, there is an urgency and a shrillness that may bespeak the author's own shrill anxiety. *The Bostonians* was the novel in which James wrote out the immediate anguish of the collapse of his old American ties, and he coupled this with a kind of vibrating anger that Boston should be so unfriendly as to let him go. It incorporated as well Miss Loring's serene and full possession of Alice. In accommodating himself to his new London life, he was in some deep underworld of emotion reliving ancient and morbid states. This, we might speculate, lay at the bottom of his inability to discipline the material of his novel, and his need to drag it out beyond its prescribed length. His next novel was to be about reformers as well, and was to contain within it also a struggle for power and possession. But in writing it he could look away from the struggle itself and focus upon its victim. What he had left out of the character of Verena, the orator, in *The Bostonians*, he was able to put into the character of Hyacinth, the bookbinder, in *The Princess Casamassima*.

While the last chapters of *The Bostonians* were appearing, there occurred a serious financial crisis in Henry's affairs. His American publisher, James R. Osgood, went bankrupt. Osgood had published James from the first; he was a man of integrity, but he had apparently managed his business poorly. He had five of Henry's books on his list, two early works, two volumes of tales and the impending Boston novel. Henry had not received a penny of the $5,000 promised him for the American, British and serial rights of that work, although Osgood had by now been paid for the *Century* serialization. The novelist acted immediately to recover his various copyrights. Ticknor and Co., which superseded Osgood, at first offered to pay James $4,000 and restore to him the English rights in the novel. These he promptly sold to Macmillan, to whom he also sold both

English and American rights to his next novel. However, at the last moment the new firm withdrew its offer and Macmillan took over *The Bostonians* for American issue as well. Not only had James not received a penny for the serial, but his advance against royalties from Macmillan did not approximate to the substantial sum due him. In a word he had little to show for his year's work.

This financial crisis lasted thoughout the spring of 1885 and produced a great deal of uneasiness and insecurity in James. He could, however, expect a substantial sum from the solvent *Atlantic Monthly* for his next work. He would have liked, on the strength of this, to proceed to the Continent. He wrote to Lizzie Boott of his yearning to surrender his Bolton Street rooms and to wander for a couple of years in foreign parts. But he was for the moment tied to England by the necessity for 'production' and by the silver cord – and the common humanity – that bound him to his sister.

Part Two:
Art and Politics

108

The Naturalist

ONE morning in early December 1884 the author of *The Art of Fiction* might have been seen standing in the damp and cold outside a dark and gloomy building with towers, on the edge of the Thames, well-known to Victorians as Millbank Prison. London no longer knows it. A more congenial climate reigns in that neighbourhood today, for some of the sprawling acres of Millbank support the Tate Gallery. The prison's walls were bare and brown; the building had ugly pinnacles; its aspect was sad, stern, impersonal. Millbank had been erected in the last year of the eighteenth century, from designs by Jeremy Bentham. Its outer walls formed an irregular octagon; and within these walls it had housed – in its accommodation for 1,120 prisoners – almost a century of human misery. The entire place seemed blighted, and the Thames at this point seemed poisonous: dreariness on this bank and dreariness across the way – long-necked chimneys, deposits of rubbish, unsightly gasometers.

Henry James, standing before the forbidding entrance, pulled hard at the bell. Somewhere within, he seemed to hear a remote stiff ring. Then the gates slowly opened, and he was allowed to go into a kind of dimness, while behind him he heard the rattle of the keys and the slamming of the bolts. After that, looking about him, fixing everything with his eyes, he was conducted through a stony court in which female figures dressed in brown misfitting uniforms and hoods marched in a circle. He squeezed up steep staircases, past circular shafts of cells, where he could see captives through grated peepholes, He edged past prisoners in the corridors, silent women, with staring eyes.

James had never felt himself so walled in – walls within walls, galleries on galleries. The daylight had lost its colour; and he lost the sense of time.

He was carefully conducted through the establishment in accordance with the arrangements he had previously made. He asked questions. But largely he looked – attentively, reflectively. The very stones on which he walked seemed sinister. 'Millbank Prison,' he was to write, 'is a worse act of violence than any it was erected to punish.' He asked to be shown the infirmary. The chambers behind the grates seemed naked with small stiff beds occupied by white faced women in tight, sordid caps.

Then bolts and keys made a scraping noise behind him once more; he was outside again, in the common London day. It was almost as if he were being released from prison, from all the sordid misery within its walls. He regained Bolton Street, the sight of familiar things, the usual movement and sound of Piccadilly. In his rooms he wrote a letter to T. S. Perry: 'I have been all the morning at Mill-bank Prison (horrible place) collecting notes for a fiction scene. You see,' he added, 'I am quite the Naturalist. Look out for the same – a year hence.'

109

The Peacock and the Butterfly

A QUEER little episode occurred in Henry James's life at this time; queer enough for him to have preserved a small relic of it – and queerer still as we look at it from this long after-time. He had sent off the first chapters – the prison sequence – of *The Princess Casamassima* from Bournemouth in June 1885; and then had come up to London early in July to find a house for his sister and Katharine Loring. They had agreed that Bournemouth could be abandoned. In London James received a letter from Sargent:

Dear James, I remember that you once said that an occasional French-man was not an unpleasant diversion to you in London, and I have been so bold as to give a card of introduction to you to two friends of mine. One is Dr S[amuel] Pozzi, the man in the red gown (not always), a very brilliant creature, and the other is the unique extra-human Montesquiou of whom you may have heard Bourget speak with bitterness, but who was to Bourget to a certain extent what Whistler is to Oscar Wilde. (Take warning and do not bring them together.) They are going to spend a week in London and I fancy Montesquiou will be anxious to see as much of Rossetti's and Burne Jones's work as he can.

This letter remained among James's papers although all the other Sargent letters were destroyed, and we can only surmise that it was perhaps James's way of reminding himself of his encounter with Dr Pozzi, Count Robert de Montesquiou and a third whom Sargent added to his group, Prince Edmond de Polignac. James had found, after a week's search, a cottage on Hampstead Heath which he took for two months. He was about to return to Bournemouth when the 'three Frenchmen', as he wrote to Miss Reubell, 'bearing introductions from Sargent and yearning to see London aestheticism', arrived. James was perhaps not the best guide to the aesthetes, to Wilde or Whistler. But to do Sargent's introduction proper honour, he put off his departure and devoted Thursday and Friday, 2 and 3 July 1885, to entertaining them.

Robert de Montesquiou was, by this time, well-known in Paris as the homosexual eccentric and dandy who had furnished Huysmans his character of Des Esseintes in *A Rebours*, a novel which, in turn, would influence Oscar Wilde. A tall thin man, who described himself as looking like a greyhound in a greatcoat, he had upward-pointed and waxed moustaches, used make-up, dressed with such perfection that the art of the tailor became invisible. 'A rare flower bloomed in his buttonhole, and also in his conversation.' The 'Prince of Decadence' cultivated exotic perfumes, and exotic colours to match the music he listened to; he called himself the 'sovereign of transitory things', and his conversation and anecdotes were as artfully contrived as his manner of life. He was allied to 'the greater part of the European aristocracy' and endowed with sufficient wealth to take care of such an alliance. Proust was to say that he 'makes a work of art of his own absurdity' and to add that he had 'stylized it marvellously'. Léon Daudet, whose bourgeois royalism could not understand that a deeply-dyed aristocrat should seek fame in letters, saw him as 'drunk with loneliness and garrulity'. The Count was some twelve years younger than James; and the only Jamesian impression we have of him was a remark to Miss Reubell that 'Montesquiou is curious, but slight'. When we recall how James had fled the Wagnerian homosexuals at Naples, it is clear that he was now less terrified – and even amused. Dr Pozzi, whom James characterized as 'charming' and whom he saw later in Paris, had been an early subject for Sargent, who painted him in his red gown; he was a society doctor, a book-collector, a cultivated conversationalist. He was three years younger than James. The third of the visitors, a man in his 60s, Edmond de Polignac, was an amateur musician and a man of considerable personal charm.

Two brief notes to Montesquiou in James's elegant French show that on the first of the two days he devoted to his visitors he took the Prince to see '*tous les Burne-Jones et tous les Rossettis possible*'. The round of galleries included a trip to Chelsea which charmed Montesquiou. On the second day James was host at a dinner at the Reform to which came James McNeill Whistler, the Prince and the Count. Whistler and Montesquiou, adepts at self-contemplation, charmed one another. The butterfly of art fluttered before adulation. Sargent had been accurate in the equation he had drawn of Montesquiou-Bourget and Whistler-Wilde. The dinner ultimately resolved itself into an obsessive desire on the part of Montesquiou to see Whistler's celebrated 'Peacock Room' in the mansion of the shipping magnate, F. R. Leyland. With Montesquiou it was the case of a dandy fascinated not only by Whistler but by his choice of the very bird that expressed his dandyism; one might risk the remark that Whistler, his painted peacocks and Montesquiou were all birds of a feather. Indeed Montesquiou wrote a poem *The Dying Peacock*, which Proust was to quote with admiration in a youthful and flattering essay consecrated to the verse-making nobleman :

> Living, he shone, and in his death he shines,
> Teaching us to die in all serenity.*

Whistler's peacock murals had an extraordinary history which may be read in the biographies of the artist. Some years before he had boldly redecorated the dining-room of Leyland's elaborate house during the owner's absence from London. Its walls had been covered with old Spanish leather brought to England long ago by Catherine of Aragon, and displaying her coat of arms – Whistler found its surface irresistible – and upon it he painted his extravagant birds in a blaze of gold and intensities of blue. Leyland had bowed before this *fait accompli*, which deprived him of his historic and ancient leather and substituted the flights of Whistler's extravagant imagination; he had even paid Whistler for this self-indulgence.

It fell to James to make the arrangements for the visit to the room, since Whistler was occupied the next day; but the painter, on the other hand, undertook to lunch James's guests on the Sunday and to conduct them personally to the scene of his handiwork. Whistler told James where to write, and late that Friday evening James sent off his 'complicated tale' to the family of the American artist George H. Boughton. In conformity with Whistler's instructions he invited

---

* *Il rayonnait vivant, il rayonne défunt,*
Il enseigne à mourir d'une façon sereine.

Mrs Boughton and Miss Boughton to lunch on Sunday at Whistler's.
'It seems odd that *I* should be inviting Mrs Boughton and you,' he
wrote to the younger of the two, 'to lunch with Whistler! – especially as I shall not be there myself, as I return to the country tomorrow.' And he added: 'But on the whole nothing that relates to
Whistler is queerer than anything else.' He apologized for this
'strange, irregular roundabout communication'. The gist of the
matter was that Whistler

has taken my Frenchmen on his back for a part of Sunday, that they
hunger and thirst to behold the mystic apartment, that he begs you and
Mrs Boughton to help him to show it to them (he speaks as if you had
all the facilities for it!) and also, if possible, to lunch with him – and
that I, to further the matter, have undertaken, to save time, to write to
you. I hope I don't bewilder or bother you too much.

We have few further details. Montesquiou wrote James an effusive 'thank-you' note and James replied with one of his large
flourishes. He told the Count that England might seem to have a dull
surface but this was, he said, a mask – *un masque trompeur des
jouissances qui vous attendent*. We now know that the American
novelist spent his two days with three of Proust's future characters.
Montesquiou would become Charlus. Elements of Polignac apparently went into the fashioning of Bergotte. Pozzi became Cottard. It
was a case of a novelist of the nineteenth century consorting with
the real-life characters of a novel of the twentieth.

110

34 De Vere Gardens

The Princess Casamassima is one of Henry James's most loosely-
written books. We may ascribe this in part to many interruptions,
his fatigue after writing a work as long as *The Bostonians*, his constant worry about his sister. During the summer of 1885 he installed
her in Hampstead; and when she seemed comfortable in that environment he left for Dover where he had worked so well before.
'*The Princess* will give me hard, continuous work for many months
to come,' he wrote in his notebooks, 'but she will also give me joys
too sacred to write about.'

He wrote steadily that summer. In the autumn of 1885 he paid the first of what would be a series of visits to the village of Broadway, in Worcestershire, then in its pristine state. Here a group of American artists had gathered around the household of Frank Millet, originally an illustrator and now painting in oils. They shared a large studio – Millet, Edwin A. Abbey, Sargent who joined them, and put up at the Lygon Arms, and certain English illustrators and painters as well, among them Alfred Parsons and Frederick Barnard. Millet had converted The Priory behind his house into a studio and here Sargent painted his celebrated *Carnation Lily, Lily Rose*. James was at ease with his 'brothers of the brush', as he had been with John La Farge long ago. The place lent itself to picturesque paintings – open doorways, brown interiors, old-fashioned gardens, the geese on the green, patches, jumbles, glimpses of colour. James explored the Cotswolds in a dogcart, walked to Chipping Camden, 'a place of rapture', and became a fast friend of Millet whose 'Yankee energy' he admired and of Abbey, whom he considered 'a pure genius' from Philadelphia.

Edmund Gosse, who visited the group on a later occasion, remembered how Henry James was at the centre of it. This was the James of the time of the Sargent sketch, done in less than an hour at Broadway, the straight-eyed profile which later appeared in the *Yellow Book*. 'Not much serious work was done,' Gosse testified, 'everything was food for laughter.' He remembered a 'rollicking day' rowing down the winding Avon from Evesham to Pershore, with much singing and Abbey twanging his banjo. James presided, his face set in his vague darkish brown beard, 'a sort of bearded Buddha, at the prow'. Out of these visits grew James's series of articles on the American illustrators, later assembled in his small book *Picture and Text*. He disliked illustrations when they were intended for his stories; but he enormously liked the illustrators. 'Ah, your illustrations – your illustrations,' he exclaimed to an editor of the *Century*, 'how, as a writer, one hates 'em; and how their being good as they are makes one hate 'em more! What one writes suffers essentially as literature, from going with them, and the two things ought to stand alone.'

Early in the autumn of 1885 he re-visited Paris, saw certain of his old friends, including the dying Mrs Edward Childe whom he had visited at her little castle at Montargis a decade earlier. She had tuberculosis, but still held court, and James predicted she would be 'agreeable, graceful, intelligent to the last'. He also saw most of his literary friends and at Bourget's met the Normandy novelist, Jules-Amédée Barbey d'Aurevilly, who had once known Beau Brummel. In October he was summoned back to Alice; she had had a neuresthenic episode. He recognized that he would have to keep himself always available.

I

He spent, after this, thirteen consecutive months in London, interrupted only by occasional country visits. He felt he should see Alice regularly. And his serial was exacting; he had left himself small margin – he was never more than two or three instalments ahead of the printer. There was however still another reason, almost as compelling. Early in December 1885 he announced that he had signed a twenty-one year lease for an apartment in Kensington. Nothing could have sounded more 'permanent'. His decision was a measure of the perspective he had gained in the two further years in Bolton Street after his parents' death. He had sought a house in St John's Wood in 1883 out of childhood memories. Now he moved into the neighbourhood consecrated by Thackeray with a sense of its fulfilling immediate needs, its agreeable 'suburban' qualities and its proximity to the centre of London life. A few decades before it had been distinctly a suburb, with a daily coach to Piccadilly, James was to characterize it as 'the once-delightful, the Thackerayan, with its literary vestiges, its quiet pompous red palace, its square of Queen Anne, its house of Lady Castlewood, its Greyhound Tavern, where Henry Esmond lodged'. For a walker of James's propensities, the distance across Kensington Gardens, through Hyde Park, to Piccadilly offered salutary exercise after hours at his desk.

His rooms in Bolton Street had been dark and small; now he had light, space and air in his fourth-floor flat in De Vere Mansions, a substantial Victorian building. A long row of western windows flooded the place with light. An enormous window, with the immensity of London spread below it, provided a place for his desk. There was a sitting-room, in addition to his study, and a 'grand salon' which served also as a library; there was a comfortable bedroom, a guest-room, servants' quarters. His windows offered a great deal of sky; some looked down upon gardens. The place had a lift, very much like a Parisian apartment. The house was located at the end of a wide street named after England's historic De Veres. No. 13 De Vere

Mansions, or 34 De Vere Gardens, became Henry's address. He gave his publisher as his reference to a landlord who appeared never to have heard of Mr Henry James. And he had the enjoyable experience for the first time in his life of wandering in shops, looking for old pieces of furniture and decorating his rooms to his taste. There would be no Chippendale, he assured his friends, and no treasures and spoils: he wanted large fat bourgeois sofas, solid tables and chairs: nothing original, 'expectedness everywhere'. For his sitting-room he chose Whistlerian blues and yellows, and in his salon the 'richest crimson'. He spoke of 'my chaste and secluded Kensington quatrième', and 'my new-and-airy conducive-to-quiet-and-work apartment'. A month after his installation he told William the place was 'perfection'. Presently he engaged a man and his wife – their name was Smith – on board-wages, for £10 a month. In the mornings Mrs Smith, wooden-faced and always with the same shy frightened manner, would interview the master, wearing her large clean white apron, to get her 'orders of the day'. Presently also he was able to have a long-wanted pet – a dachshund – upon which he bestowed the name of Tosca. She was the first of several dogs to whom he gave a wealth of affection and who offered him their disinterested devotion during his working solitude.

Henry James was finally domesticated in London. He no longer needed to dine out. He could receive friends and reciprocate hospitality. And he was sufficiently removed from the hubbub of Piccadilly to relish the tranquillity of his neighbourhood. As he emerged from De Vere Mansions and turned left, he had a pleasant view of the green of Kensington Gardens at the end of the street – as he had had the view of Green Park in Bolton Street. Near by, in all the redundant dignity of its baroque, was the Albert Memorial. And if De Vere Gardens received an eminent novelist, it was to harbour presently a famous poet as well. In the year following James's installation, Robert Browning acquired the house at No. 22, a few doors down, on the opposite side of the street. For the remainder of Browning's life Henry had as neighbour an author who had once deeply influenced him, and whom he now regarded with a mixture of respect for his genius and surprise at his worldliness.

During the early months of his residence in De Vere Gardens, James testified to his permanent establishment in the heart of Britain by writing an essay on London, as he had written essays on Rome and Florence and Venice long before. It is perhaps the best of the series, certainly the most saturated with the 'sense of place'. He wrote of the city of his adoption as a frank 'London-lover', and one who had walked it now for years, along Piccadilly or in Camden Town, in Kilburn, or in Lambeth. The city had for him 'the most romantic town-vistas in the world', and when he stood on the bridge over the Serpentine, he found that the towers of Westminster, seen from the shining stretch of Hyde Park water, were no less impressive than those of Notre-Dame rising from their island in the Seine. He expressed his affection for 'dirty Bloomsbury on one side and dirtier Soho on the other', and his profound feeling for the metropolis whose grandeur he knew and whose poverty and suffering had come to be 'a part of the general vibration'. The essay is written in a vein of autobiography – his memories of his first visits, his perception of London at its different seasons, his knowledge of its clubs and the life of Mayfair and Belgravia. As he had written his essay on *Venice* when he had emotionally taken possession of it, so his *London* followed *The Princess Casamassima* and his establishment in his own apartment. It was his way of saying that he had at last taken root in the particular spot which communicated 'the greatest sense of life'.

2

Alice, living in Bolton Row, was having the best and most animated winter of her residence in England. She had moved into small furnished lodgings with Katharine after vacating the house on the Heath. And when her companion left her for a while, she seemed quite reconciled to her brother's serving as a substitute. She had also at all times a nurse-companion. Her guests were not numerous. Sometimes Mr Lowell, when he was in London; Fenimore appears to have been welcomed; Mrs Kemble, with the infirmities of her age, came when she could, and sent flowers when she couldn't; Mrs Humphry Ward, Emma Wilkinson Pertz, Mrs Mason, Mrs John Richard Green, widow of the historian Alice had once admired, were among the others. We have but few comments on her callers from Alice, save a remark in one letter to a friend that the 'crude and unadulterated American product, Mrs Mason, comes in very often. She is a very curious study with much that is generous and fine in the midst of her undisciplined crudity.' Mrs Mason belonged to an older and perhaps more plain-spoken generation. She always succeeded in irritating Mr Hoppin at the Legation. But Alice's sharpness

was characteristic: and people and events were scrutinized mercilessly from the world of her sick-room. 'My sister is doing exceedingly well and keeping an American salon,' James told Godkin. 'That
is, she lies on her sofa, and the earnest and the frivolous alike crowd
to converse with her. She is much better, and if she should get better
yet, and remain here, she would become a great social success, beating the British female all round.' She startled him, he said, 'by the
breadth of her *aperçus* and her intimate knowledge of English public
affairs'. Alice was absorbed above all in the Irish question; it provided a generous outlet for her bile, diminished her self-absorption;
and expressed the essential Irishness of her nature.

By 1886 Alice had decided she would spend the summer in Leamington. The move was made at the end of May; and although
Alice suffered her usual fatigue and shock of the journey, she re-
cuperated rapidly. Miss Loring escorted her to her new quarters and
spent a month with her. Alice seemed quite content and urged Henry
not to take the long trip to pay visits to her – he was indeed to pay
her only one visit during that summer. In early July he dispatched
his last instalment of *The Princess*: the novel had again spilled over
into additional chapters. James offered them to the *Atlantic* without
pay, since the miscalculation was his; but Aldrich insisted on giving
him the agreed rate.

With Alice away and 'the interminable work' done, James was
free to take a holiday. He decided however to remain in London.
Since he was setting up house, 'for once in a lifetime', he had incurred a great many expenses. 'The furnishing and arranging of my
place has partly amused and partly exasperated and altogether
beggared me,' he wrote to Grace Norton. It was economical to remain in town. There was plenty of 'high air' for the hot days, and as
his rooms gradually acquired their furnishings he was pleased to
enjoy the quiet and the luxury of being in his own home. By way
of a holiday after his two years of work on *The Bostonians* and *The
Princess* he paid a number of country visits, including one to Oster-
ley Park, the home of Lord and Lady Jersey, which was an hour's
drive from Piccadilly. Lowell, who had returned to England for the
summer, was a fellow-guest. 'His whole relation to life and the world
appears to me infantine – and infantine his judgement, his kind of
observation.' Thus to Grace Norton. 'However, he is extremely
pleasant (when he doesn't publicly correct people's grammar, pronunciation, pretensions to lineage – as compared with his own – and

many other things!) and very contented and happy, apparently, as well as infinitely invited and caressed, as before.' Lowell seemed to have all the social advantages of his former position and none of its responsibilities. In midsummer old Oliver Wendell Holmes arrived and London lionized him. He struck James, who encountered him everywhere, as 'rather superannuated and extinct (though he flickers up at moments) and is moreover dazed and bewildered' by all the fuss made over him.

James's London summer was sufficiently strenuous. 'I rush off to Bournemouth for 36 hours to see a poor sick friend – and probably go also to spend a day with Alice at Leamington,' he writes to Grace Norton.

All this while I am supposed to be looking after Mrs Jack Gardner, Mrs Bronson, the Daniel Curtises and about 30 other Americans now in London, who all are holding by my coat-tails; to say nothing of polishing my periods for the purchase of my contemporaries and the admiration of posterity. So you see I am pretty well engaged.

His Venetian friends had gathered in London at this moment because of an outbreak of cholera in their water-city. Mrs Bronson installed herself in Hans Place with her big brown gondoliers and was living just as if life opposite the Salute had not been interrupted. James went often to see her and her daughter, and almost a decade later he could write to his hostess, 'I look at your little corner of Hans Place – where the house has vanished – and recall sentimentally those good months you spent there in the quiet summer time with your Venetian suite and your Italian dinners. How I used to eat them!'

He complained to William that his two major novels of the past two years had exhausted him. But to Francis Boott he was complaining at the same time that his visitors kept him from his work. After six weeks of this kind of life – during which he read proofs of the book-edition of *The Princess Casamassima* – he told his brother he felt quite refreshed. 'Now I am not tired of work, but of no work, and am again taking up my pen.' Expensive though his furnishings were, his bank account was reinforced that autumn by Macmillan's £550 advance for the English and American book-rights of *The Princess*, and this meant that the work had yielded him more than $7,000. With the writing he was committed to do, he would be able to take his longed-for holiday without difficulty. His newest problem was what to do with his flat during his absence; and how to keep his servants from becoming demoralized by idleness. He was to discover a solution for this in due time.

III

Politics and the Boudoir

DURING Christmas week of 1885 Henry James learned that his 'Voltaire in petticoats' was dead – the sharp-tongued and witty Marian Hooper Adams, whom he had known in Newport, or at Shady Hill, in Rome, in Paris, during the Adams's winter in Birdcage Walk in London, and finally in Washington. He imparted the news to Fenimore, who was living in Leamington. The nature of Clover's death was a long and well-kept secret. She had been depressed ever since her father's death less than a year before; and she had swallowed some of the chemicals she used in her photography, knowing full well how speedily they would do their work. Henry Adams was absent from the house for a brief walk. When he returned all was over. Clover's acute and morbid animus toward life had in the end been turned against herself.

'I suppose you have heard the sad rumours (which appear founded) as to poor Clover Adams's self-destruction,' James wrote to Lizzie Boott, who had known Clover almost as long as he did. 'I'm afraid the event had everything that could make it bitter to poor Henry [Adams]. She succumbed to hereditary melancholia. What an end to that intensely lively Washington *salon*.'

Clover Adams had silenced herself. She was linked with many of the novelist's old associations: his long-dead cousin Minny Temple; the springtime in Rome, when he had dined at the Adams's with Elena Lowe; and not least with the life in Washington which he had so much relished and depicted in *Pandora*. If the novelist wrote at this moment to the stricken Adams, his letter has not survived; and for good reason – for the historian destroyed many of the papers of this time. Thus we do not possess the moving tribute of the sort the novelist invariably wrote, his inevitable epistolary elegy. We can obtain a sense of what it might have been, however, from a few remarks to Godkin some weeks later: 'I thought of you,' wrote Henry, 'and how you would be touched with the sad story, when poor Mrs Adams found, the other day, the solution of the knottiness of existence. I am more sorry for poor Henry than I can say – too sorry, almost, to think of him.'

I

'We are up to our necks in the Irish question,' Henry James wrote to Grace Norton. 'The air is positively putrid with politics.' And he might have added, although he would have found more elegant words, that the politics reeked also of the boudoir and of sex. There were three changes of government during 1885–6 while *The Princess Casamassima* was being serialized. Parnell was at the height of his fame, exercising his balance of power in the House of Commons with all his political genius. Gladstone had become for James a 'dreary incubus' mouthing platitudes; and in the midst of this – with a seeming irrelevancy – Sir Charles Dilke, a monument of respectability, who had ardently wooed the middle class and been spoken of as a possible successor to Gladstone, was accused in a divorce case of having committed adultery. Mrs Donald Crawford, an infantile and reckless society belle, had pointed to him as 'the man who ruined me'.

'England is interesting at present – because it is heaving so, and crackling and fermenting. But the fissures are mainly political and the exhalations often foul,' James told Miss Norton. After Dilke there was to be the story of Parnell's relationship with Kitty O'Shea, and still later, in the mid-1890s, the case of Oscar Wilde – who happened also to be Irish. James followed the Parnell case with intense interest. He attended the trial in 1889, and used words such a 'thrilling' and 'throbbing' to describe it. Before the 1880s were over, there had been also Lady Colin Campbell's divorce suit with the naming of four co-respondents. The political *mores* of the Victorians fascinated Henry; and the unmasking of the sexual *mores* gave him a little more freedom in his tales. He could say now more casually that Victorian ladies were not always virtuous, and that Victorian gentlemen sometimes behaved like cads.

Dilke had befriended James during his early days in London. The novelist's account of the scandal throws a peripheral light on the mysterious case which seemed to be a mixture of indiscretions by the respected Dilke and perhaps, as his latest biographer believes, a conspiracy to ruin him politically. James told Miss Norton that the scandal had a certain 'low interest' for him, since he had the 'sorry privilege' of being acquainted with most of the people who were closely and remotely involved. After reporting the allegations made by Donald Crawford, he described how Mrs Mark Pattison had announced to the press while travelling in India, that she was rushing home to marry Dilke.

Meanwhile another London lady whom I won't name, with whom for years his relations have been concomitant with his relations with Mrs Pattison, and whose husband died, has had every expectation that he was on the point of marrying *her*. This is a very brief sketch of the situation, which is queer and dramatic and disagreeable. Dilke's private life won't (I imagine) bear looking into, and the vengeful Crawford will do his best to lay it bare. He will probably not succeed, and Dilke's political reputation, with the great 'middle class', will weather the storm. But he will have been frightened almost to death. For a man who has had such a passion for keeping up appearances and appealing to the said middle class, he has, in reality, been strangely, incredibly reckless. His long, double liaison with Mrs Pattison and the other lady, of a nature to make it a duty of honour to marry *both* (!!) when they should become free, and the death of each husband at the same time – with the public watching to see *which* he would marry – and he meanwhile 'going on' with poor little Mrs Crawford, who is a kind of infant – the whole thing is a theme for the novelist – or at least for *a* novelist.

The lady James did not name to Grace Norton was named soon enough when the case came to court. She was his old friend, Christina Rogerson, daughter of Mrs Duncan Stewart, at whose home he had had many pleasant lunches and dinners. James was wrong in his predictions. Dilke was crushed by the case; and never recovered from it. There was a distinct doubt whether his liaison with Mrs Crawford had occurred; but he had certainly, for a man in public life, left himself sufficiently exposed: and it is questionable whether, given his capacity for making public errors, he would have ever been a very reliable leader. James had long ago characterized him as more fortunate in birth and position than in talent. 'Not a grain of genius or inspiration' had been his verdict a decade earlier.

2

When it came to the Irish question, James did not share his sister's belligerency. Ireland was a country 'revelling in odious forms of irresponsibility and licence'. When Miss Norton wrote to say she thought the Irish a 'great people' James retorted:

I see no greatness, nor any kind of superiority in them, and they seem to me an inferior and third rate race, whose virtues are of the cheapest and commonest and shallowest order, while their vices are peculiarly cowardly and ferocious. They have been abominably treated in the past – but their wrongs appear to me, in our time, to have occupied the conscience of England only too much to the exclusion of other things. Don't think me brutal, dear Grace, or anglicized, which is the same thing.

Earlier however he had written to his friend Perry: 'If I had nothing else to do I think I should run over to Ireland: which may seem strange to you on the part of one satiated in his youth with the Celtic genius. The reason is that I should like to see a country in a state of revolution.'

The closest he had come to seeing a revolutionary setting had been that day, long ago, in Paris when he visited the barricades and ruins of the Commune. But one day in February 1886, before he had moved to De Vere Gardens, returning from Bournemouth where he had gone to pay a visit to Stevenson, he found Piccadilly littered with broken glass, and the mansions at the corner of Bolton Street boarded up. It had been a day of noisy rioting in the heart of London by the very unemployed for whom he was speaking in *The Princess*. This was not revolution; it was however still another great fissure in the decorous life of the English. James regretted missing the riot: 'I should have seen it from my balcony.' Windows had been smashed three doors away. But Fenimore, then in London, had been abroad in the streets and could supply an eye-witness account. Armed with her American innocence, and her deafness, she had wandered into Piccadilly from lodgings in Seymour Street, passing along Clarges Street; she heard distant noises and saw a mob hurry along the edge of Green Park in the direction of Hyde Park Corner. There were always processions of one kind or another in London she thought. As she turned into Piccadilly there were still groups of men, eight or ten in a group, clearly of the labouring class, moving about in a certain mood of 'larkiness'. Then it began to dawn on her that she was the only woman in sight. Traffic was at a standstill. Further along she encountered broken glass and smashed shop-fronts. Entering a picture-framing establishment liberally sprinkled with broken glass she politely inquired what had happened. 'A mob, Madam, a mob,' the proprietor said. Fenimore cautiously picked up a lonely cab in a side-street and persuaded the driver to take her home by a circuitous route. She had been relatively lucky. She learned later that ladies in carriages had been kissed or slapped and roughly handled. Some had their purses snatched. During the next couple of days a dark fog settled over the city as if to blot out the destruction. Describing the scenes to William, Henry told him there was 'immense destitution' everywhere. 'Everyone here is growing poorer – from causes which I fear will continue.' Nevertheless he felt that the usually orderly British populace had shot its bolt and would not riot again in the near future. The episode had sufficiently illustrated the 'topical' character of his new novel.

112

A Lion in the Path

DURING the summer of 1885 Henry's French visitors had included the aesthetic Montesquiou. In August of 1886, when London was empty and Henry was enjoying a sense of relief after the completion of his novel, there appeared on his horizon the figure of Guy de Maupassant, 'a lion in the path'. James would say in a memorable passage that 'those who have really taken the measure of the animal' would not make light of him. He took the personal measure of Maupassant during their few encounters that summer – it was Maupassant's only visit to England – and wrote a brilliant essay on him little more than a year later.

I

Henry James had been taking his literary measure ever since Maupassant had begun to publish his tales. He remembered Flaubert's young disciple, present at the Sundays in the Faubourg St Honoré: a sturdy young man of middle height, with a low forehead, bushy brown hair combed back, a big brown moustache and much talk of boating, swimming, Sundays on the Seine – and the conquest of women. James acquired his books with great promptness. His copy of *Une Vie* is signed and dated in his hand 'Boston, June 19, 1883'; *Contes de la Bécasse* is similarly inscribed 'Boston, August 1883'. There are other volumes – *Miss Harriet, La Vie Errante, Bel-Ami, Yvette* – all showing signs of having been carefully read. One or two descriptive passages are marked. To his friend Child, James had written of *Bel-Ami* : 'The history of a Cad, by a Cad – of Genius!'

Maupassant, when he left Paris, was apparently not certain that James remembered him; he came armed with a letter of introduction from Paul Bourget. 'I have told him,' Bourget wrote, 'that you are the only man in London with whom it is possible to talk as with the Gallo-Romans.' It is doubtful, however, whether the younger man, ten years after Faubert's Sundays, and at the height of his fame, was as interested in literary talk as Bourget. He wanted to be shown English things; he wanted above all to meet English women. James was hardly the best guide for the kind of encounters Maupassant sought. There is an anecdote, attributed to Oscar Wilde, which, even if embellished, must contain a certain grain of truth. Maupassant, dining in a restaurant with James, pointed to a woman sitting at a table and asked him to 'go over and get her for me'. James carefully explained that in England there was the matter of being properly introduced. Maupassant tried again. Pointing to another woman he said : 'Surely you know her at least? Ah, if I only spoke English!' When James had refused, with full explanation, for about the fifth time, Maupassant was said to have remarked irritably : 'Really, you don't seem to know anyone in London.'

The anecdote was characteristic. Maupassant's letters to Count Joseph Napoleon Primoli – who was his companion on this trip – suggest that the lion was a relentless woman-stalker. 'On Monday we will have several agreeable ladies, it would seem – plus Henry James,' he remarks in one missive. And in another from Waddesdon, where he was visiting Ferdinand de Rothschild, Maupassant writes : 'What a pleasure, my dear friend, to know you are in London, where I will be on Tuesday. I hope you'll be there on the 11th. I would like to present you that evening to a charming woman, at whose home you will find Bret Harte, the American writer, and also, I think, Henry James.'

The woman was probably Blanche Roosevelt. Indeed it might be said that three figures converged on Henry James during this episode: Maupassant, Primoli and Blanche Roosevelt. A handsome woman, with blue eyes and masses of red-gold hair, she had been a hunter of literary lions from the days when, at 17, she had been told by Victor Hugo that she expressed 'the beauty and genius of the new world'. In America she had visited Longfellow and made copy out of it for the magazines; in France she had visited Maupassant and made discreet copy out of her indiscretions with him. And now in London she would have liked to annex Henry James. He might indeed have invented her: she was a less conformist and more literary Mrs Headway, prepared to besiege any handsome male – if he were a writer – and James met both requirements. Born in Sandusky, Ohio, raised at La Crosse, Wisconsin, she had come to Europe to cultivate her voice – it was to her voice, probably, that Hugo had applied the word 'genius'. After studying with Pauline Viardot, she had made her début at Covent Garden. Her vocal power was judged, however, insufficient for grand opera. She had sung Violetta in *La Traviata*, a role more suited to her personality than to her voice. Her full name now was Blanche Roosevelt Tucker Macchetta, Marchesa d'Alligri. We find James writing to Francis Boott, during Maupassant's stay in London: 'I have just escaped from the jaws of Blanche Roosevelt, who used to sing in opera – didn't she? – and who is now here married to a Milanese, trying to be literary and assaulting me (with compliments) on my productions.'

Primoli was hardly another Montesquiou. In comparison with the latter's affiliation with old European aristocracy he was distinctly *parvenu*. The most that Count Joseph could boast was a direct descent from two of Napoleon's brothers: his grandparents had been cousins, the children of King Joseph Bonaparte of Spain and Lucien Bonaparte, who bore the papal title of Prince of Canino. His great-aunt was the Princess Mathilde, whose salon figures prominently in the Goncourt journals and the correspondence of Flaubert. If Primoli did not move among high French nobility he had status in the highest French literary circles. 'An odd little member of the Bonaparte family,' James called him. He was to meet him on sundry occasions in Paris and Rome and to visit him in his palace by the Tiber.

2

Whatever Maupassant's wishes in the matter of women, James felt distinctly that the proper literary honours should be paid to a distinguished master of the short story. The French writer agreed to dine with the American novelist on 12 August. Normally James would have entertained him at the Reform or the Athenaeum, but the clubs were closed in the midsummer. He remembered however that a sufficiently good meal could be obtained at Greenwich, and this was always a charming relief in the monotony of a London August. He invited George du Maurier and Edmund Gosse; Maupassant brought Primoli. The party assembled at 5.15 at Westminster Bridge and boarded one of the small grimy sixpenny steamers that plied the Thames. Maupassant was given a view of the great English river; for so enthusiastic a riverman this provided a certain picture – gave him a sense of the different civilization on this side of the Channel. The scenery was hardly that of the Seine : there were largely the backs and fronts of the expressionless warehouses, black barges, far-stretching docks and basins and a dark wilderness of masts. But once they came into sight of the Observatory, with its two modest little brick towers, he got the sense of the general English charm of the place.

It is not recorded where they dined. James had described the endless forms of fish available in the Greenwich restaurants and hotels in one of his London sketches, and had recommended a stroll first in the park, on the summit of which the famous Observatory was located, 'to get up an appetite'. In *The Princess Casamassima* the young hero and his friend spend a long afternoon at Greenwich. A letter written by James to Gosse twenty-eight years later throws a brief backward light.

Have you any recollection of once going down the River with me at Greenwich long years ago? – in company with Maupassant, du Maurier, and one or two others? One of those others was Primoli, who had come over from Paris with Maupassant; and on whom you made, you see, the ineffaceable impression. He wrote to me the other day to ask your address – it has lasted all these years – and you meanwhile – infidèle – ! I have seen him since then from time to time; he is a very amiable and rather singular person. He made on dear du Maurier, I remember, an impression that remained – though not on your sterner nature! He is a Bonaparte (exceedingly so in looks); that is his mother was a Bonaparte Princess.

We are left with the impression that Primoli charmed du Maurier, and Gosse charmed Primoli. James in all probability concentrated on his principal guest. And his verdict on the man – seen through his work – published in the *Fortnightly Review* in 1888 remains the classic essay in English on Maupassant. It shows the extent to which James was fascinated by the variety of Maupassant's subjects and the extreme brevity with which he was able to relate them. He wished very much to emulate this side of him. As for the substance of his stories, his admiration was qualified by their excessive adherence to the life of the senses – including their eroticism – and their failure to take into account sufficiently the reflective nature of man. Maupassant went in his tales to the strongest ingredients and these alone. He was an active and independent observer of the human scene, quite unashamed of any of his faculties; but his emphasis on sex, James argued, was exaggerated, or, as he put it, 'the impression of the human spectacle for him who takes it as it comes has less analogy with that of the monkeys' cage than this admirable writer's account of it'.

James wrote as a psychologist: he seized upon a remark by Maupassant that 'psychology should be hidden in a book, as it is hidden in reality under the facts of existence'. He replied that the very facts constituted the revelation. From whom were they hidden? he asked:

From some people, no doubt, but very much less from others; and all depends upon the observer, the nature of one's observations, and one's curiosity. For some people motives, reasons, relations, explanations, are a part of the very surface of the drama, with the footlights beating full upon them. For me an act, an incident, an attitude, may be a sharp, detached, isolated thing, of which I give a full account in saying that in such and such a way it came off. For you it may be hung about with implications, with relations and conditions as necessary to help you to recognize it as the clothes of your friends are to help you know them in the street. You feel that they would seem strange to you without petticoats and trousers.

James concluded that the 'carnal side of man appears the most characteristic if you look at it a great deal; and you look at it a great deal if you do not look at the other, at the side by which he reacts against his own weaknesses, his defeats'.

For all this, James argued that a healthy art had 'an indefeasible mistrust of rigid prohibitions'. And the lesson of Maupassant for him was one which was not so much influence as example. There are passages in James's notebooks which testify to this. On occasions when he wishes to tell a tale in a small compass, with a few bold strokes, we find him exclaiming to himself, 'Oh spirit of Maupassant, come to my aid'; '*À la Maupassant* must be my constant motto'; or he will say, 'Something as admirably compact and selected as Maupassant', or 'practicable on the rigid Maupassant system'. This was what Maupassant left with him beyond his shrewd observation of life. When James entertained Maupassant in London the French writer had already shown certain signs of the effects of the syphilis which killed him seven years later. 'The Frenchmen are passing away – Maupassant dying of locomotor paralysis, the fruit of fabulous habits, I am told,' James wrote to Stevenson in 1893. '*Je n'en sais rien*; but I shall miss him.' And when a friend wrote of Maupassant's end, he thanked him for 'the touching two words you had the friendly thought of sending me when the indignity that life had heaped upon poor Maupassant found itself stayed'. He added: 'My tears had already been wept; even though the image of that history had been too *hard* for such droppings.'

In the Maupassant essay James introduced a parenthetical remark. He had been speaking of the 'unpleasant' side of Maupassant's tales and his 'pessimism' and pointed to the tendency for much of English fiction to gloss over reality. 'Does not Mr Rider Haggard make even his African carnage pleasant?' he remarked. The allusion belonged to the time of Maupassant's visit. That week he had been reading Haggard's best-selling tales with a sense of horror. He had finished *King Solomon's Mines* and read half of *She*. The fact that *She* was in its fortieth thousand moved him 'to holy indignation'. He felt that 'it isn't nice that anything so vulgarly brutal should be the thing that succeeds most with the English of today'. He was struck with the 'beastly *bloodiness*' of Haggard's books.

Such perpetual killing and such perpetual ugliness! It is worth while to write a tale of fantastic adventure, with a funny man etc. and pitched all in the slangiest key, to kill 20,000 men, as in *Solomon*, in order to help your heroes on! In *She* the Narrator himself shoots through the back (I think) his faithful servant Mohammed, to prevent his being boiled alive, and describes how he leaped into the air 'like a buck', on receiving the shot. They seem to me works in which our race and our age make a very vile figure – and they have unexpectedly depressed me.

Thus in his Maupassant essay James spoke with great clarity of both sex and violence in fiction – not as one who wished to close his eyes to them, but as one who felt that in the civilization in which the artist worked it was possible to penetrate deeply into human experience without necessarily stressing the physical or carnal (as in Maupassant) or glorifying the fantastic-violent (as in Haggard). For Maupassant, the artist in James kept always a tender place.

113

The Divided Self

IN *The Princess Casamassima*, which was published in book form on 22 October 1886, Henry James wrote a large and humane work, bringing together certain of his characteristic themes into a subject unique in the canon of his writings – a 'naturalist' subject – the plight of the London working class and its nascent revolutionary impulse. The image of the depressed side of London had been with him ever since his childhood reading of Dickens. There were, however, more recent and actual memories: an old woman 'lying prone in a puddle of whiskey', for instance. His theme had been implicit moreover in his remark long ago that the English upper classes were too re-fined and the lower classes too miserable. His view of English poverty was largely from the 'outside', none the less it was the view of a profoundly sentient artist. James subtly meets the possible criticism that he was writing of conditions 'observed' outside immediate experience. His hero speaks of being 'aware the people were dire-fully wretched – more aware, it often seemed to him, than they themselves were'. James knew that poverty could brutalize the sufferers into an insensibility to their lot.

I

The novel was conceived in large terms and it ran to fourteen instalments. Within it James drew his pictures of the miseries and affluence of London, the fruit of long nocturnal walks in the city's streets, and of hours spent in pubs and probably at workers' meetings, in the manner of Zola. He had remembered how Zola had described at Flaubert's his writing down verbal obscenities heard in the Paris slums. James had followed his example – the 'rich principle of the Note' – and we find him recording 'Phrases of the People'. They seem well-worn now. 'That takes the gilt off, you know,' or the remark of a worker talking about his boss, 'he cuts it very fine'; or ' 'ere today, somewhere else tomorrow, that's 'is motto'. When he wrote the novel, he left out such words as 'bloody' and edited 'hell' to 'h –'. The language of the revised edition could be a little easier. He re-inserted the words he had censored in the Victorian period. Saturated with 'high life', thoroughly documented in his observation of the 'low', he achieved in *The Princess* what he had failed to do in *The Bostonians* – a mastery over his materials and a dense and rich texture of 'impressionism'. That the work should have had no appeal to its contemporary audience is understandable, although this baffled James at the time. He believed he had found an original theme, and one that was decidedly 'topical'. He had fancied that its novelty and its treatment would impress the critics and the public. The work conveyed, however, all too successfully the uneasiness above and below the surface of Victorian London; it came uncomfortably close to the recent riots, the bombs, the dynamiters. The Victorians tended to look to fiction for comfort and amusement, not for the anxieties of their daily lives. In America the novel fared somewhat better. Nevertheless it marked a departure from the comedies of international marriages and the adventures of American girls abroad. And then James committed the grievous error of thinking that an English version of the novels being written on the Continental side of the Channel – with due allowance for the Anglo-Saxon attitude towards sex – would be acceptable. *The Princess Casamassima* was a remote counterpart to Zola's *Germinal*, a work about the 'class war' published at the same time – before the working class itself understood what the nature of such a war might be.

Most of *The Princess* takes place on Sundays, or in the evenings. Some English reviewers expressed bewilderment at this; it did not occur to them that James was describing the impoverished Londoners during their abbreviated hours of leisure rather than at their daily tasks. The settings are dark and drab save for those Sunday hours which are spent in the parks and the streets, and the pages of contrast when the working-class hero is invited to the country house of the Princess. There is an artful chiaroscuro in the book, a large impressionism. Yet reality is never blurred. As long ago as his first year of residence in the British capital James described in one of his articles the funeral of an English radical agitator and the crowd that followed the hearse: 'It was the London rabble, the metropolitan mob, men and women, boys and girls, the decent poor and the indecent, who had scrambled into the ranks as they gathered them up on their passage.' James saw them from a hansom cab, in which he was comfortably riding. As he looked from the soft side of exist-ence he 'seemed to be having a sort of panoramic view of the under side, the wrong side, of the London world'. The 'wrong' side – and also the 'wronged' side. There were 'strange, pale, mouldy paupers, who blinked and stumbled in the Piccadilly sunshine'; the beggars' opera scene had remained with him, merging into other observed scenes of London's grimy, sooty, gin-soaked, under-privileged life.

This was the world James chose to deal with in *The Princess Casamassima* and to link with themes of the life of ease about which he had written in his earlier romantic works. At his elbow stood Balzac, Dickens, Turgenev, Zola – he drew upon *Les Illusions Perdues*, as writers of imagination draw upon their predecessors and upon the traditions of their form; he drew upon his constituted imagina-tion. Many years later, when he wished to describe the origin of this novel, he presented it in terms of his own experience of London. He had conceived of a hero, he said, 'watching the same innumerable appearances I had watched', and 'watching very much as I had watched'. The little bookbinder Hyacinth Robinson possesses Henry's visual sense – it colours his whole mind. London doors had swung hospitably open for Henry James; for Hyacinth these doors – save in one instance – remain tightly closed. Hyacinth has a conflict between 'the world of his work-a-day life and the world of his divination and envy'. In a word he is an 'outsider' and an 'observant stranger'; he looks on from the slums, not from the comparative comfort of Bolton Street.

2

James made him a craftsman, like some of the radicals of the time, a bookbinder with an urge to be a writer. He is handicapped by his origins and his poverty. He has read much, felt much; he is 'a youth on whom nothing was lost,' James wrote, echoing his prescription for young novelists. He is what someone like Henry James might have been, had he grown up without the novelist's advantages of education and travel, and the opportunity to exercise his talent. James tells us that Hyacinth has the soul of 'a genuine artist'. He is, in effect, another version of the artist *manqué* James had depicted ten years before in the pages of the *Atlantic*, the ill-formed young sculptor from Northampton, Massachusetts, Roderick Hudson. And the link with this early novel is established by the Princess Casamassima. Omnipresent and as alluring as ever, for all her world-weariness, she is the once-mysterious, once-unfathomable – and still capricious – Christina Light, some ten years after the death of Roderick. As she had crossed the path of the sculptor in the late 1860s in Rome, so now in the early 1880s in London she pulls the little bookbinder into her orbit. Christina has shed her mystery; she is now a characteristic Jamesian beauty, a woman of the world with a 'Queen complex', bent on exercising her power over her environment and over men particularly. Hyacinth's mistake (it was also Roderick's) is to care too much for her; she is interested more in men who show indifference – they are a greater challenge to conquest.

Hyacinth and Roderick were evolved from the same imaginative sources and their conflicts are similar. Hyacinth, for all his upbringing in the slums, has as much of a New England sense of duty as his predecessor. Roderick had been unable to reconcile his devotion to his art and his passion for Christina. Hyacinth feels an overriding responsibility to his class. But he aspires also to the world of case, in which he has met the beautiful princess. Like Roderick, he cannot bring together his two worlds. Their common ancestor is the volatile Benvolio, of James's New York scribbling days. Benvolio had his Countess on the one hand and a puritan maiden Scholastica on the other, and swung constantly from the grandeur of the one to the sobriety of the other. Roderick and Hyacinth are similarly divided but the stress of duty dampens the flame of passion.

Hyacinth unlike Roderick, is endowed with an elaborate and overpowering heredity, after the manner of Zola. He is the illegitimate son of an English peer and a French seamstress, who had turned on her seducer and murdered him. 'There was no peace for him between the two currents that flowed in his nature, the blood of his passionate, plebeian mother and that of his long-descended, supercivilized sire.' He impulsively allies himself with revolutionary elements; he also finds himself 'adopted' by the fine world of the Princess Christina, who is using revolution as a retreat from ennui. In her country house the little bookbinder indulges in all the luxuries of feeling James himself well knew from his visits to the great houses of England. The hyacinthine youth, however, has committed himself to revolution : he has promised to obey the shadowy but powerful Diedrich Hoffendahl, master-mind of terrorism. And the moment comes when he receives a pistol and is ordered to assassinate a Duke.

Between the time of his impulsive adherence to his cause and the arrival of the weapon he has discovered that he has no sympathy with the revolutionaries. The metamorphosis occurred when he inherited a little hoard of savings from the dressmaker who had brought him up. He used his money to visit Paris and wander in its great squares and boulevards with the recollection that his mother's father had died on Parisian barricades. What he experienced, however, was not the triumph of revolution but the *gloire* of history. Later he had an equally profound experience in Venice. In these cities of struggle and bloodshed Hyacinth the aristocrat rejects Hyacinth the revolutionary.

'What was supreme in his mind today was not the idea of how the society that surrounded him should be destroyed; it was, much more, the sense of the wonderful, precious things it had produced, of the brilliant, impressive fabric it had raised.' * These had been Henry's reflections long ago during his rides across the Campagna. From Venice Hyacinth can only write to the Princess that he has been struck by 'the splendid accumulations of the happier few, to which doubtless, the miserable many have also in their degree contributed'. The Shakespearean – and Stendhalian – phrase – 'the happy few' – is apropos. It is used once again near the end of the book, in the passage in which Hyacinth thinks how a sentient individual feels the sufferings of the oppressed more than the oppressed themselves.

In these hours the poverty and ignorance of the multitude seemed so vast and preponderant, and so much the law of life, that those who had managed to escape from the black gulf were only the happy few, people of resource as well as children of luck : they inspired in some degree the interest and sympathy that one should feel for survivors and victors, those who have come safely out of a shipwreck or a battle.

Hyacinth comes to see life as 'less impracticable and more tolerable' † thanks to 'the monuments and treasures of art, the great

---

* In his late revision of this novel James made this read 'the fabric of beauty and power it had raised'.
† Later revised to 'less of a "bloody sell" and more of a lark'.

palaces and properties, the conquests of learning and taste, the general fabric of civilization as we know it, based, if you will, upon all the despotisms, the cruelties, the exclusions, the monopolies and the rapacities of the past'. The conclusion of this eloquent letter could have been an answer to William Morris, whose socialist beliefs finally led him to exclaim : 'What business have we with art at all, unless all can share it.' Hyacinth knows how the revolutionist to whom he has pledged himself would share it. He 'wouldn't have the least feeling for this incomparable, abominable old Venice. He would cut up the ceilings of the Veronese in strips, so that every one might have a little piece.' And he adds : 'I don't want every one to have a little piece of anything and I have a great horror of that kind of invidious jealousy which is at the bottom of the idea of a redistribution.'

Had Hyacinth been a hard-headed opportunist he would have backed away, pushed open some door of escape, gone to America. He is, however, as ruthless with himself as his revolutionary mentors are with society at large and with one another. To kill the Duke would in effect be like killing his father and re-enacting the crime of his mother. Roderick in a frenzy had wandered into an Alpine storm and missed his footing at the edge of a cliff. Hyacinth circles London in his loneliness and desperation. He feels himself helpless and unwanted. He can find no footing in his conflict. In the end he comes closer to the *crime passionel* of his mother rather than the political crime. He turns the pistol on himself, upon that organ which in his sensitive and romantic young body has suffered most – his heart.

3

Readers – and critics – coming upon *The Princess Casamassima* have assumed that James's attempt to treat a 'social' subject must be factitious, or as artificial as *Romola*, a product of libraries and 'influences', and of a scant knowledge of working-class life and politics. One critic has found James politically 'naïve', another has made him out to be more documented in anarchism than he was; still another sees the Princess as derived from Dickens; and another has accused him of making his radicals more conspiratorial than they were at that time. This last is true. James did follow the newspapers, who saw an 'organized' conspiracy in sporadic acts of violence by malcontents and fanatics. For the rest, James's achievement in this novel must be seen in his belief in the novelist's capacity to deduce the unknown from the known. He had known radicals from childhood; his father was a religious radical, who consorted with Fourierists and Utopians; and James had known the dreams of a changed and new society peculiar to New England with its Brook Farm and its Fruitlands. Abroad he had met, in Turgenev's entourage, nihilists and emigré revolutionaries and had participated in their feast days. He had been an honoured guest at the Nikolai Turgenevs' on the anniversary of the freeing of the serfs. Long before, he had visited Paris during the aftermath of the Commune. And we have seen that where he had no knowledge, he sought it by visiting Millbank Prison and working-class pubs.

The rest was his artist's imagination and his humanity; he felt deeply the plight of his characters, and the as yet undeveloped class struggle. He may have met Prince Kropotkin, the theorist of anarchism, at Turgenev's bedside in 1880; he was to know him later – after he had written *The Princess* – in London. We may best judge the accuracy of the novel as observed and 'felt life' if we note that Kropotkin, arriving in London in 1881, complained that there was 'no atmosphere to breathe in'. He found the workers torpid, unorganized, inarticulate. The action of *The Princess Casamassima* is set in that year. Kropotkin said that during this visit to England there had been 'no sign of that animated socialist movement which I found so largely developed on my return in 1886'. This was the year in which the *Princess* appeared as a book. The two dates mentioned by Kropotkin fit perfectly the fictional and actual boundaries of James's novel, and help us to define the true character of its 'revolutionary' content. The politics of the novel are naïve – for the book reflects the naïveté of the workers at that time; it is a novel which records the primitive beginnings of British Marxism, and it shows the 'general muddle' which then existed. This is why James's workers are shown as helpless and confused. The Independent Labour Party and the Fabian Society were being founded during the period of the writing of *The Princess*. And the book had barely been published when the Haymarket bombing occurred in Chicago and the Piccadilly riots in London.

James had been 'topical' indeed; more, he had been prescient. And the book would have had the fate of all such 'topical' novels but for one thing: if James was not grounded in political science and the writings of Marx and Engels (Bernard Shaw was then just beginning to read Marx), he understood better than the early Marxists the dynamics of power, the relationship between idealism and the manipulation of people; and he characterized with complete accuracy the predicament of nineteenth-century liberalism which hated the violence of revolution, wanted the lot of the workers changed, and feared the self-seeking of men like H. M. Hyndman and his Democratic Federation. This was the very essence of Fabianism and the essence of Hyacinth's plight. The case of Hyacinth was to have its parallels in our century, in the young who blew themselves up while making bombs.

In the emigrés James embodied, with great affection and charm, the men he had known : their idealism, their sense of having outlived history, their chronic pain of exile. In the figure of Paul Muniment, the young worker, he foresaw the future union organizer and labour politician, in his coolness, self-centredness and capacity for opportunism. He is the cautious 'practical' revolutionary : 'Ah no; no smashing, no smashing of valuable property. There are no wrong places – there are only wrong uses for them.' Muniment lives with his sister Rosy, who like Alice James is bed-ridden (and we may judge that her asperities and hostilities portray not a little of that unpleasant side of Alice.) Hyacinth and Paul become bosom-friends; but the affection is really on Hyacinth's side. Paul can be ruthless. The portrait of the two is James's characteristic picture of the younger man who feels misunderstood by the older, to whom he is nevertheless deeply attached. There is a touch of William James in Paul Muniment.

In this group the Princess too must be considered as a kind of 'radical'; she belongs to the ranks of the exalted – those who have all the good things of life and make of their association with reform a kind of perpetual parlour game. With his usual subtle playfulness Henry creates an opposing character to the Princess. Christina Light's opposite is named Aurora. Christina has forgotten her own shabby beginnings, and is ostentatiously slumming. Lady Aurora belongs to the English aristocracy and, like Miss Birdseye in *The Bostonians*, is a humanitarian : she has the gift of true kindness. The two women offer a contrast once again between the self-interested social reformer and the dedicated and generous spirit.

4

James confessed in his notebook after starting *The Princess* that he had never found himself 'engaged in a novel, in which, after I had begun to write and send off my manuscript, the details had remained so vague'. This vagueness is muffled in calculated ambiguities and an artful 'impressionism'. Notable are the scenes of the workers who come to the tavern, the Sun and Moon, during the hard winter of 1880–81, articulate only to the point of such utterances (in his revised version) as: 'And what the plague am I to do with seventeen bob – with seventeen bloody bob? What am I to do with them – will ye tell me that?' The language James heard was probably more violent. Or such asseverations as: 'Them was my words in the month of February last, and what I say I stick to – what I say I stick to.' Articulate only to the point of general ejaculation, without leadership, the workers of the time could be rendered simply in their state of helpless despair:

They came oftener this second winter, for the season was terribly hard; and as in that lower world one walked with one's ear nearer the ground the deep perpetual groan of London misery seemed to swell and swell and form the whole undertone of life. The filthy air came into the place in the damp coats of silent men, and hung there till it was brewed to a nauseous warmth, and ugly, serious faces squared themselves through it, and strong-smelling pipes contributed their element in a fierce dogged manner which appeared to say that it now had to stand for everything – for bread and meat and beer, for shoes and blankets and the poor things at the pawnbroker's and the smokeless chimney at home. Hyacinth's colleagues seemed to him wiser then, and more permeated with intentions boding ill to the satisfied classes; and though the note of popularity was still most effectively struck by the man who could demand oftenest, unpractically, 'What the plague am I to do with seventeen shillings?' * it was brought home to our hero on more than one occasion that revolution was ripe at last.

And the following speech, with a change of a word or two, might have been a part of any revolutionary pamphlet of the time; Bernard Shaw was to endow certain of his socialist characters with this kind of eloquence on the stage:

People go and come, and buy and sell, and drink and dance, and make money and make love, and seem to know nothing and suspect nothing

* Later changed to 'What the hell am I to do with half a quid?'

and think of nothing; and iniquities flourish, and the misery of half the world is prated about as a 'necessary evil', and generations rot away and starve in the midst of it, and day follows day, and everything is for the best in the best of possible worlds. All that is one half of it; the other half is that everything is doomed! In silence, in darkness, but under the feet of each one of us, the revolution lives and works. It is a wonderful immeasurable trap, on the lid of which society performs its antics.

The most successful of the secondary characters is Millicent Henning, Hyacinth's childhood friend in the slums. She is as cockney as Shaw's Eliza, and rings true in everything she does and says. George du Maurier, whose knowledge of London was more deeply rooted than James's, wrote that she was 'the best character in the book', and 'truly loveable; and her friendship for Hyacinth, with its admirable background of foggy streets and gaslighted shops has attracted and delighted me almost more than anything else – her freedom, her readiness for a row, her potentiality for barricades or triumphal processions (in spite of her hands and feet) – and the background of London is ever there, I venture to think, as it has not been treated before'.

It is doubtful whether Millicent had a potential for barricades: but du Maurier describes her principal qualities. She is in many ways a cockney cousin of Daisy Miller, with a great deal more vitality.

5

The personal statement in this novel, in the light of James's 'orphaned' state on returning from America, lies this time near the surface. He felt himself an aristocrat by birth, who had also to labour for his bread; he could move among princesses and lords, yet at a given hour each day he was pledged to his task in Bolton Street and later De Vere Gardens – never more so than during the two years in which, month after month, he delivered instalments of *The Bostonians* and then of *The Princess Casamassima*. Feeling himself alone in the world after the death of his parents, clinging to art and civilization amid the unrest in British society, he seemed truly disinherited. He expressed this with great clarity to Charles Eliot Norton following the publication of *The Princess* [he was writing from Italy]:

The subject of the moment, as I came away, was the hideous Colin Campbell divorce case, which will besmirch exceedingly the already very damaged prestige of the English upper class. The condition of that body seems to me to be in many ways very much the same rotten and *collapsible* one as that of the French aristocracy before the revolution – minus cleverness and conversation. Or perhaps it's more like the heavy, congested and depraved Roman world upon which the barbarians came down. In England the Huns and Vandals will have to come *up* – from the black depths of the (in the people) enormous misery, though I don't think the Attila is quite yet found – in the person of Mr Hyndman.

The sense of being bereft of his parents is emphasized by the number of fathers and mothers Henry allots to Hyacinth. There had been Hyacinth's original parents, Lord Frederick Purvis, murdered by his French mother, Florentine Vivier, whom he had seen but once, in the Millbank infirmary. There is Mr Vetch, the old violinist, and the dressmaker Miss Pynsent who brought up the boy: both constitute a parental pair, advising, admonishing, helping. Miss Pynsent's savings, when she dies, enlarged by a gift from Mr Vetch, enable Hyacinth to go to the Continent. And then he has acquired still another, a disciplined and resolute father, in the person of the anarchist Diedrich Hoffendahl, seen in a nocturnal interview, to whom the bookbinder had pledged absolute obedience. Hoffendahl in James's imagination belongs with the crippled elder Henry James – for Henry endows the anarchist with a maimed arm.

Hyacinth's parents and parent-figures demand a great deal; to obey the rule of the stern 'father' Hoffendahl, he must kill the Duke and thereby re-enact his mother's murder. He is divided between a ruthless though maimed father, upon whose behalf he is called to risk his own life, and the memory of a powerful Clytemnestra mother. His immediate parent-surrogates, Miss Pynsent and Mr Vetch, want him to cut loose from his revolutionary commitment. His 'parents' have put him in an impossible position. His brother – in the shape of still another revolutionary, Paul Muniment – is of no help to him. He feels betrayed.

Thus in *The Princess Casamassima*, a novel which seemed farthest removed from himself, James wrote out the personal emotions of this period: the acute melancholy experienced in the years following the death of his parents; his 'distance' from his brother, his loneliness and depression. He seems to have disposed of a primitive helplessness and outrage in *The Bostonians*; and in his novel of London and the anarchists he re-imagined his subterranean world of feeling in terms of his hero's revolt, despair and need for action. He siphoned off into his work a lugubrious state of mind, leaving himself freer and more possessed of his mature self. One solution had been his finding a new and more permanent home. And when the last chapters, written in De Vere Gardens, were done, his thoughts turned to Italy. He had been away for six years. It was time to return.

Part Three:
Bellosguardo

114

The Lonely Friends

ON that February day of the riots in 1886 when Fenimore walked innocently through London's cluttered streets, she had been on her way to the Strand to purchase a trunk. She was returning to Italy. She had been living for three years in England writing her novel *East Angels*. 'I grow less and less of a traveller each year,' she had written to a friend. But now she craved the south, a warm sun, Italy. We have very little knowledge of her movements in England between 1884 and 1886. We know that in London she occasionally went to the theatre with Henry James; that they had paid a visit together to Stonehenge; that they met in various other places. For a while we lose sight of her completely. In September of 1885 she was at Leamington, a year before Alice James spent her summer there. She had been working quietly and making excursions – to Stratford, Coventry, Kenilworth, Oxford. She had fallen 'desperately in love' with Oxford. She was enchanted by Warwickshire; she took solitary walks, inspecting sleepy villages, with their half-timbered houses and thatched roofs, and small ancient churches with grey Norman towers. Her love of Warwickshire and of Oxford 'makes a balance-weight for my love of Italy so I shall not grow one-sided', she wrote to a friend.

In December 1885 we come upon another Leamington letter, this one to John Hay. She has just heard from Henry James about the death of Clover Adams. 'I should like to die without warning myself,' she remarks. 'But for those who are left it is very terrible.' She tells Hay she has three friends watching her work-table : three photographs. 'Mr Howells smiles and smiles; you look poetic; and Henry James cynical.' And she announces to Hay her plan to go to Italy in January.

In February 1886, as we have seen, she was still in lodgings in Seymour Street. She had accumulated a great many belongings; hence the new trunk. In March she finally left, shortly after Henry James moved from Piccadilly to Kensington. When she reached Venice, late one evening in April the air was as warm as July. Her gondola shot out into the Grand Canal; the moonlight gave the old houses and mouldy palaces phantasmal forms. 'I think I felt compensated for all my years of toil, just in that half hour.' Her destination was Florence. She put up at the *pension* on the Arno where Henry James had come calling six years before.

I

'I wonder, my dear Francis, whether you will do me rather a favour,' Henry James wrote to his friend Boott on 25 May 1886.

My excellent friend Constance Fenimore Woolson is in Florence and I want to pay her your compliment and administer to her some social comfort. The finest satisfaction I can confer upon her will be to ask you to go and see her, at Casa Molin, the old Pension Barbensi, on the Lung' Arno, which you will know. She appears to know few people there (i.e. in Florence), and though she has not made any sort of request of me touching this proposal (by which I don't mean that I want you to 'propose' to her, either for me or for yourself,) I am sure the sight of you would give her joy. She is a deaf and *meticuleuse* old maid – but she is also an excellent and sympathetic being. If Lizzie could take a look at her and attract her to the villa I should be very glad.

Boott called on Miss Woolson with some promptness, and she was made welcome at the Villa Castellani, where in due course she rented rooms in one of its wings. Her grand-uncle James Fenimore Cooper had once lived at Bellosguardo, as had Hawthorne. The Castellani had figured in *Roderick Hudson* and in *The Portrait of a Lady*, so that Miss Woolson enjoyed a sense of communion with Bellosguardo's Jamesian past – and with the friends of her friend. Before she left Italy that summer to spend the hot months in Switzerland, she had signed a year's lease for the adjoining fourteen-room Villa Brichieri-Colombi. In a letter to Lizzie Boott Henry wrote: 'Tell your father I thank him for the kindness which she [Miss Woolson] tells me he has shown her in profusion.' Fenimore had a great liking for Boott, and the sentimental songs which he composed. Boott on his side had become fond of Fenimore – indeed it is only in James's letters to Boott and his daughter that she is referred to as 'Fenimore'. Elsewhere she figures either with her full three names or simply as 'Miss Woolson'. By the end of that summer the novelist was writing to Boott: 'I have promised to go and see her after she is settled at Bellosguardo.'

2

A great change had occurred on Bellosguardo that year, shortly before Fenimore's arrival. Lizzie Boott, after almost six years of indecision, had married Frank Duveneck. The union of this descendant of the New England Bootts and Lymans with the son of a German-American immigrant had been opposed by many of Lizzie's friends; how Francis viewed it we cannot say. To judge from James's comments, he seems to have acquiesced in all his daughter's wishes. Nevertheless he was 73, and for forty years he had had Lizzie's undivided company. Now a third figure had moved into the Castellani, a stoutish, provincial-mannered, inarticulate but polite painter from Cincinnati. In congratulating Lizzie on her engagement James remarked that if Francis did not like the marriage 'he must come over and live with me – I have a room for him'. To Francis he wrote: 'I hasten to express my sympathy in all you must feel on the subject of her engagement – the apprehensions (as to becoming No. 3) as well as the satisfaction that she is to take a step that has in it so little of precipitation.' He cautioned his old friend: 'Take care lest between two easels you fall to the ground, you can so easily trip over the legs.' Later, when he saw the three together, he distinctly felt that for the time at least Boott had been 'shunted', but was making the best of it. He was to recognize that in a sense Duveneck also could feel 'shunted', for the ties binding father and daughter were strong. An observer might have said that in reality nothing had changed on Bellosguardo: father and daughter had lived there for years, and the daughter's painting-master, had now simply been added to the household. A striking snapshot of the period reveals all the ambiguities of this triangle: Lizzie stands erect in the foreground, beside her seated father; the husband is in the background, on the steps leading to the Castellani terrace; he is large and ungainly in his ill-fitting clothes and bulky beside the elderly, trim Mary Ann Shenstone, who had lived with the Bootts ever since Lizzie was born. Boott might feel that his daughter had left him; but she was still at his side. And Duveneck must have continued to feel that he was still in the background.

James had followed Duveneck's career from the first with fascination: the painter seemed so ill-matched with the 'admirably produced' Lizzie, whose education he had described in *The Portrait*. When Duveneck had arrived from Munich he was like a big child suddenly transferred from the bucolic life of a farm into that of a palace. He had not been formed for the drawing-room. He had bought himself new clothes and tried his best to fit himself into the international 'society' in which Lizzie moved. Now he had married the heiress (Boott's income was derived from certain profitable New England textile mills). He lived in a grand villa; he had to say good-bye to cherished evenings of idle drinking in *trattorias* and wine-cellars. James wrote to Lizzie that although he congratulated her, he congratulated Duveneck even more. They should become, he said, 'the *Brownings* (more or less – in a sort of way) of pictorial art'. He urged her to 'make *him* work – make him do himself justice'.

To Henrietta Reubell he described the father-daughter-husband triangle on Bellosguardo in candid terms:

I am much interested and very sympathetic, in *your* interest in Lizzie Boott's new departure. She is judging for herself, with a vengeance; but she is forty years old, and she has the right. Duveneck won't beat her, nor *la rudoyer*, nor perhaps even neglect her, and will be completely under her influence and control; but he is illiterate, ignorant, and not a gentleman (though an excellent fellow, kindly, simple, etc.) and she gives away to him her independence and freedom. His talent is great, though without delicacy, but I fear his indolence is greater still. Lizzie, however, will urge him forward and be an immense help to him. For him it is all gain – for her it is very brave.

Was it all gain for Duveneck? He could take a place in 'society', show his works to great advantage, receive commissions for portraits. He had married not only his pupil but his patroness. He was a painter of great vigour; there was something of Hals or Rubens in his brush; he had an affinity with that side of the Dutch and Flemish schools in which ruddy faces, hearty eating and lusty life are depicted. The question was whether such a native talent, a figure as unbuttoned and as primitive as Duveneck, but with a distinct touch of mastery in his palette, could fit the tight clothes Lizzie wished him to wear; whether he could adapt himself to the manners of the American gentry abroad and overcome his relaxed, easy-going nature.

James saw, and was to see, a psychological situation on Bellosguardo which he would re-imagine and re-create years later in *The Golden Bowl*, although with quite different characters – that of a father and daughter so attached to one another that the husband of the daughter feels himself superfluous. He was also, in that novel, to deal with the problems encountered by the father as a consequence of his daughter's secession from their close life together. In the real-life situation James's greatest sympathy was with the elderly Boott; and during this period we find him writing to Francis more frequently, as if to console him. When summer came, the father went north in search of cooler weather; this year, for the first time, Lizzie was not with him. He made his lonely journey through Switzerland, a country he never much liked. James asked him how he was facing 'the terrible problems' of having to be with only 'the inspiration of your own *bien-être*, a stimulus never in the past sufficient for you'. He also remarked: 'Perhaps you are not alone – I hope not – perhaps even you have met our friend Fenimore somewhere.' James had last heard from her, he said, from Geneva, where she had described herself as hanging over the balcony of the Hôtel National, looking upon the placid waters of the Lake. If he had sent Boott to Fenimore in Florence, hoping to soften some of her hours of loneliness, he seemed now to be thinking of the loneliness she might soften for Boott in his old age. This too he would, in the fullness of time, incorporate into *The Golden Bowl*.

115

The Two Villas

AFTER the publication of *The Princess Casamassima* in 1886 James decided he would break his long stay in London by a month's trip to Italy, to keep his promise to visit Fenimore and to see Francis and the Boott-Duvenecks. Alice had spent the summer in Leamington. All had gone well, save at the very end when there was an unexpected crisis, a parochial comedy. Two young clergymen, lodging in the same house, attempted to enter Alice's apartment late one evening. At first James's letters made this sound as if they had designs on his invalid sister. He said they 'pretended' they had been discussing theology; what they had discussed 'was of course whiskey'. Alice, at any rate, developed palpitations and hysterical prostration. The clergymen were contrite and offered apologies. Miss Loring wrote a stiff letter to their ecclesiastical superior. The moral of the matter, James told a friend, was that 'there are apparently strange little cads and brutes in the great Church of England'. The evidence suggests that the clergymen, if they were a trifle buoyant and tipsy at the end of their amiable evening, had simply tried the wrong door. Alice, however, could be easily upset; a simple and credible mistake, became for her, in her cloistered state, a sinister episode.

It blew over, however. In due course she returned to London, where James found small rooms in Gloucester Road, round the corner from De Vere Gardens. James wrote to Lizzie he looked forward to seeing her in her newly-married state, and to 'many a delightful and long-deferred talk'. And 'our good Fenimore must also be worked in – but I shall be equal even to this. I am very glad you are nice to her, as she is a very good woman, with an immense power of devotion (to H. J.!)' He asked the Bootts and Fenimore to keep his arrival a secret; he did not wish to be drawn into the complications of Florentine society. Before he came away it was settled that he would sublet the Brichieri-Colombi apartment from Fenimore during December, since she had her rooms at the Castellani until the new year. He would this time realize a very old dream of residing on Bellosguardo – and under circumstances that seemed to him very agreeable. The Bootts expressed concern lest he find the Brichieri cold.

It is very good of you to offer to put in *wood*, but I have an idea that Fenimore, whose devotion – like my appreciation of it – is *sans bornes* – has stacked me up a pile with her own hands. She is a gallant friend, but I am afraid she has bored you with me. Never mind, you will have your revenge; she will bore *me* with *you*.

If his arrival was generally a secret, he nevertheless informed Vernon Lee of it two days before leaving London. 'I shall come and see you very quickly,' he wrote, 'though I mean to lodge, for sweet seclusion's sake, out of town – in one of your grand old villas. The thought of going to Italy again, after a long and loathesome divorce, is absolutely rapturous to me.'

He left on 3 December 1886, promising Alice he would return within a month. He bypassed Paris and travelled via the St Gothard. On the 5th he was in Milan, 'drinking in the delicious sun'; on the 7th he was in Pisa; the next day he reached Bellosguardo. By this time he knew that he and Fenimore would be alone on their hilltop. The Duvenecks were in Florence proper. Lizzie was expecting a child.

I

The two ancient villas on Bellosguardo, the one in which Fenimore was living temporarily and the one which was to be her home at the beginning of the new year, stand near one another. The Villa Brichieri-Colombi is a substantial rambling two-storey building, the blank rear of which rises high from the wall on the winding road leading to the brow of Bellosguardo. It is situated near the summit, and a small gate, as one approaches, permits a sideways glimpse; but the high wall shuts it in and only the upper storey is visible, so that one gets no sense of its large terrace, offering a sweeping view of Florence on one side and the Arno valley on the other. Cypresses tower on either side; and an umbrella-pine stands off a little, establishing a neat balance in a warmly-human landscape. As one climbs for another two or three minutes on the steep road, following the wall, one comes to the small piazza where today a commemorative plaque lists, among others, the three famous Americans who lived on Bellosguardo – Hawthorne, Cooper and Henry James. Fenimore is not remembered, although she could have a certain claim, since the other names range from Galileo to Ouida, the Brownings to Robert Lytton. Dominating the square is the yellow façade of the massive Villa Castellani, which rises directly from the roadway, offering, through a heavy grill, a glimpse of its thick walls and noble quattrocento court. The Bootts lived in the north wing. The Castellani, however, had some fifty rooms, and here American Greenoughs and Huntingtons from the early part of the century, and others, such as Browning's friend Isa Blagden, had occupied apartments. Fenimore, standing in the Boott garden and looking across a patch of mountain terrain, could command a splendid view of the eminently practical and solid Brichieri, with its faded yellowish walls and strong tile roof.

James had never been in the Brichieri, though he knew its long history and Mrs Browning's *Aurora Leigh* with its *I found a house at Florence on the hill of Bellosguardo*. When he entered, he discovered that it gave him such a view as he had never had from the Castellani. To the north he saw a panorama of Florentine domes and towers, with Fiesole and the Apennines beyond, range upon range. On the other, the Arno side, he looked upon a soft valley in its winter dress, with sleepy white towns and the gleam of the river – old castles, towers, campaniles; and across the western end the

abrupt Carrara hills in the December sky. When there was sun he
felt well out of London. But the season was wet and cold. Fenimore
had laid in the promised store of firewood and James built himself
roaring fires. He occupied a drawing-room and a bedroom on the
ground floor, a section of the villa which had been built before the
discovery of America. Fenimore made available her cook Angelo
who acted also as his valet.

The two writers seem to have fallen very quickly into a regular
way of life. Both were industrious; their working hours were sacred.
A letter from James among the papers of John Hay shows the
novelist – otherwise consummately discreet – unbending sufficiently
to mention his neighbour. Describing the view from his windows, he
wrote that

they are not my windows – but those of our amiable and distinguished
friend Miss Woolson, and I will leave her to deal with them. She has
taken this roomy and rambling old villa, furnished, on a lease, and being
still in possession of another and not able to enter it till the first day of
January, has very obligingly sublet it to me for a month with the services of a queer old melancholy male-cook, whom she had put in to take
care of it. She dwells at five minutes' distance, and I see her every day
or two – indeed often dine with her. She has done a brave thing in settling
herself here (for two or three years) in a somewhat mouldy Tuscan mansion – but I think it clear that she will get much enjoyment and profit
from it à la longue. She will get quiet, sunny, spacious hours for work
(a prospect, on her part, in which I take an interest, in view of the great
merit and progress of her last book) and have Florence in the hollow of
her hand.

2

We know very little about the life these two writers led on their
Florentine hill-top. There are only mute witnesses. Certain books
which Henry gave to Fenimore have survived; nearly all of them
bear the dates of this time. To commemorate his tenancy he inscribed a copy of the three-volume *Bostonians* 'To his *padrona* Constance Fenimore Woolson, her faithful tenant and friend, Henry
James, Bellosguardo, December 1886.' A limited edition of Shelley,
selected and arranged by Stopford Brooke, on large paper was inscribed 'Constance Fenimore Woolson, from her friend and confrère
Henry James, 1887.' There is also George Eliot's *Romola* in a two-
volume edition; this again has her name written out in full and the
copy is signed and dated 'Florence January 1887.' Perhaps the most

significant document is the one that was most public: an article James consecrated to the work of Fenimore, in *Harper's Weekly* of 12 February 1887. Its appearance at that date suggests that it was probably written shortly after James moved into the Villa Brichieri.

During the previous year he had contributed an article to the same weekly on Howells. Thus, in writing the essay on Miss Woolson, James – who had hitherto confined himself to major continental novelists – was turning his attention to an American contemporary whom he esteemed and ranked as worthy of attention with Howells. He had told Howells as much some years before. The occasion for the essay was the recent appearance of *East Angels*, Fenimore's most ambitious novel. James's tribute was the expression of a sincere admiration for the person as much as for the writer. And yet a reader of the article in the files of *Harper's*, or in its revised appearance in *Partial Portraits*, cannot but be puzzled: that Henry should have bestowed upon work as regional and as 'magazineish' as hers the discriminating literary taste which he had hitherto reserved for the leading European writers of fiction, or upon figures such as Hawthorne or even Howells, strikes one today as curious. For Miss Woolson was on the whole rather prosy, a journeywoman of letters. Without style, and with an extreme literalness, she lacked ease and the richer verbal imagination. Her work is minute – and cluttered; she is an ardent devotee of 'local colour'. Yet Henry James threw his very considerable weight into the enhancement of her reputation. This was singular on the ground of literary criticism, although understandable on the ground of loyalty and friendship. His essay is graceful, yet laboured. He tries very hard to say the right and honourable things, and it requires effort and ingenuity. The final impression can only be that he is honouring Fenimore's dedication to letters less than her devotion to himself. Again and again what he seizes upon in her novels is her capacity for loyalty; her heroines immolate themselves for others; she has a belief in 'personal renunciation, in its frequency as well as its beauty'; she is fond of 'irretrievable personal failures, of people who have had to give up even the memory of happiness, who love and suffer in silence, and minister in secret to the happiness of those who look over their heads'. In his discussion of *East Angels* he speaks of her heroines as trying to 'provide for the happiness of others (when they adore them) even to their own injury'. This remark recalls James's words to Lizzie about Fenimore's 'immense power of devotion (to H. J.!)'.

Apparently he was reciprocating this devotion as best he could. The essay in *Harper's Weekly* contains a biographical passage of considerable critical liveliness, in which James pretends to have gained his facts from Miss Woolson's work. 'It would not be hidden from a reader of *Anne* and *East Angels* that the author is a native of New England, who may have been transplanted to a part of the country open in some degree to the imputation of being "out west",' and he goes on to tell 'so far as my knowledge goes' of her education in New York and her life in the south. He describes 'her earnest, lingering manner' in *Anne*, and speaks of her prolixity. In criticizing her for having dwelt so little on her picture of a snowbound military post at Mackinaw, he observes this is 'the only case that I can remember, by the way, in which she has abandoned an opportunity without having conscientiously pressed it out'. The effect of the essay is laudatory, as when he speaks of her liking for Florida reflected in *East Angels* – 'a high appreciation of orange gardens and white beaches, pine barrens and rivers smothered in jungles, and a peculiar affection for that city of the past, so rapidly becoming a city of the future, St Augustine'. The sketch concludes with James's wondering whether she intends to make use of her 'personal familiarity with Rome, Florence, Venice and other irrepressible cities'. Has she, he asks (not without a touch of coyness), 'a story about Europe in reserve or does she propose to maintain her distinguished independence?'

This rather strange and fulsome biographical excursion was deleted by Henry when he transferred the essay into his book. In its place he inserted a further passage of criticism, pointing out 'two defects' in *East Angels*. One defect was that Miss Woolson described in this novel a group too detached and isolated, as if on a desert island. Its members went to and fro, to New York and to Europe, but 'they have a certain shipwrecked air, as of extreme dependence on each other, though surrounded with every convenience'. The other fault, which he deemed more significant, was their total preoccupation with the famous 'tender sentiment' – the complications of the plot were all complications of love. 'Our impression is of sky and sand – the sky of azure, the sand of silver – and between them, conspicuous, immense, against the low horizon, the question of engagement and marriage.' James's criticism generalized into a belief that women-writers tend to give too much place to 'love' in a novel, and to forget that in life there were other things as well. Indeed 'in

men's novels, even of the simplest strain, there are still other references and other explanations; in women's, when they are of the
category to which I allude, there are none but that one'.

In the essay James dealt, one by one, with Miss Woolson's various
books : he praised her for giving a voice to the inarticulate South so
early after the Civil War; he professed to not having read her lake-
country sketches in *Castle Nowhere*, but in *Rodman the Keeper* he
found much 'interesting artistic work'. Miss Woolson had perceived
that 'no social revolution of equal magnitude' as in the South 'had
ever reflected itself so little in literature, remained so unrecorded, so
unpainted and unsung'. Nevertheless her pictures ended by conveying 'dreariness'. Of her popular novel *Anne* he complained that it was
her weakest work because the strong element of devotion and renunciation in her other novels was largely absent from it. The reader,
he said, builds up great hopes in a character named Tita, but 'Tita
vanishes into the vague' after an infant marriage. Miss Woolson
'likes the unmarried, but she likes marriages even better, and also
sometimes hurries them forward in advance of the reader's exaction'.
Her short novel *For the Major*, the story of a woman's effort to wear
a constant mask of youth, in spite of her being older than her husband, James found 'fantastic' but 'eminently definite'. The heroine
is aided by her husband's ill-health, 'so that she is able to keep on the
mask till his death, when she pulls it off with a passionate cry of
relief – ventures at last, gives herself the luxury, to be old'. It was
the first time, James observed, that a woman was represented as
painting her face, dyeing her hair and 'dressing young' not out of
vanity but out of tenderness for another – 'the effort usually has its
source in tenderness for herself'. Miss Woolson had done nothing
neater 'than this fanciful figure of the little ringleted, white-frocked,
falsely juvenile lady, who has the toilet-table of an actress and the
conscience of a Puritan'.

That James liked Miss Woolson for having a 'fruitful instinct' in
seeing novels as pictures of the 'evolution of personal relations' is
understandable. And yet it is difficult, in the large scale of literary
values, to read Miss Woolson's work and understand why she was
included in *Partial Portraits*. The volume consisted of several new
essays, written during that year, some on Bellosguardo, and others of
a slightly earlier time : there was the major essay on Maupassant,
and the memorial to Turgenev; his celebrated essay on Emerson,
two on George Eliot, his obituary study of Trollope and papers on

Daudet and Stevenson. The title of *Partial Portraits* contains within it a quiet pun: *French Poets and Novelists* was historical; it dealt with writers Henry had never known personally. *Partial Portraits* deals entirely with writers whom he had met and liked. The 'portraits' can be said to be 'partial' because they are not complete; and they are hardly impartial. On this ground Miss Woolson does belong in the volume; but to modern eyes she cuts a strange figure. To be sure; she is propped by Robert Louis Stevenson on one side and Alphonse Daudet on the other. The question can still be asked: why did James put her there at all? He had paid no such homage to Howells. The things he chose to say he could say sincerely enough. And the article may be a form of 'criticism by omission'. A few years later, when a friend asked him how he had come to write an article about the novels of Mrs Humphry Ward, his reply was, 'I have written no article on Mrs Ward – only a civil perfunctory *payé* (with words between the lines) to escape the gracelessness of refusing when asked.' Nevertheless he reprinted the Ward article in his *Essays in London*. This suggests the essay on Miss Woolson was largely an act of kindness. No greater pen was to commemorate her work. Posterity was to assign her a footnote in the regional fiction of America. In the life of Henry James she occupied a much larger place.

116

A Polyglot Society

Two weeks after James had settled beside his wood-fires in the Villa Brichieri, word was sent up from Florence that Lizzie Duveneck had given birth to a robust male child. To a household which already had a Frank Boott and a Frank Duveneck, there was now added a Frank Duveneck Jr. Henry wrote to William that the child was born 'very quickly and quietly'. He described it to his Aunt Kate as 'a little red worm'. Lizzie was thriving and evidently happy. 'She is much in love with her husband – who will never do much, I think, but who is all the same a fine, pleasant, polite (though perfectly illiterate) man, whom it is impossible not to like.' The baby would 'apparently live and thrive – but Lizzie will plainly be much more of a wife than a mother'. Duveneck would be a weight for Lizzie to carry for the rest of her life – 'I mean socially, and in the world. He is only half-civilized – though he is very "civil".' James thought Boott's acceptance of him at every hour of the day to be 'pathetic and heroic'. He also remarked that the new grandfather seemed 'old and shrivelled and laughs much less than in the old days'. Francis Boott's dilemma struck Henry as 'the subject of a little tale by Turgenev'.

I

Fenimore moved into her villa as planned at the beginning of 1887 and James descended into Florence where, he wrote to Grace Norton, 'I am told I went "out" a great deal. Why I don't know – as it was very exactly what I left London not to do. I am also told I was "lionized" – and the wherefore of this I know still less. On reflection, in fact, I greatly doubt it. But I did see a great many people; too many, for what they were.' James moved into the Hôtel du Sud on the Arno; and although the dusty *tramontana* and the cold were uncomfortable, he relished the winter sunshine. Florence, he told Miss Norton, 'had never seemed to me, naturally and artistically, more delightful. And the views from the villas on the hills (I was at a good many) are as beautiful – really – as your memory must tell you.'

His winter now took an unexpected turn. He had originally left London for one month. Alice wrote complaining that her lodgings were too small, and a new crisis seemed to be impending. At this moment James had the sudden inspiration to do for his sister what Fenimore had done for him. He offered her his flat, and his servants. Alice accepted with joy; it was like installing herself in 'home' instead of lodgings. James assured her that she was conferring a favour on him; she gave his servants something to do. If all went well, he would now be able to spend the entire spring in Italy. 'Foreign lands offer me better conditions of work,' he explained to his brother, 'quieter, fresher mornings, less pestered by the postman – than London does in these months, especially the forthcoming ones.' He also wrote to him : 'I have been driving the pen steadily.'

Whenever he drove the pen, he turned to society for relaxation. How often James saw his erstwhile 'landlady' we do not know. Suddenly he was dining out, paying calls, attending tea-parties. 'I won't tell you their names, or more than that they were members of the queer, promiscuous, polyglot (most polyglot in the world)

Florentine society.' Thus to Grace Norton, in a letter in which he then devotes many pages to telling the names of all his hostesses and describing them. There was Madame de Tchiatchev, an English-woman married to a rich retired Russian diplomat; there was the Marchesa Incontri, a Russian once married to Prince Galitzin, and subsequently to a Florentine, and now widowed. Madame de Tchiat-chev was 'remarkably pleasant and sympathetic' and the Marchesa Incontri was 'singularly clever and easy'. Madame de T. was 'very good and yet not dull'; the Marchesa was probably 'bad – though not dull either'. She went in for the arts. She had a salon, in her splendid villa near the Porta San Gallo, in which she received literary people and also very 'smart' folk. She even wrote novels, under pen names, rather poor things, and in English, which she spoke perfectly. James thought her on the whole 'rather dangerous'.

Near Fiesole there was the Baroness Zunch, 'a very kindly person', who was Anglo-Italian and who had James to dinner. He called on the Countess Peruzzi for old times' sake : she was the former Edith Story, whom he had known at the Barberini. 'She has grown plain, and is motherly and snobbish – and yet I liked her for she is genial and kindly and more to my taste than in her high-flying maiden-hood.' He became friendly with Dr W. W. Baldwin, an American with a wide medical practice in Florence. In particular he liked the sculptor, Adolf Hildebrand, who lived at the foot of Bellosguardo, in the former convent of San Francesco di Paola. Hildebrand had the 'feeling of the Greeks and that of the early Tuscans too, by a strange combination'. Janet Ross, the former Janet Duff Gordon, invited him to her picturesque villa of Castagnolo. A vigorous and active Scots-woman, who had been married to a man much older than herself (his name was Henry James Ross), she was a friend of Meredith and of Symonds, and had been painted by Watts and Leighton. She had lived in Alexandria as a young woman with her husband, and later they had settled near Florence where she interested herself in agri-culture. 'She wants me to stay with her – but I like you better! – and fear you less,' he wrote to Mrs Bronson. He overcame his fear suffi-ciently to spend three days at Castagnolo. Mrs Ross played her guitar, sang Italian songs and talked a great deal. 'I am not so sure of Mrs Ross's mind as of her eyes, her guitar and her desire to sell you bric-à-brac!' he told Mrs Wister. 'She is awfully handsome, in a utilitarian kind of way – an odd mixture of the British female and the danger-ous woman – a Bohemian with rules and accounts.'

A long letter of 5 February 1887 to Mrs Bronson in Venice throws more light on the extent to which James was lionized in polyglot Florence. He was just leaving, he wrote, to visit Mrs Ross for the day. He would dine with the Marchesa Incontri the next day. The following Monday he was to dine with a kinswoman of Mrs Bronson's; on Tuesday with Vernon Lee to meet an Italian critic, a Browning enthusiast '[Enrico] Nencioni, who has translated me'. The previous evening he had dined with the Huntingtons at the Castellani, and the night before that with some Americans named Loften 'in extraordinary and overdone splendour'; the night before that at the Cantagallis', in company 'with that extraordinary and most amusing woman the Countess Gamba', and the night before that with Edith Peruzzi, in company with Corsinis, Farinolas and Antinoris. He had met the McClellans, the widow and daughter of the Civil War general, at their Torrigiani cousin's, 'where I went by the latter's invitation, to see the pretended Raphael Madonna – which is no more a Raphael than Daisy Miller is Shakespeare'.

To John Hay, Fenimore wrote : 'I have never seen anyone to be so run-after as he was while in Florence.'

Vernon Lee was 'the most intelligent person in the place'. He went often to 5 Via Garibaldi, where Miss Lee received daily from four to seven, and as often in the evening as people would come. He described her as 'exceedingly ugly, disputatious, contradictious and perverse'. He liked her clever half-brother, Eugene Lee-Hamilton, formerly attached to the British Embassy in Paris but now bedridden – or rather sofa-ridden – by paralysis. There was also a 'grotesque, deformed, invalidical, posing mother, and a father in the highest degree unpleasant, mysterious and sinister' who had not sat down at table with his family for twenty years. Vernon Lee attracted to the Via Garibaldi 'all the world', discussed 'all things in any language, and understands some, drives her pen, glares through her spectacles and keeps up her courage'. She was 'a really superior talker,' he told Gosse. 'She has a mind – almost the only one in Florence'. It made James 'a little less ashamed of the stupid English race'.

In Florence he met Maurice Barrès aged 26, who brought a letter from Daudet. They lunched in the Via Tornuaboni and Barrès said years later in his memoirs he had 'explained life' to James. The novelist described him as 'very young, uncelebrated and undecipherable' and of a 'fearful precocity'. Barrès would fight duels, found newspapers, be a deputy and write novels. James deciphered him ultimately as 'a *poseur* and a mystificator'. Florentine society on the whole was 'a vain agitation of particles'. At the end of ten wintry weeks he called a halt and 'escaped from the whirlpool of idiotic card-leaving of which Florentine existence is mainly composed'.

2

From Florence he proceeded to Venice where he arrived on 22 February to find it altogether strange in its dampness and cold, with watery sunshine and the gondoliers beckoning as if it were mid-summer. He had long promised Mrs Bronson he would be her guest. Casa Alvisi, opposite the great baroque Salute, was a kind of social *porto di mare*, at the mouth of the Grand Canal. Mrs Bronson used an apartment in a Giustiniani palace attached to the rear of Ca'Alvisi for her guests. Browning often stayed there for weeks at a time; and James, hugging a big plastered stove in which a fire crackled and roared, at first found it adequate, if a bit gloomy. His hostess provided a gondolier who served as cook, so that he had total privacy.

The novelist spent 'seven unsuccessful weeks' in Venice. The 'glutinous malodorous damp' in the *calles* and *campos* bothered him. He developed a series of headaches and his state of mind was not helped by a heavy snowfall in mid-March. 'Yesterday there were sinister carts in the Piazza and men who looked like Irishmen shovelling away snow. One was almost sorry to have left Boston,' he wrote to Boott. He confined himself to the company of Mrs Bronson, her daughter Edith, and the Daniel Curtises, whom he had met long before but whom he now saw for the first time in their splendid palace, the Barbaro, on the Canal near the Accadémia. He was to become accustomed to Curtis's anecdotes ('doing his best to make the Grand Canal seem like Beacon Street') and to be fond of his wife, Ariana Curtis, daughter of an English admiral. James's social life was cut short, however, by an acute attack of jaundice. He took to his bed and ran a slight temperature for sixteen days. 'This made it,' he wrote to William, 'the *longest* illness I have had since I was laid up with typhoid fever so many years before, at Boulogne.' This remark suggests that James now took lightly his early and late claims of 'invalidism' during and after the Civil War. He had good medical attention and his gondolier was a faithful nurse. He blamed his illness on the 'insalubrious' rooms. 'The apartment is not *simpatico*,'

he said. Fenimore wrote offering him his rooms in the Villa Brichieri
again, since she occupied only the upper apartment. Mrs Bronson's
gondolier all but wept at the Venice station when he saw James off;
and his old Roman acquaintance of the *Roderick Hudson* period,
Eugene Benson, the painter, whom he had seen in the Palazzo Capello
on the Rio Marin (the palace which the novelist would use in *The
Aspern Papers*) turned up to say good-bye. In Florence Dr Baldwin
met the Venice train when it arrived on a Saturday evening in April,
and insisted on personally escorting his patient to the Brichieri. The
'breezy Tuscan hilltop suits me better,' the novelist wrote to his
Venetian hostess. 'I have the most majestic, and at the same time the
most *allegro* quarters here – and the place is more beautiful than
ever.'

117

The Aspern Papers

HENRY JAMES'S letters from his hill-top, during April and May of
1887, breathe an air of calm and release – a sense of enchantment –
rarely to be found in his correspondence. After his illness and the
winter mouldiness and decay of Venice he was living on Bellosguardo among devoted friends, canopied by blue sky and cradled in
soft light, with domes and campaniles, mountains and valleys and a
large expanse of cultivated nature as a constant refreshment to the
eye. He could sit on the great wide terrace of the Villa Brichieri or
read and write in its pleasant rose-garden. His 'vast and vaulted'
rooms offered him coolness and a sense of space. Sometimes he had
his meal out of doors, in the twilight, probably in the company of
Fenimore, with the tinkling of the little bell in a church near by
sounding its notes in the sunset. At night there would be the mournful but characteristic cry of the little Tuscan owl, and the repertoire
of the nightingales amid the pines and cypresses. His illness was forgotten: he had privacy or sociability as he wished. He had the
attentive and devoted Fenimore. He had discovered an Italian paradise.

In letter after letter he speaks of having 'the most beautiful view
in the world'. To a friend in London he wrote:

I am completely restored and have taken, till the first of June, part of a
delightful villa on this enchanting hilltop just out of the gates of Florence,

where the most beautiful view in the world – as beautiful, and somehow as *personal* – and as talkative! – as a lovely woman – hangs before me as often as I lift my head. As soon as I can stop making love to it I shall go back to England – somewhat ruefully, for I feel myself again somewhat tainted with the taste for living abroad.

To Gosse he wrote that 'at this divine moment' Italy was perfectly irresistible. In England his villa would be 'suburban', but here it was 'supercelestial'. To William he wrote, after describing his view, 'I am working very well again.'

He entered upon one of the great productive periods of his career – that interval between *The Princess Casamassima* and *The Tragic Muse* which might be called his 'Italian phase' – during which he wrote some eight or ten of his celebrated tales and a short novel. His pen seemed to take strength and power from the beauty around him and from his mode of life. He avoided this time the pitfalls of Florentine society, but descended into the city with curiosity to take part in one or two of the fêtes arranged that spring in celebration of the unveiling of the new façade of Santa Maria del Fiore, the Duomo. It had been under construction for some years. James and Fenimore could remember the tremendous scaffolding which covered the front of the church when they were sightseeing in Florence together in 1880. The King and Queen attended some of the observances and James fell sufficiently into the holiday spirit to don a crimson *lucco* and a black velvet headgear and attend the historical ball at the Palazzo Vecchio in the great Sal dei Cinquencento. 'I wish you could have seen me,' he wrote to Mrs Kemble. 'I was lovely.' Here, under Vasari's frescoes, he witnessed the royal ceremonial and costumes reflecting three centuries in Florentine life. Descendants of the Strozzis, Guiccardinis, Rucellais, Gherardescas, and others, mounted on magnificent horses and wearing 'admirable dresses with the childlike gallantry and glee with which only Italians can wear them', rode through the brown old streets followed by an immense train of citizens, all in fifteenth-century garb. It made a 'noble picture'; it testified to the 'latent love of splendour which is still in those dear people'.

I

Henry James and Fenimore were living for the first time under the same roof. For this reason, perhaps, there is no allusion to her in any of his letters, although in December he had spoken of her to his friends as his *padrona*, clearly underlining the fact that she was in another villa. He had then made it clear also – to Grace Norton and to William – that in January he had moved out of the Brichieri when Fenimore took possession of it. Now, however, he had quietly moved back in again, and merely remarked casually to his friends that he had splendid rooms in a fine old place on Bellosguardo, with a superb view. As for the Boott-Duvenecks next door in the Castellani – for they had reoccupied their apartment – they would see no special significance in his tenancy. The supremely cautious James, always careful to avoid any involvement with a woman, accepted blandly Fenimore's offer to let him have the rooms; he felt there was no danger of any public notice being taken of their contiguous occupancy. To his more intimate friends James simply suggested that Fenimore was a 'neighbour'. Thus in a letter to Mrs Bronson he speaks of meeting a Florentine kinswoman of hers who 'appeared here yesterday punctually to call on my neighbour Miss Woolson, on whom I was also calling'.

We know of one visitor who came to the Brichieri and spent an evening with James and Fenimore. This was the novelist Rhoda Broughton, whom he had encountered in London drawing-rooms. He described her to Mrs Kemble as coming up to his standard of appreciation of Florence; he liked her, he said, 'in spite of her roughness'. She was Miss Woolson's age and she possessed a fund of human wisdom and wit, and an ease and liberality in her Victorianism. From James's allusion to this evening in a letter to Miss Broughton long after, it seems that she met Miss Woolson merely as an old and valued friend of James's who happened to be a Bellosguardo neighbour.

Discreet as they were, we may speculate that they saw each other frequently, even while spending their days in solitary pursuit of their individual work. Fenimore's cook Angelo served both of them. It is equally likely that even though they were under the same roof, they lived very much as they would have lived had they been housed apart. That James in other circumstances continued to be cautious we know, for in the following year, when he kept a special rendez-vous with Fenimore in Geneva, he mentioned it only to Francis Boott: and to him he explained that they were staying in hotels a mile apart. Given James's reticences and the fact that he seems to have attached at this time no particular significance to Fenimore's devotion to him (save that it called for kindness on his part); given

Fenimore's personal shyness, for all her epistolary candour – the evidence would seem to point to a continuing 'virtuous' attachment, in which James accepted with pleasure the attention and admiration Fenimore gave him and offered a kind of disinterested and aloof affection in return. There was not a little, in this, of James's powerful egotism : why shouldn't Fenimore like him? And if she did, why shouldn't he make himself agreeable to her? That this pleasant and *méticuleuse* old maid may have nourished fantasies of a closer tie does not seem to have occurred to him at this time. If it had, we might assume he would have put distance between himself and Miss Woolson. There was a kind of truce of affection between them. And perhaps the best evidence of this is to be found once more – in the absence of correspondence – in a public document. This was *The Aspern Papers*, the most brilliant of James's tales, which he began and all but completed at the Villa Brichieri.

2

The idea for the tale was in his notebook when he came to stay with Fenimore. He had set it down one day in Florence. He had paid a call on Vernon Lee and her brother and met the Countess Gamba, whom he described as 'clever, natural, exuberant'. The Countess was the daughter of a Tuscan poet and had married a nephew of Byron's last attachment, Teresa Guiccioli. She told James the Gambas had a great many Byron letters which were 'shocking and unprintable', and James exclaimed in his notebook 'she took upon herself to burn one of them up!' In a writer addicted to letter-burning the exclamation may seem strange. But James distinguished between his own right to guard his personal privacy and posterity's duty to respect what survived. If writers did not guard their privacy, their papers were fair game. Vernon Lee's brother told James the Gambas were 'illiberal and dangerous' guardians of their Byronic heritage and refused to publish or show the letters. The Countess Gamba became angry when Lee-Hamilton told her that it was her duty to English literature to make the Byron documents public. '*Elle se fiche bien* of the English public,' James wrote in his notebook.

After the Countess Gamba left, Lee-Hamilton told James an anecdote inspired by the talk of Byron. There had lived in Florence, to a ripe old age, Mary Jane Clairmont, or Claire Clairmont as she called herself, Byron's mistress and mother of his daughter Allegra. She had a house in the Via Romana. For some time before her death a lodger lived with her, a Boston sea-captain named Silsbee. His passion in life was Shelley; Vernon Lee related that he would sit gloomily in an armchair, 'looking like some deep-sea monster on a Bernini fountain, staring at the carpet and quoting his favourite author with a trumpet-like twang quite without relevance to the conversation'. Silsbee had long known that Claire Clairmont had in her possession certain Shelley and Byron papers. He had made every effort to acquire these, and had finally obtained domicile in the very house in which they were kept. There were stories that he never ventured far from home lest Miss Clairmont should die while he was away. In one version of the anecdote he did, however, have to go to America and it was then – in 1879 – that she died. Living with her was a Clairmont niece of about 50, and Silsbee rushed back to see whether he could obtain from her the papers Miss Clairmont had hidden from the world. The niece had long nourished an admiration for the rugged Captain and she said to him, 'I will give you all the letters if you will marry me.' Lee-Hamilton said that Silsbee was still running.

James wrote the bare anecdote in his notebook on 12 January 1887. What fascinated him was the thought of Miss Clairmont's having lived on into his time; he had often passed her door. Sargent remembered her as a handsome old lady, whom he had seen once during his Florentine childhood at his dancing-class. He evoked her faded elegance and the unrelieved black of her attire. 'Certainly there is a little subject there,' James wrote in his notebook,

the picture of the two faded, queer, poor, discredited old English women – living on into a strange generation, in their musty corner of a foreign town – with these illustrious letters their most precious possession. Then the plot of the Shelley fanatic – his watchings and waitings – the way he *couvers* the treasure. The dénouement needn't be the one related of poor Silsbee, and at any rate the general situation is in itself a subject and a picture. It strikes me much,

James wrote. The interest would be in some price that the man would have to pay – a price the old woman, the survivor, would set upon the papers. The drama of the story would be his hesitations and his struggles, 'for he really would give almost anything'.

3

The Aspern Papers was an atempt by James to recapture 'the visitable past' – that past which in any generation is still within the
reach of its memory. He sought 'the poetry of the thing outlived and
lost and gone'. This he achieved in a high flight of poetic narrative.
His old woman lives beyond her time in a decaying Venetian palace
clinging to precious letters written to her by a great American poet.
The cat-and-mouse game which James devised between his Silsbee
character and this lady provides the mounting tension : and in the
tale James used his characteristic technique, that of making his hero
his own historian – writing his story with such candour and ingenu-
ousness that he discloses his own duplicity, his easy rationalizations
and his failure to grasp the fact that, in his zeal for literary history,
he is an invader of private lives. In this sense the tale is a moral fable
for historians and biographers. It has dramatized, once and for all,
their anomalous role : and it makes clear, as James's notes did not,
on which side the novelist placed himself. He might have been
shocked by the Countess Gamba's having burned a Byron letter; but
in the tale all the Aspern papers are burned – sadistically we might
say – 'one by one'. The strange tension of the story resides in the
two climaxes; so that when Michael Redgrave converted the tale into
a play he had that rare thing among modern dramas, both a second-
act 'curtain' and a powerful ending. The first is that eerie moment
when Juliana discovers the narrator trying to gain access to her desk
and turns her blazing eyes upon him – those eyes which had been
covered by a green shade – the eyes that had once looked into those
of the poet Jeffrey Aspern :

her hands were raised, she had lifted the everlasting curtain that covered
half her face, and for the first, the last, the only time I beheld her extraordinary eyes. They glared at me [they were like the sudden drench, for a
caught burglar, of a flood of gaslight]; * they made me horribly ashamed.
I never shall forget her strange little bent white tottering figure, with its
lifted head, her attitude, her expression; neither shall I forget the tone
in which as I turned, looking at her, she hissed out passionately,
furiously :
      'Ah, you publishing scoundrel!'

This is the *coup de théâtre* of the story : the narrator has been caught
red-handed; the hero-worshipper, the lover of poetry, the gallant
                    * Inserted in later revision.

gentleman, is nothing but a common thief in his quest for a memento of the man he worships. But the splendid theatricality of this scene is surpassed by the third act, in which the middle-aged niece, after the death of Juliana, suggests to the narrator that the Aspern papers could be his if he became a member of the family, 'If you were not a stranger ... Anything that is mine would be yours.' The pathos of this moment has dramatic grandeur; and it is too much for the narrator. He had been ready to steal; he had even said playfully he would be willing to make love to the younger Miss Bordereau. Now all he can stammer is 'Ah Miss Tita – ah Miss Tita * – It wouldn't do, it wouldn't do!' He flees the palace, and surrenders all hope of getting the Aspern papers.

The passage which follows is perhaps the most beautiful in this tale. The narrator's thoughts and feelings are described as he is rowed through the canals by his gondolier. The vision of the bright decaying city fuses with his personal disaster. 'I could not accept. I could not, for a bundle of tattered papers, marry a ridiculous, pathetic, provincial old woman.' He may have trifled with her affections; he now understands this; yet he is not sufficiently without principle to achieve his ends at any cost. Late in the afternoon he finds himself standing before the church of Saints John and Paul, looking up at the great equestrian statue of Bartolommeo Colleoni, the old buccaneer, who had grabbed at life with his two fists. Seldom had James combined scene and subject more artfully than at this moment when the literary narrator searches the 'small square-jawed face' of the statue and thinks of the career of 'the terrible *condottiere* who sits so sturdily astride of his huge bronze horse, on the high pedestal on which Venetian gratitude maintains him'.

I only found myself staring at the triumphant captain as if he had had an oracle on his lips. The western light shines into all his grimness at that hour and makes it wonderfully personal. But he continued to look far over my head, at the red immersion of another day – he had seen so many go down into the lagoon through the centuries – and if he were thinking of battles and stratagems they were of a different quality from any I had to tell him of.

This is all but the end of the narrator's stratagems. So tense a drama, unfolded step by step and with an inexorable logic – an old palace, two solitary ladies, and a bundle of papers as the principal

* In his late revision of the tale, James altered the name to Tina.

properties and all Venice for a backdrop – would have been nothing without the measured tread of the narrative. There is no faltering footstep in it, from the opening scene in which James introduces the all-knowing Mrs Prest (a re-creation of the benevolent Mrs Bronson) to the last scene in the old palace when the narrator learns of the fate of the papers. Once the situation had been established there had ensued a long period in which the narrator simply lived in his rooms, cultivated the garden, 'bombarded' the ladies with flowers, and found every door closed in his face. James must make the reader feel the passage of several weeks from spring to hot summer, and he does this in half a dozen pages with the beautiful assurance of one who can make the clock take the rhythm of his tracing pen. We walk the palace with the restless story-teller in his cat-and-mouse game, watching always for some move, some bit of action from the ladies who are his prey. 'Their motionless shutters became as expressive as eyes consciously closed, and I took comfort in thinking that at all events though invisible themselves they saw me between the lashes.' This brief section (it is the fourth of the nine equal parts into which the narrative falls) ends with the narrator's account of Jeffrey Aspern, the American romantic poet he idolizes: and in Aspern James evokes himself as he was, and as he would have liked to be – a kind of Hawthorne figure liberated from the parochial and from all puritan constriction – 'he had found means to live and write like one of the first; to be free and general and not at all afraid; to feel, understand and express everything'.

Such was James's flight on the hill of Bellosguardo, his vision of past and present, of a dying city, a crumbling palace, and a dying old lady who had once known a great passion for a great poet. What had begun as 'a final scene of the rich dim Shelley drama played out in the very theatre of our own "modernity"' ended in a beautifully-wrought tale which was, above all, a defence of privacy and an exposure of the unfeeling egotist who exploits others' feelings for his own ends. Nor is the old Juliana, with her green eyeshade, exempt from this predatory character; she knows her position of advantage, and on the brink of the grave clings to life with all the rapacity and cunning, as well as vitality, of that other strange expatriate-Venetian, Volpone. She knows how to bargain for the narrator's dollars or pounds – one wants to say ducats – and use her advantage to the full. If Venice in literature had been gilded by the poetry of Shakespeare, the satire of Jonson, the aesthetic of Ruskin, it was now immortally touched by the pen of fiction, by Henry James, as it would be by Proust and Mann after him. *The Aspern Papers* is a comedy raised to the level of an extraordinary time-vision, a superb play of the historic sense.

4

Henry James had transferred the scene of the Silsbee anecdote from Florence to Venice; and in the writing of it he transferred – also from Florence to Venice – certain circumstances of his immediate life. On Bellosguardo he was occupying an apartment in an old Italian villa, next to a garden, even as the narrator of the tale moves into a suite of rooms in the old Venetian palace and is given the privilege of the garden. In both the actual villa and the imaginary palace there was living a middle-aged niece – a grandniece to be exact in each case – of James Fenimore Cooper in the real life circumstances and of Juliana Bordereau in the fiction. Fenimore, too, reached back to a 'visitable past' of American literature and to the very period in which Jeffrey Aspern flourished. Aspern would have been contemporary of both Cooper and Byron and – in the re-created and re-imagined past – was on the Continent at the same time as these writers. His name, moreover, may have been selected for those further ironic overtones which James often invoked in baptizing his characters. Aspern, in Austria, was the scene of a great encounter : here Napoleon met his first crushing defeat. James distinctly identified himself with his remote fictitious poet and expatriate : we have seen how he endowed him with the same free energetic qualities he possessed or wished to possess; and he said, in his late preface, that he had '*thought* New York as I projected him', thereby conferring on him the city of his own birth.

There are other such links between life and James's imagined tale. Not only is it specified that Tita, who is referred to throughout as a 'niece', is actually a 'grand-niece'. Her name, common in Venice, is an uncommon one to find in one of Miss Woolson's own novels – that of Tita Douglas in her most popular work, *Anne*. These are but fugitive hints and perhaps matters of coincidence. Much closer and more significant is the nature of the relationship between the narrator and Tita, and the way in which he woos her sympathies and re-enacts those gallantries James bestowed upon Fenimore during the first weeks of their acquaintance. The course of this relationship in the story suggests markedly that James was – perhaps at this moment intuitively – beginning to feel uneasy about the familiar life into which he had been led with Miss Woolson. The relationship may have been propriety itself; but had he not perhaps gone too far? Of Fenimore's feelings James could never have been wholly in doubt; her letters to him, written when he was in America, had carried an implicit refrain, a demand for attention, affection, proximity : she had written to him long ago, from the very scene of *The Aspern Papers* – 'The lagoons, the Piazzetta, and the little still canals all send their love to you. They wish you were here. And so do I.' And in that very letter she had told James he was unable to portray women in love. 'If you will only care for her yourself,' she had written, urging him to pay attention to his heroines. Miss Woolson would hardly suggest to James that he should pay more attention to her, and that they should find some more intimate ground of communion, or urge upon him as directly as Tita had urged the narrator, with the Aspern papers in her hands, the need for an alliance. Nevertheless she had been saying as much indirectly ever since their first Florentine meeting. Her letters and her acts attest to her desire to be near him, not least her choice of England and its uncongenial climate in which she had lived for three years in order to have the occasional chance of James's company. The narrator in *The Aspern Papers*, fleeing the niece and the old palace, tells himself at the last that he had 'unwittingly but none the less deplorably trifled'. He repeats to himself, 'I had not given her cause – distinctly I had not.' He had been 'as kind as possible, because I really liked her', and he asks himself, 'since when had that become a crime where a woman of such an age and such an appearance was concerned?' This seems to have been James's logic as well. He treated Miss Woolson as a friendly and charming old maid for whom he had a feeling of kindness because she was devoted to him. And now, through the plate glass of his ego, he was beginning to feel that perhaps she nourished on her side, more affectionate thoughts than he suspected. The tale suggests that James had begun to wonder whether Fenimore was not expecting more of him than the presentation and inscription of books and the attentions of a discreet *galantuomo*. 'At any rate, whether I had given cause or not it went without saying,' the admirer of Jeffrey Aspern tells himself, 'that I could not pay the price.'

The narrator may have told himself 'I had not given her cause' –

but the reader knows that he has. He enlists the niece on his side
from the first by cajolery and flattery; he invites this cloistered
middle-aged woman, to whom the very sight of a man is a novelty,
to play his particular game and to betray her great-aunt : even as
James allowed his own needs for friendship, companionship, understanding, to blind him to his excessive attentiveness to Fenimore, and
what this might do to her affections. He had treated her as if she were
as old as Mrs Procter or Mrs Kemble. In the tale the unfeeling cruelty
of the narrator is softened somewhat by his dedicated artistic nature
and his sense of the past. But his cruelty is manifest. His behaviour
has in it a kind of easy innocence and egotism that does not conceal
the cad – an aesthetic cad perhaps; certainly not a sentient gentleman. In life James seems to have gained a glimmer of insight, or
sensed the danger of incurring the same charge, or a charge even
more serious – that of being so blinded by egotism that he might be
held guilty of a total failure in awareness – he the novelist who, of all
writers, could know and feel and understand.

We may carry this speculation one step further. He had probably
had an opportunity to see that Fenimore, with her innumerable
trunks and possessions, was unable to throw anything away. And
for all their promise to each other that they would destroy their
correspondence, the thought may have occurred to him that somewhere among her accumulations were impulsive, scribbled pages he
had dashed off to her, at various times, filled with his spontaneities
of affection and irresponsibilities of feeling. *The Aspern Papers* may
have been a screen for deeper thoughts, nourished by the novelist,
that somewhere, in the Brichieri, there existed some Henry James
papers that needed burning, like the Aspern papers, one by one, to be
sure that not a scrap was left to posterity.

118

Palazzo Barbaro

HENRY JAMES bade farewell to Fenimore and Bellosguardo late in
May to spend ten days with the Curtises at the Palazzo Barbaro. He
spoke of returning to Florence for another three weeks or a month,
'though not to Bellosguardo', but he lingered in Venice and his ten
days became a visit of five weeks, the longest private visit he had

ever paid. He had never lived in so princely a style. He was fond of
the elegant palace, with its gothic windows its marble and frescoes,
and its portraits of Doges; he particularly liked his quiet cool rooms
at the back, which looked into the shade of a court, through windows, set at arbitrary levels. He worked in a room with a pompous
Tiepolo ceiling (the original had been sold, this was a copy) and
walls of ancient, pale-green damask, slightly shredded and patched.
The Curtises proved congenial hosts once James became accustomed
to Mr Curtis's puns and anecdotes, and Mrs Curtis's high tone and
social fastidiousness. He found them 'intelligent, clever and hospitable'. They had left Boston in the wake of an episode of social
comedy, in which Mr Curtis had tweaked the nose of a fellow-
aristocrat and been jailed briefly for assault and battery. This had
quite soured his love for America and they had purchased the Barbaro in 1885 and become permanent Venetian-Bostonians. 'They
can't keep their hands off their native land,' James observed; this
tended to fan his own patriotism to a fever. With their great ménage
– servants, gondoliers, visiting friends, daily excursions to the Lido
– they provided James with large access to a sociable world, from
which he could withdraw to complete privacy in his princely
apartment.

Venetian society proved less strenuous than Florentine, more
indigenous. It was casual and 'exoteric'. James described it as 'a thing
of heterogeneous vivid patches, but with a fine old native basis'. One
of the most remarkable of its members was the Countess Pisani, a
lady who reminded James of the romantic heroines of Disraeli and
Bulwer. She was partly English. Her father had been the doctor who
bled Byron to death at Missolonghi. Her mother had been a French
odalisque out of the harem of the Grand Turk. The late Count Pisani,
'a descendant of all the Doges', had married her for her beauty
thirty-five years before. Now at 55 or 60, 'widowed, palaced, villaed,
pictured, jewelled, and modified by Venetian society', she impressed
Henry as the sort of woman one might have found in the early years
of the century, 'receiving on a balcony at two o'clock on a June
morning'.

Staying with the Countess Pisani was May Marcy McClellan,
daughter of the Civil War general. James had met her in Florence
and he found himself observing a character out of his own novels.
That Miss McClellan should be favoured with the hospitality of the
Countess struck Henry as bizarre. She had created a stir the previous

winter in Venetian circles by writing a gossipy letter to an American newspaper about the society which had entertained her. The letter had been, James wrote in his notebook, 'as long, as confidential, as "chatty", as full of headlong history and lingering legend, of aberration and confusion, as she might have indited to the most trusted of friends'. It had appeared in the columns of a New York newspaper. This kind of public chatter always shocked James; he had himself been a victim of it on sundry occasions – had found that charming females, who dined with him in London, later turned out to have pens in their handbags. The American habit of the public chronicling of private life had already been satirized by the novelist in Henrietta Stackpole and in the unprepossessing Matthias Pardon, of *The Bostonians*. James was to say later that 'no power on earth would induce me to designate ... the recording, slobbering sheet' in which Miss McClellan's effusion appeared; it is, however, identified in his notebooks, and a search in the files of the New York *World* reveals the offending letter in all its dull prolixity and bad English in the issue of 14 November 1886. By modern standards it is sufficiently mild: in its own day it must have been a scandalous repayment of various kindnesses. Miss McClellan had visited Varese, near the Swiss border, and had stayed in the Hôtel Excelsior, formerly a villa belonging to the Morosonis of Venice, who had sold it, she proclaimed, for 'pecuniary reasons'. Everyone she met there 'rejoiced in some sort of a handle to his or her name'. The women's jewels – and she named the women – were 'something gorgeous'. Thus the daughter of Prince Pia dei Lavvia wore sapphires as 'big as pigeon's eggs' and diamond solitaires 'which any New York millionairess might envy'. She described the 'lurching walk and excessively British garments of these Italian dudes'. The men were handsomer than the women and 'one countess who is considered something quite lovely would not attract attention in a New York ballroom'. Such had been her aimless colloquial gossip; nevertheless, the Countess Pisani 'has that foolish virgin staying with her'. James described her as 'a rather flippant, spoiled girl'. He had had some talk with the McClellans, mother and daughter, in Florence that winter and had described them to his friend Mrs Bronson, who as an American-Venetian had been profoundly shocked by the girl's betrayal of her well-meaning friends. Miss McClellan 'spoke to me of the matter with less humility – with a certain resentment, as if she herself had been wronged', the novelist told Mrs Bronson. The mother was more contrite and referred to her 'daughter's lamentable *faux pas*'. Both were concerned, however, not so much with the girl's thoughtless act, as with their fear that if they returned to Venice they might find 'every back turned to them'. James added: 'Good heavens, what a superfluous product is the smart, forward, over-encouraged, thinking-she-can-write-and-that-her-writing-has-any-business-to-exist American girl! Basta!' He also wrote: 'She is Americanissimo – in the sense of being launched as a young person before the Lord, and no wonder the poor dear old Venetian mind can't understand such incongruities. I should like to write a story about the business, as a pendant to Daisy Miller, but I won't, to deepen the complication.'

That autumn in London, however, he changed his mind. In his notebook he spoke of 'the strange *typicality* of the whole thing'. He added: 'One sketches one's age but imperfectly if one doesn't touch on that particular matter: the invasion, the impudence, the shame-lessness of the newspaper and the interviewer, the devouring *publicity* of life, the extinction of all sense between public and private.' Out of this Venetian episode James derived *The Reverberator*, a short novel published in 1888 set in Paris. The story dealt with another facet of the activities of 'publishing scoundrels'; it became a journalistic pendant to the literary *Aspern Papers*.

I

In mid-June Paul Bourget arrived in Venice, and during their many talks offered James still another theme. He told him of the suicide of a young friend, who had jumped out of her hotel window in Milan. Bourget had an hypothesis: the girl had discovered that her mother had lovers, and this had weighed upon her. He also believed that she had tried to escape into a marriage – that is, she had pressed an attentive young man to declare his intentions. The young man had been acutely embarrassed; his interest had been friendly but not marital. The girl had felt ashamed. It later developed that much of this was Bourget's fancy. James responded, however, to this new version of a woman proposing marriage to a man; and in his hands he turned the material into an Anglo-American picture – a story of a puritanical young girl, horrified by her sister's immorality who asks a young American to marry her. Before he left Venice, he was at work on this tale, to which he gave the title *A London Life* – and

for the first time in his quarter of a century of writing he found himself taking an indulgent, though not altogether approving, view of
the laxity of the married American woman seeking a divorce and a
critical view of the inflexible morality of her sister.

2

At the beginning of July James reluctantly left Venice and brought
his long Italian stay to an end. He had a final dinner with Mrs Bronson and her daughter, in their gondola, on the glassy lagoon,

in the pink sunset, with the Chioggia boats floating by like familar little
phantom ships, red and yellow and green – the impression of that enchanting hour has never left me – and I have only to close my eyes to
see you and Edith sitting there on the other side of the narrow but
abundant board and the unoccupied Domenico hemmed in behind you,
squatting philosophically on his haunches.

The Season would be over in London by the time he reached it : and
he always enjoyed being in the British capital in August. Alice James
had vacated De Vere Gardens and returned to Leamington. He had
had his fill of Italian impressions – and Italian experience. He even
thought that he might take some little apartment in Venice, create a
permanent Italian *pied-à-terre* for himself, so enamoured had he
become of the life of the place. However he decided not to force
the issue; he would let time decide. There remained only one further
promise to redeem. When on the Continent in the summer he always
paid his respects to Mrs Kemble. James journeyed from Venice to
Vicenza, Mantua, Cremona, Brescia, and Bergamo. Mantua was
dreary and pestilential; the fleas drove him away. But he enjoyed
the beefsteaks of Brescia and the beautiful bronze Victory in the
museum, 'second only' to the Venus de Milo. 'And she has wings –
and such beauties – which Venus hasn't,' he wrote to Mrs Curtis.

On 6 July he joined Mrs Kemble at Stresa and spent several days
with her. He found her an 'extinct volcano', a shadow of her former
self. 'Given the temperature, the shadow is better – and we manage
to discuss a little,' he told Mrs Curtis There were few tourists; the
hotels were empty; it was very hot and James lingered briefly. Then
he crossed into Switzerland, over the Simplon, on foot, as he had
done in the days of his youth, 'a rapture of wild flowers and mountain streams – but it was over in a flash'. After that he went straight

to London. On 22 July he was back at De Vere Gardens, his Italian holiday – with the great release of creative energy it had given him – at an end.

It had given him much more: he had never had such a sense of personal freedom. Describing his visit to Mrs Kemble he commented on the way in which she moved, as in one mass, 'and if she does so little as to button her glove, it is the whole of her "personality" that does it'. He had the feeling, however (he told Grace Norton), that it was rather 'a melancholy mistake, in this uncertain life of ours, to have founded oneself on so many rigidities and rules – so many siftings and sortings'. And then, in this letter, he suddenly exclaimed – as if he were addressing his correspondent, and perhaps all New England: 'Let us be flexible, dear Grace; let us be flexible! And even if we don't reach the sun we shall at least have been up in a balloon.'

Part Four:
Art and the Market-Place

119

The Compromises of Life

HE had, in a manner, been up in a balloon in the immensities of the Italian sky, above the beauties of the past. He had undergone the last stages of an almost imperceptible evolution begun years before – a process which had converted this hard-working, pleasure-loving, duty-haunted, sentient American, with his large and generous gifts, from an old Calvinistic inheritance of codes and rules and rigidities into a more relaxed (though still laborious) American-European. From his new altitude he had discovered new meanings in the word *flexible*. The little tragi-comedies of man engaged in his civilized round which had absorbed him seemed now less 'final' than he had ever before believed. Had it been worth-while for Roderick Hudson to tear his passion to tatters and fall over a Swiss cliff, all because of an unfathomable woman? Might not his creator have offered him certain alternatives? Was passion necessarily inimical to art? If hearts were broken, they seemed sometimes to mend. If man sinned, sins sometimes seemed to be forgiven. If man erred, he seemed some-how to have a capacity for growing scar-tissue over his errors. Even 'fallen women', as he himself knew, could sometimes make their way into society. Society actually found them a source of entertain-ment. He had pictured in his art the inflexible character of society – accurately enough – but he had also written as if everything were irreversible. He had frustrated Newman and doomed Daisy, and adhered (critically) to the *status quo*, when life seemed constantly to be built on shifting sands. Italy alone seemed to remain (so he wrote to his Philadelphia-Roman friend Mrs Wister) after other things collapsed – 'the support given by religion, the domestic affec-tions, the loss of fame, the hope of glory, the desire of fortune and various other squeezed oranges'. But to the irony and cynicism of this he might have added that a squeezed orange was not a disaster. The fruit of this earth was abundant.

These were hardly James's reflections after his eight months in Italy: but they are the implications we may read in the tales written during this period. In these stories it seemed as if James had come to recognize that people could, on occasion, defy fate – and society –

and survive. He had from the first – it was his heritage from his father's old religious crisis – had an uncanny sense of evil, not as mere wickedness or transgression, but as an eerie extra-human force, baleful and terrifying, an actuality existing beyond man's control yet capable of destroying him. This had been the meaning of the Emperor's topaz, or the unearthed Juno – disinterred relics of history which belonged to old barbarisms and cruelties and which had, quickly, to be covered up again, lest new and terrible harm be done. James had not altogether overcome this panic sense of evil. His essay on Emerson of this period shows a new and benevolent view of man's earthly weaknesses and a feeling that Emerson represented American innocence and naïveté, only half-understanding that the tree in Eden, in offering knowledge of evil, gave access to the world's wisdom. James had left London with the newspapers screaming about Lady Colin Campbell's divorce suit, and he had predicted that the case would 'besmirch exceedingly the already very damaged prestige of the English upper classes'. He returned to find that nothing had been besmirched. The perishable newspapers had had their little day, and the upper classes were as indestructible – and as unbesmirched – as ever. Moreover, they seemed to make their own rules, in the most arbitrary fashion imaginable.

James had finally abandoned his American innocence. He could still portray it as subtly as of old; but he himself now understood it as never before. He was aware that what he had pictured as 'corrupt old Europe' represented a splendid façade of civilization, formed over the centuries, behind which existed all manner of things Americans might judge harshly and regard as evil – but that this façade also concealed a life of liberty; and that it offered a veil of public decency, codes and standards and judgements, with which to protect 'the private life'. To have a private life was to have freedom; and a loss of freedom, he said, was 'the greatest form of suffering'. To be impervious to others' judgements and others' meddlings was to have freedom : and this is what James had been discovering ever since he had left Quincy Street in 1875.

I

The moral substance of his work now underwent a change. The evil in *The Aspern Papers* lay not in Juliana's ancient indiscretions or Jeffrey Aspern's 'love-life'. It lay in the invasion of privacy, the failure to enter into human feeling. The narrator had not only been a 'publishing scoundrel', but a hopeless meddler as well. In *A London Life* Henry set out to describe the sense of shock experienced by his American innocent over her sister Selina's adulteries. But what he depicted was the panic state of a girl too rigid and meddlesome to recognize that in this world adulteries do occur, marriages do break up; that people act irresponsibly – but that this is their affair, and no one else's. Moreover, the world does not thereby come to an end. All the personages in *A London Life* try to explain this to Laura. Old Lady Davenant, the charming and witty reincarnation of Mrs Duncan Stewart, says to her candidly that she has no patience 'with the highstrung way you take things' – and she speaks out of fondness for her. Laura, however, 'bristling with righteousness', pursues her sister into Belgium, after Selina has run off with Captain Crispin, as if her missionary zeal could bring her sister back. 'She exaggerates the badness of it,' says Lady Davenant. 'Good heavens, at that rate where should some of us be?' And while James the moralist does not necessarily approve of society's flaunted immoralities, he demonstrates the futility of Laura's self-righteous 'morality'. Evil is still terrifying to certain of James's characters – as terrifying as to Mrs Ambient, for whom a dead child was better than an 'exposed' living child. Laura, in her sense of her own goodness and rightness, foreshadows the anxious and panic-stricken governess of *The Turn of the Screw*.

The Reverberator was a light comedy based on the story of Miss McClellan's adventures in Venetian society, and in it James returned to the Paris of *The American*. His portrait of the two Boston sisters and their father, in the Hôtel de l'Univers et de Cheltenham, has all the perfection of his 'Daisy Miller' period and much greater maturity. The significant figure in this little Franco-American drama is Mr George Flack, the Paris correspondent of an American society newspaper called 'The Reverberator'. Mr Flack speaks for his native land. 'You can't keep out the light of the press,' he says. His conception of this light is the ferreting out of society gossip – often with the help of society.

The society news of every quarter of the globe, furnished by the prominent members themselves (oh, *they* can be fixed – you'll see!) from day to day and from hour to hour and served up at every breakfast-table in the United States – that's what the American people want and that's what the American people are going to have.

In Flack James had his vision of the future 'media'; he demonstrated that America would develop its own peculiar corruptions.
And when the journalist writes his scandalmongering letter and
endangers Francie Dosson's marriage into French society, her father
expresses surprise at all the fuss. He wants to know whether the
French were not aware 'of the charges brought every day against
the most prominent men in Boston' by the newspapers. Libel, in
other words, is routine in America. Francie, however, begins to
wonder whether the lively and chatty letters she had herself relished
in the papers had not really meant 'a violation of sanctities, a convulsion of homes, a burning of smitten faces, a rupture of girls'
engagements'. The sanctimonious side of Mr Dosson's national
character emerges when he reflects 'that if these people had done
bad things they ought to be ashamed of themselves and he couldn't
pity them, and if they hadn't done them there was no need of making such a rumpus about other people knowing'. Henry James had
seen the handwriting on the wall : he had forecast the evolution of a
press which would, under the guise of 'names make news', create
capital of people's privacy, increasingly weaken the laws of libel,
and increasingly turn themselves into journals of gossip rather than
of political and national intelligence. For the Americans in this novel
the corruption has already occurred; 'the newspapers and all they
contained were a part of the general fatality of things, of the recurrent freshness of the universe, coming out like the sun in the morning or the stars at night'.

   The Lesson of the Master, which James wrote when he had returned to De Vere Gardens, reflected the moral change in the area
closest to him. The Master in the tale, the great novelist, reads a
lecture to the young would-be writer : marriage, dressing one's wife,
educating one's children, taking one's place in the world, are costly
matters. The artist must choose. He can either marry and cheapen
his art – and be a success – or choose a celibate course, and produce
the masterpieces which the world will not understand and which
alone justify his dedication and self-denial. Success in itself, he suggests, is a cheapening process. But the Master does not follow his
own counsel. One wonders at the end of the tale what this ironic
'lesson' really is. Admirable though James's statement may be, on
behalf of the sanctity of art and the danger of worldliness, the
reader – and the young idealist – feel rather 'sold'.

   Re-examining his old high standards and their relation to the facts of existence, Henry James now pondered the extent to which an artist must be prepared to make his compromises with the market-place; and whether life itself wasn't a 'sell'. If people could sin and get away with it in society, an artist could be a 'success' – or even a humbug – and get away with it in art. The question was now for-mulating itself in Henry's consciousness in some such fashion, and it would be written out in a long novel, for which he already had the the title : *The Tragic Muse*. The words seemed to be there, seen through his high west window in De Vere Gardens as he looked out upon teeming London, and surveyed the long road he had travelled since *Daisy Miller*.

2

James was ceasing to believe that Americans were composed of finer moral fibre than Europeans. He still believed that their innocence had great charm; nevertheless, he now discerned in this innocence a claustrophobic ignorance. Worse still, a need to impose it upon others. He had set out to proclaim the forthrightness of the Chris-topher Newmans of his race and their noble gift of friendliness and egalitarianism. He had discovered that 'the first thing a society does after it has left the aristocratic out, is to put it in again' He had also come to see that perhaps the faults and virtues of the Americans and the English were 'simply different chapters of the same general subject'. We find him writing William a long and reflective letter late in 1888 when he had fully assimilated his experience of the pre-vious year. After reaching a certain age, he said, and living in a coun-try not his own, and applying to it his ironical and cynical disposi-tion, certain truths became apparent. One was that he was 'deadly weary of the whole "international" state of mind'. He positively *ached*, he said, 'with fatigue at the way it is constantly forced upon one as a sort of virtue or obligation'. He continued :

I can't look at the English and American world, or feel about them, any more, save as a big Anglo-Saxon total, destined to such an amount of melting together that an insistence on their differences becomes more and more idle and pedantic and that that melting together will come the faster the more one takes it for granted and treats the life of the two countries as continuous or more or less convertible.

From this he went on to one of the most enlightened artistic state-ments of his time :

I have not the least hesitation in saying that I aspire to write in such a way that it would be impossible to an outsider to say whether I am, at a given moment, an American writing about England or an Englishman writing about America (dealing as I do with both countries), and so far from being ashamed of such an ambiguity I should be exceedingly proud of it, for it would be highly civilized.

James not only said this privately to his brother; he published in *Scribner's*, in March 1889, a charming dialogue *An Animated Conversation*, which is an early appeal for a merging of Anglo-American cultures. This seemed to him inevitable: 'What other nations are continually meeting to talk over the reasons why they shouldn't meet? What others are so sociably separate – so intertwinedly cohesively alien?' England and America can cultivate with talent 'a common destiny', united in the arts of peace, 'by which I mean of course in the arts of life'.

In his letter to William, Henry alluded to his inability to do much reading, since 'I produce a great deal'. This was a matter on which William often touched, tied as he was to the university and his academic work. Henry observed that he had chosen early in his London life to take aboard 'an amount of human and social information' (in preference to the information contained in books) and that he would do the same if he were living his life over. 'One can read when one is middle-aged or old; but one can mingle in the world with fresh perceptions only when one is young.' He added, 'The great thing is to be *saturated* with something – that is, in one way or another, with life; and I chose the form of my saturation.'

3

Energetic 'producer' though he always was, James had never been as productive as during his eight months in Italy and immediately after in London. In sequence he had written *The Aspern Papers*, *A London Life* and *The Reverberator*, all in less than a year – and in the midst of other writings as well. The tales were held back by the editors for a number of reasons, and they appeared simultaneously, so that for the better part of the following year Henry James dominated the magazines as never before. Howells likened James's literary 'show' to an art-exhibition. What had occurred was that the magazines were now using illustrations on a large scale; and certain of James's stories, sent to *Harper's New Monthly Magazine* and the revived *Scribner's* and the *Century*, had to wait their turn on drawing-tables. Moreover he had dispatched *The Aspern Papers* to the *Atlantic* without prior consultation with the editor; and its three instalments could be fitted with difficulty into the little free space available in the current issues. Accustomed to prompt publication, James complained at the beginning of 1888 to Howells that he remained 'irremediably unpublished'. He wondered whether the failure of *The Bostonians* and *The Princess* had ruined his reputation. Editors kept his manuscripts back 'for months and years, as if they were ashamed of them'; he felt he was being 'condemned apparently to eternal silence'. The passage has often been quoted by critics wholly out of context: for if the editors were keeping back his manuscripts, it was not because they had rejected them, but because they wished all the more advantageously to publish them. James's remark, made in this letter, that 'very likely too some day all my buried prose will kick off its various tombstones at once', has been cited as prophecy of his posthumous 'revival'. He was simply speaking of delayed publication. *Louisa Pallant* came out in February 1888 in *Harper's*; *The Reverberator* ran in *Macmillan's* from February to April, although written after *The Aspern Papers*, which emerged in the *Atlantic* from March to May; *The Liar* was in the *Century* in May and June; *The Modern Warning* (then called *Two Countries*) in *Harper's* in June, and *A London Life* ran in *Scribner's* from June to September. In the meantime *The Lesson of the Master* was appearing during July and August in the *Universal Review* and *The Patagonia* overlapped during August and into September in the *English Illustrated Magazine*.

This was not all. His essay on Maupassant was in the *Fortnightly Review* in March, that on Pierre Loti in May, and a long review of the Goncourt journals in October. His appreciation of Stevenson appeared in the *Century* in April (held up almost a year whilst an artist was doing a portrait of Louis); and his since celebrated essay on *London* with illustrations by Pennell, was in the *Century* in December. Altogether 1888 was a successful and prosperous year. James's mournful complaint to Howells was that of an impatient rather than of an unpublished author.

Howells said as much in commenting on this sudden eruption of his friend's work in the journals. 'One turned,' he wrote in his column in *Harper's*, 'from one masterpiece to another, making his comparisons and delighted to find that the stories helped rather than hurt one another, and that their accidental massing enhanced his pleasure in them.' He went on :

It will certainly amaze a future day that such things as his [James's] could be done in ours and meet only a feeble and conditional acceptance from the 'best' criticism, with something little short of ribald insult from the common cry of literary paragraphers. But happily the critics do not form an author's only readers; they are not even his judges. These are the editors of the magazines, which are now the real avenues to the public; and their recent unanimity in presenting simultaneously some of the best work of Mr James's life in the way of short stories indicates the existence of an interest in all he does, which is doubtless the true measure of his popularity.

Howells said the new batch of tales constituted a series of 'master-pieces', because 'the language does not hold their betters for a high perfection of literary execution at all points'. And analysing this quality he spoke of James's 'light, firm touch', the 'depths under depths' of his characterizations and the 'clutch upon the unconscious motives'. This was a measure of discernment rare in James's day.

Howells recognized that James had entered a new phase. And indeed his entire output between *The Princess Casamassima* and *The Tragic Muse* shows him narrating his stories – even when trifles – at the top of his form; they possess an extraordinary *allégresse*. His tales coincided with the series of essays and 'portraits' also set down with the richness of a charged critical imagination. The tales of this time have an excess of charm and of high amusement; and this is far from a defect, for no tale is more enjoyable than one which the teller himself enjoys.

120

Elizabeth Duveneck

ON 31 March 1888 Henry James went to pay a visit to the Cyril Flowers, at Aston Clinton in Tring Park. He came to this Easter week-end party with a heavy heart. Sitting at a table in a room in which guests were coming and going, he wrote a letter to Henrietta Reubell. His handwriting, usually forceful and well controlled, is disorganized and shaky. 'I am writing in a room full of people talking and they make me write erratically,' he told Miss Reubell. But this was hardly the cause. He could not control the depths of his emotion. Lizzie Boott was dead. She had died that week in Paris, where she had been spending the winter with her husband and child, in a house in the Rue de Tilsit. Only a short while before she had written James a letter filled with her busy life and news of her baby: she had taken up water-colours, she said – they could be combined more easily than oils with the duties of maternity. James had replied; he had spoken of Fenimore's illness at Bellosguardo in the autumn. But Fenimore was better and was writing again. Francis Boott had been to America but was now in Paris. Then suddenly Lizzie had pneumonia. On 22 March she died, at 42, leaving her aged father, her husband and her fifteen-month-old child.

Boott had sent James the barest details. He responded by saying he was prepared to come at once to Paris if he could be of help. He had received no reply; and he turned now, in the midst of the chatter and laughter in the big house at Aston Clinton, to his old Parisian friend, Etta Reubell, for news: 'Lizzie's sudden death was an unspeakable shock to me – and I scarcely *see* it, scarcely believe in it yet. It was the last thing I ever thought of as possible – I mean before Boott's own surrender of his earthly burden.' When would Etta see Boott? Would she tell Henry what impression he made on her? What did he intend to do? What was the relation between him and Duveneck? Had Etta seen Lizzie before her death? 'What a strange fate – to have lived long enough simply to tie those two men, with nothing in common, together by that miserable infant and then vanish into space, leaving them face to face!'

Lizzie Boott – Pansy Osmond – the friend of Minny Temple in their youth, and his own friend for a quarter of a century, was gone. It was the first important loss he had experienced since Minny Temple and his brother Wilky in the ranks of his own generation, for Lizzie was but three years his junior. 'I shall miss her greatly,' he wrote. 'I had a great affection for her. She was a dear little quiet, gentle, intelligent, laborious lady.' And then he inquired whether Miss Reubell had seen any of Duveneck's work that winter. Duveneck had just painted a portrait of Lizzie. 'Is it good or interesting?'

I

A year had passed since he had been with the Bootts and with Fenimore at Bellosguardo; he had wandered with Lizzie in the deep
grass of the terrace and they looked at the view over the old parapet.
James would see her there always. He knew how deep an attachment this had been and how much the Bootts and their Florentine
villa had become a part of his life – even when years passed and he
was not in Italy. 'The quiet, gentle, loveable, cultivated, laborious
lady!' he echoed himself, writing to Mrs Curtis. 'Poor Boott – poor
Boott – is all I can say!' When he returned to De Vere Gardens
from his week-end he found a letter from Francis, and replied to it
with deep tenderness. Boott had apparently written that Lizzie had
undertaken an effort beyond her strength. In this Henry acquiesced.
'She staggered under it and was broken down by it,' he wrote to
Lizzie's father.

I was conscious of this as long ago as during those months in Florence
when superficially she seemed so happy and hopeful. The infirmity was
visible beneath the optimism – the whole thing seemed to me without
an issue. This particular issue is the most violent – but perhaps after all it
is not the most cruel – the most painful to witness – for perpetual struggle
and disappointment would have been her portion. I mean on account of
the terrible *specific gravity* of the mass she had proposed to herself to
float and carry. – It is no fault of *his* – but simply the stuff he is made
of.

There was for Henry something pathetic in all the 'little heroisms
of her plans, her faiths, her view of the future – quenched forever –
but quenched in a void – that is a soundless rest – far sweeter than
anything the hard ache of life has to give'. And James added: 'I pity
you, my dear Francis, almost more than anything else, for some of
the canting consolations that must be offered you. I am more glad
than you can say that your vision of her situation happens to be the
one which makes sorrow the least absolute. Don't answer this – I
shall write soon again.'

'What *clumsy* situations does fate bring about, and with what an
absence of style does the world appear to be ruled!' he exclaimed
to Mrs Curtis. He was thinking of Boott and Duveneck at the Villa
Castellani, strange companions, held together by the child. Twice
in Boott's long life had such a cruel situation come about. Lizzie had
been left to him when Mrs Boott died, a year after the death of their

infant son; now Lizzie was gone, leaving her child on his hands, for Duveneck promptly recognized that he – with his artist-bohemian way of life – was hardly the one to rear the boy. 'My imagination can scarcely take in Duveneck's *afloat* condition again – after his having embraced the faith that he was, for life, safe from all winds and waters,' James wrote to Boott. 'I kiss the child and shake hands with Duveneck. For you, my dear Francis, I can only repeat that I bear you constantly in the participation of my thoughts.'

2

Francis Boott and Frank Duveneck brought Lizzie back to Italy. There, towards the end of April, she was committed to the Florentine earth, in a grave in the Allori Cemetery, beyond the Roman gate, beneath a row of tall cypresses. Great masses of flowers were heaped on it; and her Florentine friends, among them Fenimore, gathered in large numbers to say farewell. It was Fenimore who described the scene for Henry: Boott calm and Duveneck sobbing. Duveneck's 'demeanour has won all hearts here', James's friend wrote. For a while the two remained in the villa, the old man and the young, and in time Francis Boott reversed the journey he had made almost half a century before. He took Frank Duveneck Jr to Boston, to rear him there among Lyman relatives, and there to pass the rest of his days. He was to live for many more years, in Cambridge, a short grizzled man who would of an evening walk into William James's house in Irving Street while the family were eating, refuse to join them at their board, but sit and chat of many things. He had lived through three generations and seen so much – his memories went back to the days of Garibaldi and to the old papal Rome, and he had had the long sweep of the Bellosguardo years.

For Duveneck the artist it was the end of the second phase of his life. The first had been his carefree days in Munich. The third would be a long anticlimax in America. Duveneck had been almost pathetically attached to his wife: she was a grand lady, whom he had had the good fortune to marry. He had painted her portrait that winter in Paris dressed for the street – wearing her hat back on her head, so that her dark parted hair is revealed; her lips are closed in a gentle smile, and her large candid eyes look affectionately out of the canvas. She is holding her muff; her arms are relaxed. If his view of her was of a *grande dame* in this painting, he imagined her also as a Knight's Lady in death – and so he posed her, recumbent with her hands folded on her breast, amid flowing drapery, on the tomb he designed and sculpted himself. It was cast in shining bronze and when James first saw it it seemed glaring and in bad taste. Time, however, would coat and soften it into a grey-green ghostliness; Lizzie lies in her eternal sleep, her eyes closed to the Italian skies. Brown, dry pine-needles sift at certain seasons gently into the folds of the metallic drapery.

Duveneck eventually returned to Cincinnati. It had beer-gardens and a certain vague feeling of Munich. He taught at the Academy of Fine Arts for many years. Sargent had spoken of him as 'the greatest talent of the brush of this generation'. He had indeed given the impression, during his earliest phase, that he would develop into a master; but he remained a talent, eventually in decline, as James predicted. And it is doubtful whether art-historians will ever settle whether Lizzie, in taming him socially, tamed his talent as well.

This was the end of the Bellosguardo chapters of James's life. More than a year after Lizzie's death Alice James wrote in her journal: 'Henry says he misses Lizzie Duveneck more and more.' She had been a certain kind of American girl – the quiet gentle Europeanized *jeune fille*, not the bold daisy but the demure pansy, and he had much affection for her. She was to remain enshrined in materials as durable as Duveneck's bronze, in the delicate beauty of Pansy Osmond.

121

In Geneva

IN March 1888, James agreed to write a serial for the *Atlantic Monthly* to run through 1889. He was to receive the same rate of pay as for *The Princess* – $15 a page. He announced that its title would be *The Tragic Muse* – 'she is an actress. But there will be much other richness, and the scene will be in London, like the *Princess* – though in a very different MONDE: considerably the "Aesthetic". There you are. It won't be improper, strange to say, considering the elements.'

That year there tumbled from the presses *Partial Portraits* in May, *The Reverberator* in June, and two volumes containing *The Aspern Papers* with two other tales *Louisa Pallant* and *The Modern Warning*) in September. 'How you can keep up such productivity and live, I don't see,' his brother William wrote to him. 'All your time is your own, however, barring dinner parties, and that makes a great difference. Most of my time seems to disappear in college duties, not to speak of domestic interruptions.' William said he had 'quite squealed' through his reading of *The Reverberator*. 'It shows the technical case you have attained, that you can handle so delicate and difficult a fancy so lightly. It is simply delicious.'

By September James had dispatched his first two instalments of the *Muse* to Aldrich. Early in October he crossed to the Continent, bypassed Paris and went straight to Geneva. He took rooms in the old Hôtel de l'Écu, those which had been occupied by his parents during the family's stay in Geneva in 1859–60. 'I am sitting in our old family *salon* in this place,' he wrote to his brother on 29 October,

and have sat here much of the time for the last fortnight, in sociable converse with family ghosts – Father and Mother and Aunt Kate and our juvenile selves. I became conscious, suddenly, about October 10th, that I wanted very much to get away from the stale, dingy London, which I had not quitted, to speak of, for fifteen months, and notably not all summer – a detestable summer in England, of wet and cold. Alice, whom I went to see, on arriving at this conclusion, assured me she could perfectly dispense for a few weeks with my presence on English soil; so I came straight here.

On occasion Henry – even at 45 – felt that he had to explain his movements to William. It was not however a matter of being away from Alice – from whom he had been away much longer the previous year. He had some need to justify his presence in Geneva at this moment for quite another reason, one that he did not mention to his brother. He was keeping a scheduled rendezvous with Fenimore. She had, as usual, passed her summer in Switzerland. Not wishing to go to Italy that winter (because of the serial) he was meeting her in Geneva to pay her a promised visit, before she travelled south.

In his tale of *Louisa Pallant*, written during his Italian phase, Henry had described how the elderly narrator and the love-smitten youth, on their way to Baveno on the Italian lakes to see the heroine, found it more decorous to stop at Stresa 'at about a mile distance'. They would not inhabit the same hotel as their friends, and 'nothing would be easier than to go and come between the two points'. The only record of the Geneva rendezvous is in a letter from James to Francis Boott. 'You have been a daily theme of conversation with me for the past ten days, with Fenimore,' he wrote.

That excellent and obliging woman is plying her pen hard on the other side of the lake and I am doing the same on this one. Our hotels are a mile apart, but we meet in the evening, and when we meet she tells me, even at the risk of repetition to which I am far from objecting, the story of your last months, weeks, days, hours, etc. at Bellosguardo. We often talk of Lizzie and it is a great pleasure to me to do so with one who had entered so much into her life in so short a time.

James's letters written at this time – to William, to Henrietta Reubell, to Mrs Curtis – create the picture of a writer who has fled society and is enjoying a solitary three weeks, contemplating Mont Blanc and taking quiet walks to observe the 'admirable blue gush of the Rhône', as he had done in his 16th year when he was attending Monsieur Rochette's preparatory school. Geneva seemed both duller and smarter than in 1859. The Academy had now become the University (he was to interpolate this fact into his revision of *Daisy Miller*) and was housed in a large, winged building in the old public garden. All the old smells and tastes were present. But what his relatives and friends were not told – save Boott – was that his stay was less solitary than it seemed.

Of Fenimore there is only one more mention. It is again in a letter to Boott, written three months later, on 18 January 1889: 'On leaving Geneva I parted with Fenimore – she went back to Bellosguardo and I went (through the Mont Cénis) to Genoa and the Riviera. I spent two or three weeks at the delicious Monte Carlo and the month of December in Paris.' He then reiterated 'She cherishes the mystical survival [on Bellosguardo] of dear Lizzie.' There is also one silent witness. Miss Woolson's copy of the two-volume edition of *The Aspern Papers* is inscribed with her name 'from the author, Geneva, October 16th, 1888'.

Of this entire Continental trip we know very little. It is perhaps the least documented of James's journeys. There survive some fragmentary pages of notes which show that he planned later to write a comedy with Monte Carlo as a setting, but nothing came of it. He stayed at the Hôtel des Anglais; and before that was briefly at Turin as well as Genoa – 'such a little whiff, or sniff, of Italy'. Our only clues to James's visit to Paris are three *pneumatiques* from Paul Bourget to the Grand Hotel. On 18 December James seems to have been at the salon of Madame Straus (Geneviève Halévy), thus most certainly encountering, if not the young Proust himself, some of his future characters. One of the messages from Bourget expresses regret that he was not able to accompany him on this occasion, but that he was certain this 'adorable and exquisite' woman would receive him cordially.

In addition to Bourget he saw Miss Reubell. And his notebook records that he visited the Théâtre Français backstage and had a chat with the comedienne Julia Bartet in her *loge*, an experience re-created in some detail in *The Tragic Muse*. Paris struck James, 'after a long intermission of habit there, as bright, charming, civilized, even interesting'. He was back in London in time for Christmas.

122

The Expense of Freedom

HE had captured in Italy in 1887 a true sense of freedom – that freedom which the artist in a pressing, interfering, demanding world can seldom attain. Now it seemed to him that the time had come to embody the conflict of 'art and "the world"' in a novel which he had begun to plan as far back as the winter of 1886 when he was moving into De Vere Gardens. The novel seemed to him later to be framed by the wide west window in his flat, where he sat writing day after day during fog-filtered Kensington mornings or in the short winter afternoons with near and far London sunsets, 'a half-grey, half-flushed expanse of London life'. He had first thought of it as a short work, a study of the nature of an actress, her egotism, her perseverance, her image as a creature for whom reality is illusion and illusion reality. He had discussed such a case with Mrs Humphry Ward, whose novel *Miss Bretherton*, based on the success of the American actress, Mary Anderson in London, he had carefully read. In the summer of 1887 he told Grace Norton he was beginning *The Tragic Muse*, that it would be half as long as *The Princess*, 'thank

God!' and that it would not be serialized. But by early 1888 the design had grown much more complicated; he had committed it to the *Atlantic*; in spite of his 'thank God!' it became his longest serial, running to seventeen instalments, from January 1889 to May 1890.

What had happened to enlarge the work was his desire to present an antithetical case to that of the actress enslaved by the conditions of the theatre. This may very well have offered itself to him in the spectacle of the Cyril Flowers, in whose home he had been a visitor, and where he found an intensely political environment. Flower, an amateur of the arts, a man who moved among poets, painters, musicians, had married a Rothschild wife whose memoirs reveal how much she cherished political rather than artistic power; and Flower – who had even made friends across the Atlantic with Walt Whitman – found himself a Member of Parliament, and later (after *The Tragic Muse* was published) a member of the House of Lords. We may speculate that this 'case' interested James; and the coincidence that within the domain of the Flowers was a village named Sheringham, in which they at one time contemplated living, may have given him the name of the diplomat-theatre-lover, Peter Sherringham. At the home of the Flowers James encountered Gladstone again, and found the political ambience upon which he drew for his novel; although we must recognize that his various visits to Lord Rosebery and *his* Rothschild wife also furnished him with ample material for the creation of Mr Carteret, the crusty politician of *The Tragic Muse*. And then he was always meeting political figures and statesmen at his clubs.

These instances may be mentioned if only to illustrate that James – who could hardly be said to have had an intimate knowledge of English politics – nevertheless found in his path sufficient examples to yield him his 'political case' which he could use as a parallel to his 'theatrical case'. Of the theatre he had had ample observation during his entire European career: he knew intimately the playhouses of England and France and to some extent of Italy. At the time that he was sketching out the *Muse* he had renewed his acquaintance with Coquelin, who came to lunch at De Vere Gardens. Henry delighted in his art and found 'a rare magnificence' in it; his personality he considered 'insupportable', though he was 'an admirable talker (on his own subjects)'. Struck again, as he had been many times, by the self-centredness and 'self-exhibitionistic' character of stage-folk, James felt he had all the materials at hand for his novel and he began it with an excitement and interest which he carried with him to his Geneva meeting with Fenimore.

The book is a large cheerful mural of English life and art; it is filled with witty talk; and parts of it read as if James were writing one of his critical papers rather than a piece of fiction. The novel has a hard dry essay-like quality. It incorporates a picture of the English stage, the Parisian theatre, the life of a comedienne attached to the Théâtre Français, the high bohemia of London on the very edge of the nineties; it offers also in the anomalous character of Gabriel Nash a glimpse of the Montesquiou-Whistler-Wilde aestheticism. With this we are given a picture of solid English upper-class Philistinism in the struggle of a young man to resist being pushed into parliament by his family and by the ambitious woman he thinks he loves. He would much rather be a painter.

Henry James had never undertaken a work so crowded with characters and so split in theme. He was, in reality, trying to put together two novels in one and sometimes the seam shows. But it is a work rich in portraits of people and pictures of contemporary life. In it James at last wrote out, on a large scale, that duality which existed within himself and which he had long ago depicted in *Benvolio*.

I

There are four central characters in the book and they serve to illustrate the problem at the heart of *The Tragic Muse*. First there is Miriam Rooth, the half-Jewish, half-English girl, who wants to be an actress and who dedicates herself to this goal with the ferocity of her egotism and the discipline of her art. The divine spark is not evident when we meet her, but she is single-minded in her ambition. Nowhere in all his work has James given us a more carefully documented picture of the evolution of a certain type of artist, and of an artist-nature, and of its implacable selfishness and self-assurance. The 'theatrical case' fascinated him, for he had been fascinated by the stage from his youth. And Miriam's history in the art of performance was learned during long evenings with Mrs Kemble – she the archetypal actress who believed in her art and abhorred the stage; during evenings at the Théâtre Français, whenever he was in Paris; and his meetings in certain London homes with Henry Irving, Ellen Terry and other of the stage-folk dominating the late Victorian theatre.

His political case is drawn with a less firm hand: but the in-gredients are familar to him – Nick Dormer's powerful mother, his deathbed promise to his father to keep the family name in parlia-ment (he is again a second son who must assume the responsibilities of the first-born, in this case a titled brother whose sole interests are hunting and shooting). The family fortunes of the Dormers are negligible and Nick is expected to make an advantageous marriage with Julia Dallow, who aspires to Downing Street. Nick is to inherit a fine fortune from his father's old friend, Charles Carteret, an elderly politician. Everyone sees Nicholas Dormer, not as he is, but as what they want him to be. He is totally rejected for himself – the quiet thoughtful artistic young man – and is offered a public self he does not want. Only his sister understands him.

The opposite to Nick Dormer is Peter Sherringham who expresses the dilemma at the heart of the book – and of its author. Sherring-ham is Julia Dallow's brother and a successful diplomat. His passion is the theatre; and it is a true passion save that it will not be per-mitted to interfere with his career. He 'discovers' Miriam Rooth and helps her take her first steps towards the stage. He has not allowed for his falling in love with her. Nevertheless an actress will not do as an ambassadress, and (as with Basil Ransom and Verena in *The Bos-tonians*) Sherringham asks Miriam to marry him and give up her career. Miriam and Nick Dormer face the same predicament. Nick is asked to be a politician rather than a painter: Miriam is asked to be a diplomat's wife rather than an actress. Sherringham believes in 'a passion exercised on the easiest terms', and he will keep the drama as a 'private infatuation'. He does not understand the 'professional-ism' of art. What he is saying is that one can trifle with one's passion, whereas his friend Dormer holds that this is impossible. Sherringham discovers before the novel is over that there is no halfway road to art: if one is committed to it, one must face it, as Dormer does, when he throws over the chance to marry Julia, rejects Mr Carteret's money and the solicitations of his electorate, and resigns from parliament. Miriam puts the case with consider-able force to Sherringham. She tells him that the stage has 'a deep fascination for you, and yet you're not strong enough to make the concession of taking up with it publicly, in my person'. And again: 'You consider that we do awfully valuable work, and yet you wouldn't for the world let people suppose that you really take our side.' Miriam does not marry the diplomat; she marries an actor, and at the end of the book is well on her way to becoming a great figure on the stage.

Nick Dormer's decision is more difficult than Miriam's, for James distinguishes between the 'performing arts' and those involving creation. His choice, James makes amply clear, is not only that of throwing over wealth, public office, status, society; it is that of finding himself face to face with the trials and joys of his art – he must accept loneliness; his faith is his only companion. This is the expense of freedom – the price an artist must pay. The actress, by the very circumstances of the interpretative art, is involved in a gregarious existence. The painter – or the writer – is alone with his canvas – or his blank sheets of paper. It is for this statement, the reader feels, that James wrote *The Tragic Muse* : his picture of Nick, in his studio, closing the door as Miriam leaves and taking up his palette to rub it with a dirty cloth.

The little room in which his own battle was practically to be fought looked woefully cold and gray and mean. It was lonely, and yet it peopled with unfriendly shadows (so thick he saw them gathering in winter twilights to come) the duller conditions, the longer patiences, the less immediate and less personal joys. His late beginning was there, and his wasted youth, the mistakes that would still bring forth children after their image, the sedentary solitude, the clumsy obscurity, the poor explanations, the foolishness that he foresaw in having to ask people to wait, and wait longer, and wait again, for a fruition which, to their sense at least, would be an anti-climax.

Going to the great galleries and seeing historic paintings, Nick was made to feel that the artist works unknown, misunderstood, a fool in the public eye; he casts away the gains of the market-place for some cherished ideal that is his own and no one else's, some creative urge that he cannot explain to anyone else. Before great portraits in the National Gallery he has a vision of a posthumous triumph which for him may well be the only triumph :

As he stood before them sometimes the perfection of their survival struck him as the supreme eloquence, the reason that included all others, thanks to the language of art, the richest and most universal. Empires and systems and conquests had rolled over the globe and every kind of greatness had risen and passed away; but the beauty of the great pictures had known nothing of death or change, and the ages had only sweetened their freshness. The same faces, the same figures looked out at different centuries, knowing a deal the century didn't,* and when they joined hands they made the indestructible thread on which the pearls of history were strung.

This is Nick's vision as it had been Hyacinth's, and Henry James was to cling to it during the coming years as he created the enduring masterpieces of his art which in his own time would be misunderstood or ignored.

2

In the sprawling and uneven novel into which James put such high skill, the figure of Gabriel Nash has understandably attracted the attention of many readers. He is a 'Gabriel' – hardly angelic, but much addicted to trumpeting. And he is an aesthete whose performances tend to be those of word rather than act. In certain ways he is a distraction : for James intended some of his trumpetings to sound loudly his own beliefs. He describes, with Jamesian wit, the predicament of the dramatist who is asked to place the 'exquisite' on the stage of a theatre between dinner and the suburban trains. He speaks with all the Jamesian warmth for sentience and high ideals : 'Where there's anything to feel I try to be there.' The reader senses, however, that this makes him too ubiquitous. His business is 'the spectacle of the world'. He 'talks' Henry James; and in appearance he even resembles his creator. But he is far from being the novelist. He belongs rather with those characters in James's fiction whose sole existence depends on their having an audience. Nick Dormer discovers this when Nash comes to sit for his portrait. He finds Gabriel increasingly uncomfortable and finally catches a glimmer of what this discomfort means. It was 'simply the reversal, in such a combination, of his usual terms of intercourse. He was so accustomed to living upon irony and the interpretation of things that it was strange to him to be himself interpreted, and (as a gentleman who sits for his portrait is always liable to be) interpreted ironically.' James hammers this home : 'From being outside the universe he was suddenly brought into it, and from the position of a free commentator and critic, a sort of amateurish editor of the whole affair, reduced to that of humble ingredient and contributor.' That such an individual's portrait should start to fade, and become

* In the revised version James made this read 'knowing so many secrets the particular world didn't'.

ghostly, after the manner of portraits in some of Hawthorne's tales, is understandable. It is the fate of most aesthetes and critics who talk but never *do*; who spin their theories but never adhere to them. Nick says to Nash that he wishes 'very much you had more to show' – but all Nash can show are his trumpetings. He is much more the Count de Montesquiou than Oscar Wilde or Whistler – but he is also Henry James's father who spent his life in talk.

We know the actual model for Nash. James kept his promise to himself of his first Venetian days in 1881 and used the image of Herbert Pratt, who had talked so well and been consistently anecdotal during James's long stay in the water-city. 'He was a most singular, most interesting type, and I shall certainly put him into a novel. I shall even make the portrait close and he won't mind.'

3

Re-reading the novel many years later, James felt that he had not succeeded with his young politician-artist Nick Dormer. The better part of him is 'locked away from us'. This is true. And it is strange. For it is Nick who carries the burden of what James most deeply felt: he enunciates the message of the artist and the solitary refuge of his art. He shows how much the true artist must be prepared to sacrifice. One cannot be half artist and half something else; he must strip himself of the easy compromises society exacts. The 'lesson of the master' is stated with much less cynicism than before and therefore much greater force. But the reason for Nick's elusiveness did not reside altogether in James's 'outsider' of English political life as he believed; it was his paradoxical failure to identify himself with this character. He is more identified with Peter Sherringham, Nick's 'double', who doesn't want to make the supreme sacrifice. James's own worldliness – his old Benvolio self – stands between him and Nick. Sherringham, at certain moments, is our old friend Benvolio: even the words of the old tale recur – 'there were two men in him, quite separate, whose leading features had little in common and each of whom insisted on having an independent turn at life'. The personal statement in this novel is that of the James who on the one hand was strongly pleasure-loving and who without his vaulting ambition and genius might have been an easy-going Herbert Pratt, an aesthetic Gabriel Nash. He had not yet reconciled himself to the loneliness of which he wrote: he wished, like Sherringham, to eat his cake and have it. Sherringham did not succeed, and James knew he couldn't, but he was still willing to try. He knew that he had an enormous facility; he could, like so many other excellent writers, have continued to spin some of his more thin-blown tales, as he had done with his minor 'international' stories and the exploitation of his inter-continental Daisy Millers. He had, however, always been artist enough to override this temptation, even after yielding to it for a while. And yet there he was – established in De Vere Gardens, with the look of 'success' and prosperity, and still condemned to scribble away his time so that he might capture occasional vagrant moods in Paris or in Venice. The plan which he was nursing, and which he publicly debated in *The Tragic Muse*, now took firm hold. There was a possible solution in this middle-aged choice which he found himself still forced to make, for he was thus constituted – a choice of quite a different order from the one of his youth, when he had turned to Europe to find freedom. What he needed now was a double freedom : that of the great place of art and that of the market-place, and these two 'trumped' each other, in a kind of grim, ironic game. The paradox of success was that it cheapened everything while offering him the expensive solution. It put money in his pocket, and somehow created a clinking dissonant sound beside the rhythm of prose and the sonorities of 'style'. There was, however, a possible issue, he told himself, and he would seriously test it. He could descend into the market-place and try to be a playwright – an honourable and income-producing career for a man of letters – while at the same time preserving his art of fiction from all violation by the money-changers, keeping it for his sacred creative hours. James the play-wright would 'bail out' James the novelist. It was not the same as his taking a job, say as secretary of legation as Lowell had wished to make him a decade before. If he succeeded as playwright he might very well incorporate the stage into his distinguished literary career. There had been a time when the greatest poetry had been associated with the actor, and England's finest genius had been wedded to the apron-stage and the groundlings. Times had changed. Victorian England had produced no dramatists to speak of, and its poets – Browning, Tennyson – had foundered when they approached the theatre. Wasn't this precisely, then, the moment for someone like himself to seek an entrance? He knew, from far back, that he could launch a scene and create a drama; his artist's sense told him that in his pen there was a great ability to dramatize. What had *Wash-*

ington Square been but a series of dramatic episodes. And in the very novel in which he discussed the stage he had boldly put together his story by scenic alternation, not by telling the reader everything, but by letting the scenes explain themselves, as in a play. He had even perpetrated an anomaly in fiction – been an omniscient author who boasted of his lack of omniscience. This occurs in the very middle of *The Tragic Muse*, when James pauses to explain to the reader that his method of telling the story prevents him from imparting certain facts. The passage must be noted:

As to whether Miriam had the same bright, still sense of co-operation to a definite end, the sense of the distinctively technical nature of the answer to every question to which the occasion might give birth, that mystery would be cleared up only if it were open to us to regard this young lady through some other medium than the mind of her friends. We have chosen, as it happens, for some of the advantages it carries with it, the indirect vision; and it fails as yet to tell us ... etc. etc.

This is the artist calling attention to his own method, and by the same token to his own virtuosity. It presents us with the anomaly of a novelist who has chosen 'the indirect vision' intruding in the most direct fashion possible to explain his indirection. On the stage James would not be able to intrude. The play would have to explain itself. James the artist would try. He was not yet ready to be an anchorite of art – the happy hedonist still had the upper hand.

123

The Gallo-Romans

IN the late eighties and early nineties, Henry James was increasingly linked with a group of Gallo-Romans – Bourget liked to characterize himself in this way – various Frenchmen, in London and Paris, who represented all that the American loved in the Gallic and the Italianate spirit. In the many years of his association with France he had never found close French friends. Bourget was the sole exception. He had become fairly intimate with Daudet, but the author of *Tartarin* was an invalid, and there could not be with him that camaraderie James had with Bourget when they met on either side of the Channel or in Italy. Now, however, there arrived in London a brilliant young diplomat, Jules Jusserand, Counsellor of the French Embassy; and also a young student from the French provinces who had written verses and attracted Bourget's attention, Urbain Mengin. With these two men – Jusserand, alert, swift, active, and Mengin, quiet, modest, studious and poetic – both moving on different levels of London life, James had new resources of Gallic friendship, and he responded warmly. 'A remarkably intelligent and pleasant little Frenchman,' Henry said of Jusserand. He wrote to Grace Norton in the autumn of 1888:

I am going in half an hour (this is a decent Sunday afternoon) to pick up a very nice and accomplished little man of whom I have lately seen a good deal, Jusserand, the French *chargé d'affaires*, in order to go with him up to Hampstead. We often do this of a Sunday afternoon when we are in town, and having scaled the long hill, which used to be so rural and pretty, and now is all red brick and cockney prose, we go and see du Maurier and he comes out and takes a longish walk with us – usually, or sometimes, with his pretty daughters (one of them is very pretty indeed) and his two little dogs. Then we go home and dine with him *à la bonne braquette* and walk back to London at 10 o'clock. Du Maurier is an old and good friend of mine and has a charming Anglo-Saxon mind and temper.

James added that Jusserand was

a little prodigy of literary and diplomatic achievement effected at an early age. He is alive to his very small finger-tips, ambitious, capable and charming – and if he were a few inches less diminutive, I should believe that Europe would hear of him as a diplomatic personage. But he is too short! Up to a certain point, or rather down to it, shortness, I think, constitutes a presumption of greatness; but below that point not.

Jusserand was to overcome his shortness, quite beyond James's prediction, and to be an important French Ambassador in Washington during the presidency of Theodore Roosevelt. In his memoirs the French diplomat describes the Sunday evenings at du Maurier's and remarks that the James of the late 'eighties 'enjoyed and spread merriment and showed a disposition to sarcasm and raillery which did not spare the British, at least as a nation'.

Urbain Mengin was destined to have a less spectacular but a quiet and distinguished career in education, and to be an early authority in France on Shelley and the English romantics. He had turned up one day at De Vere Gardens with a letter of introduction from Bourget. He had a delicacy of spirit and a temperament which James liked. He was a mere youth, in his early 20s when he came to London to teach French and study English. James received him with a cordiality and a warmth that Mengin remembered all the days of his long life. 'I passed almost an entire Sunday with Henry James. One drinks excellent claret at his table,' he wrote to his parents. 'I've just left Henry James, after a long walk in Hyde Park,' he told them on another occasion, 'where bands of Amazons on horseback constantly passed us'. In an unpublished memoir Mengin remembered James as wearing

a beard neatly trimmed and still dark, his hair at the temples was just beginning to turn grey, he was bald and his forehead was very fine; his glance expressed kindness and was at the same time distinctly analytical. He spoke French admirably, with a slight hesitation, sometimes repeating twice the same syllable of a word.

Bourget, the young French tutor and James were to form a triangular friendship in which James expressed to Mengin his unhappiness with certain of Bourget's novels which he could not say to Bourget himself. When Mengin, who became tutor to a future Duke of Sutherland, told James that he was reading him, the American rejoined: 'Don't read me -- when you have all English literature before you -- for heaven's sake.' His letters to Mengin are written in a mixture of English and French. There is a charming one in which James urges him to apply himself to his study of the English language: 'One's own language is one's mother, but the language one adopts, as a career, as a study, is one's wife, and it is with one's wife that *on se met en ménage*. English is a very faithful and well-conducted person, but she will expect you too not to commit infidelities. On these terms she will keep your house well.'

The most notable of his letters to young Mengin is the one he wrote on receiving the French scholar's work, *L'Italie des Romantiques*. Mengin had taken a walking-tour, scrupulously visiting all the scenes which had figured in the lives of Shelley, Byron and their circle. The letter is of a much later date; it shows admirably the benign yet critical eye James kept on his friend. After telling Mengin he had read his book attentively and had found much entertaining matter, well represented, he went on to say he especially liked his pictures of Lamartine, Chateaubriand and Madame de Staël.

How little they all *saw* compared with *nous autres*! And to have had to become *romantique*, and break a thousand window-panes, to see even that little! The only thing one can say is that they saw more – (more beauty) than the Président des Brosses. But we could kick their posteriors today for what they *didn't* see – especially that big yellow-satin *derrière* of Madame de Staël.

He went on to regret that Mengin had treated a poet of 'a vertiginous lyric *essor*' like Shelley without indicating his quality and splendour:

He is one of the great poets of the world, of the rarest, highest effulgence, the very genius and incarnation of poetry, the poet-type, as it were. But you speak only of the detail of his more or less irrelevant itinerary, and put in scarce a word for what he signifies and represents. I regret it for the reason that French readers have very rarely occasion to hear of him, so that when by chance they do I can't but be sorry that the case isn't stated for him more liberally as *poet*. He was the strangest of human beings, but he was *la poésie même*, the sense of Italy never melted into *anything* (*étranger*) I think, as into his 'Lines in the Euganaean Hills' and *d'autres encore*. 'Come where the vault of blue Italian sky ... !' is, for *me*, to *be* there *jusqu'au cou*! And *de même* for Keats, the child of the Gods! Read over again to yourself, but *aloud*, the stanzas of the *Adonais* (or I wish I could read them *to* you!) descriptive of the corner of Rome where they both lie buried, and then weep bitter tears of remorse at having sacrificed them to the terrestial *caquetage* of A. de Musset! Forgive my emphasis.

Jusserand, Mengin, and the Anglo-French du Maurier offered James that elegance of spirit, delicacy of expression and fertility of mind which he sought periodically in the French capital. And he was never more aware of this than on the day in May 1889 when Jusserand arranged a little luncheon in honour of Hippolyte Taine, and invited James to meet his distinguished guest. The American had never encountered the French critic and historian, whose major work he had reviewed during his young Cambridge days. He speaks of finding Taine 'remarkably pleasant'; and much more good natured than his 'hard, splendid, intellectual, logical style and manner had led me to expect'. He was a charming talker and gave James a renewed feeling 'of the high superiority of French talk'. After describing his 'obliquity of vision', his fine head, his straight strong regular features, 'a fine grave masculine type', he recorded that Taine rated Turgenev higher in form even than he himself had done. Taine used a very happy expression, James noted, when he said that Turgenev 'so perfectly cut the umbilical cord that bound the story to himself'. He recorded in his notebook that Taine's talk about the Russian novelist

has done me a world of good – reviving, refreshing, confirming, conse-crating, as it were, the wish and dream that have lately grown stronger than ever in me – the desire that the literary heritage, such as it is, poor thing, that I may leave, shall consist of a large number of perfect *short* things, *nouvelles* and tales, illustrative of ever so many things in life – in the life I see and know and feel – and of all the deep and delicate – and of London, and of art, and of everything: and that they shall be fine, rare, strong, wise – eventually perhaps even recognized.

The summer of 1889, when James was working at *The Tragic Muse*, had its usual interruptions. He wanted to go to Paris to see some plays; but June and early July were devoted to entertaining in De Vere Gardens his old friend E. L. Godkin, who had been his host in New York during James's last visit to America. Godkin had begun his career by emigrating from Ireland to the United States; now he gazed upon the Old Country through American eyes. His fresh impressions interested James, who was struck by how much Godkin found that was unfavourable to the United States – in spite of his own irreducible Americanism. Godkin was barely gone when William arrived to attend a psychological congress and to see Alice. He stayed briefly in De Vere Gardens; they had a day at Leamington together, where Henry first lunched with his sister, prepared her for William's sudden appearance (they had not told her of his coming so as to avoid creating needless excitement and tension), and then tied a handkerchief to the balcony of 11 Hamilton Terrace as a signal that William might safely enter. The episode is humorously recorded in Alice's journal. She writes that Henry had a queer 'look on his face' as he said to her, 'I must tell you something.' Her assumption had been, 'You're not going to be married?' He had quickly told her that William was outside, after visiting Warwick Castle, and was awaiting the appointed signal in the Holly Walk. Alice fortified her-self with some bromide; Henry tied the handkerchief.

Later that summer he went to Whitby, where Lowell was staying. He found his friend with undiminished powers of 'walking, talking, joking, smoking, drinking and playing host and guide – in the kind-est, gayest most fifteen-year old way'. They had a ramble on the wide moors after a rough lunch at a stony upland inn; they made an excursion by rail to see Rievaulx Abbey, a graceful fragment of a ruin. They wandered on the great curving green terrace in Lord Feversham's park overhanging the Abbey and visited a battered bit of castle where they saw young Yorkshire folk playing lawn-tennis. He missed him in London when he called to say good-bye, before Lowell's return to America, and penned a hasty note wishing him 'a winter of fine old wood fires and a speedy return'. A day or two later Lowell left. This was his last journey to England.

In September James went to Dover, planning to move on to Paris. Katharine Loring was with Alice and he could allow himself a comfortable absence. He found Dover so comfortable and quiet, however, that he lingered, walked, worked, enjoyed solitude and exercise and decided he would cross the Channel later. He returned to London, dispatched further chapters of the *Muse*, and after three or four weeks went to the French capital on 24 October.

By now he had still another task to perform. He had agreed to translate Daudet's new Tartarin novel, *Port Tarascon*, and was to work on it from the printers' galleys. Between this chore and the writing of the final chapters of the *Muse* James visited the last days of the Exhibition of 1889, spending his mornings and early afternoons in his room at the Hôtel de Hollande. To re-read the final chapters of his novel, he wrote later, was to remember how the 'tone of the terrible city seemed to deepen about one to an effect strangely composed at once of the auspicious and the fatal'. Paris was 'terrible' because it was distracting. Nevertheless, he saw his job through; the last chapters of his longest serial were sent off early in December. He had an evening with Daudet, and they talked novel and theatre. Daudet, in the naturalist tradition, was taking notes on the progress of his disease. In the midst of this he was writing his 'new, gay, lovely' *Tartarin*. The serial would be profusely illustrated and James was to 'represent him in English, a difficult but with ingenuity a pleasant and amusing task'. He saw much of Bourget and something of François Coppée. He dined twice in the company of the dramatists Meilhac and Ganderax, the drama-critic Sarcey, Blowitz, the Paris correspondent of *The Times* and Edmond de Goncourt. He distinctly cultivated the theatrical side of the city. His French confrères were still, however, besotted mandarins, when all was said and done. 'Nevertheless I've enjoyed it, and though I am very tired, I shall have been much refreshed by my stay here,' he wrote to William. Early in December he returned to London.

124

The Private Life

TWELVE days after James's return, word came that Robert Browning had died in Venice. The poet had spent a part of the late autumn with their friend Mrs Bronson at La Mura, her summer home in Asolo. He had dedicated a book to her – his last, *Asolando*. 'To whom but you, dear Friend, should I dedicate verses,' his epistle began. At the massive Palazzo Rezzonico, on the Grand Canal, where he had gone in November to stay with his son – who was also the son of the long departed Elizabeth Barrett Browning – the poet contracted a chill, and bronchitis followed. On 12 December, as San Marco's clock chimed its ten bronze hours in the evening, another of the great Victorians was dead.

Little more than a year before, James had been in the same carriage with Browning, at the funeral of their ancient friend Mrs Procter. He had seen him occasionally, and Browning had lunched with him, chatting as always about mundane things in a mundane way, without the remotest suggestion that this was the poet James had read and loved in his youth. They had never become friends; they had always been the pleasantest of dinner-table acquaintances.

The novelist went to Westminster Abbey on the last day of 1889. It was a day of deep fog that seemed to make St Margaret's bell toll even more deeply. Browning was laid to rest – he, one of the most 'modern' of poets – among the ancients in the Poets' Corner. The boy-voices of the choir soared and descended, 'angelic under the high roof'. The obsequies were in every way national. 'His funeral was charming, if I may call it so,' James wrote to Mrs Bronson, 'crowded and cordial and genuine, and full of the beauty and grandeur of the magnificent old cathedral.' And to Francis Boott, who had known the poet in his earlier Florentine days, when Elizabeth Barrett was still alive, James wrote: 'The great Abbey grandly entombs him.'

As always, the novelist's elegiac note was capable of a high flight. 'We possess a great man most when we begin to look at him through the glass plate of death,' he wrote in a brief memorial article contributed to a London journal which he entitled *Browning in Westminster Abbey*. It was a simple truth 'that the Abbey never strikes us so benignantly as when we have a valued voice to commit to silence there.' He said it would have taken the author of *The Ring and the Book* to render all the 'passion and ingenuity, irony and solemnity, the impressive and the unexpected' of the occasion. 'A good many oddities and a good many great writers have been entombed in the Abbey; but none of the odd ones have been so great and none of the great ones so odd.'

Browning had been a magnificent master of poetic emotion. He took into the Abbey, Henry wrote, a great expression of life and a very genuine modernity, 'rendered with large liberty and free experiment'. He was unmistakably in the great tradition, a wonderful mixture of 'the universal and alembicated'. He had never been more powerful than when he had voiced the things best liked by his race – 'the fascination of faith, the acceptance of life, the respect for its mysteries, the endurance of its charges, the vitality of the will, the validity of character, the beauty of action, the seriousness, above all, of the great human passion'.

Years before, when he had first met Browning in London, James had been struck by his double personality – the poet incarnated in an individual as hearty and conventional and middle-class as any of the numerous privileged with whom he and Henry dined out constantly during the late seventies. Again and again in various letters James had expressed his sense of this paradox. Now that Browning was gone, James allowed his imagination to play over the image of a great poet who could be deadly prosaic. To meditate on such a matter was to seek some opposite case : and the opposite seemed to him to exist in the President of the Royal Academy, Sir Frederic Leighton, a painter who had all the gifts and all the versatilities of his art; he could make graceful after-dinner speeches, was charming and inventive so long as he had an audience. He was, so to speak, the poet of diners-out – and James imagined that he evaporated into thin air the moment he had no audience.

These reflections led to James's writing a little tale, *The Private Life*. James called it a 'conceit' – his picture of a playwright staying at a Swiss inn who has promised an actress a play, but who seems quite incapable of writing it. The narrator discovers, however, that the playwright has a double, who stays in his room and does his writing for him. The 'playwright's opinions were sound and second-rate, and of his perceptions it was too mystifying to think. I envied him his magnificent health,' the narrator observed. On the other hand Lord Mellifont, also staying at the inn, is a man whose personality pervades English life. 'He *was* a style.' Where the playwright's talk suggests 'the reporter contrasted with the bard', Lord Mellifont is 'the host, the patron, the moderator'. He puts more art into everything than is required.

The tale describes the adventures of the narrator and one friend who discover the strange natures of their fellow-guests at the mountain inn. But above all the tale is Henry's picture of Robert Browning as he had known him. The world had seen always the commonplace Browning. The genius was in his books. Browning had been all 'private life' and had no life in public, save the usual and the expected. Lord Leighton had been all public, and had no corresponding private life. James remembered that when he had heard Browning read, it had been almost as if he were reading the work of another.

Such was Henry's little fantasy about the poet. It was also a fantasy about himself; it reflected the dichotomy which he envisaged in his own life: his dedication to art and to privacy; his eagerness at this moment to set this aside, and seek the worldliness and publicity of the stage.

Index

Works by Henry James

MENTIONED IN THIS VOLUME

Novels

Tales

Other Writings

MORE ABOUT PENGUINS
AND PELICANS

Penguinews, which appears every month, contains details of all the new books issued by Penguins as they are published. From time to time it is supplemented by *Penguins in Print*, which is our complete list of almost 5,000 titles.

A specimen copy of *Penguinews* will be sent to you free on request. Please write to Dept EP, Penguin Books Ltd, Harmondsworth, Middlesex, for your copy.

In the U.S.A.: For a complete list of books available from Penguins in the United States write to Dept CS, Penguin Books, 625 Madison Avenue, New York, New York 10022.

In Canada: For a complete list of books available from Penguins in Canada write to Penguin Books in Canada Ltd, 41 Steelcase Road West, Markham, Ontario.

Peregrine Books

THE LIFE OF HENRY JAMES
VOLUME 2

Leon Edel

'The greatest literary biography of our time' – A. L. Rowse

Since 1953, when the first part was published, Leon Edel's life of Henry James has been the subject of increasing critical acclaim. It now appears in Penguins in a 'definitive edition' of two volumes.

Volume Two carries on the story from 1889 until the death of the 'Master' in 1916. James had settled in England, latterly at Lamb House, Rye, and his reputation as one of the leading literary figures of his generation was assured. After a brief dalliance with the theatre which, although unsuccessful, profoundly influenced his later writing, his output of novels and stories continued, and this period saw the publication of *The Spoils of Poynton*, *The Turn of the Screw*, *The Ambassadors* and *The Golden Bowl*. Like Orwell and T. S. Eliot, Henry James was reluctant to open his life to biographers, but Professor Edel, in what amounts to an object-lesson in the art of biography, has masterfully uncovered the life of a man whose contribution, by precept and practice, to English literature was enormous.

Peregrine Books

THE FICTION OF HENRY JAMES

S. Gorley Putt

'Putt's book is much more than a "reader's guide" to the one truly great artist we have produced in American literature : it is a demonstration that there is nothing like approaching a text with a fresh and open mind, free of critical clichés and critical subjectivities. His book brings a clean strong wind into Jamesian studies, which have grown stale and repetitive' – Leon Edel

'On the long shelf of books about Henry James – all too much of it esoteric balderdash – *A Reader's Guide* will stand out as a sensible workmanlike volume' – *The Times*

This critical study is the work of an Englishman who has also lived and studied in the United States. He is well equipped, therefore, to understand that special blend of European and American experience which is peculiar to Henry James. He comments here on the whole corpus of James's novels and tales with a sensitivity to literature and social comedy which is unusual. Drawing out the main themes of his fiction, Mr Putt points to the kindness, sanity and wit which irradiate all James's writing.

'Mr Putt's appreciation of . . . James makes him a stimulating cicerone through the Jamesian labyrinth' – *Times Literary Supplement*

'His enthusiasm for James re-kindles one's own, and his book makes one want to argue – an infallible sign of merit in a critic' – Walter Allen